Date: 9/30/21

BIO HWANG
Hwang, Sŏg-yŏng,
The prisoner /

The Prisoner

The Prisoner

by Hwang Sok-yong

Translated by Anton Hur and Sora Kim-Russell

VERSO

London • New York

**LITERATURE TRANSLATION
INSTITUTE OF KOREA**

This book is published with the support of the Literature
Translation Institute of Korea (LTI Korea).

First published in English by Verso 2021
Translation © Anton Hur, Sora Kim-Russell 2021
Originally published in Seoul, Korea, in two volumes:
수인 1−경계를 넘다 (The Prisoner 1: Across the Border) and
수인 2−불꽃 속으로 (The Prisoner 2: Into the Fire)
© Munhak 2017

1 3 5 7 9 10 8 6 4 2

Verso
UK: 6 Meard Street, London W1F 0EG
US: 20 Jay Street, Suite 1010, Brooklyn, NY 11201
versobooks.com

Verso is the imprint of New Left Books

ISBN-13: 978-1-83976-083-9
ISBN-13: 978-1-83976-085-3 (UK EBK)
ISBN-13: 978-1-83976-086-0 (US EBK)

British Library Cataloguing in Publication Data
A catalogue record for this book is available from the British Library

Library of Congress Cataloging-in-Publication Data
A catalog record for this book is available
from the Library of Congress

Typeset in Sabon by Biblichor Ltd, Edinburgh
Printed and bound by CPI Group (UK) Ltd, Croydon CR0 4YY

"You're putting your fate in someone else's hands," said my mother, to discourage her son from becoming a writer. Your son as a young man wore you down, and now as an old man dedicates this book to you.

Contents

Editor's Note

This book is published with the support of the Literature Translation Institute of Korea (LTI Korea), which the publisher gratefully acknowledges.

The short excerpt from Hwang Sok-yong's novel *The Shadow of Arms* is from the translation by Chun Kyung-ja, published by Seven Stories Press in 2014, and appears here with permission.

Readers should note that in order to bring the original two-volume Korean text into one English volume, this translation is a slightly shortened version of the text, abridged in collaboration between the author, translators, and editor. All Korean and Japanese names are set in the Asian style, that is, family name first and given name second.

Prologue

I was eating my last lunch in the underground room. Not the usual cafeteria food on a tray but *seolleongtang* beef soup from a nearby restaurant. The head of the investigation, as he waited for me to finish, had divided thick reams of statements into manila envelopes to give to the Prosecutor's Office. He began to speak.

—We'll all be going home at five on the dot once you're gone. You've been through a lot here, haven't you?

The investigator standing by him spoke up.

—What do you think your sentence will be, sir?

I answered as if I were talking about someone else.

—I don't know. Three years?

The head of investigation looked surprised.

—Really? So little?

—They give smaller sentences to the instigators than to the followers.

I must have been thinking about Moon Ik-hwan, the pastor who was pardoned after three years in jail, when I made that joke.

—But you've gone to North Korea and met Kim Il-sung several times, so they've got to put you away for at least seven or eight.

I replied again as if it were some other man's business.

—Oh my, what a bother that's going to be.

—Or maybe not. Isn't this meat and potatoes for you writers, your "material," if you will?

The other investigator agreed.

—We know you're going to write about us when you leave . . .

—You gentlemen sure know how to make me feel important.

I kept on joking, pretending to be unfazed. It was a skill I'd mastered during their interrogations, an acquired habit of keeping my cool no matter what, so as to not lose in the battle of nerves. In the last few days, I was beginning to feel more like their coworker than a prisoner. These twenty days of the investigation by the Agency for National Security Planning (ANSP, formerly the Korean Central Intelligence Agency) were coming to an end, but I had only cleared the first of the gates of hell. Now I would be up against the Prosecutor's Office.

I was never tortured. I was arrested several times during the Yushin dictatorship of the 1970s and once jailed for disobeying martial law declared after the assassination of President Park Chung-hee, but I never got so much as a slap across the face. Was I lucky, or were my stunts too tame to make it worthwhile? My fellow writer friends used to joke that one of these days my luck would run out and I would get my comeuppance. Thinking back, luck had something to do with it, but it probably helped that I was also a famous young novelist with a large, mainstream following, one who had serialized a saga titled *Jang Gil-san* every day for the past ten years in the pages of a daily.

When I was first arrested at the airport and dragged, blindfolded, to this underground room, the anti-communism investigators tried to intimidate me by shoving me into a corner and having a phalanx of investigators bark questions at me. A skinny man with piercing eyes cursed at me as he swung his fists. I had readied myself for this. I ducked the blows, pushed him away, and tore off my shirt.

—What, the law isn't enough for you? Fine, torture me. Hit me!

The investigators tried to calm the other man down and pulled him away, calling him *"Siljangnim,"* which allowed me to guess that he was the section chief. I still remember what he said to me before he left.

—You bastard, you think the world has changed? You think all you got to do is bullshit a little and we'll let you go? We're gonna flay the skin off your ass!

The painter Hong Seong-dam was once arrested and severely tortured for sending slides of his murals to the World Festival of Youth and Students in North Korea. He later drew a portrait of his torturer and published it in a newspaper; it turned out to be the same face as my own would-be torturer.

But whenever an investigator tried to use their usual violent tactics against me, another would stop him.

—Hurting him is more trouble than it's worth.

On my first day at the ANSP headquarters, I had been asked to take off my clothes. I looked askance at the investigator before removing my shirt.

—Do I have to take it off for you? Strip!

The irritation in the investigator's voice made me tense at the thought that the torture was about to begin. I reluctantly took off my pants. Another investigator standing by tossed a military uniform on a chair and left with my clothes. I gritted my teeth and proudly stood up straight while the remaining investigator looked on indifferently.

—You'll get your clothes back when you leave. Put those on for now.

I put on the worn, loose army uniform. In the middle of my first interrogation, I was dragged into the corridor and made to stand with a sign that had my citizen's registration number on it as they took my picture. A doctor came down to the interrogation room and performed a quick checkup. I had to stamp my thumbprint on numerous documents saying that I agreed to everything I was subjected to and that I would take sole responsibility for whatever happened. I had expected verbal abuse and humiliation to be part of the investigation process, but what was unbearable was the lack of sleep. Scores of investigators took turns questioning me in groups of three or four, and for the first few days I was confused by the hourly flow of new faces. Whenever there was a change in investigators, the questions started over from the beginning. The walls and ceiling of the interrogation room were of perforated soundproofed particleboards, and there was a desk, four chairs, a military-issue cot in the corner, and a bathroom. As time went on, I learned that the interrogations were also being watched from the outside. I realized this when I happened to say something inconsistent in my statement, and a higher-up came running into the room to hound me about it. There were some fluorescent lights on the ceiling and a vent, as this was underground, but the lack of windows made it impossible to tell whether it was night or day. There was, of course, nothing like a clock. All I could do was measure the hour by the fatigue on the investigators' faces and guess at how many days had passed. Sometimes, when I went into the bathroom and dozed off on the toilet, an investigator came in and dragged me back to my chair. More than once, someone clasped me by the shoulders and gently rocked me, saying, "What a pity if something terrible were to happen to this important person," before waving his fist in the air as if nothing would make him feel better than to let it fly into my face.

One time, probably late at night when everyone would have been itching to leave work, a man sauntered into the interrogation room. He looked older than the other investigators and stank of alcohol.

—Why are we wasting time questioning this worthless bastard? In my day, we'd just order the younger guys to deal with him. They'd take him out with one blow to the head.

The investigator interrogating me got annoyed.

—Why don't you go sleep it off upstairs? You don't need to be down here.

—We should toss all these bastards into the East Sea and let the seaweed do the rest.

He wandered out of the interrogation room. The young investigator muttered under his breath.

—Those old farts, always a pain in the ass. He's retiring in a few months.

The older man's words chilled me more than any act of physical violence, for I had just realized what he meant. I thought of the motorboats in the Korea Strait that were used to transport pro-democracy politician Kim Dae-jung after he was kidnapped in his Tokyo hotel room and forcibly returned to South Korea during Park Chung-hee's dictatorship. How many people had been drowned on that Cold War sea border?

Around the time I decided to visit North Korea, I'd set myself a steadfast rule: I was going to make my thoughts and actions as transparent as possible. I believed that the only way for my deeds to be interpreted objectively and escape distortion was for my every word and gesture to be made completely public. Since I knew I would be arrested as soon as I returned to South Korea, I tried to document every event and meeting I attended, in either interviews or my own writings beforehand. Thanks to this, they already had a wealth of information on me, and the first thing they did was to verify all of it. Or, to be more precise, they began by making me repeatedly write and rewrite my "statement," an unending repetition of testimony designed to lead me into making mistakes or revealing new facts or contradicting myself. But I was confident that I had all my facts straight from beginning to end. No matter how many times I rewrote my statement, my memory never wavered.

The investigators would break down my statement into smaller units of time by chronology and grill me on them. Each broken-down statement became another plethora of episodes that were recreated in detail through repeated questioning. When it seemed like nothing more could be gleaned from my memory or statement, that was when the real wringing out began. Interrogators entered in shifts and asked over and over again about the section of the statement they had been assigned. This part was the toughest. I'd reassured myself that I had nothing to hide since I'd already made everything public, but I wasn't prepared for the distortion and the sheer manufacturing of facts. And yet, how could I have prepared for that? They were the ones writing the script designed to drive us toward one foregone conclusion, while I was the clown at the center of their comedy, helpless to stop any of it from happening no matter how clever I thought I was.

My mistake was to assume that people would understand the truth from facts alone. But it turns out that facts are treacherous things that can be twisted and used to distort the truth. I see now how naïve I was, how clueless about what was coming my way. The investigations were like a foundry, and the National Security Act was the mold. While I was out bouncing from place to place and dodging them, they had been sharpening their knives for four years, discussing how they would cook me up upon my return, and at that point, "flaying the skin off my ass" wouldn't have been enough for them. As it was, I fooled myself into thinking that I emerged from the investigation with my writerly dignity intact; later, I came to realize that all I'd really succeeded in doing was learning to roll over and play dead on command, like a well-trained dog.

To get this out of the way, I do not support the ideology of the North Korean communist regime, and all I wish for is the peaceful reunification of the divided North and South. The same was true for the journalist Chung Kyung-mo and the pastor Moon Ik-hwan, who accompanied me, not to mention the activists that supported our visit to North Korea. More specifically, we believed that when South Korea became a truly democratic society, we could change North Korea for the better. I still believe this, although I have since become more of a pacifist than a reunificationist, as the concept of reunification has become vague and misused for political marketing over the years.

Created from the division of North and South, the National Security Act is a Procrustean bed, a torture rack on which those who don't conform are stretched or chopped down and made to fit. This law, modeled after the internal security laws during the

Japanese occupation, was unilaterally legislated by the ruling party after the formation of separate North and South governments in 1948. It is built on the premise that North Korea is not a sovereign nation but an "anti-governmental" or terrorist organization, a premise long discarded in practice since North and South Korea simultaneously joined the UN in 1991. The act itself, however, was never struck down and remains the law of the land to this day. Even the most vaguely positive-sounding mention of the North Korean regime can be construed as a crime of "praising" terrorists; the only way to stay legally safe is to criticize North Korea unconditionally. To meet with a North Korean is to "consort" with the enemy, and if the meeting place happens to be overseas or in North Korea, it is seen as an additional attempt to "infiltrate and escape." Even if that North Korean is a parent or a sibling, it is absolutely illegal to meet with them. Receiving any kind of money or goods from a North Korean constitutes "bribery," and telling them any news about South Korea is a "breach of confidentiality." The Supreme Court even ruled that sharing news that has already been broadcast on the airwaves or in the press with North Koreans is considered a breach, as "any information deemed to be advantageous to North Korea falls into the category of confidentiality." Moreover, any gathering of North and South Koreans is deemed a terrorist organization and a conspiracy to foment unrest, a conclusion that is easy enough to reach when it comes on top of the other, previously mentioned crimes.

When I was blindfolded and walked down the steps to this room where I opened my eyes to the dark, I was sure that I would be laid on the bed of the National Security Act and my limbs would be hacked off. Every single statute of the act would be brought down upon my head.

After lunch, the head investigator had me change into civilian clothes and took me to the reception area on the first floor. It was an ordinary room with a sofa and a desk, but the sunlight shining in from the south-facing window was too bright for my eyes after twenty days of darkness. I had to wait a moment for different colors and shapes to emerge from the blinding white.

The division manager told me to sit. He was usually sharply dressed, but today he'd gone with the casual look of T-shirt and windbreaker. He offered me a warm cup of coffee and a cigarette. The coffee wet my tongue and spilled down into my soul, followed immediately by a lungful of nicotine, which together woke a repressed craving for freedom that spread to the very ends of my body. It was the first coffee and cigarette I'd tasted since leaving New York some twenty-odd days ago. Later, in prison, I would learn what "going to Hong Kong" meant, but for now the few puffs of tobacco left me feeling light-headed and weak, and I felt I would do anything in that moment if asked to. The manager spoke.

—You see how we're all human beings here. I feel that we've treated our writer guest with the utmost respect. You did not experience any torture or violence during the investigation, am I correct?

I was so relaxed that I couldn't help feeling moved by the words "we're all human beings." I quickly shook my head, as if it were unimaginable that I could have been treated as less than human in a place where all were human beings.

—Never, never.

I was thinking that being deprived of sleep while being questioned was barely comparable to the other kinds of torture that went on. The manager nodded and went on with the rest of it as if following a script.

—I'm afraid there's more hardship still ahead of you, but I'm sure you're ready for it. After all, you brought it on yourself. In truth, we both love our country, only in different ways, do we not? We may contradict each other during the trial process, but if you deny any of the facts that you confirmed and signed off on . . .

He trailed off and glanced at the head of investigation, who completed the sentence for him.

—Then we'd have to meet up again.

—Oh, not that that will happen, of course. That was all in the authoritarian past, and we didn't even press charges on everything we know about you. The government will help you for the next few years to get resettled; when you're ready to start working again, you must resume writing. I hope we can then meet again as writer and reader.

This conversation marked the end of the investigation, and as I had no idea their words were only a meaningless formality, I felt a gratitude so powerful that it melted my resentment. I even shook hands with them and posed for souvenir pictures. The head investigator and division manager put me in a car and drove me to the Prosecutor's Office in Seocho-dong. The forests of Nam Mountain passed by outside the window. The trees had been budding when I arrived and were now green with leaves. Oddly enough, after that day, whenever I was arrested and being transported as a prisoner, I stopped noticing people's individual faces or attire. They were just meaningless blurs to me. Instead, the only thing that filled my eyes was natural scenery—clouds, mountains, forests, trees. Each time I pictured the outside world from inside my cell, I would recall the blur of passing streets and think about how the only thing missing from them was me. And since I didn't exist in the real world out there, I was as good as dead.

The prosecutor in charge of my case was an ambitious young man in his thirties. He reminded me of a first-year officer who had been assigned to my regiment in the last year of my military conscription. Painfully aware of his own lack of experience, he was tense and overbearing during the month he spent raking me over the coals with the written statement I'd made for the ANSP. But I'd already testified to the facts and had no wish to argue with him. I was so obliging from the beginning that it must have scared him, as if I would soon change my mind, which made him push on with the interrogation day and night.

When I was brought to the Prosecutor's Office from prison, they put me into a waiting room that was no better than a chicken cage. Tucked into a dark corner was a small bucket that I was to use for a toilet. It had gone unemptied for days, filling the cramped space with the stench of human waste. The room was so narrow that I couldn't even sit down and had to stand for hours with my face poking through the bars in the little window in the door. The prosecutor often stuffed me into that coffin of a space and left me there for hours, just to rile me up. But what really tested my patience was how this overgrown brat would lecture me in informal Korean as if he knew something of the world. I had no choice but to listen in silence; I was amazed by the extent of my own endurance. His sheer ignorance made it clear that he hadn't read a single book beyond the legal text-books needed to pass the bar.

His family, like my own, had apparently fled North Korea and settled in the South during the war.

—All that divided-family crap is such sentimental bullshit. Those so-called relatives and blood relations are all commies by now, what kind of conversation would you have with them? My father refuses to go back. He doesn't want to lay eyes on any of them ever again.

My family used to spend Lunar New Year making dumplings together and reminiscing about our loved ones left behind in North Korea. But this man's father would rather die than go back home.

—You're a fool, you're just being used by the commies. Everything you've done is bullshit. Reunification? You think America wants that for us? Singing that nursery rhyme about "Our Wish Is Reunification" is for babies. Typical sentimental crap.

He disguised his self-pity with arrogance and cynicism. If, instead of being from a refugee family, he'd had the least bit of family backing in the South, he wouldn't have been assigned to the notoriously thankless and tedious national security division, despite having passed the difficult bar. He must have known that the thawing of North–South relations meant his days were numbered, because he kept boasting about how he might move out of Seoul, get himself a place in a smaller city or country town and live like a king. Or, failing that, ditch his job at the Prosecutor's Office and set up a private law practice where he'd rake in the cash, and other nonsense that I had zero interest in hearing about. Twenty years later, I came across an article about him online and found out what had become of him. Nothing about it surprised me. He was in his sixties, obese, aging badly, and still ignorant of how he'd been a puppet of the system, still using red scare tactics and calling progressives, activists, and opposition politicians "commies."

Once my time with the prosecutor was over, I was transferred to Seoul Detention Center in Uiwang. I was given a blue uniform and black rubber shoes, and my clothes and personal possessions were put in storage. I had become prisoner #83; my name, Hwang Sok-yong, disappeared. Visitors often teased me about my number, saying that I'd earned the 83 for having gone back across the 38th parallel that divided North and South.

The prison covered a wide, flat plot of land and was surrounded by two tall, white perimeter walls. The building itself was structured like an airport terminal, with a long central corridor branching out into three-story prison hives. It was the end of the day when I arrived, the work halls and corridors were empty, and all I could hear was the murmuring of the prisoners. Most of them were roomed in groups of about ten, but as a political offender, I was given my own cell. At the head of each corridor in each hive was a guardroom occupied by two guards, followed by four single cells, with multiple-inmate cells further down the hallway. My space measured about three meters square and had a window with a covered toilet beneath. Next to the door was a little slot with a wooden panel that opened. We called it the "food hole," but it was used for delivering goods sent to us from outside, as well as our prison-issued meals, usually by other prisoners who'd been assigned to cleaning or miscellaneous chores.

They shaved off the hair of all except political prisoners. On top of which we enjoyed the further distinction of a red badge sewn above the number on our uniforms. Whenever I passed an ordinary prisoner in the corridor, they would see my red badge and mumble, "Commie bastard." A few months after I arrived, they stopped shaving prisoners' heads and color-coding our badges by crimes committed.

My first night in prison, I couldn't sleep. I turned toward the wall and thought about everything I'd been through. It was a lot, but at least I was alive. This suffering couldn't possibly last forever. I was good with people and an optimist. Prison would surely be an important life experience; I was going to make the best of it. I whispered to myself: *Let's live through this!*

I soon grew used to the fluorescent lights that never went out, but in the beginning, I had to put a towel over my face to fall asleep.

~

I see a field of green barley spread before me. A path winds through it trimmed with dandelions and milk vetch that bob in the breeze, and the tall wildflowers, radish, and shepherd's purse sway with the wind that ripples through the barley. Father, who has walked on ahead, is wearing a fedora and carrying a rucksack while my two older sisters are in summer dresses cut from identical fabric. Their feet are clad in white socks and they, too, carry small rucksacks. Father does not look back as he strides. My sisters skip and run after him, stopping to pick the occasional flower and add it to their bouquets. Mother is carrying me on her back as we follow. I'm itching to walk on my own and want to be near my sisters, so I lean sideways and wave my arms. For some reason, they pretend not to notice. I'm so frustrated that I call out.

Sisters, wait for me!

They don't look back. My mother shushes me and shakes her shoulders.

I told you to ignore them . . .

None of it makes sense, and I'm growing more frustrated by the moment. My father and my sisters walk farther and farther ahead of us.

Mother told me later that this was a memory of our crossing the 38th parallel. My sisters explained it to me too. They said our parents had told them to pretend we were going on a picnic, and that I wouldn't remember because I was too little. But I do remember, or at least, I remember this much.

Like so many others at the time, my parents believed that they would someday return to the land of their birth. But neither was ever to step foot on home soil again.

1

Leaving

1985–86

Some forty-odd years after pretending to leave on a picnic, I returned home for the first time, in 1989. But before going into my North Korean visit, I should begin with my very first journey overseas, which took place a few years earlier in 1985. That trip was what inspired me to go to the North.

We used to be able to sail to Manchuria or take a train to Siberia and even to Western Europe. That was during the Japanese occupation. But ever since the division of the Korean peninsula, those routes have been blocked. South Korea might as well be an island. We think of North Koreans as isolated, but even South Koreans weren't allowed to travel as tourists until 1989, and it was difficult for us to get a permit to go abroad before then. There existed, however, a new, single-use "cultural passport" enabling artists and employees of large conglomerates to attend international events. The trickiest part of obtaining such a passport was the background checks—you were rejected if there was even a single thing off about your application. Once you did pass the background checks, you still had to attend national security training with intelligence officials and attach the certificate to your application. The US was especially strict about granting visas. It took months to obtain one after submitting tax receipts, financial guarantees, invitations, and going through a grueling interview process at the American embassy. Still, getting a passport was in itself a great privilege.

I had the luck of applying when the process had been some-what relaxed, just as Korea was beginning to open up. The background checks were still in place, and while a notoriously anti-government person like myself couldn't normally dream of obtaining a visa, it so happened that I had published a contro-versial book of testimonials of the Gwangju Democracy Movement, titled *The Kwangju Uprising*[1]—and, counter-intuitively, this helped me obtain a passport to leave Korea for the first time.

Back in 1979, then president Park Chung-hee had attempted to stay in office indefinitely only to be assassinated by the Korean Central Intelligence Agency director, Kim Jae-gyu, after which military officials seized power in a coup d'état and declared martial law. This triggered a groundswell of calls for democratization. In May of 1980, the military government massacred thousands of Gwangju citizens who were protesting against martial rule. Barricading themselves in the city's provin-cial administration building, the residents of Gwangju had battled against the soldiers to protect their city.

Many people tried to tell the country and the world of the truth behind the slaughter at Gwangju. The whole of the Korean media was censored at the time under the government's report-ing guidelines. Only a few were able to learn what had happened, thanks to certain religious groups that had obtained news reports by foreign correspondents.

Having moved to Gwangju myself, I launched a cultural activist movement in the 1970s that included students, teachers, writers, and artists, and eventually expanded to bring in work-ers and farmers. Our first mission was to use as many tools of dissemination as possible to publicize the resistance movement in Gwangju. We could not afford modern staging and equip-ment, so we resorted to a traditional form of drama known as

---

1   This is the title of the new English edition. The original title was *Kwangju Diary: Beyond Death, Beyond the Darkness of the Age.*

madanggeuk or "courtyard play," which we performed outdoors in village plazas and empty lots, and created music to go along with it that we recorded on cassette tapes. Painters made posters, and young people with new skills used photography, 8 mm film, and video to create rough but affecting images. These activists went on to become famous directors, playwrights, writers, composers, singers, actors, painters, and filmmakers.

We decided something big had to be done to commemorate the upcoming fifth anniversary of the Gwangju Democracy Movement. Three teams in Gwangju collected news reports, photos, and videos created by Korean reporters, but more importantly, recorded the testimonials of participants and witnesses.

Hong Hee-yun, my wife at the time and the mother of my two children, was in charge of the Songbaekhoe Gwangju women's group made up of activists, wives of political prisoners, teachers, and citizen group workers. They raised funds and provided support to the material collection team. My task was to summarize and streamline the collected records into a concise narrative. The young people gathering the testimonials discreetly forwarded the material to me via the Modern Cultural Research Center, to prevent the authorities from manufacturing a fake spy incident out of our efforts. The center had been established in 1979 by me and Yoon Han Bong, who went into exile in America two years later, and was secretly still in operation after the Gwangju Uprising.

I came up to Seoul with the materials, rented a room near the publisher's office, and worked on editing the book for a month. The initial pamphlets were distributed in universities, and a select few college activists staged a protest inside the American Center. It was an attempt to highlight the fact that our military rulers could not have been able to seize power without the tacit approval of the US, which officially held operational command over the South Korean military. The book was published on schedule in May by a brave printer, and 20,000 copies were distributed to bookstores. The publisher, Na Byung-sik of Pulbit Publishing, had been arrested twice before, during the National Democratic Youth and Student Alliance incident. This time he went into hiding for ten days before turning himself in. I was on the run for about a month, until his interrogation ended and the facts of the case were established.

The world seemed to do a somersault once the book was released. A police raid turned my house in Gwangju inside out, even digging up the flower garden. My clever wife had already stashed the Gwangju materials under the slate roof of an old shed in the corner of our yard. The police went through the shed, but they didn't think to rip off the ceiling panels.

I went underground, moving from house to house of my younger writer friends on the outskirts of Seoul. The books were seized after about half of the first printing had been sold, but photocopiers were becoming mainstream and pirated copies entered the market. I called to turn myself in after a month and was taken to the police instead of central intelligence. The station was close enough to the Agency for National Security Planning (ANSP) Nam Mountain headquarters for intelligence investigators to come down and question me. They were trying to avoid a direct ANSP investigation, because the military dictatorship felt threatened by the rumors surrounding Gwangju. Lockup was full of students protesting against the government; they no doubt thought I would be a bad influence if I were in there with them, not to mention the number of famous and powerful people who came to the station demanding to see me. They quickly ended their interrogation and squirreled me away in a remote police station before putting me in the border customs detention center near the airport. The day I got there, a British woman in the next cell said hello. She had come in from Hong Kong. Someone had paid her to pass on something, a packet she had put into her bag without much thought, that turned out to be drugs. She wept with regret. Another cell held two people from the Middle East.

I was brought out of my cell for questioning a week later. The ANSP agent, a man of few words, said the government was treating my case as rumormongering, and even the highest sentence for this kind of misdemeanor was only twenty days in custody. My trial was set for two days later. He handed me two pieces of paper, which turned out to be invitations in German and English. Apparently, I'd received an invitation from West Germany, and the ANSP was getting heat for not letting me leave the country. But if I agreed to keep my mouth shut and leave Korea for a bit, the government would be willing to let me go. He visited me one more time. I wrote up my passport application in my cell, stamped my thumbprint, and even had my passport photo taken there. The day I was released, I received my passport and a plane ticket sent from Germany.

My wife Hong had come up from Gwangju to meet me. We spent a night in Seoul and bought clothes and a suitcase for my trip. She had to go back the very next day to relieve our neighbor, who was babysitting for us. We were exhausted. She and I had been housewife and novelist, but we'd also been working as political activists for years. We practically took turns being interrogated and investigated, miraculously avoiding arrest every time.

We had moved to Gwangju in 1976 at the beginning of our national movement for democracy. I was away from home several times a year, from a week up to a month. Hong kept herself busy by putting together a women's group composed of the wives of our imprisoned younger friends. They did things like knit socks and gloves for the prisoners and take up collections for their prison allowances.

When I was home, I was so taken up with the novel I was serializing that we never once went out for dinner. My habit of working at night and sleeping during the day also made it difficult for us to have more than one meal at a time together. It was my fault. Even when we did sit down face-to-face, an uncomfortable silence settled between us as we ate. It wasn't long before we both stopped bothering to do anything about it. That day, after my release, I should have escorted her to the bus terminal in Gangnam, but I took her to a restaurant instead and reluctantly told her over dinner, "I'm sorry, I'll try to write often."

Aside from my general hopelessness with the paperwork involved, we had no telephone at home. Getting a landline installed in any house outside of Seoul was complicated. My colleagues used to joke, "What's the point of having a phone? The police will just tap it anyway."

Hong must have felt some premonition at that moment, because her eyes suddenly grew red and she quickly turned away to wipe her tears.

"What's wrong?" I asked, surprised. "Are you worried for me?"

Her usual calm and cool demeanor returned. "I think you'll be away for longer than you think. But have a good trip. And don't drink too much."

She left in a taxi while I stood there on the pavement staring after her. I had no idea that that was the beginning of the end for us. Even now, when I think back on that moment, my heart is seized with sorrow and I feel swept away by a wave of regret.

~

West Berlin in 1985 was like a desert island in the middle of East Germany. In essence, it was a city under occupation by the forces that had won World War II. No one could imagine that the wall looming over Berlin's gloomy, peaceful cityscape would fall in a few years. Whenever I visited Berlin afterward, I would always find it odd that there was still no direct flight between Seoul and the German capital, and remember the gray walls towering above.

I was a country bumpkin on his first overseas trip, and as the Europeans I met kept asking "Who are you?" I naturally began asking myself the same question. Who was I? I was forty-two. I had written four novellas and a volume of plays and had just published the tenth volume of my popular novel *Jang Gil-san*, which I had serialized since 1974. My work, however, did not exist outside of Korea. I promised myself on the plane that I wouldn't even bother mentioning literature: I would only talk to as many people as possible about the plight of the citizens of Gwangju and our democracy movement.

When I arrived, I was met by Korean students living in Berlin who were charged by the event planners with taking me around. These students were sponsored by the Korean Germans who had come over as coal miners and nurses in the 1960s. Some of the students had been miners and nurses themselves and had remained in Germany for school or other jobs when their contracts ran out. Some of them married Germans or became local doctors, teachers, technicians, or businesspeople. They learned about trade unions, human rights activism, and social engagement through German activists on the ground, and became aware of Gwangju and the Korean democracy movement through the Korean students studying abroad. They were well organized and in some ways more radical than the students who had to go back to Korea after their studies. And they were, from the perspective of the Korean embassy representing the military dictatorship, troublemakers all.

The novelist Yun Heung-gil and the cultural activist Im Jin-taek were already at the hotel when I arrived. Berlin was staging a cultural event called "Horizonte," to highlight little-known emerging nations. According to their brochure, the event before ours had dealt with Latin America, and the one before that, Africa. Asia was in focus for Horizonte '85. I remember that the program included the Jindo *sitgimgut* shamanic ritual, classical and folk music, and art exhibits, as well as the three of us.

Our event featured Im Jin-taek and Germany's Wolf Biermann in the first act, and readings by Yun Heung-gil and me, followed by a Q and A, in the second. Im Jin-taek was a first-generation cultural activist along with Kim Chi-ha and me. For the event, Im Jin-taek repurposed Kim Chi-ha's ballad "The story of sound" into modern *pansori*. The original poem was a famous satire that directly criticized the Park Chung-hee government and had led to a death sentence for Kim Chi-ha. The incident had the opposite effect to that intended by the South Korean dictatorship, inspiring instead an international campaign of writers and intellectuals to save him. Kim Chi-ha was finally released, but his poetry remained banned and he continued to be hospitalized from the aftereffects of torture.

Wolf Biermann was born to communist activist parents, and his Jewish father had been incarcerated for years by the Nazis before being executed at Auschwitz. He became disenchanted with the failure of East Germany to achieve the real ideals of communism and wrote about these thoughts in songs and poems, which branded him as "unfriendly" in the eyes of the East German authorities. His first collection of poetry, *The Wire Harp*, was regarded as anti-national, and Biermann was censored and put under house arrest for eleven years. Then he won the West German Offenbach Prize in 1974. When he performed in Cologne by invitation of a metalworkers' trade union in 1976, East Germany deprived him of his citizenship and banned him from the country. This sparked criticism against the East German government, and twelve writers signed a petition condemning the decision. I happened to meet three of those twelve: Sarah Kirsch, who had left East Germany for good, in Hamburg; Christa Wolf, whom I met the very winter the Berlin Wall came down, during my German exile days after my visit to North Korea; and Stefan Heym, at a literary event for the Nobel Peace Prize in Norway's Tromsø. Biermann's ban was a shock to East Germany, the effects of which lasted for a long time. Some even considered it the trigger for the fall of the Wall.

The only East German work I had read at the time was Uwe Johnson's *Speculations about Jakob*, which had been published in Korea. Christa Wolf's *Divided Heaven*, published in East Germany in 1963, only appeared in South Korea in 1989. Their works made me think that South Korea was more similar to

East Germany than West Germany. Much like Gwangju, the June 1953 workers' uprising had been cruelly suppressed by Soviet tanks. And echoing South Korea's restrictions on foreign travel, East Germany built a wall around itself and maintained tight control over its citizens while keeping them under constant Stasi surveillance. I kept remembering the strangely familiar mood in Brecht's poetry collection, *Buckow Elegies*.

If the South Korean military dictatorship seemed East German, the North Korean system was even more extreme than East Germany's. It's been said many times before, but North Korea's constant state of emergency—justified by the decades-old isolation promoted by the Americans—has enabled the endurance of its political system of control and tension. I know very well that North Korean society could never produce work that criticizes the government as East Germany's could. But my thinking was that, as long as South Korea was unable to establish a democratic society like West Germany's, we could hardly afford to criticize North Korea or even hope to change it. My experience of visiting a Germany that was divided like Korea, and then spending several years in a Germany where the Wall fell during my exile there in 1989, would inform my worldview forever after.

After the Horizonte event, a man who had come to Germany as a miner and ended up getting his PhD there told me there was something I needed to see. He drove me to the composer Yun I-sang's house outside Berlin. On the street in front of his house, the city had posted a sign that read "Artist at work, please do not honk," which left me feeling very impressed with the German authorities. I would later spend the first months of my exile in this house.

"I am not a communist." This was the first thing Yun I-sang said to me after shaking my hand.

I was taken aback. "You don't have to worry about that with me," I replied.

After he was arrested in 1967, someone had written about him saying how he couldn't possibly be a communist because his music was too modern. The Soviets and the Eastern Bloc had believed any modernist music or experimental art to be reactionary.

Yun I-sang had quit his job as a music teacher at the age of forty to study in France, and later moved to Germany. His wife, Lee Suja, had lived apart from him for five years before joining him in Germany, while their two children grew up in a relative's home and did not get to see their father for close to ten years.

In the 1960s, the North Korean embassy in East Germany regularly sent pamphlets and propaganda to South Korean students studying in Europe. These proved fascinating to the young intellectuals who had spent their lives in the echo chamber of the South Korean dictatorship. Yun I-sang visited the North Korean embassy, which happened to be a few subway stops away. Around this time, the painter Yi Eungro, in an incident that broke the hearts of his family and friends, had been lured from Paris to North Korea with a promise that he would be allowed to meet his son who had gone North during the Korean War. Yun I-sang was considered one of the world's five best contemporary music composers in the West, and Yi Eungro had been famous for combining Korean ink-brush paintings with Western methods and was popular on the biennale circuit.

There had been others in the so-called "East Berlin Spy Incident," some of whom were implicated for merely visiting the North Korean embassy out of curiosity; others actually took up the North Koreans' offer to host them in the country. The territory remains inaccessible under the National Security Act, and the Cold War did not make things easier at the time. In contrast, West Germany cultivated a policy of engagement that encouraged its citizens to contact and interact with East Germans. If anything, it was the East Germans who were wary of contact, but they were authorizing four-day passes for those who had family living in the West—a far cry from South Korea's policy of total separation. They even allowed single-day visas for foreign visitors.

Yun I-sang was not really a political person to begin with. He became a pro-democracy advocate after his run-in with the South Korean government made him realize the extent of our plight. He has always said that his visit to North Korea was for two reasons. One was that he wanted to catch up with his friend, the leftist composer Kim Sun-nam, from whom he had been separated since the war. Kim went North just before the Korean War broke out and later studied at the Tchaikovsky Conservatory in Moscow, where his work was lauded by Dmitri Shostakovich and Aram Khachaturian, famous for composing the ballet *Spartacus*. Khachaturian in particular urged Kim to request asylum in the USSR at the time of the state purge of the Workers' Party of South Korea, but he refused and returned to North Korea where he was stripped of his privileges and died of an illness soon after. Yun I-sang, who was the same age as Kim, never forgot Kim's talent and legendary social engagement following Korea's Liberation in 1945 from Japanese occupation, which was why he wanted to see his friend one last time. Of course, once Yun I-sang arrived in Pyongyang, not only could he not see his friend, but he discovered it was forbidden to even mention Kim's name in public.

The other reason he went to North Korea was that he wanted to see the ancient Goguryeo murals with his own eyes; a Japanese publisher had just brought out a book of vivid color pictures of these tomb paintings. Yun I-sang understood modern Western music as a deconstruction of the past and a recombination with Eastern influences. He attempted to expand Western music by introducing into it the rhythms, improvisational character, and five-tone scale of Korean folk, classical, and court music. The photographs of the Goguryeo murals had instantly inspired new musical forms in his mind. The blue dragon, white tiger, red phoenix, and black tortoise were turned into variations on a theme, the music capturing the dance and flight of these fantastical animals.

I completely understood what this old artist meant when he said he had only wanted to meet his friend and see the wondrous murals. Unlike now, when South Koreans are allowed to freely travel the world, anyone stepping out of the de facto island that was our peninsula back then experienced something akin to a panic attack, brought on not by homesickness but rather the overwhelming sense of freedom that we encountered on foreign soil. And yet this freedom has the effect of isolating the traveler from their normal space and time. In an intellectual, moreover, it triggers a feeling of humiliation and defeat. In your attempt to escape the consciousness of the peninsula, you suddenly begin to think you are no different from the Europeans around you. You forget, strangely enough, the virulently anti-communist country you came from. That is how a perfectly sane and worldly intellectual can take one look at a piece of North Korean propaganda and cross the border, heart aflutter, despite the threat of prison or execution back home. Those who had family in Japan or happened to have a relative who was forced into labor during the war, or those who crossed the sea border by mistake while fishing and spent time trapped in North Korea before being returned, or those who drunkenly mouthed off about politics at a bar, their tongues loosened by *makgeolli*, an everyman's rice brew—all kinds of people have served time and later successfully sued the government for imprisoning them under fabricated charges. I consider myself fortunate, but nothing can compensate me or my family for the years we lost in suffering.

The East Berlin Spy Incident came about when a South Korean youth, studying in Germany, visited North Korea and then turned himself in when he came back to Seoul. South Korean operatives trussed it up as an organized espionage effort. They carried out a secret investigation and concocted a list of people, some of whom they lured to one location only to haul them off to the South Korean embassy and others whom they called on in person to invite them to a fake Liberation event being held in the home country, going so far as to accompany them on the plane ride back to Seoul, where they were promptly arrested. Many people's lives were destroyed in this way like so much tissue paper—just the few stories here are tragic enough. This is the net we have woven under the North–South division, a net that traps us to this day.

Yun I-sang said to me before we parted, "Thank you for coming to see me. I'm aware that even calling me on the phone is grounds for interrogation when you get back to Korea."

"I couldn't leave Berlin without seeing you. I would have been too ashamed to face my friends back home."

"Don't take this the wrong way," he replied in a low voice, "but I do intend to help North Korea . . . as people of the same blood. They need to open their doors and step out into the world."

I thought I would never see him again, but Yun I-sang called me the next day, asking to meet for lunch. He was seated with an old German couple when I got there. The woman was the novelist Luise Rinser, who would have been in her mid-seventies at the time. Her eyes sparkled with mischievous curiosity and her firm lips and high cheekbones gave her an air of formidable will and perhaps stubbornness. I knew her, of course, from reading contemporary German literature. Her novel *Nina (Mitte des Lebens)*, published in 1950, had been translated into Korean by Jeon Hye-lin, who worked as a translator and essayist after returning to Korea from her studies in Munich but committed suicide just as she turned thirty. Many young, bookish women who read this translation ended up applying to German literature departments for college. But Rinser's life was not as glamorous as they may have thought. Her first husband, an orchestra conductor, died on the Russian front, and she herself had been incarcerated while resisting the Nazis. Her third husband was the contemporary composer Carl Orff, but they had divorced. Orff and Yun I-sang were friends, and Rinser even published a book of her conversations with Yun I-sang, titled *The Wounded Dragon*.

Rinser visited Korea for the first time in 1975. Her impressions of that trip, compared to her account of her North Korean visit in 1980, were extremely negative. Korean conservatives still call her a communist and a puppet of Kim Il-sung's regime, but she really wasn't a communist. If anything, she was an extreme environmentalist who once ran as the presidential candidate for the German Greens. Her *Nordkoreanisches Reisetagebuch* (North Korean travel diary) remains a controversial work in South Korea to this day.

Rinser visited Korea after Park Chung-hee had abolished term limits for his presidency in 1972 and declared a state of emergency in 1974, arresting students and activists left and right for protesting these measures. Universities were closed indefinitely. Arriving in the midst of such trouble, it's obvious that Rinser would not have derived a good impression. She managed to elude the agents trailing her and met with many activists and conscientious intellectuals. She also seems to have explored the red-light districts that operated openly in the back alleys of central Seoul and the bars where women wore traditional *hanbok*, places she referred to as "geisha houses."

Rinser visited North Korea in 1980 when South Korea was in the throes of a terrible, tragic time. The mere mention of "Gwangju" inspired anger among the world's media and artists. Of course, we now detect all sorts of prejudice in her travel writing about North Korea, which tries to treat the socialist idealism of the dictatorship objectively, making it somewhat different in tone from, say, André Gide's conclusions in *Return from the USSR*. I will say more about this later. But, whenever someone asked me what it was like visiting North Korea, I always said, "I was moved, and I despaired." Then I would add, "I was moved by the resilience of the North Korean people who created a self-sustaining way of life out of the ashes of war, and I despaired over the viselike control of the North Korean government."

Rinser asked me if I was going to return to Korea, and, as I had no other plans, I said yes. She suggested I apply for asylum instead.

I was adamant in my refusal. "I have to go back to where they speak my mother tongue."

It was not until much later that I realized how naïve and preposterous those words were. She was silent for a moment after Yun I-sang interpreted for me, and then said in a cheerful voice, "Well, if you want to spend some time overseas, you ought to learn some German or English first."

I met her again on the summit of Paektu Mountain during the First Pan-Korean National Conference in 1990. Even then I would never have dreamed that the world was about to grow worse. But a crueler age was headed toward us, an age of widespread and indiscriminate bloodshed brought on by ideological and religious conflicts, by imperialist desires disguised as civil wars.

About a week into my sojourn in Berlin, I was hailed at an event by Jochen Hiltmann and his Korean wife, the painter Song Hyun-sook. They had visited me in Gwangju a year before, on their way from visiting Song's home in Damyang. Song had read my novels and wanted to meet me.

A professor at an art school in Hamburg, Hiltmann was also working as an editor and critic at an art magazine and had quit sculpting in favor of photography and videography. He demonstrated against the Vietnam War when he was young and had lost his job because of it, and also used to be a Maoist. He was shy when I teased him about it, and said the most he did as a Maoist was sew himself a corduroy version of their distinctive jackets. Hiltmann was his wife's biggest supporter and promoter. He loathed the contemporary sculpture in the streets of Germany and went as far as to say, "I quit sculpture because of those horrors." He used all sorts of amusing words to express his hatred of the random pieces of steel and stone that stood in for sculpture in front of the buildings of Seoul.

Song Hyun-sook graduated from a girls' high school in Damyang and, like many other women intent on helping their family, trained as a nurse before being sent off to Germany. Instead of directly supporting patients, though, she was assigned to various kinds of menial labor around the hospital. Her teachers had praised her drawing ability in elementary school, and she once won an art contest in middle school for a painting. But she could not afford the pencils and watercolors to keep it up in high school. In the German nurses' dormitories, she kept a sort of diary by drawing pictures with a ballpoint pen to mitigate her homesickness and work stress. One day, she boarded a train to visit a nurse friend of hers in a nearby city, and Jochen happened to be sitting next to her. They became friends. When Jochen saw her drawings, he convinced her to apply to his art school in Hamburg. In any case, they seemed determined to help the Korean democracy movement any way they could after having visited Gwangju and listened to people's stories. They were a great help to me later on.

My first stop after leaving Berlin was Hamburg. They were renting an apartment there near Jochen's school, but it was too small for all their books, to say nothing of workspace, so they'd also bought a farmhouse on an island near the Danish border. From Hamburg you had to drive or take a train north for about an hour and a half before boarding a ferry from Dagebüll to the island of Föhr, where the house was in the village of Oevenum. The Hiltmanns stayed in this hundred-year-old farmhouse every term break, fixing it up. There was a large library and studio with a living room in the middle, and a loft that served as a bedroom and storage. There were many little empty spaces throughout the house, as if designed for hide-and-seek. Each spot was equipped with comfy chairs and small tables perfect for reading or drinking tea. The house had a thatch roof nearly half a meter thick, made from a mixture of coal tar and the tall reeds that grew all over the island.

The poet Sarah Kirsch visited Oevenum for lunch one day. She had left her husband in East Germany in 1977 to come to the West. Her poem about the husband left behind suggests she had abandoned him on the spur of the moment. Her poetry was melancholy but beautiful; critics later called her the Sappho of East Germany.

She brought with her a younger man who was her lover, a composer, and together we discussed the problem of borders. Song Hyun-sook did not know much about literature at the time and her German was also limited, but this curb on our German–Korean communication stripped the conversation down to its essentials, much like children and their simple metaphors, prompting our imaginations to fill in the blanks and use symbols to express the unspoken. Kirsch said her poetic theme was winter, and though we couldn't share much about what she meant, her words were enough to make the day-to-day of socialist society seem palpable. I wondered what kind of society would go so far as to prohibit lyric poetry. Perhaps if I had met her a little later, I would have been even more interested in her work. At the time I thought of Heinrich Heine's poems; this colored my thoughts on Kirsch. I couldn't help but ungenerously think, what freedom could she possibly lack here? I also did not have the wherewithal to consider how important lyric poetry might actually be to a fighter like her. Later in my Berlin asylum years I would slowly read through Brecht's *Buckow Elegies* and Kirsch's "At the White Pansies," and find the means to dream for myself a different life in Korea.

~

When I arrived in France from Germany, the first thing I did was call my poet friend Choi Min. He said he couldn't make it to Gare du Nord, the train station in Paris I was arriving at, because he had class that day, but he had asked Hong Sehwa's wife to pick me up. Hong Sehwa, an exiled dissident who would later become a writer and politician, was making a living as a taxi driver.

I was having a simple breakfast of a baguette and coffee at Hong's house when his young son and daughter, both in elementary school, began talking to me. The son approached with pencil and paper and asked if he could draw my portrait. After he was done with that, he drew every animal I asked him to with a good likeness of the real thing. His bright, innocent eyes made my heart break, the eyes of this boy who had to live in a foreign land because of his father's exile. I thought of my own two sons waiting for their father in our Gwangju home.

Hong Sehwa finally came in. He still gave off the air of a melancholy literary youth, as wordless and brief with his smiles as he used to be in the music cafés of Seoul. He had just lost his job at a restaurant owned by someone known for being pro-North, and the tongues of all the Koreans in France had been wagging about him. The exiled are never free.

It was almost the end of summer when I returned to Paris from my travels through Italy and Spain. Friends told me Seong Nak-young had called from Göttingen, so I went from Paris back to Germany to his Korean acquaintance's house in Düsseldorf where he suggested we meet. The couple living there had met as a coal miner and a nurse and had just managed to leave the world of manual labor to open a dry goods store. The miners were beginning to leave the pits of Bochum for Dortmund, Düsseldorf, Essen, and Cologne, where they could pursue new lives. Whenever Koreans of note visited, they would set up events for them and help them get around.

Seong Nak-young told me at the Düsseldorf house that Yoon Han Bong had called several times from Los Angeles in the hope that I would visit the US someday to help him there. Seong Nak-young also had a fax page with him, an invitation from a Christian organization in America. I had only a single-use passport and no American visa. Still, I thought it was worth a try, so I applied for a visa at the American embassy in Berlin. The embassy man at the counter looked askance at my application. He said the rules stipulated that I had to go back to Korea to apply for this visa. I was about to give up, but Seong Nak-young launched into a whole spiel in English on my behalf as he handed my passport back to the staff member. When I asked him what that was about as we left, he said he had suggested they call the organization in America themselves.

We went back to the Düsseldorf house and contacted the Korean Resource Center in Los Angeles. For the first time in five years, I was hearing Yoon Han Bong's voice. He happened to be with a group of my friends living there. They passed the phone around. During Yoon Han Bong's drastic exile to America, my friends had visited him at an event and told him they were happy to help any friend of mine. Such is Korean society: it's always easy enough to find someone who knows someone, and it made me feel that Korea was indeed a small country.

When I went to the American embassy the next day, a staff member handed me my passport with the visa stamped in it and said, "Your application was accepted. We made an exception for you."

At the airport in Los Angeles, my old friend the poet Lee Se-bang and the playwright Jeon Jin-ho were there to greet me. Lee Se-bang's father was a leftist who had gone missing during the war. The poet had been raised with his younger sister by his single mother, an elementary school teacher. The family managed to immigrate to the States when the sister got a job as a nurse there. Lee Se-bang had ceased being a poet and become a photographer, while Jeon Jin-ho had fled the South Korean dictatorship of the 1970s by marrying Lee Se-bang's sister and settling in the States.

We arrived at a house in Koreatown that bore signs saying "Korean Resource Center" and "Young Koreans United," where we were met by young members and some adults who had prepared a spread. The house had an outdoor deck and a wide backyard. Yoon Han Bong still looked like a day laborer in his jumpsuit and sneakers, with his hair cut short. We did not hug each other like Americans but clasped each other's hands and shook them firmly. He was smiling but there were tears in his eyes. I had to turn away to wipe my own tears.

Right after the Gwangju massacre, I had helped several younger friends who'd fled from there to get settled in Seoul, placing them with acquaintances in the capital who had the space to hide them. Yoon Han Bong did not believe that the military dictatorship would ever surrender power to a civilian government and was predicting another bloodbath. Yoon Han Bong, Choi Kwon-heng, and I were all in Seoul that spring ourselves, and we helped Yoon scout out a place to hide just in case his fears were realized.

I found another sanctuary at the artist's studio of my ex-wife Hong Hee-yun's friend. It had the advantage of being down an alley in a nonresidential area, away from prying eyes. Yoon Han Bong was wanted by the police. The assumption was that he would be tortured to death if caught. We hid him in the studio for almost a year, but he was recognized by a visiting literary couple who happened to be related to the landlord. Since he was unable to live there any longer, a plan was hatched to spirit him out of the country. A handful of people got involved, and finally contact was made with the crew of a ship that sailed international waters. On the night of April 29, 1981, Yoon boarded the *Leopard*, a ship registered in Panama. He hid in the bathroom of the ship's infirmary, a space about four meters square where, during his thirty-five days at sea, he almost died from fear and starvation. A sent package needs receiving, and Gwangju's church leaders had made contact with their counterparts in America. A Korean pastor was to meet him at the dock with an agreed code: the pastor would ask Yoon, "Do you like roses?" and Yoon would answer, "No, I like azaleas." The Korean church informed the Americans that "the package has been sent," and asked the Robert F. Kennedy Human Rights organization for protection.

The infirmary bathroom was next to the boiler chimney, which made the room as hot as a sauna, and the sailing route included an Australian detour. In the process of crossing the equator twice, Yoon became a ghost of his former self.

When the pastor arrived to meet the stowaway, he hesitated because a group of Americans in trench coats were loitering about the dock. He learned later that they were from Robert F. Kennedy Human Rights, and had come to escort Yoon to safety. The Korean pastor snuck onto the boat and found Yoon, who was near death, and asked him the code, but Yoon wasn't conscious enough to answer. Thinking it was a trap set up by the Korean government, the pastor left the ship and went home. It was only when his Korean informant on the phone urged him to return, insisting that the man in the bathroom was "unmistakably our package," that he went all the way back to the ship to rescue him—a mere hour before the ship was due to sail.

Who could have guessed that, after all that trouble, we would meet each other again in this foreign land?

I should say a little about Yoon's nickname. He entered the Chonnam National University College of Agriculture after his military conscription duties, which made him four years older than the other first-years. He also looked older than his age, and was such a country mouse that the students called him Hapsu, a Jeolla dialect word for a kind of manure made from combining urine and excrement. This actually pleased him, as he declared it was the most precious kind of manure to a farmer and that he hardly deserved such a title, although he marked each of his textbooks with large Chinese characters for *hapsu*. By contrast, the poet Kim Nam-ju's nickname was Mulbong, after the Haenam-style soft-boiled potato, for her accommodating nature and generosity toward others.

Hapsu was truly a born revolutionary. I was in awe of him, but I was also at times exasperated. I often criticized him for his strictness about rules, intolerance of any deviation from the Party line, and combative way of making his point, saying his attitude was not conducive to a mainstream political movement.

But despite his constant suspicion of my liberalist tendencies in managing the cultural movement, he always took my side in the end. I used to joke that he was the politician among us cultural activists. He created the Korean Resource Center in Los Angeles and met young Korean Americans through South Korean students studying abroad, giving talks at youth groups in major cities along the East and West Coasts. He was more effective in informal talks with a dozen people than in large lecture halls filled with an audience.

The student groups met once a quarter to go on team-building trips and hold debates. Centers were established and run by both full-time workers and volunteers. They printed newsletters and gathered clippings on the South Korean democracy movement. The Korean Americans also dealt with community issues such as the lack of documents, unpaid wages, and insurance and tax consulting. I was especially impressed with how they worked in solidarity with different organizations—including religious, human rights, and feminist groups; they even participated in protests going on in different states. Young Koreans United brought together incoming South Korean students, who had a clear political consciousness of what was going on in Korea, with 1.5- and second-generation Korean Americans, who, as US citizens, were able to draw in non-Korean volunteers to help with the organization's many projects. This was how one person managed to spark great change in the lives of people living in a faraway country.

The organization was keenly aware that it still needed its elders, who were the foundation of Korean American immigrant society. These were first-generation immigrants who followed North–South relations closely and had left South Korea during the dictatorship-led development phase of the 1960s and '70s, people who had by this time settled down in the States. They had all sorts of jobs—professors, doctors, lawyers, pastors, businessmen, shop owners, technicians, farmers—and what drew them together was Korean churches.

Maybe the only thing that truly made them feel like they belonged somewhere was to meet other Koreans at church once a week.

Yoon Han Bong exerted a persuasive influence on young people from the start of his period of asylum, but the older Korean Americans shunned him. He hadn't been famous and was not even a Christian, much less a pastor. They called him a troublemaking *demo-kkun* (a term akin to today's "paid protestor"), having bought the Korean government's line that the "Gwangju Incident" was no more than a commie riot.

My American visit was special to both of us in many ways. I had credibility as a democracy activist and could vouch for the fact that Yoon Han Bong had been sent to the US by our movement. My name was fairly well known thanks to the serialization of *Jang Gil-san*. As a record keeper of what had happened in Gwangju, I could discuss it with authority, so our appearing together at events was a good opportunity for him to become better known in the Korean American community.

We gave a lecture in LA and toured the country, talking to other Korean American groups. The Korean Resource Center had connections across the US, and we easily attracted audiences in San Francisco, San Jose, Seattle, San Diego, Dallas, Houston, and Denver. After resting in LA, we flew east to New York where more lectures and local talks followed. For the next three months we also toured Philadelphia, Washington, DC, Boston, Chicago, and Detroit. Inspired by our tour, Yoon Han Bong created the One Nation Korean American Alliance with a network of first-generation Korean Americans.

I had known Yoon very well before, but I got to observe him up close during this time. He had certain rules when it came to his life. First of all, he did not consider himself an immigrant but an asylee in exile, and he made no effort to adapt to American life. He did not try to learn English and he did not take on American manners. Second, in deference to the poor and imprisoned in Korea, he did not sleep on a bed but on a futon spread on the floor. Third, he did not spend money on frivolous things. He relied on the funds of the main office and always submitted receipts for housing and meals. Furthermore, he did not want to impose too much on the Korean Americans who put us up while we were on tour, so he tried to use their bathrooms as little as possible. He showered or bathed only once a week.

The Korean Resource Center in LA was a house with a wide backyard that had been donated by a Korean American. Yoon got rid of the grass and planted a vegetable patch instead. He told me that the lettuces, mugwort, perilla leaves, and chilis he grew there halved their spending on food. Many guests who stayed there complained good-naturedly about being woken up early by Yoon to help with watering and weeding the garden. Kim Yong-tae and Yoo Hong-jun, who stayed after I did, made the same joke as me before the table full of greens: that here we were in the Land of Plenty but without a shred of meat or any of the LA *galbi* (marinated ribs) that were so ubiquitous in the city. As Yoon crisscrossed the country meeting people and giving advice, he carried, just as he had in Korea, a small plastic suitcase, like a traveling salesman. It was a dark chestnut color, so that his acquaintances called it "the shit bag," after what appeared to be Hapsu's favorite shade. The case contained underwear, socks, writing implements, a Swiss army knife, nail clippers, and other items that might have come in handy should he have found himself marooned on a desert island. I referred to this as his "prisoner mentality."

At the American PEN Center in New York, we reported on the status of imprisoned writers such as Kim Nam-ju and Lee Gwang-ung and requested solidarity in the efforts to have them freed. We also visited the Human Rights Commission of the American State Department with an American pastor who was a lobbyist at the Korean Church Alliance in DC. We discussed the human rights situation post-Gwangju. We visited the Robert F. Kennedy Human Rights center and the offices of legislators interested in Korea.

Among the Korean Americans I met and came to know well were some who had written about their visits to North Korea. They had family there, had traveled to meet them several times, and had recorded their experiences in a book published in the States that was circulating in South Korea. I wasn't the only one who was moved by this book.

We had finished our tour and were resting when I suggested that a cultural activist group should be established in the US. The first thing I did when I'd gone down to Jeolla Province had been to create such a group to help educate and mobilize people. Yoon Han Bong knew what I was talking about from his years in Gwangju. He approached people at Young Koreans United who might be interested and tried to attract students who could be active in the cultural sphere, even if they weren't members. I decided to write a courtyard play first; I finished it just as we were gathering members and beginning rehearsals. I felt it was necessary to share a "people's history" of the Korean peninsula with audiences, especially younger Korean Americans. The first scene was of Jeon Bong-jun, leader of the 1894 Donghak Peasant Revolution, being tried and executed. The play ended with the citizen uprising and the final night in the provincial administrative building in Gwangju. It was told mostly in *pungmul*-style percussion and dance, with spoken lines compressed as much as possible. The flow followed the structure of a shaman *gut* ritual. We found someone who could choreograph and another who could play *samulnori* drums.

The Young Koreans United New York chapter meeting room became our rehearsal space, and we occupied it for almost a month. Rehearsals were grueling. Students were skipping classes to attend, and members who had jobs either quit or went on leave. They were bound to be penniless by the end of the performance, but fortunately, the Korean American community got wind of this and collected food donations, raised funds, and helped sell tickets. We titled the play *Reunification* Gut: *The Blue Mountain Calls for Us*, and the performance marked the establishment of the Young Koreans United cultural movement group. The members continued to request instructors from Korea to teach them *pungmul*, dance, *talchum* mask dance, folk songs, *pansori* opera, and *gut* rituals, and passed their knowledge on to other youth. They became both artisans and activists. They appeared at international solidarity events and protests, making a joyful racket with their drums and gongs, and quickly became famous. Years later, after I came back to the States from my visit to North Korea, I would attend the performance of the fully matured, professional troupe, now named Binari.

New York was now into winter. Someone came looking for me in the Young Koreans United office in December: Professor Wada Haruki of the University of Tokyo. He had heard that I was in New York and decided to drop by on his way to a conference in DC. Based at the University of Tokyo Institute of Social Science, Wada Haruki was an authority on Russia and North Korea. He had been a student activist as part of the Japanese postwar (Ampo) Struggle generation, had protested against the war in Vietnam, and was now actively supporting the Korean democratization movement. He even chaired the Japan–Korea Solidarity Committee. In short, he was yet another figure held in contempt by the South Korean government. There were quite a few foreign intellectuals similarly labeled as subversives, such as Bruce Cumings, who differed from other American scholars in his view of the Korean division and North Korea, and whose work was banned in South Korea. Wada Haruki asked me to visit Japan on my way back home.

When I arrived in Japan on Christmas Day, Cho Seong-wu, who had been contacted by Yoon Han Bong, was at the airport to greet me. Cho Seong-wu had been imprisoned several times for his involvement in the student movement at Korea University before finally managing to re-enroll and earn his diploma. He was then falsely accused of the serious crime of "conspiracy to commit a rebellion" and was imprisoned again, but by a stroke of good luck was pardoned and went on to continue his studies in Japan. Through Professor Wada Haruki's Japan–Korea Solidarity Committee, I got to meet Japanese writers, journalists, professors, and leaders of citizens' organizations, and attended their talks.

My friends in Japanese civil society have always won my respect with their modesty, work ethic, and dedication. It is my belief that their work not only contributes to peace in Asia but to democracy in Japan. A perpetrator of war in Asia, Japan had managed to rise from the ashes thanks to the sacrifice of Korea's division, but even that success was undermined by the oppressed lives of the Japanese underclass. From Japan's imperial heights to its postwar lows, social change remained an impossible dream. Japan was instead stuck in a never-ending state of "modernization."

Wada Haruki introduced me to Yasue Ryōsuke, the editor of *Sekai* magazine. The Korean Japanese community remember him fondly. Some Koreans who had been dragged overseas through Japanese military conscription or forced migrant labor during the war had managed to return to Korea after Liberation, but many were already settled in Japan and were unable or unwilling to leave. Koreans living in Japan were a united community up until Liberation and national division, both in 1945. Suddenly freed from colonial penury, the Korean Japanese, most of whom belonged to the lower working class, had to find a new place for themselves within Japanese society. They created the Alliance for Korean Japanese People, which, reflecting the ideological division of North and South, soon split into the pro-South "Korean Residents Union in Japan" and the pro-North "General Association of Korean Residents in Japan." For half a century after Liberation, both the North and South Korean governments used the Korean Japanese for political gain without ever doing anything for their brethren in return.

With the transports of Korean Japanese families to North Korea that began in 1959, and the fingerprinting of registered foreigners that began in 1955 and only stopped in 1993, Korean Japanese people began identifying as *Zainichi*. They divided themselves into three nationalities: Republic of Korea (ROK), Democratic People's Republic of Korea (DPRK), and "Joseon," alluding to the Korean peninsula's name prior to Liberation. Intent on waiting for reunification, this third group refused to choose between North and South. As Japan did not have diplomatic ties with North Korea, the Korean Japanese who were either of North Korean nationality or Joseon allegiance were effectively considered temporary residents and subject to all sorts of discrimination, such as being forbidden to travel overseas without first acquiring a re-entry visa. Six hundred thousand Korean Japanese had been divided into Northern and Southern, with 300,000 eventually becoming naturalized Japanese citizens, unable to endure the oppressive discrimination of Japanese society.

I mention this history of the Korean Japanese to explain the deep relationship between Yasue Ryōsuke and Korea. He had worked at the Iwanami Shoten publishing house when young, and was volunteering as an aide in Tokyo governor Minobe Ryokichi's office when he learned the Korean Japanese were trying to establish their own school, so he helped them found Korea University (not to be confused with the school of the same name in Seoul). Some years later, when I visited Japan before my trip to North Korea, I saw that he had become the CEO of Iwanami Shoten, which was a progressive publisher that had been anti-war during World War II and continued being a beacon of peace and good conscience for Japan's intellectuals.

Yasue's interest in Korea began with the 1960 April Revolution, an uprising led by labor and student groups, and continued through the social unrest of the next two decades. From 1973 to 1988, he published a column called "Communiqué from Korea" in *Sekai* written by someone calling himself "TK

Seng." Korean intellectuals of that time may not have known Yasue Ryōsuke, but they did know TK Seng, the faceless Korean who wrote about the things no one in the South Korean media dared mention. Yasue also interviewed Kim Il-sung in North Korea, a first in the history of Japanese journalism. It was, therefore, obvious what the South Korean government thought of him. He maintained good relations with Japan's ruling and opposition parties and cherished a dream about the future of Asia as an Asia-Pacific peace community, a dream which we in Korea were beginning to share with him.

He was very lighthearted and funny in person. When criticizing his enemies, he sounded more like he was chastising a friend who had made a mistake. I never got from him the sharpness that I experienced with other Japanese intellectuals.

Yasue Ryōsuke invited me to lunch one day. When I arrived at the offices of Iwanami Shoten, he introduced me to the novelist Ōe Kenzaburō. I assume he arranged this meeting because he thought that, as a novelist myself, I might enjoy talking to a fellow writer, rather than being limited to conversations with Wada Haruki, who was a sociologist. It was a nice gesture. I was surprised but happy to meet Ōe. Eight years older than me, he was just a boy during World War II. I, meanwhile, had been born in Manchuria and spent my own boyhood during the Korean War after crossing the 38th parallel. I was the first generation after the Japanese occupation to receive a Korean education, and I experienced the student revolution of April 1960. Just as Japan was swept by protests against the security treaty between Japan and the US, Koreans objected to the Korea–Japan talks at around the same time, allowing students and intellectuals of both countries to connect with each other. The Korean War split Korean literary society into North and South, with North Korean literature degenerating into propaganda for Party and leader and South Korean literature reduced to anti-communist screeds or blinkered fictions completely cut off from reality. The April Revolution that deposed President

Rhee Syngman ushered in a spate of foreign books and ideas, and most of what came from the West came through the break-water that is Japan. Around this time, Japan's classical and contemporary literature, including genre works, were being widely translated into Korean and appearing in women's maga-zines, fashion glossies, literary journals, and art periodicals. With foreign publications being imported from Japan, book peddlers and bookstores specializing in these titles proliferated in the small streets off downtown's main thoroughfares, where the cost of rent was a little cheaper and bookstores clustered.

A great variety of world classics collections and series on Western thought were published, as well as dozens of pocket editions. During the postwar years, it was through Japanese contemporary literature that I had my first glimpse of the modernity of a literature open to the world, and it was that window that allowed me to see beyond the society that boxed me in. We used Japan as a stepping stone to jump back and forth between the lives depicted in the faraway West and our interior-ity as it existed on the Korean peninsula. This was part of the process of overcoming our own internalized colonization, as well as the beginnings of a literary magazine movement that attempted to find Korea's own place in the context of world literature.

Ōe Kenzaburō had protested against the Vietnam War and supported incarcerated writers around the world, including Kim Chi-ha, in solidarity with efforts for peace in Asia and Japanese civil society. He was unassuming and of a quiet nature, but remained consistent in his mission and actions as a writer into old age. Ōe once said to me that he envied Koreans for living in a country so rich in narrative. I probably answered with something cynical, along the lines of "That's just a nice way of saying we've had nothing but trouble." I added that I envied Japan's freedom. Ōe demurred: "We're not strong at all, we're just getting by from day to day." He and his wife had a child with a developmental disorder, he added, and daily life was not easy. But it was also this child that motivated him to keep on working at his literary career. His quiet words moved me deeply and I was ashamed of my cynical retort.

I felt the need to visit the Kansai region, which was in many ways a more important place to the Korean Japanese than Tokyo. I went on a tour of Kyoto, Kobe, and Nara while based in Osaka, giving talks sponsored by Japanese civil groups. Yang Kwan Soo, who was married to a second-generation Korean Japanese and studying for his PhD, contacted Cho Seong-wu and together the two of them organized everything for me. During his student years at Seoul National University, Yang had been imprisoned for demonstrating against President Park Chung-hee. He'd gone abroad before the Gwangju Democracy Movement, but as his home was in the same province as Gwangju, he always felt guilty about how he lived in comfort and safety far away from it all. He had brought together a group of students who were proficient in Korean to translate *The Kwangju Uprising* into Japanese. The book was already being circulated by Korean Japanese civil groups on both the left and the right, as well as through local organizations. Each region's talk naturally arranged itself around the Gwangju Democracy Movement.

I worried that the Korean government would never let me get away with engaging in political activity in Japan. But when I thought of the people of Gwangju, I shook off my fear. I couldn't shirk the responsibility of revealing the truth behind Gwangju, just as I couldn't ask someone else to put the book of testimonials together.

In the audience were many people who had read the book and many who hadn't, but every talk turned into a moment of sadness and anger. There's one question in particular—an ordinary one, perhaps—that has stayed with me. What did I think of North Korea after twenty years of post-Liberation division? To a Korean, answering this question in a public space presents a conundrum: do I answer according to my conscience, like someone professing an unpopular religious faith, or do I prevaricate? At the very least, I couldn't choose one side and *not* heavily criticize the other. My other option was to avoid answering altogether, which no one would have minded. The audience was well aware of Korea's National Security Act.

But I did answer. "I'm not pro-division. But I've never been to North Korea myself, so I can't really talk about it. The only real answer I can give you is that my writing and I are products of South Korean history and that South Korea is my destiny."

The person who had asked the question suddenly shouted: "So you'll spend the rest of your life accepting division? If a writer from the motherland gives up like this, what are we supposed to do, living as outsiders in this foreign country?"

The moderator, Yang Kwan Soo, managed to smooth things over and move on to the next question. My answer was a canned response I'd developed in Berlin. Another hand shot up to ask why I was so thoroughly negative about South Korea but unwilling to voice a single criticism of North Korea. I answered without hesitation that I wasn't criticizing South Korea per se but the military dictatorship that ruled it. Having seized power through a coup d'état, they were not the government of the people. I had never been to North Korea and knew nothing about it, so there was nothing I could really criticize. I asked him if he was implying that I should visit North Korea. The questioner's face went red with fury, but he sat down in silence and the audience burst into applause.

"So you'll spend the rest of your life accepting division?"

I thought about this question for a long time. I had never really accepted division as permanent. But it was true that I had attempted nothing, and let my fear of the National Security Act limit my activities and actions and writing. Was it enough, to avoid "praising" the North Korean regime, to say that communism was evil and that we had to destroy the communists if we wanted reunification? I thought of the people who had died in both North and South during the Korean War, the people who had broken the taboo of this border and were imprisoned or executed, and all the people in Gwangju who died while demanding democracy. If I did not try to cross this border myself, then I was not a writer. I wasn't anything.

In order to adapt our American performance of *Reunification Gut: The Blue Mountain Calls for Us* to the Japanese stage, we created a preparation committee, led by Lee Hoesung, filled with Koreans of different nationalities and Japanese activists. We did a press conference for publicity and started to assemble young performers. The sole requirement was to be a Korean Japanese resident of any nationality. We borrowed the space of the Japanese troupe Kuro Tento and opened an audition where about a hundred Korean Japanese showed up.

We were accepting of any Korean with an appreciation for Korean culture, and so we picked the cast based on passion and talent, and the rest who wanted to volunteer were hired as stagehands. We became a family of fifty. Some of the young members had come from as far away as Osaka and Kyoto.

Before going into rehearsal, we held a ceremony where we hung a sign that said "Uri Cultural Center" (Our Cultural Center) by the office door. We decided to call our group Hanuri ("One Us") after the composition of our group. Osaka's Yang Kwan Soo was also readying the launch of another Uri Cultural Center. In the Kansai region, the organization would stretch from Osaka to Kyoto, Nara, and Kobe. After two months of practice, the Tokyo performance was held for four days in March at the Japanese Trade Union Confederation auditorium. There was an unprecedented spring snowfall on opening night and traffic was jammed, but the auditorium was packed. The stage was on the same level as the audience, and there was practically no division between players and watchers, much like it had been in Korea, where the traveling troupes would simply find an empty spot in a factory or village and put on a show.

The lobby of the auditorium was bustling with all sorts of civic groups handing out pamphlets and newsletters. After every performance we danced a festive *nanjangchum* with the audience and shared ceremonial rice cakes, meat from a roasted pig's head, and *makgeolli* rice brew. These performances continued in Osaka and Kyoto. A kind of "reunification shaman *gut* ritual" was being held all over Japan.

I could sense a yearning for change in Japan. Though it was much freer than Korea, people did not feel that they'd achieved a mature form of democracy. Since the Meiji Restoration a hundred years before, Japan could say it had gained the appearance of modernization, but this modernity had not come from below, through the values of freedom, human rights, and equality, but from above—through a fascism centered around the monarchy. Since its imperialist days, Japan's power and capital were concentrated in the elite, and it managed to rebuild its economy by leaning on America's Cold War tactics in East Asia. Japanese democracy itself had not been achieved by its people, but was granted to them by the American occupying forces. Never having had a chance to confront its national shame and use it as an opportunity for inner growth, Japan's twisted modernity was headed toward a society that was dangerous even to itself. Its strong ruling party, which never gave up power, ruled the country unchallenged for decades, and its press, while seemingly free, never managed to cross a certain limit. Korea's developmental dictatorship in pursuit of capitalist modernization tried hard to catch up with Japan, but because of national division, Korea and Japan ended up on very different trajectories.

~

I returned to Korea on May 9, 1986. My activist friends Lee Myoung-jun, Choi Yeol, and others were waiting at the gate, as they were worried I'd be taken away, but the ANSP arrested me anyway and took me to their headquarters on Nam Mountain in Seoul. There, with the Council of Writers for Freedom and Practice holding a protest right outside, I was grilled about my activities in Europe, America, and Japan over the past year. The PEN International annual congress was being held in Hamburg at the time, and as there were German, American, and Japanese writers in attendance with whom I'd become acquainted, the conference turned into a "Free Hwang Sok-yong" movement. Unlike the PEN branches in other countries, PEN Korea tends to take a government-propaganda line to this day, to say nothing of what they were like back then. When the chair of PEN Korea, Jeon Sook-hee, declared that "Hwang Sok-yong is being investigated for political, not literary reasons," an enraged Günter Grass, the chair of PEN West Germany, leaped onto the stage and grabbed the microphone from her. Perhaps because of this international support, or the government's unwillingness to stir up any trouble regarding Gwangju, I was not charged and ended up being released.

When we were preparing for our performance in America, I had hired Kim Myoung-su to teach us Korean music and dance. She was a graduate of the Martha Graham School and was active in the US. She had learned ballet as a child and modern dance in college, and after graduating had apprenticed in Korean dances such as *seungmu, salpuri,* and *taepyeongmu*. With her knowledge of Korean rhythms and traditional courtyard narratives, she had helped make our courtyard play in New York a success. For our "reunification *gut*" performance in Japan, Cho Seong-wu invited her to help make that event a success as well. She and I worked closely together for another six months there, during which our friendly relationship turned into a romantic one.

When the Japan performance was over, our colleagues worried that we'd be arrested as soon as we returned to South Korea. We put our heads together and decided it would be safer for Kim Myoung-su to go back first, as all she was guilty of was helping us with choreography. I would follow after a good interval of time. When she arrived in Korea, everything seemed quiet. Later I heard that she wasn't taken in for interrogation, but asked to come to a downtown café to answer some questions from a CIA agent. That was the extent of her troubles.

I emerged from the basement of the ANSP headquarters and went home to Gwangju for the first time in a year. Hong Hee-yun greeted me warmly as if nothing had happened. But the next day, when the children had gone to school and we were alone, she informed me that she knew about me and Kim Myoung-su. She said she'd been contemplating divorce for the past year, and wanted to focus her energies on the children: our daughter Yeo-jeong was still in elementary school, but our son Ho-jun was a middle-school student and entering the sensitive waters of adolescence.

I told her the honest truth about Kim Myoung-su. The rumor confirmed, disappointment and devastation deepened on her face. I felt like the world's biggest fool—or maybe it was closer to despair, a sense that things had played out beyond my control. It wasn't in me to make dramatic denials, and had she wanted a temporary separation, with me retreating into the countryside alone to write for six months, I would have been up for it. But now that she had reached a decision, after so much worrying and suffering over a man who was always wandering about and unable to be a responsible husband to one woman, she didn't want to change her mind.

The children were very happy to have me in the house after my long absence. Hong Hee-yun stopped talking to me and wordlessly gave me my meals before retreating into the bedroom alone. Soon I couldn't bear it any longer and accepted her proposal. I should have tried harder to understand her. I knew that giving me the silent treatment was the only way she could control her feelings of betrayal and anger and resentment, but I was weak.

We agreed that the proceeds from my most lucrative work, *Jang Gil-san*, would go to the family, and I would move out.

Hong Hee-yun got the divorce paperwork and we filled it out before going to the courts together. The judge reviewed our papers in a dry, bureaucratic fashion, confirmed that we both consented to the divorce, and registered our application. Throughout the whole process he spoke down to us in *banmal*, the informal form of Korean, which left me barely able to suppress my anger. Hong revealed her own anger in a consoling way by saying, as we left the building: "That's how they let us know what they really think of us."

Before moving out again, I went to the public baths with my son Ho-jun. He was grown now, and I didn't have to wash him anymore like I did when he was little. I explained to him as we walked down the street together that his mother and I were parting and that he needed to protect his sister and his mother now. Ho-jun had had little patience as a child. My son asked if I was really leaving, and whether he would ever see me again. I said that I was going to live apart from them but would visit from time to time. I also told him that I loved both him and his sister.

As I packed a few of my things, Hong Hee-yun said she would send me the rest along with my books when I knew for sure where I'd be living. She tried to seem indifferent but when I looked back at the house before turning at the end of the alley, I saw that she had come to the gate and was watching me. That's how I left my family. It was 1986, the summer of our fifteenth year of marriage.

A month later, the painter Hong Seong-dam contacted me. He was such a close friend that, at home, my children called him Uncle. Seong-dam took down my new address, and a moving van arrived that evening. All of my books, notes, albums, and furniture had been carefully packed; Hee-yun was ever the perfectionist. I was seeing Seong-dam off at the entrance to my apartment building when he suddenly grabbed my arm and burst into tears, saying that he thought it was only a marital spat and how could I do this to my family. After he left and I was back inside, putting my things away, I noticed that Hee-yun had cut her image out of all our framed photos and albums. That gave me pause for a long time. She so wanted to be erased from my memory, and now I had to begin living a new life.

2

Prison I

There was another month of interrogations when the Agency for National Security Planning handed me over to the Prosecutor's Office in mid-May, after which I was finally able to take a breather in the detention center. I'd been arrested as soon as I got off the plane on April 27, 1993, and already I was entering my third month as a detainee. Prison life so far had consisted of being summoned immediately after breakfast to be handcuffed and have my arms and legs bound for good measure with rope, in preparation for transport to the Prosecutor's Office along with other detainees for more questioning. Though I was already familiar with the route, which led from Seoul Detention Center past the Seoul National University of Education intersection and up the hill towards the Prosecutor's Office, everything looked different through the grille covering the bus windows. The crowds waiting to cross the street and the young people taking smoking breaks in front of office buildings looked like scenes from a movie, like they lived in some other world that I could never be a part of.

The prosecutors went over every line in my statement for the ANSP, trying to squeeze out as many allegations as possible. I mostly answered yes to all their questions, but sometimes they went too far. Around the time the ANSP was nearly finished with their interrogation, a night-shift investigator came to see me. He said he had a favor to ask and presented me with pen and paper. He wanted me to write down general information on certain activists in the opposition group, the National Association for Democratic Activism (Jeonminryeon). With his short stature and soft voice, I couldn't help thinking that he would have made a great elementary school teacher. I asked him what he was going to do with the information, and he said it was just for himself, a souvenir. The request was so unusual that it threw me off a bit, since I knew so little about them that I couldn't recall a single name. But then I remembered seeing a few activists profiled in a newsmagazine when I was living in New York: Lee Bu-young, a former reporter with a gentle demeanor and a strong intellect; Kim Geun-tae, a democratic youth group organizer with firm principles but generous in his leadership; and Chang Ki-pyo, who had quick political reflexes and a deep understanding of mainstream activism. I wrote down a couple of lines for each person, but the investigator pushed for fuller profiles. I refused, as the official interrogation was over and I was only waiting at that point to be taken to the Prosecutor's Office. The mild-mannered investigator badgered me for a long time before giving up. But when I got to the Prosecutor's Office, I found that this "souvenir" had been entered into my statement as part of a nonexistent interview with the North Koreans during my visit. I forcefully objected to this fraud.

The prosecutor became irritated at my tone.

—You've said worse things on record, so why do you care? You told them Korea has a thousand nuclear warheads or something.

—I said that because I didn't want to see two countries of the same nation annihilate each other. And everything I said is public knowledge and printed in newspapers.

—It's still minor compared to what you're really being accused of.

My North Korean visit was being milked by the prosecution so that they could wield every last statute of the National Security Act against me. Moreover, the simple fact that I had been spokesperson of the Pan-Korea Alliance for Reunification was being interpreted as my founding a terrorist organization under North Korean orders.

Exhausted, I gave in. *Fine, execute me, that's what you really want.* I didn't learn until much later, during my trial, that writing these character profiles fell under the National Security Act's "dissemination of secrets" statute, constituting the clearest evidence of espionage.

My days consisted of three meals and up to one visitor and attorney's consultation a day, plus an hour of exercise. I had a team of three lawyers headed by Park Sung-kwi, who took care of my welfare in the detention center and kept my family and colleagues informed of any progress. I got to know Park Sung-kwi when he tapped me as a witness for the publisher Na Byung-sik, who had printed my Gwangju book and was later arrested for his publication of *Hanguk minjungsa* (A People's History of Korea). Park Sung-kwi initially had nothing to do with political activism but was a loyal and trustworthy friend from Na's home in Jeolla Province. Park didn't really have political leanings despite the cases he took, and though sharp as a tack when it came to defending clients, he knew so little of the activist sphere that I had to explain to him who everyone was. No lawyer in his right mind wanted to take on a National Security Act case, as there was almost no way to win against the state and it only hurt your reputation. Park however was steadfast and did everything by the book, qualities that never changed the entire time I was detained. My new wife, Kim Myoung-su, who had remained in the States, had hired Park after Na Byung-sik's recommendation and paid his fees on my behalf.

Another lawyer on my team, Han Seung-heon, was the first to come running to demand an interview when I was arrested by the ANSP. He was a famous human rights lawyer and later headed the Board of Audit and Inspection during Kim Dae-jung's administration. Han took on National Security Act cases of every magnitude and had even been arrested in court by the

military dictatorship. He specialized in Korean Japanese defen-
dants with mainland connections, who had been visiting Korea
for study or tourism and ended up falsely accused as spies under
the act. He volunteered for my defense and even cracked a joke
at our first interview: "The National Security Act is unbeatable,
which is why everyone calls me the Sure Loser. But at least I
might get you a lighter sentence." We both laughed.

Park Won-soon, who would later become mayor of Seoul,
also aided me pro bono. I knew him from before his Institute for
Korean Historical Studies days. Two months into his freshman
year at Seoul National University, upperclassmen brought him
to his first protest. The protest leaders gave rousing speeches to
get everyone fired up and then advanced toward the school gates
with the lower-year students positioned at the front, as per
tradition. Park was among them, of course. As soon as they
started to move, the riot police, who'd been waiting for them at
the school gates, cut into the crowd and threw the students at
the front into police buses. These fifty or so students were
expelled to set an example. Park Won-soon had been hoping to
declare as a law major but found himself kicked out of school
with a criminal record instead. Reflecting on it later, he had to
ask himself why he'd joined the protest in the first place and
why he had to be expelled. Deciding he needed to learn more
about history, he entered Dankook University as a history major
and later took the bar and became a prosecutor. Not long after,
he opened his own legal practice. He took on human rights
cases and founded the Institute for Korean Historical Studies
and the People's Solidarity for Participatory Democracy, as well
as the Beautiful Foundation. He stayed with me for a time when
I was in exile in Berlin and New York, unconcerned about what
others might have thought.

Lawyers like Han Seung-heon and Park Won-soon wrote
books about how the National Security Act went against democratic principles and human rights and called for its abolishment.
The ANSP would quote Socrates during interrogations, saying

"Harsh is the law, but it is the law," whenever the subject of the National Security Act came up. But the act still persisted through the introduction of two democratically elected administrations. This warped framework branded anyone speaking out against it as a "North Korea–loving commie." Both the United Nations and the US State Department have recommended striking down the act for years, on grounds that its statutes provide too much scope for abuse. The excuse of a North Korean threat seems outdated, now that South Korea has far outpaced its neighbor in terms of political and economic success. If anything, repealing the act would further highlight South Korea's advanced democracy compared to the system in the North. Current criminal codes dealing with national security are sufficient, and this separate act needs to be struck down to prevent political abuse in the future.

Han Seung-heon and Park Won-soon each attended the trial, but Park Sung-kwi was the one who visited me every week. My literary friends also came, and politicians visited under special privileges. Many who came to the detention center were turned away, because each detainee was allowed only one visitor a day.

If I didn't have anything else to do in the afternoons, I'd be called up by a special division that used to undertake the political conversion of leftist activists but by that time simply managed the political detainees. When National Assembly legislators came to meet me, they usually allowed us the privilege of using this special division's office. A guard with a three-hibiscus insignia was in charge. He was said to be a rigidly devout Protestant and an elder of some church. The first time we met, he asked me to allow him a moment to pray for my soul. I'd grown up in a Christian household, so this imposition didn't bother me. I even mumbled "Amen" after him when he was done. When I was sentenced to life after my first trial, he clasped both my hands and genuinely tried to comfort me, calling upon God to give me strength, and I was sincerely moved, even though I hadn't been fearing or despairing of the future—to be honest,

I couldn't at the time fathom having to spend the rest of my life in prison.

If the government had let me write while detained, my sentence would have been much more bearable. I had nothing to fear as long as I had pen and paper. But that was wishful thinking on my part.

The *Hankyoreh* newspaper printed an op-ed on June 29, 1993, describing the international movement led by PEN chapters around the world to free me from jail. By August, I had heard that a committee devoted to my release had indeed been founded, consisting of 412 artists, politicians, and activists. They also petitioned for the repeal of the National Security Act, the pardoning of conscientious objectors, and the right for political prisoners to write and engage in activism. My record of my North Korean visit, *Sarami salgo isseonne* (They're Just like Us), was also published. The 60th PEN International Congress was held in Spain from September 6 to 12 under the theme "Roads of Literature." There, the representatives unanimously voted on a resolution to campaign for my release. They declared that the Korean government needed to stop persecuting me with the National Security Act for what had been a sincere effort toward peaceful reunification.

I had the absurd expectation early on that I would be allowed to write in detention. Had that been the case, then my cell would not have been a place of confinement but a space of unfettered imagination, free from the tedious distractions of daily life. After all, look at all the classics, from both East and West, that were written in prison. But decades of military rule had left Korea's prisons devoid of paper and pens, let alone freedom to write. Even letters to our family had to be written on single sheets of regulation stationery that folded into envelopes. We would fill them to the margins with the aid of arrows and tiny writing. Any paper we wanted for statements or appeals had to be bought, a ream of twenty red-lined pages at a time, and if you ran out, you had to purchase more separately. We were given a single Monami ballpoint pen with the guard's name stamped on it. This meant that if the pen was discovered elsewhere, the guard would be held responsible. The only time we could use the pen was from after lunch until the guards changed shifts in the evening. The pens were then retrieved and locked away in a desk drawer in the guards' room. Writing was strictly forbidden beyond letters home and documents submitted to the courts. I had to give up my daydream of our new civilian government reforming the prisons and granting us the freedom to write. Once I was transferred to prison, I went on a twenty-day hunger strike for the right to write, but to no avail, or at least, not in any meaningful way. It was true that I'd been more of an activist than a writer during my four years of exile after visiting North Korea, but they understood very well that preventing a writer from writing was a punishment in itself.

The guards' room at the entrance of each cell block was like a gatehouse built into the corridor. The guards, or corrections officers, took shifts in there. The rank insignia of the regular corrections officers bore two leaves, while the senior corrections officers' insignia bore three. The ones on the day shift during the week were all senior guards. The ones who fetched us for visitors' meetings or took us out to the yard for exercise were regular guards, who also took the night shifts. A senior guard oversaw an entire block and was assisted by a group of regular guards. Past the block and through the big corridors that connected each block was another small office. This housed the chief inspector, with two hibiscuses on his insignia. One rank below them were the regular inspectors with their single hibiscus. A group of blocks was called a jurisdiction. Each detainee's cell was referred to by its jurisdiction, block, and cell number, with this number stitched on one side of their uniform and their prisoner number on the other for easy identification. I happened to be locked up with many famous political and white-collar criminals, probably for easier management.

My cell had formerly belonged to the poet Park Nohae, detained here before his sentencing for being part of the Socialist Labor League of South Korea. I recognized many of the people I bumped into in the halls: seemingly every politician, university president, and retired general who'd been showing up in the news. According to the jailers, there had been so many political prisoners up until the last administration that sometimes the prisoners would visit each other, and prison reform seemed imminent. But now that we had a civilian government, it was like the end of a party. The guards predicted that life in prison would soon return to normal.

We usually think of political prisoners as activists, arrested for demanding change or for struggling against the government, but by and large the detention center also treated as political prisoners the ruling-party stalwarts who'd been arrested for corruption. We were all lumped in together, probably for administrative convenience, but the detention center employees looked at it more simply. They joked with me that, left or right, we had all broken the law and were thieves. As political prisoners, we were kept away from the other inmates to avoid "indoctrinating" them, so I had no choice but to share the exercise yard with a bunch of right-wing criminals. And whenever we had a court appearance, or even when we simply had a visitor or our lawyers had come to see us, we were taken out in groups. Whether I liked it or not, I had to cross paths with a politician or a corrupt businessman at least once a day.

One time, I was sent to the visiting room along with the former defense minister, Lee Sang-hoon. He was a stout man who looked up at me and said:

—If you like North Korea so much, why did you come back?

I knew he wasn't genuinely curious. I wasn't angry, and my reply was sincere.

—I went to North Korea for the sake of South Korea. Because I'm South Korean.

He had nothing to say to that, but I doubt he understood what I meant. The guards told me his wife came to see him every day. They would return him to his cell along with a stacked lunch box all wrapped up in a cloth, which they referred to as a special care package. That was what we called a "foul" in our prison terminology. I wish there were a more satisfying word to refer to someone that two-faced, but I'll settle for call-ing him a *yangban*, like an arrogant civil-military official from the Joseon dynasty. Another person I thought of as a two-faced *yangban* was the former head of the Supreme Prosecutors' Office. He was rude to the guards and antagonized all of them. Whenever he went out to the exercise yard, detainees in the other blocks would start shouting his name and cursing him. The guards would run up to the cells and shout right back, rais-ing quite the ruckus, but when this kept happening, he was given his own special exercise time.

Among the detainees who made a lasting impression on me was former defense minister Lee Jong-gu, a dyed-in-the-wool soldier. He never slouched or equivocated, but was straight as an arrow all the time. I often rode in the bus with him on the way to court. He once told me:

—I may be a soldier, but I'm against war. Even *The Art of War* says it's best to avoid war.

For a soldier like him to slip up made it clear to me just how flawed the Korean military was. In fact, a slew of starred generals were thrown in jail after the civilian government took power. Talking to former and current navy and air force chiefs of staff and a commander in the marines left me feeling anxious on their behalf as they awaited their sentence. I remember once, when Lee Jong-gu and I were on our way to court, he lifted his handcuffed wrists and offered me his hand, which I automatically shook.

—It seems this is where we part ways. I'm pretty sure this is my last day in detention. Please take care of yourself, and I hope to see you on the outside.

He was released that day on probation.

Kim Chong-in, unlike most other detainees, wore a traditional *hanbok* outfit printed with a funny pattern. He spent his exercise hour kicking a volleyball against the wall. If I kicked the ball back to him, he often stumbled, his foot slicing the empty air. I once stroked the tunic of his *hanbok* and joked:

—Why, isn't this silk?

He answered with mock pride:

—Only the finest from my family!

I'd bought a *hanbok* from the commissary myself. Our normal blue uniforms were fine for spring and summer, but in the winter it was cold even with a sweater on underneath. At least the gray trousers and white tunics of the official prison *hanbok* were warmly padded with cotton.

One day, I saw him sitting off to the side while the others were basking in a sunlit patch in the corner. I wondered aloud:

—Isn't he kicking his ball today?

Someone replied that he had just received a five-year sentence. Seeing him there alone with his back turned made me feel bad for him, so I went and sat with him. The prosecution was seeking a life sentence in my case, so I was hardly in a position to try to console someone else, but I carefully suggested to him that his sentence would probably be reduced. Surely by half, I added, judging from what happened to other inmates. Indeed, his sentence was reduced to two and a half years before he was transferred to prison. I went out to the yard one day and was told he was gone.

Years later, a mere week after I had been released from my own five-year sentence, I bumped into him at a bar in Insa-dong. "Well, look who it is," said a tipsy Kim, but I didn't recognize him at first. I wasn't pretending, either. I honestly didn't recognize him, which is why I cautiously asked, "How do we know each other?" He just grinned and left the bar. Only later when I came to my senses did I realize it had been Kim Chong-in. I remember Kim and his volleyball to this day, but even I needed some time to readjust to the outside.

~

In the winter I was moved to the southeast block—I think because it got more sunlight. The jurisdiction chief and the middle-management guards all seemed to like me, and while they claimed it was because they'd read my books, I apparently had a reputation for getting along with regular and political prisoners alike, making no fuss, and being good for morale in my block. This was probably thanks to the regular guards who spoke well of me. One of the ways the guards did us favors was to leave our cell doors open so that we could hang out in the hallways, the washroom, or around the guardroom. After being locked up all day in less than a *pyeong* of space only to learn that your one hour of scheduled exercise had been canceled due to rain, you'd find yourself pacing restlessly in your tiny cell. According to the guards, the lawyer Lee Don-myoung used to get heart palpitations and would kick the door and scream that he couldn't breathe.

An even bigger favor from the guards would be when one of them opened the food hole and passed on a lit cigarette before silently disappearing. Smokers used to joke that "smoking after a meal isn't a matter of digestion, it's to prevent sudden death," which was how much we craved a smoke after eating. In prison, we called cigarettes "puppies," matches "heads," the striking surface "the floor," and the flame "a flower." Penniless detainees were "dog hairs" and rich ones "tiger hairs." Dog hairs had to use the batteries from the electric shavers sold in the commissary to create a flower, while tiger hairs flagrantly used disposable lighters. These lighters were hidden in a "safe" inside the floor. Once or twice a month, the jurisdiction would designate a cell block for room searches. If an inmate was caught with something, he was moved to a different room. The common prisoners hated to be moved, because hierarchy in their shared cells was determined by how long they'd been there. Moving meant starting over again from the bottom.

Cigarettes were the most prized commodities in prison. A pack usually cost around 100,000 won, but the price went up to

200,000 whenever a crackdown compromised the supply. A carton easily fetched 1 million or even 2 million won. The next most precious commodity was the "pigeon." This was a mode of communication in which information too confidential to be shared during attorney visits was passed on afterward to family members or co-conspirators. The guards passed these messages back and forth between the prisoners and people on the outside. Since every piece of communication in the detention center was censored, pigeons were invaluable. The price went up to several million won depending on the urgency and importance of the message. These days, guards lending their cell phones to detainees are the new pigeons. Later, when I was in Gongju Correctional Institution, all of the guards, from the officers all the way down to the lowest-ranking, ended up being punished because a mob boss had been using their cell phones to call outside.

Getting moved to the infirmary wing or even out to a civilian hospital was possible if you had money, making prison a microcosm of capitalist society. The principal of an exclusive Gangnam high school was occupying the cell next to mine. He'd been arrested after he made the airwaves for putting his wife on the board of directors, oppressing the teachers and students, and committing all manner of fraud. I had no interest in him and wouldn't have known who he was if the guards hadn't kept talking about how he had stolen pocket money from children. Night after night, he would pound on his door until the night shift guard came running, and then he would shout at him about how he felt like he was having a heart attack.

One time he saw me receive a visit from a National Assembly member. Using the window of his cell, he called me over and asked how well I knew my visitor. He begged me to introduce him, as the National Assembly member was apparently on the education committee. I answered that while I knew him, I was hardly in a position to introduce him, and asked why he needed his help. He went on and on about how difficult it was to run a school and that his heart condition was very serious and that he was desperate to be under house arrest instead of detention while awaiting trial. I knew he was being disingenuous, but he made such an annoying racket and he just seemed so pathetic that I decided to give him some advice. Unless he was somehow cleared of all charges, the only way he could leave was to be at death's door. And the fastest way to destroy your health, according to what I'd seen of prison life, was to starve. A week of fasting weakens you and changes the way you look. Do that, I told him, and the center's doctor would diagnose him with the heart condition he kept yammering on about. He would need that diagnosis to get moved to the infirmary wing. As for making it out of there to a civilian hospital, he'd have to figure that part out himself.

He listened carefully to my advice and from the next day on I heard nothing more out of him, other than the occasional plea that he was too sick to eat, and sure enough after a week he was moved to the infirmary wing. I don't know if he managed to get out of there or not, but I did read in the papers long after I was transferred to prison that he was alive and well and suing for control over his school.

One night, a guard in his twenties pushed one of my short story collections through the food hole and asked me to sign it. I did, including a little note, and after that he dropped by now and then at night to chat with me through the food hole. His home was in Gwangju. He knew that I had lived there and in Haenam. He seemed surprised that I wasn't from Haenam myself, that I'd been born in Manchuria but had grown up in Seoul since the age of four. The young guard had taken the Level 9 civil service exam after high school and was just two years into his job. He was enrolled in Korea National Open University and told me he was going to change jobs as soon as he graduated. He wanted to become a teacher. Nowadays the Level 9 civil service exam is as competitive as the bar exam, but back then a prison guard did not make much money and was tied to military-style rules and interminable night shifts. He liked my books, so I contacted my publisher and had them send over the ten-volume set of *Jang Gil-san*, which I signed for him. He was so delighted that he slipped me a full pack of cigarettes. To have an entire pack was, in the parlance of prison, "a light sentence." But he didn't have the means to get me a "flower," so I had no way to light my smokes. Being locked up in a cell is like having no hands or feet.

Each cell block had a designated *soji*, whose origins dated to the Japanese occupation era—even the Japanese pronunciation of the term was still in use, rather than the Korean *soje*. The *soji* cleaned, distributed meals, and delivered commissary purchases. They tended to be young, jailed for relatively minor offences, with shorter terms. The *soji* were free to roam up and down the corridors and were not restricted as to the number of cells they could visit, a kind of power in itself, but more than anything, they could tip the guards off about anything going on in their block. The detainees bribed the *soji* by buying them underwear or food from the commissary. Since the detention centers had more of these goods than prisons did, this was a chance for *soji*, who were invariably dog hairs, to stock up before transferring.

Since I was a political prisoner in a private cell, I never needed to curry favor with them; if anything, they had to behave themselves around me. Pro-democracy activists tended to wield more moral power than the warden, which made us unwelcome in any block. Death row inmates were likewise given private cells and kept at arm's length by everyone else. Each block's entrance had four private cells side by side where death row inmates, political prisoners, and notorious white-collar offenders were held. There happened to be two death row inmates next door to my own cell.

I summoned a *soji* and discreetly asked him how I could obtain a flower. His eyes lit up and he asked if I had a puppy. I said I did, and he said he would tell me how if I gave him half of it. I snapped one in half without hesitation and gave it to him. He gave me something that felt like hairs from a paintbrush.

They were fibers from a piece of steel wool used for washing dishes.

—You know those electric razors? Take out the battery and touch the ends of this to the plus and minus signs. You'll get a spark. Use that to light it.

He gave me some extra advice.

—You can make them last longer if you split up the tobacco and roll it really thinly in pieces of toilet paper. You get four sticks out of one that way.

He said that it would be hard to light them by holding them directly to a flame and that I should pinch the end of the toilet paper into a wick first and light that. Some of the other detainees bought an English dictionary at the commissary and used its pages to roll cigarettes. When I tried it myself, the spark lit the wick in one try. It had been so long since my last cigarette that the first inhalation immediately plunged my brain into a dreamlike state and my arms and legs went limp. In prison we called that "going to Hong Kong." Back then, Hong Kong was considered the finest foreign destination among Koreans. The slang used in Seodaemun Prison during the days of martial law under Park Chung-hee had followed us into Seoul Detention Center and was still current.

In any case, I could make four cigarettes out of one, and smoking them made a whole month fly by. My endless stream of visiting friends brought books for me, and my life in detention grew much calmer as I passed the time reading the classics that I hadn't got to before. But once I ran out of cigarettes, I became more anxious than I'd ever been outside. Smoking had become my one true happiness by then. At a meeting with my lawyer Park Sung-kwi, my hand automatically reached into his suit pocket and stole his cigarettes. "Hey, if you get caught I'm done for," he said. Nevertheless, he slipped me a lighter, too, and advised that this was my chance to quit cold turkey. Those cigarettes helped extend my lease on my addiction, and even the *soji* got a cig or two thanks to me. When they ran out, I kept nagging my *soji* about finding me some more. One day, he brought me a butt and told me how lucky he'd been to find it. The guards were not allowed to smoke inside the cell block, but I knew that they secretly smoked in their bathroom near the entrance to the corridors. Some of them didn't throw the butts out the window but dropped them on the floor instead. The one he gave me still had half the tobacco left in it, but he warned it was drenched.

As he'd instructed, I peeled open the cigarette butt and spread the remaining tobacco on top of a plastic container filled with hot water to dry overnight. In the morning it was crisp and curly, and I wrapped it, lit up, and took a puff. It smelled terrible. I can only assume it had been soaked in piss. I was disgusted with myself. I dropped the rest of the cigarette into the toilet and flushed it. I decided then and there to quit smoking, and I managed to stay strong for the rest of my time in prison. I learned later that political detainees' nicotine cravings were often exploited. It was rumored that clever guards would provide or confiscate cigarettes to manipulate the mood of each block and cell. And once a political detainee became dependent on those cigarettes, he would stop agitating for prisoners' rights or better treatment.

There was another infraction that many political detainees were familiar with: moonshine. All you needed was a pack of Yakult, some sliced bread from the commissary, some pills called Wonkiso that were used as digestive aids, and vitamins from the pharmacy. (Back then, you could buy all manner of things from the commissary, but a year after the civilian government took power, the selection was reduced in the name of preventing corruption; we joked that our sentences had "doubled," as our food became limited to regulation tray food.) First you wet the bread and put it on a sunny windowsill until mold grew. Then you placed that mold in an empty plastic bottle, filled it the rest of the way with the Yakult, and threw in a couple of Wonkiso pills. Then you corked the bottle loosely with tissue paper and left it by the toilet for about five days until it fermented into a sweet-and-sour brew. An incarcerated student I talked to through our windows by our toilets advised me not to throw away the dregs in the bottom but to use it as a starter to make more, a method that saves much time and effort. If you put some in a can of grape juice, you eventually end up with actual wine.

Just as we spent the first half of the year marking each major resistance anniversary—March 1, April 19, May 18, and August 15—with shouting and hunger strikes, we always took time to commiserate with or congratulate those who had just come into detention, were being transferred to prison, or were being released, by singing together. Then we would drink whatever moonshine we'd managed to create, and while it wasn't as strong as what was available outside, the rare taste of alcohol was enough to get us flushed and tipsy. This was the kind of sentimental thing that was only possible in detention, because once you got to normal prison, all bets were off.

I must have moved cells three times while in detention. They always put me into the third cell from the entrance of each block. The fourth cell was right next to the regular detainees, with whom they didn't want me to have contact. And the first and second cells were close to the guards' rooms, which was too close for comfort for either of us. There was a small lavatory next to the guards' room and a fairly spacious washroom. The regular detainees had a full shower once a week. The shower room was also where the *soji* washed dishes and stored their cleaning implements. Next to the bathroom was the first private cell, the second one, and then mine. They normally put death row inmates into the first and second, with political prisoners in the third and white-collar crime detainees in the fourth. The remaining cells along the corridor were group cells for regular detainees. Each room had a window, high enough so that you couldn't see into the windows of the other blocks. The regular detainees would talk to each other while doing dishes or on their way back from the exercise yard. You could also talk to the cells above and below through the window over your toilet. The guards overlooked most of these conversations, but if the jurisdiction officers showed up or it was getting too loud, they'd stick their own heads out of a window and growl at us about cell-to-cell communication being grounds for punishment.

There were so many head counts that we used to joke that doing time was just a matter of being counted over and over until you got out. There was one when you woke up, one before each shift change, and one after breakfast when that day's court attenders had left. There was another after coming back from exercise, another after all the court attenders were back and visits had ended, and another before the night shift took over. Then the jurisdiction officer in charge would come in for a final check. My detainee number was 83, but since I was always in the third cell, I shouted "Three!" One, two, three . . . Everyone shouted their number; those in the group cells called out the row they were sitting in. Hanging by the door of each cell was the cell number, the number of detainees inside, and the prison number assigned to each occupant.

From my cell window, I was able to chat now and then with Hwang In-seong and Lee Chang-bok of the National Alliance for Democracy and Unification of Korea, both nice fellows who told me about their visits to North Korea and to whom I passed on what people abroad were saying. The Buddhist monk Beopta, in the end cell of the lowest block, was especially talkative. He had been the abbot of a temple in Los Angeles until his arrest for violating the National Security Act by contacting someone in North Korea about One Korea Buddhist Movement affairs. I told him about a Jindo dog I'd had in New York. My son Ho-seop, who was about five at the time, had envied our next-door neighbors for their dog. I was downtown and happened upon a pet shop that had a cute yellow puppy in the window. Hanging outside the cage was a breeding certificate typed in Korean: it was a purebred Jindo born in the States. We took the puppy home to our house in Queens and named it Dolswe. After six months it had grown into quite a handsome dog. Apparently, after I left the US, Dolswe would wander the neighborhood looking for me. When my family moved to Manhattan, they gave it to Pastor Kim Hyo shin in New Jersey. But the loyal creature could not give its heart to its new family and kept biting the other neighborhood dogs. My children's mother had no choice but to send it to her mother in Korea, who hated dogs. I knew that Dolswe was in danger of being sent to the pound to be euthanized. When I related the story to Beopta, Dolswe was still being held in quarantine at customs. Beopta found this highly opportune, saying that the monks in his temple would be willing to take good care of the dog, this was all Buddha's will coming to fruition. But by the time arrangements were made, my former mother-in-law had already given Dolswe away to another family. It grieved me to think about my failure as a patriarch, when I couldn't even take care of the family dog, much less my own children. It felt like an omen, portending yet another family breakup. I was going through at least one trial a week at that point, and I was exhausted from answering the same questions over and over again, my spirit completely conquered.

A new detainee moved into the cell directly below mine, a young man, from the sound of things. I didn't know he was on death row at first. Whenever we came back from dinner, he would stick his head out of his bathroom window and sing at the top of his lungs. He always sang "Morning Dew." Even the best singer can ruin a song by repeating it too often, and this boy was tone-deaf to begin with. He droned straight through to "more precious than pearls is the morning dew / that clings to each leaf, awake through the long night" in a monotone, no rhythm at all. He might as well have been reading aloud from a phone book. Then, at the part where it goes "This is my trial, I go forth now into that wilderness," his voice suddenly turned high-pitched and sappy, and from "I cast off sadness and make my way now," it changed again into a fast-paced marching song. He got the lyrics right each time, but the tune and the beat were never the same. I'd grip my book and lie with my face buried in my bedding, just waiting for it to stop, but no sooner would he finish than he'd begin another round. At last I couldn't take it anymore, and shouted out the window:

—Not that again! You can't seriously be singing the same song over and over, day in, day out. At least learn *how* to sing. Good god, how am I supposed to live with that racket?!

There was silence for a moment and then he started up again. The guard on shift must have heard me, because he stuck his head out of his window.

—Something wrong?

—That guy downstairs, he won't stop singing "Morning Dew," and it's annoying as hell because he can't even sing properly.

—He's a red tag. Probably has a lot on his mind.

I understood immediately. Death row inmates had their prisoner numbers stamped on a red patch of fabric, to distinguish them from the regular detainees. Next door to me was a heavyset man with a thick beard, and beside him was a pale young man as delicate as a woman. They had both been sentenced to death. The former, who was in his midforties with the last name of Hur, had been awaiting execution for the past eight years.

Funds were tight at the detention center, and so we had no heating, let alone air conditioning. The painted cement walls were a burning hell in the summer and a freezing hell in the winter. The hot-water radiators, which were little more than a formality, were only run on the coldest days, lending the cell block a tiny bit of warmth. On bath day, the regulars took showers in the shower room, while the private-cell detainees took turns bathing in the guards' bathroom at the entrance to the cell block corridor, where two large rubber tubs made from recycled tires had been filled to the brim with hot water. Hur and I shared the same bath time. He'd been around longer than me and taught me the trick of keeping the tub lids open so we could enjoy the steam. The steam would turn the tiny room so hot that we could barely breathe. We'd throw towels over our heads to work up a sweat and then open the windows to let fresh air in and begin to bathe. We scrubbed each other's backs. Hur was so strong that he did a good job on mine. I did my best scrubbing away at the wide expanse of his back, but he sometimes seemed dissatisfied, turning to reposition the scrubbing towel wound around my hand. Then, before we soaped up, we soaked for a bit in our respective tubs. Hur chanted Buddhist scripture every morning when he woke, and sometimes he chanted while he bathed. As spring approached, he grew quieter and more depressed. There was a rumor that executions would be carried out once winter had passed. He'd told me that he wasn't worried about death so much as about his daughter, whom he'd left in the care of a Buddhist temple. I tried to comfort him, saying,

—They've waited this long, don't you think they'll end up pardoning you?

His sad face broke into a smile and he murmured casually, as if talking about someone else:

—It's time to be off. Best not to be such a burden on everyone.

The other death row inmate, Choi, was a well-mannered and clever young man. His mother, a widow, had come to visit one time and left him a bracelet of Buddhist prayer beads that she had carved herself from sacred fig wood. I will never forget Hur and Choi, because I learned of their executions only a day before they happened. I was called to one of the offices for something, so I went during my exercise period and found the chief inspector sitting with his chair turned away from his desk, staring at some documents. He was so intent on them that he didn't notice me approach. I glanced over his shoulder and saw a list with two names. The chief inspector suddenly sensed I was there and quickly flipped the papers over and swiveled his chair to face me. I asked him what was up. His face was still tense as he looked around the room before quietly raising one hand. He made his hand stiff as a blade and mimed it coming down on his neck. I understood what he meant. *When?* I mouthed. *Tomorrow*, he mouthed back.

My heart was heavy as I returned to my room. Choi called out to me from his window, wanting to talk, and I reluctantly went to the window next to my toilet. He babbled about the future that he had put together for himself from a fortune-telling book. He went on about the things that would happen in decades to come, and all I could think of was how he had only hours to live. That moment lingered for a long time in my heart. The following dawn, at wake-up time, Hur struck his wood block as usual as he did his morning chanting. I had my morning exercise first, while the others had theirs just before lunch. Maybe it was the mood of the guards, or maybe just a very human premonition, but everyone, the condemned men included, gave off a strange anxiety as silence settled over the whole block. Lunch passed quietly. There were no bustling cross-cell conversations, no friendly urgings to each other to eat their fill. Only silence filled the air.

As soon as lunch was over, a special team wearing red caps marched in. The rooms kept their hush. I could hear Hur complaining as he was brought out:

—You're going to hang me with my stomach full. If I'd known this would happen I would've just drunk water.

He stood at the inspection slot in front of my room.

—Mr. Hwang, I'm going first. I hope to see you on the other side.

Hur disappeared, and now Choi stood before my door.

—Sir . . . please take this. And write my mother a letter if you can.

He held out his prayer beads carved from sacred fig wood. I still have them to this day.

Their executions were the first at the center in years.

Afterward, all of the private-cell detainees were made to change rooms. I was moved closer to the administrative center. It was still a private cell, and I didn't think much of the change, but once I turned in bed to face the wall, I saw a line of writing along the white cement: "To exist is to be happy." The cell had belonged to a death row inmate.

A month later I rode next to a guard in a van on the way to court. Apropos of nothing, he started talking about executions. He told me about Hur and Choi's final moments. The scores of prison employees drew lots, and he along with a few other guards were the unlucky ones. "Unlucky" was his choice of word. Korean executions are done by hanging. The prosecution, the head of the detention center, and religious representatives, among others, come in to observe. Behind a lattice stands the gallows, about two stories high, while the device that operates the trapdoor is in a control room at the back—the execution cannot be seen from that spot. Three people are posted there. The guard had wanted to be in the control room but was assigned to a front seat instead. The condemned man was brought in, handcuffed and tied, a black sack put over his head, and the noose hung around his neck before the curtain was drawn before him. That was all the observers saw, even after the floor opened up and the prisoner dropped, as the lower part was blocked from sight by a wall. They waited for about twenty minutes before a guard, a doctor, and the religious representative went to the lower room to confirm his death.

Choi was so scared that he was unable to walk to the gallows and had to be supported by a guard on either side. Hur was calm in comparison and started loudly reciting Buddhist scripture even before they put the black sack on him.

While in college, Choi had taken a job tutoring an elementary school student. He'd just completed his mandatory army service and was renting a room downtown while preparing to return to school. The mother of the child he tutored had borrowed money from him, promising to pay it back with interest. When the new semester was about to begin, he asked for the money back several times, but the woman said that he had no proof that he had ever loaned her any money. When the child stopped showing up for tutoring sessions, he went to the child's school, picked him up in his car and drove around, demanding that the mother pay her debt. It turned into a full-blown hostage situation that ended with Choi taking the child out to a quiet country road, killing him, and burying his body in the mountains.

Hur was a produce dealer. During kimchi-making season, he would drive his truck out to the countryside and buy up entire fields of cabbage to resell in bulk at the market. One day, he went to a field where he had prepaid for a load only to discover that the cabbages had been sold off to another bidder. The farmer said he had sold it at a higher price and would pay Hur back, but that meant Hur would miss the all-important kimchi-making season. They got into an argument and, in a fit of frustration, Hur swung a pickax that had been lying around on the ground and accidentally killed him. When he came to his senses, he loaded the body into the back of his truck and buried it on a hill. He had thought no one else was around, but it turned out there was a witness to the argument and Hur was quickly apprehended.

I heard these stories from the guards as if they were legends from the distant past. Yes, both men had committed dreadful crimes, but they weren't evil people to begin with. Circumstances had conspired against them. That winter Hur and I spent scrubbing each other's backs would stay with me always. Whenever I rubbed the prayer beads Choi left me, I always thought of his pale face and the love he had for his widowed mother.

The Kim Young-sam administration executed fifty-seven people over three rounds. Since the last one in 1997, South Korea has not carried out another death sentence.

~

I was sentenced on October 25, 1993. The court still ruled that

North Korea was an anti-government or terrorist organization under the National Security Act, but what interested me was how they redefined what "national secrets" meant. The court went against a previous Supreme Court ruling on this point. Of my alleged disclosure of the personal information of leftist activists and discussion of activism with North Koreans (a completely fabricated claim in any case), they declared that national secrets needed to have some degree of actual value as secrets and hence the allegation against me did not apply here, acquitting me of this charge at least. As I mentioned before, this supposed information had come from me falling for an ANSP trap, and the trumped-up charge had persisted despite my protests. I sensed it was a highly sensitive matter as, under the National Security Act, accusations of spying stemmed from leaking intelligence. The prosecution had also tried to frame me for espionage by insisting that the 200 million won from the South and the 250,000 dollars (about 200 million won at the time) from the North—payment for my North–South collaboration movie deal for *Jang Gil-san*—were my operative fees.

At the end of my first sentencing I received eight years in prison and eight years of suspension of qualifications. The prosecution and defense both appealed, the former because my sentence was too low, even if some of the charges had been dismissed, and the latter because the court had ruled on the grounds that North Korea was a terrorist organization.

The PEN America president, Louis Begley, sent a letter to South Korean President Kim Young-sam protesting my continued incarceration. He urged President Kim to deliver on his promised democratic reforms by immediately releasing me, and by recognizing the National Security Act as a tool used to suppress free speech. He further argued that my incarceration and my restriction from writing were inevitably damaging South Korea's international image as a rising democracy. He added that the cruel treatment I'd received during the initial interrogation should also be investigated. The letter criticized the fact that I was being punished for visiting North Korea, because any law that indiscriminately penalizes someone's freedom of movement would never be up to the international standards of human rights.

My first winter in detention felt especially cold and long. As I despaired over how many more winters I would have to spend under lock and key, the new year began. On January 18, 1994, Pastor Moon Ik-hwan passed away. He had been a friend of both the poet Yun Dong-ju, who died in a Fukuoka prison during the Japanese occupation, and the activist Chang Chun-ha, who had died in suspicious circumstances during the Park Chung-hee administration. Chang's death had inspired him to become an anti-dictatorship activist. Pastor Moon used the pen name Neutbom ("late spring") to symbolize his late entry into the national democratization movement. He was jailed six times during the military dictatorship and spent a total of ten years in prison. I couldn't help the wave of regret I felt upon hearing of his death, as I recalled the last time I had seen him when we met in North Korea. He could have led a life of placid contentment, guiding a congregation, but he dedicated his life to the cause and was met with a heartbreaking ending. But he wasn't the first, nor the last, to suffer such a fate in this country.

In February 1994, the appeals court amended my custodial sentence from eight to six years, with six years of suspension of qualifications. But in May, the Supreme Court dismissed the previous verdict of not guilty on the charge of leaking intelligence and sent the case back to the High Court. They declared:

"It has been the Supreme Court's consistent ruling that even if a fact had already been widely disseminated through newspapers or books, any information that is useful intelligence to the anti-government organization that is North Korea and can put South Korean interests at a disadvantage pertains to this charge."

In other words, even widely distributed information can be

considered "national secrets" if it happens to be advantageous to North Korea. The activist lawyers vociferously objected to the courts' retreat into Cold War thinking.

Around this time, the US and North Korea reached a stalemate regarding nuclear disarmament talks, and the US was readying an airstrike against the North's Yongbyon nuclear facilities. It is a well-known fact that during the Korean conflict, President Rhee Syngman relinquished wartime operational control to General Douglas MacArthur, a control which we never took back, so that the ability to decide war or peace on the peninsula lies with the United Nations Command in Korea. In other words, with the commander of US forces in Korea. Any military movement or the right to declare or stop war belongs to the US commander, and there is nothing the South Korean people, their president, or their government can do about it. The Pentagon had already completed war simulations. According to President Kim Young-sam's memoirs, he was unable to sleep the night he heard about this. Those few weeks were like a very taut tug-of-war. It was then that former president Jimmy Carter stepped in to visit North Korea.

There are some who argue now that it would have been better to go to war, and that Carter was used by Kim Il-sung. They claim that his visit only bought the North more time to develop nuclear weapons. But let's look back at the roots of North Korea's nuclear development for a moment. Our division has persisted for seventy years since Liberation. Our war is both a civil war and an international war, part of a Cold War system that formed from Europe all the way to East Asia. When the Cold War ended in 1990 and Germany was reunified, Eastern Europe's socialist system collapsed. North and South Korea eventually joined the UN as separate, sovereign nations. In other words, Russia and China finally accepted South Korean sovereignty, while the US and Japan approved of North Korea's. Russia and China in turn normalized diplomatic relations with

South Korea, but the US and Japan decided to delay doing the same for North Korea. A disappointed North Korea then turned to nuclear development as the trump card to force America to the negotiation table. The ultimate goal of such a negotiation was the stability of their regime and a peaceful reunification, which could only come about if a formal end to the Korean War was declared.

South Korea's Kim Dae-jung administration pushed their "Sunshine Policy" by drawing North Korea, the US, South Korea, and Japan to the negotiation table and tried to make international society more inclusive for North Korea. Their idea was to pursue a one-nation, two-systems arrangement, and guaranteed peace was essential to this vision. The rules had been laid down with the September 19, 2005, agreement in Beijing; but due to America's failure to lift sanctions, among other things, the deal fell apart. America then embarked on a protracted war in the Middle East and neglected North Korean relations, leading to North Korea firing long-range missiles and going ahead with their fifth nuclear test. Meanwhile, South Korea's conservative governments were completely ineffectual in taking the lead and dealing with America and Japan's attempts to curb China's influence. With US cooperation and approval, Japan moved to rewrite its constitution of peace, which it had maintained since the end of World War II, and upgraded its national defense force to globalize its reach. The Japanese Armed Forces had long defined China as enemy number one and the Korean peninsula as its foremost theater of war. This was a continuation of the Japanese military class's traditional mindset regarding Asia. Today, the US is attempting to bind Japan and South Korea into a Northeast Asian Cold War system, with China as the enemy. It is more important than ever, as we stand on the brink of war, that international forces work together to turn the peninsula's state of armistice into a state of peace.

~

In June, the South Korean media reported extensively on former US president Carter's prospective talks with Kim Il-sung. As a North–South summit began to seem like a possibility, my writer and politician friends went as far as to congratulate me during their visits. They no doubt thought that once the summit was held, I would be pardoned. Around this time, one of the guards told me that there was "someone who came down from North Korea" in our block. I asked if he had breached the National Security Act, and he replied he was a "plate." We were in the habit of using flippant terms to refer to different types of criminals, like "water gun" for rapists. "Plates" referred to con men—I assume this came from the jester-act of spinning plates in the air while con men move through the crowd to steal money from distracted spectators. The guard also told me the plate was claiming to be related to Kim Jong-il. I wasn't interested, and figured it was just a defector who was not adjusting well to South Korea's capitalist lifestyle. Many North Korean defectors claimed to have been important people back home.

One day, a crowd of regular prisoners was walking past my door on their way to exercise when my food hole opened and a bright, energetic young face appeared in it.

—Hello! Nice to meet you. I am from North Korea.

I had my suspicions about him, so I simply smiled and said:

—I hope things look up for you soon. How did you end up escaping?

He smiled back and dodged the subject.

—Long story. Anyhow, my wife collected your North Korea travel writings and sent them to me here.

I feigned modesty at the interest from this supposed North Korean.

—I only described what they were willing to show me. They did seem to be a very hardworking people, so I tried to keep it positive.

—It's the same here, no? There is light and dark everywhere. You captured the bright parts for the sake of reunification.

This young North Korean man seemed a simple soul, and yet he spoke to me as if he clearly understood what I had meant to write. For a while after that, we only exchanged quick greetings, until a guard who trusted me came in for duty and I asked him to let me talk more with the young man. We would sit in the washroom and talk comfortably while the others were out in the exercise yard. I realized he wasn't fake when he guessed right away where I had stayed while in North Korea.

—If it's near Pyongyang Station, it has to be the visitors' center in Seojaegol, and you said you fished at a reservoir, which means it's the Cheolbongri VIP visitors' center. That's where the actress Choi Eun-hee and director Shin Sang-ok used to live.

We had several shower room conversations like this where I got to hear his whole story. His name was Ri Il-nam. He was the only grandson of Song Yu-gyeong and Kim Won-ju. His grandfather had studied in Japan during the occupation and become a socialist. Right after Liberation he was put in charge of fiscal affairs at the Workers' Party of South Korea, despite the fact that his family, the Changnyeong Songs, had been landowning aristocrats throughout feudal times. His grandmother, Kim Won-ju, was a "New Woman" who had been a reporter at *Gaebyeok* magazine. In 1948, she participated in the North–South Conference as the South Korea Democratic Women's Federation's representative. Her eldest son, Song Il-ki, was conscripted at the age of seventeen and operated as a partisan in the South Gyeongsang Province branch of the Workers' Party of South Korea. He became a prisoner of war after the armistice and was left behind on his own in the South. Song Yu-gyeong fled to the North, but his fortunes fell with the end of the Party, and he died in sorrow. His eldest daughter Song Hye-rang raised her children, Ri Il-nam and Ri Nam-ok, alone after her husband died in a car crash. The second daughter, Song Hye-rim, graduated from the Pyongyang University of Dramatic and Cinematic Arts, became an actor, married, became famous, and was awarded the People's Prize, catching the eye of Kim Jong-il, who was younger than her. Her husband reluctantly gave her up in light of Kim Jong-il's interest, and in the late 1960s Kim Jong-il and Song Hye-rim started living together in the infamous Residence No. 15, a secret kept from Kim Jong-il's father, Premier Kim Il-sung. The couple later gave birth to Kim's eldest son, Kim Jong-nam. It was around this time that Kim Won-ju lived with Song Hye-rim at the residence, helping to raise her grandson.

When Kim Jong-nam entered elementary school, Ri Il-nam and Ri Nam-ok moved with their mother into Visitors' Residence No. 15. Song Hye-rang had been a physics major, but under her journalist mother's influence, she also developed a talent for writing and was publishing short stories.

Around the time I was released, a friend of mine brought a copy of Song Hye-rang's memoirs, *Deungnamu jip* (Wisteria House). This was long after the scandals of the sisters Song Hye-rang and Song Hye-rim and Ri Il-nam's death, and so the book was overlooked by the general public and quickly fell out of print. What moved me deeply about this memoir was how it maintained a politically impartial perspective regarding the North and South and, while it was a personal record, it still contained many valuable details otherwise forgotten by history. The first part was about the revolutionary activities of her journalist and socialist activist mother, Kim Won-ju, and the son of a feudal lord, Song Yu-gyeong, continuing on to the war they experienced in North Korea and its aftermath. The second half offered a calm and objective account of Song Hye-rang and Song Hye-rim's life in the Visitors' Residence and their relationship with Kim Jong-il, against the backdrop of the changes in North Korean society.

Ri Il-nam told me about life in Residence No. 15 with his mother, aunt, younger sister Nam-ok, and Kim Jong-nam, who was technically a cousin but as close as a younger brother. The family was segregated from the other citizens of Pyongyang and they were indeed treated like "visitors" in the residence. They called Kim Jong-il, who came to the house every few days, "the Chief," and because they were not allowed to play outside or have any friends, the three of them stuck together. In an annex to the residence lived a driver, a cook, and a middle-aged assistant. Ri Il-nam said that every day there would be transcripts delivered to Kim Jong-nam's office of phone conversations with higher-ups in the Party, like O Jin-u or Kim Yong-sun, and the Chief would look through them and then feed them into a shredder. No matter how august an official came to visit, the young Kim Jong-nam always spoke to them in informal Korean, and while Kim Jong-il said nothing about this, Song Hye-rim would admonish him and say he needed to use the polite form to adults. Ri said that more than once he had seen the driver and the assistant stack boxes of dollars and gold ingots into a cabinet taller than a person inside the office. If the Chief mentioned a dish at dinner, it would invariably appear on the table a few days later, and even a dish that wasn't available in North Korea would be served at least a week after it was invoked. There was a screening room in the house, and the family watched a European or Hollywood movie once every few days.

Ri studied at Mangyongdae Revolutionary School, then went to Moscow, and then to Geneva with Kim Jong-nam when the latter was sent abroad. Their lives were the same overseas, as they were stuck at home all the time, and Kim Jong-nam started to get into the new pastime of video games. An assistant took them to and from school. That was in the early 1980s, and Ri, nineteen at the time, wanted to visit America. He had grown up watching Hollywood movies in the residence, his video game equipment was from the States, and he loved American pop music. When he talked about this to his friends at school, they said he would need a visa to go to America and that he would have to contact the Korean embassy. Ri, like his Swiss classmates, didn't know much about the North–South division of Korea, or maybe he just didn't think about it. He hesitated a few times before calling the South Korean embassy from a pay phone. The person who picked up managed to grasp who the caller was and offered to help him get to the States. When Ri called again a few days later, he was instructed to not tell anyone and come to a place where he would be given a passport. Ri met the contact at a café and then got into a car with him, supposedly to go pick up his passport together.

—I don't know how many days went by after that, but when I came to, I was in a two-story house in Seoul, South Korea.

That was September of 1982. Ri said the people who had brought him to South Korea seemed disappointed. They had thought he was one of Kim Jong-il's children and were excited that he had voluntarily contacted the South Koreans, but he was only the nephew of Kim Jong-il's mistress, a nobody.

Ri lived for years in the ANSP residence. He changed his name to Yi Han-yong—meaning "I will live forever in South Korea"—and had plastic surgery. It was said that, whenever there was contact between the two governments, North Korean officials would ask if the South had him. He earned a degree in drama from Hanyang University, and the South Korean government got him a job as a producer at KBS. He began to brag a lot about his best days. The ANSP helped him as much as they could, and he even got married. His wife was a demure young woman from an ordinary family who worked as a model. He drove a Grandeur complete with a car phone, his wife drove an SUV, and they lived in a huge eighty-*pyeong* apartment (about 265 square meters) in the most expensive complex in Gangnam.

He had never had to strive for anything in his life and had been protected and cared for, in both North and South, like a hothouse plant, which might explain why he was even more naïve than he looked. His cheerfulness and simplicity came from being clueless and always doing whatever he felt like. It was no wonder con men couldn't leave him alone. He flaunted his wealth, drawing the attention of a group of con artists who proposed a real estate development project, in which they negotiated with apartment owners to knock down and replace their old apartment buildings. Ri invested all of the resettlement money given him by the South Korean government into this scheme, and mortgaged his own apartment, but the buildings that were constructed were shoddy. The proprietors refused to move into the new buildings, on the grounds that they were not up to par, and sued the developers. These promptly disappeared with the money, and Ri found himself in prison. He worried about his wife and daughter, sighing that they had nowhere to go but his mother-in-law's house.

One day, on the way out to the exercise yard, Ri opened my food hole and urgently blurted a question.

—Mr. Hwang, do you happen to know anyone at the *Hankyoreh*?

—Why? What happened?

He was agitated and breathing hard.

—They're going to blame me for everything at the trial.

I told him that civil suits like his were hardly in the purview of a newspaper like the *Hankyoreh*'s interests, but he went off on a tangent.

—Bastards! They dragged me here against my will and now they've washed their hands of me. If they don't intervene, I've got a lot to say for myself, I'm telling you. I'm going to talk to the press!

I finally understood what he meant. I said that he must have had a handler before, and that he should get in touch with him and explain the situation.

—My wife says everyone's positions shifted after the change in administration.

I reasoned with him, saying the country could not take responsibility for every last individual's life; he had an unusual story and if he went public with it he would only harm himself, and he should learn not to abuse that secret. Things went quiet for a while until one day, passing by my cell, he opened my food hole again.

—I think I'm headed out now. My old handler said he would take care of it.

I understood. His situation would have been a pain in the neck for them. As he predicted, he was out on probation a week later, but he was like an innocent little boy to the end. He was carrying his things down the corridor, so I asked a guard to let me out to say goodbye to him at the entrance of the cell block. He was ecstatic at the thought of getting out.

—Mr. Hwang, I am indebted to you in many ways.

—I hope you live diligently in the future.

He bowed and shook my hand.

—Yes, I will work diligently for reunification.

I didn't let go of his hand but patted his shoulder with my other hand, saying:

—Don't even think of doing such a thing. Just concentrate on making a living.

And I added, insistently:

—You are in a very special situation and therefore must be extremely careful. Live quietly and happily with your family, because your life won't be like it was before. Be frugal and live earnestly.

Years later, in perhaps the winter of 1995 when I was at Gongju Correctional Institution, the *Chosun Monthly* started to serialize Ri's memoirs and included a transcript of phone conversations with his mother Song Hye-rang, who was living in Moscow. For weeks the papers talked about Song Hye-rang and Song Hye-rim and Kim Jong-il's private life, speculating that the Song sisters would go into exile. Ri looked as if he would never go back to the kind of life he'd led before. According to the reports, he was running a chocolate shop in a department store (I suspect this was also thanks to some outside help). This would have been a great favor by the standards of ordinary South Koreans, but to him it was perhaps not enough. That's why he sold his story to the magazine and published a book. There was a rumor that, after his phone calls with his mother, Song Hye-rang, he had sent his wife to Hong Kong to meet with her to receive some money, or that Song had wired some to him.

Song Hye-rang and Ri Nam-ok managed to leave Moscow around that time, but they did not end up in South Korea.

I had already predicted as much. Ri was a major liability on either side of the 38th parallel. Under lurid headlines like "Taedong River Royal Family," the newspapers ran stories about his plastic surgery and name change and how he had been kidnapped into South Korea. Ri was later killed by two operatives in his home in Bundang, in the suburbs of Seoul. A witness stated that, before dying of gunshot wounds to the head and chest, Ri held up two fingers and said, "Spies." He fell into a coma and was declared dead a few days later. The spies were strangely sloppy. They had found his current address by contacting the Seoul Detention Center and giving his prisoner number and name, leaving a clear trail for investigators to follow. His address in Bundang was actually just a room in his sister-in-law's apartment. The Bundang Police had clear jurisdiction over the case, but the ANSP immediately took over the investigation. All the head of the Bundang Police could do was to lodge a formal complaint. There was also a news report quoting a coroner who complained that the ANSP had reported only one bullet casing on the scene, but another had been discovered in the pocket of the victim during the autopsy. A few months later, the ANSP claimed to have arrested a husband-and-wife spy team. According to their statements, Ri's killing had been carried out by North Korean operatives who had already returned to North Korea. For the longest time, I could not shake the thought of this young man's death. It made me wonder how many things had happened because of that dark and ominous border over our long, long years of division.

Meanwhile, Jimmy Carter had visited North Korea and proposed to Kim Il-sung in person that he meet with President Kim Young-sam, and Kim Il-sung immediately accepted. For a month afterward, the South Korean media was abuzz with the upcoming North–South summit. It was reported that Kim

Il-sung personally examined all the preparations in the visitors' residence that Kim Young-sam was to stay at.

In July there was an unprecedented heat wave, and I had no way of battling the heat bouncing off the concrete walls except to sit on the toilet in my underpants with a wet towel over my face. Then, one day, the ballooning expectations surrounding the North–South summit burst at the news that Kim Il-sung had passed away. The cause of death was a heart attack. The news reported it a day after it happened. I spent that day in an unsettled state of mind, stripped down and tossing and turning on a bed of wet towels that I'd spread out on the floor. It looked like I was going to be in for the long haul, and our state of division would continue indefinitely, dark thoughts that left me sleepless from anxiety and suffering.

3

Visit to the North

1986–89

After returning from Japan and splitting from my wife, I began a new life with Kim Myoung-su. We had been living in an apartment in Seoul, but we decided to build a house on the outskirts so that I could have a better writing environment. The painter Yeo Un, who had helped me find my house in Haenam, also happened to find my next abode. Our families were picnicking together in a scenic part of Gyeonggi Province's Gwangju (not to be confused with Jeolla Province's Gwangju, of the Gwangju Democracy Movement) when we came across an abandoned house on a hill overlooking a wide stream. It was pure coincidence that I came to live in a new town also called Gwangju. Yeo Un connected me to a contractor, and I cobbled together some advances from publishers to build a house. I was planning to write a twenty-volume narrative history of Korea, to be published in serial form at first.

It took about six months of living with Kim Myoung-su to realize that our marriage was a mistake. She didn't seem to understand what I was trying to do or what I was trying to say with my work or how it related to the difficulties of our age. She knew what it meant to be an artist: her father had been one, she had been a dancer all her life, and now she was a choreographer. But her values were also typical of Seoul's middle class, and while intelligent, she possessed little patience. Her sense of victimhood, of sacrificing her own artistic path for her husband's writing, took the form of constant complaints. A part of me was already subsumed with the guilt I felt toward my ex-wife and children, and I was struggling under a debtor's pressure to write because I'd already spent my large advances on building the house. The extent of my selfishness and egocentricity was laid bare every time I blamed her during our arguments.

Even as I sat writing in my room, my mind felt like it was treading water at the thought of my children left behind in Jeolla Province's Gwangju. Sometimes I'd write long letters to Ho-jun and Yeo-jeong in the middle of the night, only to hide them in my desk from Myoung-su, and later destroy them. At one point someone passed me a message telling me to call the Jeolla house. My ex-wife picked up and said that the children kept asking for me. Ho-jun had tried not to make a fuss, but Yeo-jeong kept nagging her, saying she wanted to see me. My son and ex-wife must have wanted to hide the fact of the divorce from Yeo-jeong, who was still in elementary school. I decided to take the children out to see *The Goonies*, which was being shown in film theaters in Seoul. Ho-jun seemed to have grown up a lot in the past few months. When we went to dinner after the film, Yeo-jeong kept saying we shouldn't eat anything expensive— her way of being considerate to her poor father who had to live away from them for the sake of his writing. At the bus terminal, I wanted to hop on the bus after them and follow them back to Jeolla Province.

On May 3, a mass demonstration of students, labor, and democracy protestors was staged in Incheon against the dictator Chun Doo-hwan, leading to a charge of sedition against the organizers. This incident continued to reverberate into the next year, as college student Park Jong-chul died during his interrogation at ANSP headquarters. There had been numerous suspicious deaths before, which the military dictatorship had managed to gloss over in the past. But this time it was different, and the people continued to demand to know the truth. The sexual torture of a female college student, Kwon In-suk, by the Bucheon Police Department was also exposed around that time, while the Catholic Priests' Association for Justice revealed that the officials had tried to cover up the fact that Park Jong-chul had died under water torture. As these incidents fueled more protests, another college student named Lee Han-yeol was hit by a tear gas canister during a protest and declared brain-dead. President Chun Doo-hwan informed the nation that the next president would be determined not by a democratic vote but through a National Conference for Unification, in the style of Park Chung-hee's administration, just as his own presidency had been decided. It signaled his lack of interest in constitutional, democratic reform.

A nationwide protest began on June 10 with the participation of activists, students, and ordinary citizens, continuing until June 29. The slogan of the protests was "Down with the Constitution, down with the dictatorship." Activists set up a National Headquarters for Protecting Democratic Constitutional Rights, and students and citizens held a sit-in at Myeong-dong Cathedral. The "March for Peace" that the headquarters proposed was attended by over a million people; the police were unable to disperse the crowds. President Chun Doo-hwan was ready to mobilize the military but had to back down in the face of strong American opposition. I marched, as well, because the Association of Writers for National Literature and the People's Cultural Movement Association was of course affiliated with the headquarters. We were given daily updates on where and how to protest, leaving early in the morning and returning late or spending the night in Seoul. My clothes stank of tear gas all the time. Naturally, my newspaper serialization had to be suspended.

The June Democratic Uprising did not end with the fall of the dictatorship but with the June 29 Declaration by the ruling Democratic Justice Party's successor-in-waiting, Roh Tae-woo. In essence, it was about changing the presidential election into a national vote. This was the compromise between the people in power who wanted to keep something of the old rules and the progressives who yearned for any semblance of democracy, and optimistically expected that the old system would inevitably be overcome.

The national crisis quickly shifted into presidential-election mode as Kim Dae-jung and Kim Young-sam split ways and created separate parties with their respective followers. The activist space and the People's Cultural Movement Association that I had organized were also in danger of fragmenting. Having received a call from the human rights lawyer Cho Young-rae, I was all up for a unified candidate: it was obvious to anyone that the "two Kims" together could just barely win the election, but we had no chance at all with them apart.

In my old home of Jeolla Gwangju, unresolved despair over the Gwangju Democracy Movement ran deep. The local people had pinned all their hopes on Kim Dae-jung. My phone rang off the hook with calls from there, ranging from accusing me of being a Kim Young-sam supporter because of my support for a unified candidate, to outright cursing. The calls all amounted to demands for the People's Cultural Movement Association to do something. Kim Yong-tae and about half of our executive committee were pushing Paek Ki-wan as "the people's presidential candidate." This was another way of unifying the field, but it also showed the political limits of the two Kims. If support for Kim Young-sam symbolized unity, and support for Kim Dae-jung signified reluctance, you could say most of the young people of the Association of Writers for National Literature were reluctant. I half-jokingly dubbed Paek Ki-wan supporters a "purist sect." Ten days before negotiations for a unified candidacy fell apart, I gave up my stance and supported Kim Dae-jung as a reluctant supporter, making a speech on television to that effect. The presidential election ended in thorough defeat, with the opposition vote split and Roh Tae-woo elected with little more than a third of the popular vote, unleashing a sense of disgust and disappointment with politics that swept the nation. We had just barely managed to win a democratic system, and then spoiled it with division. The democracy movement would be deeply wounded by this division between the two Kims for years to come.

After the election, the poet Kim Jeong-hwan and his followers demanded that the leadership take responsibility as they vowed to bring the People's Cultural Movement Association back to the center of on-the-ground activism. They had a point, so Kim Yong-tae and I created an arts organization that was truly centered on artists and experts. Almost every day for about a year, we went around meeting artists from different fields. People from the fields of literature, fine art, architecture, photography, Eastern calligraphy, theater, and film gathered to hold discussions and fill leadership roles, resulting in the Korean People's Artists Federation that launched on November 23, 1988. Each division was led by an elder artist, with Kim Yong-tae as secretary and me as spokesperson.

Democratization activists, having failed to bring about a transition of power with the past election, organized themselves into a national movement to work against further divisions. My work in the Korean People's Artists Federation and the Association of Writers for National Literature brought me closer to the new National Association for Democratic Activism, which covered the activist, religious, and political worlds under one wide umbrella.

As the 1988 Seoul Olympics approached, each group pressured the government to improve relations with North Korea and allow exchanges between the two countries. The Roh Tae-woo administration took power, a democratically elected government in form but the same old system of military dictatorship in content, while the country was swept up in preparing for the Olympics to be held in September.

PEN International decided to hold their conference in Seoul that year in honor of the Olympics. PEN America's president

Susan Sontag and vice president Arthur Miller sent a joint statement to the South Korean leader, saying that they had accepted the poet Kim Nam-ju and journalist Kim Hyon-jang as honorary members of PEN America, respectfully requesting their release, as well as that of the publisher Lee Tae-bok. I've mentioned this before, but since joining PEN in 1955 during the Rhee Syngman administration, the Korean branch of PEN had been no more than a propaganda arm for the South Korean government during two dictatorships. It made no effort to even talk to the various writers whose freedoms had been curtailed since the 1970s, a state of affairs that continues to this day. I visited PEN America's headquarters in 1985 and corresponded with them through Young Koreans United in New York. That summer, the Association of Writers for National Literature called up, saying that a guest from PEN America was looking for me.

It turned out to be Karen Kennerly, sent to Korea by Susan Sontag. She had lived in Japan for years and knew quite a lot about Northeast Asian politics. Kennerly told me that PEN America's aim in Korea, more than anything else, was to express its deep concern over the incarceration of Korean writers and the restraints on freedom of expression. She was on a reconnaissance mission to meet writers who were fighting for democracy outside of the literary mainstream, quite a contrast to the PEN Korea propaganda machine. The Association of Writers for National Literature promised to hold a parallel literary event with world writers during the same period that the PEN International congress was being held.

The visiting writers came to Korea for the conference and visited the Association of Writers for National Literature, with Ko Un, Paik Nak-chung, and I attending. Susan Sontag was there, along with twenty writers from the US, UK, Germany, and France, all crowded around a table in a Korean restaurant in the Sinchon neighborhood. They informed me that they were at the Seoul conference for the express purpose of passing a resolution for the release of imprisoned Korean writers.

Sontag had been translated several times into Korean and was well known among Korean literati for her writings on a wide range of aesthetic topics, as well as for her social activism. She was in her midfifties and had just survived a bout with cancer when we met in Seoul, but she was as passionate and curious as ever. Whenever a foreign writer spoke, she leaned toward me and introduced them in a low voice, informing me of how good they were. I understood her a little but could only answer in single words, my English being, then as now, the jury-rigged kind learned during my Vietnam War days. But Sontag was patient and took care to speak slowly, in easy sentences. She listened to Paik Nak-chung's opinions on literature and realism for several minutes before giving me a thumbs-up: his thoughts had met with her approval.

My memory is hazy on which Korean writers they were supporting, but I do remember they were especially interested in the poet Kim Nam-ju and asked many questions when someone mentioned I had worked alongside him for many years. I gave them a brief summary of his life and work. Sontag immediately understood Kim Nam-ju's reasons for participating in the South Korean National Liberation Front when I mentioned that he had translated Heinrich Heine, Pablo Neruda, Bertolt Brecht, and Frantz Fanon. She seemed on the verge of tears when I explained how he was forbidden from writing in his cell and had secretly sent out poems written on milk cartons and the silver foil in cigarette packets. The Korean People's Artists Federation and the other mainstream arts organizations that acted like propaganda outlets would put out a declaration of support for the government every time there was some political prompting under the military dictatorship: when Kim Nam-ju was imprisoned, they proclaimed him a "leftist communist" who should never be released. Then as now, any criticism of the government got you labeled as a communist. The PEN International congress held in Seoul's Grand Walkerhill hotel descended into farce, as the foreign delegates tried to pass a resolution for the release of political writers while PEN Korea tried to block it. Nevertheless, Susan Sontag and the Western writers went back into the conference hall to inform and try to persuade the Russian writers and other delegates who were unaware of the situation.

The day before the conference, Ko Un, Paik Nak-chung, Susan Sontag, and other writers from PEN along with myself held a press conference in Myeong-dong. Sontag had spoken for the foreign writers, and the Korean writers were speaking in turn, when suddenly a young man started reading aloud from a letter he claimed had been sent from prison. The gist of it was that this prisoner objected to the Seoul Olympics because it was a foreign powers' showcase for the success of Korea's division; he likewise rejected PEN America's liberalist, human-rights approach to imprisoned Korean writers. He had a point in a way, but the argument left no room for rebuttal with its emphasis on "self-reliance," a concept in vogue among young people at the time. In any case, it was my position to regard the citizenry of Western powers like the US, UK, and France separately from their imperialist governments, and to stand in solidarity with their people even as we fought their policies.

Ko Un pulled at the young man's arm, trying to get him to stop, but he kept on reading the letter as the foreign writers caught on to the awkward mood. Years later, when I met Sontag in New York, she told me she still found the situation utterly baffling and their efforts at the Seoul PEN conference a complete failure.

After the press conference, I joined the foreign writers at a bar in Myeong-dong, where we ordered a dish of *sannakji*, or live octopus. Sontag let out a playful yelp at the sight of the writhing tentacles, her face full of curiosity and amusement, but couldn't bring herself to take a bite. Perhaps because of the bar's cover fee, the bill was much higher than expected. Later in New York, Sontag told me she had been surprised first by the chopped-off, still-writhing octopus tentacles, and then again by how much that dinner cost.

I was able to read a fairly objective account of what happened at the PEN International congress held at the Walkerhill thanks to the *Hankyoreh*, a brand-new independent newspaper that was established with the help of funds from activists and ordinary citizens. The resolution failed to garner enough votes despite the valiant efforts of the previous evening's group of writers. Sontag and the other writers shed tears of anger. The reporter from the *Hankyoreh* wrote: "I was profoundly confused by the Korean writers at the conference, overjoyed at defeating a resolution that would have called for the release of their fellow writers." Despite this setback, the foreign writers announced the resolution outside of the conference hall at the Association of Writers for National Literature and the '88 Seoul National Literature Festival in Yeouido.

A long time later, in early September of 2001, I was invited to the literary symposium commemorating the centennial of the Nobel Peace Prize in Norway's Tromsø. The theme that year was "War and Peace," and the posters printed the word *war* very large and *peace* very small, reflecting the state of the times. I met Israel's Amos Oz and also Stefan Heym, a venerated East German writer. My friendships with the German writer Hans Christoph Buch and Norway's Halfdan Freihow have continued ever since that time.

I was sitting at the hotel bar one evening when someone came up and greeted me. It was the Russian poet Yevgeny Yevtushenko. I had first read him in the 1960s, when he was introduced to the Korean audience as a new, avant-garde poet influenced by the anti-Stalinism of the Khrushchev era. He was no longer a young poet but in his late sixties. He seemed to have something he really wanted to tell me. Yevtushenko said he had once visited Seoul, around the Olympics in 1988. I had very clear memories of that time and asked him if it was for the PEN International congress. He nodded, saying that there had been talk of petitioning the Korean government to release imprisoned Korean writers. He was now thinking that those writers had been my friends.

Yevtushenko said that when he arrived in Seoul, the head of PEN Korea and an assistant came to his hotel room to say hello. They briefly explained the atmosphere of unrest and expressed their concerns about a literary event being turned into a political one. They left behind an envelope containing $5,000. Later, the day before the vote on the resolution, someone visited Yevtushenko's room and asked him again not to support the resolution, leaving behind another envelope of $5,000. The Soviet writers, after Yevtushenko discussed it with the Soviet group chairperson, decided to abstain from this vote and also from the independent events outside of the conference, choosing a path of non interference and silence. He did not know what had happened with the other participants. But at the time, with economic liberalization underway in Russia, $10,000 was a lot of money. Yevtushenko's wife bade him to take this secret to the grave, but the decision had haunted him ever since. "As soon as I heard you were from Korea, I wanted to tell you what had happened back then." When I asked if I could quote him in the press, he said that his telling me at all was permission to do so, which I did in a brief article for a Korean daily when I returned to Seoul.

Right before the Seoul Olympics, the Korean government announced the July 7 Declaration, a document that hinted at the shifts in the Cold War era since Perestroika in the Soviet Union and Deng Xiaoping's "Black Cat, White Cat" liberalization policies in China. But democracy activists never forgot how the previous July 4 North–South Korea Joint Statement, the most progressive since the division, had been used by the South Korean government as an excuse for getting rid of term limits and by the North Koreans to abolish all checks on the Great Leader, Kim Il-sung—demonstrating that the reunification issue was politically exploited in both North and South, resulting in a kind of hostile symbiosis. We used to call these unrealized reunification campaigns "political marketing." In any case, the

July 7 Declaration was at least a step up from outwardly hostile North–South relations vowing mutual destruction, a result of the nationwide upswell in sentiment for reunification after Roh Tae-woo's election. On July 7, 1988, Roh's government announced the "Special Declaration for National Self-Esteem, Unification, and Prosperity," expressing the administration's willingness to promote diplomatic relations for the sake of peaceful reunification. Its points were as follows:

- Allow exchange between North and South Koreans and freedom of movement for foreign-national Koreans to both North and South Korea;
- Allow divided family members to confirm the status of their families across the border, along with the exchange of letters, and family-reunification visits;
- Open trade and cultural exchanges;
- Pursue balanced economic development and allow non-military goods to be exchanged with North Korea and allied powers;
- End confrontational diplomacy and the all-consuming war between North and South, and begin cooperating on the international stage;
- Improve relations between North Korea and the US, and South Korea and the Soviet Union and China.

By the spring of 1989, writers' and arts associations were gearing up for a year full of North–South exchanges. There had been many moments during my tour of Europe, the US, and Japan a few years before where I was infused with much hope for the future by overseas Korean democracy activists and foreign artists and politicians. I began talking about the specific logistics of North–South cultural exchange with Kim Yong-tae, who had begun to manage the Korean People's Artists Federation. Kim Yong-tae and I came to the conclusion that if there was going to be progress in North–South exchange, someone had to visit the North and talk with the North Koreans. We were sure that the South Korean government would pretend to help us but would, in the end, use all kinds of excuses not to follow through. I felt an obligation to further North–South cultural relations, but a big part of me also wanted to write my own objective take on North Korea. Even if it meant being prosecuted under the National Security Act, it would be a good opportunity to show the world that writers as well as politicians were subject to this heinous law. What worried me was the "non-notification" statute of the act, meaning that if friends or family knew that I was going to break this law but didn't report me to intelligence, they also could be criminally prosecuted. It meant that not only would I be thrown in jail but that the newly minted Korean People's Artists Federation and the Association of Writers for National Literature would also suffer persecution.

I came up with a plan. I had been helped by friends in the art world when I set up the Modern Cultural Research Center in Gwangju with Yoon Han Bong. During the Park dictatorship, artists had also supported the Council of Writers for Freedom and Practice when it was rechristened as the Association of Writers for National Literature. We brought together famous painters and brush calligraphers to decorate pottery and sold the completed pots in an arts bazaar. It was a way to gain the support of companies, individuals, or politicians who found it difficult to directly fund an arts organization that was critical of the government. The association successfully raised enough funds and sold the leftover ceramics for a long time afterward. The Korean People's Artists Federation used the same method to approach a National Assembly member, Kim Sang-hyun, who had ties to both Kim Young-sam and Kim Dae-jung's followers; he donated a painting to raise funds for the Korean People's Artists Federation's founding. After much discussion, Kim Yong-tae and I decided to ask Kim Sang-hyun for help as well. We were riding on the Korean People's Artists Federation's coattails, but we were sure Kim Sang-hyun would understand our situation. We had realized that the government would be much more cautious in deploying "non-notification" if the problem involved not just people in the arts but the opposition party as well. Kim Sang-hyun agreed to meet us for breakfast.

Kim Sang-hyun was waiting at a hotel restaurant when we showed up rubbing our eyes. Kim Yong-tae acted as a witness of sorts while I pled our case. I was going to visit North Korea, and it would be good if the honorable representative informed Kim Dae-jung's people and Kim Young-sam's people first. Kim Sang-hyun was unreadable. We exchanged a few jokes over breakfast before we parted. Kim Yong-tae telephoned me saying that Kim Sang-hyun had called him several times afterward, and that he seemed rather tense. Kim Sang-hyun had cloaked his feelings at breakfast, but he must have felt tricked into helping us. Nevertheless, he did reserve a place close to the Korean People's Artists Federation for our next meeting—a *bangseok-jip*, a lower-end hostess bar that was trendy at the time, where the female employees wore traditional garb and the patrons sat on floor cushions, from which the place derived its name.

When we got there, he exclaimed, "For goodness sakes, how could you think I'd be able to undertake such a thing on my own? I've brought along a friend to help us."

Kim Yong-tae and I had no idea who to expect when another man, wearing indoor slippers and a dress shirt and tie without a jacket, came into the room. It was National Assembly member Lee Jong-chan, secretary-general of the ruling party. Lee seemed to have strolled across the street from his party's headquarters at Kim Sang-hyun's call. Although a member of the conservative ruling party, he was the grandson of Lee Hoe-yeong (founder of the legendary Shinheung Military School of the Korean independence movement in Manchuria), and the grand nephew of Yi Si-yeong (vice president of the Provisional Government of Korea led by Kim Koo), and was thus a cut above the snarling dictatorship-holdover generals and colonels of his party.

Kim Sang-hyun introduced us and explained the role of the Korean People's Artists Federation. Lee Jong-chan seemed bemused by the situation but reassured by the fact that I was a well-known novelist.

Kim Sang-hyun patted my knee and said, "These people seem to be planning something. I'm not sure if I'll be enough to help."

I quickly added: "Actually, I'm trying to visit Pyongyang. How do you feel about that, Mr. Speaker?"

He looked surprised but smiled. "Well, I imagine that's good for the country," he said. "Have you received permission from the government?"

"We should get official permission, of course."

Lee Jong-chan seemed reassured by my answer. He observed that, ever since the Lunar New Year, it seemed like every arts organization and civic group was floating plans for North–South exchanges.

He told us about how he got into the Korea Military Academy as a student. President Rhee Syngman had adopted Lee Ki-poong's son Lee Kang-seok when he had no children of his own, having him enter the academy with Lee Jong-chan. As we listened to his family stories, we hoped that someday we'd be able to talk about that meeting as the beginning of a friendship, not just of a strategic alliance.

We had mentioned at the Korean People's Artists Federation meetings that a certain Mr. Hwang might be visiting North Korea, hoping the rumor would spread. There was an ANSP handler I met frequently who happened to be the regional police station's intelligence detective. Along with the police who mobilized the intelligence division detectives whenever there was a big public incident, the ANSP called and met me at restaurants or hotels about once a month. I had an ANSP handler exactly my age and practically a friend, who was fond of saying, "Life is one big insult." I imagine that what I ended up doing must have upended his life afterward. He showed up punctually after I called and asked him to come to my house, instead of meeting outside. I said that my book *The Shadow of Arms* was coming out in Japan next month, and I wanted to be there for the launch. I also hinted that I might sound out while I was there if it were possible to visit North Korea. He replied that it would be a fine thing if Mr. Hwang visited North Korea. When I asked why, he said it was because writers could see and hear things ordinary people couldn't, and went so far as to add that I should go and see as many things as possible, and write about it. He advised me that for now I should only check out if it was possible, and to come back to South Korea and discuss it with the government once I had secured an invitation. Our thinking on this differed, but I answered that of course I would discuss it with the authorities.

In any case, I had notified them of my intention to visit North Korea.

~

I left for Japan on February 28, 1989. I met with Professor Itō Narihiko, a critic and a long-time, politically savvy activist. It was important to figure out whom to tell about my intention to visit North Korea. Telling a Korean Japanese or Korean could make things legally complicated for them, not to mention the danger of more fabricated spy incidents. I concluded that I should tell someone who had connections with Japanese politicians and wasn't shunned by the General Association of [North] Korean Residents in Japan, someone who more than anything else was trusted by the North. That would be the former editor of *Sekai* and current head of Iwanami Shoten, Yasue Ryōsuke. My thinking was that I should inform him of my intentions but not tell anyone that I had. As I mentioned earlier, Yasue had serialized the "Communiqué from Korea" for years in the pages of *Sekai* and was persona non grata to the South Korean authorities. His role as a bridge between the Koreas was crucial. I needed to decide beforehand whom I was to credit with connecting me to the North when the official invitation arrived and my North Korean visit was settled. I followed Professor Itō's suggestion to designate Doi Takako of the Japanese Socialists. She was internationally known, and regarded helping a South Korean writer to visit North Korea for cultural exchange a rightful part of her duties as the leader of a neighboring country's political party.

I met Yasue Ryōsuke to explain the civilian exchanges between North and South and my intention to visit the North, and he immediately agreed to help. Next, I went to Chung Kyung-mo's offices for *Ssiarui him* (Power of a Seed) in Shibuya. Chung grinned when I told him my plans and teased me, saying, "You think you can just walk in there like it's your living room!" He came to the point as we got drunk after dinner. He had himself visited North Korea recently, and talked of his impressions of Pyongyang and the taste of the old-fashioned grilled mackerel they served in the visitors' residences. "I must be getting old, I kept wanting to break down in tears." He looked around at the Japanese people in the bar and added in a low voice that Pastor Moon Ik-hwan was also preparing a visit to the North. I'd heard a rumor to that effect, but I was still surprised by this evidence that we weren't the only ones planning on visiting North Korea. Chung was as excited as a child, saying he never dreamed he'd be going to North Korea with the writer Hwang Sok-yong on one arm and the pastor Moon Ik-hwan on the other.

I cautiously asked if my North Korean trip could be separated from Moon Ik-hwan's. Being involved in the National Association for Democratic Activism, Moon was visiting the North for the sake of political negotiations toward reunification; I was on a cultural exchange with no other agenda. As a writer, I had to be more flexible and able to move about freely and widely, my actions more geared to the mainstream. I was also considering publishing my travelogue in a South Korean newspaper or other formal media. I was too naïve at the time to consider that the National Security Act would not care about the exact nature of what I was doing in North Korea, or that when it came to it I would often overstep my prerogative as a writer.

Chung understood what I was saying and asked no more questions when I responded with a silent smile to his query of who was handling my visit. He advised, however, that I should not tell Itō or Wada Haruki about what Moon Ik-hwan was planning. He did not trust Korean Japanese organizations, and he was worried that Japanese people would blithely tell the Korean Japanese of our plans, unaware of the sensitivity of the issues.

About two weeks later, Yasue Ryōsuke delivered to me an invitation letter from Baek In-jun, chairperson of the Korean Federation of Literature and Arts. Yasue also wrote me an invitation letter himself. Itō Narihiko accompanied me to the Chinese embassy where I was granted a transfer visa. Before I left Japan, he asked the assistant, Gotō Masako, to set up a meeting with Doi Takako. I'd first met her at a publishing event a few years ago, during my six months in Japan; she had a briskness about her and a forthright way of meeting one's gaze that seemed different from other women. When I explained to her that I was going home to North Korea after forty years away, she wished me a safe journey and said she envied me, adding that she could foresee changes in the current Cold War situation. I had Itō take a picture of us together, as she was to be the official mediator of my trip. I wrote up a statement for Professor Itō and the director for the Japan–Korea Solidarity Committee, Professor Takasaki Sōji, to give to the media once my visit North was announced.

On March 18, about twenty days after leaving for Japan, I boarded a commercial airliner bound for Beijing. Most of the passengers were Chinese, officials and executives and the like, with few Japanese tourists at that time.

Once we had crossed the sea, the rugged peaks of a continental mountain range appeared from between the clouds. It reminded me of how young people would sign off petitions with "X years of yearning for reunification." Indeed. Forty-four years had passed since the division. I'd been unable to fall asleep in the hotel the night before and had bumbled about in the airport, briefly losing my passport and finding it again. Professor Dakasaki pretended to rap my head with his knuckles, warning me to pull myself together. I kept thinking of mysterious North Korea as a land of mischievous *dokkaebi* or a den of witches and got paranoid about eyes in the crowd watching my back. I felt disembodied as I sat in my hotel room, staring at myself from the outside. I was feeling the aftereffects of breaking a half-century-long taboo.

The plane descended as if on a staircase, dipping sharply at intervals. The customs official looked down at my transfer visa on my passport and cocked his head. China and South Korea did not have diplomatic relations at the time. He said something to me in Chinese, but I couldn't understand him and didn't answer. He called for someone and a woman approached. She looked through my passport and asked me in English:

"Where are you headed?"

I had no answer prepared, so I improvised. "It hasn't been confirmed yet."

She tilted her head as well. "Isn't this a transfer visa?"

"It is. Your government authorized it."

"What is your next destination?"

I could only smile like an idiot. She shrugged and gave me back my passport.

The airport was a bit of a mess, especially around the baggage claim area. It was dark inside, like some bus terminal out in the country. The passengers milled about in the small space, waiting almost an hour for their luggage to emerge. The conveyer belt looked filthy, made of repurposed tires shabbily fastened together. I sat down on the lowest step of a stairway, ready to wait it out until the crowd thinned.

Finally, a short man in a windbreaker who appeared to be searching for someone came up. He looked at me and said, in clear, North-accented Korean:

"Are you Mr. Hwang?"

I said I was.

"Do you have much luggage?"

I said it was all so chaotic that I was waiting for more people to leave.

I wasn't surprised the man was North Korean. He looked nervous, so I teased him a little. He must have been a section chief in the Committee for the Peaceful Reunification of the Fatherland, and, perhaps trying to disarm me with friendly intimacy, had showed up conspicuously chewing gum. I'm sure it was intentional, because I never saw him chew gum once we were in Pyongyang. I was probably the first South Korean he had ever spoken to. His hair was slicked back like an actor from the 1930s, and his hitched-up collar against his deeply tanned face made him look like a country mouse who had smartened himself up for a jaunt in the big city. I heard later that, every Friday, the Party administrators went to the communal vegetable farms outside Pyongyang to do volunteer labor.

"Please wait while I bring the car around." He slipped away. I sat there alone again, thinking that there was no turning back now—I really was headed for North Korea. He grabbed my bags without asking and put them in the back of a waiting Benz. The man sitting behind the wheel grumbled in lieu of greeting: "We've been here every day since Wednesday. You're not an easy man to find!"

He was quite different from the first handler. There was a sharpness about him, a touch of frost. It was he who recognized me first, apparently, when I was crouched in the corner of that airport.

"Since when do you wear glasses?" he asked, as if he'd known me for years.

"I've had these about a year now."

"You're more handsome than in the photographs."

The handler next to me said, "Today is Saturday so we must stay for two nights in Beijing. Is that all right?" He explained that the only flights to Pyongyang departed on Mondays, Tuesdays, and Fridays.

The shadows of poplar trees along the avenue whipped past in the car's headlights. We reached the Beijing Hotel, which had been enlarged three times since it was first built in 1915 and was bleak and empty-looking compared to the cozy compactness of Japanese hotels. In any case, my mind was running so far ahead to the land of the North that I barely paid attention to the foreign land around me.

In the oddly stark atmosphere of my room, the handler and I clinked glasses filled with some alcohol he had brought with him. I listened to him rant about China, because we didn't have much else to talk about. But amid his complaints about the chaotic social changes and the revolution that had lost all meaning, he repeatedly exclaimed: "You have to admit, it's not easy keeping this many people fed."

The next day was a Sunday. I was taken to see Tiananmen Square and the Forbidden Palace, but historic tourism had never really interested me. It was more fun people-watching: young people kept coming up to ask if I had any US dollars to exchange, and a young woman trailed us for a while, nagging me to hire her as a sexual companion. I saw many young people who looked like they were trying to imitate Western fads and seemed embarrassed to bump into a foreigner. I wasn't a psychologist, but I too was born in a place rife with self-consciousness, which made me recognize it right away. On my way back from North Korea, I would see the same vaguely anxious faces during the demonstrations that would later grow into the Tiananmen protests. The protesters had made a model Statue of Liberty to lead a march with, and I couldn't help feeling cynical about this, given my serious reservations about capitalism at the time. It was only when I was in exile in New York and heard the news of the ensuing disaster that I understood: what I had dismissed as naïveté was the longing of Chinese youth for a freedom that lay beyond the world they knew.

~

The next day at the airport, I saw many Korean Japanese waiting for our flight; a few young people in neat suits were no doubt North Korean students studying abroad. There was also someone who seemed to be a Korean American. I could tell which regions they were from by their accents.

A tall, demure North Korean woman in a blue uniform greeted us inside the plane, her face as softly pale and round as the moon.

"Would you like a drink?"

"What do you have?"

"Pear soda, spring water, and beer."

I ordered spring water. The label said Shindeok Springs. A little later I was offered a stick of chewing gum on a tray, Jindallae brand. It was stamped with an intricate logo of an azalea, just like the ones on old cigarette cartons, and wrapped in some sort of paraffin paper instead of foil. The gum crumbled to pieces as I chewed but it softened after a long while. It turned out to be all right. These cheap products, so confidently offered by the crew, felt like a sneak peak into the North.

It took about an hour and a half to fly from Beijing to Pyongyang. Just when I thought we'd had enough drinks and candy we were presented with a meal. My tray contained two slices of Castella sponge cake, some thick sausage from a government-run farm, and a boiled egg with some salt. It was like children's picnic food or a sports day lunch. I peeled the egg, thinking of train trips where I would have offered an egg like this to the person sitting next to me. Soon my handler tapped my arm and said, "We are now in the airspace of the Fatherland."

I rushed to look out the window. The valleys of the rugged mountain range stretching down from the north looked like wrinkles, and the places the sun didn't touch were still covered in heavy blankets of snow. Something hot rose up in my throat, and tears spilled down my cheeks. Our land! The native soil I'd been unable to set foot on for so long unfurled below me. As we dropped in altitude on our approach to Pyongyang, I could see villages and hills. Much of the mountains had been cultivated into terraced rice fields and orchards, and the straight lines of irrigation canals crisscrossed and converged in large man-made reservoirs. It was still early spring, the branches were bare, and the stretches of yellow earth were seemingly endless.

~

The plane landed at Sunan Airport north of Pyongyang. I had to wait inside the plane with my handler while the other passengers disembarked. "Your visit is not to be made public until Pastor Moon arrives with his team. I hope you don't mind a modest welcome."

Outside the window I could see a little girl in a blue coat holding a bouquet of flowers, a knot of people standing behind her. As I came down the stairs, the girl took a step forward and raised one arm in the Young Pioneer salute, hand angled over forehead, that I would grow accustomed to seeing.

"We welcome you, Mr. Hwang Sok-yong, to your father-land," said the girl in a clear, confident voice.

"Why, thank you," I murmured as I accepted the flowers and kissed her cheek. "You remind me of my daughter."

A man who seemed to be in charge of protocol gestured to a tall old man standing nearby. "This is Comrade Baek In-jun, chairman of the Korean Federation of Literature and Arts."

Baek In-jun patted my back as he hugged me. "Welcome! It's been too long!"

I was embraced in turn by the novelist Choi Seung-chil and the poet Choi Young-hwa. My heart was fit to burst at the thought of them being my fellow countrymen and, furthermore, writers who shared the same love for our language. We were driven into the city. The first thing I noticed was a painted slogan at the entrance to an orchard that read "Let's live our own way," which would more or less sum up my impressions of the North.

I was brought to a visitor's residence on the outskirts of Pyongyang. It was surrounded by fruit trees, and beyond that was a lush forest, making it hard it to tell where we were. Later I guessed it was only about ten minutes from downtown Pyongyang, somewhere in the northwestern suburbs. I was told it was an artists' retreat as well as a visitors' residence, used not only by writers but composers, screenwriters, and playwrights who needed to concentrate on finishing a piece of work. In my later visit to North Korea with my family, we would once more stay here in Seojaegol, where some of the houses had foreign flags flying out front, as if diplomats lived there. I also stayed for a long time in Cheolbongri, where there were four or five residences for foreign VIPs spaced widely apart around the reservoir.

This one was a single-story Western-style house. A carpeted hallway led to a large room with a piano that doubled as a parlor and movie screening room. Beyond that was a dining room, a row of bedrooms, a study, a bathroom with a tub, a recreation room with a pool table and table tennis, and a library with three walls of shelves filled with books. My own spacious quarters lay closest to the foyer. The vestibule led to a living room and study, and another room led to a bedroom with a bathroom attached, much like a hotel suite. The study had a shelf of reference books, including an encyclopedia; an easy chair; a television; and a refrigerator in the corner with a Chollima logo. Inside a stationery box on the desk were a fountain pen, pencil, ballpoint pen, a ream of papers, a thick notebook, and a notepad.

I opened the fridge: pear soda, tangerine juice, omija berry juice from Mount Kumgang, blueberry juice from Paektu Mountain, Ryongsong Beer, Geumgangsan Golden Ale, mineral water, and Shindeok Springs. There were some plain cookies, sandwich cookies, gummy candies, and sticks of taffy that I remembered from my childhood. The spring water and omija juice were the best and the taffy was good. It was made in the traditional way, by boiling down barley malt, and was not too sweet. The floors were neatly covered in woven straw mats from Kaesong. Kaesong was known for traditional handicrafts and light manufacturing, and these mats had been their designated product since the Korean War armistice.

The bedroom had a wooden bed, a built-in wardrobe, two chairs and a little table with coffee, ginseng tea, Chinese jasmine tea, black tea, and an electric kettle. There was a dresser with a bottle of toner, creams, lily perfume, pomade, and camellia hair oil. There was pine-scented soap and ginseng toothpaste in the bathroom. Only one thing stood out in contrast to hotel rooms around the world: framed pictures of Kim Il-sung and Kim Jong-il. I'm aware that this was hardly a reflection of how ordinary, or even high-ranking, North Koreans lived, but I've gone into detail about the room and its objects because it reveals North Korea's aspirational ideal of a rich life, dreamed up outside of the world market and made of homegrown, domestic products.

They kept my room stocked with sweets, as well as snacks and chocolates. The North Korean author Choi Seung-chil, our companion in the residence, always slipped handfuls of sweets into the pockets of visiting professors or researchers from Kim Il-sung University or the Academy of Social Sciences, bidding visitors to give them to their grandchildren. He whispered to me that such items were rare in North Korea: children got to eat candy only on Kim Il-sung's birthday, or as holiday rations once or twice a year.

There was a small banquet on my first day at the residence. Seven of us gathered: Baek In-jun, Choi Young-hwa, Choi Seung-chil, my handler from Beijing, the people who worked at the house, another handler who assisted me with outside events, and myself. I never asked my handlers from the Party for their names or rank, and they never disclosed them to me. The Workers' Party of Korea was said to have 2 million members, which was about a tenth of the entire population. I gave them nicknames in my usual teasing way, because I found it a little awkward not knowing what to call them. The man who met me in Beijing had said he was from the mountains of North Hamgyong Province, so I called him Mountain Man; the short and neat housekeeper said to have previously headed a middle school was Headmaster; and the man in charge who sang folk songs in a deep voice and who was, to quote the others, "a man of the people," became Comrade Farmhand.

There were two more men who assisted Comrade Farmhand and me with outside events. One of them was a handsome fellow with a pale face who had majored in French literature in university. I wondered if I should nickname him French Actor, but when I heard that his sixteen-year-old eldest daughter was good at the violin, my teasing took a new tack and I suggested that we betroth her to my son, the idea being that they would get married after reunification. We half-jokingly fretted that our children might wither into a spinster and a bachelor if reunification didn't come soon, and we vowed that we would do whatever it took to make sure it did. He therefore became My In-law, a nickname that he reciprocated. His team helped with my tour of North Korea with the other artists, putting up with endless hassles as they took care of our housing, transportation, and food. Sometimes at events, when I got so emotional that I'd well up, they too would start crying as they stood behind me.

The novelist Choi Seung-chil was a Hamju native who had graduated from Kim Il-sung University and worked as a reporter at *Rodong Sinmun* before his debut on the literary scene. After Liberation and peninsular division in 1945, his two daughters, college students at the time, had protested the establishment of what would become Seoul National University and had fled north across the newly demarcated border along with an aunt. Choi Seung-chil began writing fiction and became a full-time author affiliated with the Joseon Writers' Alliance. He was earnest, warm, and ten years older than me, born in 1933. I used the honorific *seonbaenim* with him. He never attempted to force his ideas on me, and would instead wait patiently until I understood him. We often talked late into the night about life and its complications. He told me stories about what had happened to some of the Southern writers who had disappeared in the North, talking of their fates in a grim, sometimes regretful tone. He also criticized the formulaic way of writing that some of the North's writers insisted on. I visited his apartment and met his family, and up until my last visit to Pyongyang in 1991, he always stayed with me as a companion at the visitors' residence. Later, when I was imprisoned in South Korea, I heard that he had died of a brain aneurysm.

Baek In-jun, a tall, wide-shouldered man with neatly combed hair and a back that was as straight as a rod, was seventy at the time; he had attended Yonhee College (now Yonsei University) and Rikkyo University before being conscripted into the Japanese military. He said he had roomed with the poet Yun Dong-ju during his Rikkyo days in a boarding house in Takadanobaba, Tokyo. Arrested for participating in the Korean independence movement, Yun Dong-ju died after being subjected to live medical experimentation in a Fukuoka prison. Baek In-jun knew by heart some of the poems Yun Dong-ju had written in their boarding house. One evening, perhaps a bit drunk, he recited Yun's "Easily written poem" in a low voice:

Night rain whispers outside the window.
The six-tatami room is another country.

To be a poet, I know, is a sad calling,
but here I go scribbling down another line of poetry.
Carrying an envelope sent to me, heavy with
tuition money and the scent of sweat and love,

I clutch my college notebook
and head to the old professor's lecture.

When I think about it, I lost first one, then two,
then all of my childhood friends.

What more could I wish for
than to settle to the bottom, alone?

Life is difficult, they say.
That writing a poem should come so easily
is a shameful thing.

The six-tatami room is another country.
Night rain whispers outside the window,

I light a lamp and hold back the dark a moment,
the last of me waiting for the dawning of an era.

I extend a small hand to myself,
a first handshake in tearful solace.

The poet and vice-chairman Choi Young-hwa was a thin, frail-looking man in his sixties who surprised me with his strength. I'd heard that he sometimes snatched his grandchildren's candy for himself but if any of his writer friends got into trouble, he would run around, heedless of the consequences, trying to get them out, even voicing his objections directly to the Party. He accompanied me to many of my events despite his wife being hospitalized for cancer. He was known to buy a whole case of beer when a group of younger writers came to call late at night, which they would drink "until they fell over," arguing over literature and bellowing songs until dawn.

The permanent staff included the cook, the driver, the Headmaster in charge of housekeeping, the women who took care of the meals and cleaned up after us, and the writer Choi Seung-chil. The other staff came and went as required. The chef was a young man who had just turned thirty and had served in their equivalent of the marines, where he had learned to cook, presumably Chinese cuisine, based on the flavor of his food. He had once been a weightlifter and bragged about how he used to clear up to ninety kilos. When drunk, he liked to dance to the fast Western dance music popular with young people. He had a tattoo on his bicep but was an otherwise simple and uncomplicated young man.

And then there was Hye-sook. She was a young woman of twenty, assigned to the visitors' residence with her mother. She said her home was in Nampo by the western coast near Pyongyang. Her mother seemed to go home every two or three days, but Hye-sook almost never left. Her father was a technician and her younger siblings attended middle school. Hye-sook had graduated high school and had not gone to college yet. She said she wanted to go to teacher's college if she had the chance. I wondered if she played an instrument, because I'd heard that North Korean youth studied at least one performing art in school. Hye-sook said she specialized in artistic gymnastics and had performed many times. She mostly served our meals, made our tea, collected our laundry, and saw us out of the residence or welcomed us back at the gate. She didn't say much but was a very warm person nonetheless. Whenever she read a book or set the table, she put on electronic music with a fast beat that she said was all the rage in Pyongyang. She once escorted us to a circus performance; after I complimented her on how pretty she looked in her formal *hanbok*, she spent the rest of the evening hiding from us in shyness.

My first night in the North was unforgettable. The release of the tension of the past months must have caused me to drink more than I normally would at the reception—I have no memory of going to bed. I was awakened by thirst around two or three in the morning. My surroundings were silent except for the cries of a scops owl in the distant forest. Its call sounded no different from what you would hear coming from Bukhan Mountain in Seoul, or the hills of Gwangju or Haenam; even the barking of dogs made me realize that the whole peninsula was one large village. My memories of life in the South flowed into the dark of the night like a memory of some faraway place. Scops owls do not divide themselves into communists and capitalists, but we Koreans had lived as separate countries for the past four decades. I could not believe I had crossed such a wide expanse of time to be here. Sleep fled at the fearful thought of our children inheriting the same fate.

Drawn by birdsong, I opened the window and put my head out, staring toward the dark forest. The sky was turning blue. A thin ribbon of light appeared on the horizon, and the rich scent of loam filled the air. A new day was dawning over Pyongyang.

I felt very much at home in Pyongyang, as it was my mother's hometown. When we were growing up in the South she told us many stories, again and again, of her childhood, our family's customs, the food, our relatives. While watching the Taedong River flow past, I could imagine my mother as a high school student skating over it when it froze in the winter. In any difficult moment of her life as a widow raising four children on her own, my mother would say determinedly, "I am a Pyongyang woman. Put me anywhere in this world and I could still raise all of you." Through these repeated assertions, Mother was teaching us about the strength of Northern women and making sure we knew that as no one was going to help us, we had better help ourselves. My mother also taught me the taste of *noti* rice cakes, extra-large dumplings, and buckwheat noodles in *dongchimi*, a pickled radish broth, during the long winter nights. She would often lament that nothing in the South tasted as good as food in the North.

From the time we fled to the South until the day she died, Mother kept all of her old land deeds and Japanese-era bonds in a battered briefcase. Sometimes she would secretly take them out to look at before bed—not so much to confirm her assets as to reminisce about the house and lands that she had grown up in. My memories of Pyongyang, where I lived until I was four, are as vague as a dream, but my mother remembered the place clearly. Its traces remained with her for a long time.

Pyongyang was utterly different from Seoul and even more different from Tokyo or New York. If I had to compare it to a foreign city, it reminded me of Berlin. Both Pyongyang and Berlin had to be rebuilt over the rubble of intense bombing. When I visited East Berlin after the Wall came down, I thought of how the apartments there, built in the 1950s after the aerial bombardments, were shaped and structured exactly like those of Pyongyang's Botonggang district. According to one theory, this came of imitating Moscow's speedy rebuilding of its showcase capital. Foreigners criticized Pyongyang for its hodgepodge of architectural styles, but the eclectic nature of the buildings probably stems from the changes that followed the North's ideological and social advances from the postwar era up to the 1980s. There were buildings and gardens that were Korean in style, but also plazas, bridges, and memorials that gave a Western impression. The more recent constructions were super modern, with the suspended construction of the Ryugyong Hotel, due to lack of funds, looking positively avant-garde. Pyongyang was not the Pyongyang of thousands of years of history, but a new city rebuilt from the ashes according to socialist urban planning. About a million South Koreans visited the Northern tourist and industrial attractions of Kaesong, Mount Kumgang, and Pyongyang from the end of 1990 to the early 2000s, when North–South exchange was at its height, and street views of Pyongyang are now broadcast regularly on South Korean television. But back then, during my first visit, the Soviet Union and the Eastern Bloc still existed, and North Korea managed to maintain its economic system of self-sufficiency and redistribution despite the difficulties. The country would fall into real peril a few years later, and from prison I would watch on TV what later became known as the Arduous March.

Pyongyang was organized around its centers of employment. People who worked at the same company lived in the same apartment zones. Later on, black markets would appear first in the regions and then, when things got worse, in the back streets of Pyongyang, but all I saw then was foreign-currency shops (the equivalent to our duty-free shops), department stores, and the various amenities that one would expect to find alongside those places.

In the accounts of Western journalists at the time and still today, Pyongyang tends to be described in the same terms: few people, cars, or shops on the street, many placards with slogans or statues and buildings dedicated to Kim Il-sung, pedestrians wearing drab clothes, a limited choice of products in department stores, shoddy goods, and a citizenry with no idea what is going on in the rest of the world. It's true that everyone went to school or work at the designated time, traffic cut off at the designated time, and there were no bars or nightlife, which made the city seem dead after rush hour. The North did seem poorer than the South on that first visit, but it still seemed to be more or less maintaining its self-reliance. You could see many young people and families out and about on weekends, relaxing on the banks of the Taedong River or near Moranbong, changed from their old work clothes into weekend wear. But their lives did seem dull and over organized. They could be free only within limits, and any individual deviation was strictly forbidden. Even at the visitors' center, the workers seemed to have weekend classes and gathered in a meeting at the end of every day. I once found Hye-sook sitting at the kitchen table, absorbed in writing something in a notebook. She was copying some "Words of instruction from the Dear Leader and Comrade Kim Jong-il" into it. It must have been homework assigned by the Party. I wondered if the high-ranking officials of the Party and its leader Kim Il-sung ultimately led boring, monotonous, and lonely lives themselves. In truth, my own life in Pyongyang was an example of such monotony. While awaiting Moon Ik-hwan's arrival, I unofficially visited downtown Pyongyang, following the guide to the Mansudae Art Studio, the Pibada Theater, the Grand People's Study House library, Pyongyang Maternity Hospital, Mangyongdae Children's Palace, Pyongyang Department Store, the subway, the Chongsanri cooperative farm, the Juche Tower, Moranbong, and Mangyongdae where Kim Il-sung was born. Around March 25, I was informed that Pastor Moon had finally arrived in Pyongyang via Beijing. His visit was made possible by the help of the National Christian Council in Japan, Chung Kyung-mo, and the Korean business-man Yoo Won Ho. Before this, the head of the Hyundai Group, Chung Ju-yung, had visited North Korea with the permission of the South Korean government and had announced plans for his Mount Kumgang development. The North called for a joint committee toward holding a North–South summit and invited the leaders of the South's ruling and opposition parties, Cardinal Kim Sou-hwan, Pastor Moon Ik-hwan, and Paek Ki-wan. But the South Korean government decided that Chung Ju-yung's visit was legal and everyone else's illegal; they alleged we were being used as pawns in North Korea's reunification tactics. The government's attitude was fundamentally a self-contradictory stance that went against the July 7 Declaration of 1988. South Korea's broadcast news reported frantically on Moon Ik-hwan and me visiting North Korea, while some other media outlets were content to calmly record the facts.

On the morning of March 27, one of the handlers came in look-ing nervous and said, "There's an important event today." He told me to put on a suit and tie, which made me anxious about the day ahead. The visitors' residence people usually let me sleep in after a night of drinking and did their best to delay any other event I might have, so I could rest. I didn't ask, but guessed it had something to do with Moon Ik-hwan and his group. I was driven to a house surrounded by forest; it took me a while to get my bearings. When a young man in a black suit and tie opened the car door for me, the handler whispered that we were at the residence of Chairman Kim Il-sung. In the foyer, I saw the familiar face of Chung Kyung-mo. We gladly greeted each other, and when I looked around for Moon Ik-hwan, Chong told me that he was currently meeting the chairman. Moon had been invited as a guest of the Committee for the Peaceful Reunification of the Fatherland to discuss with Chairman Kim, in a political negotiation of sorts, the North's proposal for federation-style reunification and the South's proposal for a pan-Korean community. In other words, Chairman Kim Il-sung was discussing the different forms reunification could take with civilian reunification activists from South Korea. Roh Tae-woo's pan-Korean community was an answer to Kim Il-sung's proposed Koryo Federation, the contents of which would be reconfirmed in 2007, through the October 4 Joint Declaration between Roh Moo-hyun and Kim Jong-il. Reunification activists such as Moon Ik-hwan did not oppose Roh Tae-woo's reunification plan at the time. They tried to convince Kim Il-sung that certain aspects of the North's proposed Koryo Federation would be difficult to implement in practice, meaning that smaller steps were needed at first.

The Southern activists' plan for a federation was based on the idea that if either the South or the North made their own ideology or political system an absolute condition for reunification, it would only result in conflict and deepen the divide. The most reasonable solution seemed to be that each side accept the other as it was and create a national reunification government in which they would share the same rights and obligations, while maintaining political autonomy in their respective territories. This proposal for a reunified republic was suppressed all throughout the 1990s. Thousands of people were arrested at National Liberation Day events in 1994 and 1996, with over 400 being sent to prison. And yet all either side wanted was to pursue reunification through peaceful coexistence, with the North proposing reunification with both systems left intact and the South likewise respecting each other's existence via their concept of a pan-Korean community. This was the proposal's most important point of commonality with the North's proposal: that the peaceful reunification of North and South was held to be the sacred duty of the nation.

On June 15, 2000—two years after I was released from prison—President Kim Dae-jung of the Republic of Korea and Chairman of the National Defense Commission Kim Jong-il of the Democratic People's Republic of Korea met in Pyongyang to proclaim what would be called the June 15 North–South Joint Declaration, expressing their desire to come together to take ownership of and resolve the reunification issue, including humanitarian matters, social and cultural exchanges, and the question of political prisoners.

The second point of the declaration indicated that the South's community proposal and the North's low-level federation proposal had something in common, and that reunification could be pursued along these lines. Of the three stages of South Korea's plan, the first stage of a united Korea would require North and South to remain independent nations with their own defense structures and diplomatic corps, while cooperating through United Korea summits and cabinet meetings, maintaining a "one nation, two countries, two systems, two governments" approach. On the other hand, the North Korean "low-level" federation was similar to the South's proposal in that it would maintain one nation, two countries, and two systems by allowing each region to handle their own defense and diplomacy, but differed in suggesting a single, unified government. In recent years, South Korea's conservative governments have insisted on the total breakdown and absorption of North Korea into the South, but this is wishful thinking that deliberately ignores the influence of the US and China, which both claim ownership over the Korean peninsula.

There were tall, intimidating men wearing black suits standing around the lobby and reception area, who I later learned were part of the North Korean secret service. Before I went in, they instructed me to answer every question the chairman asked me, to speak in short phrases and in a loud, clear voice, to never interrupt him or bring up anything I wasn't asked, and to speak only of light matters, along with a bunch of other nonsense that, true to form, I promptly forgot the moment I stepped into the room. My "liberal" way of speaking left the men visibly disconcerted, while Kim Il-sung, who must have found my odd behavior amusing, laughed often during our talk.

Chairman Kim stood waiting by the door as we stepped into the meeting area. He was tall and had a hoarse voice. He shook the hands of my companions, but at my turn he embraced me instead. He was bigger and broader than I was, and I felt as if I was being buried in his chest. I heard later that when he receives guests from far away, such as Koreans from overseas, he hugs them and pats them lightly on the back. He always used courteous language; in a more intimate moment he would ask in a low voice a question in informal Korean. He called me Comrade Hwang or Writer Hwang in private, but in public he always used the proper honorific of Mr. Hwang. He was, as in photographs from his youth, a handsome man with gray hair swept back and long, thick eyebrows that made a formidable impression. We sat at a round table with Pastor Moon to his left and me to his right. Also present were Chung Kyung-mo, Yoo Won Ho, and Yun Gi-bok and Chong Jun-gi from the North's National Committee for the Peaceful Reunification of the Fatherland and the Party's United Front Department. The chairman asked after Pastor Moon's mother, who was nearing one hundred, and talked of his memories of Longjing and Bukgando.

Many independence fighters had stayed at Pastor Moon's house while he lived in Longjing; he said his mother had even taken care of the martyr An Jung-geun there. Chairman Kim also talked about Manchuria and his alliance with the Chinese resistance against the Japanese, how they used to give him goods or lodging, and how he signed off on IOUs with "Korean People's Revolutionary Army Commander Kim." He smiled as he recollected how Zhou Enlai, his closest friend in the Chinese government, had told him that any landowner who happened to have one of these IOUs was pardoned. He emphasized that old records and the family names of Manchurian people, such as the Gaoli, indicated that Manchuria was an ancient Korean land. In parts of China that used to be Korean territory, he added, they still drink what we in Korea call *sikhye*, which Deng Xiaoping especially enjoys; he lamented the failure of our ancestors to hold on to that huge territory. He also said that the Jurchen peoples used to live in North Hamgyong Province and that the Aoji Coal Mine and Jueul hot springs all got their names from Jurchen, as *aoji* means "fiery stone" and *jueul* means "hot water" in that language. There were still people in that province with old Jurchen surnames that had had to be changed to Korean ones. Whenever he spoke of some region, he would say something like "There was that woman from Myongchon who lost all three of her children during the war. Her oldest grandson should get married this year. Then she'll feel more at peace." He accurately remembered who lived in what neighborhood, and always turned the conversation toward his concern for the people.

Out of the blue, Chung Kyung-mo asked the chairman whether his mother had been an evangelist. The chairman did not understand at first, but one of his men explained that Chung was asking whether his mother had been a Christian.

He smiled and said, "My mother had a hard life, so she used to go to church to catch up on sleep." Later I asked Chung why he had asked the chairman about his mother. He replied that Kim's maternal grandfather had been a Presbyterian pastor and had an uncle on his mother's side who was also a church elder, and that Kim's father had attended Soongsil School, which was part of the Presbyterian church. Kim's mother's given name was

Pan-sok, the old Korean translation of the name of the apostle Peter, so he had wondered if it were a Christian name. Come to think of it, my own mother's family was Christian, as were most enlightened intellectuals in the North at that time. Chairman Kim's father, Kim Hyong-jik, ran church-style night classes while organizing young people and participating in the nationalist independence movement. Later, as he learned about the Russian Revolution and imbibed modern ideas, his eyes were opened to the proletarian struggle. This was probably when he left his family in Pyongyang to fight the Japanese as a communist guerrilla in Manchuria.

Kim Il-sung spoke of the church for a bit before shifting to a new topic. "We were active around Paektu Mountain at the time. There was almost no one living around there. Aside from us, there were some locals who believed in Cheonbulgyo or something. They were slash-and-burn farmers who lived in tiny hamlets made up of a handful of log cabins. You know, religion is an amazing thing. Those people believed in Dangun and the Buddha and the mountain spirits, all mixed up, but they were a fine people. There's nothing to eat in that primordial wilderness. The Paektu tundra has harsh winters, it's nothing but snow and wind. We would come across these people during our marches from time to time. But even they had to abandon the place in the 1940s, when foreigners kept invading. We were the only ones left in the end."

I remember him as a natural storyteller who spoke through metaphors and his own experiences, rather than in abstractions.

After the audience with Chairman Kim, Moon Ik-hwan's team was scheduled to leave Pyongyang on April 3. I was going to stay behind for twenty more days researching the countryside. I called on Moon's team the morning they were due to leave. Their lodgings were a visitors' center on the banks of the Taedong River. The car entered a wide garden before stopping by a gazebo. Moon was sitting there alone, gazing down at the Taedong River.

He said he had just written a poem, which he read to me in a ringing voice. We were all hopeless optimists in those days, but even so, I was particularly moved by the purity of his passion that enabled him to face so peacefully the imprisonment that surely awaited him upon returning to South Korea. We reminded each other that our trips to North Korea had been planned separately. We also worried over the businessman Yoo Won Ho, who had accompanied us without either party having had time to prepare. He was the weakest link and so would endure the worst of the interrogation. If he returned later than we did, he would be even more isolated and his position uncertain. In any case, he had chosen this path for himself, and despite our misgivings he handled his situation with aplomb. Pastor Moon advised, "We don't have to arrive together and be arrested all at once. Mr. Hwang must write his travelogue of North Korea. Finish that, and then return. But you're going to have a hard time of it. The longer you delay, the worse it's going to be."

This old man in his seventies was more worried about me than I was about him. I went into the residence, where Pastor Moon told me Chung Kyung-mo would be. As soon as I stepped into the living room, Chung wordlessly raised a hand in greeting but kept his seat. He had earphones on and was concentrating on something. When I asked what he was doing, he put a finger to his lips and handed me an earphone. It was the eighteenth song of Schubert's, titled "Winterreise Der stürmische Morgen" ("The Stormy Morning"). It begins: "See how the storm has torn apart / Heaven's gray cloak! Shreds of clouds flit about / In weary strife." The first song of the cycle is "Gute Nacht" ("Good Night"), which includes the words "A stranger I arrived; a stranger I depart," depicting the feelings of a man who must leave the woman he loves on a frigid winter's night to wander alone. As I listened, Chung said, "Isn't that exactly how we feel?"

I know that we had all thought long and hard about risking prosecution to visit North Korea, but it was absurd how cool and calm they were acting. As I mentioned earlier, while South

Korea insisted on a "community of nations" system and the North pushed its "federation," these were just words that in the end meant the same thing. Pastor Moon had managed to convince Kim Il-sung that South Korea needed a transitional period because of its particular circumstances, which is why the chairman had retreated a step and come up with his "loose and low-level" federation proposal. Our efforts would later be enshrined in the June 15 North–South Joint Declaration.

I wish to take a moment here to address the politicians who call this "loose" reunification a sentimental take on the issue. I say to them: Don't mistake a hypothetical future for an actual one. Kim Il-sung is dead, his successor Kim Jong-il as well, but North Korea is still intact. A political power that has managed to preserve itself for the past half-century cannot be so easily toppled. It's been twenty years since Kim Il-sung's death, and we cannot maintain a North Korean policy that relies on simply waiting for the North to implode. It would be a very dangerous situation if it did implode, for then we would be at the mercy of the world's superpowers, just as we were on Liberation Day when division was foisted upon us, unless we take control of the situation. It is my opinion that, for North and South to survive, we must take ownership and lead the change ourselves.

After seeing the others off, I spent twenty more days in the North, touring the Paektu, Kumgang, and Myohyang Mountains, and the Tumen River. I also attended the April spring festivities, held around Kim Il-sung's birthday on April 15.

~

On Kim Il-sung's birthday, the chairman and his wife Kim Sung-ae invited me and some others to a dinner with Cambodia's Norodom Sihanouk. The setting was the chairman's building. Kim was waiting for us in the lobby. At the reception next to the banquet hall, he sat down next to Minister of Armed Forces O Jin-u, with me and Secretary Yun Gi-bok across from them.

The Sihanouk couple and Kim Sung-ae were not there yet. The reception area was wide enough for each seat to have its own side table.

Kim Il-sung pulled no punches. "The Japanese bastards spread rumors of my death several times when I was a resistance fighter. A few years ago, the Western media and newspapers in the South suddenly reported that I was dead, that Comrade O who sits next to me now had shot me, and that the People's Army had revolted. Long ago, when the May 16 coup happened in the South, one of my people said it was one of our people's doing, but I didn't believe it. I told everyone to wait and see. Of course, the new South Korean government became even more hostile to North Korea. I spent my whole life plagued by infighting. When I launched the armed resistance in Manchuria, many of the independence fighters left or broke away when the situation worsened. If they weren't going to fight, they could at least have stood aside, but they instilled doubt in the minds of young people who were determined to risk their lives, and created conflict among comrades. It wasn't enough to be nationalists or socialists, they had to draw even more lines among themselves and fight it out. Koreans love dividing themselves so much that if you put two Koreans together they'll create three parties: my party, your party, and our party." To his way of thinking, these party schisms were where the enemy had slipped in to create chaos.

Kim Il-sung finally got to his point. "Pak Hon-yong helped us significantly as the theorist of the Party, but he created much division both inside and outside the country. I've fought in armed resistances overseas since I was young, but it must be understood that there are quite a few spies and reactionaries even among those who fought their battles at home rather than abroad. I appointed Pak Hon-yong as my deputy prime minister and introduced him to his wife, but he did not manage the people around him properly. During the war, we held meetings on the move, and each time we changed our lodgings, too. And yet, each time, the American planes would bomb us very precisely where we were. This was how I knew there was a mole in our midst."

I had the impression that he regretted executing his political rival Pak Hon-yong for being an American spy, this man who had entered the resistance movement from a different angle and was affiliated with a different group. There was a theory among scholars that Kim's 1953 purge of the former members of the Workers' Party of South Korea was to shift the blame of war, and the 1956 removal of Kim Tu-bong and others after the August Faction Incident was to avoid political interference by China and the Soviet Union and strengthen his standing. Later, when I talked to Yun I-sang in Berlin about our impressions of Kim Il-sung, he described Chairman Kim as usually displaying a genial demeanor save for a sudden, cruel expression that would cross his face if something displeased him, his gaze turning as ferocious as a tiger's, a recollection that made us think about Kim's two faces. It was thanks to this hidden cruelty that he could efficiently kill the many competitors who had formerly been his comrades.

Kim Il-sung affirmed that the people loved him very much. He went on, "In Manchuria there were other Korean regiments carrying out armed resistance against the Japanese whose leaders were more experienced than I was, like our comrades Kim Chaek or Choe Hyon. I had many shortcomings, but my comrades encouraged me and tolerated me, which is how I ended up with the great responsibility I have today."

The Sihanouks and Kim Sung-ae arrived. Yun Gi-bok introduced me to them. The couple spoke a few words in greeting to me and continued to speak in French for the rest of the evening, aided by an interpreter who sat on a folding chair between them.

King Sihanouk had received a French education from a young age and attended university in France. He was eighteen when he ascended to the Cambodian throne and also served as president, premier, speaker of the house, UN representative, and head of the provisional government in exile, making him one of the most titled kings in history. During World War II he was inspired by the Japanese to declare Cambodia's independence from France, but when the French returned after the war, he waited until their defeat in Indochina in 1953. He was young but benevolent and wise. His wife, born Paule-Monique Izzi, was Cambodian-French-Italian and his sixth marriage. Sihanouk was outwardly restrained and for fifteen years ruled with a soft touch that spared Cambodia the disorder that reigned in some of the other Southeast Asian countries. His neutral stance regarding the Vietnam War did not sit well with the US. While North Vietnam did not support Cambodia's communist Khmer Rouge, he overlooked Vietnamese communists using eastern Cambodia as a secret base of operations. He was deposed in a coup d'état staged by General Lon Nol with the aid of the US in 1970. Pol Pot of the Khmer Rouge had used Sihanouk to gain the backing of the Cambodian people and discarded him once they were done. The king initially fled to China, until Kim Il-sung granted him exile in North Korea. He went back and forth between China and North Korea, became interested in directing and producing movies, and made a film with North Korea's help. He regained his crown in 1993 after peace talks in Paris with the Cambodian coalition government. A happy ending; but the road to postcolonialism for the prince of this small Asian country had been long and hard.

Kim Sung-ae wore a modest gray *hanbok* and looked like an ordinary, elderly housewife. It was said that she was never mentioned or shown in North Korean media. As a People's Army soldier during the war, she had come down as far as the Nakdong River front but had fallen behind and marched a thousand *li* to rejoin her troops.

Queen Monique was a middle-aged, mixed-race woman who wore a gentle smile the whole time as she looked from one speaker to another.

King Sihanouk was a small, stout man with slender fingers. His large eyes made him seem like a sensitive soul. He had lived in China since losing his throne but spent his springs and autumns in North Korea. Kim Il-sung, who once served as vice chairman of the Non-Aligned Movement, had many close friends among third-world leaders. He was helping the unfortunate Sihanouk like he would a younger brother.

A peaceful resolution to the Cambodian problem was being discussed in Geneva at the time, and naturally our conversation arrived at this topic. Sihanouk was worried that Pol Pot and Heng Samrin were leaning on their respective backers, China and Russia, and were refusing to come to terms despite his own mediation. He wondered if Chairman Kim could step in to mediate as an elder statesman. Kim responded:

"The smaller the country, the harsher the sectarian conflicts. These leaders rely on the strength of powerful countries because they do not trust the power of their people. I suffered because of sectarianism for forty years. There are many countries in this world and many nations, and of course each wants to live in its own way. Koreans must live in the Korean way, Cambodians in the Cambodian way. We cannot live like the Americans or the Soviets. I hope for good results from these talks, but the people must come together if Cambodia's problems are truly to be solved. These problems will not be solved by someone else telling them what to do. But do bring those two to me, Your Majesty. If I succeed in mediating peace, Your Majesty must buy me a drink."

He then consoled Sihanouk. "I visited Indonesia once when President Sukarno was alive. We took a detour through Cambodia then as well. Indonesia had many poor people and beggars. But under your rule Cambodia was prosperous in comparison. Any country is livable if the rulers are not greedy and they work hard with the people. The problem is that strong countries do not allow them to do that."

Sihanouk dabbed at his eyes with a white handkerchief. Queen Monique looked moist-eyed too.

I had visited Paektu Mountain, the highest mountain on the peninsula and considered sacred in Korean mythology, a few days before and could still recall the awe I felt while looking upon the endless Kaema Plateau rising from the mist. I spoke of how the peaks beyond the lake in the crater were Chinese land, so we could not stand on that side to look down at Manchuria, but it was moving to see, from the North Korean side, how our land flowed from the top of this mountain to beyond what the eye could see.

Kim Il-sung began to talk about borders. "Our borders were decided with China after the war. The trickiest part was Paektu Mountain. The border problem came up not long after China's revolution, so it must have been around 1950. We had already resolved this problem during the Joseon era with the Qing. A border marker was supposed to have been placed on Paektu Mountain, but when I ordered a search for it, we found that it had been left somewhere in the foothills of Nampo Taesan instead. The mandarin in charge of setting the stone had obviously gone no further on his palanquin. Hiking into the primordial wilderness would have been too much work for him, so he just tossed the stone there and left. China knew what had happened, yet still insisted on the misplaced stone as the basis for our border. There was no talking sense into them. Zhou Enlai and Peng Dehuai said they would come. Zhou was, of course, not someone you could talk sense into. I was in hospital at the time, and the two of them came to visit me there. I brought up the border problem. They didn't want to speak too long with a sick person. We decided then and there to divide the Amlok River in half, with the northern half on their side and the southern one on ours, Paektu Mountain and all. The Tumen is a mere stream upriver, but the northern part of it became China and the southern, Korea."

Sihanouk turned the topic to health, and Kim had this to say: "What other secret can there be to good health, except to follow a good routine and be optimistic? People like us are young at sixty and sixty at ninety, so I'm not even sixty yet. There are many people older than ninety in the countryside. Maybe if I've lived so long it's because of all the rumors of my death when I was a resistance fighter. The Japanese supposedly arrested me, assassinated me. They put my face on Wanted posters. But if you want a revolution, you have to be optimistic, like the people."

Indeed, Kim Il-sung's teeth were straight and white and he had hardly a wrinkle on his face. He was slightly hard of hearing in his right ear, so his assistants talked a little louder and each person in official meetings with him was given a small speaker in front of their seat. But normally, guests would be seated right in front of him.

He discussed Korean reunification for a bit with Sihanouk, then handed me a photograph. "This was taken last week. I was in the garden one morning when I saw a white bird I'd never seen before, sitting on the grass. I thought it was a pigeon at first, but it was a white magpie. I had my aides quickly fetch a camera and take a picture."

Just as he said, the photograph showed a white magpie, long-tailed and nimble-bodied, sitting underneath a pine tree.

"It flew there twice. I asked Hong Ki-mun if there was any precedent. There are several such instances in *The Veritable Records of King Sejong.* It's an augur for a country's good fortune. Maybe our countries will be one again. You take good care of that photograph, Writer Hwang. Be that white magpie that brings the happy news of reunification to our nation."

During my time in North Korea, Kim Il-sung invited me to several personal meetings where he spoke of many things. He said that he was glad my family was to join me in Germany the next year, and broached the subject of Pastor Moon's sentence being commuted from life imprisonment to ten years. "That National Security Act . . . Without it, you would be much safer . . . I don't think the people of the South feel ready. I met Pastor Moon twice. Not two hours in all. How much of my 'red dye' could have rubbed off on him? Sending an old man to prison for ten years is a death sentence. Pastor Moon is a man of God and a patriot. We need people like him to stay around for a long time. I even asked if there was anything I could do for him. The cold is not good for old people. I should send him some herbal medicine."

The student protester Lim Su-kyung had come to Pyongyang to represent South Korean college students at the World Festival of Youth and Students. Chairman Kim spoke regretfully of what had happened to her since. "Lim is a true daughter of the nation and a hero. I tried to convince her not to cross back through the Demilitarized Zone. My officers went to her and asked how old revolutionaries like them could sit by while a young female student walked into the maw of a tiger. She answered that if they didn't let her, she would jump off the thirtieth floor of her hotel. No one could eat properly while she was on her hunger strike in the DMZ."

He talked about his imprisonment for agitating against Japan's building of the Gilhoe Line railway during his days at Yuwen Middle School, and how lucky he was that his sentence had been shorter than that of other comrades, who were imprisoned for decades, if not executed. He spoke of the good and bad things about prison. "I've met so many people that I can read their fates in their faces. Writer Hwang is a man of multiple talents and he'll do great things. You must use your talents for the good of the nation. Look how Yi Kwang-su's early talent gave so much hope to the youth of Korea. Although he sold out to the Japanese bastards later on, which harmed our nation. Writer Hwang must write many masterpieces, even after reunification. I used to read a lot during my instruction tours of the country, but now my eyesight is failing and I can't read for long. If there is a book I really want to read, I have a pair of actors record it for me. I listen to these recordings when I can. I also have the letters on my documents enlarged."

I'd heard from an aide that Kim Il-sung had listened to the whole of *Jang Gil-san* in a recording and had praised it. Kim

Il-sung had read numerous books since he was young and, like revolutionaries in other countries, had experience in the arts himself, which naturally gave him an interest in literature. He was fluent in Japanese and Chinese and could speak some Russian. His books displayed in a museum of the revolution were above all translations into Japanese and Chinese. He seemed to have read mostly Japanese books on Western thought early on.

"The first time I was introduced to such books was in Manchuria, when my father gave me Japanese translations about the October Revolution and the Paris Commune. I also read Nikolay Chernyshevsky's *What Is to Be Done?* and was moved by it. I didn't read many novels at first, but I read as many books on modern thought as I could. I left Wusong for Huadian, where the nationalists had founded a two-year school called Hwasungeuisuk to educate young people. It had about sixty students. Among them were two twenty-years-olds who were attending on the recommendation of the resistance fighters. Some of the students went on to fight alongside me. One of my father's friends in Huadian lent me plenty of books, which I then discussed with my comrades. *The Communist Manifesto*, *Capital*, *Wage Labor and Capital*, I read all of those then. My reading expanded in earnest when I entered Yuwen Middle School. I was always picked as the librarian at student council. Yuwen had the most progressive library at the time. The works of Lenin on the question of colonized nations and imperialism were especially helpful. The book club created at the time became the start of the Down-with-Imperialism Union. I spent all night devouring books like Maxim Gorky's *The Mother* and *The Song of the Stormy Petrel*, and Nikolai Ostrovsky's *How the Steel Was Tempered*. I read Tolstoy's *Resurrection* and Alexei Tolstoy's *The Road to Calvary*. I read Dostoevsky and Shakespeare as well, but while they were great writers, from the perspective of the people, they were reactionaries. We couldn't get hold of any books when we were guerrilla fighters in the mountains, so we made a mimeographed newspaper where we'd read the writings of our colleagues. We had someone in the Korean villages keep their copies of the *Dong-a Ilbo* and Japanese papers, which we consumed in fortnightly stacks. Comrades who had gone on missions to Seoul sometimes returned with books and magazines. We were so eager to read anything in our language that we absorbed every word, even the ads. I once read a short story by some writer, the title had something to do with toes. I was infuriated for our people when I finished it. The writer was in Seoul, so he obviously would not have known about us fighting in the middle of snowstorms, but surely he must have seen other people suffering around him. You must not make literature or art of that sort."

As we ate noodles for lunch, he said, "We call these frozen potato noodles. I asked Luise Rinser if Germany had something like this when she visited from there some time ago, but she said North Korea was the only country to cook with frozen potatoes."

The noodles were black, thick, and delicious. The starch came from frozen potatoes that had been kneaded, sliced, and boiled, perfect for dunking in cold soybean soup. There was a sprinkling of black sesame seeds on top, and it came with a side dish of Hamgyong Province–style charlock kimchi.

"Many people around the Tumen River helped us when we fought. The subsistence farmers were hungry themselves, but they would bury potatoes near the roads where we would pass and leave marks for us to find them. The earth was frozen underneath the thick snow, and the potatoes were like black rocks. You couldn't roast them or boil them. The Japanese bastards had successfully cut off our supply lines at the time. They expected us to freeze or starve to death, and were going to kill off any guerrillas that were left. We did not want to throw away anything the people had given us, so a comrade who had once been a slash-and-burn farmer thought of making noodles from the starch. Poor people know how to survive. How delicious those noodles were with only salted water for flavor."

Another day, once I had seen something of the country, Kim Il-sung asked whether I could suggest any improvements. I remember speaking freely then as well, unlike the other visitors.

"I was very surprised at the resilience of the people. But I couldn't help thinking that North Korean society has no joints."

"What do you mean by joints?"

"I've read that the chairman goes all the way to the backwaters of Chagang Province to deliver his on-site teachings. But how could it be possible to see everything? There are problems of all sizes, from the tips of the country's toes to the head, all converging at the center, the heart. Wouldn't it be better to allow certain regions to solve their own problems? Those are the joints. They're like fuses that break at a power surge. When the joints are inflexible, you're in danger of paralysis."

What I meant was that if the Party's center held all the decision-making powers, the system would become fraught with the dangers of bureaucracy, such as mindless processes, corruption, and results that looked good only on paper. Perhaps the League of Socialist Working Youth or the General Federation of Trade Unions of Korea or Socialist Women's Union of Korea could be given a bit more autonomy. I had been in a village that was preparing for a visit from Kim Il-sung and saw them hastily transplanting fruit trees and being given more rations to make them seem better off than they were. There were places in Hamgyong Province where I saw signs that read "Topsoil Battle." I cautiously asked what this meant. Apparently, despite localities reporting successful achievement of their productivity targets, upon actual inspection, productivity was found to have fallen. In the absence of fertilizer the quality of the soil was declining, the topsoil becoming unsuitable for farming. Research revealed that vast areas of land would no longer be arable in a few years. Soil from the mountains had to be hauled in for topsoil. While the isolation of North Korea played a significant role in the nationwide famine during the 1990s, this kind of bureaucracy and red tape had surely compromised the "self-reliant agriculture" that depended on the farmers' motivation to work. The wife of a famous foreign visitor once told me of how the chairman had entered a farmer's house on a whim and opened the rice pot, only to find a layer of white dust. The chairman had crouched down on the dirt floor and burst into tears.

"That is a very good observation. The people must fight against bureaucracy. The Party should not always try to do everything directly. Being so poor, we have tried to do so much, perhaps too much. In the end, we can only rely on the strength of our people."

The South Korean activist sphere had not taken kindly to Chung Ju-yung's visit. Some Hyundai laborers had been beaten up by hired thugs on the very day he entered North Korea. Koreans living overseas became highly critical whenever Chairman Kim met a far-right figure such as Moon Sun Myung.

But Chairman Kim had an unexpected take on the issue. "What do young people in the South call Hyundai's Chung Ju-yung or Daewoo's Kim Woo-choong?"

One of his aides replied, "Ah yes, monopoly capitalists."

"Monopoly capitalists. I don't see them as that. Moneymaking is a talent. Not everyone can do it. We must take a broader perspective. Mitsubishi or Mitsui belong to other people, but Korean companies belong to us. It is a good thing if they use their riches to benefit nation and country. In my speeches after Liberation, I told the people that those who can give money should give money; those who possess knowledge, their knowledge; and those with strength, their strength for us to build our nation. I still think so. We're a divided nation with foreign powers right under our noses, so we should not have division among us. Of course, our relationship with production will change as well once we achieve a peaceful union."

As Kim Il-sung said himself, his life had been a long process of fighting against sectarianism while expanding the membership of the pro-reunification club. He mentioned Choe Chang-gul many times when talking about these struggles, from the years in Manchuria where he allied with anti-Japanese Chinese forces to when he shook hands with right-wing nationalists who were often more intent on crushing communism than on fighting the Japanese. Choe Chang-gul was the principled squadron leader of the nationalist right-wing group, Gukminbu, who had brought reinforcements to Kim Il-sung at the latter's desperate request, before being assassinated by one of his own men. As Choe succumbed to his injury, he bade his army not to punish the assassin. This was his way of making them realize that, despite their ideological differences, the resistance must stand together to fight the Japanese.

The chairman used many interesting turns of phrase, saying that "turning left leads to a narrow road"; that public activism needed to be "like a peach, mouthwatering from the outside, soft flesh on the inside, a hard pit in the middle, and a soft kernel in the pit" (the skin was mainstream politics, the flesh was the masses, the pit was the central organization, and the soft kernel was the love and trust among the people of the organization); or that theories of revolution that were "as cold and hard as ice" needed to be "melted down in the flame of experienced wisdom." I called this his "people's rhetoric."

The spokesperson for the German Greens, Rainer Benning, told me an amusing story about what Kim Il-sung said when asked about liberalization and opening up the country. "Well, it is a bit stuffy, so we should open the window. We'll get a fresh breeze if we open it just a crack, but we'll have flies and mosquitoes and other insects flying in if we open it too much. We'd need a screen."

His words on the North–South division left an impression on me. "South Korea is like the horsehair *gat* hat the nobles of old used to wear. The *gat* is the reunification problem. It stays on the head because of the two ribbons tied under the chin. One string is the American empire, the other, the Japanese. Just one loose string can take the whole *gat* off."

He was quite a conversationalist and said many such interesting things to me whenever we met. I was always impressed by how much he read and by his unexpected intellectual depth.

If someone were to ask what I thought of Kim Il-sung (and this question was inevitable at the end of my talks, usually posed in an accusatory tone by someone who knew I'd been to North Korea), my first answer would be another question: can we really talk of modern Korean history without Kim Il-sung? We need to look at his life objectively. He was born in 1912, just as Russia and Europe were gearing up for their imperial wars and revolutions, and he had started his own revolutionary work in 1926 with the Down-with-Imperialism union. He could be seen as part of the first generation of socialist revolutionaries that includes Lenin, Stalin, Tito, Mao Zedong, and Ho Chi Minh, leaders from other countries who are fairly famous in South Korea. Our own modern history frequently mentions the patriotic Enlightenment movement or the Reformist movement, but almost never talks about the socialist movements of the 1930s or the armed resistance against the Japanese. Kim Il-sung was alternately relegated to being thought of as dead or fake—and at best a puppet of superpowers like China or Russia. Until the beginning of the revolution in Asia, the Comintern's central ruling powers directed revolutionaries in Vietnam, which had lost its country, and Korea was forced to be part of the Chinese Communist Party under the "one party per country" rule, to be deployed in China's revolution first. Kim San's *Song of Arirang* shows us that countless young revolutionaries who sacrificed themselves in the Guangdong and Shanghai communes were Korean. André Malraux's *Man's Fate* depicts the "Canton Commune" around the same time that Ho Chi Minh worked as a member of the Chinese communists. This was why Kim Il-sung was affiliated to the CCP and had to move his base of activity to the Tumen River to overcome the conflict between the Comintern and the issue of the Korean communist revolution. The unfortunate circumstances besetting the Korean revolutionaries are reflected in Kim San's own frustration at being a hanger-on in Yan'an. Having given his whole life to the revolution, in the end he was accused of espionage and executed. Hong Bum-do, who had also been a legend in the Russian Manchurian armed resistance, was forcibly moved to Central Asia where he spent the rest of his life as a janitor in an obscure theater.

There is a theory that Kim Il-sung's resistance group against the Japanese was nothing but a puppet army of the Soviets, and that our own armed resistance was negligible in the 1940s. Japan's war of conquest was heating up around that time, and anti-Japanese guerrillas did work mostly in small groups. It was only just before Liberation that the US and Soviet Union struck alliances with the resistance and coalition forces of various Asian and European countries. The American Office of Strategic Services trained guerrillas and the resistance in France, Italy, Greece, and Yugoslavia, as well as Vietnam's Ho Chi Minh and the illustrious commander of Dien Bien Phu, Võ Nguyên Giáp, who were subsequently drafted into Allied forces and used in the war against the Japanese. We know from the memoirs of Kim Jun-Yop and Chang Chun-ha that it was the same with the Korean resistance, who were also given military training by the OSS for deployment on the Korean peninsula—only to be dismissed when Japan surrendered after the nuclear bombs fell. It is not unknown that Kim Il-sung's army, which enjoyed intimate knowledge of the Tumen River region and the trust of its people, were part of the Soviet section of the Allies. We can see from US State Department files that Japan's Guangdong forces and Koreans in the North were aware of Kim Il-sung and his soldiers. As the only armed Korean forces to be acknowledged and accepted by the Allies, they are proof that there was armed Korean resistance in eastern Manchuria. It is not good history to deny even the most objective facts about Kim Il-sung, just because he stood on the other side of division. We need to be able to talk about Kim Il-sung's achievements and faults, just like we need to have a balanced perspective on Park Chung-hee.

I have always maintained that speaking of peace and communication while twisting the facts and attacking the other side would never lead to a better relationship, which is why I've tried to be as generous as I can with North Korea. I have written about the things Kim and I discussed because there was a compassionate dimension to his words, very different from his policies, which I could never agree with. It is undeniable that his many errors of judgment have brought misery to the North Korean people, especially his role in dividing Korea. The American policy of containment shares some of the blame, but it was indisputably Kim Il-sung who imposed isolation on North Korea and the basis for a hereditary rule that has extended to his grandson. This is why history will continue to remember him as an internationally notorious dictator.

~

I know that everyone has childhood memories, and there's nothing inherently remarkable about reminiscing over them. But being able to look back, albeit dimly, on the old days in a land that I thought I would never see again was an absolutely unforgettable feeling. And maybe it was that feeling that nudged me in a certain direction. I am confessing this now to explain the reasons for my generous interpretation of the state of affairs in North Korea. First and foremost, it was because of my childhood family memories. But maybe my reasons went beyond that, into the political. Pastor Moon told me in Pyongyang that Chung Kyung-mo said to him: "If the North Koreans insist they are making soybean paste out of black beans, just play along. Isn't that the way to get them talking to us? Hasn't every other outside visitor gone against them, saying 'no,' 'we object,' 'that is not the case'?"

I thought it only right to praise the resilience of the North Korean people. General Douglas MacArthur, from his headquarters in Japan, had written in his report of the war against North Korea that there were no targets left in the territory after they had bombed every harbor, railway, and minor reservoir. The North Koreans had restored what, to borrow an American expression, had been bombed into the Stone Age, and had become self-sufficient—an achievement no Western nation has the right to look down on. To criticize the official Juche ideology or the dictatorship centered around the Great Leader is something else, and my thinking was that we needed to give them the leeway to develop trust and communication, for the sake of reunification, before we could "lead" North Korea to change. I know that to say anything in the slightest way positive about North Korea is to violate the National Security Act, but I was glad to see that the fields and forests along the Taedong River remained undeveloped and looked just as they had in the past.

Moranbong is really a small hill, and like Nam Mountain in Seoul, it serves as a park in the middle of the city, dividing Pyongyang into east and west. From there you can see the Taedong River and the plains east of the city. The famous pine trees of Moranbong were almost wiped out by bombing during the Korean War, but trees and bushes had been replanted since and were filled with blooms when I visited in the spring. The Japanese-style two-story house where my family lived when we moved down from Manchuria had stood between the stadium and the arch memorial that was built after the war. My old neighborhood had vanished, and now there were tall apartment buildings built at intervals over areas of green. I stood on the western side of Moranbong, which we would have seen from our house, in order to guess where it had been. I was about three at the time, so my memories were fragmented like dreams at dawn. They were memories my mother and sisters and I had rehearsed many times over the decades, so parts of them were very clear. A Soviet officer and his wife lived on the first floor of that two-story house; we lived on the second. His wife adored me and gave me things to eat and hung colorful epaulets and medals on my clothes. The rooms all had tatami mats and large *oshiire* (built-in closets) that were so cozy I would climb into them and fall asleep. My family would become frantic, thinking I had disappeared.

We could see Moranbong from the second-floor window. A row of traditional *hanok* houses had lined a hill that was now all memorials and murals. We could see my younger aunt's house (she died in South Korea in the 1970s). In the mornings I would see her busily moving about in her courtyard. I can clearly remember my older sisters leaning out the window and calling, "Auntie!" whereupon our aunt would look up and wave to us.

The path up the western slope of Moranbong led to Chilseong Gate. Every morning I would hold my father's hand and pass through the gate to walk to the Ulmil Pavilion. Occasionally the caramel candy seller would be there, and if I were lucky, I'd get to enjoy a treat that morning. Looking out from Chilseong Gate and a little off from our neighborhood was a main road where the tramline ended. My sisters and I would play all day and then go to the tram station to wait for our mother to return from work. I can still see my mother smiling and running toward me with a bag of Japanese cookies or rice crackers in her hands, and then lifting me up in her arms.

I went through Chilseong Gate and up Moranbong, like I used to as a child. The gatehouse, old walls, and stone steps were still the same. It had seemed like such a tall mountain when I was little, but now I saw that it was only a small hill. The winding stone steps led up to the base of the pavilion, and on the corner of the steps of Ulmildae itself was a small crag. My father and I would rest our legs there for a bit when we reached it. Ah! That crag was still there. There was a photograph of my father and me at this very spot, which was how I remembered it so well. I sat in that spot that had been a faint memory these past forty-odd years and had a photo taken of myself, a boy who had returned as a middle-aged man now older than his father. I turned away and cried. Not from happiness or sorrow, but maybe for the harshness of this life.

Born and raised in Pyongyang, Mother was one of the "New Women," having received a higher education in Tokyo. My maternal grandfather joined the Donghak Peasant Revolution as a youth before becoming a Christian and graduating from divinity school to become a pastor. He was imprisoned for helping to organize the 1919 March 1 Movement against Japanese colonialism in Pyongyang, which was followed by another prison sentence for speaking out against compulsory Shinto worship. My mother's older aunt and younger brother became socialists under his influence, which resulted in their family being divided into North and South.

It was my mother whose memories of youth were in Pyongyang and Tokyo. She went through hell and back after becoming widowed not long after the war was over, raising and educating her four children. I grew up listening to her say over and over again that our family would thrive only if reunification happened and that we must, someday, return to where we came from. Of all her children she loved me the best, and all her hopes were pinned on me. But I did not meet her expectations. She had not wanted her son to become a novelist.

The first thing I did in North Korea, of course, was to seek out my North Korean relatives. I was thinking of how difficult my mother and oldest uncle's final years had been in the South. I also remembered how my younger aunt, who had worked as a teacher in South Korea and died alone, would often sit with my mother and sing the songs they'd learned as schoolgirls in Pyongyang, harmonies and all. I gave my handlers a list and was told that my mother's youngest sibling, my third aunt, was living in Sariwon. The children of my oldest uncle, my cousins, were living in Myongchon in Hamgyong Province. They had all been born and raised in Pyongyang, but my uncle's wife wasn't able to raise the family in the city after my uncle had gone to the South, which is why they ended up as Myongchon people. According to a North Korean escapee who called me on the phone one day in 2000, my oldest and youngest cousin in Myongchon both starved to death during the Arduous March.

I recognized my youngest aunt immediately when I met her in the reception hall of the Koryo Hotel; she was just like my mother when she was alive. My aunt also recognized me and called out, "Sunam-ah!" My baby name. We hugged and cried for a long time, before going through the introductions to her children and the stories of what had happened to our relatives on both sides of the armistice line.

When we had settled down a bit, my aunt looked into my face and said, "Your demeanor has changed quite a lot. You used to be so handsome, and smiled easily . . . Now you seem sharp and frightening."

My youngest aunt's words would stay with me. I had been through so much with the Park dictatorship and the Gwangju struggle that my face could no longer be the carefree one that she remembered.

My youngest aunt told me that after my grandfather was imprisoned again for agitating against compulsory Shinto worship, my mother brought her to Manchuria and sent her to school. My aunt took care of me when I was little, and after Liberation, when we settled in Pyongyang, she would still carry me on her back when she needed to go out. Before my family fled to Seoul, she married a socialist who had graduated from Japan's Meiji University.

When my mother lived with us in Haenam in South Korea's Jeolla Province, she once told me she had a dream in which my Pyongyang grandmother visited her. My youngest aunt was well off and had taken care of my grandmother. According to her, my grandmother had died in 1978 in Sariwon, around the time that my mother was dreaming about her.

Not only did the war and the North–South division tear apart many families this way, Korean literary history was split in two as well, and the work and lives of countless writers were destroyed or lost. Writers persecuted by the dictatorships in both North and South were thankfully able to recover their work somewhat with the advent of democratization in the South, which worked as an indirect pressure on the North's authorities. We can overcome our division, not with prejudice or violent language—calling us "leftie whiners" or telling us to "go live in North Korea"—but by the establishment of a genuine democracy in the South.

I asked my handlers about the most senior and still-remembered writers who had ended up in the North, namely the novelists Hong Myong-hui, Ri Ki-yong, and Park Taewon, as well as for news of their families. The novelist Choi Seung-chil, who was in the residence with us, also told me stories of the North Korean writers. Camaraderie between writers is inevitable and transcends ideology and writing style. Speaking in euphemisms, Choi Seung-chil told me that poets and novelists were provided with housing and a stipend, but if they did not produce results within a few years, they were cautioned by the Party, and if they still couldn't produce, they were reassigned jobs. Much later, I heard a little more about what had happened to the poet and translator Jeong Ji-yong, through the critic Cho Jung-ho of the North Korean literary magazine *Tongil munhak* (Unification Literature), at the August 15 Pyongyang Reunification Festival, which I attended with Do Jong-hwan and Jung Hee Sung in 2001. The North Korean novelist Seok In-hae (who died in 1990) had finished a cultural mission in the South and was returning to North Korea on September 21, 1950, when he met Jeong Ji-yong in Dongducheon. Seok and Jeong crossed over the mountain north of Dongducheon together. When Seok said the mountain was called Soyosan, Jeong joked that the name had a certain elegance to it and laughed. Suddenly, an American fighter plane shot rockets and fired its machine guns at them. After the plane was gone, Seok found Jeong with his chest riddled with bullets. He and his party had to hastily bury him by the road, unable to even mark the grave before they departed. (A similar incident to this is described by the poet Kim Soo-young in his incomplete testimony, *Uiyonggun* (Conscripts). Writers, actors, and other artists were frequently bombed or machine-gunned on their march up North. Kim Soo-young also described how Grumman fighter planes would follow lines of people walking North to attack them, so this was probably the same time and place.)

The life of Park Taewon offers one illustration of what writers faced in North Korea. Park Taewon sat on the executive committee of the Korean Writers' Alliance when it was formed in 1946 and was a literary activist for the Workers' Party of South Korea. But while living in South Korea in 1948, he attempted to avoid arrest by joining the Bodo League, created by the South Korean government for the "reeducation" of leftists. Its members were being executed when the Korean War broke out, but Park Taewon had already escaped death by then. When I first visited North Korea, Park Taewon had already passed away in 1986, and his widow, Kwon Young-hee, was living alone in a small apartment in the Pothong River region. The floor was inlaid with wood, and the layout was in the open kitchen style of the West, with radiators instead of *ondol* floor heating. Though he died before my first visit north, I did meet his widow, Kwon, who told me it was a little cold in the winter and that she used a coal stove in the living room for extra warmth. She showed me the bedroom where she had taken down dictation for Park Taewon. There was a bed and a small desk.

The entire family had gathered for my visit, and as I was there from midday to dusk, we talked of many things. Park Taewon, Yi Sang, and Jeong In-taek had formed a group of "modern boy" dandies in colonial Seoul. "New Woman" Kwon Young-hee went out with Yi Sang at first, but when Jeong In-taek fell in love with her and threatened to commit suicide, their friends intervened and got the pair to marry. The novelist Jeong In-taek was the son of the journalist Jeong Un-bok, who had planned the exile of the Prince Imperial Uihwa. Though born in Seoul, he had been such an ardent collaborationist that, like Choi

Jae-suh, he had received the Japanese Government-General's literary prize in the final years of the occupation. At the mention of her first husband, all Kwon would say was that "he was a reporter," apparently reluctant to acknowledge his literary works. Jeong In-taek joined the Korean Writers' Alliance with Lee Tae-jun and Park Taewon right after Liberation, and then the Bodo League, in order to survive before fleeing North during the war. He had immediately been arrested, according to Park Taewon's "survival legend" told by the Northern writers. Everyone in the Bodo League had been blacklisted, and Rhee Syngman's government executed each regional branch as they retreated southward. It is said that the South Korean government was in such a hurry to vacate Seoul that they had not managed to execute the Seoul branch. According to Kwon Young-hee, the North Korean army had quickly taken the prisons in Kaesong and Seoul where many prisoners were saved, Park Taewon among them. Jeong In-taek had also been part of the Bodo League, so to them, escaping North was the last hope of survival. Cho Young-man, an English literature scholar and Park Taewon's friend, was the last to have seen Park in Seoul. It is assumed that he went North, like many of his literary colleagues before him, with a group of war reporters who were sent into Pyongyang.

The later life of Park Taewon and Kwon Young-hee played out like a soap opera. In September of 1950, during the Battle of Incheon when Seoul was on the cusp of being retaken, many intellectuals, artists, and noted persons headed to the North with their families following later. Kwon Young-hee and her two daughters tried to hitch a ride in a transport truck during a brief stop in Hwanghae Province, but the eldest, Tae-seon, found herself accidentally left behind. A North Korean soldier carried her on his back up to Pyongyang, where he passed her on to the care of another soldier, who brought her over the Chongchon River to the final gathering place of refugees along the Amlok River. There was a bridge covered in white notes, messages searching for lost family members. This was where she was miraculously reunited with her mother. Kwon Young-hee said that Jeong In-taek had been killed during an aerial bombardment of the road. According to records, Workers' Party of South Korea writers such as Pak Hon-yong were being purged beginning December of 1952. Up until 1954 there was a wave of "self-criticism" in which writers from the South were inter-rogated and forced into reeducation. Following the Workers' Party of South Korea affair, the further purging of the Yan'an and Soviet factions in 1956 affected many more writers, such as Lee Tae-jun. Park Taewon was banished to a communal farm in Kangso, in South Pyongan Province, before working as a princi-pal in a country elementary school in Hamhung and being allowed back to Pyongyang in 1960.

Park Taewon's Seoul family had no idea where he was until he arrived in the North. His eldest daughter, Seol-young, from whom he'd been estranged since she was in middle school, went North during the January 4 Retreat in 1951 to look for him, but the most she could do was ask after his whereabouts around Songdo School in Kaesong, where there were many students from the South. She found a job in the city and was finally able to reunite with her father when the war was over and Park Taewon had returned to Pyongyang.

One fall day in 1956, Park Taewon visited Kwon Young-hee's house with his eldest daughter in tow. He had been friends with the poet Yi Sang and Kwon's late husband, Jeong In-taek. They'd known each other since their youth. Park was closer than family to Kwon, who knew no one in Pyongyang. She was teaching at an arts university at the time and lived on campus with her two daughters. He was probably dragged there by his daughter, but he was the one who proposed to Kwon: "What do you think of uniting our two households?" His vision had already narrowed so much by then that he could only see two letters at a time. He was in trouble politically and now his health was also in peril. Their marriage seemed to have been made possible through Park's daughter, Seol-young, and Kwon's daughter Tae-seon. They recalled that Park had reasoned, "It's not as if we were complete strangers to each other." The evaluation and reeducation of writers from the South were already underway, and Park was desperate to write a new piece of work to exonerate himself. She had been his friend's wife, he had been her husband's friend, and now the two were reunited in a strange land where, one by one, their friends were disappearing. Kwon was not entirely confident that she could help a man who was losing his sight to write a novel. A few months after they started living together, he gave her an old Japanese newsletter printed in an archaic style and asked her to read it out loud. When she did, he yelled, "That's it, that's it!"

"This was how our life as a couple, no, as a pair of war buddies began," she wrote in a letter later on. "On top of everything else, his optical nerves failed and he became blind, then came a mental breakdown, an aneurysm followed by paralysis in half his body, another blood clot leading to full-body paralysis and serious language impairment, with only his hearing remaining intact. The hospital called him a miracle. He continued to work with superhuman strength throughout all these circumstances, and the fact that this most singular invalid's wife didn't have to stand before other people's kitchen doors with an empty bowl in her hands is only thanks to our regime."

When they took walks along the Taedong River, he had to hold her arm because he could not see. Mischievous youths unaware of his disability would break them apart and run away laughing. She always prefaced her stories about him with the words "Our comrade Park Taewon . . ." It was clear from only a few details of her story how difficult it had been for them in his final years. Along with her younger daughter, Tae-eun, she stayed by his side through every banishment and new appointment.

His eyesight suddenly worsened after he had finished the first volume of *Gyemyeongsancheoneun balgaoneunya* (Is the Dawn Coming?) and was embarking on the second. The diagnosis was of optic nerve atrophy and retinitis pigmentosa, incurable conditions at the time that he was told would likely lead to blindness. Before losing his eyesight completely, Park Taewon gathered material from all over North Korea, reading old texts from libraries and museums and hand-copying books that he couldn't easily get. He rushed to write one more, just one more page before his eyesight gave out. He prepared for the worst by acquiring the biggest magnifying glass he could find, but one day in 1965, while reading new material in Pyongyang, his vision went dark and he collapsed. He was nearly at the end of the second volume when he suffered a brain aneurysm and lost function in half of his body. He had a special gridded frame made to fit on top of a sheet of manuscript paper so that he could continue to write legibly. After his second aneurysm in 1976, his *Gabo nongmin jeonjaeng* (The Peasants' War of 1894) which had been planned as sixteen parts, was shortened to three while he continued to work on it. Kwon took dictation and managed to complete the second part, but in 1981 Park lost his language functions and could no longer speak. Kwon ghostwrote the ending by going through Park's notes and materials, reading aloud to him what he had written, and relying on his gestures and eyes to register approval. He died in July of 1986. Two years later, in 1988, the South Korean ban on works by writers who had gone to North Korea was lifted. Was it really the North Korean Communist Party's guidance that drove him so strongly to write, or was it the struggle of an artist whose existence is vanishing, to try to overcome the illusion of time? This was the stark reality of Korean literature under division.

If South Korean literature attained modernity in a global sense by resisting dictatorship and insisting on freedom, North Korean literature leaned more toward state propaganda, closely managed by a dictatorship of the proletariat. After the June Democratic Uprising of 1987 in South Korea, the ban on North Korean writers born in the South was lifted, and North Korean books of literature, history, and other fields became widely available to a previously unimaginable degree thanks to the valiant efforts of publishers. University colleges and public libraries also began stocking North Korean newspapers and materials.

North Korean literature largely falls into four categories. First, there are the chronicles of the Great Leader's historic deeds and accomplishments. Second, books propagating the policies of the Party. Third, historic novels that raise national-istic morale. Fourth, fiction on the daily lives of the people, written to encourage good behavior. It is the third and fourth categories that are interesting. Historic novels and insights into daily life in North Korea are like the escape valves of this liter-ature. In 2004, South Korea's Manhae Prize was awarded to a North Korean writer for the first time since the division. The prize money was wired to the winner, Hong Sok-jung, and his books were published in South Korea; one was made into a film. This work was based on the *kisaeng* artisan and poet Hwang Jin-yi, who lived during the Joseon era. I myself introduced Paek Nam-nyong's *Friend* and Nam Dae-hyun's "Hymn to youth" to our literary world. In 2005, a North–South Korean writers' convention was held in Pyongyang for the first time since the division, with about 800 participants from South Korea and abroad and about 100 from the North. The hope was that the exchange would help North Korean writers. I have personal knowledge of the real difficulties that they face. This publishing of their work in South Korea and bestowing prizes on it was designed to exert implicit pressure on the North Korean author-ities. But all civilian exchanges became once again forbidden with the advent of successive conservative administrations in the South and the freezing of inter-Korean relations.

~

On paper it says that I'm from Sinchon in Oncheon-myeong, Onjeong-ri, Hwanghae Province. That's where my father is from. I was not born in Sinchon and had never set foot there, until I was guided for another reason to my father's birthplace where he had lived before leaving for Manchuria. There was a Museum of American War Atrocities in Sinchon (now moved to another location) testifying to a massacre of North Koreans by US soldiers during the Korean War. We drove out of Pyongyang on the Kaesong Expressway, and there the town was in the middle of a wide plain. In addition to Chaeryong and Unryul, the vast fields of Namuri and Eoruri Plains stretched to the west coast and Gyeonggi Province, forming the granary of the northwest. In North Korea, where 80 percent of the land is mountainous, this region was what fed the North Korean people.

The Sinchon Massacre is largely unknown in South Korea, but it was internationally infamous enough that socialist countries, and even Western countries with legalized communist and socialist parties, sent fact-finding missions to learn more about it. It is the incident depicted in Pablo Picasso's *Massacre in Korea*, just as his *Guernica* describes the Nazi and Fascist atrocities of the Spanish Civil War. I saw this painting at the Musée Picasso in Paris. The picture looked like a cubist reinterpretation of Goya's *The Third of May 1808*, composed of a machine-like, murderous gang and women and children being slaughtered.

North Korea's official position, having built this museum of American imperialist genocide, is that the US military slaughtered Koreans in Sinchon in great numbers, with women and children making up more than half of the victims. The museum was formerly a military building that had been the main location of the killings. The guide used a pointer as he read aloud to us from the texts that explained the reason behind the museum's founding:

During the recent Korean War of Liberation, the US invaders exposed their beastly nature as twentieth-century cannibals by unleashing mass murder on our soil on a scale unprecedented in human history. In accordance with the orders of Harrison, the blood-thirsty commander of the US Army at Sinchon, they carried out a massacre that far surpasses the bloody devastation of Hitler's Auschwitz in the Second World War. The American imperialist invaders demanded that every living thing in Sinchon be buried under dust and ash, and during those fifty-five days, they butchered 35,383 innocent people, one-fourth of the population, in the cruelest and most savage way, an unforgivable, demonic atrocity.

Most of the exhibits were photographs and were accompanied by posters or foreign news reports from the era. There were also objects on display. I saw a pile of shoes—the first that caught my eye were the white rubber slip-ons that women used to wear. There were two pairs of them, one with the soles broken in half and the other yellowed from age. There were crumpled shoes, shoes with rusty nails sticking out where heels should be, little black slip-ons for children, a single black sneaker with a broken shoelace. There were some telephone lines and wires that had been twisted into bracelets and used to bind someone's limbs, objects that all the more revealed the absent, vanished body. They had probably been dug up along with the human remains from the pit they'd been tossed in. I could see the seeds of our tragic division in the Sinchon Massacre, and felt strongly that to unearth this seed would be the true purpose of my North Korean travelogue.

When I returned to North Korea to get physical therapy for a slipped disc during my Berlin exile, I stayed long-term at a residence in Sinchon so I could visit the nearby Samcheon hot springs. I never entered the museum again. I did not feel easy in Sinchon, despite its being my official ancestral home. It was a beautiful place, but there was something dark about that town, especially on rainy days, that made me reluctant to go out. After leaving the North, I went to Japan and asked around about the Sinchon Massacre. A few academics told me that the incident was a "tragedy between Christians and Communists" and later sent me some information. I then found out more from two Korean Americans from Sinchon, whom I met when I moved to the US. One lived in New York and the other in Los Angeles, but they had something in common: both insisted that the massacre had been committed "by Koreans against Koreans."

The province of Hwanghae, where Sinchon is located, boasts the largest plains in the central region. It lies just north of Seoul where once the royal palace was located, and traditionally there were no major landowners there. Of the three great plains of Korea—Honam, Yeonbaek, and Chaeryong—the latter two are both in Hwanghae, which made the province the largest site of arable soil on the peninsula. Its annual rates of both sunshine and precipitation were the optimal for agriculture, its soil quality was excellent, and the temperature conditions ideal, which lent a good terroir to its produce. Consequently, the palace's own rice was tithed from here. Unlike in the Jeolla region, there was no big landowner because the land was owned by the royal family. The Joseon scholar and politician Jeong Yak-yong observed, while passing through the region at the turn of the nineteenth century, that the compulsory labor of the people in Hwanghae was even more problematic than in Jeolla, where the tyranny of petty officials was rampant.

The province had many poor tenant farmers, as well as thieves, and civil unrest was frequent. Instead of *yangban* nobility, there was a middle class called *mareum* that ruled the peasants. This middle class attempted to use the *hyangshi* civil service exams assigned to these regions to obtain political influence toward the end of the Joseon era. Kim Koo was a regional *hyangshi* and a leader in the Donghak Neo-Confucianist movement of the later nineteenth century, and the independence activist An Jung-geun's family joined the Catholic faith and mustered soldiers to crush Donghak followers. Hwanghae Province was where Protestant evangelicals, based in China, built their first churches to begin spreading the Christian message during the Enlightenment era.

The people of the western coast and the northwest had been discriminated against throughout feudal times and were forbidden to occupy any position of administration or government, which is why they were generally indifferent to traditional rules and norms. To them, Christianity and the West's new concepts were the fruits of an Enlightenment that would raise them above the indignities of feudalism. It was inevitable that during the years when old Korea was being subsumed by Japan, Christianity spread widely in Hwanghae and Pyongan Provinces. When the Japanese invaded the region, they appropriated the palace's lands in Hwanghae and gave them to the Oriental Development Company and the Industrial Bank of Chosen, their colonial exploitation apparatus. This was where the greatest number of tenant-farmer revolts occurred during the Japanese occupation. Land reform became the first item on the agenda after Liberation, when a socialist government took power in the North. The leadership must have felt that they were pressed for time given that similar reforms in Vietnam and China had occurred with much more violence. The fundamental principle behind their land reform was uncompensated confiscation and free redistribution as part of the transition toward communism.

Around the time of Liberation, Protestants in the North were either landless urban citizens or middle-class, while in the countryside they usually owned some land. The temples and churches also possessed a great deal of land. The North Korean administration clashed with them as it undertook the reform, and many large landowners and business owners moved south before the outbreak of the Korean War. In Sinchon, where there were many small landowners, land reform centered on tenant farmers or day laborers, exacerbating the situation. These lower-class villagers were sent to Pyongyang for a brief training and then sent back home to be at the vanguard of expropriation, making them enemies of the landowning Protestants. In South Korea, which had installed Japanese collaborators in key positions and embraced American rule, youth from the disenfranchised classes gathered to form right-wing organizations. The Korean War broke out just as they went back and forth across the poorly guarded 38th parallel, trying to restore the old order. North Korean forces invaded all the way down to the Nakdong River in June of 1950, and at the end of September, the Americans retook Seoul at the Battle of Incheon and began pushing back north.

The Protestants of the North had been at odds with the North Korean administration in the run-up to war because of their refusal to participate in the March 1 Movement memorials and in the elections, and as the Americans approached, the Christian youth of Sinchon and Chaeryong fought against the right-wing youth. At first, the North Korean army and Party officials executed Christians before retreating. The young right-wingers rose up in Sinchon in retaliation and massacred the communists and their families who had not managed to flee before the Americans arrived. The Americans finally entered the region on October 18, but there was no battle with the Northern army. Some have testified that the Americans provided the right-wing militia and youth groups with captured weapons and gunpowder. It was on the 18th, as the Americans were stationed outside of Sinchon, that the massacre began.

According to eyewitnesses, the Americans did not order or oversee the killings, and historians have found no American records showing US forces to be responsible—though North Korea claims that one Lieutenant Harrison was the key figure of the massacre. But a petty officer did file a report mentioning the presence of a Korean right-wing militia and a massacre, revealing that the Americans had known of this incident from the beginning.

It is clear that, if the American forces did not instigate or actively take part in the massacre, they had passively condoned it and also provided weapons and gunpowder. North Korea's story, that the massacre was wholly the fault and doing of the US, can perhaps be understood in light of the fact that the Americans were in operational command of the region at the time and had already carpet-bombed North Korea, killing 2 million people and devastating the land, in addition to threatening the use of nuclear weapons. While the American forces were not directly responsible for the Sinchon Massacre, they had clearly breached the fundamental rule of war followed in the East and West, past and present, stating that armies, whether friend or foe, have an obligation to protect civilians under siege. This is why the North Koreans are unable to see the Korean War as a civil war, like we do; for them, it is a "war for the liberation of the nation."

I realized that these contrasts showed how difficult reunification would be for both sides. That's why I thought we needed a transition into a system of peace, and for that, we needed to begin with cultural exchange, hence my visiting the North. As I counted down the days until the end of my trip, I kept reminding myself of my purpose here and what I could do for the cause as a writer.

I wrote about the Sinchon Massacre in my novel *The Guest*, completed after I was released from my five years in prison. I began in 2000 on the fiftieth anniversary of the outbreak of the Korean War. As soon as it was published, I was alarmed by how fragile peace on the peninsula was despite the end of the Cold War, when North Korea was branded as part of the "axis of evil" after the 9/11 attacks. North Korea, thwarted in its petitions for peace, began concentrating on nuclear development as Northeast Asia returned to the Cold War system. Thus, as I watched the Wall come down in Berlin, my first place of exile, and saw the world change once more, I felt even more determined to craft a deliberately Korean narrative that would depict reality from our point of view. The truth is, that terrible massacre was committed "by Koreans against Koreans," and the guilt and fear it engendered lies at the root of the manic hate that continues to this day.

I had collected material and witness testimonials, but during my imprisonment, I was not allowed to write. This turned out to be good for the book, as the work had time to ripen in my mind while I sat in my cell. I thought of it as a study of how Christianity and Marxism had been filtered through colonization and division, forms of modernity that we had been saddled with instead of developing our own. I started with the concept of the *sonnimgut* shamanic ritual, which used to be held in response to outbreaks of smallpox. Smallpox, colloquially referred to as a *sonnim* or "guest," was regarded as a Western import. I then depicted Christianity and Marxism as "guests," that is, the opposite of the owner of the house. My resulting novel, *The Guest*, borrows for its basic form the twelve scenes of the Hwaghae *jinogwigut* appeasing ritual. Just as in the ritual, the living and dead appear simultaneously in scenes of the past and present and voice their individual memories and stories. I used "time travel" as the weft and each character's perspective and experience as the warp to weave multiple narrators into a single, tapestry-like story.

If memories have a way of growing more real the more we try to forget them, then neither the living nor the dead can ever be free from the ghosts of the past. Yet those horrors are not illusions, but the traces of war that we must still resolve. The *gut* rituals that keep the god of death at bay, allowing the dead to reconcile with the living, are also performed by my novel, dismantling the mindless force of history that has sacrificed human lives to that same god, and returning us to a more human time.

I received news from South Korea every few days in the form of a correspondence packet, stuffed mostly with translations of foreign articles and photocopies of Korean newspapers. The envelope was stamped "For official use only" and marked with the name of whoever was in charge. But we were always about two or three days behind the news. I had gotten advice about how this could be remedied, so I dropped several hints, and one day a handler said: "You've been given permission." From then on, the packet was waiting on my desk every morning when I awoke. Magazines, even women's magazines, were delivered monthly. I naturally learned how Pastor Moon had been arrested as soon as he touched down, along with what happened to him subsequently, in fairly good detail.

The North–South writers' conference, scheduled to meet on the border at Panmunjom, on the Northern side, was canceled when the South Korean authorities arrested all of our programmed writers. The North Korean writers had spent the night before in nearby Kaesong and were waiting by Panmunjom, but they gave up, dejected, when they heard the news. It had partly been expected, but now that even the slimmest hopes had been dashed, the specter of what was to come weighed more heavily on me. I knew that the Korean People's Artists' Federation had released a statement regarding my North Korean visit. The KPAF affirmed that "Hwang Sok-yong's visit to North Korea represents the will of every artist in the nation," adding, "We are outraged that the authorities are criminalizing our representative Hwang by default . . . If Hwang and others are prosecuted through the National Security Act and other unreasonable regulations, every artist in the nation shall fight against it." As soon as reports appeared that I was in North Korea, the Democratic Party's National Assembly member Kim Sang-hyun called a press conference. Here he revealed that I had told the Democratic Justice Party secretary-general, Lee Jong-chan, of my plans and had also informed a handler at ANSP. Lee confirmed this and added, "I assumed he would get permission first. I did not think he would actually go there on his own." The authorities insisted: "We told him to obtain permission before visiting North Korea."

Later, in Japan, I met some reporters and reaffirmed that I had told the secretary-general of the ruling party and my ANSP handler of my plans. In fact, Kim Yong-tae, Cho Seong-wu, and others had been arrested because of me, while my ex-wife, Hee-yun, and my second wife, Myoung-su, were interrogated by the ANSP. In the case of Pastor Moon, Lee Bu-young, Kim Geun-tae, and Lee Jae-oh were questioned by the authorities. The fact that Pastor Moon had met with Kim Dae-jung—member of the National Association for Democratic Activism executive committee, and then National Assembly member—before leaving was also under scrutiny. The authorities were trying to apply the charge of "non-notification" to all these individuals and organizations, but the political opposition and the activist sphere took my side, emphasizing that I had indeed informed the ruling party's secretary-general and my ANSP handler of my visit. They further argued that the authorities' feigned ignorance could only be interpreted as weaponizing the National Security Act, constituting a move toward authoritarian rule.

Before I left Pyongyang, I had a public meeting with North Korean writers at the People's Palace of Culture and signed an agreement toward the reunification of national and literary arts in the South and the North. It opened with this declaration:

1. Both sides, as our most sacrosanct duty to our nation as literary artists, will actively contribute to the sacred national cause of the reunification of our country under the principles of self-reliance, peace, and national unity through literary and artistic activities, and will oppose all acts that perpetuate division and harm the unity of our nation.

2. The literary artists of North and South shall pursue meetings of groups and individuals toward the realization of a pro-reunification position in our nation's literary arts.

3. In order to surmount the ignorance of literary artists on each side regarding the realities of the other, an ignorance imposed by the division of our nation's territory and people in the last half century, progressive literary works created in the South and those created in the North are to be gathered and published in both South and North under the title *Contemporary Korean Literature*, an endeavor to be eventually turned into regular periodicals.

4. Although divided, the two sides shall as one develop creative activities in literature and the arts and contribute in all possible ways to the development of a national literature and arts as one nation.

4

Prison II

The first thing that changed with the advent of the civilian government was the introduction of daily newspaper subscriptions. We were supposed to be allowed television access as well, but the detention center authorities held off on that, saying they didn't have the resources yet. The regular detainees were entitled to one newspaper subscription per room; I requested two. The morning paper and exercise hour became my great joys. The papers reported endlessly on Kim Il-sung's death at the time, predicting an inevitable cooling of relations between North and South until his successor was established. South Korean broadcasters showed scenes of mourners at the Kim Il-sung memorial and derided them as brainwashed, but I thought it must have been like mourning a parent for the North Koreans. While the South Korean press mocked the supposed "forced mourning of the people," every foreign media correspondent in Pyongyang reported that the sorrow seemed genuine. One correspondent wrote that a cashier at a shop was crying too hard to sell him anything. World leaders like the UK's John Major, France's François Mitterrand, Japan's Hosokawa Morihiro, and Russia's Boris Yeltsin expressed their regrets, while the South Korean government kept its distance. If anything, President Kim Young-sam strongly objected to the American government sending a highly placed official to North Korea to transmit their condolences. It was quite a change in attitude for someone who had agreed to a summit with the deceased a mere two weeks before. The conservative media and politicians threw a fit when Lee Bu-young, of the Democratic Party, suggested on the floor of the National Assembly that the South Korean government pay its respects, considering it was the death of a summit counterpart. The claim by Sogang University president and Catholic priest Park Hong that there were hundreds of thousands of pro–North Korean *Juchesasangpa*—supporters of North Korea's political ideology of *juche*, or self-reliance—living in South Korea became popularly accepted as fact and set off a panic. There were sudden investigations of universities and civic groups, and 120 people were arrested. Park's statement turned out to be as baseless as the boy who cried wolf, according to a later prosecutorial report, and the matter faded into the background.

I knew my trial would be affected by the panic, but more than that, I was disappointed because I had thought that the summit was the best opportunity since the start of the Cold War to declare the end of the Korean War and inaugurate a regime of peace. Kim Young-sam was a conservative, but I hoped against hope that the man who had worked with Kim Dae-jung to fight dictatorship for the sake of liberal democracy would advance North–South relations in a peaceful direction. If only Kim Il-sung had managed, with Kim Young-sam, to turn the de facto state of war into a state of peace before he died! Then he would have been remembered primarily as "a nationalist and a socialist revolutionary and ruler who had been part of the armed resistance against the Japanese," and the Korean peninsula would have a very different place in international society today.

One day I heard a cricket chirping outside my cell window, and then every night after, a cool breeze blew in. I'd been in the detention center for over a year and a half. People had left one by one as their sentences were handed down. There weren't many political prisoners left save for the occasional late-caught youth involved in the Socialist Labor League of South Korea incident, whom I bumped into during exercise hour.

The Norwegian Author's Union (NAU) announced that they would send a fact-finding mission to further the release of five of the "seven oppressed writers" designated by PEN International. NAU President Thorvald Steen reiterated this intent, declaring in his keynote speech at the Stavanger International Festival of Literature and Freedom of Expression that NAU and PEN International "shall endeavor to never let the world forget the people who have been arrested or threatened for expressing their views," and that they would "send fact-finding missions and establish a managing committee for cases in South Korea, Nigeria, Cuba, Turkey, and Yemen."

At the appeal hearing, my sentence was amended to six years. Then, after the Supreme Court sent the case back to the lower court, the judge in my final trial, held on September 27, 1994, sentenced me to seven years' imprisonment with seven years suspension of qualifications, declaring that the charge of leaking state intelligence could be applied to me according to the precedent that "public knowledge can still be considered secret." I had made my sentence worse by appealing. The ruling stated that "while the court acknowledges the defendant's literary achievements and that the intention of his visit was to help end the state of division and bring about a swifter reunification, we find him guilty based on the Supreme Court's jurisprudential ruling of the crime of leaking intelligence."

Now that my sentence was confirmed, all that remained was to wait to be transported to prison. Around this time, Ōe Kenzaburō won the Nobel Prize in Literature. I read that Ōe and Yasue Ryōsuke, of the Japanese publishing house Iwanami Shoten, had visited Kim Young-sam on their tour of Korea to appeal for my release. Ōe wrote me a letter that he sent in a hotel envelope. He consoled me, saying he was sorry he couldn't be of more help and that we should work together for a peaceful Asian community in the new century. I heard later that Ōe had written many times to international writers' organizations and notables calling for my release.

Soon after I changed cells again, a new rule was created for single-cell prisoners like me to exercise individually in a special facility, not in the yard with the regular prisoners. This facility was like nothing I'd ever seen; it was Jeremy Bentham's panopticon made reality. I'd experienced a half-circle cell when I was imprisoned by the military for violation of martial rule in Gwangju a few years before, but this new structure was an almost perfect panopticon. Bentham's idea was inspired by the zoo at Versailles, cages where each occupant can be seen while they themselves cannot see anyone. The precinct was surrounded by a long, tall circular wall, and the inside was divided like cake or pizza slices. Each section had its own door; when it closed behind you, you were left alone inside a wedge of concrete walls. There was a two-story circular tower in the middle. From the top, the guards could look out in all directions. I never actually saw anyone watching us from above, though. The guards were probably sitting somewhere comfortable, chatting or having a smoke. But they could look out at any time to see which prisoner was doing what. In any case, the windows of the watchtower were tinted so the prisoners could not see the watchers. It was truly a symbol of some kind. The prisoners walking around their cells must have looked like rats in a lab.

One prisoner kept kicking a ball against a wall and muttering to himself. Another walked in circles in the narrow space, counting as he went. Still another stood still and stared out at the mountains or the sky. I mostly looked back and forth between the sky and the ground. Clouds drifted by, and sometimes birds flew past. Passenger planes plied their routes. I could tell which were headed south and which were headed southeast, and guessed at whether they were international or domestic by their shapes and sizes. I pictured the people inside those planes. A passenger with their seat reclined, taking a nap, a passenger rustling through a bag of snacks, another soothing a child, another reading a magazine or a newspaper, still another listening to music, the flight attendants going up and down the aisles. Someone using the lavatory. Someone turning their head to kiss their lover. All the carefree individuals of the world . . . And here was I, an animal trapped between concrete walls.

I had a game I liked to play back then: taking care of plants and ants. Little weeds grew resiliently, from spring to summer, along the light and shade of the concrete walls. The most common plants were dandelions, *sseumbagwi*, and violets. I watered the prettiest ones. I brought the water in an empty milk carton, carrying it all the way there to quench their thirst with it.

I would rip out a handful of other weeds to write on the cement wall, words that faded after a day. Their whitened traces nevertheless persisted through rain. Students and laborers who were detained for political reasons wrote slogans and objectives or messages for each other. I once found a message that said: "Be brave, Mr. Hwang Sok-yong!" *Down with the fascists, power to the workers, hooray for democracy, hooray for reunification.* The guards washed these off whenever there was a Ministry of Justice inspection and weeded the sections bare— not just with their hands but with hoe-wielding groundsmen, no less. Alas, even my preciously kept flowers were pulled out by the roots and left to shrivel. The flowers were so delicate that nothing of their form remained.

Many kinds of ants lived within the panopticon: small, black ants; ants with black thoraxes and thick red abdomens; slightly larger, quick-moving ones; and the rare, truly big ones. I liked the small black ants the best for their facility at digging tunnels and their passion for work. It was the insects flying in from the outside that made me an avid ant-watcher. Many of these insects flew into the panopticon cell by mistake and died as they struck the walls again and again, unable to fly high enough to escape. There were grasshoppers, locusts, a variety of beetles, and once, oddly enough, a perfectly healthy dragonfly. Like most of the other prisoners, I felt sympathy for these poor creatures. I would carefully pick them up and help them fly away over the wall.

Sometimes I'd suck on some candy and drop it by an ant hole. From time to time, the guard at the watchtower would see me crouching for a long time and ask what I was doing down there. I'd look up and show him my beaming face. They already knew what single detainees did inside the panopticon. The ants would discover the candy and suck on it for hours, melting it down, or cover it with dirt before digging a tunnel underneath to break it apart from there. Their little jaws would clamp down on a speck of sugar as they carried the candy away piece by piece. In the fall, I saw the young queen ants fly up into the air to start their own colonies. The beauty of nature shone even in the cement boxes of the panopticon, while I felt myself growing stronger inside.

I experienced the beauty of life in the earth's smallest and commonest creatures and imagined the freedom of a different world through the sky above the panopticon where airplanes flew past. That was where I thought up my novel *The Old Garden*. It was a paradoxical take on utopia. I took the title from an old Eastern legend of a hidden world with a beautiful garden in a valley. I had gazed upon the changing world in my place of exile in Berlin and whispered to myself, *The revolution is over.* And: *This is a new beginning.*

After the breakdown of the Cold War system, a sense of bitter disillusion swept over the world. Environmental destruction worsened, there were brushfire wars and strife between religions and races, and a fight for world domination in the name of terrorism and anti-terrorism plagued the world. The so-called peripheral countries still experienced dictatorship, resistance, and disappointment in turn, suffering once more from war, poverty, and hunger. The capitalist world order ran rampant with the fall of socialism; anyone with common sense could see this could only lead to a terrible ending. All we could pin our hopes on was the fact that the future was not set in stone. The democracy movements of the 1970s and 1980s under national division successfully brought down the dictatorship, but as we entered the 1990s the major players of those movements found themselves torn between their passion of the past and the realities of the present. This crisis worsened with the dissolution of ideologies after the breakdown of socialism, and the realization of how much we had lost in the process.

My plan was to write *The Old Garden* as a love story. I thought that the lives of a man and a woman separated from each other during this period of crisis would be an appropriate frame for what I wanted to express. The two would narrate the years gone by through their own internal monologues. Their internal lives, which would serve to disrupt the organic flow of narrative, would offer differing visions of reality. Two narratives that ought to succeed one another chronologically would instead run parallel until the end, never leaving the confines of the first-person perspective of each. The purpose was to express the severance of time and space and the isolation that comes from the man being in prison during the eighteen years that the woman is living her life. He will only be able to reconnect with her through letters and diaries discovered after her death. But this rupture is overcome with the participation of the reader, who reads the text from a third perspective, and the characters' thwarted love and time are thus given back to them in the here and now.

Around the Chuseok holiday of that year, the world was set aflame by the Chijon gang horror. In July of 1993, six youths ganged up to murder five people in an organized serial spree lasting a year. They were day laborers at construction sites who had all been born in poor farming villages and dropped out of middle or high school. Kim Ki-hwan, who at twenty-six was the oldest, had lost his father when he was only three years old, and later dropped out of middle school. His mother was bedridden after a stroke, while he went from site to site for work. They observed the following gang rules, which the media took from the police report: 1) Kidnap wealthy people and take their money. 2) Always kill the victim. 3) Don't stop until each member has amassed a billion won (equal to $1,250,000 at the time). 4) Whoever quits the gang must be pursued to the ends of the earth and killed. 5) Trust no women, not even your mother.

They kidnapped, raped, and murdered a woman in her twenties for practice and buried her body on a mountain. They hunted down and murdered the youngest member of their gang, a teenager who had felt guilty about what they'd done and fled with 3 million won stolen from their collected funds. Under their plan to rob and kill the rich, they obtained a list of 1,200 Gangnam Hyundai Department Store customers. Kim Ki-hwan, who had experience in construction, dug up the basement in an empty house his mother used to live in and created a death factory by installing a cage and crematorium. The gang said they went on taking their orders from Kim Ki-hwan, after he'd been locked up for rape, by visiting him in prison. They kidnapped a young couple who had gone for a drive in the countryside in an expensive car, but it turned out that the man was a nightclub musician and the woman a café waitress, and the car just a used one. They forced the man to drink a lot of alcohol, killed him and made it look like a drunk-driving accident, raped the woman, and told her she had to join the gang if she wanted to live.

The gang had swords, axes, steel pipes, tear gas guns, shotguns, and dynamite. Around Chuseok, hoping to raise more funds for their crime spree, they kidnapped a middle-aged couple who were weeding their family burial plots deep in the hills. This couple was also not rich; the man was a small business owner who had only graduated from a trade high school and previously worked in a factory. They locked the wife in the basement and took the husband outside to receive the tens of millions of won one of his employees had brought for him. As soon as they returned, they made the kidnapped waitress, surnamed Lee, kill the man with a shotgun. Before the man died, he begged them to spare his wife, but the one named Kim Hyun-yang later testified that they killed her with knives and axes and added defiantly that he had cut some flesh from her corpse and eaten it. He went on to tell reporters that his only regret was not murdering more people, and that he should have killed his own mother as well. The gang went so far as to hold a barbecue as a literal smokescreen when they cremated the bodies of the couple.

A few days later, some of their dynamite accidentally exploded while they were experimenting with it, and Kim Hyun-yang was taken to hospital by the kidnapped waitress, Lee. Lee managed to escape in a taxi, reach Seoul, and report the gang to the police, who then arrested the members near their hideout. All the newspapers reported the sordid details, which sounded like something out of a crime novel, and the TV news played clips of the crime reenactments on a loop. The gang blamed their cruel serial killing on society, raging against people who drove expensive cars, spent large sums of money in department stores, and bribed colleges into accepting their children. But they had never even come close to hurting any upper-class people, despite their claims. All those they harmed had been as disadvantaged as they were: a helpless young woman, their own gang member, and three ordinary, hardworking people. Under South Korean capitalism, the gap between rich and poor increased during the dictatorships from the 1960s to the 1980s, and the corruption and cheating that ran rampant during those two back-to-back military dictatorships enabled the rich to disproportionately succeed. The South Korean middle class that emerged from this period had obtained material wealth under those dictatorships, but they were far from being "citizens" in the modern sense. The press mockingly referred to it as "pariah capitalism." The Chijon gang members all had criminal records dating back to their teenage years and were human garbage from the perspective of South Korea's cliquish, competition-heavy society. But we were the ones, living in this era, who had turned them into "garbage," and their terrible crimes were ultimately the waste products of our society. Their crimes were, in the end, evidence that it was our society that was diseased.

One day, I heard a sudden noise in the corridor. The special red-cap team came in with a handcuffed prisoner further restrained by ropes. Though the one-person cell next to mine was empty, they put him in with the regular prisoners. The *soji* were quick to pick up the rumors: the new inmate was the Chijon gang boss, Kim Ki-hwan. He had been in the Gwangju Correctional Institution for the past few months for rape but was transferred to Seoul when murder and creation of a criminal organization were added to the charge sheet. We could all see that he was headed for a death sentence.

Death row inmates, or "max sentence" as we called them, were normally put in one-person cells if they were well behaved, but if they were thought to be at risk of self-harm, they were put in group cells and kept shackled around the clock. The regular prisoners would complain that they were being punished unfairly when they had death row inmates housed with them. These inmates automatically took the highest place in the cell hierarchy, and the former top dog would find himself relegated to silently sulking in second place. There was nothing to be gained from provoking a death row inmate, as that would only get you punished or transferred to another cell. If you messed with him, you might end up with a chopstick in your eye—he was going to be executed anyway, so he had nothing to lose. That's why there was nothing scarier than a dead man walking. And if the prison authorities did not permit him to remove his shackles at mealtimes, that only meant the other inmates had to feed him by hand. Even when there was already a guard in the office at the cell block entrance, a young conscript guard was stationed separately in front of the cell where Kim Ki-hwan was. I thought this young guard would shout his "*Chungseong!*" military greeting only during shift changes, but he shouted it every time someone of higher rank came down the hall—even in the dead of night, which made sleep difficult. When I complained to the head guard, he said he would ask the younger man to not shout so loudly at night. But he added that we had probably lucked out by having the boss in our cell block, while the accomplices were scattered through the rest of the prison, because at least the boss would have no need to shout.

A few days later, I agreed to a suggestion by a guard to have a talk with Kim Ki-hwan. I informed the *soji* that we would have *jjajangmyeon*, or black bean noodles. The food that was served rotated between pork, beef, curry, and *jjajang*, and that day it was *jjajang*. Normally we were just given the sauce with barley and rice, but the *jjajangmyeon* I ordered was a special treat made with ramen noodles. I went to Kim Ki-hwan's group cell entrance and asked for him. He jumped to his feet. He said the guard had told him I was coming. I invited him to eat lunch with me. The guard said I could take Kim Ki-hwan and a *soji* to have lunch in the shower room, but that he was not authorized to unshackle Kim. We didn't have much to say while waiting for the *soji* to finish serving the other prisoners and join us to cook the noodles over a portable gas burner. I did not forget that, unlike Hur or Choi, so recently executed for crimes committed on impulse, this was someone who had organized a gang and planned his killings. He eagerly ate the noodles that the *soji* fed him with chopsticks. The awkwardness between us relaxed a bit as I helped myself to the delicious noodles I hadn't tasted in a long time. I spoke first.

—So, how are you doing in here? Been making an effort to get along with the others?

—I've been in prison before, I know the drill. I just want to go as soon as possible and not make any more trouble for anyone.

He said this so decisively that I couldn't think of what to say next. He suddenly spoke up again.

—Those kids who were with me, they were really hard up.

—If only they hadn't harmed anyone . . .

I spoke cautiously but he answered as if talking about someone else.

—Me, them, we're all the same, we lost hope a long time ago. We don't care when we die.

—But that Kim Hyun-yang, why must he speak so harshly? That he ate a human body and regrets not killing his mother. It was horrifying.

—He's doing that on purpose. He hates the world so he's trying to scare everyone, trying to look like a tough guy. I really am sorry for the dead people. Hyun-yang, he wasn't always so bad, he used to go to church and was a hard worker.

I told him about my old neighbors Hur and Choi, and how they had been executed not long ago.

—We all die, young man. Me, you, everyone. But it's better not to die with such hate in your heart. You have to let it go.

—Better for whom?

—For yourself, who else?

After that, whenever he had to go to court or went out for exercise, he would open the food hole to my cell and say hello. As my transfer date approached, the detention center authorities moved me to a south-facing cell block with lots of sunlight and a view of the hills, and I never saw him again.

In November of 1995, exactly a year after I was transferred to Gongju Correctional Institution, I read in the news that the Chijon gang had been executed. Kim Ki-hwan smiled cynically when asked for his final words and said, "Shouldn't a man keep his word to the last?" He probably thought the manly thing to do was to show that he wasn't afraid of death. Couldn't anyone have taught him better? While the outside world knew him as the devil incarnate, up close he only seemed like another poor boy caught in the snare of fate. I had seen many kinds of people in that place and was depressed by the pity I felt for them. Thankfully, time keeps passing for the living. To the outside world I was confined, as if trapped in a freeze-frame. But life goes on no matter where a person is, and gradually I was learning how to endure the monotony of our days.

5

Exile

1989–93

I left Pyongyang on April 24, 1989, and landed in Beijing. I had to go through Japan again, retracing my entry route in reverse, because there were no direct flights between Seoul and Beijing. China and South Korea had not yet normalized diplomatic relations. I was going to apply for a Japanese visa once I dropped off my bags at the hotel. But as soon as I got to my room, a South Korean reporter—who knows how he found me—telephoned to ask for an interview, which I reluctantly agreed to on condition that it would be just the two of us. He wrote for the *Dong-a Ilbo*'s sports page but scented an exclusive when he heard I was staying at the hotel while he was on assignment for a feature on next year's Beijing Asian Games. I only agreed to the interview because I felt I owed them for stopping the serialization of a novel in the magazine *Shindonga*, the newspaper's sister publication, and also because my friend Seo Joong-seok, who later became a historian, was a reporter there. I also had the idea of publishing my North Korea travelogue in *Shindonga*. I knew the editor-in-chief, and he seemed like a reasonable gentleman. I use *reasonable* here to refer to the ability to deal with one another despite fundamental differences; it's a more reliable word in Korean than *conscientious*. Too many unreasonable things kept happening in South Korea for conscientiousness to survive. While the *Dong-a Ilbo* was one of South Korea's most notoriously right-wing publications, *Shindonga* magazine was somewhat more moderate. They would publish me provided I maintained a neutral stance. A progressive publication like the *Quarterly Changbi* or the *Hankyoreh* might have been easier to deal with, but my thinking was that the reunification problem, more than any other issue, needed to be discussed in the mainstream if it was to go anywhere.

The next morning, I came down from my room with the North Korean handler who had accompanied me from Pyongyang and met the North Korean embassy worker who had guided me from the airport the last time I was there. He said the plan had been to let me rest for a day and take me to the Japanese embassy the following day, but the mood in Beijing was becoming agitated. Students and workers had been protesting for the past two days, mourning the moderate politician Hu Yaobang, who had passed away on April 15, with thousands gathering at the Monument to the People's Heroes and Tiananmen Square. At Hu's funeral in Xi'an two days before my arrival in Beijing, protesters charged at local authorities, with workers and farmers demanding the fall of tyranny as they set scores of cars on fire. Deng Xiaoping ordered a violent crackdown, and the *People's Daily* declared the incident a riot. I had no idea what the story behind it all was, but my two North Korean handlers were adamant that we were looking at capitalist fallout from China's liberalization policies. I learned later that 150,000 students from eighty Chinese universities had showed up at the protests demanding democratization and freedom.

On April 26, I requested a month-long visa from the Japanese embassy in Beijing but received a fifteen-day visa instead. There was an endless procession of young people holding banners and picket signs on the road from the hotel to the airport, all headed for Tiananmen Square. I got the North Korean handlers to drive me there as well; the square was already filled with people. I learned later in Japan that the protest had been organized by a student government coalition of twenty-one Beijing universities.

The situation worsened during the two weeks I was in Japan, the protests continuing even through June, when I was about to leave for Germany. When the Tiananmen massacre finally broke out, I thought of Gwangju in May of 1980, the beginning of my long journey to where I was now. The implementation— or otherwise—of democracy was a question being asked all over the world. But the world would change very slowly, and in a very different way from what we'd imagined. Such is life.

On my commercial flight from Beijing to Japan, a *Shindonga* reporter took a seat on the plane next to me, under orders from his editor. Lee Ju-ik and a representative of the publishing house Iwanami Shoten, Okamoto Atsushi, were waiting for me at the airport. They whisked me off before any other reporters could approach and drove me into downtown Tokyo. I ended up at the Yamanoue Hotel, which Yasue Ryōsuke had booked for me, on the hill of an obscure residential neighborhood that not even many Japanese people knew about.

I dined with Ryōsuke and Professor Itō Narihiko as we discussed what I was to do in Japan. They knew I was going to write up my North Korea travelogue, and that I'd gone so far as delaying my return to South Korea with Pastor Moon's party in order to do so. The most urgent matter was the extension of my Japanese visa. A lawyer managed to open a case, effectively delaying deportation proceedings for the time being. Second on the agenda was to give a press conference, a rite of passage I had to undertake if I didn't want to be constantly hounded by foreign correspondents. The Japanese government had used the Kim Dae-jung kidnapping incident as a pretext for putting me under surveillance, not to mention the Korean government also keeping tabs on my every move, which made the current hotel unsafe; we needed to find better long-term accommodation. I decided to hold my press conference just before I left the hotel. The authorities also had people come spend time with me in shifts, saying it was dangerous for me to be alone.

Itō met with Harada Shigeo about my housing problem and together they decided to lend me an apartment with a large office and a private bathroom not far from Harada's realtor office. Lee Ju-ik, who was working on his PhD at the University of Tokyo under Wada Haruki and reporting for the *Hankyoreh* as a foreign correspondent, alternated morning and afternoon shifts with Seo Dong-man to watch over me.

The morning I checked out of the hotel, Seo Dong-man moved my bags while I held a brief press conference in the lobby with Professor Itō. A Japanese police officer had greeted me with his business card on my first day there, informing me that I was under surveillance and that his team was taking shifts to make sure I was protected. The Japanese police made it clear that they had an obligation to ensure my safety as long as I followed Japanese domestic law, and that any problems I had with the South Korean authorities were none of their concern.

The Tokyo-based South Korean correspondents, who had come running at the call, were waiting for me in the lobby. What interested them most, besides my impressions of North Korea and Chairman Kim Il-sung, was whether it was true I had notified the secretary-general of the leading party Lee Jong-chan, the opposition party's Kim Sang-hyun, and my ANSP handler before visiting North Korea. I stated that I was well aware that no politicians of either party were in any position to authorize my North Korea visit, but as long as the crime of "non-notification" existed in the National Security Act, I thought it would be better if the responsibility were shouldered by the politicians who represented us and not just the Korean People's Artists Federation, the Association of Writers for National Literature, or the other ordinary people in my life.

I informed the reporters that I had risked violating the National Security Act in order to write a North Korea travelogue, to be titled "They're just like us," and that I had every intention of returning to South Korea once I was done. I added that as it would take a month to write up, I needed an extension on my fifteen-day visa and would finish it in another country if the extension were denied. The South Korean police had interrogated my family and acquaintances, who had nothing to do with my visit, and seemed to have expressed their consternation to them. To my relief, the next day, the reporters printed my words exactly as I had spoken them.

I came across an interesting story in a magazine once, a sort of modern folk tale from somewhere, maybe the Philippines or a country in South America, I don't remember exactly. There was a village of indigenous people living in a jungle. A taboo had been passed down for generations forbidding them from climbing the "big mountain" behind the village. There was purportedly a scary demon king living on the summit, and a great disaster would befall the village if any of the villagers looked upon him. A curious little boy from the village secretly went up the mountain. He scrambled through the jungle, climbed up the rock face, and after much difficulty reached the summit where there were strange machines and foreigners about. It was a missile launch site. The boy was shocked and overwhelmed by what he saw, came down the mountain in a fright, and told his discovery to only one friend when he could no longer hold the secret in. But the rumor of his transgression spread, and the boy was summoned before the village elders. He stammered out his story, but nobody believed him. The villagers disputed his claim that there was no demon king but only machines and foreigners at the summit, and insisted that he must have seen the wrong thing. He had broken the village's taboo and needed to be punished. Then one elder shook his head. "None of us have ever climbed that mountain," he said. "Therefore, none of us have ever seen what the boy saw. We don't know if a demon king lives up there or not and have no way of knowing whether the taboo is right or wrong. Therefore, we cannot punish this child."

While I was living in exile after my visit to the North, I thought about this story every time I came across other Koreans, especially reporters. If there is any oppressive taboo about the unknown, a writer will violate it if only to confirm its truth. Anyone who has seen migrating birds fly over borders, walls, and steel fences will have realized the fundamental nature of life and questioned the meaning behind the hodgepodge of rules humanity has come up with. My exile schooled me into distrusting the notions of "nation and country" and seeded my ambition to become a citizen of the world. By that I mean that I would share my problems with the people of the world, and consider the world's problems my own.

I had parted from Professor Itō and was following Seo Dongman's directions on the subway back to the apartment when a strange feeling came over me. I looked back to see a Japanese man following me. He looked familiar; thinking he might be a plainclothes detective, I slipped into the crowd and hopped on whatever train had just arrived. At the next station, I jumped off at the last second and leaped onto the train on the other side of the platform as a young Japanese man, panting, just managed to get on the train himself. This was a different detective from the one I first spotted. He said in broken English: "We are protecting you. You are a VIP. Please cooperate." I bowed and thanked him. His teammates must have missed the train because of me. I figured they would sort it out amongst themselves, but still felt sorry about it. I joked later that I had just taken part in a scene from a spy movie.

The apartment Harada Shigeo was loaning me wasn't ready, so I had to stay for a couple of days at a hotel in Takadanobaba. Harada welcomed me warmly when I went to see him and told me to stay as long as I needed to finish my North Korea travelogue.

While I was there, the two of us often went out drinking. Among our many topics of conversation, Harada mentioned his hometown and family, how his grandmother would make kimchi and perilla leaves preserved in soy sauce. He was ten years older than me, so those were probably memories from the Japanese colonial era. Harada's grandmother was Korean. He smiled as he spoke of a quarter of his blood being Korean, but his eyes were tearing up. Later, when I left Japan and lived in exile in Berlin, Harada's son spent a night in my apartment at the Bundesplatz. I took him to the just-fallen Berlin Wall and Checkpoint Charlie, which had demarcated the border between East and West Berlin, all of which he studiously captured on camera. His father had instructed him to meet me in Berlin and to take as many photos as possible of the fallen barrier. Years later, as I lay staring at the walls of my prison cell, I thought of what Harada had said about a quarter of his blood being Korean. Many people had left an impression on me in Japan, but thinking of Harada and his son made me realize how important it was to form true connections with people in this world.

Once I was alone in my hotel room, the tension of the past days drained away and I couldn't be bothered to do anything anymore. While unpacking, I took out a long box that had been handed to me just as I was leaving the Visitors' Residence in North Korea. I was told it was a gift from Chairman Kim himself. I opened it to find wild ginseng from Paektu Mountain and a pair of deer antlers—used in traditional herbal medicine—for Pastor Moon and me, but Moon said they would end up confiscated under the National Security Act's "reception of goods" statute and that I should just leave them in Japan. Later, when I was in Germany, Chung Kyung-mo, worried about Pastor Moon's health in prison, discussed with me how to turn wild ginseng and antlers into pills, but I don't know if Moon's family succeeded in getting him the medicine.

I opened the box, removed the lining of moss, and stared at the three fresh wild ginseng roots. They still had green leaves and their stalks were thin, but the roots were long. Each branch of the root was secured with tape. When I snipped off a bit at the end and chewed it, the fragrance filled my mouth and the soft texture was easy to chew. I had assumed until then that I would simply return to South Korea when my transfer visa period was over. But now that I thought about it, I would be dragged directly from the airport to the ANSP basement and all my belongings would be confiscated. The head of the ANSP would probably eat one of the wild ginseng roots, and the remaining two would be delightedly consumed by the South Korean president and the first lady. There was no point in letting something good go to waste on someone else when it was me who was facing the gauntlet. And wasn't "finders keepers" the first rule of wild ginseng? I picked up one of the roots and slowly began chewing it raw. It tasted like, well, any other kind of ginseng. I finished one root in a few bites, picked up another, and ate that one, too. I picked up the last one and thought, Oh, what the hell, and finished it off. Most people go their entire lives without ever tasting wild ginseng; there I sat, having scarfed down three Paektu Mountain wild ginseng, washed down with some water. I waited for something magical to happen, but nothing did.

About an hour later, I began feeling drowsy and a kind of chill went through my body, like I was about to catch a cold. I crept into bed and decided to sleep until the afternoon. I didn't know how many hours had passed when I woke up thirsty and drank half a bottle of water from the fridge. I had just come out of the bathroom after using the toilet when someone banged on the door. Lee Ju-ik stood outside.

"Everyone is frantic because you're not answering your phone! How could you have slept so deeply?"

I was nonplussed. I asked him what time it was; he said it was after 8 p.m. I said I'd lain down at three and taken a five-hour nap, but he shook his head.

"You've been out of contact since yesterday."

He told me the date. I realized I had slept through the previous night and most of the next day. How many hours was that? I tried counting with my fingers and gave up.

"I ate three wild ginseng roots yesterday," I said, and told him the whole story of Kim Il-sung's goodbye gift.

He slapped the desk and wailed, "How could you eat it all by yourself? You have no loyalty, Mr. Hwang. You should've shared it with me! Because that can only be real wild ginseng!"

"What makes you so sure?"

"It's wild ginseng tithed to the chairman. If anyone dared offer up a fake, that person would be sent straight to the mines in Aoji. So of course it's real. Since you've eaten three of them at once, about eighty percent of it is going to pass right through you. Well, I guess you'll still have twenty percent left."

I joked that I had just been to the toilet and that my stool had come out a lustrous golden color.

This three-ginseng incident became a long-running joke that even the ANSP interrogators and prison wardens would tease me about for years. The guards would dismiss any complaints I made about the cold. "Why are you shivering?" they'd say. "You're the lucky man who ate three wild ginseng roots!" Well, they had a point: throughout my four years of exile and five years in prison, I never did catch a cold.

I had made public my intention to write, but I found it hard to concentrate. I had just finished the first chapter of my travelogue when the novelist Jeon Jin-woo contacted me through my wife, Myoung-su. He had been fired from his journalist job in the 1970s and somehow managed to return to the *Dong-a Ilbo*. He interviewed me about my impressions of North Korea, stayed in my apartment for a few days, and returned to Seoul with the first part of my manuscript. *Shindonga* had agreed to serialize the work.

Itō Narihiko and I met with the Japanese human rights lawyer Niimi Takashi about my visa, which was set to expire on May 11. We visited the Ministry of Justice and requested an extension, but the Japanese authorities officially turned me down the next day. Niimi submitted another request for a special stay, mainly because processing the paperwork took forever and it would buy me a month or two more. Professor Itō was in contact with the

German embassy, just in case. He had studied in Germany when he was younger and received a degree for his work on Rosa Luxemburg. I heard later from him that West Germany had immediately accepted my request and expressed their willingness to protect me as a member of another divided nation. Meanwhile, Japan's Ministry of Justice sped up their paperwork so efficiently that it took them only a week to officially deny me my stay.

There was a press conference scheduled for the afternoon I was to fly out of Japan, but I decided to give my petition to Professor Takasaki Sōji, of the Japan–Korea Solidarity Committee, and leave quietly. We threw a small goodbye party in a café in downtown Tokyo, where Wada Haruki and some of the committee people came to see me off. Professor Itō was to escort me all the way to Berlin. At the airport gate, someone came up to the professor and me, begged our pardon, and took a picture. Professor Itō let him, saying that he was probably just a Japanese agent who needed photographic proof that I was leaving Japan. It was May 19, 1989, when I got on that Lufthansa flight and left Japan for Berlin.

~

We were transferring at Frankfurt when someone again jumped in front of us and took our photograph in the transfer corridor in the airport. He was Asian, and after two snaps, he stepped aside for another Asian man who asked me, "Are you Hwang Sok-yong? Where is your next destination?"

"And who are you?"

He smiled as he walked next to me and said, "You know very well who I am."

"I'm going to Berlin next. All right?"

"Be well." He fell behind.

Professor Itō, who had been walking ahead, looking nervous, asked me if he were a reporter. I said no.

"Then he must be one of your biggest fans," he joked. We both laughed, and the tension lifted.

There were more suspicious people waiting for me at Berlin's Tegel Airport. It was a small place and the parking lot was close to the exits, making it easy to pick them out. They didn't approach and would slink away after taking a photograph. We decided on a downtown hotel. Professor Itō telephoned Yun I-sang. Itō and Yun were old acquaintances. They had both been in a worldwide campaign against Kim Dae-jung's death sentence, with Yun I-sang being the main contact in Germany. Itō and Japanese civic organizations provided much help to Yun when he was sentenced to life in prison for the East Berlin Spy Incident. Yun led a petition effort in the European Parliament for Kim Dae-jung, as well as directly appealing to West Germany's minister of foreign affairs, Willy Brandt.

The Yun couple welcomed me gladly but cautioned against staying in Berlin. They thought it would be better if I went to the countryside until Moon Ik-hwan's trial had advanced further and the waves we'd made with our North Korea visit had calmed down. I mentioned Song Hyun-sook and Jochen Hiltmann to Itō the next day—the couple I'd met on my first Berlin trip—and he offered to appeal to them personally on my behalf. I was feeling bad about the trouble I was causing him and assured him he didn't have to, he should feel free to return to Japan since I was a grown man who really ought to take care of himself. But Itō insisted that he could not go back before I was properly settled somewhere.

A mere thirty minutes after I had called a Korean German mutual acquaintance, who had been a nurse alongside Song, and explained the situation to her, Song Hyun-sook herself called me back. She said she was in their Oevenum house over the weekend, but they would be back in their apartment in Hamburg on Monday. Itō and I went to Hamburg and spent the weekend swanning about like tourists and frittering the time away.

Jochen Hiltmann and Song Hyun-sook knew of my North Korea visit thanks to all the hoopla in the Korean press, and

they were quick to offer their Oevenum home as a writer's residence for me. Itō and Hiltmann, whether because they could
converse in German together or their mutual interest in politics,
quickly became friends. It was decided that Itō and I would
spend a night in Professor Hiltmann's house before Itō went to
Frankfurt by train and flew back to Japan from there. Hiltmann
had classes on Monday, Wednesday, and Thursday but decided
to cancel his Thursday class so he could take me to Oevenum.

The next morning, the Hiltmanns and I saw Itō off at
Hamburg Station. Itō and I hugged before he got on the train. I
saw he was in tears. I was in tears as well. Hiltmann patted his
back and said not to worry, that they would take good care of
me, and Itō boarded the train with reddened eyes and stood in
the door and said, "Write well," to which I replied, "We'll see
each other soon." I felt as if I were parting from an older brother
as I watched the train pull away.

Jochen, Hyun-sook, and their five-year-old son Han-song
and I went to Dagebüll Harbor from Hamburg as planned.
Jochen drove while Hyun-sook sat next to him and nagged
him about speeding. If there was a car in front of him, he would
lean on the horn as he accelerated around them, which for
me—famed as I am for my impatience—was a secret delight
every time.

We took a ferry from the harbor. Oevenum, where Jochen's
country home stood, was in the middle of Föhr surrounded by
forests and fields. We rode bicycles all weekend and explored
the island, bought fish at the docks to grill, and spent time on
the beach. In a tidepool after the tide was out, I felt something
squirm beneath my foot, and when I gripped it with my toes and
brought it out, I saw it was a flatfish the length of two of my
palms. Jochen and Hyun-sook also prodded around with their
feet but only caught a few between them. The sight of me pulling up flatfish after flatfish with my feet must have made me
seem like some oriental mystic with magical powers, because
they couldn't stop exclaiming about it. They could not guess it

was from my childhood years of playing in the streams in Yeongdeungpo, Seoul. I brought this up later, when Jochen and I were wrangling over stereotypes: I told him that his ideas about Asians being more instinctual than intellectual, having more highly developed senses or being closer to nature, were all stereotypes. It was only a matter of our different childhood experiences.

I was left alone in the village of Oevenum when the Hiltmann family went back to Hamburg. Actually, another family member stayed behind with me, by the name of Kowalski. Kowalski was a jet-black cat. Jochen had adopted him from Sarah Kirsch as a kitten, and the poet had been the one to name him as well. Song Hyun-sook asked me to take care of him. There was nothing to it; all I had to do was feed him twice a day and bring him in at night.

I had never had a cat before and wasn't too fond of them. Kowalski immediately picked up on this and kept his distance from me as well. They say cats are independent, and this proved to be true. But if I happened to be napping, he would come up to the foot of the bed and meow for food. If I grew too absorbed in my work and missed a feeding time, he was apt to crawl right up my leg and loudly meow for his meal. I ended up with a nick on my knee from him. His meal consisted of cans that Hyun-sook had bought at a supermarket. All I had to do was fill his bowl with one along with a bowl of water. After his breakfast, Kowalski would disappear somewhere. There was a neighboring farm next to the wide lawn and another house over the hill by the road. If I couldn't spot him around dusk, I would walk all the way up this hill, calling out "Kowalski! Kowalski!" And when I came back, he would always be standing by the back door of the house, waiting patiently for me to let him in.

I continued to work on my travelogue in Oevenum and felt calmer in body and mind as I settled into a simple routine. I would wake in the morning and take a walk in the woods or go to the bakery for a brötchen, eating it as I came back. I sometimes borrowed one of the Hiltmanns' bicycles to ride along the peaceful coastal roads. I wasn't great at bicycle-riding but had fun tooling around the empty roads outside the village where there wasn't a cultivated field or human being in sight.

The Hiltmann couple returned to their country home when the semester ended, and I was about halfway done with my travelogue. A Korean student going back home for vacation delivered the manuscript to my wife, Myoung-su, in Seoul. *Shindonga* had published the beginning of it, but they deleted so much in their edit that I decided to cancel the serialization, after arguing fruitlessly in a long-distance phone call.

An activist friend in Berlin called me in early July. The National Council of Student Representatives in South Korea had sent delegates to the World Festival of Youth and Students in the North. He said that he had cried at the sight, caught on TV, of a young female student entering the stadium, energetically waving her arms. This was the twenty-one-year-old Lim Su-kyung from Hankuk University of Foreign Studies, who had had to cross continents, going via Japan and Berlin, to reach Pyongyang. After the event Lim had wanted to return to South Korea through the North–South armistice line, the most heavily guarded border in the world. The Catholic Priests' Association for Justice sent Father Moon Kyu-hyun to protect Lim, who was a Catholic. After days on hunger strike, Lim held Father Moon's hand and was arrested by South Korean agents as soon as she stepped across the border at Panmunjom. These dramatic scenes were captured by the foreign correspondents who were in North Korea for the World Festival, and were splashed all over TV screens and newspapers.

Being all too familiar with the situation between North and South Korea, I thought that Lim Su-kyung had acted with bravery and wisdom in how she conveyed the determination of South Korea's university students. She switched North Korea's slogan "Joseon is one" to "The Fatherland is one," and wrote it on a sash; she asked for watercolors to paint a South Korean flag, which she wore as a cape. It all showed that she was part of South Korean society and that she would never forget her friends at the Jeolla Province chapter of the National Council of Student Representatives. I heard later that she never accepted North Korea's requests unconditionally. She sang the well-known children's song "Our wish is reunification" over the militant songs popular among the activists, even teaching the North Koreans to sing along. I believed that Lim's explosive appeal among the North Koreans was due to the strong individuality of this twenty-one-year-old from the South, her vibrant sense of unfettered freedom and her tireless energy that bowed to no one. She made extemporaneous speeches that moved tens of thousands of people. No doubt the sight of a young woman acting with personal agency was a shock to North Korean youth, accustomed to mass games and collective behavior. The North Koreans are sensitive to mass emotion, which they use to their advantage, and soon Lim was being paraded as the "flower of reunification." The South Korean leadership, on the other hand, was harshly critical of her and cut her off from public view as soon as she was arrested on her return. Such prejudice and disapproval have never fully abated, but Lim herself lives on well enough in the second half of her eventful life.

~

Berlin's summer, which wasn't that hot to begin with, had already given way to autumn by mid-August. On August 13, amid the furor accompanying Lim Su-kyung's visit to the North and return to South Korea, thirty-six elder writers including Kim Tong-ni, Hwang Sun-won, Jeon Sook-hee, and Kim Nam-jo announced a "Proclamation on the current state of affairs." In it they stated that "we abhor certain purposeful literary organizations that produce propaganda for violent revolutionary forces," and urged the government to "make the consequences of their divisive actions clear to Moon Ik-hwan, Hwang Sok-yong, Lim Su-kyung, Moon Kyu-hyun, and others of their ilk."

Most of these writers, who had become the mainstream of South Korean literary society after the war, were fond of claiming that they were above politics while standing in for the authorities in their own "literary associations." In response, the *Hankyoreh* published an op-ed by one of their readers:

A proclamation by certain veteran writers was published on the 18th calling Pastor Moon Ik-hwan, author Hwang Sok-yong, and others "impure forces," complicit with the communists and lackeys of leftist ideology, goading Korean society into chaos. I can't but be surprised at such a simple-minded lack of logic . . . Today's social unrest is not because of visits to the North or the spread of *minjung* ("people's") literature, as claimed by establishment writers, but the result of our enduring dictatorship and the political paradox of our system . . . *Minjung* literature is writing that expresses the lives and emotions of the people, who make up most of our citizenry, and unless literature goes against the flow of history, a literature that fights for the survival of its people and aims for the overcoming of division will continue to be popular with the masses. It is regrettable that in these difficult times, the only thing our elder writers can come up with is the national security argument and justification for far-right positions.

I had moved from Oevenum to Yun I-sang's house, where I stayed until early September. Yun introduced me to the chief administrative officer of the Academy of Arts, Berlin, and they promised to support me in establishing my status and finding a place to live. I met many members at an academy event and was introduced to its president, the novelist Walter Jens. Later, the DAAD (German Academic Exchange Service) Berlin office connected me with Dr. Joachim Sartorius, later head of the Goethe-Institut. The director of DAAD was Barbara Richter. I became an Academy of Arts invitee with support and residency supported by DAAD. They had received information about me from the South Korean embassy in Germany and were aware that I was being persecuted by my government for violating the National Security Act. A house was assigned to me, but I had to wait a month because the current tenant still had time left on their contract.

I often socialized with the Korean European Council for Democratic Activism folks on my outings to downtown Berlin. They were mostly former miners and nurses, plus some students, who had organized themselves into groups like the Jeon Tae-il Memorial Group, Labor Class, Women's Group, and the Korean German Cultural Association. The council was a coalition of these groups, as per the political trend in South Korea to merge groups. They even published a newsletter, entitled *Minjujoguk*.

In early October, my novel *The Shadow of Arms* received the Manhae Prize. I was contacted through the poet Lee Si-young of Changbi Publishers and sent my acceptance speech via fax. The jury considered that I had "clearly exposed the fundamental truth about the model capitalist state that is the US through a measured, realist depiction of the oppression of a third-world nation."

About a week after the news of the award, I was finally able to move into my DAAD apartment, located in a complex on the corner of the Bundesplatz. It used to be a factory but had been converted into studios and spaces for artists. My apartment had been formerly occupied by a female Romanian composer. There were a few other invitees like me living on different floors. Across from my room was the widow of a Berlin painter. Judging from the strains of flute and cello that I heard from time to time, a musician lived downstairs. The apartment was a studio and, true to its industrial design, the ceiling was two stories high. A floor-to-ceiling window filled one of the walls, and it had a sleeping loft. Beneath the loft was a good amount of office space, and the living room was wide enough to be used as a painter's atelier. There was a kitchen and a bathroom to the side. The unit came with a sofa, bed, shelves, and utensils. All I had to do was call the superintendent if I needed anything fixed. Most invitees stayed from six months to a year, but it was possible to ask for an extension.

Berlin is sufficiently northerly for dusk to fall at 3 p.m. in November. For the first few days I kept missing the daylight, having woken around 1 or 2 p.m. after reading late into the night or dozing off while writing. I soon got used to it, though, and began to enjoy the depressingly dark loneliness that one might read about in Russian novels.

On the evening of November 9, 1989, the telephone rang when I was deeply absorbed in writing my North Korea travelogue. It was Yun I-sang, who rarely called. I could hear his voice trembling down the line.

"I was wondering if you were home. The world has turned upside down. Haven't you heard?"

"What on earth do you mean?"

"East Germany has called for the fall of the Berlin Wall and declared free movement." He began to sob into the phone.

I was overwhelmed by the news, even as I felt the grief of my old artist friend. "We, too, will be as one. You see? No power can keep a nation divided."

Yun told me that scenes of national reunification were playing out on television at that very moment, that the Berlin Wall was coming down and Germans were pouring into either side.

I tossed aside my pen and got to my feet. The phone wouldn't stop ringing. Everyone found it hard to contain their tears. A Korean student brought a newspaper with the headline "THE BERLIN WALL HAS FALLEN," and underneath, in red: "Berlin is Berlin again!" Uh Soo-gap called me, sounding excited, and said he was at the Korean European Council for Democratic Activism offices but would come and pick me up. First he went ahead and took photos of Brandenburg Gate for the newsletter. Kim Sung-kyung and Yang Young-mi arrived to take me to the site.

We had seen some advance signs. Countless East Germans had requested asylum in the West over the summer, and groups of asylum-seekers kept arriving to the West via Hungary. There had been a demonstration demanding free movement in Leipzig, and just a month before, another march of hundreds of thousands in East Berlin.

The street, usually empty in the middle of the night, was backed up with cars trying to make their way toward the city center. Kim Sung-kyung skillfully drove through back alleys, trying to get as close to Tiergarten as possible. The cars were filled with young people cheering and tooting on horns like at a soccer match. The whole city seemed awake. Waves of Berliners moved toward the city gates. Whenever the cars stopped, the people in the vehicles smiled and waved peace signs at each other. These were not the cold, staid Germans we'd grown used to. We decided to park the car and join the tide of people instead.

The thin fog soon turned into a light rain. We passed the Reichstag, which still bore traces of the fire in 1933, and came upon a section of the Wall that had been torn down. People and vehicles from East Germany were pouring through, to the loud welcome and applause of the West Germans who made way for them. In the churning crowds were people handing flowers to each other, young couples with children on their shoulders, lovers holding each other close, and old people looking around with amazed smiles on their faces. The boxy cars of the East mingled with the sleek sedans of the West amid echoing cheers.

Some impatient West German youths were attacking the Wall with sledgehammers, taking turns, crowds of them perched on top of other sections like birds on a wire. The people brought out wine and champagne, pouring glassfuls for each other and sprinkling them over the Wall. I looked around. We three were the only Asians in the crowd. I kept wiping my eyes with my sleeve; like the song goes, I couldn't tell if my eyes were wet with tears or the misty rain. Why did I weep? Any Korean with a heart would have wept in that moment. The three of us walked for hours among the intermingled West and East Berliners flowing through the streets, all the way to Breitscheidplatz where Europa-Center was. Kim Sung-kyung didn't worry about his car abandoned in the street. Who cared about that stupid piece of junk right now? We came to Kurfürstendamm in the middle of West Berlin around three in the morning. The plazas and roads were still crowded with people, and every café was full to bursting.

Walter Momper, the mayor of West Berlin, was broadcasting a moving speech. "Today is the very day we have dreamed of for twenty-eight years. Borders can no longer divide us." He praised East Germany for opening its borders to both East and West Germans. "No one needs to travel to a third country anymore. Many of us will now visit East Germany, and there will be much to discuss. That is why I beseech all citizens of Berlin to extend a warm welcome to our East German guests. We are now going for the first time to a country we have only seen on television."

We got to the bar where we had promised to meet Uh Soo-gap and shouted over the noise as we discussed what had happened. Everyone said they had started crying before realizing what they were feeling. East Germany was not an ideal society, but at least it served as a counterweight for West Germany, and now wouldn't the West lose its caution and do whatever it wanted? No, hadn't the West patiently put in the effort over the years toward changes in the East? But look at what South Korea was doing with the National Security Act, whereas West Germany's government had allowed its citizens to visit East Germany and to meet as much as possible with East Germans, in a bid to encourage East Germans to gradually change and find it impossible to continue without opening their borders. The arguments went on and on. In any case, watching the limits of humanity crumble is always a wonderful thing. If flowers are blooming in the valley over there, might they bloom in this valley, too? But

East Germany was not North Korea and West Germany was not South Korea. I had a lot to drink that night and ended up quite tipsy.

Berlin DAAD's Barbara Richter said we needed to meet, as she had something urgent to discuss with me. Barbara was a cultural administrator in her fifties, a heavyset woman with a kind smile, your typical German auntie. She visited me when I first moved into my apartment to check whether I needed anything, and even took me out to dinner to congratulate me. The moment I stepped into her office, she began talking about the fall of the Berlin Wall in her accented English and said that change was sure to come to Korea as well, her eyes pink and welling with tears. She said that the Korean president was going to visit and that there were things we needed to discuss. The gist of it was that their invitational program normally included the family of the invitee, meaning that my family should come to Berlin and stay with me. They, along with the Academy of Arts, had tried to invite them, but the Korean embassy responded that they were forbidden from leaving the country. They therefore wanted to ask the German president, Richard von Weizsäcker, to mention my family's situation to the Korean president. Their proposal and my petition would be sent to both the South Korean president's chief of staff and the Ministry of Foreign Affairs. I was deeply moved by her offer. I wrote down the names and birthdates of Myoung-su and our son, and promised to write up a petition.

President Roh Tae-woo, who was on a European tour, was visiting Germany from November 20 to 22. His North Korean policies were being put into effect. After the visit, I received a letter from President Weizsäcker's office: the German leader had been informed of my situation and had asked President Roh to allow my family to leave the country, which he had agreed to. I called Barbara. She shouted with joy that her offices had received a similar letter. She said the German embassy in

Korea was going to begin the process of bringing my family to Germany.

In Korea, the Manhae Prize ceremony for my novel *The Shadow of Arms* was held without me. But the very day before, the ANSP announced that they had arrested, searched, and were interrogating the poet Lee Si-young, publisher of the *Quarterly Changbi* that had run my North Korea travelogue in its winter edition. Intending to quash any further publication of my travelogue, they even arrested my editor Kim Igoo along with Lee Si-young. The ANSP also carried out a search of the Changbi Publishers offices. This raid deployed seventeen agents to confiscate my manuscript pages and galleys, contracts for the book version and receipts, the airmail envelope I had used to send the manuscript from Germany through Professor Takasaki Sōji, and my acceptance speech for the Manhae Prize that I had faxed over.

Changbi published a statement that said: "This investigation is a gross interference with the people's right to know and with freedom of expression"; many newspapers published op-eds about the North Korea travelogue and the arrest of my editors. They opined that the South Korean people had the right to know the objective truth about life in North Korea and that the freedoms of the press and academia could not be interfered with by the one-sided judgment of the government. The Association of Writers for National Literature, which had entered protest mode with the imprisonment of the poet Lee Si-young, also put out a petition saying that sections of the travelogue had already been published by *Shindonga* and that to arrest Lee was an inconsistent application of the law. The ANSP retorted that the first and second parts in *Shindonga* had heavily edited out the positive aspects of North Korea, but the third part "praised North Korea" to the point of *Shindonga* refusing to publish the travelogue. The newspaper op-eds were suspicious of how much a work can be altered by mere editing, and asserted that it was difficult to tell whether the *Quarterly Changbi* was being prosecuted for bad editing or for threatening the security of the government and the survival of the nation simply by printing and selling a North Korea travelogue. The press also highlighted the fact that arresting Lee Si-young for "aiding in the creation, distribution, communication, and contact of works that benefit the enemy" was inviting controversy regarding freedom of expression and equality under the rule of law.

To make matters worse, I learned that my son, Ho-jun, had been arrested and interrogated by ANSP agents for trying to organize a "politically impure organization" at his high school. I had worried that my visit to the North might have consequences for my ex-wife and children but was hoping against hope that their lives would remain peaceful and that they would not be affected by my political activities. When I phoned her to find out exactly what had happened, Hee-yun burst into tears, and my own emotions became so intense that I could not find the words to speak. The National Association of Teachers for Democratic Education, which had started in Gwangju when teachers had entered the democracy movement, had inspired high school students to create a high school student representatives association and elect nine national representatives, of which Ho-jun was one. It emerged that all of the organization's officers had been taken in for interrogation and some of them arrested. All had been expelled by their schools. Ho-jun was in second year at the time. He took his high school equivalency exams after his expulsion and entered university but, like his father's, his teens became his lost years.

I discussed Ho-jun with Barbara Richter and she suggested adding him to the invitee list, as it would be better for him to study music in Germany. I talked it over with his mother, but he was not allowed to leave the country anyway, and he did not want to be a burden to me. Maybe it was because he had grown up among Gwangju activists, who were constantly in and out of the house, but Ho-jun was always deeply considerate of others and was, as they put it, a conscientious soul.

I began to see many visitors in Berlin as the year ended and the dismantling of the Cold War gathered pace with the fall of the Wall. First came a call from Chung Kyung-mo. Lonely in a strange land, my heart stirred at the prospect of his visit, as if I were about to be reunited with family. Choi Young-sook drove me to Schönefeld Airport to pick him up. Chung wore a thick coat and a dashing beret. He carried no luggage. He had taken the Russian national carrier Aeroflot but his bags had not arrived at the Moscow transfer. They did not arrive in Berlin for the whole time he was there and, in the end, he had to make arrangements for them to be sent on to Tokyo. Choi and I showed him around Berlin, taking him to the broken Wall and East Berlin, and in the evening held a welcome party with the Korean European Council for Democratic Activism and the Women's Group members.

After Chung returned to Japan, I received a call from someone speaking carefully into the phone. To my surprise, it was Yeom Mu-ung, the critic. We had been close friends ever since we were young. Yeom was two years older but a decade ahead in terms of patience and consideration for others, qualities entirely absent in myself. As good a friend as he was, it had taken a lot of courage for him to ask if he could come out to Berlin to see me. For one thing, this was right after Lee Si-young had been arrested for publishing my writings, under the crimes of meeting and corresponding with and giving comfort to the enemy. He was joining one of the many university professor groups who were coming over to witness the changes in Moscow and Eastern Europe. He was only passing through Berlin but made sure to obtain my phone number through Lee Si-young because he really wanted to see me. I immediately agreed to meet up when he was in the city for two days.

We met in a second-floor café at Berlin's Zoo Station on the first day. I was so excited I couldn't remember anything we talked about. He came to my apartment the next day. When I opened the door, we awkwardly shook hands as if we were meeting for the first time. He looked around my room, sat down on a chair, and said, "It's a bit like prison." Of course, he didn't mean just the room but the fact that I was cut off from the outside. He brought out a bottle of whisky that he had purchased duty-free for the express purpose of drinking it with me. We were able to talk in more relaxed terms than the day before, when we'd met at the café. He asked me when I was going to come back, and I said I had three more years left on my passport and planned to return before it expired. Yeom Mu-ung mentioned the prison sentences handed down to Moon Ik-hwan and others, saying that I had achieved my goal and shouldn't go about making more trouble. We agreed, at least, on the fact that so long as democratization didn't advance further in South Korea, we would never obtain the capacity to bring about reunification. He got up when it was time to go. I saw him off only to the bottom of the stairs, where we threw our arms around each other at the same time. He patted my back and bade me stay healthy. I tried to wish him a safe journey home, but my throat was closed with tears.

Professor Itō Narihiko contacted me a few days later to tell me he was in Berlin. I was so happy to hear from him after seeing him off in Hamburg that I immediately went downtown to meet him. He was well acquainted with the Korean Germans thanks to their solidarity work with Japanese civic organizations, which was why Choi Young-sook came out to see him as well. Professor Itō was waiting with a professor who worked at Humboldt University in East Germany and his wife. To think that an East German professor could now take the train to West Berlin really brought home how much the world had suddenly changed.

Over dinner, the East German professor, who had apparently heard about my North Korean visit, asked me about Kim Il-sung's fight for political power. He wanted to know how I felt about the purge of Pak Hon-yong and the Workers' Party of

South Korea. I said I was only interested in how today's North and South Korea could meet as one; I was totally uninterested in the past internal politics of the North. In truth, I regretted the faction-related disputes within the left in North Korea that had once been unified in resistance against the Japanese, and I was also critical of how Rhee Syngman had gotten rid of his competitors in the South. This was not some phenomenon unique to Korea. Stalin killed countless political rivals such as Trotsky. As we had just seen in the East German example, sociopolitical change does not come about because a dictator gives permission but because the people take action. I asked him whether the East Germans would want reunification. He replied that the Honecker administration had succumbed to the will of the people, there could be no going back, and the only possible future pointed to reunification.

I tried to suppress my disgust and changed the subject. Throughout our conversation, I detected a typical European sense of superiority over Asian society in his cynical take on not only North Korean socialism but also South Korean capitalism. Thenceforth I felt a strange reactionary vibe from East German intellectuals that I couldn't quite put my finger on. This was, in part, a matter of disappointment in the East German Communist Party and also an allusion to their own ideologies. At a symposium I once looked through the biographical notes of a German presenter who was harshly critical of North Korea. It turned out that he had once studied there. They seemed to be radically veering right. Years after Germany was reunified, these same people would again express feelings of alienation from and disharmony with West Germans.

Itō Narihiko had come to Berlin to look for new Rosa Luxemburg manuscripts and said he would soon travel to Moscow for the same purpose. He would go on to write a book based on these rediscovered manuscripts. He brought with him some royalties, payments from magazines, and my contract fee for the Japanese edition of *Jang Gil-san*, all of which were of great help to my life in exile. Professor Itō said before he left that I was a "lucky guy," that the world was changing dramatically, the Cold War was ending, and we would soon be free of the burden of the National Security Act. His prophesy, however, stopped short of coming true where Korea was concerned. Our political situation would seem to improve, only to turn out to have been a false hope or something even worse.

The DAAD offices contacted me with the news that my family was set to leave South Korea. I wanted to call home, but I didn't know what the situation was like over there and decided to wait until they called first. I believed that it would happen, as it had been promised by both the Korean and German presidents.

Then one day in December I received a call from a woman in Korea who told me that she worked for the German embassy and that my family had left that day on a Lufthansa flight. I gave a Korean student in Berlin the flight number and my wife's name, asking him to find out her booking details. He managed to obtain her arrival time in Tegel Airport and the information that she was transferring from Frankfurt. I got to the airport on time. I didn't see the intelligence official from before, but I did recognize a Korean restaurant owner standing there with a camera. I pretended not to have seen him and kept my distance. I'm sure he took photos of me being reunited with my family and sent them to the South Korean government.

Soon a crowd of passengers emerged, and I saw Myoung-su holding little Ho-seop by the hand as he toddled out. I lifted him up, but the little guy must not have remembered me because he twisted away toward his mother. We acted like we hadn't been apart for a long time and calmly made it back to my quarters.

DAAD had promised from the beginning that they'd come up with a different apartment more suitable to our needs once my family arrived. The current one was fine as an artist's studio, but a little bare for a family to live in. Ho-seop, unused to the new surroundings, kept telling his mother, "I want to go home,

I want to go home." It hurt my heart to say to the little one, "This *is* our home." Myoung-su said that the ANSP had taken her in for questioning for a few days and that her younger sister had cared for the child during that time. Her sister said he had turned to the bedroom wall and cried for a long time after Myoung-su was taken away. That was only the beginning of Ho-seop's troubles. The child would continue to undergo separation from his family for years to come.

Myoung-su had been invited to meet with the German ambassador and consul general a month previous. After checking if she was willing to leave the country, they told her to pack up and be ready to travel by the departure date. The consul general drove her to the airport himself and made sure Lufthansa would take care of them for the whole journey. The German government had done so much for us in so many ways.

A few days later, we moved to an apartment in Berliner Strasse, a stop away from Bundesplatz. It was on the first floor of a corner building right next to a public park; anyone walking down the wide sidewalk could look right in. They probably thought that it was safer for our family to be next to a big road than in a quiet, secluded place. It was a large space with a living room and three bedrooms. Myoung-su had sent our things ahead to my address, most of which were books from my library. The cargo arrived almost a month later, after the start of the new year.

Around Christmas, a call came from the North Korean embassy in East Berlin. Secretary Yun Gi-bok was visiting the city and wondered if I could meet with him. My memory is vague here, but I believe the North Korean embassy was closed after East and West Germany declared reunification in October the following year and North Korea changed its diplomatic mission to united Germany. Looking back, he was probably coming to determine how to respond to Europe's swiftly changing political climate and to retool their reunification policies.

Berlin had become one city after the Wall fell. I simply crossed town to have lunch with Yun Gi-bok at the North Korean embassy. This was the first time we were seeing each other since the previous spring in Pyongyang, when I was there with Moon Ik-hwan. He mentioned Pastor Moon and Lim Su-kyung, and informed me that there had been other emissaries from the South leading to various ideas for cultural exchange. He first proposed a North Korean edition of my historical novel *Jang Gil-san*, and I readily accepted, having been among the first to argue for North–South cultural exchanges. Yun Gi-bok then said that General Secretary Kim Jong-il had approved the North Korean production of a movie on the Gwangju Democracy Movement, and wondered if I could help. When I asked how, he explained, "We don't know the realities of the South very well, and so we need help with the script." I didn't think much of it and said I could probably pick out a mistake or two of whatever they sent me.

My next novel, "Stagnant river," was supposed to begin serialization in February in the pages of the *Hankyoreh*. The idea for this novel had come to me during a conversation with the co-manager of Pyongyang Department Store when I was in North Korea. The co-manager was a white-haired old man but tall, and his back was straight as an arrow. He spoke in an old-fashioned Seoul cadence that I recognized immediately.

"Where are you from?" I asked. He smiled and said he was from Seoul. "Where in Seoul?" "Yeongdeungpo." I was so glad to meet someone from home that I mentioned the name of my neighborhood, and his face lit up as he said that he had lived across the street from me. We walked past the display cases as we reminisced about Yeongdeungpo. There had been an elementary school nearby and a wooden building from the Japanese occupation that burned down. The outhouse had burned, and the stench of boiling feces put the whole neighborhood off their food for days. I was nine at the time; he would have been close to thirty. We felt an instant closeness at the fact that our memories were the same and made a promise to meet up again soon.

My schedule had been so tight that it was difficult to find the time, but I managed to convince my handlers at the residence to free up an evening for me. Choi Seung-chil led us to a fish market near the Taedong River. We had seasoned pollack and grilled flatfish as side dishes to our soju while I listened to the old man's story. He had worked in a railroad factory in Yeongdeungpo. As a teen he was apprenticed to his father—a train conductor on the Seoul–Hsinking line during the Japanese occupation—before becoming a conductor himself. He spoke endlessly of the wildflowers blooming by the small stations of Hwanghae Province past Seoul and Kaesong, of the country folk and familiar itinerant sellers getting on and off the train, the gradually roughening northwestern accent, the sorghum as far as the eye could see, the great plains of Manchuria where the loam was rich and a red sun as big as a washbasin set over the horizon, the flocks of ducks flying over the Amlok River in the winter, and the snowflakes as big as children's heads crowding down from the sky. After Liberation he joined the National Council of Korean Labor Unions. Then, during the 1946 Daegu October Incident, he left for North Korea with his middle school son. I decided to base my novel "Stagnant river" on these three generations of railway men. The story was all the more significant for me because there were almost no Korean novels about laborers from the era of modernization. Railways and trains were symbols of modernization. I came to the story with the awareness that we had forgotten our memories of being part of a continent, ever since the division turned South Korea into a de facto island. I was going to use that middle school student and first-person narrator to begin the story from right after the war. But when the *Hankyoreh* sent a reporter to Berlin to discuss the prospect of serialization, I began to have my doubts about the "three generations of railway men" story. I was standing at the center of a wildly changing world. My writerly instincts were telling me that the world was about to be very different, and my own narrative methods would have to change accordingly.

In retrospect, the very title of "Stagnant river" foreshadowed how the work would not be completed. Looking at the title now, I feel a determination to say something meaningful in the face of my North Korea visit and the shock of the Berlin Wall. What a blatant allusion to division my title was! I began to think that it was a bad idea as soon as I started writing the work, I hated the form I had chosen, and I felt as if I had pushed myself too close to reality and got burnt by it in the process. My status as a man in exile did not allow me enough distance to think like a writer. In any case, I was still tied to North and South Korea and felt like they were standing behind me, left and right, looking over my shoulder.

~

I had gone to North Korea again after my first visit, because I'd agreed to attend the Pan-Korean National Conference that was being held simultaneously in North and South Korea in 1990. The overseas representatives who attended the planning conference in Seoul earlier that year officially requested my presence at the events to be held in the North. I had no initial plans to go, as I was certain that some other representative from the South would be there. I was also deep into writing the "Stagnant river" serialization. But I began to feel ashamed about limiting my activities to shutting myself in a room and writing a travelogue when Moon Ik-hwan, Lim Su-kyung, and countless other political activists were in jail. I felt my own responsibility was that much greater if no one else was able to show up on the South Korean side. I had no choice but to accept the invitation. This would take me further from the path of return to South Korea, as I was an exile with an uncertain future, and the personal damage I had to accept was also significant. But once I had decided what to do, I thought I ought to be even more outrageous in my activism, to not only infringe the National Security Act but to render it absurd.

At the end of June, a little before the Pan-Korean National Conference, I received news that my youngest aunt was on her deathbed. She had spinal cancer. She'd already been in the final stages when I met her in 1989. When I told Myoung-su, after some hesitation, that I wanted to visit North Korea again, she threw a fit. Her emotions had been in turmoil ever since she had arrived in Berlin, the unfamiliar surroundings and the constant stream of visitors setting her teeth on edge. It was my fault for bringing her to Berlin, but I was discovering, day by day, just how difficult it was for someone in exile to maintain a happy home.

I called the newspaper and informed them that I was canceling my serialization. Then I hopped on a plane that flew from Berlin to North Korea every Thursday. The novelist Choi Seung-chil and an unfamiliar handler were waiting for me at Pyongyang airport. The handler, a Party worker in his late fifties, had a sense of humor and a deep knowledge of Western society. They had prepared my quarters in Seojaegol. Deputy Minister Han Si-hae was waiting for me there. He was a man of the world, as one would expect from a diplomat who had spent seven years in New York as the North Korean envoy to the United Nations. The handler informed me that my youngest aunt had already passed away a week prior at Pyongyang Hospital. She had already been buried in a cemetery in Sariwon. In effect, I had confirmed that the older generation of my dispersed family were all dead. My maternal eldest uncle, mother, and younger aunt had died in the South, and my maternal eldest aunt, younger uncle, and youngest aunt had died in the North. My generation would be next.

I went to my younger cousin's house in Sariwon the following day, escorted by my handler. I'd heard that my aunt had four children, and that day I met three of them at a family home, where a full meal had been carefully prepared.

One of the eldest took me to the outskirts of the town. We stood before my aunt's grave, a mound of soil on a hill covered with rocks and stones. Judging from the other mounds nearby, the hill was a graveyard. My aunt's grave was one of the few that were marked with a tombstone. My cousin said, "Mother bade me to put your name on it as well."

The gravestone had her immediate family's names engraved on the back, with mine at the very end. It was a physical marker, left to our blood relatives in the North through me, of my mother's lifelong yearning to see them again. The handler nodded, adding that the people's committee was likely to have treated the deceased well because she had once been the manager of a state-run farm. I laid down the flowers I'd brought and did the three deep bows.

My maternal grandmother's grave was nearby, someone said; it was suggested we visit it. I had never met her but had heard so many stories that I had a clear picture in my head of what she was like. My grandmother's grave had no tombstone and was almost completely obscured by overgrown weeds. The eldest son, perhaps ashamed of the state of the grave, mumbled that he would come back on a less busy day to do some weeding. We stood for a long time in respectful silence. Whenever my mother was having a rough time, she used to say, "Mother came to me in a dream." I wonder if my aunt and grandmother's graves are still there, among the rocks and stones of that hill. The prospect of ever visiting them again seems as remote as ever.

At the Seojaegol visitors' residence, during a dinner with Yun Gi-bok and Han Si-hae, I abruptly declared that I would attend the upcoming first Pan-Korean National Conference with my family. They understood what I meant by that: I would be actively participating in the reunification movement overseas from now on.

I returned to Berlin and notified the Korean European Council for Democratic Activism that I was going to the Pan-Korean

National Conference. Myoung-su was completely against it at first but then decided she would attend with Ho-seop, saying if I was going to do it, we might as well go all the way. As an overseas Korean, she wanted to perform at the event herself. She discussed it with Choi Young-sook, who managed the cultural part of the event, and I came up with some ideas of my own. Yun I-sang's daughter-in-law also happened to be a North Korean dancer, so Myoung-su added a number to the overseas Koreans' *gut* ritual that she choreographed and planned to perform in.

In early August, I headed back to Pyongyang from Berlin with my family. We were assigned to the Seojaegol visitors' center. Overseas Koreans began to arrive as the date for the Pan-Korean National Conference approached. They were put up at the Koryo Hotel. Roh Tae-woo's administration in the South proclaimed on July 20 that they were officially allowing the Pan-Korean National Conference to proceed in the South, only later to cancel the tripartite meeting between North, South, and overseas representatives at Panmunjom, in the Demilitarized Zone (DMZ). The overseas organizers, who had entered the country in anticipation of the talks, managed to pass on the South's terms, return to the North, and create some semblance of a three-way agreement enabling the opening of the Pan-Korean National Conference.

On the day before the opening ceremony, Chon Kum-chol, the arrangement committee chair of the North, came to visit me in Seojaegol. He asked me whether I expected to get into trouble, now that the South Korean government had officially forbidden South Korean representatives from participating in the meeting at Panmunjom. I answered that it did make it difficult for me to participate if I did not have public backing, and that I was probably making my Southern cohorts uncomfortable because I was wanted for violating the National Security Act. Still, I wasn't exactly out for glory. Anyone could see that I was only making trouble for myself as an asylee. Chon

Kum-chol tried to convince me by pointing out that the North and overseas representatives had already agreed, so we would have a three-party agreement retroactively. I'd decided myself that it would be pointless to go back without having attended the Pan-Korean National Conference, when I'd come determined to see it through despite the dangers to myself, and it would be extremely difficult to hold it again in the future if we failed now. I informed him that I would be a symbolic representative of the South but would not present any opinions, and only act according to what the South had publicly proposed. I took on that role on my own. I had always been one to see things through to the end, and my thinking was that if I was going to be martyred for this, I might as well go all the way. I did not discuss this with Myoung-su beforehand. This would leave a lasting wound on our relationship.

The opening ceremony was to be at the new Kim Il-sung Stadium, built on what used to be the end-of-the-line tram station at the foot of Moranbong. It was attended by hundreds of thousands of Pyongyang citizens. Representatives from the US, Europe, Japan, China, and the Soviet Union had gathered at the entrance and entered the stadium like Olympic athletes, guided by *hanbok*-clad attendants holding signs with the names of where they were from. Once I had rushed through the welcome of the city of Pyongyang and was about to join the "Parade of Peace," I was led to a reception area near the entrance where there was a Northern-style café. As I stepped inside, I was surprised to find it filled with old women wearing white *hanbok*. The handler introduced the women one by one. I don't remember all of their names, but they were family members of famous people in South Korea. This was where I first learned that Choi Eun-hee, the first female journalist in South Korea, had an identical twin. This twin sister was still alive, as were Seoul National University's Im Seok-jae's two older sisters, almost one hundred years old. His two daughters were there too; also Dr. Chang Kee-ryo's wife; the novelist Park Taewon's eldest daughter, Park Seol-young; and Lyuh Woon-Hyung's children—except for his eldest daughter, Lyuh Yeon-gu, as she was an officer of the Party. The old ladies, upon hearing I was from the South, wept as they clasped my hand.

The parade began. The Northern authorities had placed League of Socialist Working Youth propaganda officers left and right on the sidewalks among the masses. The officers, following instructions, leaped out of the crowds and hoisted the representatives, including myself, on their shoulders, shouting "Reunification of the nation! Reunification of the nation!" I hadn't expected this and was disconcerted at first, but soon I was shouting along with them. The crowd was getting more and more excited. I saw that the old ladies in white had been moved out to the front of the masses, who overflowed the sidewalks and were spilling into the street by the time we reached Kim Il-sung Square. As we moved closer, the crowds pushed the line of old ladies further onto the street. One of them fell down, and I pointed at her from my position atop the shoulders of the young man and cried, "She's going to get hurt, she's going to get hurt!" I saw a video later on of that day. In their edit, the North Korean narrator proclaimed that I was "South Korean author Hwang Sok-yong calling to join the struggle." The South Korean edit featured the most dramatic examples, labeling them as "the megalomania of a leftist pro-communist." I'm told that this latter edit, which included footage of my visits to the North, was used in military education in corporations and army reserve training to illustrate the dangers of leftist pro-communists.

The North had never worked with overseas activists or even with South Koreans before, which made for many conflicts from the get-go within the Pan-Korean National Conference. It wasn't easy to find consensus, despite the shared determination to act as a united coalition.

The South overcame their government's blockade and went ahead with their half of the first Pan-Korean National Conference, with sixty-six representatives from twelve regions, including Seoul, and 20,000 participants. On August 17, the South's executive committee successfully voted to form a united reunification campaign group. Following this, the overseas Korean representatives left Pyongyang to form the European branch of the Pan-Korea Alliance for Reunification, grouped into organizations in each of their regions with their delegates assuming leadership roles.

On October 3, 1990, Germany was reunified as the East German states joined the West German Federal Republic. This was the result of East Germany's consistent democratic reforms since the fall of the Berlin Wall; also, during this period, East Germany abandoned its one-party system and held free elections. West Germany's democracy and unchanging reconciliation toward the East had finally changed East Germany. The Pan-Korea Alliance for Reunification ("the Alliance") was a response to the encouragement we received from these developments.

In early November, Cho Seong-wu, the political exile and student activist who I'd met in Japan, came to Berlin. He stayed at our place and sat in on the preparation process with the Korean activists of the Alliance in Europe. After an intensive two-day discussion that ended on November 20, it was decided that representatives from the North, South, and overseas would hold a conference to form a national reunification organization (Joguktongil beomminjok yeonhapche). My role was to bring the conflicting Southern and overseas Koreans into alignment, while the North Koreans sat out the argument, claiming neutrality.

For the duration of the South Korean military dictatorship, overseas activists suffered all sorts of oppression, as they were seen as anti-governmental or pro-communist. The Korean Democratic Unification Union (Hanmintong) in particular, which started in Japan, was often condemned as an anti-governmental organization. But its members were foreign residents in no danger of being arrested, and this allowed their activism to be more radical. What made activism in Japan more irksome to the South Korean authorities was the presence of Hanmintong in Japan and the fact that the national security incidents of the 1970s and '80s had mostly occurred with Japan as a backdrop. During South Korea's two periods of military dictatorship, activists in American and European immigrant communities were organized into the Democratic Koreans United (Hangukmin juminjok tongil haewoe yeonhap). But Yoon Han Bong in exile in the US and the Koreans studying abroad in Europe after the Gwangju Democracy Movement felt greatly disconcerted by the radical turn the older activists were taking and the pressures it exerted on South Korean activism. It had been decades since these older activists had left Korea, which made them out of touch and more ideological. The center of the scene should always be Korea, and it was South Korea's changes that would decide the direction of North Korea's metamorphosis.

The point of contention in the three-way talks in Berlin was that the South Korean side sought to change the name of the Pan-Korea Alliance for Reunification, and modifications in the organization itself, but the overseas Koreans refused to give an inch. In the end the name was retained, which was the name used in the declaration at Panmunjom as well, while the organization would maintain its separate seats in the South, North, and overseas with a general headquarters to coordinate them. The South Korean representatives also requested that I move to the US, specifically New York City, where the UN was. We were to use the general headquarters to check the Northern and overseas branches and to mold the movement's direction to the advantage of the South.

The conference was over, and it was time for everyone to leave. Pastor Cho Yong-sul and Lee Hae-hak from South Korea, along with Cho Seong-wu, were to be arrested immediately upon their return. I had a talk with Cho Seong-wu over drinks before he left. "Actually," he said, "I spoke with Yoon Han Bong before I came here. He said we needed to convince you to leave Berlin. I think so, too."

They must have been worried about how much the North was reaching out to me because I happened to be in Berlin. I too was feeling the need to distance myself, and told him I was thinking of going back to Korea anyway, after helping set up the general headquarters.

"A South Korean has to be the head of the general headquarters no matter what, even if we have to send someone from South Korea," said Cho Seong-wu. We agreed that if this proved to be impossible, Yoon Han Bong, who was well connected with the South Korean activist sphere, would use the American branch to lead the general headquarters.

There's another point I need to mention: all the members of the North Korean branch of the Alliance were Party officials from the United Front Department and the Committee for the Peaceful Reunification of the Fatherland. When we objected to this, the North stubbornly stood their ground, telling us that "the people and the Party are one, there is nothing wrong with what we're doing." I told them that if they persisted in this, we would be obliged to concede that the Alliance was indeed being manipulated by the North Korean government, just as the South Korean authorities were saying. After some discussion, the North Korean branch of the Alliance was almost completely re-staffed by artists, intellectuals, religious leaders, journalists, workers, and farmers, and its new chairperson was the writer Baek In-jun, of the Korean Federation of Literature and Arts.

At the beginning of January 1991, I was washing my face when I felt my back give, sending me to the floor. The pain was so bad that I could not take a single step and I had to spend that day in bed. I thought I'd be better after a couple of days' rest, but the pain grew worse and I was unable to even bend my knees. The doctors at a university hospital in Berlin took an X-ray and diagnosed a slipped disc. There it was, clear as day on the plate: the cartilage between my vertebrae had protruded and was touching the nerves. My German doctor recommended immediate surgery as the only solution. I was afraid of putting my bones under the knife and said I'd need to think about it first, and came home. Yun I-sang called. He heard me out and replied that he was glad I'd hesitated, for it was better to tackle a slipped disc through physical therapy. He reckoned it would be best if I was treated by North Korean doctors, who had a lot of experience combining Western medicine with alternative therapies like acupuncture. I wasn't looking forward to sitting in a plane for that long but figured it outweighed the risks of surgery, so I quickly made plans to leave.

On January 17, 1991, I boarded a plane for Pyongyang via Moscow. The German doctors injected me with something the day before and urged me to find a doctor as soon as I landed. I remember the exact date of the flight because the main headline on an English-language newspaper was about the start of the Gulf War. Saddam Hussein had invaded Kuwait and was threatening Saudi Arabia the previous summer, while I was in Pyongyang preparing for the Pan-Korean National Conference. It was the background to this conflict in the Middle East. I was therefore not surprised to find the airport in Moscow emptier than usual. I couldn't read the Cyrillic alphabet, but I could tell from the photographs and video footage that the media was focused on Iraq.

My family and I were taken to the visitors' residence in Cheolbongri. The houses were spaced far apart from each other around the reservoir. I went to Bonghwa Hospital to get examined, but they said it would take much longer if they used non surgical methods. Bonghwa Hospital catered to North Korea's Party officials and their families; Kim Il-sung and Kim Jong-il's private doctors worked there as well.

I received alternative treatments that included a paraffin heat poultice and cupping. The residence bed was too soft, so I placed a thick sheet of plywood on the mattress and a thin blanket over that. It was uncomfortable at first but helped with the back pain. Two weeks later, we moved to Hwanghae Province. We stayed near Sinchon, and I went to the Samcheon hot springs about half an hour away for physical therapy. It had a military hospital as well, and was near the Dalcheon hot springs, reputed as a vacation spot for the people. Samcheon was where those who had been injured during training would enter the building in wheelchairs and walk out of it on crutches. The baths were in individual cubicles in a large hall, each containing a private tub with physical therapy equipment. For an hour every day, I used a device that applied traction to my ankles as I held on to the bath by my armpits. I soaked in the hot water and slowly had my body pulled until I was stiff as a plank, then slowly relaxed. I had no idea fifteen minutes was such a long time; my face and shoulders were above the water but drenched in sweat. I got out of the bath and rested for a bit before repeating the exercise three more times. Within three weeks the pain had gone and I could walk normally again.

I had reckoned on a month for the treatment, so I got to spend an extra week with my handlers touring the locations for my novel *Jang Gil-san*. We went to Paeyop Temple and Woljong Temple on Mount Kuwol. The Buddha statues in Woljong Temple were all gone and only the paintings remained; I was no expert, but even I could tell they were from the Goryeo dynasty. There was, of course, no head monk, and the temple was maintained by the people's committee in the village below. The women took turns keeping the place clean. There must have been a lot of humidity because the mold on the walls had spread all the way to the paintings. In Pyongyang, I told the writer Choi Seung-chil that the murals were neglected and in danger of rotting; they needed to be taken away and preserved, perhaps in a museum in Pyongyang. I later heard that he made a phone call to the relevant department.

I went to Pongsan and Chaeryong nearby as well, but it was difficult to find anyone with knowledge about the *talchum* mask dance. After that, I went to Jangsan Cape, out past Monggumpo, adjacent to the armistice line. From there, I had a clear view of Baegnyeong Island. It reminded me of my trip to Mount Kumgang, when I'd gone to the end of Haegeum River and could see all of Goseong. Seeing the South from the other side of Panmunjom had been very moving, and now looking down on Baegnyeong Island from Jangsan Cape was like gazing upon another country.

We were resting at Monggumpo on our way back when something fluttered in the shrubs below the slope. I didn't know what kind of bird it was, but it was big. Its wings were caught in some branches. The driver and the handler went down to catch it. The driver reached out and tried to grab the bird only to get his hand scratched. The handler threw his jacket over it before extricating it. It turned out to be a hawk. The handler, a Party worker from the Hwanghae Province region, informed us it was a *haedongcheong* hawk—what the Chinese refer to as a Korean hawk. The handler pointed to the gray feathers and the smudge of blue under its neck and said the name *haedongcheong*, or "ocean blue," came from these colorings. My heart was beating fast. My novel *Jang Gil-san* begins with a preface centered on the legend of the Jangsan Cape hawk.

Back in 1984, in lieu of a publication launch, we had held a memorial *gut* with the shaman Kim Keum-hwa to celebrate the release of the ten-volume edition of *Jang Gil-san*. I received the *gongsu*, the words of the gods channeled through the shaman during a state of possession. What came out of my mouth at the moment was, "I vow to enter the North Korean land that lies beyond the armistice line." People joked to me at the afterparty that I'd turned the ritual into a reunification *gut*.

The driver put the hawk in a paper box at the visitors' center. I heard later that he entrusted it to the Pyongyang Zoo. I never visited the zoo myself, but Ho-seop said he had gone to see it with his mother. Apparently, the North Korean authorities had thoughtfully put my name on the plaque, as the donor. I wonder if I should have just let the hawk go.

I wrote the novel *Princess Bari* while living in Paris in 2006, and sent the complete manuscript to Changbi Publishers via email. The two chief editors immediately went into the office to work on it, despite the fact that it was a Sunday. The publishing house was in the Paju publishing complex on the northern outskirts of Seoul. A large bird suddenly flew in through the window and smashed against the walls and glass, fluttering on the floor. They assumed it was a pigeon at first but one of them observed that it was a little too big to be a pigeon. It turned out to be a hawk, a creature they had only seen in photographs. On a phone call to me in Paris, they mentioned how they'd had to open all the windows to let the hawk escape. The shamans say hawks are messengers of the gods; perhaps I share some kind of fate with them.

I still felt a little pain, maybe because I had worked too hard despite my back not having properly healed. The doctors examined me and said that my vertebrae were still a little out of alignment. So I decided to leave my family behind in Pyongyang and go alone to the Kyungsung hot springs for three weeks. I received a mud bath treatment there, which involved sitting in a tub up to my chest in water as black as mudflats. It wasn't too hot, but my upper body would be soaked with sweat to the point of severe discomfort after just twenty minutes. After I got out of the tub, I'd have cupping done on my back. By the time I returned to Pyongyang and had follow-up X-rays taken at Bonghwa Hospital, the cartilage that had been nudging my nerves was back in its proper place and I was proclaimed completely healed.

Pyongyang was entering spring. The weather was still chilly and white patches of snow still clung to the mountainsides, but the ginger and the pussy willow were budding and yellow flowers began to bloom. Around this time, the head of North Korea's Munye Publishing visited the Cheolbongri visitors' center with publication contracts for *Jang Gil-san* and *The Shadow of Arms*. He explained that there was no system for paying royalties in the North, and all intellectual property belonged to the government. Instead, a manuscript fee was paid and you could count on a print run of hundreds of thousands, as there was a printing distribution center in each region. I turned down the manuscript fee and asked them to spend it on food for the laborers at the Tongil Street construction site at the time. Later, in New York, I heard from a North Korean official that *Jang Gil-san* and *The Shadow of Arms* had been published. Kim Il-sung had told me on my first visit to North Korea that he had read the first two volumes of a large-print version of *Jang Gil-san* and had a pair of male and female voice actors record the rest. It was said that he took a keen interest in my descriptions of North Korean geography and its specific traditions.

Another portion of my visit was spent working with the cultural exchange between the Korean People's Artists Federation in South Korea and the Korean Federation of Literature and Arts in North Korea. At the time, I was commissioned by the Korean People's Artists Federation chairs to draw up an agreement with North Korea's Korean Federation of Literature and Arts poet Choi Young-hwa. South Korea did not manage to keep up the exchange, but Japan and the US staged performances, exhibitions, and film festivals. I proposed that we create a new literary magazine to which both North and South Korean writers could submit work. We titled it *Tongil munhak* (Unification Literature) and went on to publish many South Korean poets and novelists, including Park Kyung-ni, whose historic saga *Land* we printed in installments.

A few days later, I had a goodbye lunch with Chairman Kim Il-sung. I went with my wife; the screenwriter Ri Chun-gu also came with his spouse. When Chairman Kim asked Ri Chun-gu how many children he had, Ri leaped to his feet and shouted, "I have three children, sir!" which made Chairman Kim refrain from talking to him again. It showed how highly North Korean citizens esteemed the Chairman. Kim started talking about his own family, which led to stories about his mother in Manchuria. He must have heard that I was moving to the US, because he asked worriedly, "Why are you going to that den of gangsters?"

He had some interesting thoughts on Koreans based abroad. "Even after reunification, not all of our countrymen living over-seas will be able to come to Korea to live. No one looks for their roots anymore, they want prosperous lives now. Overseas Koreans shouldn't prioritize reunification activism, they should work to strengthen their rights in the countries they live in. That's how Japan's General Association of Korean Residents in Japan moved leftward. They were desperate then."

With regard to recent events in Europe, he mused, "The whole world is changing, and as long as our feet are on the ground instead of stepping on clouds, we have to change with it." He said that, in his time, socialism was the only ideology that could fight against the Japanese for the good of the Korean people. I still clearly recall what he said next. "I believe that even if our Workers' Party became just another progressive party in the bourgeois-style Western legislature that South Korea has right now, that would be reunification enough for me." Before we parted, he embraced me and expressed his regret, saying, "Writer Hwang, don't go anywhere, stay here with us."

Strangely, not a single Party officer or any of my handlers, who normally dropped in a few times a day, came to the visitors' residence after we returned to pack our things that evening. We'd had to give up our passports when we entered North

Korea; we couldn't leave the country if they weren't returned to us. I had to call for the handler many times until he finally showed up, very late. He said that Deputy Minister Han Si-hae had gone overseas on business and that we must wait to leave until after he'd returned. I had a strange feeling about what was going on. I managed to persuade them to send my family on to Germany first, so they could prepare for our move to the States, and I would stay behind for a while. They gave Myoung-su her passport, and she left Pyongyang first with our son. I waited alone for about ten days and remembered how Yasue Ryōsuke in Japan had given me a letter of introduction to Kang Ju-il, first deputy minister of the United Front Department, and asked to meet with him. He had been the student council president when Kim Jong-il was at Kim Il-sung University and was known to have advised the younger Kim. The North Koreans referred to him as "an old friend of our Dear Leader." Kang was five years older than I was. He gave me the impression of being reasonable and warm. When I asked him why my passport wasn't being returned, he looked as if he'd never heard of such a thing before.

I was getting more and more angry as I spoke. Staying in the North was not an option for me. I could not live apart from my South Korean readers, and I had a duty to my fellow activists in the democratization and reunification movement. I was a product of South Korean history and therefore would never be anything more than a houseguest in North Korea. Such houseguests, whether they are in the North or the South, only serve to perpetuate division by being used by the divisionists. I was determined to go back to South Korea after my exile, to receive the punishment that awaited. But ultimately I was determined to win back my freedom and live as a writer who contributes to the good of his own community.

Kang listened to me calmly, but his eyes grew increasingly moist. Finally, he nodded. "You are right to think that way, little brother. We must live for the good of the nation wherever we end up. Have a farewell drink with me before you go."

My passport was returned to me the next day, and I left Pyongyang. This was in May of 1991. I imagine that Chairman Kim's parting words—"stay here with us"—had been taken rather literally by his overzealous underlings.

Back in Berlin, I called PEN America in New York and the Young Koreans United offices. PEN America's Karen Kennerly gave me the news: artists' programs in Minnesota and Wisconsin wanted to invite me. I looked up these places on the map and saw that they were in the Midwest, making me imagine endless fields of wheat and corn. If I really wanted to write and take care of my family in a quiet environment, I should have taken up those offers. But I had a clear reason to be in New York.

My title was Spokesperson for the Pan-Korea Alliance for Reunification, but since the second Pan-Korean National Conference preparatory meeting in Berlin during June of 1991, I hadn't really done anything for the Alliance. I held temporary roles in the Alliance overseas headquarters and general head-quarters at the European regional headquarters, but it had been decided that the overseas headquarters should be in Japan, considering its "eldest sibling" place in the history of the move-ment. The South Korean Alliance was still in its preparatory stages, and the South's chairperson Moon Ik-hwan was still in prison along with Lee Chang-bok, who had been on the prepa-ratory committee. It was up to me to go to New York and set up the Alliance general headquarters.

My passport was only for three years, and by this time I had just four months left before it expired—less than the six months that was required for me to receive a visa. To make matters worse, Myoung-su had just been diagnosed with a gallstone and needed an operation. DAAD understood our plight and extended our invitation period to three years in an effort to help, but the Korean consulate in Berlin notified me by phone that they could no longer grant me a passport extension. I requested that they state their official reason in writing, but all they could do was repeat that there was "no further guidance on the matter" from the authorities.

As I waited for news of New York's Young Koreans United, Dr. Chee Changboh, a sociology professor at Long Island University, sent me an invitation. He could not provide funding, but he could give us a place to stay. I was in no position to look a gift horse in the mouth. What most worried the young people at Young Koreans United who helped me was that I wouldn't have enough time on my passport to be able to receive a visa. The paperwork for the invitation went through relevant channels in DC before arriving at Young Koreans United, who sent it on to me by express delivery, but I now had only three months left on my passport. I had all but given up, as I knew my visa would be refused, when I received a call about four days later. A man said, in fluent Korean but with a somewhat awkward accent, "I am an American. You received the invitation and papers to an American university? I can help you, Mr. Hwang."

He said he wanted to meet me. I was surprised and glad, and immediately agreed to see him. He told me when and where, so I called up Choi Young-sook who drove me to the appointed place. It was a bar and restaurant beside an overpass and was almost empty because it was a weeknight. The man would only say that he was employed by the US government. He had worked in Korea, and had a black belt in taekwondo. I had brought my passport and papers with me, but he didn't even glance at them. He only asked if I was able to get to the American consulate with my family the next day to receive my visa. I said my family's passports were fine, but I only had three months left on mine: wouldn't that affect my chances of getting a visa? He simply answered, "Ah, that passport is the concern of the South Korean government. It has no bearing on the US government's visa." I got the message loud and clear. We enjoyed a drink or two and parted.

The next day, we went to the American consulate where we passed the long lines of people and headed straight to the side entrance, as instructed. Most of the people in line had come after the fall of the Berlin Wall and were from Eastern Europe, with relatives in the US. Our man arrived, and we followed him inside to the consulate chambers on the second floor. Our visa processing did not take even a minute. The man said to someone who seemed like a consulate officer, "This is the person I told you about. And this is his family." The officer grinned at us and immediately issued us visas. Our man escorted us to the front entrance of the consulate and said once more in Korean, "Goodbye."

I left Germany on November 14, 1991. Myoung-su was to follow me after she had undergone surgery under Germany's health insurance for invitees. I went ahead to New York to make my start date on the Long Island University invitation.

~

Dr. Chee picked me up at the airport and drove me to his home in a forest near the university, where he lived alone in an old wooden house that was said to be a hundred years old. Dr. Chee had argued for the peaceful reunification and political neutralization of the Korean peninsula since the Cold War, along with the former UN ambassador Lim Chang-yong and the Washington dentist and composer Noh Gwang-wook. All progressive students during the time of Liberation from the Japanese, they were unable to pick a side in the great conflict between left and right.

Dr. Chee was born in Pyongyang and was a graduate of Kwangsung School, which had been founded by my maternal grandfather. When the division came, he was studying abroad in Chuo University in Japan, avoiding Japanese conscription by putting off his return to Korea, and wound up unable to return. By the time he was back on the peninsula, he had to cross the 38th parallel to go home. Not knowing where his family had moved, he had wandered aimlessly around Pyongyang Station until fortunately bumping into his aunt and mother, who had been going to the station every day in the hope of finding him. He crossed the 38th parallel again and entered Yonsei University, from which he was expelled for participating in the movement against the establishment of Seoul National University. He worked at a Christian nonprofit for a while before going to the US to study with the help of a Christian missionary. After he obtained his doctorate, he taught at different American universities before joining the sociology department at Long Island.

Meeting him made me realize that Yoon Han Bong's ability to come to the US and create mainstream activist organizations was thanks to such elders of conscience who kept themselves impartial. Dr. Chee cooked his own meals every day and expertly served rice and side dishes to his visitors. I did not ask him why he never married. He'd painted Eastern-style ink paintings as a hobby since his younger days and had far surpassed any amateur level. I remember two paintings in particular that hung in his living room: "Tufted heron" and "Persimmon." The lone heron standing on one leg with its head down looked like him, and "Persimmon" was inspired by a woman he'd known in his younger days. It was a long story, but she was part of the Korean Alliance for Democratic Young Patriots and was killed at Mount Jiri during the war. I used the story he told me as an episode between a father and daughter for my novel *The Old Garden.*

The first thing I did was go to Long Island University to meet their president. After that was over, I came out to find a white man in his fifties with gray hair waiting for me by the door. Dr. Chee greeted him and introduced us. "This gentleman wanted to meet the famous Hwang Sok-yong." The man gave me his card. The moment I saw it I thought, *Ah!* I'd realized who he was. The Korean-speaking man in Berlin who helped me get my American visa had given me a similar card. This gentleman had been part of the American education center in Berlin, the one now affiliated with the American education center in Moscow.

He took us to a Japanese restaurant he had booked before-hand. My English was rough, so Dr. Chee helped. Unexpectedly, our conversation consisted of my experiences in the Vietnam War and the changes in Europe. He asked after my family as well. On our way home, Dr. Chee joked, "Look at Mr. Hwang, he's such an important person now!"

I opened a bank account and applied for a social security number, which I was later told meant I could get a job and work in the US, and that it was unheard of for someone with a tempo-rary visa and an expired passport to receive one. Having this number meant that my family and I were guaranteed official residential status in America.

After a long time had passed, I began to think that neither the American in Berlin who helped me with the visa or my meeting with Dr. Chee were coincidences. It seemed that the Americans had used stealthy means to keep me under watch. I had experi-enced this kind of surveillance before, in Seoul, Pyongyang, and both sides of Berlin, all symbolic cities of the Cold War era. During the third Pan-Korea Alliance for Reunification confer-ence in Berlin, I once spotted a familiar car from the South Korean embassy across the street from the Berliner Strasse house toward the Bundesplatz, as well as another car next to the entrance to a park near our house. The second car had a red license plate belonging to the East German diplomats—this meant North Koreans. There was also a van with tinted windows to the left where the subway station entrance was, and that would have belonged to the West Germans. They had probably been moni-toring who went in and out of my house for the four days of the North, South, and overseas three-way meetings. A couple of days after each of my visits to North Korea, a young and cheerful German couple would visit the house and ask if we were having any problems with the gas or electricity. These were incidents that made me feel like I was under protection.

After we had settled down in the States, I was leaving a small event at Long Island University when a young American greeted me outside the classroom. He explained in fluent Korean that he was a graduate student married to a Korean and that he lived in Flushing as well. He offered to drive me home, which I accepted. We became friends and had drinks at my house once. I asked him where he'd learned his Korean, and he said it was in the US, though he'd also served in the military in Korea. I asked him what his work had been, and he replied with honesty, "Mostly North Korean surveillance." His wife worked in the UN; I was told she enjoyed her job very much.

He once visited our home with his wife and brother-in-law. He said his brother-in-law was studying in the US, was one of my readers, and wanted to meet me in person. This brother-in-law, once he got drunk on the wine they'd brought, pointed at him and said to me, "Mr. Hwang, do not be friends with this person. In your situation and all, shouldn't you be more careful?" To his brother-in-law he said, "Hurry up and finish your degree and find another job." I smiled and said nothing. The graduate student came to see me another time, with a second-generation Korean American who had just returned from Desert Storm. But once I became busy, he gradually stopped coming over or calling.

A few months later, the subject of the man who helped me with my visa came up when Choi Young-sook's son came to New York to study English. Apparently Choi had met with the American one more time, right before Myoung-su left Germany. After a few beers, she had asked him outright what his job was, saying jokily, "Are you CIA?" to which he answered simply, "Department of Defense." Our suspicions confirmed, I felt a little sad at how it went to show that the Korean peninsula was still really a war zone. They had wanted to surreptitiously show me that I, too, was under their system.

Yoon Han Bong called me at Dr. Chee's house and congratulated me on arriving in America, assuring me that our Young Koreans United family was doing their best to set up a place for us to live. I moved to the Young Koreans United offices a week later. I managed to find a rental house, thanks to the director in charge of the region, and bought the furniture and other household goods that we needed. The house was a little distance away from Flushing, where many Koreans lived, and the landlord was a Chinese immigrant from Hong Kong. Yoon Han Bong came to visit me one day from Los Angeles.

The first thing Yoon Han Bong, who was wanted for his part in the Gwangju struggle, had done after getting on a ship to the States was to set up a Korean school in Los Angeles, which had a significant Korean population. The Korean Resource Center aimed to organize and educate full-time activists, and indeed it had produced hundreds of young members and adult sponsors in just a few years. Young Koreans United USA brought about a new era in the Korean community in the US, thanks to the volunteer work of young full-time activists who engaged with ordinary Koreans in the mainstream. First, they went beyond the initial, exiles-based activism of the Korean community in America, by valuing the dedication and day-to-day persistence of youthful contributors. Second, they promoted national education and cultural activism, traditionally ignored by older activists in the US. Third, they expanded efforts in international solidarity and maintained relations with peace and human rights activists in Asia, South America, and Europe. Fourth, they set peace as the main agenda for Korean activists in the US, working toward American nuclear disarmament on the Korean peninsula, the withdrawal of American troops from Korea, the signature of a peace treaty with North Korea, and lowered military spending in both North and South. Fifth, they engaged in more systematic and continuous publicity than other organizations. Yoon Han Bong brought together the Korean American mainstream in 1987 as his sponsor base and launched the One Nation Korean American Alliance. If Young Koreans United is an organization for youths, One Nation was founded for the same purpose but geared toward those who were over thirty-six years old, including middle-aged and senior citizens. Young Koreans United in the US was extremely well organized, with specialized subgroups for older activists (One Nation), publicity (One Nation US PR), culture (Binari), and education (Korean Resource Center), enabling them to put down deep roots among the Korean community in the US.

I told Yoon Han Bong about my days in Germany and the Pan-Korean National Conference, as well as the tripartite talks. He knew some of the facts, but there was much he needed to be filled in on. I asked him if I could set up the general head-quarters in New York and have the Young Koreans United run it, and he smiled wryly and said, "Everyone in Korea is busy shedding their blood and being thrown into prison, but here there is no end to these organizations. It all ends up as positions and power."

I knew that any movement or organization will become a bureaucracy burdened with power if it goes on long enough. The Korean Democratic Unification Union (Hanmintong) in Japan was founded in the 1970s and was, in a sense, the vanguard of overseas organizations, existing precariously between the General Association of (North) Korean Residents in Japan and the (South) Korean Residents Union in Japan. Democratic Koreans United had been founded in the US and Europe with the aid of that organization, and the North American Association for Reunification of the Fatherland, the self-designated North Korean communication channel in the US, was also primarily composed of personnel from Democratic Koreans United. At the beginning of his exile, Yoon Han Bong had been accused many times of being a South Korean spy by the older generation of activists. It followed that he could only, in his words, work hard "with steam coming out of my nose" to build out his base on his own.

Yoon Han Bong in turn filled me in about what had happened since I last saw him, and we discussed the current state of Korean political organizing in the diaspora.

"The other organizations will not accept it if we propose to lead the general headquarters," Yoon Han Bong argued. "Cho Seong-wu basically shunted off the work to us before going to prison, but that's because he's not aware of how things are here. We can't just do whatever we want. It's the South Koreans who will end up suffering."

I said that the matter of the general headquarters had already been decided at formal meetings, meaning it had to be seen through, but Yoon Han Bong was adamant: "There are elders in One Nation who have joined the Pan-Korea Alliance for Reunification. Talk to them about it. Young Koreans United still hasn't come to a consensus over the Alliance and have no desire to take part in the general headquarters."

This was followed by a long and awkward silence. Yoon Han Bong broke his severe expression with a bright smile. "But I'm glad Seong-wu got you here. I feel like someone has my back." He said he had scolded the overexcited youth who had returned from the peace parade, and that the festival had been just that, merely a festival. "We are not a country, but weak individuals gathered according to their conscience. No matter how tough things get, we can't allow ourselves to be used like pawns by those in power."

Myoung-su arrived with Ho-seop almost a month after I had come to the States. In the interim, I met with the One Nation people who had joined the Alliance and Lee Hang-woo, who had been at the three-way talks. They were of the same opinion as Yoon Han Bong. The North American Association for Reunification of the Fatherland people I met in LA were interested in the general headquarters and were eager to establish it in the US. But it would be in a different direction from what I had talked about with Cho Seong-wu. It made me wonder how I would ever be able to work in solidarity with these people.

~

Another year went by, and it was 1992. I heard some news from Berlin. The overseas headquarters had already moved to Japan, and a meeting of the overseas leadership in Berlin, which had been

the site of the Alliance overseas headquarters and general headquarters, had decided that the general headquarters would likewise
be moved to Japan until it was properly established in the US.
Therefore, if I failed to set it up in the US, Japan's Hanmintong
and Democratic Koreans United would naturally co-opt the
Alliance's activities. Yoon Han Bong's prediction had come true.

One day, Yoon Han Bong called me up, saying that he had
come to participate in the Young Koreans United East Coast
meetings. They boiled tofu-and-kimchi stew in the office and
put out some soju for me. This modest dinner took place three
months after we had last seen each other, as I had been on a
lecture tour of American universities. "What did I tell you?"
Yoon Han Bong said. "They'll never allow us to open the general
headquarters here. We saw it was impossible because of the
situation on the South Korean side."

"You were right. The reunification movement should be
mainstream. What's going to happen if they continue on their
radical path?"

"Choose the mode of activism that's right for you. You did
teach us about cultural activism in Gwangju."

I told him I had actually been meeting with professors, intellectuals, and artists in New York, and that we were interested
in communicating with Asian immigrant youth from China,
Taiwan, Vietnam, and Japan. Yoon Han Bong offered to introduce to me some youths who had been in Binari and a couple of
people who used to be in Young Koreans United until they grew
old enough to be moved to One Nation. "We need you to do
your work. These are good, hardworking people. If you build a
house, at least its traces are sure to endure, no matter what
hardship befalls it."

Observing the LA Riots that broke out not long after I had
arrived in the States, I realized that the first order of business
was to forge sociopolitical unity among the Korean community.
In a sense, this was a bigger problem for the Korean American
community than reunification. I came to think during my

meetings with the Koreans in various spheres that helping 1.5- and second-generation Koreans establish their identities was crucial, that this had to be at the center of social activism in Korean American society. Not only that, we needed to have some kind of solidarity that extended to other East Asian youth. I created a committee chaired by Dr. Chee to establish the Institute for East Asian Culture, with me as the head. We had an opening and sign-hanging ceremony and hosted talks between youths every weekend. Kim Jong-ho, who led the Philadelphia branch of Young Koreans United, was the director, and two second-generation Korean women worked there full-time. They were highly educated housewives who took turns helping out. We decided to publish two monthly newsletters—"South-North-overseas" in Korean and *Mother Bamboo* in English—which would connect Koreans in all three territories.

In August of 1992, the Third Pan-Korean National Conference opened in Pyongyang. But without a passport, I was unable to leave the US and could only follow the conference secondhand. Around October, I finally heard the news that unification negotiations were in progress between the LA-based West Coast division of the Pan-Korea Alliance for Reunification associated with the North American Association for Reunification of the Fatherland and the East Coast–based Alliance associated with the Young Koreans United/One Nation. They wanted me, as the spokesperson for the whole Alliance, to arbitrate, which was why I went to the meeting for unification in LA on October 23. But just one day before, Young Koreans United/One Nation suddenly proclaimed the disbanding of the East Coast part of the Alliance without giving so much as a reason. Having no other choice, we spent a nervous month reorganizing some East Coast Koreans through New York's Reuniting Dispersed Families Committee and managed to come to a "unification" of sorts at the American headquarters Alliance general meeting on

December 5 in LA. But we failed to pass a resolution on the matter of the general headquarters at the Alliance's New York meeting. I submitted my resignation as spokesperson, via the European branch, to the overseas headquarters and general headquarters in Japan.

I was contacted around this time by Joo Dong-jin, who said he lived in New York. I couldn't recall who he was by his voice or name alone but recognized him on sight when we met at a Korean restaurant in Flushing. He had been a film director and owner of Yeonbang Movies, the company that produced the dramatization of my short story "The Road to Sampo." The final scene had initially shown Baek-hwa being sent off on the train and the two laborers getting on their own train in a snowstorm. Then, when the censors objected, Joo changed the ending to the laborers seeing Sampo developed into a tourist attraction and cheering, in a kind of "New Village Movement" propaganda ending. This had bothered me for a long time.

As Joo Dong-jin spoke of what happened, he added that the censorship and political harassment had been so harsh that even he, who had filmed over 150 films in Korea, was forced to leave the country. What most complicated matters was his eldest brother in the North. He, too, worked in movies: Ju Dong-in was the head of the state film studio and served as a standing committee member in the Joseon Writers' Alliance in the 1960s. Mere coincidence; but the fact of the brothers being in the same business was enough to rattle South Korean intelligence. Joo immigrated to the US, where his wife found work managing a shopping mall and he set up a film export company, called Cinema Empire. He produced the first North–South Korean film festival in New York as executive committee chair, with great success.

Now he was negotiating with the US State Department to produce a seminar and film festival toward a North–South film collaboration. He asked after the *Jang Gil-san* movie dramatization project, and I told him what had happened in Berlin. Sounding determined, he proposed to represent me as my agent to produce the North–South collaboration himself. Every few days or so after that, he visited me at home or at the Institute for East Asian Culture offices in Manhattan to update me on his progress. Considerable interest was expressed in South Korea, on the part of former *Korea Times* CEO Jang Gang-jae, Samsung, movie production houses, and broadcasters. Then he informed me that the film actor Kim Bo-ae was coming to New York to sign for the South Korean side. Kim Bo-ae, wife of film actor Kim Jin-kyu, represented Samsung for the agreement. She also happened to be the sister-in-law of Lee Duck-hwa, the man who had once sent someone to Berlin to negotiate with me.

It was the day of the seminar and film festival, but this fell around the time that South Korea, about to enter a presidential election period, was preparing for a "wind from the North"—a local term for how the situation up there can influence the outcome of an election. I learned later that Jung Hyoung-geun, who led the ANSP investigative branch, was preparing what would later be called the Lee Sun-sil spy incident, as the South Korean ruling party had determined that having good relations with North Korea would not benefit them in the elections. All events and contact related to North Korea were canceled. Therefore, many South Korean filmmakers and actors reached LA but didn't make the connecting flight to New York, with only Kim Bo-ae flying over directly from Seoul. The North had sent the vice chair of their state film studio, a male and a female actor, and screenwriter Ri Chun-gu. I got Joo Dong-jin's call and had dinner with them. Ri was very glad to see me. The deputy minister of the propaganda ministry, who headed all of North Korea's entertainment and film, was not at that dinner but transmitted the news that Kim Jong-il had already signed off on the North–South collaboration over *Jang Gil-san*. Kim Bo-ae signed for the movie companies in the South, and a state film company was the signatory of the North, with Joo's Cinema Empire producing.

Myoung-su confirmed through her mother in Korea that the money for the rights had been transferred to my bank account. I had been concerned that my period of exile would last a long time, or I'd need funds for the Institute for East Asian Culture, and had requested 200 million won from North and South producers, which according to the 800:1 conversion rate at the time was about $250,000. The North Koreans hadn't brought the cash with them this time but promised to send it through the mail in two weeks. Later, the North sent over their share of the fee through their representatives at UN headquarters.

Joo Dong-jin, as my agent, revealed the *Jang Gil-san* North–South collaboration agreement details to the reporters. Later, when I returned to South Korea and was arrested, the ANSP announced that this contract fee was my payment from the North Korean government for acting as their spy. I called up the actor Kim Bo-ae as a witness. She clearly stated in court: "I left with the express permission of the South Korean government for a collaborative film production. If you wish to rescind that permission now, I will cease working on it." Before the reporters, I demanded to know how anyone could be paid as a spy and then hold a press conference about said payment; but, according to the National Security Act, any kind of exchange in money or goods with North Korea is illegal, and that includes any measures of hospitality or even the wild ginseng that I had devoured.

One day, the novelist Yi Mun-yol called me saying he was in New York. Despite our political differences, I was lonely, and it had been such a long time since another writer had visited me that I was glad to meet him. I borrowed some cash from an acquaintance who had made their fortune through shopping malls and went out to Manhattan. My pride demanded that I, as the senior writer, be the one to buy him a drink, even if I was in exile. Yi showed up with the director Yun Ho-jin and the future Korea Theater Association president Jung Jin-su. They were planning the musical *The Last Empress* and were writing up the play on which it was based, "The fox hunt." They had come to see some Broadway shows for research.

After we'd had a few, Yi asked when I was coming back to Korea. I said I was biding my time. He talked about the breakdown of the socialist Eastern Bloc and railed against the unreasonable socialist system of North Korea. I listened for a while and said I agreed with him. The North had entered a "system of protest" for stronger unity and regulation as they went through the Cold War, taking them far from the fundamental principles of socialism, and in reality they were a dictatorial system with elements of both socialism and militant fascism. He asked why I'd visited North Korea then, and I repeated my standard answer that "we can't have true democratization without reunification." A mature democracy in South Korea would help to spark change in North Korea, and that would open a path to peaceful reunification. I suspected that my previous statements had been twisted by the mainstream press ever since I'd visited North Korea. But this was probably like when a bus driver veers right and the passengers lean left in order to keep their balance. I remember saying then that we should work together to keep our balance.

When he was drunk, Yi began talking about his father who had fled to the North. He had tried to track him down several times through the authorities. He wondered if I could find out anything more about him. I had an idea and asked if he were coming back to New York soon; he said he'd be in Washington for a week before returning to fly back to Korea. I told him to call me then. I knew a Korean American who ran a travel agency-cum-"dispersed family reunion service" in LA, but I was also in contact with the North Korean UN delegation in nearby New York, so I called them instead. I faxed them the specifics of what Yi knew about his father and the time period in which he would have gone North. I received a fax and an answer after exactly four days of waiting. The fax contained a simple CV of his father and a description of his relatives, as well as his current address. The North Korean diplomat also disclosed a few more things over the phone.

As scheduled, Yi Mun-yol returned to New York in a week, and this time he bought the drinks. I brought out the fax. I still remember what it said. His father, Yi Won-chul, changed his specialization from agricultural economist to mechanical engineer. This was probably after 1956 when there was a slew of reeducation and political killings, like the Workers' Party of South Korea incident, and during the time Pyongan Province was undergoing extensive postwar engineering and repairs. Even judging by Yi's father's very short CV, the man was an accomplished intellectual. That's probably why he'd survived. He took a job at some industrial university in Wonsan, remarried, and had five children. There was a long list of the names of Yi Mun-yol's younger half-siblings and their jobs. Yi stared at the paper for a long time then suddenly bent over as if he were about to collapse, clamped his mouth shut, and began to sob. I couldn't bear to see him so devastated and had to turn away as I wiped my own tears. A long time after, when he'd regained his composure, he drank another glass and tried to smile. "That old man, my mother knew he had remarried." I told him about the additional details the North Koreans had shared with me. They said that if he ever visited the North Korean embassy in Beijing, they would allow him to talk to his father over the phone. But I had my own thoughts on that. There was a famous soccer player who'd become a coach; he was in Beijing for an international match when he heard news about his father. He went to the North Korean embassy and cried his eyes out while talking to him on the phone, then illegally visited North Korea to see him. The incident was covered up and he wasn't arrested, but he was sacked from all official positions. I probably told Yi that this looked like bait thrown by the North Koreans. And I told him in New York, before we parted: "Forgive your father. Back then he was no older than your son is now, a young man who didn't know enough about the world."

Three or four days after Yi returned to Korea, I got a phone call from an intelligence consulate officer. No sooner did I pick up than he said in a nasty voice, "Mr. Hwang, don't you care about what will happen to you when you return to South Korea? Why are you going around telling people to go to North Korea?" I had a bitter moment where I simply declared that I had never said anything of the sort, neither in the past nor would I ever. At the same time it made me want to shrug off this burden of the oppressions of division, both on myself and my art, and just live as an anonymous exile for the remainder of my days. I had been turning down numerous offers from the American government to request asylum, choosing instead to live as a stateless being. But I easily understood Yi Mun-yol's fear. I hoped he would someday exorcise the ghost of ideology from himself and free himself as a writer.

At the end of that year, Kim Young-sam was elected president. Almost immediately, he expressed a willingness to improve North–South relations, stated that "nation trumps allies," and claimed that he was "willing to meet with Kim Il-sung any time to discuss matters of our nation." Bill Clinton's administration also took power. Among the Korean delegates to his inauguration was National Assembly member Kim Deog-ryong, who sent a mutual acquaintance to say, "We wish to hold a North–South summit and would like to know if Chairman Kim is amenable." I knew of a Korean American businessman in Philadelphia who visited North Korea to buy raw materials; he agreed to pass on the message. He came back from Pyongyang after ten days and said that he'd been staying at the Koryo Hotel after having passed on the letter when he was suddenly moved to the visitors' residence in Seojaegol. He ended up having lunch with Kim Il-sung. Chairman Kim gave him his answer verbally.

First, the meeting place had to be Beijing. Second, it had to be a closed meeting, at deputy-ministerial level. Third, the topic was to be a North–South summit. Fourth, they wanted to begin negotiations without the Americans knowing about it. I had already been assigned to contact a certain person about the answer, namely Ban Ki-moon, an acquaintance of mine, who was at the South Korean embassy in Washington. He asked me to come to Washington when I told him there had been a response. I said I couldn't, upon which he said he would think of another way and hung up. The next day, I was told to come to a rendezvous where there were two people waiting for me. One was an intelligence officer I had seen before and the other a diplomat. I passed on to them, in spoken words again, the four points Chairman Kim had proposed. They tilted their heads at the fourth stipulation.

Park Hyoung-seon called me from LA after that. I was surprised to hear his voice. He had been imprisoned with Yoon Han Bong after the National Democratic Youth and Student Alliance incident. He later married Yoon Han Bong's sister and had asked me to officiate and for the poet Kim Nam-ju to emcee. Park's younger sister Gi-soon had tragically died from overwork; while a student at Chonnam National University, she had obtained a job at a factory in order to help organize the workers. I created the musical *Imeul wihan haengjingok* (March for the Beloved) based on a "spiritual marriage" between her and Yoon Sang-won, who had been killed by state forces as part of the citizen's militia that had taken the provincial administrative building during the Gwangju Democracy Movement. Park said he could not come by New York on that trip and that he had called just to hear my voice. "You should come back, older brother, and write your good works," he said, adding: "Your brothers and sisters in Gwangju are begging you to return before the May eighteenth anniversary." Yoon Han Bong had decided to end his ten-year exile and return to South Korea; only later did I learn that he had asked Park to pass that message on to me.

He couldn't bring himself to tell me directly that he was leaving me behind in exile.

The poet Kim Nam-ju called me out of the blue the next day from the Association of Writers for National Literature offices. He, too, wanted to talk about my return to Korea. He said that as important as my writing was, my being imprisoned and the activism to get me out of prison would bring international attention to the issue of the National Security Act. After all, there were plenty of other people in the States who could do what I was doing. Later, when conditions improved, I could write a good book in prison. By a strange coincidence, the novelist Choi Ihn-suk visited New York to discuss the movie and came to my house. He announced that the Association of Writers for National Literature was formally asking me to return.

I decided to return to South Korea and began getting my affairs in order. I informed the Pan-Korea Alliance for Reunification overseas headquarters and the European branch of my decision. This was to show them that I had fulfilled my obligations to them and was finishing up. They were extremely upset on my behalf. The director Im Min-sik cried as he said, "You've worked hard for us. I'm sorry our own circumstances made it difficult for us to help you. When you're interrogated over there, blame everything on me. Tell them I made you do it."

I had expended so much energy in Berlin struggling to stay balanced in the volatile Cold War between North and South Korea that the tension had almost literally broken my back, and in America I felt like the vast continent itself was an enormous entrapping force. When I left Berlin, I had been determined to return to South Korea after setting up the general headquarters for the Alliance, but the realities I faced since coming to the US had turned me cynical and helpless. The fear that my life had become more that of an activist than of an author was also beginning to rear its head.

I wanted to go home. And my home was literature. Even as I

wandered the world in a constant fog of anxiety, what I missed most, in moments of clarity, was that home.

I discussed many things with Myoung-su after deciding to return to Korea. She too had realized that we couldn't sustain our unstable life in a foreign country for too long. It would take about fourteen months after returning to South Korea for the investigation, trial, and sentencing to take their course. We decided that the family would not follow me back until then.

On April 27, 1993, we went to the airport together. As I approached the departures door, Ho-seop must have felt some kind of premonition as I heard him cry out, "*Appa!*" The doors slid shut behind me, his cries ringing in my ears as I made my way to the security check.

6

Prison III

About a month after my final sentencing on September 27, 1994—that is, sometime in late October—the security officer brought me into his office for a meeting one week before my transfer to prison. He gave me a few words of advice before telling me where I was to be held.

—The Gongju Correctional Institute. It's a good place.

—Why do you say that?

—Gongju is not a big city. It was a small township until a few years ago. It's known for having good schools, which makes the people very genteel. And you wouldn't want to go to too small a prison, as they have to get by on smaller budgets. A midsize prison such as Gongju's will be more than tolerable.

It had been a year and a half since I'd entered Seoul Detention Center. I transferred out in the reverse order that I came in. I was given a physical first, then my belongings were searched, my pre-imprisonment belongings confirmed, handcuffs fastened, ropes tied around my arms, and then we were put on the bus. It was the usual chicken-cage bus they used to transport prisoners to and from court, much too large for just the senior guard, two senior corrections officers, and me. The bus left Uiwang, went past Cheonan and Onyang, over the Charyoung Mountains, and through the Yugumagoksa ravines. The valley was aglow with autumn colors, and I felt as light as if I were on my way to a picnic.

We reached Gongju Correctional Institute in the afternoon, and my pre-imprisonment belongings were locked up again. My cell was behind a steel door at the end of the first-floor corridor of a two-story building. The door was numbered and bore a wooden plaque that said the cell was for one person and was 0.8-*pyeong* wide. A junior corrections officer greeted me and said Father Moon Kyu-hyun had been incarcerated here before his pardon. The single cells were about a third of the size of the regular cells that held ten inmates.

There were three single cells in a row, but the one next to the stairs was being used to store supplies. The one next to mine was for the *soji* inmates, and the next two were regular cells for "exam prep" prisoners. The rest of the cells in the building housed the prisoners who were hired out as laborers. The exam prep prisoners were being supported by the prison to take their middle and high school equivalency exams, and I thought this system to be a good one. These prisoners were provided with textbooks, workbooks, and desks made by the carpenter inmates, and were taught by visiting schoolteachers and cram school instructors. I helped them in my own way as well, writing to publishers and getting hundreds of books donated to them.

I was moved to a second-floor cell a month later. That floor was filled with prison laborers who left for work in the morning and returned at night. I was alone during the day, put in de facto isolation. Gongju Correctional Institute was comprised of four rows of two-story buildings; my block was in the very back. The building in front was the special block that held students, officer-level and work-release inmates on the second floor, leader and model prisoners, and gang bosses. But the gangsters and leaders could choose whether they wanted to be in that block. Most chose to be in the regular cells. The first floor held problematic inmates who resisted rehabilitation, or inmates with light mental issues who were held in solitary confinement before transferring to a psychiatric ward in Jinju if their symptoms did not improve, from which they would return if they got better. I was supposed to be on the second floor of that block, but as a "person of interest," I was incarcerated alone in the exam prep and prison laborers' block.

The first winter I experienced in prison proper was much harsher than at the detention center. The cell block was not heated. Gongju Correctional Institute had originally been used as a courthouse and prison since the Japanese occupation, and there had been a mass execution of political prisoners there during the Korean War. The prison moved to its current location in the 1970s, into cement buildings, but the facilities were old and the sewage, running water, and electricity were unreliable. During winter a coal stove was placed in the middle of the corridors where the guards' desks were, but the heat didn't reach the prisoners at all. When I woke on cold mornings, I saw how my breath had frosted over the cement walls and ceiling. I lodged formal complaints and stuck thin sheets of Styrofoam on the walls, but nothing helped.

Serving a prison sentence in the winter is so harsh that there's a separate term for it. This "winter penance" begins early in October, which is when the winter supplies are provided. All they consist of is padded blankets with unevenly bunched-up cotton batting and a kind of hot-water bottle called *yudamppo*. The young *soji* prisoners would spread the padded blankets out in an empty cell to try to even out the batting and mend any rips or tears before distributing them.

The *yudamppo* had been passed down since the days of the Japanese occupation. It consisted of a rubber pouch and a cloth wrapper, but the cold was so acute that the water never stayed warm until dawn. The prisoners preferred the military-issue gunpowder containers, but these were granted only to the "barking mouths," meaning financial criminals, gangsters, and long-term prisoners. The gunpowder containers could hold a lot of water, and the rubber lining around the lid made it safe. Upon request, I also was issued one, and every night I put in hot water boiled on the coal stove in the hall, slipped it into a sleeve made of blanket material, and slept with it under the covers.

My second wife, Myoung-su, was still in New York at the time and delaying her return to Korea, so there were few people to help me outside of prison. My eldest son, Ho-jun, visited regularly, and Ho-jun's mother, experienced in supporting prisoners of conscience, passed on via him the things I would need for winter penance: thick socks, gloves, sweaters, hats, and underwear. A few of my women writer friends, who had somehow understood what I needed, also sent me socks and underwear through the post. I gave away the excess to the other political prisoners.

There was a student inmate and a young man from the South Korean Socialist Laborers Alliance when I entered, but the political prisoners really began arriving the following year. At one time there were a little over ten students and youths held for various offenses of organizing and protest.

Not a single ray of outside light entered the solitary cell, making the inspection slot on the steel door seem little more than a wall decoration. The food hole, locked from the outside, opened only three times a day for meals. There was a narrow space next to the door where a tiny, low desk was placed, requiring one to edge past sideways when leaving the cell. A fluorescent light bulb hung over the desk, and for 365 days of the year, it was never switched off. If it ever went out, the guard on shift would take a look and get it replaced. The prisoner needed to be visible at all times, whether eating, on the toilet, sitting, or sleeping.

The walls and ceiling were of cement. The floor, however, was laid with wood. The prison-issue bedding, once spread, left a palm's width of space on either side. Whether sitting or standing, when I stretched out my arms, my hands hit both walls before my elbows had fully straightened. Lengthwise, it left about three palms' worth of space at my feet, which I used for storing my toiletries and personal belongings. And then there was a wooden frame wrapped in clear plastic with a door: the toilet. The inspection slot had a good view of the prisoner squatting over the toilet. It was so narrow that my leg muscles would cramp when I used it. A bucket of water was provided for us every day; it took one gourd-full to flush urine, two for the other thing. We were expected to wash our dishes and ourselves with the bucket of water provided, so we had to use it sparingly. Extra water could also be stored in a couple of plastic bottles and used for heating or drinking.

The toilet wasn't quite a flush toilet. It smelled so bad that we had to half-fill a plastic bottle with water and plug the hole with it when it wasn't in use. A stopper against the smell, if you will. The more experienced inmates filled rubber gloves with water until they were as taut as rugby balls, tied off the ends, and used those. All you had to do was pull a string to get the stopper out. (I personally found the plastic bottle method more convenient, regularly swapping out the bottles until my release.) I assume the waste traveled down the cement pipes into a cement tank underground. The smell would permeate the whole prison on the days the tanks were cleaned.

The toilet had a window of sorts with plastic panels for panes if you were lucky and an opaque plastic sheet otherwise, as glass was forbidden. It was the only place that looked outside, and a cell with a good view might let you see faraway mountains. It was the only space where you could glimpse a corner of sky, a wedge of mountain, a fragment of the path of the moon, and a handful of stars. Those imprisoned in the single cells spent many hours in there. The toilet window was also the only place we could communicate with the other prisoners. But unlike in the detention center, most of the people communicating this way were gangsters, who tended to be the leaders in their regular cells. Around mealtimes, they shouted through the windows for their bosses to have a good dinner, and the bosses shouted back that their underlings should eat up as well. The financial criminals were not so blatant in their cell-to-cell communication and preferred to keep within their own groups at the infirmary or during religious services. They do say capitalist class differences are even more conspicuous in prison than on the outside.

Since my time at the detention center, following the advice of an experienced ex-prisoner, I started every day with push-ups and a splash of cold water. Getting out of my warm bedding on freezing mornings took some serious willpower. But daring myself to endure the cold water helped me survive the chill, mentally and physically, for the rest of the day; after I left prison, I graduated from splashing myself to taking cold baths. In the mornings, we had an hour of exercise time in between breakfast and lunch, after which I would head to our block's showers. My block was empty from the other prisoners having gone to work at the factory inside the prison. Theoretically I was supposed to have my own guard, but the guard in charge of the exam prep cell on the lower floor happened to be responsible for me as well, and he allowed me to be on my own in the corridors until lunch time. At lunch, the *soji* brought up my meal. I would enter my cell afterward and shut the door. Then the guards would come around for the first afternoon checks. In other words, for my hour of exercise and an hour after that, I could wander the empty halls of the block and stare out the window at the mountain behind the white wall of the prison.

The showers had a big tank that was always full of clear water. There was no washing machine, but a nonprofit had donated a spin-dryer that removed most of the moisture from our hand-washed laundry. The Gongju Correctional Institute water came from an aquifer hundreds of meters underground and was said to have received good inspection ratings. I would douse myself with cold water, scrub my body with a towel from head to toe, jump into the big tank, and count to 100. Soon, I could count up to 500 in there. I ran laps no matter what during exercise hour. Half an hour of running was about four kilometers, and I would talk to the young political prisoners during the ten minutes before and after while I warmed up and cooled down. Sometimes, the urgency of the current events outside of prison made us extend our discussions to half an hour, cutting into my exercise time.

There was also a tennis court that the convicts had made in the corner of the exercise yard. They had put down earth, sprinkled salt, tamped it down with a cement wheel, and sprinkled ash for lines. They even installed steel pipes to hang a net. There were many clever and creative prisoners; it was often said that, given the right materials, the inmates could have built themselves a plane. At a mid-level prison like ours, building a tennis court was a piece of cake. During the regular prisoners' exercise hours, I'd see inmates wearing flashy, expensive exercise clothes and swinging foreign-made rackets as they played tennis. There was a separate maintenance team that covered the court with plastic on inclement days, sprinkled salt, took care of the earth, and ran the cement wheel over it from time to time. It didn't take long for me to learn that most of the tennis court users were gangster bosses. I had no interest in tennis myself, but the young inmates in the political prisoners' cell block asked me to register a complaint. Was this court created for the convenience of a few? Why were political prisoners not allowed to use it as well? The prison authorities were taken aback. They asked if we wanted it shut down, but I suggested that if it was too difficult to open the tennis court to all prisoners, they should at least take applications from those who showed good behavior.

The internal rules for treating political prisoners were never made public, but since the military dictatorship we had always been subject to special disciplinary measures. We had to be incarcerated singly, our exercise hours were kept separate from other inmates', all of our letters and books were vetted, limitations were set on the number and manner of visits, audiovisual education (movies or TV) was restricted, and no labor was allowed. We were treated at the most restricted levels with improved conditions by default, depending on how hard we fought for them against the warden, upon whose authority treatment was decided. Whenever a new warden was appointed, everything went back to square one.

In this case, use of the tennis courts became allowed for the political prisoners. I had begun to see that the "war on crime" the authorities had waged in the past few years, which resulted in the wholesale incarceration of the gangsters that had once proliferated in every city in the land, had introduced a new predator class into the prison ecosystem. One particular boss who headed a nationwide crime organization was said to have received a "king's sentence"; he even had his own cell phone. There was another by the name of Jang who had made the papers with the Seojin room salon scandal; a former judo champion, he was mild-mannered and silent. Another gangster who left an impression on me, named Lee, was the "chief of operations" of the World Cup gang in the provinces, doing life for launching a surprise attack on the boss of a rival gang and sneaking into a hospital to revenge-murder an enemy. These two were serving the heaviest sentences in the prison, and they would always greet me or chat when we met during exercise hour. Lee, in particular, I found striking. He was a voracious reader and I was often surprised by his insightful commentary on books. Thanks to his influence, the other gangster leaders got along well with the political prisoners.

A little after my arrival, I went out to the exercise yard and was greeted by all the young inmates, who jumped up and bowed to me at ninety-degree angles.

—Good morning, Chancellor Hwang!

I found the use of this honorific amusing and kidded them about it.

—So, is a college president higher than the warden or what?

—I believe it's higher by a hair.

—But why?

—Were these grounds not once a public university?

As they knew everything about what went on here, they advised us political inmates whenever we planned collective action against prison conditions. They updated us on newly appointed wardens and national security officials and had a comprehensive understanding of the workings of the mess hall and commissary.

I had been getting used to the place, more or less, when a writer friend came to visit and told me some unexpected news: just before I left Seoul Detention Center, the Ministry of Justice had announced that they were going to allow writing in prisons. I had no idea what had been going on since I'd just been transferred, but apparently the ministry had proclaimed this after the UN Commission on Human Rights, Amnesty International, and PEN International announced they were sending a fact-finding mission to determine my imprisonment situation and writing conditions. The ministry had even declared through the press that, starting November 1, "All prisoners may obtain writing implements using their own money, use them during the day, store letters and literary works in the prison, and with permission, publish them in newspapers or magazines." They further stated that "Hwang Sok-yong, serving a seven-year sentence, has been permitted to write his screenplay for *Jang Gil-san* and is currently writing it"—effectively proclaiming that I was writing something that even I wasn't aware of. I complained about this to the warden. His immediate response was simple: I could write whenever I wanted. But there were conditions. I could use pen and paper during the day, but at the end of the day, I had to hand them back to the guard on shift. "The day" here meant civil servant hours. If a National Security Act violator like me wanted to write something, I needed to submit an application first detailing what I was planning to write, and the warden and prison committee would evaluate it before sending it up to the Ministry of Justice for approval. Once approved, I was to submit a set amount of manuscript pages every week to determine whether my writing fit the proposal, and these pages were to be stored by the prison. Once the work was finished, the prison would hold on to the manuscript until I was released, but it would be up to the correctional committee and the Ministry of Justice as to whether the work would be allowed to go with me. They were basically telling me not to write. I was enraged by the underhanded scheming of the authorities. Their announcement granting me the right to write in prison was just a show put on for the outside world.

I had no choice but to give up writing while in prison. Right up until the end of my sentences, these conditions never changed. Once, when I tried to pass on to my publisher an author's note for a new edition of *Jang Gil-san*, the prison demanded that two of the lines be rewritten, which I refused, and so the author's note never made it into the edition. Their control of me was this stringent, so I could only imagine how much worse it was for the regular prisoners.

Around this time, there were reports that international human rights organizations had begun demanding investigations into rights protection in South Korea, having found the government's violation of such rights and relevant international treaties problematic. The UN Commission for Human Rights notably passed a resolution that my incarceration under the National Security Act was a case of arbitrary imprisonment and demanded that South Korea honor its human rights agreements. These events came to my attention when Amnesty International, which had petitioned UNCHR on my behalf, revealed the UN resolution to a South Korean human rights organization after nothing was done by the government despite being notified of their human rights agreement violation by the UN in October of 1994. On January 25, 1995, a resolution by the UN Commission of Human Rights' Working Group on Arbitrary Detention was made public, in which "the detention of Hwang Suk-Yong [*sic*] is declared to be arbitrary, being in contravention of article 19 of the Universal Declaration of Human Rights and article 19 of the International Covenant on Civil and Political Rights, to which the Republic of Korea is a Party." The resolution also noted that the South Korean government had refused to respond to the UN's requests for consideration on this matter and had declared the UN's intervention to be egregious.

Most inmate complaints were related to the mess hall and the commissary, so much so that we used to say that fully half of the misery of doing time was the food. Mealtime began after the prison laborers left for the factory in the mornings. A shout of "Ready provisions!" would prompt a response shout from the *soji*, the clatter of their carts, and the smell of approaching food. Despite the enticing meal schedule posted in the hall, the dishes we received were pretty much indistinguishable, consisting largely of unidentifiable broth with scant meat or vegetables. Most of the time I could only tell whether it was supposed to be a soup, a stew, or something braised, by the dregs that had settled to the bottom. Any day where a piece of tofu, pike, or pork made it onto your tray was a good day. Something about the food coming through the food hole in the door made my throat close up with tears at first. The fact that I was like an animal kept in a cage, fallen to the bottom of life, and the prospect of doing this for years to come, filled me with despair and frustration.

The daily budget for inmate meals was less than 1,000 won per person, which meant only about 300 won—roughly 25 cents—was spent per meal. When I mentioned to the prison officers how we'd been given more food at Seoul Detention Center, they told me that Gongju was allocated a smaller budget because it had fewer inmates. With the civilian government coming into power, the kinds of goods inmates could purchase were curtailed as well, in order to deal with corruption among subcontractors.

The prison had a carpentry workshop, a sewing and knitting factory, and a work-release factory, which doubled as trade schools. The prison laborers ate at the factories, and the work-release prisoners, according to the policies of their work-places, could get whatever food they were allowed there. The block I was in was all prison laborers. It was quiet all day and bustling in the evenings. After I became acquainted with the chief of the cell next to mine, I began getting surreptitious snacks slipped in through the food hole. They were mostly items not found on the commissary list that could be hidden away from the physical inspections they received coming back in: blood sausages, dried meat, or smoked pork trotters, flattened inside workbags. Around Lunar New Year, a plastic soda bottle popped through the hole as the next-door cell head shouted, "Enjoy a cool, refreshing soda, Mr. Hwang!"

A cool, refreshing soda in this weather? I grumbled a bit but took a polite sip, seeing as he'd gone to some trouble to get it for me, and was surprised and delighted at what I tasted. He had dumped out enough of the soda to mix in a bottle of soju. A kind gesture, enabling me to have a drink in honor of the upcoming holiday. A gangster from Mokpo, he lived next door for a year before transferring to the cell block across from us. The soju, I realized, was from the boss of bosses, Jang, who was something of a leader of all the gangsters in the prison. In the winter, the other lifer, Lee, sent me a change of thermal underwear, and in return I sent him some thick socks and a cap.

There were normally two *soji* per block, and the prison authorities assigned one of them to me. He was to keep me company, and keep an eye on me, since I was alone during the day. They tended to trust political prisoners more after our third year, when they would leave our door unlocked and allow us to roam about the block during the day. I would even go and have lunch with the other young political prisoners.

People behind bars think about food all day long. We were given our three meals, but the menu hardly varied within each season and neither did what was available at the commissary, causing us to crave the delicacies we loved when we were outside. Aside from those working overtime shifts, the inmates had to stay cooped up all day in their cells on the weekends. This is when they would "dine out," "go out," or "sleep out." Just what kind of a prison sentence is that, you may think, but it's the kind of dining and sleeping out that's all in the imagination. "Dining out" means talking about all the delicious things you used to eat outside of prison; to a single-cell inmate like me, it was like reading a cookbook or a collection of essays on food.

One time, guards had to charge into one of the group cells and pull apart two inmates who had gotten into a fight. I heard later that they were arguing over whether *jjajangmyeon* or *jjambbong* was tastier, which escalated into whether sweet-and-sour pork or *japchae* noodles were tastier, whereupon one of them apparently couldn't take it anymore and shoved the other guy, thus starting the fight.

Dinner in prison was normally served at five. That was followed by checks, then the day guards went home, just like any other civil servant. The night guards took over then. By nine, the meager dinner would have been digested and I would already be too hungry to even lie down. I tried not to snack at night myself, but this was the time the regular inmates would eat their instant noodles, dried squid, or the single brand of crackers available at the commissary. I could ask the *soji*, if they were walking about in the halls before lockdown, to boil some water for me for instant noodles, but I could hardly ask that of the lone night guard. The dried squid sold in the commissary was so tough that it took a long time to chew and swallow just one arm, and my jaws and chin would ache so much the next day that I'd have difficulty eating. I learned to soak the squid in water before eating it.

I borrowed cookbooks from the library. The supplementary booklets from women's magazines with their precise instructions proved to be the most popular books checked out by inmates. The first thing I wrote when I came out was an essay on food, the result of all my yearning over food while I was in prison.

If that's "dining out," then what's "going out"? I also learned about that from the regular prisoners. It required a few different books. First, an atlas. Then, anything on driving, hiking, and fishing, along with travel guides—which were just then beginning to come out in South Korea, following the easing of restrictions on overseas tourism. There were travel guides for Europe, the US, South America, Southeast Asia, Japan, and China. For domestic travel, you picked the car you wanted and opened a map. Soon you were motoring over the Daegwanryeong ridge and following the East Sea, or down the west coast and onto a ferry at Mokpo, where you would cross to Jeju Island, drive across the island past Mount Halla and arrive at Seogwipo or zoom along the coastal road. You went hiking, or angling for parrot fish, or you struggled to reel in a bonito. When you were tired of Korea, you went overseas. If I asked the next cell for reading material, they might answer: "I just left Paris and am headed over the Pyrenees," and offer to loan me the book once they'd finished their tour of Spain.

"Sleeping out" required interior decoration magazines or a copy of *Country Home*. I used to secretly tear out pictures of interesting materials or decorations that caught my eye. First, I planned a two-story house, but thinking it would be better to separate home and office, I divided the house into living quarters and an annex for work. Time flew by while I drew up these plans. Once they were done, I stuck the tear-outs on top of them and constructed the buildings in my mind. I poured concrete for the foundations, put up the walls, and placed the roof, all the while constantly changing the construction materials.

The interior required more attention to different textures. I didn't like wallpaper, so I finished the walls with something that had a more natural feel, like stucco or plaster. The colors took a long time to choose. In the end I decided that the whole house should be painted in the same color but with a warm, bright shade for the children's rooms. The study should have rough stucco walls, befitting a workspace. The kitchen had to be to my wife's taste, with consideration for efficiency of movement, and various bathroom fixtures, faucets, and doorknobs all clamored in my mind to be chosen. The more I looked into it, the more there was to be done. It didn't take months, like a real house, but I could easily fritter a month away just rolling it over in my mind. Best of all, I could always knock down the house mentally and start again from scratch.

I really wanted a fireplace. It would be nice to roast sweet potatoes and chestnuts with the family; but it was the thought of sitting alone by the fire and doing nothing, not listening to music or reading, that made me feel sweetly drowsy and happy. Oh, and I wanted a Jindo dog. I had a picture of one cut from a magazine but thought it would be better to have a pair, so I found another to cut out and put beside it.

Some called it point-blank "going home" instead of "sleeping out." Prisoners dreamed of returning to homes they would never be able to build in real life, but once they awoke, they only found themselves surrounded by concrete walls. I once read about a long-term prisoner who dreamed he left his cell to frolic in a meadow filled with wildflowers, then rushed back to the cell to make it before checks and waking; I myself had a similar experience many times. Once I dreamed that I had "gone out" and was going home, only to find that my house wasn't on the street where it was supposed to be, so that I woke up in my cell. This was devastating. Another dream had me released from prison to find that my wife and child were gone and another family was living in our house. Yet another had me as a child losing my whole family during the Korean War evacuation and finding our house bombed out. I sat in the yard and cried for my mother until I woke up. At that moment, I realized the child wasn't me but had the face of my son Ho-seop, whom I had left behind in New York.

I played this house-building game for a long time before tiring of it. As the days passed, I began to doubt that I would have any home to return to by the time I was released. Would the house I dreamed of ever really exist? Maybe crossing the 38th parallel on my mother's back at the age of five was the moment I lost all hope of ever having a home to return to.

7

Childhood

1947–56

The great division began as political change swept the peninsula. By May of 1947, it was only a matter of time before two separate governments were established. I was five years old. One night, we grabbed some of our belongings and went to my youngest aunt's house. My mother never so much as hinted to her other siblings that she was planning to flee to the South. We had already entered the days in which people questioned each other's "ideology."

My youngest aunt had just gotten married. Her husband was an "ideologue" who had studied law in Japan. When his Japanese student conscription notice arrived, he headed first for Pyongyang before fleeing to Manchuria. They say that later, upon Liberation in 1945, he entered the newly founded Security Cadres School, then became a high-ranking political aide during the Korean War. He was also an ambassador to some country or other, but I am not sure which. I heard more stories about him years later from his children, after I'd become reacquainted with my aunt. His last days were spent as a caretaker at a government-run farm in Sariwon, until dying sometime in the 1960s.

My mother brought her husband and children to this aunt's house because she was the only person in the family in whom she had confided about fleeing to the South. My aunt's husband pretended he knew nothing about it but actively helped us by hiring a driver to take us to Hwanghae Province, just north of the border. My mother suspected he helped us because he considered her an educated person, unsuited for life in the North. In any case, all I can recall of that drive is us getting out of the car and pretending to go on a picnic.

I think we had dinner at an unfamiliar cottage. There was soybean paste stew with whole baby potatoes boiled in it and a side dish with little crabs marinated in soy sauce that I can still picture. Those tiny creatures had even tinier claws and beady little eyes, and their bodies were bright red from being cooked. I picked one up with my fingers and examined it closely, but I could not bring myself to eat it. That was in the boatman's house.

I also remember taking a boat at night and sailing down the river to the sea. Everyone had to lie flat against the wet boards and not make a sound, because we did not want to get caught by the patrols along the 38th parallel. At the time, the patrols were still relatively lax, and riding in the boat with my family were peddlers who regularly went back and forth between North and South. I was too preoccupied to be scared, fascinated as I was by the shaking of the stars as the boat rocked from side to side.

We reached a building, something like a school, which was filled with people. It was a refugee camp in Kaesong; we must have stayed there for about four days. On the hill behind the schoolyard were mounds of red dirt shaped like graves and flanked by soda bottles sprouting wilted flowers. There were many Japanese families that had come down from Manchuria and the northern regions in the midst of the war and its aftermath. The long journey had left their children vulnerable to even the slightest cold or bout of dysentery. The little red mounds were where they were buried. These emotive scenes are what is left of my childhood memories of walking those mountains and rivers during the first days of the North–South division.

I have almost dreamlike recollections of moving from neighborhood to neighborhood once we reached Seoul in the South. I remember a wide backyard and an apricot tree and a cherry tree. The garden had been neglected and the ground was thick with soaked, rotting leaves. I picked up a fallen apricot and bit into it. The fruit, wet with dew, melted on my tongue.

For several months we lived in a two-story house in Hyochang-dong. It was a Japanese colonial-style building with tatami mats covering every floor. Some cunning person must have snapped it up for an absurdly low price the minute the Japanese owners left, just like in Pyongyang. The landlord lived on the first floor and we on the second. My mother had to cook our meals on the stove on the first floor before carrying them up with my sisters' help. Each closet door revealed a wicker trunk filled with bedding and clothing that smelled of mothballs.

My mother liked to frame our flight south in apolitical terms, telling people that we'd simply moved to Seoul because my father was looking for a job. My parents must have brought gold and other valuables with them from Pyongyang to help us get established. My father had a nest egg saved up to open a business or buy a house, but one day, when the upstairs living room had been briefly left empty, someone stole all the money. According to my eldest sister, the culprit was surely the land-lord's newlywed daughter, who visited the house often. We never saw this daughter again. A successful businessman during the colonial era, my father tried his whole life to recover the standard of living he had enjoyed in Manchuria; but there was only so much he could do after losing all his savings so soon after being uprooted.

For the longest time, under my mother's influence, my siblings and I grew up believing deep down that our life in Seoul was temporary. We assumed we would return home someday. We were "refugees" for years. We all were: Northerners who had waited out the Korean War only to endure the long reconstruction period and continuous military dictatorship; rural migrants who'd given up on tilling the land and crowded into the city from every corner of this end of the peninsula, which was so tiny that if they so much as tripped they'd be back home already;

emigrants who couldn't survive here and were pushed out into foreign countries; and everyone who could never go home or see their loved ones again because the Cold War had us living under different political systems. Every Korean was a refugee. For years my mother could not take a bite of a fruit in season or some vegetable without lamenting: "This tastes terrible, the cucumbers back home were so much better."

In my memory, *kimbap* seaweed rolls were the fare of vagabonds. You may think that *kimbap* would have been a luxury in those times, and I suppose there's truth to that. There were other wartime foods, from *jumeokbap*—lumps of cooked rice molded into a ball the size of a fist—to *gaetteok* cakes and *beombeok* porridge and *sujebi* soup, all made from cheap wheat flour. And, later, *ggulgguli jook*, or "pig slop stew," which was made from food scraps found in the trash outside of US military bases and looked about as appetizing as it sounds. But *kimbap* was always the street food of refugees. Or at least the barley rice smeared on low-cost sheets of seaweed, unevenly stuffed with sour kimchi or pickled radish, that passed for *kimbap*.

Such are the wisps of memory that remain: the tatami rooms, the smell of mothballs wafting from built-in closets, lumps of rice wrapped in dried seaweed, and our family's solemn prayers as we sat before our meals.

I've already mentioned that my grandfather was a pastor. My mother was one of four girls and two boys. Her father started out in the Methodist ministry but moved on later in life to teach at a divinity school. Like most of the early members of the school of Enlightenment before him, he was a pro-education nationalist. My grandfather was prominent enough in Pyongyang to have established a medical school and a high school. Whenever I asked my mother why a pastor would found a medical school, she replied with a mixture of pride and resentment in her voice: "Back then there were very few hospitals, and many people died because they couldn't find treatment." The resentment came from having to return home from studying in Japan, despite having made it through vocational school. After Grandfather was jailed for joining the March 1 Movement in Pyongyang, and then spent another seven years in lockup for refusing to submit to mandatory Shinto worship, there wasn't enough money left for her to continue her studies. Around this time my mother received a marriage proposal through a matchmaker, and this is how she met my father.

My father was from Sinchong in Hwanghae Province. He had an older sister but was otherwise the only son for three generations and apparently monopolized the hopes and affections of his parents. He lacked my mother's expressive way with words. In fact, he was downright taciturn. I have no memory of ever hearing him tell stories about himself. According to my mother, he had a happy childhood, but it didn't last long. His parents died young, in quick succession. His sister married a man from the Baek family in Yonan, and my father spent his dark adolescent years in that household. His brother-in-law was not an honest man; once he got into gambling, he sold off parcel by parcel the family lands that had been passed down for generations. One night, Father waited until everyone was asleep, grabbed the land deeds hidden in the credenza in the master bedroom, and ran away. He came to Pyongyang, sold off the land, went to school on this money until it ran out, and left for Manchuria with nothing in his pocket at the age of twenty. There he worked in a factory owned by a Japanese man, where he ripped apart and reassembled hundreds of car engines until he was able to go into business for himself, setting up his own body shop, which he eventually grew into a big company that manufactured tires.

Photographs from this time show him decked out in a trench coat and a fedora, or a fur-collared coat and a Russian-style fur hat, with round-rimmed glasses. The very picture of a colonial bourgeois. Shanghai and Harbin were cosmopolitan, modern cities, so his sporting a leather jacket as he stands before a car doesn't seem odd at all.

My father was already in his midthirties when he met my mother. Before then, he had lived with a Japanese woman—which I only found out about at some point after he died, when my widowed mother brought it up as a complaint. I don't know if he had any children with the Japanese woman, but upon succeeding in business in the Manchurian capital of Hsinking, he ended his affair with her and returned home to Korea in search of a wife. When my older sisters wondered why he had to get married to a Korean woman, my mother would reply with something like, "How should I know? He probably wanted to carry on the bloodline."

My mother used to jot her thoughts and memories down in a notebook whenever she had time. According to her journals, she herself seemed to have been interested in someone else before she met my father. He was a friend of my eldest uncle and was on the Pyongyang High School soccer team with him. They spent weekend afternoons playing practice matches at school. One early summer afternoon, my mother was home alone doing her homework when she suddenly heard a ruckus. A crowd of Pyongyang High School students rushed in through the front gate. She found her brother and the whole soccer team soaked with sweat and clamoring for water. Mother filled a clean porcelain bowl and brought it out with both hands. A male student grabbed it from her and drank it down in one gulp. Someone laughed and said, "Your mouth touched the side where the *bok* character for 'good fortune' is, so now you're soulmates!"

After meeting that boy, my mother joined the Cheondo students' association with him, around the twentieth-century religion of Cheondoism, despite being from a Christian family. (She remained a devout Christian and never let a day pass without prayer, from the day she married my father until the day she died.) The two got together at student meetings, took walks along the Taedong River, and occasionally went out together for cold *naengmyeon* noodles or snacks of *hotteok* pancakes. Mother was also talented in sports like table tennis and track and field, often representing her class in competitions, and was the only one of her sisters to learn how to ice skate, which she did with my oldest uncle on the frozen Taedong River. The student she liked often came out on the ice, and the two would glide up and down the river to their heart's content. But seeing how Mother once told my oldest sister in passing, "If you like someone, never introduce him to a friend," I have a feeling her love was stolen by a friend of hers.

Father had a hard time understanding Mother whenever she shared something she'd read in a book, or made a literary allusion. Beginning her adult life as a married woman in Manchuria, Mother enjoyed books and American and Japanese movies, whereas my father was more the pragmatic workhorse type. He stayed out late entertaining his customers and often returned home exhausted and drunk from evenings spent in clubs or teahouses. She wrote that the winter nights were so long and cold that she sat next to the Russian stove and read books until late in the night. Mother was also more interested in political issues: not only was Father completely unconcerned with any politics outside of business, he had absolutely no curiosity about it. This was why, when times grew turbulent later on, he had no choice but to rely on his wife.

I have no memories of Manchuria. Liberation happened just two years after I was born, and Manchuria, which like Korea had been controlled by the Japanese empire, became a battleground, invaded by Russian forces and ultimately ceded to Chinese Communist control. My parents had to leave behind their land, factories, and the fortune they had amassed through their colonial business, pack only a few bags, and depart. Father would never recover the vigor of his days as a self-made man or the lifestyle of that time.

Mother brought the family into her parents' home in liberated Pyongyang before finding a rental house near Moranbong at the end of the tram line. It was a Japanese-style house, which was common around that time. She had also obtained several thick Japanese books containing a range of clothing designs and patterns, to open what became a successful clothing store downtown. Designing, patternmaking, and operating a sewing machine were a small sample of her many talents, and she fed our family with her efforts. Her clientele consisted mostly of the wives of the occupying Soviet military. Father went out every day, but I don't think he ever found a job.

When I was about four, I played with my older sisters cutting and folding colored paper and drawing pictures with crayons. They would make me epaulets and medals made of silver paper and paste them on my shirt, and I would puff out my chest and strut grandly about the neighborhood.

A Soviet officer and his wife lived downstairs. I recall now that they never managed to have children. Whenever the wife saw me on the stairway, she would come running and hug me and rub her cheek against mine and kiss me. She often gave me fermented herring and rye bread to eat, to my mother's horror.

During this period after Liberation, Soviet soldiers drunk on vodka would spill out into the residential areas at night looking for women. Young women smeared their faces with coal dust and covered their hair with ratty fabrics to repel them. Every house had a brass basin, and if any drunken Soviet soldiers appeared in the night, people would bang on those basins to alert the neighborhood and scare off the soldiers.

Around evening, my sisters would lead me by the hand to the last tram station to wait for our mother to come home. Sometimes we were lucky and met her just as she was getting off the tram, and sometimes she didn't show up until long after the sun had gone down and it was dark, making me cry.

My memories now move on to the "tree of heaven house" in Seoul's Yeongdeungpo neighborhood, the home my father bought and fixed up himself with the help of a carpenter. We settled there after we had left Pyongyang for South Korea and had already moved around a bit within Seoul. The house was close to Yeongdeungpo Station and the market. Between them was a rotary with a street that branched off toward Dangsan-dong; the house was on that street. Formerly a bicycle store, it had a storefront and living quarters and a fairly wide lot in the back. Father bought the lot as well, expanded the house into it, installed a plank fence, put in plumbing, and built an outhouse next to the fence. The reason we thought of it as the "tree of heaven house" was because of the trees of heaven planted along that new street. A rare tree now, they were heavy with tiny oval leaves like acacia trees and strung with fruit the size of bean hulls in the fall. They grew in the street outside our home, and there was also a grove of them in the empty lot Father had bought. Perhaps the previous owner of our house had planted them, or they just happened to sprout there. They were all cut down during Mother's remodeling, when she put the house on the market after the war and my father's passing.

Trees of heaven and sycamores lined the streets by the station, rotary, and market, but the Yeongdeungpo district itself was really a factory zone built up by the Japanese. Just a few steps beyond this district and you were in a countryside with rice paddies, but the towering smokestacks still stood out. Because of all the freight, railroads crisscrossed the district from all directions, and the roads were properly paved with cement. There were empty lots here and there with coal dust mixed in with the soil, where the rain created puddles of black water. Sometimes cement tubes and steel supports lay piled up in these lots. The corner of the elementary school's sports field opposite our house had an entire hill made of coal. Children climbed to the top to fly kites.

The center of Yeongdeungpo began at the station to the south past the rotary and stretched to the tracks that led to the re-developments in the west. Around the center were Japanese-style houses and shops from colonial times; Korean-style houses were more common around where our house was. Near the factories stood the company accommodation, cookie-cutter Japanese-style bungalow housing built by companies for their administrative staff and factory workers.

Looking back, the "tree of heaven house" was neither Japanese nor Korean in style; it was simply strange. It was shaped like a box, with a master bedroom used by my parents on the right-hand side and a kitchen behind. Near the stove was a little door leading to the master bedroom and another door that opened to the backyard. Next to the master bedroom on the left was the living room, and in front of that was the foyer with several glass windows. Behind the living room was the left-side exit and the spare bedroom next to the kitchen. The house faced southwest. Strong sunlight shone through the back windows every morning.

In the summer, balsam pear blossom, sponge gourd flowers, and morning glories on their delicate vines would climb up the cords my sisters had tied by the wall and peer into our windows with their pretty yellow and blue faces. In the winters, frost bloomed thickly over the windowpanes; forests, palaces of strange countries, and the sharp peaks of mountains would appear as the sun shone through. Late at night, I was woken sometimes by the sound of trains whistling and wheezing out plumes of steam as they rumbled past.

A little further up from the stream was a dike, and often when the Han River overflowed, the tributary stream would deluge Yeongdeungpo. Beyond the dike lay a long sandy beach and grassland, and across from the stream was the island of Yeouido, which had been an airstrip since the Japanese occupation. Before the Korean War, there were just a few planes there for flight instruction, and my whole family would wake to the sound of propellers firing up.

A crumbling industrial road led from Yeongdeungpo's center to the factories; the layers of oil and gasoline coating the asphalt would turn the rainwater in the potholes into puddles of rainbows. So many factories shut down after Liberation that the road was all but deserted. It later became a strategic corridor during the Korean War, and I got to watch military trucks and tanks pass by right in front of my nose. Across from our house was a *gobanso* (the Japanese Korean word for "police station" that was used for a long time even after Liberation). Next to it was the *gobanso*'s separate interrogation room, a carpentry workshop, a butcher's, and a restaurant. On the left side of our house was a cabbage patch, and across from that, a big Chinese restaurant called Two Star Pagoda that was built from brick. Toward the market rotary to the right was a barbershop, a few houses, and the home of a family workshop that produced funeral biers.

Father worked at Kyongsong Electric for a while after we moved down South, but I think he soon quit and looked for other work. One day, he went inside the gates (the four old city gates of Seoul—we used to say "going inside the gates" to mean "going downtown" in those days) and met Mother's cousin once removed, who had come to the South first and opened a shoe store in the Samgakji neighborhood. There was an American military base nearby, and his business was flourishing. This relative introduced Father to a supplier for shoemakers and other goods, and so Father's shoe store in downtown Seoul must have been thanks to the experience passed on by the cousin.

Mother, being much better educated than Father, found work more easily. A girls' school called about a teaching job, along with a few other offices responding to her résumé. She eventually became a teacher at a weaving factory nearby, where factory girls lived in dormitories and took classes in the evenings. Mother became vice principal, in charge of managing the educated, middle-aged matrons who guided the factory girls.

Mother put on Western clothing every morning before going to work. I had no choice but to entertain myself alone after my parents and older sisters had left for their jobs and schools. I sat in the shade of the trees of heaven and drew white lines on the ground with talc and dark lines with nails. I mumbled stories to myself as I drew. When a new character appeared in my head, I quickly erased what I had drawn and drew a new picture.

My younger aunt had lived on a hill across from Moranbong in Pyongyang and arrived in the South about a year after we did. She was an elementary school teacher before, which helped her get a teaching job as soon as she arrived, due to the shortage of skilled workers. They had a daughter named In-ok who was two years younger than me and perhaps born a bit frail. She was often sick. Her hair was as listless as stray thread and yellowish in the sunlight. My aunt's husband usually stayed home with In-ok. For several years, until he eventually opened a store in Namdaemun Market, it was my aunt who kept them fed. I was annoyed and bored with how In-ok refused to share anything and yet insisted on following me around. The few times my aunt's husband talked to me was to scold me for not playing with her more. I can still hear her calling after me, "*Oppa-ya*!" If I was on my tricycle, she would run to me, grab the handlebars, and demand that I give it up to her. I pedaled hard toward the rotary to get away, and In-ok wept as she ran after me. If only I'd let her have a ride. The child died not long after.

Mother took me to my aunt's house the day of In-ok's death. They didn't live far from us; her neighborhood was the two rows of Korean-style tile-roofed houses past the large rice mill near the market. The alleys were so similar that I remember I kept getting lost whenever I went to my aunt's house on my own.

My aunt lived in a *hanok*-style house that had a courtyard surrounded by a master bedroom, spare room, and another room by the entrance. When we came through the gate, Father and my uncle were drinking *soju* together on the edge of the veranda that lined the courtyard. My aunt burst into tears as soon as she saw my mother. She had planted daisies by their courtyard walls just like we did, and I remember there were many red flowers in bloom. The door to the spare bedroom was open, and I could see a small wooden box tied with cotton ropes that looked like suspenders. I stared at the box in fear, knowing what it was.

A bearded man arrived and was carrying the box out on his back when my aunt ran toward him and tried to stop him. My mother and uncle had to restrain her as she screamed and cried.

My mother went to the cinema on weekend afternoons, just as she had in Manchuria. She never changed out of her vice principal suits beforehand, though. Instead, she called me over as I played outside with the other children, spat on a handkerchief from her handbag, and hastily scrubbed away at my dusty face. The strange smell disgusted me. Mother would take me by the wrist and lead me to the Yeongbo Theater, which used to present kabuki shows, samurai plays, and oper-ettas during the occupation. Hollywood films were not yet common, and *yeoseonggukgeuk* performances, with their all-female casts, would become popular only after the Korean War, so we mostly saw plays and operettas during that time.

"The self-playing drum," depicting the tragedy of Prince Hodong and the Princess of Nakrang, dated back to that time, and "A tale of two sisters" gave me nightmares. When I pretended to be one of the ghosts by covering my head with a towel and moaning, "Mother, why, oh, why did you kill me," my sisters, who had not seen the play, would run away from me, shrieking with laughter.

I drew scenes from the plays in the dirt and built a barrier of stones and bricks around them so they wouldn't be trampled on by passers-by. Unless there was rain or wind in the night, the scenes were still there in the morning. One day, my mother came upon my little gallery and its little shapes scratched into the dirt. She called me outside and asked me what this was. As she pointed to each part of the drawing, I explained which charac-ter and scene it depicted.

"I see . . . Well, I think you should be reading books instead of doing this."

Mother had taken the decision, right then and there, for me to start learning to read instead of waiting to do so at school. Nowadays it's common for children to learn to read and even learn a foreign language before they start school, but back then even kindergarten was considered unusual. I attended church kindergarten for a while but grew tired of having to dance and sing with girls, my hands and feet fidgeting with boredom. Mother liked having someone to take care of me as she worked and hoped I would take to it, but I soon insisted on quitting.

Mother wrote out the vowels and consonants of Hangul in large brushstrokes, posted them on the walls of my room, and taught me whenever she had a free moment. I memorized them naturally enough and could soon put them together to read. I read my sisters' books first and then the ones Mother bought me. I especially liked *Gulliver's Travels*, *A Little Princess*, *Treasure Island*, and *The Man in the Iron Mask*. My favorite time of day was when everyone in my family had left the house and I got to read all by myself. Later on I pestered our babysitter, Tae-geum, to take me to the bookstore near the rotary so I could read new editions of the children's magazines. Now, not only did I draw pictures but I also painted my face with my sisters' watercolors, wrapped myself in fabrics, and dressed up in adult clothes to look like the characters in the novels, muttering to myself as I acted out the scenes alone.

I have a memory of those days that had been submerged for a long time but has recently broken through the surface. I once followed my mother to the Changgyeongwon Garden and met a stranger there with whom we spent a sunny afternoon. My mother had put on a pretty Western dress and scrubbed me clean and given me a neat change of clothing. The man and I bought a bag of feed for the fish, and we sat by a pond and threw the feed to the colorful koi that gathered with their mouths protruding from the water. This memory would come back to me from time to time like a wordless scene from a movie before being forgotten again. I remembered this scene when, as an adult, I read my mother's notebooks and realized that this man was my mother's first love, the student who had drunk from the bowl at the *bok* character for "good fortune."

There were other children my age in the neighborhood; they were either the poor children who were born there or the offspring of laborers who lived in the factory housing across the street. The children of the funeral bier house were known for being little troublemakers. The eldest was three or four years older than me, the middle son was my age, and there was a girl who was five. The girl always had a sty in her eye. She couldn't look directly at people but had to glance at them sidelong, prompting my sisters, who didn't know her real name, to call her "Lobster."

The funeral bier house employed a number of craftspeople, including one who made all of the wooden decorations that went onto the biers and another who painted them with intricate and colorful patterns. Whenever a funeral was held, they'd get drunk and have screaming fights late into the night, making my mother shake her head and say, "This is a bad neighborhood." Father tried to reassure her, arguing it wasn't bad enough to force a move elsewhere.

The poor children had their own games. For instance, if they found a straw effigy in an irrigation ditch, they'd hitch one leg up, stand on their toes, and spit three times to inoculate themselves before removing the money or food from inside. It was all strange to me, so I hopped on one foot and spat as they did, but I couldn't bring myself to put my hand into the straw dolls to take out the money and food. Around then it was common to see effigies tossed into the irrigation ditches or the gutter after a shaman *gut* ritual, along with pieces of rice cake or other food.

The children of the funeral bier house were more brazen than most. One time, the boy who was the same age as me took me into an outhouse and touched my crotch, made me take out my penis, and put his against mine. He started rubbing them together. When I asked him what he was doing, he said it was what grown-ups did. He sometimes did the same thing to his sister. I was scared and felt like I was doing something wrong, so I went home and hid inside the closet for a long time.

Once the war had come and gone, the neighborhood became vibrant with more houses being built and children moving in. It was exciting to explore strange new worlds with them, rather than stay at home or go to church. Outside was a whole unknown universe that made my heart beat fast, as if something great was about to happen.

The new road in front of my house toward Dangsan-dong led to more factories, the largest of which was the Yeongdeungpo railway engineering works. It had the most laborers. The Gyeongin, Gyeongbu, and Honam Lines split into their respective destinations from Yeongdeungpo Station, and the railway ran past the center of the neighborhood and into the factory area, with the engineering works where they maintained the trains somewhere in the middle. This was the second largest of its kind after the one in the Yongsan district. Whenever we heard the sound of exhausted trains creeping and sighing into their berths, my mother said it reminded her of Manchuria. At dawn we heard bicycle bells and the footsteps of workers going to work; by dusk the streets were filled again with workers leaving, the sound of metal chopsticks rattling in the empty tin lunchboxes that hung from their handlebars.

That part of the city maintained how it looked after the armistice and all through the years of modernization and military dictatorship. The trees along the avenues grew tall but gaunt, their leaves covered with thick dust. The cinder blocks in their faded camouflage added to the desolate atmosphere, the same old patches of paint over obscured, scrawled slogans. The tiled *hanok* roofs still looked as if they had been crushed, and the empty alleys and the blackness of the dirt remained as they had always been.

In a neglected and crumbling lot that had once been factories, weeds grew as tall as children and rotting water pooled in ditches, sometimes giving off green foam. But the stars at night were much clearer and cleaner than they are now, and the sunsets were beautiful. The weeds were dotted with dark berries like black pearls; two cupped palms' worth of them filled the mouth with sweetness like a blessing. All the children used this lot as a playground, where praying mantises and band-winged grasshoppers would befriend more familiar insects, like mole crickets or earwigs.

There seem to have been frequent clashes at the 38th parallel the year before I entered school. I knew all the words to the song "The ten human bullet warriors" that my sisters learned in class. There were truckloads of sand at the construction site where they were building an elementary school, and this became a playground for the neighborhood children. I followed around the older boys who split into teams to play capture the flag. The little ones like me were too young to be soldiers, so we sat on the side and watched over the piles of the older boys' coats and shoes. Military trucks carried loads of soldiers past our neighborhood every day, heading for the western front. We heard the shout of marching songs as the trucks passed at night: *Before us lies the bright road, a gun in one hand and love in the other, the wide, wide heart of man has forsworn his youth and fears nothing . . .*

We learned these songs and sang them at the top of our lungs without knowing what they meant. My sisters, playing with a Chinese jump rope or tossing *ojami* balls (fabric pouches filled with grain), often chanted Japanese songs they didn't understand—songs like the legend of Momotarō, or how a great man named Ninomiya used to sell straw sandals as a child. We kept on learning and forgetting songs whose meanings escaped us, every time the world changed.

~

I was finally old enough for school. One cold spring day in 1950, Mother brought home a leather satchel and school supplies I'd never seen before, like notebooks, a pencil case, pencils, and crayons. Father sharpened my pencils for me and laid them side by side in the pencil case.

On the first day of school, I put on a woolen sailor shirt, a pair of shorts, and white socks, and slung the leather satchel over my shoulders. I looked like the son of a rich family. I had always hated wearing new clothes my mother made for me, because then I was forbidden to roll around on the ground or play in the dirt. Mother was angry if I got new clothes dirty. I wore altered shirts that used to be my sisters' or my mother's or made from worsted fabric, along with shorts and long socks, and I hated how I was always dressed like a girl. Having my hair grow from its short buzz and getting it parted with a comb made me look just like my sisters when they were younger.

I kept fighting with my mother about my appearance even as I reached my teens. She would say, "Looks matter," and I would retort that comfort mattered more. She must have wanted to assert her modern education and middle-class values, having been forced to move to a new milieu.

School was my first experience of things that were "not me." I was assigned to a teacher and her class at the playground. My teacher was a tall, pale woman in her late twenties, probably a newlywed. Everyone shouted along to her whistle—one, two, three. As I took my seat in the classroom, I was swept up in the noise of other children. I was only used to my own face, having looked at it in a mirror. Everyone else was so strange, their voices so different, and nobody sat still. One child was already crying for his mother, others were hitting each other and fighting, and another was grabbing other children's things. I plugged my ears with my fingers. But the sight of children moving and crying without a sound was even stranger. I repeatedly plugged and unplugged my ears. The resulting ringing was like the hum of machines.

I told my mother I hated school as soon as I got home. When she asked why, I replied, "There are too many children I don't know."

"You'll be friends with all of them soon. School is not just for studying, it's also for making friends."

It had been three or four months since I'd started school. One day, I heard loud claps of thunder, and the mood among the adults turned tense. When I got to school, our teacher ordered us to return home. I had reached the front of Yeongdeungpo Station when the crowd suddenly began to scatter, sirens wailing from the nearby fire station. Sirens sounded every noon and midnight in those days, but this time they were accompanied by the roar of propeller planes. A man on a bicycle stopped underneath a tree and gestured at me, saying "Child, come here and hide or you'll get shot!"

Not knowing what else to do, I ran and stood with him beneath the tree. Planes swooped down with a clamor like bamboo poles banging on a hardwood floor. When the noise receded, people quickly moved along under cover of the canopies of the storefronts that lined the street. I ran past the rotary to home. My sisters said they had heard in school that war had broken out. Airplanes from the North had bombed Yoeuido and fired machine guns. We didn't have to go to school anymore. The neighborhood kids said they'd climbed the embankment of the tributary and seen twin-prop Australian planes dogfighting with Northern ones.

A stream of refugees began to flow past our house. My father stopped one to question him and was told they were from the northern part of Gyeonggi Province and had just crossed the river. Truckloads of soldiers moved in the opposite direction. When evening descended, we anxiously listened to sporadic cannon blasts, sounding like the portents of a storm.

I'm not sure whether we joined the stream before or after Seoul was taken. All I remember is that one night we heard a series of blasts that shook the earth. It turned out to be the bombing of the Han River Bridge. All the cars hastening southward fell into the water, and many pedestrians also died in this brutal way.

The Rhee Syngman administration continued to broadcast a recording on a loop that proclaimed, "We shall guard Seoul to the end, our citizens must not panic," while anyone with a modicum of political connection had long fled further south. Despite there still being soldiers who had not retreated from the North, the South Korean government had bombed the Han River Bridge to keep Northern troops out. When the mood of the people turned against the Rhee administration, some colonel or other took the blame and was executed by firing squad.

Our family left the house one early, rainy morning. This was after my younger aunt had already gone south to Daejeon, where my uncle knew someone. I packed my books and notebook into my satchel, but my mother had to convince me to leave it behind. We got together with the family of a distant relative of my father, his cousin's child, whom we referred to as Haeju Aunt. Together we went past the station where a few train cars stood empty on the tracks, and began walking toward Incheon. I believe the plan was to catch a boat. Haeju Aunt's family had fled Haeju to Incheon on a fishing boat. They say this method is why, to this day, there are so many people from North Korea's nearby Hwanghae Province living in South Korea's Incheon.

Our progress was slow because we were mostly women and children. On the way, we met with other refugees coming from Incheon, and upon hearing what was going on, we had to turn back. It was rumored that North Korean troops were already there. Our hesitation had resulted in our being stuck between the front lines of the North and South Korean forces.

The sun had set when we reached Oryu-dong in southwestern Seoul. Haeju Aunt's husband went to a farmhouse that was visible from the main road and managed to buy us a night of shelter. We sat in a room with straw mats, facing each other as we ate our dinner by the bright light of the petroleum lamp. The gochujang stew made with tiny whole potatoes with their skin still on was delicious. Our family spent the night crouching in the dark, and all night we heard the sound of cars driving past outside.

The next day, I was outside by the road with my mother, watching military trucks go by. The driver and ranking officer sat in the front and the soldiers in the back, a couple of men with rifles at the ready sitting at the head of the soldiers' rows. They were all armed to the teeth and had grass and leaves for camouflage stuck to their helmets. A passing jeep stopped in front of us to ask my mother something. The ranking officer gave me a bag of army biscuits before going on his way. He had told my mother that the Noryangjin neighborhood was the front line and that we should retreat south toward the city of Suwon. But the adults seemed to have given up on fleeing and were planning to return to Yeongdeungpo, reentering the district once the two front lines crossed each other. Planes flew overhead, and the sound of guns and bombs was incessant. We decided to crawl into an irrigation tunnel with another family that we'd met on the way and spend the night there. The tunnel had been dug to let out water during the rainy season and was big enough for farmers to pass through. We spent two nights in that tunnel.

Soldiers found us at our first dawn there. It was too dark to see whether they were Northern or Southern; they shone a flashlight into each of our faces and disappeared. Another group of soldiers appeared early the next day. They were probably police or reconnaissance teams, whether from the North or South we still couldn't tell. We heard hours of gun fighting that night at close proximity. I was young, and the shock of what happened next would continue to haunt my dreams as an adult. The soldiers shone a flashlight into the tunnel again and gestured for us to come out. My father carried me on his back. My mother gripped my sisters' wrists and stuck close by my father. I had my head against Father's back and could hear him breathing loudly.

The soldier who seemed to be in charge stepped forward. "Who do you follow? Dr. Rhee Syngman or General Kim Il-sung?"

No one dared to answer at first, but then someone said it was General Kim. That person was quickly taken away into the dark by another soldier, and we were summoned to answer again. When we remained silent, the commanding officer barked, "Shoot them all!" and we heard the sound of guns reloading.

My father spoke up then. Mother repeated his words so many times later on, I can hear them to this day. "We are only peasants and know nothing of politics. Teach us which side we should follow."

It worked like magic. The soldier delivered a long speech, told us to keep hiding where we were, and the men scattered into the night when the sound of gunshots broke out nearby.

We hunkered down again inside the tunnel. There were a few other children aside from us, but strangely enough, none of us cried or whined. Mother told me later on that although the soldiers were dressed in South Korean uniforms, they were doubtless North Korean reconnaissance troops in disguise, as the man who had said he supported General Kim was found the next morning having breakfast at a nearby farmhouse. It was still early in the Korean War, and even the most excited of soldiers did not dare harm the peasantry.

We returned home a long time after the front lines moved south. On our way back, while approaching a bridge in Guro-dong, where you could see the railway cross the Siheung River and curve toward Suwon, I saw a man die for the first time—and at close proximity, no less. We were walking toward the bridge when someone grabbed my wrist. I looked up to see a man in padded cotton trousers. My mother had to help me get away from him.

"What a mess your clothes are!" she exclaimed, as she pretended to hoist up my trousers while the man moved safely past. Right ahead was a North Korean checkpoint where people coming from the direction of Incheon were being interrogated. The soldiers wore sand-colored uniforms with wide epaulets and bore rifles punched with holes along the barrel.

We were filing by in obedient lines when we heard a shout up ahead, and in a split second, someone was running down to the irrigation ditch. Everyone swiveled in surprise, and I saw it was the man who had grabbed my wrist. He jumped into the green rice paddy, and two soldiers standing side by side on the dike fired off several shots. The man fell into the rice paddy and did not get up. Later, my mother said he had been ordered to lower his trousers and that he had probably been wearing a Southern army uniform underneath.

We crossed the bridge and entered the factory zone where we saw the devastation left behind by the bombardment: exposed steel bars twisted like human hair, walls riddled with bullet holes, shattered windows, and a collapsed roof that still gave off a plume of smoke. By the side of the road was a damaged truck. A tank lay absurdly on its side, its long cannon bent. On the tank was a black lump of a human body, clothes burnt off and limbs barely recognizable. Behind this was another object that looked similar. Mother covered her mouth with a handkerchief and pushed me forward, saying: "Only look forward, just follow your sisters," but I kept looking back.

My feelings as we returned home that day overlap in my memory with how I felt when we returned home after our second retreat from Seoul. I'd kept a diary during the second retreat, and I followed my mother's suggestion to rewrite that day's entry into an essay titled "The day we returned home," which won me a commendation in a national elementary school writing contest. The shattered windows and the shards, the bedrooms with the footprints of people who had broken in and made a mess of our possessions, the torn wallpaper drooping from the ceiling, the floors soaked from the rain, the earwigs and millipedes that dared to crawl into the house now, the spiderwebs in every corner, even the silly graffiti I'd secretly drawn—everything looked abandoned and pitiful.

~

One rainy morning, I woke to find my father staring out at the street. He stood where we would later install a floor to expand our house, but at the time it was just dirt with a roof over it. The building had once been a bicycle shop; the earth was black and often yielded rusty nails and bits of metal. This was the space where my father, along with a cobbler he had hired, made shoes to sell to stores. Next to the piles of shoes and leather pieces and shoe trees was a row of windows where he would often stand and watch the rainwater flow over the street, or observe what was happening in the neighborhood.

A formation of soldiers was marching toward us. They each carried Soviet rifles as long as they were tall or submachine guns with perforated barrels. The officers wore long trousers and sand-colored leather boots and sported pistols at the hip. There were female soldiers with bobbed hair and a boy who was so short and young-looking that he reminded me of one of the older kids in my neighborhood. These North Korean soldiers marched past our house for a long time. A group of children and I ventured as far as the train station and saw even more soldiers and tanks from up close. The soldiers in the tanks invited us in one by one and showed us the interior of the tanks and gave us army biscuits.

The rice mill woman was named the new neighborhood captain. She was fat and had a perpetual, disarming smile. She sought out my mother, saying the neighborhood needed someone with an education to be her assistant. Mother reluctantly accepted the position but on condition that it was only for a month, and indeed she resigned a month later. She was pregnant at the time and getting closer to her due date. In fact, it was thanks to her obvious pregnancy that my father was safe from harassment the whole time we fled from Seoul.

The American air raids occurred more and more frequently, and Yeongdeungpo, an industrial zone, was hit especially hard. Whenever the bombing started, it was as if the explosions were going off right next to me. Father would make my sisters sit in a corner and throw a thick winter blanket over them, while Mother pushed me underneath her Singer sewing machine.

One time, after Seoul was retaken, a fire broke out at an ammunition depot nearby. My mother and sisters were ironing the old-fashioned way, using heated coals stuffed into the cover of an old blanket, when we heard a thud, and a lump of metal crashed through the roof and landed in the middle of the spread fabric. It was long like a sweet potato and had sharp sides like a knife. My parents said it was probably shrapnel from a bomb.

Father was a survivor. His wisdom helped us survive in the midst of strife. Even during the war, we almost never went without a meal or came too close to death. But perhaps the effort to keep his wife and children alive through the long years after leaving Manchuria was too much in the end. Because just a few years into the armistice, he would suddenly sicken and die.

There was great pressure on the people of our neighborhood for volunteer labor. Many things needed to be done, such as restoring bombed roads and railroads and putting out fires that still burned from the previous night's bombing. Mother took me to one of these initiatives in Yoeuido once. She said Father was in the country trying to get us food and so she'd stepped up on her own to help. We saw many people from our neighborhood, including the fat captain woman. She told my visibly pregnant mother and me to go sit in the shade of the trees with the food vendors, who peddled corn, sweet potatoes, and bran cakes. One old woman had brought a load of melons, and the sweet smell of this fruit was enough to drive both of us crazy. I begged my mother to buy us one, but she would only open her eyes wide and make a scary face at me. Subsequently she would reproach me for this incident. "How foolishly insensitive you were, to think of eating melons in the cool shade while everyone else sweated in the sun carrying rocks and soil!"

After some discussion, my mother and father decided to move us to "Gwengmei" for a while. This was what is now called Gwangmyeong, but Seoul slang at the time tended to soften the "uh" and "ah" sounds. Still later we moved into temporary lodgings in "Naggul," on the road to Mount Gwanak. This turned out to be Nangok, near Sillim-dong.

Our new place was like somewhere a student would play hooky, like a watermill or the market clearing on the way to school. We stayed in our Yeongdeungpo house for a bit, letting people see that we were there, and then after an appropriate amount of time we moved to the little house in Gwengmei. Once there we acted like refugees from the city for about ten days, returning to the Yeongdeungpo house before they got too used to us being there. This enabled us to keep to ourselves in both places. It was probably part of Father's survival plan.

I'm not sure which part of Gwengmei we were in. It was an utter backwater. A clear stream flowed through it, and the cluster of houses was surrounded by rice paddies. In one of those houses, we rented a room that hadn't been used in a long time. We stayed in the cowshed until Father and the landlord were done putting down new flagstones and redoing the floor with a mixture of dirt and straw. The cows had disappeared during the chaos of war. We swept it clean with a large broom and put down a mat on the floor, but the stench of cow dung was incredible. After a few nights' sleeping there, though, it smelled downright savory. We nailed a mosquito net to the wall and pillars and slept side by side.

There wasn't much to do for food in the city, other than my parents taking turns to go out and trade their belongings. The shoes we had sold in our store must have been useful for bartering, and the sewing machine, bicycle, clothes, and jewels would have been the last to be traded away. When the wave of refugees reached far down south, my father ended up converting all of our gold into cash and rented a truck so he could sell things to them.

I played in the stream nearby with the village children, catching little fish and frogs. I learned how to rip the legs off frogs and cook them using a branch as a skewer. In the summer the village children ran around naked except for cotton pants held up with elastic bands. Of course, my mother was not one to tolerate this. She never allowed me to leave the house without a shirt on.

There was a girl next door who caught my eye. She seemed to have come from the city; I've forgotten her name. Her parents had left her and her younger brother with her grandmother. The house had a melon field, and as summer deepened, the grandmother spread a mat in front of her house and sold melons and steamed corn.

My mother took me and my sisters to buy some melons one evening. That's when I met the little girl, sitting next to her grandmother. She wore a dress, like my sisters, instead of black linen bloomers and little rubber shoes. The grandmother told stories about her life spent following her late miner husband in the mountains of Hamgyeong and Pyeongan Province, and my mother talked about Manchuria. They became close, and we children would play together into the night on a mat near the mosquito fire in the grandmother's backyard. Amid the scent of burning mugwort, the night sky with its flood of stars seemed to land very gently on my head. We lay on our backs and looked for the Big Dipper and the trails of comets.

My friend once called me over when I was playing hide-and-seek with the other children. She took out what she was hiding in the folds of her skirt. It was a large piece of scorched rice from the bottom of the rice pot. Not the hard kind, but the toasted kind with some unburnt rice still stuck to one side, round from the curve of the pot. The exact kind of treat that every child likes, the kind where you bite down into both soft rice and crisp crust. As I ate it, my heart beat fast and I felt a bit shy. I had a naughty feeling of doing something illicit.

There were red dragonflies in the air, so it must have been the end of August. We'd been going back and forth between Yeongdeungpo and Gwengmei when my mother sat down in the middle of the road one day and murmured, "If only I had some cold noodles . . ." But my father could not do anything for his pregnant wife.

One day, we came to Gwengmei to find the mood had changed. Young men wearing armbands were walking about, and the girl I knew now kept herself at home with her brother. We spent a few days in Gwengmei and returned home, never to go there again.

The fighting worsened a little after our return to Yeongdeungpo. Every day, bombers and fighter planes swooped in like wasps to bombard downtown Seoul across the river. Father heard from somewhere that the Americans had landed at Incheon. All night we heard the sound of nearby cannon and the whistling of bombs flying overhead. The next day, Father took us out on the road again. We had reached the rotary when we saw a camou-flaged North Korean army truck on fire, and a completely black fighter plane called a Grumman flying low in the sky. Father bowed low by instinct and kept pushing me on in front of him. A North Korean soldier stood underneath the tree in front of the photography studio, firing at the fighter plane.

Our family reached the new road going to Suwon. Near Seoul Usin Elementary School, on a railway bridge, was a North Korean fort, a wall of sandbags guarded by a machine gun. I heard my father urgently say to my mother, "We have to get out of here, this is an ammunition depot. The planes will be attack-ing it soon."

We rushed across the street, and sure enough, as we climbed a hill, we saw the planes bomb the fort. We were used to the sound of machine guns from the fighter planes, and the rockets might as well have been farting noises to us. A ball of fire drew an arc in the air and exploded with a flash of light. My sisters, used to it now, didn't bother to block their ears, only cringing at the explosion.

The "Naggul" house was very shabby, a thatched-roof hut surrounded by a bush clover fence. There was a low hill behind it. A young farming couple lived there with their newborn, and the wife's face was dark from the sun. There was a child about my age living next door. It was chestnut season, and I did what the child did and got a long stick to knock chestnuts off their branches. We peeled the still unripe husks with our shoes, revealing the little chestnuts with their white fuzz inside. Scraping off the bitter skin with our teeth, we finally reached the flesh inside, tasting of raw sweet potato. As we knocked the chestnuts off the branches, we stopped for long moments to stare at the planes flying overhead on their way to bomb the city.

The North Korean army had split up, and their troops came through Naggul to cross the hill behind the village. They sometimes entered the village to ask for a drink of water before going on their way. Their uniforms were ragged and soaked in sweat. Some of the recruits were very young, and the sight of teenage girl soldiers made my mother discreetly wipe away tears. Once a girl and boy soldier, who looked to be about high school age, asked for water. Mother gave them the sweet potatoes she had been steaming in the rice pot instead. They scarfed them down in a hurry. Mother patted the girl's back, telling her to take the time to chew, and in a South Jeolla accent they told her without prompting that they were brother and sister. Whenever my mother reminisced about this moment, she would add, "How their mother must have worried about them!"

Mother's fearless generosity would get my father into trouble. This was still early on, and some North Korean troops that had been marching by happened to come to our house. Their commanding officer singled out our family and a few other households across the street and offered us provisions in exchange for cooking for them. An entire division's worth of soldiers seemed to have been allotted to us alone. They never dared enter the house itself, and instead sat talking and smoking in the shade of the tree of heaven out front, or on the edge of our store when the tall doors were open. An older soldier who was probably a petty officer always seemed happy to see me and reached into the pouch on his shoulder to give me a handful of stir-fried beans. He even rubbed them between his hands and blew on them to unpeel them. Perhaps I reminded him of his own son, for he wouldn't leave my side and kept annoying me with questions like how old was I, what was my name, what grade was I in, did I know the words to "The song of the general" or "The morning shall shine."

With the help of two neighborhood women, my mother placed rocks in the yard to make a firepit and set the iron rice pot over it to make rice for all the soldiers. All we had for side dishes were soybean paste stew made with greens and some kimchi we'd obtained from our neighbors, but they ate their fill. Breaking the silence of the meal, a young soldier asked my mother where she was from. My mother, somewhat tense, asked him why he wanted to know.

"Well, ma'am," he said in a Northern drawl, "you sound like you might be from Pyongan Province, is that right?"

Mother reluctantly admitted she was from the city of Pyongyang.

"Then why do you live here?"

Not missing a beat, she replied, "I see that your own mother never married?"

The soldiers roared with laughter.

~

We returned to Yeongdeungpo after the front lines had swept over Seoul, and the Americans that had landed in Incheon had crossed the Han River at many points. There were still buildings on fire and many fallen telegraph poles, their lines stretched to the ground. For days American trucks and tanks and amphibian vehicles passed our house.

Mother learned that the rice mill woman and neighborhood captain had been arrested by the security forces, and that the carpenter had killed several people before he fled to the North.

The carpenter's shop was across the street from us. It was always noisy with the sound of electric saws and trucks arriving with wood. There was a child my age there, who was very clever, and spoke with a Gyeongsang accent. When we needed sticks to play soldiers with, he would let us pick whatever we wanted. We made wooden swords and spears out of them. His father and an uncle had been stationed at a naval shipyard and were now community leaders, so we called him "the leader's son."

Their house was abandoned after the retaking of Seoul. According to my mother, the carpenter had gone around executing people when the North Korean retreat seemed imminent. Mother had once gone to Yeongdeungpo Market and glimpsed him from afar as he loitered around the linen shops. His expression was so fearsome that she had almost fainted next to the fried foods stall. "People did all sorts of terrible things whenever either side invaded or retreated," she would say. "It takes two hands to clap and make a sound."

When the police returned to Seoul, many people in our neighborhood and factories were arrested. My father was briefly taken into the police station across the street for questioning when they learned we had once fed a group of North Korean soldiers. My pregnant mother paced for half an hour before going in there herself and arguing with the police, who subsequently released my father after taking a statement. Mother told them that our family had deliberately left Pyongyang and crossed the 38th parallel because we hated the North so much. She said the North Korean soldiers had offered us rice in exchange for cooking it, that she had to accept if she was to feed her children in the middle of a war, and what person in their right mind could say no to men with guns?

According to many postwar memoirs and autobiographies, Seoul had divided into those who crossed the Han River and fled and those who had to stay behind. But the ones who fled, and bombed the Han River Bridge behind them, came back after the retaking of Seoul and accused those who had been stranded of being traitors. It was a time that drove home the fact that, to live in the divided South, one had to be able to express one's reasons for choosing a side and to be able to loudly condemn the other.

The chaos continued, but our neighborhood went on as usual, and as before the war, the children called each other out to play. There were piles of abandoned ammunition and shell casings lying about in bombed-out buildings and empty lots. The children would open the bullet casing, take out the bullets, and gather the gunpowder inside the casing. The 50 mm machine-gun bullets were the most popular; they were about as thick as a small turnip. Putting in a wick and some petrol and placing a can over it made for a very handy lamp. The machine-gun bullet casings were filled with gunpowder that was like the lead inside thick pencils. The children cut pipes and fastened wooden handles to make guns.

There were many accidents. One intrepid child tried to take apart a trench mortar by knocking it with a rock and went flying, along with all the children around him. I also experimented by punching a hole in the bottom of a tin pail, putting some gunpowder into it, and lighting the bottom—I almost fainted when the pail exploded into the air with a loud bang. For a while I thought my eardrums had burst. Playing at war was very different from when we played capture the flag on a pile of sand. Finally, the adults took action, and the police went around and confiscated all the explosives.

The schools were not open yet, and the South Korean army and allies had reached the Amlok River on the northern border of North Korea, but as the weather turned cold, we heard some depressing news. The Chinese had entered the battle on the North Korean side, and the Allies—South Korean, American, and United Nations forces—were in retreat.

One cold day in December of 1950, our family were once again refugees on the road south. My father had gone to the train station for the past few days to look into transportation. My mother made me wear a thick coat, balaclava, and large women's shoes that came up to my ankles. My feet couldn't feel a thing through the three pairs of socks I wore. Mother and Father both wore simple clothing and carried suitcases. The quilts and other household items were moved for us by a man with a wheelbarrow. The sun hadn't risen yet. Everything around the market rotary was still dark. Footprints in the ice made the roads bumpy. Shards of frozen mud splintered beneath the hard soles of my shoes.

As early as it was, Father was rushing our departure because of what we'd experienced last time. He figured it would be better to get a head start on going somewhere safer and finding a living. We had spent days preparing, as we dug a hole in the corner of our courtyard and buried our more precious belongings, but I had no idea what was going on. The passenger trains at the time had either been destroyed or were being used to transport troops, with refugees and supplies now being moved on freight trains.

Fewer trains were running as the Chinese forces pushed the Northern front lines toward the 38th parallel. What Father had managed to negotiate was for us to join a military family on their train. Since the trains were filled with supplies, refugees had to sit on the roofs of the carriages. But occasionally there were open freight cars in between the other carriages, with sometimes two linked end to end to carry artillery or tanks. To ride inside an open-air freight car was a special privilege at that point. It was safer than riding on the high, narrow roof of the carriages, and there was plenty of space for a family to lie down.

There weren't many refugees when we arrived at the station, and the railway itself was fairly empty. Someone in charge of seating designated a spot on the train for us, and we put down thick quilts and canvas to sit on. The day began to break once the people who had seating had finished boarding, and evacuees began crowding in. They crawled up to the roof of the carriages and perched there like birds on a wire, bundled together in layers of blankets. This was during the second taking of Seoul by the Northern forces, the so-called January 4 Retreat, in other words; but fleeing had already begun in the middle of December.

It was a train that normally delivered munitions instead of people, so it was slower than what we were used to, and it would pause for half a day whenever it came to a stop. By the time we saw the sign for Osan, we were having cold *kimbap* for dinner. All we had to eat were *kimbap* and rice balls. It must have taken over a day to get through Gyeonggi Province and reach Cheonan.

The train sometimes left late at night. Whenever that happened, the people on the carriage roofs would shout the names of their family members who had gotten off. Some ran after the train as fast as they could, only to be left behind. They might eventually be reunited after a long struggle or be parted for a long time. It took ten days to go from Seoul to Busan. Among those who grew exhausted from the journey, sleeping on the roofs of the carriages, some fell to their deaths.

A friend of mine was one who missed his train. At the time, people in Seoul were going to Yongsan Station to catch the trains going south or paying for seats in military transport. My friend had lost his family in the station among the crowds of refugees when he went to relieve himself, jumping over a few tracks to squat next to a fence; by the time he came back, the train had left. This child who was no older than me cried as he went around the empty tracks and had no choice but to return to the house his family had abandoned.

My friend's chronically ill grandmother was at home, lying in the master bedroom. She had insisted on staying behind, preferring to die at home than on the road. It enraged him that his family would leave both him and his grandmother, and he never forgave them for the rest of his life.

Seoul was almost empty. Winter that year of 1950–51 was especially cold. The country was split into North and South, and the children who had been left behind by their parents joined forces with each other. My friend's mission was to keep the fire that heated the floor burning for himself and his grandmother. He went around the empty houses, gathering what kindling he could, and struggling to obtain the least morsel of food.

The children like him who were left behind fell into an age hierarchy like they had when playing soldiers. They divided into groups and went foraging in the empty houses for scraps. The cities in both North and South were mostly piles of ash by then. The grandmother did not survive that winter. He called together the children when she died, and they dug up the frozen earth of the yard and buried her wrapped in a blanket, like they would a jar of preserves.

It was a cruel time for adults, but on the outside at least, the children did not seem to have felt too frightened or sad. If anything, the gangs of youngsters in the middle of a war zone seemed almost happy with their laughter and games. As long as they had something to do and didn't starve, there were many things more fun than going to school. All you needed was a good cry in those brief moments of hunger or sickness or sadness, and that was that. Once you wiped your tears and got up again, the mere fact of survival was enough to electrify you. But was it really that easy? Just as frostbite returns without one noticing, I've seen how such children later grow up floundering in pain, unable to handle the scars of war. My friend was like that. He has passed away, but to the end of his life he was distant from his family and unable to adjust well to society.

The brief winter sun had set by the time we finally pulled into Daegu Station. We didn't go all the way to Busan, because of my mother's reasoning: she was sure that the southernmost port city would soon overflow with refugees from all over the peninsula. Finding a place to sleep would be difficult and the struggle to survive would be brutal. And people were saying that the Northern forces would surely not make it over the Chupung-nyeong mountain pass easily—not this time, anyway.

At the station we moved away from the flow of the crowds and sat with our luggage against the window of the cargo handling offices, waiting for Father. He had left us at the station to find a room. An endless river of soldiers and refugees passed before us.

Father came back with news late in the night. The main street that started at Daegu Station was lined with Japanese-style houses and modern buildings, but each alleyway contained many thatched cottages. We found a room in an old house in Deoksan-dong, near the Central Market and past the Red Cross Hospital. There was a well in the middle of the cramped courtyard and an empty pigpen in the corner. A widow lived there with a son and daughter who went to middle school; her older daughter had married but lived nearby and visited often. She was constantly getting into screaming fights with her brother, and the mother would have to intervene. We started off renting the big room in the house, and once my younger brother was born, we rented one more room in the annex next to the gate.

Father disappeared without a word a few days after we'd settled in. I learned later that he had taken a train back to Seoul. He seemed to have forgotten something at home. My older sister reckoned it was to gather some means to open a business in Daegu, as we had no idea how long the war would keep us there.

I slept by my mother's side while my father was gone. I would wake in the night to the sound of her mumbling prayers. Father returned home safely, but he'd had to change trains three or four times and walk quite a bit of the way, risking his life several times. He sold goods off a truck he drove between Daegu, Busan, and Masan, spending the other half of the month in

South Jeolla Province. Sometimes he made a profit, sometimes he didn't, but he managed to keep our heads above water.

Mother thankfully gave birth when Father was home. It was Daeboreum, the first full moon of the lunar year, so he had probably rushed back to be with the family. The new baby was already sleeping in my mother's arms when I woke in the morning. Nowadays people act as if both mother and child would surely die if the baby wasn't delivered in a hospital, but back then it was common for babies to be born at home and for husbands to pitch in during childbirth. Not to mention we were lucky that we could welcome the baby into a warm room despite being at war.

Even in wartime, Mother managed to find a big bookstore in the marketplace where she bought me books. I read things like *Pauvre Blaise*, Bang Jeong-hwan's "Stories for boys and girls," *The Adventures of Tom Sawyer*, *The Count of Monte Cristo*, the works of Plutarch and Hans Christian Andersen, and so many others in the midst of all that turbulence.

On the streets of Daegu everyone was being rounded up, including refugees and students, for interrogation and conscription, but despite the war they opened the schools in the spring and admitted refugee children as well. I enrolled at Jungang Elementary School near our home, but the building had already been appropriated for use by American forces and classes were held in a makeshift schoolhouse instead—namely, a Japanese-style house whose inside walls had been knocked down to turn the small rooms into one big classroom. There were, of course, no desks or chairs. I only got to sit at a desk after the war, mere months before I graduated from sixth grade.

Each student had to bring a mini chalkboard, a bag for their shoes, and a cushion. We went to class with our chalkboards slung on our shoulders by the strings we'd tied on them and rested them on our knees as we wrote our letters. The best place to sit was on the patch of wooden flooring; everywhere else was either cement or bare dirt. In the rainy season, our cushions would turn damp from the water seeping up through the ground or cement, and the roof leaked.

We ran into my old teacher from Yeongdeungpo at the school's entrance ceremony. She burst into tears as she greeted me, and my mother clasped her hands as they sobbed together. Just the fact that we had made it alive through so much chaos was reason enough for gratitude.

I was bored with what they taught at school, having already conquered books at the middle school level. My mother always said to me, "No one can match our family in learning and teaching. That will serve you well later."

Boys and girls had to sit on opposite sides of the classroom from each other, but at least I finally got to meet girls my age to whom I wasn't related. It was fun to be able to call out their names and talk to them. The front lines ran red with blood, but we carried our chalkboards to the orchard hill and drew trees and flowers with our crayons. Meanwhile my father wasn't home for half the month, running around in other parts of the country, trying to make ends meet.

Every time I walked down the main street that started from Daegu Station, my heart pounded and I squirmed with longing. That was because of all the huge, painted movie billboards hanging in front of Munhwa Cinema. My memories of going to see operettas and movies in Yeongdeungpo with my mother only added to my excitement. In Daegu they were advertising a Tarzan movie and *The Adventures of Tom Sawyer*. Of course, I knew better than to pester my parents for movie tickets, since most children at the time couldn't even afford to go to school and had to shine shoes or sell loose cigarettes. But every time I passed the theater, my throat ached from the effort of keeping quiet.

One day, on that very street, my father and I ran into my oldest uncle on my mother's side, who had fled from the North alone. There were many vendors as well as shops on that street, stands where they displayed lighters and timepieces in glass boxes and refilled lighter fluid or fixed watches, not to mention stores selling military gloves, sweaters, army jackets, red bean pastries, fried rice cakes, and sweet potatoes, all of which I was gazing at greedily as we walked, when suddenly my father came to a halt. The tall man about to pass us also stopped in his tracks. The two men stood there for a moment, before loudly whooping in unison and embracing each other.

"My brother, when did you come down?"

"The January Fourth Retreat . . . And Gyeongdo, where are you now?"

"We have a house here, in Daegu!"

They spoke rapidly to each other. People stopped in the street and formed a circle around them, smiling broadly as if it were something happening to themselves as they watched and listened to the conversation. My uncle was very stylish. He was tall like my mother and had long, wavy hair, slicked back, with the occasional unruly strand that he would smooth away. He wore a long black coat with wide lapels and underneath it an olive-green sweater from the American army. My uncle immediately hurried with us to our wartime refuge in Deoksan-dong, and I heard, for the first time, my mother crying out over and over again, "Brother, oh my brother!"

Uncle was a doctor who had studied in Japan and had been a medical school professor in the North. He was well read, could answer any question, and was a gifted storyteller who could utterly beguile us with a tale. This was how our aunt and uncle became our only relatives from the North who made it to the South, and my mother got to have her older brother and next younger sister live close by. My aunt had divorced after she lost her only child, the little girl In-ok, and never remarried. It turned out that her husband had had a son with another woman.

My uncle withered away as he fought for survival in the 1950s. A fake doctor hired him for his medical license and then falsely accused him of treason over a few words spoken at a drinking session with old school friends, which led to torture under what was aptly nicknamed the "Makgeolli Anti-communism Law." Then he was accused of something else, and sent to prison, after which he lost all zest for life and turned to alcohol. He remarried twice and in his later years had only his daughter to take care of him. My aunt and uncle were of the first generation of Korea's divided families. They both passed away as the world entered the 1980s.

I wrote a novella, *Hanssi yeondaegi* (Mr. Han's Chronicle), based on my mother's memories of the dark despair and relentlessly dispassionate survival of that time. It was my uncle who provided many of the stories in it—the stories he'd told me as a child.

Seoul had been retaken, but by then many of the refugees who had managed to settle in southern areas were reluctant to uproot themselves again. My own family left Daegu to return to the capital. But the blood sausage stew in hot earthenware bowls, the taste of black-market chocolate and the colorful gumdrops, the milk porridge my sisters and I stood in line for at the Red Cross Hospital, my classmates and the temporary schoolroom to which I carried my cushion every day—how could I forget any of it?

My aunt, who'd gone alone to Busan, joined us on our journey back to Seoul. Father rented a truck that would take us up to Daejeon. He said we could hitch a ride with a military truck from there to Suwon. I don't remember how long it took for us to get back to Seoul. I only remember how there were places to eat that appeared along the way, where we ate wedged in among a crowd of other people. Whenever a military convoy loomed, we had to move off the road to let them pass. As the dust of the paved roads settled, we would hum along with the military songs that faded into the distance. *Walk over the bodies of our fallen friends, to the front, to the front, goodbye Nakdong River, we're going to the front . . .*

We weren't allowed on military transport without a permit past Suwon, so it was decided that Father would drive our luggage home to Yeongdeungpo and the rest of us would walk. It can't have taken more than a day, but it feels to me like it took longer. My mother and aunt sang hymns, and my sisters sang along. After I heard them a few times, I was able to sing along, too.

We had come to a tunnel underneath a railway track when an American soldier in his undershirt, riding the train above, tossed something toward me. I picked it up; it was a can of food. I looked back up to see the soldier waving as he disappeared into the distance.

~

School was held in Yeongdeungpo's abandoned factories or houses that had been gutted of all but their roofs and walls. Most of the floors we sat on were of course dirt with a mat thrown over. We were vaccinated several times a year, and the American military's civil volunteer services sent trucks to spray DDT. A rubber tube was put into our sleeves or down the backs of our clothes, and a white powder was sprinkled on our skin. We giggled because it tickled. A long time later we learned that this was a very toxic chemical, but the children seemed to have survived all right, on the outside at least. On the other hand, I was oddly sensitive to vaccines, and I'd lie in bed for a few days after each one. Back then we got shots for typhoid, smallpox, and tuberculosis, and I was particularly weak against the typhoid shot. I got chills all over, and at night the fever made me feel like my body was growing as long as a telegraph pole, then shrinking to the size of a bean, then falling off a high cliff before bouncing on the ground below.

Walking to school, I'd sometimes see hanging from the doors of hastily built shacks a rope with bits of red paper twisted into it. This meant a patient was quarantined inside. Outbreaks tended to hit certain parts of the country first and peak there before spreading to the rest. I assume that our neighborhood had had a typhus outbreak—though the term adults used back then could refer generally to any infectious disease. Later, cases of encephalitis began to go around as well.

Thinking back on it now, it's surprising how, despite the disarray of the times, we had more or less continuous running water and electricity. Of course, the electricity went down for a few days in the fall when war swept over the country, but there still was running water. Once the front lines moved on, electricity miraculously returned, although the lights automatically blacked out at ten to conserve power. All the family, except for my father, sat under our single light bulb for a certain nightly task: taking off our long underwear and spreading them over newspapers to catch lice. We'd find their nits lain along the seams. Mother used a special comb to get the nits out of my sisters' hair. This was a common scene right after the war. I don't know if there's a connection, but once coal briquettes became the most popular source of heat, we no longer had to deal with lice. Perhaps it had more to do with the general improvement in our standards of living.

The people who had fled were coming home. The ones from the North tended to settle in Seoul rather than the countryside. There were also many from the countryside who, having survived the conflict of left against right, were looking for new ways of life in the city.

The market began to revive. So many vendors appeared that a little guy like me could barely push his way through the crowds. They brought with them foods we'd never heard of. Whenever my sisters and I bugged our mother for snacks, she would give us a big sack of grain and send us off to the market to see the puffed rice man. He popped corn, rice, and barley for us. The grain popper he used was round like a bomb and had a pressure gauge with a face like a watch. He'd place the popper on top of a brazier and rotate it until the pressure had built up nice and high. Then he would assume a safe position and use an iron rod to open the mouth of the popper and release all the pressure at once. When we saw him take that position, we would plug our ears and take a step back, and all the people passing by would plug their ears, too. Bang! With that sound, steam billowed out, and the popped grains spilled into a finely woven metal net. We carried sacks of the stuff home over our shoulders, proud as farmers returning from harvest.

And so many medicine sellers! Beneath the weeping willow near the rotary or in the station plaza, these peddlers with their monkeys or little girls or trained dogs would be surrounded by onlookers watching their antics. One played "Yangsando" and "The old walls of hwangseong" on violin, another did magic tricks, another played "Nights in Shilla" on accordion, and another beat a large drum on his back by pulling a string tied to his foot as he played the harmonica. Their gimmicks were one thing, but their storytelling was quite another and pedestrians would forget where they were headed and join in the laughter.

"And who am I, you ask? My surname is The, my given name is Real Thing, I am The Real Thing! Of the Tokyo Imperial University pharmacology department, which I didn't get into but I did brush past its back gate once. And does The Real Thing come to this alley every day? Look for me tomorrow, and I'll be gone! But maybe I'll be in the next alley over. And what have we here, ladies and gentlemen? This is from a tiger shark."

It was perhaps thanks to my fascination with these "snake-oil salesmen" that I later became known as quite the comedian among my friends.

The war left many people mentally shattered. I wrote about them in *Moraenmal aideul* (The Children of Moraenmal), but one memory that has never left me is of the singing homeless couple dubbed the Gombaes. The man's hand curved in toward his wrist, so we called him a *gombaepal* (bear claw), which was shortened to Gombae. For about two years, alone, he came to our neighborhood every morning and begged for food as he sang and danced. He never begged in front of the same house or neighborhood twice in a row and instead skipped a house every time, following some kind of order. Naturally, when they heard him singing, people thought: "That Gombae has come to our house, it must be our turn," and they would come out with food for him, as if paying their taxes.

His real job was snake-catching, for which purpose he carried around a military-issue lunch tin and a stick with a hook. One day he showed up with a female partner, and instead of coming to each house and begging, he claimed a space for them both on the sidewalk by the vegetable market and collected money as the fat woman sang. In contrast to her size, her voice was so delicate that people said she sang "The Tears of Mokpo" better than the original performer. She was said to be a Hamgyeong Province refugee who had lost her entire family in a bombing and had met Gombae on the road. I saw her once standing in a corner of the market in her wide military jacket dyed black and her tattered, loose trousers, her hands gathered gently before her as she sang. The song was "Be strong, Geumsoon." Gombae provided percussion by drumming his chopsticks against his metal lunchbox.

Gombae built a dugout against a dike. I was familiar with dugouts because I'd made them with other children; we called them our headquarters. They were easy to build and easy to conceal. You dug out a ditch, crisscrossed some branches over it, and covered it with straw. Inside you put down some sand and straw sacking for a carpet. You had to bend low to crawl in, but once you were inside, it was cozy and warm even on the coldest days of winter.

Gombae's partner became pregnant, but she died before the baby was born. The neighborhood children had set a nearby reed field on fire while playing *jwibulnori*, imitating the farmers who would scorch their fields by lighting a fire inside a container and spinning it around on a cord. The blaze spread and torched their dugout. All through that night the village nearby heard Gombae's tearful cries. "You bastards! Are we not human, too? Are we not human?"

Alone again, the devastated Gombae lingered for a time around the burned dugout. Then one day he built a wooden bridge over the stream near his old home and disappeared. The stepping-stones the villagers had put down tended to disappear under the water as soon as there was any rain, and people had to take their shoes off before crossing the river. Who was the first to call the new construction "Gombae Bridge'? The name persisted even when another wooden bridge was built for military use, until finally some American army engineers replaced it with a strong, concrete structure.

The only large, modern buildings at the time were schools. Across the street from our neighborhood was an elementary school built after Liberation, but an American regiment had commandeered it. The same was true of the school buildings near Mullae-dong, which I attended.

The Chinese restaurant Twin Star Pagoda was a two-story brick building large enough to be used, later, as a wedding hall. The Americans turned the second floor into a dance hall, and the prostitutes who catered to them—called *yangsaekshi*, "western brides"—moved into houses across from us and in the back of our neighborhood. In essence, the area turned into a red-light district. The children bragged about what they'd seen. Someone said they'd witnessed an American soldier doing the deed with a *yangsaekshi*, naked on a sheet of tent canvas spread beside a military jeep in the school playground surrounded by a wire fence. Someone saw another pair kissing on a porch and doing it standing up; someone else would rush to a peephole whenever an American soldier entered a certain house, affording a good view of what would turn out to be as good as a movie. The adults were too busy trying to survive to worry about the children looking or not looking. No wonder we all grew up so fast.

Mother had two sewing machines in the spare room and made dresses for the *yangsaekshi*. She obtained parachute fabric from somewhere, which was perfect for party dresses. The fabric was high-tech, light and smooth, and never wrinkled. You could dye the white parachute fabric all sorts of fancy colors. Haeju Aunt and my younger aunt helped Mother with the sewing for a while.

The boogie-woogie and the swing were in fashion, with men and women dancing with their hands clasped as they spun and rocked their hips and legs. The second floor of the Twin Star Pagoda was a nightly racket of band music and lights. Mother used to say that our nanny Tae-geum became loose under that influence. Carrying my baby brother she would dance with him to the music that flowed out of the Twin Star Pagoda, jiggling him up and down, chanting "One-two-three, one-two-three" in time with the beat as my brother giggled.

I should have suspected it when I caught Tae-geum surreptitiously putting on my mother's face cream: she had fallen in love with a policeman who worked across the street and one day said goodbye to us, awash in tears. Only when my mother told me did I realize that whenever I saw her lean against the wooden fence by the trees of heaven and stare over, she had been looking toward the police station every time.

I can't forget to mention Pomade and the Advisor, two characters who appeared in our neighborhood after the war. I don't remember Pomade's original name. He always had his hair slicked back, stuck to his scalp, with long sideburns. He must have been nineteen or twenty at the time. He always had a comb and mirror on him, and kept combing his already combed-back hair.

He knew the lines to a lot of melodramas and was always reciting them, imitating the cadences of silent-film interpreters. One time, he gathered the neighborhood children to put on a play that he'd written himself. The location was a house with a water pump in one of the back alleys. All of the houses flanking the main street had glass fronts like stores but were built like traditional *hanok* in the back. The house with a pump also had a large backyard and porch. People sat in the courtyard, and the porch served as a stage. Pomade lived with an older sister who was a *yangsaekshi*, one of several occupying the shacks built on the edge of the courtyard.

The Advisor had a lisp that made everyone laugh, no matter what he was saying, even when he was angry. This made people disrespect him despite the medal he kept bragging about. He imitated a battalion commander shouting commands or giving a speech before going out to battle, but despite his solemn words, everyone just collapsed into laughter at his lisp. He'd received his commendation after being hit by shrapnel during combat and being honorably discharged. He once proudly explained the rank system when we were playing soldiers and taught us the correct way to salute.

Someone sneered, "So what if he was in the war? He was just an advisor, judging by the way he talks." An advisor was what bureaucratic American liaison officers stationed with Korean troops were called, and the term came to refer to stupid soldiers who failed to understand instructions and harmed more than they helped. The term was passed down to my generation and was still in use around the time my son was conscripted. Pomade was particularly quick to make fun of the Advisor's war stories. It was he, in the end, who made the nickname stick.

The Advisor lived with his older sister and her boyfriend, an American petty officer. The original people of our neighborhood tended to despise or ignore the incomers, and treated the *yangsaekshi* and their families especially badly, despite extorting high rent from them every month. The adults didn't bother using the polite form of address with the Advisor as they mocked him for being a parasite who lay around all day, to the point that his sister was forced to sell herself to make ends meet. The children had already agreed among themselves that he'd been a nothing in the military, too.

But an unexpected incident made us admit that he had some merit. Across from the Twin Star Pagoda were two neighborhoods divided by a big road; they sat on slightly higher ground than us. Haeju Aunt lived on that side, so I was pretty familiar with its ins and outs. They had a kindergarten, a church, and also a rice mill, which we had too, only ours was smaller. To those who grew up in the country, *rice mill* conjures up a pestle and mortar attached to a water wheel, but this one was all cogwheels and belts, more of a factory.

The street across from the Twin Star Pagoda also had a small barbershop and a cotton gin, and the yard of the rice mill was ruled by a courageous pair of geese. If we ever dared to go into the yard, the geese charged at us with their long necks darting like snakes, their honks sounding more like barks. They were indeed as scary as guard dogs, and no kid ventured in there twice. One day, my friend Guk-weon, whose family ran the dye shop, rushed into our house and said something was going on in the big rice mill. A child had gone up on the roof to fetch a stray ball and had been electrocuted by a loose wire.

There was already a crowd gathered when we reached the barbershop. A policeman blew his whistle and struggled to keep the gawkers at bay. There were people with loaded bicycles craning their necks, people sitting in a row on the wall opposite, and children squeezing in between the adults, trying to get a better view. Guk-weon and I decided to go up to the roof of the Twin Star Pagoda. We detoured around the crowd through the carpenter's and went up a pile of planks, climbed the fire escape, and reached the roof. But we were immediately disappointed by what we found.

"Why are you guyth doing up here?" lisped the Advisor. He had thought of the place first and was already occupying it. We said we wanted to see what was happening on the rice mill roof, and to our surprise, he allowed it. "But don't you dare call me 'advithor' again. Come, take a look."

Guk-weon and I ran over like little mice and crouched next to him. We could see directly down to the rice mill roof. There was a thick cable wound around a child who had fallen unconscious, with smoke coming off his burnt clothes. A rubber ball hung from a downspout. A few rice mill workers were trying to untangle the cable with a long stick but every time the split wires scraped something, there was a flash of blue light.

An old man managed to make it to the roof despite people's efforts to hold him back. His hands were wrapped in torn car tire tubes. He grabbed the cable and yanked, but it wouldn't release its victim. The child twitched with each shake of the cable. The old man gave the cable another strong pull, but it writhed like a living snake and wrapped itself around his left arm. The old man stumbled left and fell, and the cable coiled around his leg. He trembled as he worked to extricate his leg, and succeeded, but now it was bleeding. The old man pounded the slate roof with his fist and shouted, "Did anyone call the electric company? Two people are dying up here!" The policeman only looked at his watch, his expression tense.

The Advisor jumped to his feet. We stared up at him.

"You bathtards . . . you're juth going to watch? Inthtead of thaluting a thuperior offither when heeth going into battle?"

We sensed that he was not joking, so we stood up and saluted him.

In an instant, the Advisor reached the roof of the rice mill accompanied by the murmur of the crowd. He was completely barehanded. First, he went up to the old man and began pulling the cable off of him. His body shook violently, his muscles swelled, and his eyes bulged like those of a dead fish as he was wracked by the electric current. The places where the cable whipped him bled, and soon his entire body was bleeding. The Advisor finally succeeded in extricating the old man, who was carried down carefully from the roof by some onlookers.

Next, the Advisor began to free the boy. Blood and sweat poured down his face. Guk-weon and I could hardly bear to see the Advisor in such agony. He managed to get the cable off the child's back and legs, but as soon as he did, he toppled backwards. The cable snaked around the Advisor's body as he flapped around with the rubber tube in his hand. The child was pulled down from the roof, and the crowd cheered. But the Advisor was still wrapped in the cable like Tarzan caught by a carnivorous plant, his body writhing. He rolled, and his legs slipped over the edge of the roof. The crowd roared in unified concern. He was still hanging there when an old truck chugged down the street. The policeman seemed to have come to his senses as he ordered everyone to make way. The truck had been sent by the electric company. They climbed the telegraph pole where the cable was coming from, but then the Advisor's legs flailed again and he fell all the way down to the ground, the cable breaking his fall. He rolled off of it, all the way to the front of the barbershop.

Guk-weon swallowed and murmured, "He's dead!"

As the people gathered to carry him away, he suddenly shook them all off and jumped to his feet. He then raised both of his bloody arms and waved to show everyone he was fine.

I remembered that incident with awe for a long time. It was only later I realized that people who don't have anything don't have any choice, either, except to survive using desperate means. In any case, heroes like him would appear in difficult times, only to fade away as the years passed.

Once the war reached a stalemate and armistice was declared, the American forces moved north of Seoul along with the people who followed them like migrating birds, and peace returned to the neighborhood. The adults were relieved and regretful at the same time. We had quiet now, but it was also the end of our war economy.

The bustle of the Yeongdeungpo Market made us forget that we'd been at war for the past few years. At first, a few used book vendors appeared with their wheeled carts only at night, but then someone got the idea to set up shelves and lend out books for a fee. You paid a deposit, which was about the cost of a new book, and a small fee was deducted each time you borrowed a book. These vendors also bought old books; they probably became bookstore owners later on. The books were mostly from private collections that were broken up for sale after the war. They were likely once owned by people who disappeared or died in the conflict, volumes pawned by family members who needed to eat. There were all sorts of genres, from classics collections published during the Japanese occupation to ideological tracts and mainstream novels. There were even socialist or North Korean books, the kind that later South Korean military dictatorships would have more time and resources to persecute readers for owning. In fact, this proliferation of books published during the post–World War II era into Liberation space was still selling in dusty bookstores in the Insa-dong and Cheonggyecheon neighborhoods of Seoul, as late as the 1970s.

My eldest sister loved books as much as I did, and we fought over them regardless of their age-appropriateness. We read Dostoevsky's *Crime and Punishment* and Tolstoy's *Resurrection*, not to mention mainstream novels for adults.

I used to read lying on my stomach in the living room, but I grew so annoyed by my family's interruptions that I got an army flashlight, climbed up to the cramped attic, and read in there. Thanks to my mother's influence, as an elementary school student I was reading the kind of classics people usually didn't encounter until their teens.

~

In the summer of 1953, after three years, millions of casualties, and 10 million people separated from their families, the war reached an uncertain armistice. A fourth grader at the time, I continued to take my classes in an abandoned factory with a leaky roof. The surrounding grounds, however, had beautiful fields and streams where, except for the winters, the children could freely enjoy themselves in nature's classroom. We had what the children from the countryside called *kongseori*, where we snapped off beans and barley from the vines as they ripened and cooked them over a fire in a dry irrigation ditch. We tied up grasshoppers in foxtails to roast or cooked them in empty soda bottles, and roasted frog legs as a snack. We learned to catch fish using a bowl covered in cloth with soybean paste as bait, and caught sparrows by disturbing their roosts under eaves.

I met my friend Yeong-shik when we were in Daegu; we began going to elementary school together when his family came to Seoul and moved into a Japanese-style house next to the police station across the street. He was the youngest, with three older sisters. The whole family was a very devout Protestant household that went to dawn prayers every day.

Yeong-shik's mother spoke with a Hwanghae accent in a high, thin voice. His father was a detective. At the time, we used the Japanese term "surveillance" to describe his division, but now he'd be called an "intelligence" officer. He had wide, deep-set eyes that made him look like a Westerner.

One time at his house, Yeong-shik showed off a bunch of things that he'd taken out from their built-in cabinets. Along with some photographs, there was a katana sword with its handle wrapped in gauze. I remember being awed by the shining silvery blade of the katana when it was unsheathed, coveting it for myself. He said it had beheaded many people. His father had been a policeman in Hwanghae Province during the occupation and had killed countless rebels during the Jeju Island "anti-operatives" campaign. The photos showed Mount Halla in Jeju, some military officers posing with guns and scores of prisoners in *hanbok* tied up in front of them. I still remember the haggard face of a young female captive in the front row with a baby on her back.

Yeong-shik and I accompanied each other to school and went fishing in the streams together. He was a frail child, perhaps from being the youngest, but he would end up taller and stronger than me. We once played at an empty lot that had a stack of railway supports that I lightly jumped over, but when he followed me, his foot caught and he fell, breaking a few ribs. He always tried to keep up with me despite his fragility. Later, I taught him how to swim. After school we used to play in the water under the railway bridge that crossed Siheung River, beside which our temporary school building was located.

Much later on, when my family had long left the neighborhood, I ran into Yeong-shik as a college student and spent the night at his house. This was because Yeong-shik made an earnest request: he said his house was haunted. His second brother-in-law had been the first to spot the ghost.

The second floor of Yeong-shik's house had been assigned to the surveillance division of the police station. On the first was a spare room above the basement, a big room with a built-in closet by a hallway, and a large living room at the front. The second brother-in-law had been sleeping in the spare room when he woke to the feeling that someone was standing over him. When he half-opened his eyes, he saw a woman with an emotionless expression looking down at him. He was too surprised to do anything but stare back. She slowly opened the room door and left. The brother-in-law followed her into the hallway, shouting, but there was no one there.

Yeong-shik's mother was the next to see the ghost. The living room was wide enough to have been covered in tatami mats, but it was not heated, so they curtained off a section of it to use as a storage space. One day his mother noticed that the curtain wasn't fully drawn, so she went to check behind it and saw a woman standing there. His family saw this woman several times.

By the time I spent the night at his place, the surveillance division had moved out and the second floor was empty. Yeong-shik's family was also about to move out. He was using that wide second floor all by himself.

When we were little (around the time of the second recapturing of Seoul), Yeong-shik used to brag about watching the surveillance detectives interrogate prisoners. They would tie their hands and feet, hang them on a pole, put a handkerchief over their faces, and pour water over that. Or they would hand-cuff a prisoner, sink their hands in a water bucket, connect telephone wires to their thumbs, and pedal the generator. Or twist their fingers with wrenches. I was more curious than afraid, so I kept getting him to tell me about it.

After I looked around the empty rooms on the second floor, I asked Yeong-shik: "Do you think it's the ghost of one of the people who were tortured?"

He nodded, serious. "Probably."

We were just beginning the summer vacation of our first year in college, and Yeong-shik would have a few more ghost sight-ings before the summer was over. He used an old spring bed from a military hospital. He woke up on his side one night to the faint sound of cackling laughter, and right before him was a white hand shaking the bed. Another time, he opened the door to the stairway leading downstairs and saw the woman staring up at him from the bottom step.

In the wake of the war, the adults' remorse continued to hurt them, like an open wound. The children felt its impact, too. I remember Yeong-shik's pale mother who, upon sitting down to any table, even at our house for a cup of tea, would bow her head in prayer. Then there was his brother-in-law, whose face peered out from a window when I went to their house and called his name. With a curt "Yeong-shik is not here," he glared at me with a cold hostility that somehow stayed in my memory for a long time.

Tae-gyun was a boy who lived across from the cabbage patch, to the left of our house, in a *hanok* that shared a wall with the Twin Star Pagoda. The *hanok* roof was tiled like ours, but the main gate was topped with beautifully curved eaves made of galvanized iron. His grandfather's workshop was right next to the gate. His father had gone missing during the war; I don't recall if he was conscripted by the Japanese or kidnapped by the North Koreans. Tae-gyun's mother was an extraordinary woman, much admired by my mother, who remarked on her demureness and dignity—so different from the Southern women who didn't hesitate to remarry when they lost their husbands. Her hair was always combed back and secured with a long hairpin. She wore an apron over her black skirt and white top, cooked three meals a day for her widowed father-in-law, and grew her own vegetables to save money. The immature children that we were would complain about her whenever we fell into the pits where she'd buried the compost. Tae-gyun's grandfather wore his hair in a traditional topknot and horsehair headband, and he carved water buffalo horns. I had been inside his workshop a few times and admired the strange, beautiful crafts on display.

Tae-gyun was a couple of years older than me, so I called him *hyeong*, "older brother." Normally I never dared to question him or pick a fight, but he was the rough type and teased and bullied the younger children when he was with the neighborhood captain's son, a boy about his age. Once, I was so angry at his teasing, I threw a stone and it hit him bang on the forehead. He came running after me with one hand on his bleeding forehead. I'd just managed to reach the house when I happened to slam into my father who was coming out. "Watch where you're going, you rascal," he said, giving me a light rap on the head, and that's when I saw something odd. Tae-gyun stopped in his tracks, looked up at my father, and his mouth began to tremble. My father gave him a nonchalant glance and went on his way. Tae-gyun started to cry and went back to his own house. At that time, the rules of engagement were that whoever gets a nosebleed or cries first loses, so while I was perplexed by this development, I felt proud of myself, too.

That afternoon, my mother summoned me outside. I saw Tae-gyun, his eyes swollen and his forehead bandaged, standing in front of our house with his mother. This was unexpected. He was a little too old to be escorted by his mother over something like this. Mother told me to apologize, and I awkwardly said I was sorry. A few years later, my own father passed away when I had just entered middle school, and I began to comprehend why Tae-gyun had burst into tears.

What I remember best about Tae-gyun was what a passionate cinema nut he was, like the main character from *Cinema Paradiso*, and I followed in his footsteps. When his grandfather died, his mother opened a clothing shop in Yeongdeungpo Market, and Tae-gyun, an only child, was left to spend all day alone.

Yeongbo Theater had stood near the market since the Japanese occupation. Another cinema, named the Disabled Veterans Hall, appeared near the railway works after the war, and yet another, the Namdo, opened near the industrial zone. In other words, three movie theaters had appeared within blocks of each other, each changing their movies once a week. Tae-gyun's mother's shop was right at the corner of two streets, perfect for movie posters. His mother was given free cinema vouchers whenever a poster was put up, which you could redeem around the end of a run when empty seats became more readily available. Cigarette shops and snack shops that doubled as *manhwa* comic book outlets also took posters, and often sold their vouchers half-price. Tae-gyun and I saw plenty of movies. I used my occasional allowance to buy poster vouchers from him.

Once, I had managed to save for a voucher ticket toward *Gunga Din*, a movie about colonial India that I had much looked forward to seeing, but my mother tasked me with watching my brother until my older sister got home. That was the last day I could use my voucher, and all my careful planning was about to go down the drain. I decided to take my brother with me to the cinema. He was a toddler, about four years old. We had sat down and the lights had gone out for the movie to begin when, scared of the dark perhaps, my brother started to snivel. A man sitting next to me gave him some soda pop to soothe him, but after sucking on it like a milk bottle for a bit, he began crying again. I had no choice but to take him out to the lobby, but I really wanted to see the film. I let go his hand outside the theater, stared fiercely at him and growled, "Go home on your own!" Then I went back to my seat until the end of the movie.

Once it was over, dusk had begun to fall. Only then did I begin to worry whether the little one had managed to find his way home. The path past the busy market and around the rotary would have been complicated for a child. Oh no, what if I'd lost him? I have thought of this many times over, even into adulthood, and the regret still breaks my heart.

I ran home. Thankfully, my brother had made it, and the sight of the little one asleep with his face toward the wall and his feet blackened by dirt was so pitiful it brought tears to my eyes. Even when my mother hit my legs with a stick and I was sent outside to the yard without my dinner and I was staring up at the stars, all I could feel was relief at the thought of my brother returning safely and the sight of him sleeping soundly.

I'm not exactly sure when my mother started to be very strict with me, but it was probably after Father moved his shop from Chuncheon to Yeongdeungpo and was consequently home less and less. Before that, I'd taken a month off of school here and there to go spend time with him in Chuncheon, and despite my being a good student, my grades inevitably suffered. There were also students returning from the countryside who were a few years older or had been schooled with relative stability throughout the war, and they got better grades than I did. Sometimes I even fell to the bottom ten of the class. That was when my mother began using the rod. I was still more interested in reading or doing other things than studying. Around that time, I was also caught stealing money from her purse. I was given a thrashing and sent outside the house in the middle of the night. She didn't let me in until it was almost curfew-lifting time.

One day I decided to run away from home, like Guk-weon. Unlike Yeong-shik, who went to school with me, Guk-weon had gone to an elementary school near his house before dropping out. He lived with an older brother and his widower father until a stepmother entered the picture. She wasn't wicked, like in fairytales. If anything, when the children were being beaten she would try to intervene and get hurt herself. Guk-weon's father would mercilessly punish his sons whenever he got drunk. I've been hit by my mother wielding a rubber shoe in her angriest moments, but Guk-weon was beaten with a belt on his back, legs, head, and every other part of his body.

After running away from his odious father, Guk-weon spent about a year and a half at an orphanage. There, he was assigned to play a bugle to signal wake-up and sleep times. He brought the mouthpiece of this bugle back with him when he returned home and sometimes blew on it, making a thin, sad sound like a baby's cry. Having read *The Adventures of Tom Sawyer* and *Huckleberry Finn* by then, I thought Guk-weon was just like Huckleberry Finn.

I planned it all out. White acacia was blooming in the warm May air, but the nights were still chilly, so I found a serge jacket among our winter clothes. At the time only orphanage children wore colorful secondhand clothing; children raised at home wore the black national school uniforms once they reached fifth grade. Mother used her sewing machine to convert American uniforms into good jackets for Father and me. Thanks to her skill, I once had a beautiful pea coat made from one of my older sisters' long coats. I packed socks and clothes and, in case of rain, a raincoat and a towel. If rucksacks had been the fashion before, now duffel bags had taken over, carried by every adult and child on trips and picnics, later to be replaced in turn by messenger bags. I packed my things in a dark blue weekender, ran home on Saturday afternoon before my sisters came back, and took off.

I knew my eldest sister was saving up pocket money, so I dug through her bag. It contained a booklet of train times and a red vinyl wallet. Inside the wallet were the stiff bills she had squirreled away.

I had heard you could see the ocean in Incheon. I didn't do anything foolish, like try to buy a ticket at Yeongdeungpo

Station. Instead I headed for Seoul Station, as I knew from my sisters, who took the tram or used train passes into downtown Seoul, that there were student commuter trains from there to Incheon four times a day.

In those days the passenger trains were modified freight cars. There were corridors connecting the cars, but otherwise passengers had to get on and off using the wide doors. As there were no windows, the passengers tended to cluster around the doors. I had heard from other children that if you wanted to ride the train for free you needed to stand near the connecting corridors, so that's what I did. I heard the endless rhythm of the steel wheels going over the seams of the tracks. I avoided the conductors by staying ahead of them and getting off on the platform and moving to a rear car whenever the train stopped.

As we approached Incheon, I could smell the salt air. Then, when we passed Ju-an, I saw wide tidelands and salt fields. We reached East Incheon Station, the train's final destination. I followed some other kids my age through the freight exit at the opposite end of the platform. A flock of birds sitting on a grim cement wall took flight. Seagulls!

I could guess what was beyond that wall. As soon as I passed it, I could see mudflats and the sea beyond. Later, visiting Mallipo Beach in middle school, I looked at the white sands and blue ocean and realized how bleak and dull my first glimpse of the ocean had been; but in that earlier moment, the faint line of water in the distance foreshadowed a new world. Even the cargo ships on the horizon seemed to mock the fact that I was standing still on land.

How long did I sit there, staring at the ocean? The western sky started to turn orange, and the layers of clouds shifted into different shades and colors. As twilight fell, I instinctively thought of my mother.

I wandered around the darkening town. I suddenly felt tense and scared. I bought some red bean pastries from a street vendor, went into a market where the sellers had gone home, and found a panel leaned up against a wall in an alley. There were only occasional pedestrians, and the stalls were empty. It stank of fish, but I crawled into the dark, cozy spot behind the panel and curled up. With my weekender as a pillow and my zipper up to my neck, I tried to fall asleep. I could hear the voices of people nearby, the blare of a locomotive in the distance, and the chugging of a ferry engine. I must've fallen deep asleep.

"Ah! What's this?"

I heard a woman's surprised voice; the panel was moved aside and someone was staring down at me. I rubbed my eyes to show I had been awakened from sleep and clumsily sat up.

The woman, wearing loose trousers and long rubber gloves, crouched down. "Child, who are you? Why are you sleeping here?" She smelled of fish.

I didn't say anything but felt her slowly looking me up and down.

"Where do you live?" When I kept silent, the woman grabbed my hand and tried to lead me out of there. "Fine, I'm taking you to the police."

I blurted out: "I have a home. I live in Yeongdeungpo."

Later she would explain that she'd guessed straight away that I was not an orphan and that I'd run away from a nice, middle-class home after being scolded. *He had a student buzz cut and a beautiful serge jacket and even a duffel bag.*

She asked me if I'd eaten, and when I shook my head, she clucked her tongue as if she'd suspected as much. She had been on her way home after salting some fish she hadn't managed to sell and storing it under the panel. The fish peddler took one more look at me and, her groceries in one hand and my wrist in the other, pulled me along, saying, "All right then, it's late, so you're coming home with me for now."

She brought me to a new neighborhood filled with refugees. The shacks built on the hillside were practically stuck together, and the alleys were all twists and turns. Particleboards and boxes from the American army bases had been repurposed for walls, and the roofs were painted with black tar. Large stones sat on the roofs so they wouldn't fly away in the strong winds coming off the water. There was of course no plumbing or electricity in the whole neighborhood. Many similar dwellings had been built right after the war in my own neighborhood, and, having visited school friends who lived in them, they weren't unfamiliar to me.

Somewhere I could smell pike being cooked. Hunger made me more melancholy, and this in turn made me want to go home. Ever since then, I always think of home when I pass the gladly familiar scent of a fruit shop while traveling in a faraway land, or smell fish cooking over a charcoal fire in the back streets of a poor neighborhood where children run and play.

The fish peddler had a husband and three children. Her husband was a good carpenter, and he had no shortage of work because there were so many people building houses at the time. But, like many other manual laborers, he suffered from a bad back. Later, when she and my mother became friends and called each other sisters, we came to learn more about their family history. Her husband had hurt his back when he fell off a scaffold at a construction site, and she blamed "that damned drink" for it all.

The eldest daughter made a stew from the fish her mother brought home. Everyone sat around the tiny table, rubbing shoulders, the stew in the middle accompanied by fresh kimchi that still had green in the cabbage. The lamp on the wall was bright but gave off quite a smell. The fish peddler complained about it to her husband. "I told you to snip the wick! It won't stop smoking."

How delicious the food was! My forehead and neck were sweating. The fish peddler ripped the kimchi cabbage into strips and deposited a coil of it on each of the children's spoons, and we opened our mouths extra wide to shovel it in. The fish stew was sprinkled with red pepper powder and just one spoonful made the mouth hum with heat.

The whole family lay down in a row, side by side, and soon I heard the snoring of the adults. I slept at the end of the row next to the son. In his sleep he occasionally dropped an arm on my head or a leg on my stomach, waking me up. I can say that as I slept for the first time with someone else's family, in someone else's house, I realized that my family and home were not the whole world.

The next day, the fish peddler took me to the station and bought us both train tickets. She sighed as I stammered about my family. "You silly child. Your mother must be sick with worry right now. I bet she didn't sleep a wink last night."

The journey back was so short and quick that we were in Yeongdeungpo before I knew it. My heart began to race. It was nice to see those familiar streets, but I oddly resented it a little that everything seemed to be business as usual despite my absence.

Mother didn't scold me once that day. Instead, she took the fish peddler out for lunch. All she had to say about it was, "I think I've made a lovely friend." Mother and Father visited them in Incheon later. Every spring, during the croaker drying season, the fish peddler would send us a whole box of Yellow Sea croakers. Mother only gave me one punishment. She ordered me to write down everything that had happened, from the moment I left home to the moment I came back.

My grades kept slipping. As spring finals for fifth grade approached, Mother forbade me from going out and playing with my friends after school. I did all right on my exams, but math was still a disaster. Mother knew this was because my extended sojourn in Chuncheon the year before had made me miss some fundamentals, but she still decreed that I was to have no vacations from then on. She even got my eldest sister to tutor me in math. My mother and sister took turns sitting next to me at the desk as I pored over my textbooks and workbooks, testing me. They beat me mercilessly if I dozed off or daydreamed out of boredom.

It was summer, but I lost track of how many days had passed since I'd last been outside. Our neighborhood was by a stream, and we children loved the water and ran to it as soon as the chill broke. Once we became wet, the slightest breeze felt so cold that we crouched on the sandy banks clutching our balls and warming ourselves in the sun. The fishing net I had begged my parents for never went three days without being dipped in the river. Yeong-shik and Guk-weon each held a side of the net while someone else chased the fish into it. We caught carp, mandarin fish, minnows, and once a catfish that had lost his way. We imitated the adults by cooking these trophies in a pot with red chili paste, soybean paste, green onions, and garlic. I had been longing to join them again, but that damn report card had dashed all my hopes.

I heard a low voice calling me by my childhood name. "Sunam-ah! Sunam-ah!"

Mother happened to be out, and my eldest sister, having assigned a math problem, was in another room chatting with my other sister. I crept into the backyard, leaned against a tree of heaven and peered over the fence. Guk-weon stood there, holding a pail.

"Let's go fishing."

I listlessly shook my head. "Can't. I'm stuck here."

"How stupid of you not to grab your report card before your mother saw it. Lend me the fishing net, then. We're going camping."

Guk-weon's eager face was burning a hole in my stomach. I grabbed the rolled-up net, two military-issue ponchos that Father used in the shop, a blanket and a raincoat, and set off. Guk-weon, seeing me outside the house, was beside himself with joy.

Jeong-sam and Ho-shik were waiting for us in front of the school. Jeong-sam was the junkyard owner's son, and Ho-shik lived in the back rooms of the barbershop next door. Ho-shik had followed his brother to the South and was a couple of years older than us, but two years below in school. The children in his class were still babies, but Ho-shik was taller than us by a whole handspan, and the skin above his top lip was darkening. His voice was the first of ours to change.

We pooled what we'd brought: three blankets, two military-issue raincoats, the fishing net, a pail, pots, dishes, a pocketknife, red chili paste, soybean paste, and spices. We were set for adventure. We followed the tributary where the water level had shrunk to a trickle between occasional isolated pools, walking on the sands with Yangmal Mountain in sight. The Yeouido flight strip's barbed wire fence followed us on the right. The fence cut through the middle of a wide grassy field, and at the end of the weeds was a long peanut patch. We walked across the field until we could see the shore of the Mapo district.

Guk-weon suggested the water level might rise if it rained that night, so we set up our tent where the grass ended and the sand began. We cut poplar branches, stuck them in the grass as poles, and hung the raincoat over them to make an excellent tent. Inside we put down another raincoat and a blanket over that. There was plenty of space for four children to sleep under the remaining two blankets.

We went down to the water and splashed around, prodding the sand and bringing up clams with our feet. Fishermen gathered every weekend at a wide pond under a hill with a pagoda, so we knew there were many fish. In the rainy season, the Han River overflowed to the foot of Yangmal Mountain and left behind a pond the size of a sports field when it receded. This made that spot as good as a fish farm.

Guk-weon and I held the net on either side as Ho-shik and Jeong-sam herded fish into it. The little pools where waterweeds floated among the pebbles were obviously good places to fish. We moved slowly through the waterweeds, bowing over the surface, while Ho-shik and Jeong-sam splashed around and made a ruckus on the other side. At the right moment, Guk-weon and I locked eyes and spread the net at the same time. A couple of carps the size of our palms came up flapping against the net. We tossed them into the pail.

We gathered large stones on the sand to make two stoves, put rice on in the small pot, and the cleaned fish and spices in the big pot. Ho-shik, in the meantime, snuck into a nearby field and grabbed some zucchini, peppers, and even a couple of ears of corn.

"When the tears fall from the rice, it's almost done," said Guk-weon, pretending to be wise. The rice turned out well, and the fish stew was even tastier than it was at home.

Dusk slowly fell on the riverbank. The peaceful silence right before a summer sunset was somehow sad and beautiful at the same time. The cries of the birds bedding down for the night in the reeds of Yeouido sounded as plaintive as babies settling down to sleep. The sudden moon hung low in the still blue sky, and a few vagabond stars followed in its wake. The insects in the grass began their throaty songs, and darkness descended rapidly. We made a fire on the sand with some branches we'd gathered. Just when we were feeling hungry again, Guk-weon and Ho-shik came back from a raid with an undershirt full of peanuts. We roasted them in the ashes near the fire.

Guk-weon used the bugle mouthpiece he wore around his neck to play a sad lights-out tune. The stars looked ripe for the picking, as if they would all shimmer to the ground if you shook the sky. There was a rustling sound as Ho-shik took out a cigarette, lit it, and very calmly inhaled and exhaled. He must have filched it from his brother's barber gown. Guk-weon held out a hand and Ho-shik handed the cigarette to him. It was my turn after that, but one inhalation left me coughing and teary for a long time. I don't think anyone was thinking of home that night.

My eyes opened of their own accord the next morning as light slanted into the tent. The fog over the water was evaporating in the sunlight. We joked around as we woke each other and dug holes in the sand to do our business. Then, still naked, we jumped into the river and swam out to the middle before flipping over on our backs to swim back to shore. The fish we caught were still moving their gills inside the pail while the more hotheaded ones were already belly-up.

Time flew by so quickly that once we'd had our light breakfast of turnip pickles, the sun was already high in the sky and the river water was lukewarm. We ran back into the river and gathered clams and got our fishing net out again when we saw a school of freshwater shrimp. Guk-weon and I had sunburned noses, and Ho-shik, who was on the pale side, was red all over.

As evening fell, Ho-shik and Jeong-sam began to get anxious. They said in despondent voices that they hadn't told their families they were going camping, and now they'd be in trouble if they went back. I too had been dreading this moment. Guk-weon shook his head. He said that if we went back now, we'd get thrashed and sent to bed without dinner, followed by days of having to endure everyone's contempt, so it was better if we went home the next evening. By then the family would have grown too worried to be anything other than relieved to see us, and all we'd have to do was beg for forgiveness. And if that didn't work, we could strike back with the declaration that we would only run away again. It seemed like a good plan.

We spent another night camping, and at dusk the following day we headed back to the neighborhood and split up. I carried my blanket, fishing net, and raincoat under my arms and slowly walked home. Ho-shik would probably be beaten to within an inch of his life by his older brother. More than once, over the fence, I'd heard his sister-in-law egging his brother on during these beatings. That was why he had wanted to stay with Guk-weon a little longer and creep back in after his brother was asleep.

I leaned against the plank fence outside our backyard and listened for the sounds of the household. My sister seemed to be cooking in the kitchen, and no one was out. I screwed up my courage and walked in the front door. My middle sister, who was sitting in her room next to the door, looked wide-eyed at my appearance and called for Mother. Thankfully, Father was away. Mother gave me the once-over and said, "Put those things down. You're coming with me."

She didn't ask where I had been or who with, but only took my hand and led me out of the gate. "You hate school and you hate studying and you hate home, am I right?"

I didn't answer. Mother walked me over the dike and past the wooden bridge built by the American military engineers, all the way to "Ghost Rock" by the hill with a brick house. It wasn't completely dark yet, because a remnant of the sunset still lingered on the horizon and the stars were beginning to shine. Mother began dragging me by the hand into the river. "You and me, we're better off drowning here together!"

Ghost Rock had once been a sand quarry, and there were many pits concealed under the water. Even children who were good at swimming avoided that spot. There were a lot of waterweeds, and a number of people drowned there every year. As the water came up to our waists, I kept fearing that something would grab my ankle and pull me under. When I stopped in my tracks, Mother jerked my arm. "I'm going to die and take you with me. Only then will our family be at peace!"

I strained against her grasp and kept saying that I would stop misbehaving. My sisters later reported that, according to Mother, I'd begged for my life, but that's an exaggeration. Mother told me herself, when I became an adult, that she had read a scene like this in a short story in the Japanese magazine *Bungeishunjū*. Whenever she went downtown to Myeong-dong, Mother would visit "Dollar Alley" and buy a copy of *Bungeishunjū* or *Shufu no tomo* (The Housewife's Friend). In any case, this extremely literary and melodramatic scene was the source of much chaffing from my sisters for years to come.

Middle schools were selective at the time, condemning my generation to suffer "entrance exam hell" in elementary school. My fourth and fifth grades were spent moving between temporary schools, which made me largely self-taught during those years. The long stays with my father in Chuncheon did not help, resulting in spotty attendance and a poor grasp of the fundamentals—a calamity that immediately revealed itself in the sixth grade. My reading comprehension and rote memorization skills were fine, but my math and science scores were so bad that even I could not understand how things had come to this. I had to buy textbooks from lower grades to catch up. Mother and I stayed up almost every night, making up for lost time. I soon crept into the top ten in my class and, by the end of sixth grade, had finally retaken the top spot.

The last winter vacation of my elementary school days ended, and I turned thirteen. By then my father's health had been irrevocably damaged. I went with my parents to the middle school entrance exam results announcement, on the school sports field, where posters were already up with our test numbers. My father found my name first and shouted out, "*Aigu*, you're in!"

I looked up at my father and was surprised by how old he looked, his eyes filled with tears and his sideburns and temples so gray. On the way back we stopped at a grill in Jongno and had *tonkatsu*, but Father only drank some soup and gave me all his meat.

"Are you feeling all right?" Mother asked, but Father merely said that his breakfast wasn't sitting well. Looking back, I suspect that Father had been to the hospital a few days before and knew why he felt so weak and exhausted on the day of my entrance announcement. He did not live for more than six months after that day, and the summer of the year I entered middle school, he suddenly passed away.

8

Prison IV

It seems like South Korea celebrates a national holiday or memorial day every month: March 1 Movement Memorial Day; April 19, the April / Revolution; May Day on the first; Buddha's birthday in April or May; May 18, Gwangju Democracy Movement Memorial Day; June 10, Democratic Uprising Memorial Day; July 17, Constitution Day; August 18, Liberation Day; November 3, Student Independence Movement Memorial Day; and Christmas Day in December. These days had extra significance for political prisoners, as they gave us a mandate for protest. We ended up agitating every month of the year except January and February. The reasons for our agitations were different each time, but the point was to commemorate the dates with some kind of struggle.

In March came the spring labor protests and the March 1 pardons, just in time for the universities reopening for spring term. Next, the student inmates who had been arrested for protesting would never let April 19 go past without a fight. Political prisoners had an obligation to teach the regular prisoners the meaning behind May Day and May 18. The commemoration of the June Uprising and the beginning of the Korean War on June 25 were also essential as educational opportunities, reaffirming why we were fighting for democracy. Constitution Day was to remind ourselves of the spirit of our Constitution as we battled against tyrannical laws, and Liberation Day was for demanding fairer pardons and remembering how we had lost our country to foreign forces. On Chuseok, the Korean harvest festival, we rested as we meditated on our gratitude toward our ancestors. And by the time we had finished our preparations for winter, it was already November 3; there was no way the student activist prisoners could overlook a day commemorating the student independence movement. Lastly, Christmas marked the point where we would rally to campaign for better pardons.

Resistance in prison almost always began with hunger strikes, because there was basically no other way to resist. (I undertook nineteen hunger strikes during my five-year sentence.) The prison authorities were obligated to report to the Ministry of Justice any political prisoners on hunger strike for over four days, and the prison wardens, whatever the specific circumstances, would face reprimand for negligent management. But you really had to hunger strike for at least a week, because in practice four days were not enough to get a response.

You notify the fact of your strike to the prison authorities, read out your petition, lean out of your bathroom window and shout a two-line, four-syllable slogan, and sing songs of struggle. When your throat closes and your mouth gets dry, you bang your utensils against the window frame to let the other political prisoners know what you are doing, and finally, you begin kicking the door to your cell. If your heel begins to hurt or you become exhausted, you slam the door with a broom or pail. A decorous public figure like me would desist when he heard the pounding of guards' shoe soles on the cement floor, but the student protesters would throw feces at them, shove a mattress against the door to keep it from opening, or hold up their chopsticks and threaten to stab the guards in the eye. Eventually, five or six guards would enter the cell, drag the political prisoner to the hall, handcuff their hands behind their backs, tie up their arms with rope, and fasten a leather-strapped muzzle with a bit made of wood. The bit fills your mouth and presses down on your tongue, making you drool, and you're thrown into punitive confinement in one of the sensory deprivation cells. Regular prisoners are thrown in six or seven at a time into that space less than a *pyeong* wide, where they can barely move, but political prisoners were normally confined alone.

They dared not put a muzzle on me, but I could not avoid the sensory deprivation cell. The thought of the young inmates thrown into the cells next to mine along that dark hall made me determined to persist in my hunger strike. There was a tap, a defecation hole, cement everywhere, and a vent about two palms wide at the very top of the tall cell wall. Handcuffed and bound with rope, I could only tell the time of day and how long I'd been in there by the angle and intensity of the light seeping through the vent.

It would take at least two hours for a youth with a bit in his mouth to realize how his situation had changed and to become aware of the cell, the hall outside, and the space next to the cell block that was outside the window. His tunic would be drenched with saliva from the bit, driving him to the brink of insanity. One young man told me that words would boil like porridge cooking in his chest and throat, bursting to get out. No matter how hard he tried to scream, all he could manage were *uh, ee, uh, ee*, sounds that barely reached the tip of his tongue before collapsing in his throat. After a day, the inspection slit on the steel door would slide open with a clang, and the eyes of the punishment cell guard would appear. The slit would mercilessly slide shut if the prisoner's eyes were still hostile, but by the time the guard looked in, the prisoner would usually be lying on his side, spent of fury. The door would then open and the free air of the corridor would blow in.

The guard would state, in a businesslike tone:

—If you promise to be quiet, I'll take the muzzle off. Will you be quiet?

The prisoner nods. You don't need to hear a pleading voice to tell his nods mean *Please, please*. The hand that removes the muzzle is like the hand of God. The prisoner opens his mouth wide and takes several deep breaths and licks his liberated teeth and lips. The steel door slams shut once more.

I bent my tied legs to my chest and leaned against the wall with my hands tied behind my back. How strange, the punishment cell was the size of my regular cell, but the lack of a window made the whole world shrink. I could feel a sharp pain when I pressed down where the handcuffs were fastened. My back itched, my wrenched shoulders strained, and my breath moved in and out of my nose and mouth. There are moments when just being alive is in itself humiliation and suffering. I couldn't do anything because of the restraints. I couldn't lie down, couldn't lean forward, and I needed to distract myself with something if I wanted to forget my current state. I needed to loosen my hands a bit.

Most prisoners who have experienced the punishment cell know to search for a nail or a piece of wire in the ground as soon as they are thrown in. It could be one that a previous prisoner has left behind, or a nail pulled out of the floor through long and careful effort. Or you could negotiate with the guard during interrogation to have your handcuffs refastened to the front of you instead, or beg to have them temporarily taken off. When they put them back on, you make an angle with your elbow so as to make a wider space in the cuffs. Once in the cell, you rub your hands with as much dry soap as possible and wriggle your hands out of them. You can always put them back on when you hear footsteps.

Unlike the regular prisoners, I had no opportunity to negotiate, so what I did was crawl around in the dark as I tried to sweep the floor with my hands. I'd keep pressing down with my feet the slightest bit of elevation or edge in the wooden boards. I could feel the head of a nail popping up after about an hour. Sometimes I could immediately pull it out, sometimes it took a whole day. Getting that nail out of the plank becomes the most important project in the history of the world. *Ah, finally! It's out.* This tiny piece of metal was the key to changing me from an animal into a thinking, working human being.

The long, thin beam of light seeping through moves slowly to the left, shrinking gradually shorter as it inches back toward the vent, then narrowing still more before turning into a faint smudge near the corner of the vent, and soon disappearing altogether. Around this time, I smell the savory scent of fermented soybean paste stew and hear the squeak of the steel wheels of the food cart. My handcuffs are still not released. They won't be released until the administrative office calls for me in four or five days. I hear the turning of the key and the whole door, not just the food hole, opens. With a practiced air, the guard puts down a tray with three white plastic bowls, one for rice, one for stew, and a side dish. With a sneer he says:

—Eat your kibble.

I've already declared my hunger strike, so I kick over the tray instead. The guard curses me from afar as the *soji* assigned to the sensory deprivation cell comes to clean up the mess. The regular prisoners have to bend over with their hands tied behind their backs to eat their food in a hurry, getting it all over their faces. The prison authorities will sometimes attempt force-feeding if a hunger strike continues. I once was sent to the infirmary during a hunger strike, and the doctor threatened to force-feed me like in the old days if I did not comply. I threatened him right back. I warned that I knew his name and rank, that force-feeding was officially a form of torture, and that he would never be able to shake off the repercussions of having tortured a political prisoner—something that would rebound on the warden and the minister of justice as well. Thwarted, he mumbled something about having done so in the past with no problem. Indeed, I heard they were still force-feeding regular and student prisoners on occasion.

In this process the doctor grasps the prisoner in the sensory deprivation cell, with the help of some guards, and pumps watery rice gruel into a rubber hose shoved down the prisoner's throat. It's as suffocating as having an endoscopy, and the gruel ends up coming out of the hunger-striker's nose, but that's not the worst of it. What brings tears to the prisoner's eyes is how humiliating and degrading a violation it is. He vomits again and again, but the texture of the rice grains in his throat and the savory taste at the tip of his tongue are already unforgettable. His bodily resistance begins to break down.

The sensory deprivation cell rips away that symbol of humanity from the prisoner: his very freedom of thought. You could not bear to have any thoughts at all in that place. The only way to affirm that you were alive in your own body was to have a goal and to concentrate on that goal.

Right, I have a tool. The goal is to remove my handcuffs. I lift the nail I've hidden in the cracks of the floor. I explore the nail with my fingertips to become comfortable with its detailed structure and motions, the circling, lining, crossing, and so on. Then, I slip the tip into the keyhole of the handcuff and try to learn its structure. You have to remember when you feel something catch. You turn, dig, and pull scores of times, making a mental note of how much strength to apply in which direction. You try again, you keep on trying. The motion of your fingers becomes ever finer, and even as you concentrate, you close your eyes and all kinds of thoughts grab at you and come after you.

There is a wide field of green barley, rippling in the breeze. I see pine trees bending on a hill across the field, the path I am walking on winds next to the hill, continuing over the bridge that spans the stream, and curving toward the mountain beyond. Tall willow trees grow along both sides of the path, and their branches dance, leaves fluttering and sparkling in the sun as though clapping and laughing. I am walking along but can't feel any bumps of rocks or stones beneath my feet. The dirt road is damp, the soft, cushiony soil tickling my soles. The moment I feel I'm about to reach my destination, my feet tickle more than ever. I glide along the path in silent motion like in a dream.

Click. The saw-toothed claw of the inner cuff pops out with a clear metallic sound. I slip my hands out. Now for the ropes. It takes a long time to release the first knot and at least an hour more to untie the others and free my wrists from the rope. If I keep pulling and relaxing and pulling again at the ropes, I can create a hole big enough for my hands to escape. Exhausted, I collapse to the ground with the remaining rope tied around my elbows. I clench and unclench my fists, scratch my itching nose, and enjoy a respite on my back. The moonlight from the ventilation window creates a faint parallelogram-shaped stain on the cement wall.

I must have fallen asleep. I hear the steel doors open on the floor below as the night shift make their last rounds before changing out, hearing the "No problems during shift!" call of the guard, low and curt. My eyes pop open, and I quickly sit on the handcuffs and rope, turn to hide my back and arms from the inspection slit, and pretend to be asleep. I can see the visor of the guard on shift go by the slit. I'm completely awake now and put the handcuffs back on. I slip my hands into the loops of the rope-harness and tighten the knots like before. I slip the nail back into the plank where I found it. As long as I can be free whenever I want, I've won. Not even the darkness of the sensory deprivation cell or these narrow cement walls can get me down.

It's always at the beginning that prison is hardest. Like anything else, even the worst situations become tolerable after a week or so. But there are long-lasting side effects to being dragged out of the sensory deprivation cell and into the sunlight for a "consultation" with the prison administration or security officers. First, you can't open your eyes as soon as you step into the yard. Yellow light fills your vision under closed eyelids, and the dizziness of vertigo makes you swoon. The guard knows this is the case, which is why he doesn't urge you on but waits for you instead, speaking in a cold voice.

—So, what's it like "going to Hong Kong"? Two months spent rotting in that box will turn into a model prisoner.

When I open my eyes and start walking again, the white light dims as if the colors were being drained out of it, and I'm back to normal. But even then, the trees and sky and the whitewashed cement walls of the yard itself seem like full-color slides projected in the dark, crystalline and spectacular. The prospect of returning to sensory deprivation is horrifying. When I am dragged back to the dark solitude of the cell, like on the first day, and the steel door slams shut behind me, I fall into despair like a man who has lost everything.

There are different stages of "punishment" inside the sensory deprivation cell. First come the days of struggling like an animal to adjust. Then, a period of being let out and forced back in that serves to underline how there's nowhere lower you can sink from where you are now. When you're past this time of stagnation, tedium, and loneliness, the guards release the handcuffs and ropes and try to make you see it their way, to make you an offer conditional on your willingness to write a statement admitting fault. There is still a point where the inmate feels wronged and insists, full of hate, that there is no possible compromise. In this case the administration resets the punishment to its original conditions, or grants you more time for reflection and outside exercise. If both sides refuse to bend, the prisoner really does go insane or is sent to an even worse place of confinement. In any case, he's broken in the end. All such days are present in the accepting gaze of the long-term prisoner.

A guard came to fetch me after a week on hunger strike in the sensory deprivation cell. They were probably conducting a preliminary interrogation because they were afraid that I would make waves on the outside. I left the young inmates behind and didn't look back as I returned to my normal cell. I should have refused and demanded that the others be freed before me, and that is my lasting shame. But I was still denied visits, and so my strike continued. I think that was the hardest period for me. No wonder I carved the warden's name on the wall so I would never forget it. But I do not remember his name anymore. After five years in prison and the return to daily life in the outside world, the bad things I experienced behind bars became as foggy as the fragments of a bad dream. The things I've managed to recall for the first time while writing this are enough to surprise even me, making me almost question whether they really happened.

My first winter in prison, the twenty long days of my hunger strike took their toll on me: two of my teeth fell out as I brushed. I stared at the spat-out teeth on my palm and couldn't bring myself to throw them away, so I put them in a plastic container. I went on further hunger strikes during my time in prison and lost fourteen more teeth after I was released. This meant years of misery getting implants.

The regular prisoners tried their damnedest to become "mad dogs." They searched out the guards' weaknesses, made violent threats, and tormented the officers every chance they had. Those whom sensory deprivation could not tame would find themselves back in those airless cells over and over for six months, driving everyone crazy. The most effective measure was self-harm: swallowing things like needles, nail-clippers, carpentry nails or glass, or slashing themselves in the stomach with can lids, or even, as a protest against the hideousness of the world, sewing their eyelids shut. One prisoner sewed his lips together into a bloody mess because a guard castigated him for talking back. This is usually enough for the guards in charge to give up and allow some leeway. Most "mad dogs" would never dare act like that at the beginning of their sentences, because they would simply be shut down and transferred to another cell or a more remote prison; but those in their last year were normally left alone. Once they got a permit to grow out their hair, you could say the world was their oyster from then on. Although all it meant was getting put into easier workstations, being given more morsels at meals, or being moved into a wider cell with fewer people.

Prison life resets when you change prisons, or even just change cells. And no matter how peaceful or reasonable your sentence has been up to that point, all those conditions disappear when the people around you change. Political prisoners continued the struggle inside because of important developments outside, or their moral mandate, but when it came to the living conditions of prisoners, especially, there was a rule that all must fight for the good of all. Things that were as inconsequential as dust on the outside took on life-or-death meaning inside prison: a decrease in the pork that was served once a week, or guards using violence or violent language toward the regular prisoners, became important points of struggle.

The Gongju Correctional Institute brought in two pigs a week. Each prisoner was entitled to one hundred grams of pork, but it cooked down to eighty. In contrast, the Seoul Detention Center served beef stew once a week and the morsels were minced, which meant the bottom had to be stirred for prisoners to get some. The "mad dogs" there would receive more bits of meat, thanks to the tricks of the *soji*, and put them in ramen or cook them separately. But there were so many things you could purchase from the commissary in the detention center that no one really complained about it. In prison proper, where the conditions were worse, everyone looked forward to pork day. However, eighty grams of steamed pork should be the size of a man's palm, and the prisoners complained that it was blatantly obvious that they were only getting half that. It was a miracle that we ended up with anything at all, after the prison's executive officers took home the best cuts, then the guards, and then the mess hall workers, who served it boiled to the leader-level prisoners. There were many other complaints about food: for instance, we were entitled to three pieces of nori but only received two—and of such poor quality that we said we were better off getting a few more vegetables instead.

The political prisoners received the regular prisoners' complaints in written notes, and on memorial days we used our political mandate to issue demands related to matters like "the pork problem." Negotiations would begin after about a week of hunger strikes, and the young student activist would face off with the security officer in charge, in this case verifying with scales whether we were indeed receiving eighty grams per head. These were problems that would be bad publicity if they got out, so the prison tried to resolve them internally. The victorious prisoners, rejoicing over their palm-sized piece of pork, cursed those who had taken half of their meat before. But over six months, the serving of pork slowly shrank to half its regulation size again. Then we fought, nagged, and complained until conditions seemed to improve, before turning bad once more, repeating ad nauseam as time went by.

A harrowing experience led me to read books about alternative medicine, where I learned that fasting was so dangerous it is referred to as "knifeless surgery." You're supposed to work up to it with a preparatory fast, and ideally request pills called Magmil (magnesium hydroxide) from the pharmacy in order to completely empty your digestive system, which will help avoid side effects. You fill plastic bottles with water and drink at least two of these every day. Emptying yourself quickly will cut down on withdrawal, so in the evening you get a bowl of lukewarm water and give yourself an enema. This involves poking a straw into a plastic bag, wrapping the opening with a rubber band, and filling the bag with warm water through the open end of the straw. You insert the straw into your rectum and lie on your side as you squeeze the water in little by little. Soon, your stomach rumbles and gurgles. You lie still until you can't stand it anymore and go to the toilet to evacuate your bowels. After a few rounds of this, your stomach will feel much more comfortable, and your desire to eat will also lessen.

A day of fasting is very different from a day divided by three meals: for prisoners who spend their days waiting for breakfast to turn to lunch and lunch to turn to dinner, the tedium in between can become unbearable. With fasting, the hardest part is making it to the fourth day. There's an old saying that three days of starvation will turn anyone into a thief, and the third evening of fasting is that point where every thought and sense is attuned to food, so much so that reading becomes impossible. Your senses of hearing and smell turn painfully acute at the creaking of the food cart's wheels, and the heavenly scent of rice steaming in the kitchen makes your nerves sing. I could tell not only when bean paste soup was being served, but also the exact kinds of side dishes on offer.

The clatter of the cart reaches our corridor, and the other cells begin to murmur as they accept their food, which is when I close the food hole and sit with my back to the door. I hear the sounds of laughter and eating in the other cells. I recall a memory from when I was sick as a child. I was staying home from school, either from flu or indigestion, and my family ate at the table while I lay alone in a corner. They talked amongst themselves about what had happened that day and the food they were eating, and the sound of their cutlery clanging on bowls made me feel lonelier as I lay there, listening.

Finally, the cart stops in front of my door and the food hole opens. When the *soji* asks if I'm eating and I answer no, he shuts the food hole without another word. I take a deep breath and pour some of the water I've stored in the plastic bottle into a bowl and drink it slowly, rolling the water around on my tongue. My hunger subsides after about three bowls.

The fluorescent bulb is so old that there are black stains at its edges, and I hear a buzzing from it that normally doesn't register. It's getting louder. When I'm too restless to fall asleep that night, it feels like the metallic sound is making long waves as it passes through my head. The perpetual light of the fluorescent bulb has converted to sound energy that overtakes my cerebrum. Like in the darkness of the punishment cell, my body disappears little by little and all that's left is my consciousness. That's the borderline between the third and fourth day. After the fifth, and around the end of the first week, the seething demands of the body are easily ignored and begin to subside. I stop eliminating and, later, all that comes out is a bit of clear water. This is when the smell of food becomes repulsive.

I dream. I see a wide, green field and trees. As in my dreams inside the punishment cell, I tread the field or pass over it lightly like clouds or the wind. After two weeks of this I begin to feel cold, yet the slightest bout of fever and chills leaves me feeling like I've just returned home from being caught in a storm and have dried off and snuggled warmly down in bed. I begin to sleep less and my mind grows clearer. I wake in the middle of the night and spend hours sitting upright. And like an old man, I am flooded with memories. I just sit on the bedding and follow the path the memories take me.

Why is it that fasting makes the past more vivid? Having three meals a day creates clear demarcations of time and brings one back to the world of the fully alive. Without regular meals, the body leaves the present. Memories burdened by excess activity in the brain cells are slowly freed, their forms becoming clearer in the mind's eye. But of all those memories, I could summon only the ones that I thought were insignificant and therefore had forgotten, or else incidents where I'd done something wrong.

At two weeks of my hunger strike, the infirmary sends someone every day to measure my blood pressure, which is, of course, much lower than normal. Water tastes extremely good. I grow a beard and my skin becomes rough, but my eyes seem clearer and brighter.

The guards take turns leaving things like apples, and one holds out a thermos full of bean paste soup, bidding me to smell it. Right before afternoon lockdown, I go to the cell block office and return the food untouched. They threaten to force-feed me, and I retaliate by saying I will publicly disclose such an act as torture.

Eighteen days in, we come to not quite a victory but a

compromise of sorts. But this is the final test. If I want them to accept my terms, I must make it clear that I will continue with the strike until my last breath. And yet, the thought that there are only two or three days left to go makes me impatient, the urge to get this over with rising from the pit of my stomach, making this last hurdle a truly high one to clear. Time suddenly stops then. The days become endless and the night seems to last forever.

The cold forces your body to work harder, and you risk frostbite on your hands, ears, or toes where they are exposed to the cement walls. There's a numbness at first, followed by pain and itching. I discover my toes have frozen stiff when I take my socks off. I rub my hands together to warm them and rub my toes one by one. I stroke my ears, up and down, countless times. Sleeping in a fetal position all night stiffens my body so much that I can't easily uncurl myself in the morning. Only when I slowly jump up and down for an hour in front of the steel door do my joints recover from their stiffness.

But the hunger strike isn't over just because your demands have been met. After having endured it for over three weeks, now comes the battle against yourself. This is the hardest part of fasting: recovery. The kitchen *soji* delivers thin rice gruel twice a day on orders of the infirmary. I also get some soybean paste broth with two leaves of lettuce floating in it. How fragrant the smell of rice and soybean paste! All my past memories disappear and there is only the present. A present filled with the aroma and taste of food. I write down a list of things I'd like to eat and follow the cooking instructions for them in my mind. I am in the process of reentering the world of the living. The fast has lasted for about three weeks, which means I'll need about ten days to recover.

Once recovery is over and I return to the usual prison routine, my appetite returns to normal and I still feel hungry after every meal. I've spent the coldest month here passing from hungry to freezing and back again, which makes my body think it is in danger. I've lost seven or eight kilos and feel like a deflated balloon. Lunar New Year approaches, a time when the saltiest of last year's kimchi is bottoming out.

At feeding time, I take out my white plastic rice bowl, stew bowl, side dish bowl, and the sleek wooden spoon and chopsticks that I asked the carpentry inmates to make for me, and I sit in wait by the food hole. The cart comes, the food hole opens, and the steaming rice and stew and side dishes are served. There's nothing more to come, but I don't close the food hole right away, waiting a moment just in case. Then, I start eating. I sit with my face to the wall and shove a spoonful in my mouth, chewing without a thought in my mind. As a courtesy, the guard on shift puts on some music. It's just an old cassette player on the desk that plays the same tracks over and over again, but no one complains. Because no one can hear it. I hear only a low murmur and the sound of eating from the other cells. It's a sacred moment, as in a house of prayer.

One snowy evening, I was eating my bowl of rice mixed with lukewarm stew when I suddenly gasped and began to cry. What did I see? A calendar with all the months printed on one page hung on the wall in front of me, the kind distributed by religious organizations to the prisoners. Under the picture of a sheep-herding Jesus with a halo and staff were the words: "The Lord is my shepherd; I shall not want. He maketh me to lie down in green pastures: he leadeth me beside the still waters."

What made me sob was not the words or the picture but the countless X-marks on the calendar. The days I had spent in there was time that had no meaning. There were so many crossed-out days where I had struggled with all my might to make something happen, to protect something at all costs. But what had I really managed to protect? A shred of meat in our stew, a little bit more time for exercise, loosening the censorship of our letters, allowing forbidden books to be checked out without special permission, demanding that officers punish a guard for assault, putting on a show of resistance every holiday or memorial day—all of these gains were struggles to hold on to the least of what made me myself. But even these new conditions, procured sometimes through hunger strikes, would fall away and things would return to what they used to be each time the seasons, and the people of the prison, changed.

9

Lost

1956–66

Where did I get my tendency to distance myself from other people and things in general? I was capable of showing different versions of myself to different people, much like the Monkey King, who can pluck a few hairs from his sideburns and blow on them to create doppelgängers of himself. As a child, I'd enjoyed playing alone, whispering characters into life and dressing up in order to see new people reflected in the mirror. I read all sorts of books on the sly while keeping my impressions to myself. I spent a lot of time alone because I didn't feel as if anyone in the house shared my interests—not my mother, my two older sisters, or my much younger brother.

The Gyeongsang Province kids used to tease me with a sort of rhyming curse, "*Seoulnaegi damanaegi*," which literally meant "city slicker onion," but referred to the fact that I was a lazy fool whom they could not figure out, no matter how they peeled at my layers. I still remember an upperclassman in middle school named Shin Wu-seok, whose eyes flashed as he hissed, bewilderingly, "You can't fool me, you're an Eleven-Faced Guanyin." But I was neither an onion nor a Guanyin. Just a coward who'd realized he could never truly connect with anyone. The me that I showed to the world was whoever I thought the other person wanted to see. And sometimes I surprised them by showing the opposite of what they wanted. It was, in a sense, my way of avoiding hurt.

One day at school, I was informed that my father had passed away. I left class early, and as my train crossed the Han River, I burst into tears. My poor father . . . He never had managed to rebuild the nest egg that was stolen from us before the war, but he did leave enough for all four of us to continue our studies. He must have exhausted himself, never letting on to anyone, in the effort to keep us fed and alive during the war years. I still remember the tears in his eyes when we stood in the middle school sports field and they announced my school admission. It was for him, perhaps, a moment where self-pity and the anxieties of his responsibilities toward his family collided.

The first thing I felt in that exclusive Seoul school was the self-consciousness of having come from the margins, at least in terms of education. The boys enrolled there had all come from top schools in Seoul and were better at their studies than I was, clever as hell and good-looking to boot. I felt intimidated throughout the first semester, and my grades confirmed my mediocrity—I'd been buried in the middle of the class rankings, invisible and insignificant. I became the class clown around this time. I made my classmates laugh and practiced making funny faces in the mirror. Anytime I was absent from class, my friends would say to me the day after, "Class was boring without you."

But the class clown is always in a precarious position. If he stops working on his act, he may find he's become a tedious has-been overnight. He might win a sympathy laugh or two, but the class clown isn't thought of as important. His loneliness is frequently ignored.

When my voice began to change, I yearned to become a real man. This longing also came from not wanting to be the child of a widow—I wanted to be my father's son. A male adult with a strong sense of self who didn't show others what he thought or felt, someone who, depending on the listener, might utter a few effective words, but no more.

As the chaos of postwar reconstruction began to abate somewhat, the availability of book sets and pocket editions soared. I collected books instead of borrowing them from the market shelf. There were many translated world literature series, as well as various nonfiction classics of Western and Eastern philosophy. I also began reading magazines.

Around the end of the year, stationery stores would sell thick daily planners with childish inspirational quotes at the bottom of each page. I used those to jot down short thoughts or poems. But I never showed my writing to anyone. The schools were enforcing a one-student, one-talent educational program where you could enroll in a special class during special activities hour, but I never joined the literary club and instead chose swimming or water polo. I never went within arm's length of the literary club in high school either, opting for the hiking club. I just felt that the more you cared about something, the more you needed to keep a certain distance from it. More than anything else, the thought of gazing at the moon or a flower and striking a pose as I held my pen aloft, poised to write, made my flesh crawl. Later, when I entered the real world, this developed into a yearning for the act of writing and the act of living to become one and the same.

I wasn't naturally antisocial. Student life, from the middle-school entrance track in the sixth grade through all three years of middle school, consisted of taking monthly exams to compete for a higher class ranking. On top of which I was forced to wear a Japanese-era school uniform and cap over my hair, shorn to a regulation stubble, and every morning we were required to meet with the upperclassmen prefects and disciplinary teacher for instruction. We had to do inspection parades in military formation as part of the Korean National Defense Student Defense Corps every Monday.

One evening during the second year, my monthly exam ranking was so bad that my mother demanded I go back to school that very minute to write down the names of all the students above me. "You seem to have no idea how badly you're doing!"

344

It was already dark outside. I was starving, exhausted from the hour-long commute home, and dying to lie down for a moment. Returning to school at that hour meant multiple bus and tram transfers. The school's steel gates were closed. The guardhouse light was on, but the injured veteran who was our groundskeeper had gone out on patrol and was nowhere in sight. After staring up at the three-story brick building that loomed like a monster before me, I went to the small shop in front of the school and bought some matches. Whenever I recall that night, I wonder why I thought to buy matches but no candle.

I slunk along the wall around the school trying to find a good spot to climb over, when I spotted a wheelbarrow leaning up against it; on the other side was the swimming pool. Standing on the wheelbarrow, I managed to hoist myself to the top of the wall, but landed badly on the other side and scraped my palm on the cement. Sucking at the graze as I passed the swimming pool, I pushed at the main door only to find it opened easily. Finally, I stood in front of the results posted by the teachers' lounge. There was a column of mimeographed names and rankings; I figured my name would be somewhere at the end of that long sheet of paper. Why didn't it occur to me, like it would have for any sensible kid frustrated at the school's authorities, to just tear that stupid thing up then and there?

I took out paper and pencil, struck a match, and read the first names on the list. I managed to scribble them down in the dark, strike another match, and read the next name and rank. Once I got the hang of it, almost burning my fingers several times, I got into a rhythm of memorizing and writing down the names of two students per match.

"Who's there!"

I heard a shout and saw the groundskeeper limping towards me with a flashlight in his hand. He shone the light over me from head to toe, glanced at the rankings list, and said, "What are you doing here?" No wonder he thought something strange was going on: from outside he'd seen a faint light going on and off in the school corridor.

"I'm writing down the rankings and scores. My mother told me to."

He shone his flashlight at the paper in my hand and the name tag on my chest, and sighed.

"Your mother, she must be some lady. D'you have any idea what time it is?"

We moved after I passed my high school entrance exams. Mother worked hard to eke out the money that Father had left, trying out businesses and selling things. She was planning to build a new house for us, and go to newly built neighborhoods to buy or rent market lots. Every night she would stay up late drawing plans for the house. It was on a hill and had five whole bedrooms. My sisters had graduated from prestigious all-girls' high schools and were now attending prestigious universities, almost completely independent as they earned most of their tuition and expenses through part-time work.

My siblings and I got separate bedrooms once we moved into the new house, and mine was a quiet room at the far end of the hallway. I read many books in those days. I rediscovered the Western classics of the nineteenth and twentieth centuries, and I also began writing fiction. I wrote in a college spiral-bound notebook with a ballpoint pen; sometimes I stayed up all night writing. At first, I got worried about going to school when my window started to grow light, but eventually I just didn't bother with sleeping at all and would go directly to school. This led to constant dozing off and jolting awake during morning classes. Mother picked up on it eventually and barged in one night, snatching away my notebook. She read some of it and set it on fire in front of me. I watched the notebook burn, feeling my heart about to explode. My mother, widowed early with four children to raise, had set my rebellion ablaze with her expectations of how an eldest son should behave.

I began going to school with only the books I wanted to read, rather than with my textbooks. During lessons I would secretly read a book spread open on my lap. My grades were a mess at the end of the year, but the first short story I submitted won an award in a student literary journal, and after that I got another story into a college literary magazine. Soon, everyone in the school knew I was a fiction writer. But Mother, far from praising me, became ever more adamant that I should not do the one thing I really wanted to do.

"Look at your eldest uncle. Even that spineless man can get by, despite how hard things are right now, thanks to his medical skills. Writing is a hobby for children. You're supposed to drop it when you grow up, or else you'll end up a loafer, ruin the lives of the people around you, and destroy yourself with drink."

The first short story I wrote was titled "Lamenting fate," about Tae-geum, the girl who had worked for us before leaving to start a family of her own. My next story was called "The day I got out of prison," based on the story of the older brother of one of the kids in our neighborhood. I wrote it from the point of view of a boy who returns home after being in juvenile detention for some minor offense. I wrote many other short stories and observations of varying lengths in notebooks throughout my high school years.

As I mentioned before, it was on the swimming and water polo teams in middle school that I made full use of my experience playing in the waters of the Mapo River and its tributaries every summer. I even won awards and set records in national competitions for the hundred- and two-hundred-meter freestyle. There was a swimming pool at school but it wasn't regulation size for water polo, so I mostly went to the Han River to practice, which involved taking a rented boat out into the middle of the river and floating about for two to three hours. My face and body tanned dark as a seal, and kids started calling me "Mr. Dark."

The Literary Club kids were soft and quiet, like girls, calmer and more mature than I was. Most sports clubs are the same in how they attract students who like getting into trouble. I naturally had more friends among the sporty kids than the literary ones. We went site training at natural pools in Anyang and Gwangnaru, and later went to Mallipo Beach together as well; it was the first time I had gone on a ten-day trip with friends, which made it feel like freedom.

My high school hiking club, like many others at the time, still followed the Japanese occupation–era tradition of upperclassmen escorting lowerclassmen on rock- and ice-climbing trips. I befriended two very different boys around then. There was a hill to the right of the school gates that we called Oriole Hill. From early spring to early summer, golden orioles would fly from branch to branch and sing their bright and beautiful songs. In May, students brought their lunch boxes to picnic on benches near where the acacias bloomed. After lunch, I would stretch out on the bench and read. One day, a boy in the same year as me came up to my bench and asked what I was reading. It happened to be Albert Camus's *Nuptials*. "You mean that guy who hates everyone?" he said, which told me that he'd read Camus, too. I was surprised, but I immediately got what he meant. "Yeah, he's like that. His short stories, too."

He was holding Rilke's *Notebooks of Malte Laurids Brigge*, a piece of semi-autobiographical fiction. "Westerners must all live alone, or something."

This was Ahn Jong-gil. Jong-gil later introduced me to his close friend Gwang-gil, who was short and so wrinkled that he already looked like an old man. Both of them had been in literary clubs since middle school and wrote poetry that they published in school newsletters and magazines. He asked me why I wasn't in the Literary Club, and I replied that it looked boring.

Gwang-gil was not only part of the Literary Club but also on the staff of the school English-language newspaper. His older brother was a reporter, one reason why he knew so much about what was going on in the world. He talked about the dictatorship of the Liberal Party administration and their repression of the opposition, the execution of Cho Bong-am, who had once been a presidential candidate, and Dr. Chough Pyung-ok's Democratic Party.

Their parents, like mine, had been educated in the colonial era, but now they were living in poor neighborhoods on the outskirts of Seoul. I didn't see Jong-gil or Gwang-gil that often, but when I did, we traded books or went to the library after school to check out books together.

There was a boy I befriended in Hiking Club named Taek. At this club, the upperclassmen trained the new members in rock climbing on Saturday afternoons. The first route they took us on was the rock face on Mount Inwangsan. You went up an incline that kept getting steeper, becoming almost vertical at one point, and then, past a short chimney where two walls split, there was a brief overhang. You had to get over the overhang to reach the relatively easy track that led to the summit.

The freshmen, out on their first training expedition, were often defeated by this part of the course. The upperclassmen put a lot of slack into the belay line on purpose and wouldn't pull the rope taut until the trembling climbers, arms and legs outstretched on the rock face, became exhausted and started sliding down. If a freshman couldn't make the summit after three tries, the day would end with a group punishment and they would have to attempt the mountain again the next week.

Taek, who was a year above me, joined me on my way home one day. He was nicknamed "Pig" because his prominent forehead and thick lips made him look like a wild boar. His father worked in construction and stayed many nights outside of Seoul; later a stepmother moved in and gave birth to a little stepsibling. After the first day of training, he took me to a tavern near the shack he lived in with his family by Seoul Station. We drank two kettles of *makgeolli* together. I picked up on the fact that

Taek was interested in literature, too. I had the impression that he wrote poems in his spare time.

"Hey, that story, 'The day I got out of prison,' whose experience was that?" he asked.

"I heard it from an older kid in our neighborhood."

Taek nodded and said, "I'm glad you joined the Hiking Club."

I didn't say anything. He added, "Because home and school, it's all a mess, but the mountains are always good."

Taek and I were a year apart in school. We didn't talk much but somehow became good friends. We went rock climbing every weekend in the mountains near Seoul. It was always a relief to get away from school and camp in the mountains with friends. There were nights I couldn't sleep because of the moonlight glowing through the tent or the pattering of rain on the canvas. The clouds would rise slowly above the trees and wrap themselves around the peaks before scattering when we woke at dawn, shivering with cold, and lit a fire to make breakfast. Once, I woke on a summit to a sea of clouds beneath my feet and almost took a flying leap into them.

My Hiking Club upperclassmen would kill me if they knew this, but there was a winter evening when heavy snow fell as I climbed Suninbong Peak. Like magic, I could see every crack and hold of the rock. The rock never felt cold, even when I was grabbing it with bare hands, and the wind was also warm. The moon hung high above Suninbong. The snow-covered forest looked as if it were under a white blanket. I climbed that rock face without a belay, and if my upperclassmen knew, they would've ripped me a new one.

During lunch one day on Oriole Hill, Taek brought another upperclassman to see me. His name was Kim Seong-jin. He made an impression with the dyed, big-pocketed American military pants he wore instead of uniform trousers. As soon as Taek introduced me he said without preamble: "Look at his eyes. He looks like a troublemaker." I just smiled, and he demanded:

"Why are you doing that bullshit mountain climbing? Are you getting something for it?"

Taek and Seong-jin had formed a club of their own. They tracked down books, wrote on the sly, debated, and generally studied things that were not taught in school.

Seong-jin was an artist; his drawing skills were so good that he won many awards around the beginning of his high school career, even ranking in a national competition. He always had a sketchbook with him and would draw whatever he saw, whether person, street, or scenery. He had liked his middle school art teacher, Mr. Choi, a contemporary of the painter Lee Jung-seob. Whenever Seong-jin spoke of Mr. Choi, he referred to his style as *insaengpa* (life movement) instead of *insangpa* (impressionist movement). One night, Mr. Choi had gotten drunk and was killed by a passing bus as he walked up the hill road outside Jahamun Gate. Seong-jin was quick to embrace the new in most areas, but hated avant-garde artists. He seemed very confident of his skills. His father had left his mother and him a long time ago and was living with another wife somewhere. His mother struggled to make ends meet. His two older brothers worked their way through school by being live-in tutors, and Seong-jin had no choice but to live with his younger sister and irritable, nagging mother.

My friends were mature for their age and given to reflection, but they were far from model students. They weren't bad kids, but they were delinquent in the eyes of the previous generation. Taek, doubtless due to the neighborhood he lived in, had "graduated" from the local brothels when he was just a middle school student; he said that whenever he spotted a woman he knew on her way to the bathhouse with her plastic basin under one arm, he'd get an itch that wouldn't go away until he'd gone to her place to wait for her to return, fresh and clean from the bath.

Whenever we visited the foreign bookstores that dotted the path between Gwanghwamun and Jongno, Seong-jin would make a beeline for the Japanese photo books and pocket editions.

He liked to shoplift the photo books, which were the most expensive in the shop due to their high-quality paper and color printing. He would take two down at a time, slip one into his bag, and reshelve the other. When the store owner was distracted by another customer, he would sweep into his bag two to three volumes from a display just out of sight. He put books into my bag as well. My heart pounded and I wanted to run out of there as fast as I could, but Seong-jin took his time, leisurely perusing other books on display near the owner and even saying goodbye as he left.

Later, Taek and Seong-jin took turns running away from home with me. My mother never forgot their names, not even in old age, and whenever she happened to see a photograph of them, she would launch into curses. "Those little punks! Are they even making a living these days?"

Compared to hanging out with these upperclassmen, my Literary Club friends Gwang-gil and Jong-gil seemed nice and sedate, to the point of boring. But Gwang-gil frequently sought me out; through him I often saw Jong-gil as well, and we'd discuss books. I was reading the only monthly newsmagazine, *Sasanggye*, at the time, and we talked about the old critic Ham Sok Hon, who had been arrested for his writings.

~

April 11, 1960. The discovery of the body of the student Kim Ju-yul, found by a fisherman in the waters near Masan with a tear gas canister embedded in his left eye socket, turned the world upside down. He was seventeen years old, a year younger than I was, and had gone missing during the protests in Masan against Rhee Syngman's rigged election. He'd entered Masan Commercial High School on March 14, the day before he died. Every newspaper talked about this incident, and the entire country, not to mention all middle and high school students, knew about it. The discovery led to more student protests against Rhee's election and demanding a change in power through democratic means. After Korea University student protesters were attacked on April 18 by a group of thugs calling themselves the Korean Anti-communist Youth, 30,000 students took to the streets the next day. They managed to reach the presidential residence, Gyeongmudae, which wasn't far from our school, marched past the stone walls of Gyeongbokgung Palace, were met with resistance at Jeokseon-dong, and made it to the last stop on the tram line in Hyoja-dong.

That April 19, I had been dozing off all morning, and third period was about to end. Two upperclassmen came into the classroom during the break, their faces grim, and made an announcement. "We're teaming up with our fellow college students to protest all over the city. They're at the Central Government Building already and are headed for Gyeongmudae. We need to be there, too. Please join us in front of the school gates after lunch."

As we sat through fourth-period chemistry, waiting for class to end, we heard gunfire. It was one or two shots at first, no more alarming than a popgun, but soon we heard the *tak-tak-tak-tak* of continuous fire. Someone kept yelling, "Let's go, let's go," but the chemistry teacher was a young man in his first semester on the job. He still looked like a college student and kept dabbing his forehead with a handkerchief, disconcerted by the situation. "We have to finish class. No matter what happens in this world, students must study."

But despite his attempts to stop us, the trickle of students slipping out the back door suddenly turned into a river. Soon, half the class was in the corridor. We weren't really thinking of joining the protests, but the sound of guns roused our curiosity and the upperclassman's speech had stirred our hearts.

Outside, a wave of students was surging toward the school gates. But as we came down the hill, we found the steel gates firmly shut and teachers standing in front of them. "Go back, everyone, go back to your classrooms."

The upperclassmen and alumni, who wore college uniforms, were arguing with the teachers on one side and trying to galvanize us on the other. "Our friends are bleeding to death this very moment in front of Gyeongmudae! The enemy is firing at innocent citizens and students. We can't just stand by and watch!"

They pleaded and begged the teachers standing guard to open the gates, but the head disciplinarian and his colleagues did not budge. "We have an obligation to protect the students. Just look outside the gates!"

Outside the road was blocked by a barricade of woven steel poles. A jeep and some policemen were standing nearby. Undeterred, a few students had already begun to jump the brick wall some distance from the school gates.

We spent our lunchtime murmuring among ourselves and went back to our classrooms to wait it out. Finally, at around 2 p.m., we were allowed to go home—hours earlier than was normal. The teachers came out to block the streets that led to Hyoja-dong and made us go through Jeokseon-dong toward Gwanghwamun instead. We were in our usual groups of three and five when Gwang-gil spotted me. Jong-gil was by his side. Jong-gil lived near Seodaemun and Gwang-gil probably lived in Mapo.

"We found you! Wanna go see a demonstration?"

I didn't know if Gwang-gil was serious, but I immediately agreed. "Yeah, let's see what downtown is like right now."

"Those assholes, they're shooting people in broad daylight now . . ." This was from Jong-gil, normally so quiet and calm, now enraged.

The students who had been pushed toward the train tracks of Jeokseon-dong could be seen in the alleys, and as we came out to Gwanghwamun, we saw that the whole neighborhood had been overrun by protesters. They were ordinary citizens, college and high school students, and even the boys who sold newspapers and shined shoes. The sidewalks and roads were filled with people. To the left of the Central Government Building in what is now the Central Government Complex were police on horseback, standing next to the old Gyeonggi Province administrative offices, not far from the Anti-communist Youth hall. That hall was giving off black smoke as it burned, while overturned jeeps and trucks were on fire in the middle of the road. The old National Assembly building was besieged by protesters, and the *Seoul Shinmun* newspaper building across the street was aflame.

As we made our way through, the crowd of protesters kept spilling off of the sidewalks and pushing us into the roads. Occasionally, a jeep or army truck commandeered by protesters would streak by with a bloodied Korean flag fluttering from the open windows. There were can-shaped taxis remodeled from jeeps and military trucks standing in for ambulances, transporting medical school students in white gowns. A few of them carried dead bodies, while others bore injured young people wearing bloody bandages and shouting protest slogans.

A sudden roar of the crowd came from the direction of City Hall, and we were swept toward it. Protesters started throwing rocks at a police station near the stone walls of Deoksugung Palace. That station was where the police were posted every time the Liberal Party illegally dismissed the National Assembly. We started hearing gunshots as the protesters advanced. The shooting began that day from two directions in front of City Hall, and random gunfire rained down from the roof of the Seoul office of the Counter Intelligence Corps.

At the sound of gunfire, the protesters ducked and scattered in all directions. We ran as well, and I saw Gwang-gil grab Jong-gil's arm as Jong-gil fell. Suddenly, Jong-gil's head jerked back and blood splattered across Gwang-gil's shirt. Gwang-gil tried to staunch the blood with his cap and shouted, "Get a car here!"

I ran into the swiftly emptying street and waved both arms at an approaching jeep. It came to a screeching halt and someone gestured and shouted, "Get the casualty inside the car!"

Gwang-gil and I carried Jong-gil's limp body to the back of the jeep and got in. One side of my uniform was soaked in blood. The jeep sped to the Severance Hospital near Seoul Station, where a couple of college students, who had been standing by with a military-issue stretcher, quickly carried him in, only to return with him moments later.

"Why isn't he being treated?" Gwang-gil demanded.

"Can't you see?" One of them jerked his chin at Jong-gil, whose legs had already gone stiff.

We went with them to the corridor where the dead bodies were laid down in a row and sat on the floor. In the sudden shock and grief of losing a friend, we lacked the words to console each other. All we could do was sit a distance apart and wipe our tears with our fists.

Things moved quickly from that point. Martial rule was declared in Seoul and every other city in the country, protests continued all night in the outskirts, and in some places, citizens fought the riot police with stolen weapons. Politicians resigned in droves because of the rigged election, Vice President Lee Ki-poong among them. When college professors joined the protests, all of Seoul's citizens took to the streets, night after night. Rhee Syngman finally stepped down as president, and Lee Ki-poong's entire family, including the son Lee had Rhee adopt as his own, committed suicide. Rhee himself was exiled to Hawaii a month after stepping down. Jong-gil's death and the citizens' protest that day in front of City Hall affected me greatly for the rest of my life.

We put together a posthumous poetry collection for Jong-gil during the long break in our studies. It was published under the title "Spring, night, stars." Seong-jin, the artist, drew the cover, which I still remember to this day. He described it in these terms to me: "This hand, emaciated to the bone, is the poet's hand. Above it is the crushed moon, symbolizing the world of the ideal, and the hand is outstretched toward it."

It was summer vacation. College students volunteered at farms, like during the Japanese occupation, but high school students went on "penniless trips." Because the country was still quite poor, most students couldn't travel very far and would end up close to where they lived.

When I proposed to Gwang-gil that we take a penniless trip, he upped the ante by suggesting we plan together with some cohorts, upperclassmen, and graduates, which would allow us to travel further.

I told Mother about the trip, and to my great surprise she immediately gave her assent and even told me to let her know if I needed anything. I was planning on going with or without permission, of course, but I had not expected her to end up giving me some emergency cash for the journey.

Gwang-gil slept over at our house the night before we left. The day had been humid and overcast, and sure enough, monsoon rains began to fall. Even now, I get restless before leaving on distant journeys. I woke at dawn to the sound of rain and tossed and turned for a while before getting up to go to the bathroom. There was a banging sound coming from the kitchen. I opened the door a crack to find my mother sitting on the floor and pounding away at something in the iron mortar. She had risen at dawn to make *misutgaru* roast grain powder and *injeolmi* rice cake for our trip.

In the morning, I packed the food she had made and set off with Gwang-gil. Our plan was to ride the train for free by avoiding the rail workers. The whistle-stop that was Noryangjin Station was surrounded by empty streets, making it easy to hitch a ride as long as you avoided the platform. Although transport in those days was obviously better than during the evacuations of the Korean War, when it took several days to get anywhere, trains were still almost the only way to travel outside the city.

We hopped aboard the Gyeongbu Line all-stop train, which indeed stopped at every tiny station and was slow to start. The cars were so crowded that people were stuffed into the passageways, and one person was even perched on an empty luggage rack above the seats. We sat on the steps in the doorway of the train.

There were other college and high school students dressed for penniless trips. We gazed at the passing scenery, wanting to remember every moment. We saw wide fields, steel bridges over rivers, little thatch-roofed villages against faraway mountains, farmers at work, children splashing around in irrigation ditches, the rickety shacks congregating on the outskirts of towns, and the ruins of old factories destroyed during the war.

We still needed a nominal destination, so Gwang-gil and I decided to take a tour of the historic Baekje sights and go down to Jeolla Province to visit Gwang-gil's country folk in Sunchang. Nearby in Namwon was Seong-jin, who had told us he was staying with his grandmother there. Further down south in Mokpo, we planned to take a boat to Jeju Island, then return to the mainland through Busan, see the historic Silla city of Gyeongju, and take the Gyeongbu Line back to Seoul. A very academic, historical trip.

It took us all day just to reach Daejeon; we jumped off the train as it slowed down coming into the station. The rain that had fallen since the afternoon was still pouring down, so we threw on our army-issue ponchos. The rain soaked into our student caps, making our heads stink with old sweat.

There weren't many cars on the road to Gongju. Gwang-gil and I sat on the stoop of an empty farmhouse, with our legs poking out from under the eaves, and ate the *injeolmi* my mother had made us. Frogs were croaking all around as the rain mercilessly drenched our legs.

We were lucky to find a place to stay that night at another farmer's house. It was past dinner time but the farmer's wife gave us barley rice, radish kimchi, and pickled shrimp to eat. While we poured water into the rice and scarfed it all down, the farmer sat next to us and kept saying things like "That Dr. Rhee Syngman, why did he have to go all the way to Hawaii? It would have been better for him to stay here. Oh well, those young students died, a lot of them, too, I suppose he can't stay in Korea now."

We would continue to bump into older or old men in places such as barbershops or noodle stalls who would bring up politics in a condescending or critical way. They were probably asking us, as young students, what our political leanings were— but we didn't read the papers too closely either, so we didn't really have precise opinions. Because there were so few educated people outside the cities in those days, I guess they expected high school students to know more about what was going on in the world than they did.

I don't know why we were so passionate about visiting each historic spot. It must have come from some desire to know every corner of the country. We went on to Buyeo, where we climbed Nakhwaam Rock, and on to the battlegrounds that were said to still be haunted by the ghosts of dead soldiers. Then we headed to Nonsan, to see the Eunjin Mireuk statue of Buddha in Gwanchok Temple. The sound of the wind as we sat under the crumbling stone towers of Baekje was so sorrowful and lonely that Gwang-gil and I sat on the grass for two hours without exchanging a word.

One day we walked for miles down a darkening, deserted national highway where poplar trees flanking the unpaved road looked like brooms planted upside down. Our upper bodies were dry thanks to the ponchos, but our lower bodies were soaked to our underwear. The heel of Gwang-gil's army boot came off, but he limped on. Whenever we passed the small, poor villages by the road, we felt ready to follow the light of any faint lantern and fall asleep atop a pile of straw.

We walked and walked and finally reached Jeonju, where we spent the night at the house of one of Gwang-gil's uncles. The sound of train horns in nearby Jeonju Station was so forlorn that I couldn't fall asleep.

Gwang-gil and I dropped by Namwon for Seong-jin to join us. We had already let him know by postcard that we were coming; he said he'd been counting the seconds until we arrived at his grandmother's house. He grabbed a simple box of water-colors and a few sketchbooks, and we set out. After the somewhat heavy mood of being alone with Gwang-gil, having the hyperactive artist Seong-jin around was like seeing a black-and-white world turn Technicolor.

Gwang-gil's Sunchang country home was bubbling over with cousins who had come visiting for the summer. Gwang-gil's father was the eldest son, but he had left home early on and not been back once since the war. Seeing how he had never managed to land a job and relied completely on his poor wife's support, I wonder now if Korea's history of colonialism and war had left him traumatized. I also remember meeting Gwang-gil's deranged uncle in that house. He grew his hair and beard long, like a wise man of the mountains, and went about the fields and hills in traditional *hanbok* clothes. He had studied in Japan like Gwang-gil's father, and it was said he had "gone crazy because he was too smart." He would return home at night, and his perfectly sane and kind wife or sister-in-law would make him dinner; once he'd eaten, he'd go out and sleep in any old place. He had been a partisan in the war, and Gwang-gil's grandfather had to liquidate a good deal of his fortune in order to save his life. I once jumped out of my skin when he crept up on us and suddenly stroked our hair and cheeks.

Gwang-gil's grandfather presided over a household of scores of people, and he spent all day in a corner room of the men's *sarangchae* annex looking through old books written in *hanja* characters. But he was also curious about new things and once asked me to read him one of my short stories, which I did by the light of a lantern. He listened to the end, and said, "Good writing, of course, should be short and clear."

One day, the three of us took a fishnet from the house to a tributary stream of the Seomjin River. The water didn't reach over our knees in most places, but there were spots where it was one *gil* deep. Only Gwang-gil knew how to throw this particular net, but even he wasn't very good at it. After a couple of awkward attempts by Gwang-gil, Seong-jin, who was quick on the uptake, took the net and threw it in a wide arc into the air. When we pulled it up, we found three or four sweetfish trapped in it. Seong-jin got better and better at casting the net. Soon, our pail was filled with sweetfish and minnow, and we picked perilla leaves from a nearby field and ate the fish sashimi-style along with garlic, bean paste, and chili paste we'd brought with us. All we had to do was slice off the heads and tails of the sweetfish, wash out the innards, and dip them in the paste.

Seong-jin groused about drinking, so Gwang-gil went to a little store near the entrance of the village and brought us bottles of soju. We got drunk and jumped into the stream and ran along its sandy banks naked. We saw groups of people passing by across the stream—voters on their way to the July elections after the events of the April Revolution. The entire village and even the neighboring ones immediately began talking about a group of boys running around by the stream, sloshed and naked in broad daylight. Gwang-gil's uncle heard the gossip, as did Gwang-gil's grandfather.

We had passed the long hot summer afternoon and returned to the house for dinner when the women of the house, whispering in fearful tones, said Gwang-gil's grandfather had been calling for us. We had to kneel down with Gwang-gil at the *sarangchae*'s porch and be roundly scolded by the old man.

After dinner, we were sitting on the straw mat in the yard and talking when Gwang-gil's uncle approached us with a bottle of *makgeolli* and said, "If you want to drink, you've got to drink at home. Out here in the country, people are always watching. Also, out of respect to the good nourishment that is drink, please keep your clothes on when you do."

We drank several bowlfuls into the night and stretched out on the bench and mat as we gazed at the stars and sang a few songs before falling asleep. But the night air was a little chilly, and the swarming mosquitos made it impossible to keep sleeping. We crawled into the grandfather's room at dawn, grabbed the mosquito net, and fell asleep on the heated floor again.

Seong-jin's face was quite a sight when we woke up in the morning. It was so swollen from the bites that his entire face looked flattened. We all wondered aloud who this stranger could be as we roared with laughter.

A few days later, along with boisterous country folk and their pigs, chickens, wooden bowls, and baskets radiating the smell of fish, we boarded the train to Mokpo that traveled as slowly as if it were caught in time. Seong-jin held a sketchbook half the size of a notebook in one hand and drew the passing scenery with the other. We fell in love with the sea. At a food stall on the ferryboat dock, we had a few shots of soju along with some grilled clams and sashimi.

The waves were so strong when we crossed the Jeju Strait in the boat from Mokpo that almost all the passengers were delirious from seasickness. Inside the wide, auditorium-like space reserved in the hold for third-class passengers, everyone rolled this way and that like so many stockfish. The first- and second-class cabins weren't much better, just a few rooms tacked on to the crew members' space on deck, where the passengers sprawled out flat on tatami mats. The three of us weren't seasick at all; on the contrary, we digested our food so well that we were unbearably hungry in the middle of the night. Seong-jin and I rolled with the pitching boat and snatched up food that had been dropped by those too ill to eat. There was soju, some bread, and even a cracked watermelon. Once we'd crossed the dark ocean waves into dawn, we could make out the faraway triangle of Mount Halla. We could see it clear as day, but it must have been farther than it looked because the boat didn't pull in to the western docks until well after sunrise.

The harbor has changed a lot since then with the construction of breakwaters, but at the time the tide surged right up to the docks like river water. An old junk, sailed in and summarily abandoned by Chinese refugees, tilted and wavered in the water. Farther inland, Jeju's freshwater, which came from underground, running through the gigantic water filter that is Mount Halla, attracted women who washed laundry and dishes wherever there was a spring. One of the young women fetching water was so beautiful that Seong-jin and I talked about her for a long time afterward.

The whole country was in postwar ruins, but it was worse the further south you traveled. The only people eating regular meals were salaried workers in the cities or salespeople. Many farmers were tenants who did not own the land they worked, and their families would go hungry every spring.

Jeju was populated by many refugees who had come during the war and not managed to return. A few years before the Korean War, there was a violent suppression of communist guerrillas at Mount Halla. I myself did not learn of the Jeju Uprising until the 1980s, when I saw the evidence and heard eyewitness accounts of the revolt and massacre, and how the fighting had continued right up to the final days of the war in 1953.

I still can't forget a certain female high school student we met in Gwaneum Temple. That rascal Gwang-gil insisted we climb Mount Halla, so we ended up hiking for a whole day up to a pavilion at Gwaneumsa. The arid, rocky path seemed almost flat, but apparently we were over 1,000 meters above sea level. I got so thirsty that we stopped at a hut near a watermelon patch to buy a melon and rest our legs. This gave me an upset stomach and I was ready to collapse by the time we reached the temple. Gwang-gil, of course, was eager to make the summit, and even the normally lazy Seong-jin was game, which left me waiting for them alone at the temple. Just a little while later, the sky suddenly darkened and a mist-like rain began to fall. I was too exhausted to move from the muddy floor of the pavilion.

I saw someone heading toward me through the mist. The figure was taller than me, wide-shouldered, carrying a backpack, and wearing a military-issue jacket with the hood drawn firmly down. They'd obviously just come down from the peak.

"What are you doing here by yourself?" I had assumed it was a man, so the female voice caught me off guard. I told her I was waiting for my friends, and she asked if I was sick. I replied that I had an upset stomach. She said the water was the only good thing around here and that I should drink a lot of it. It turned out she was a year older than us.

"Something big just went down in Seoul, huh?"

"Yes. My friend died. He was shot . . ."

"It's all bullshit when they say the history books will talk about it. The people must make an effort to remember."

Though I didn't understand what she meant at the time, her words stayed with me. She seemed as mature as any proper adult. I asked her if she came up here often, and she said she climbed Mount Halla once a week. We talked about the mountains and the sea. Her family had once lived here in the mountains but after their neighborhood was destroyed in the fighting, they moved to the city. When we finished talking, she reshouldered her pack and disappeared down the slope. They say that experiencing a tragedy takes away your innocence—she was clearly grown up. I learned later that everyone from Jeju is separated by only one or two degrees from people who lived through unspeakable suffering.

By the time we reached Gyeongju, having taken the ferry back to Busan from Jeju Island, the station and administrative offices there were struggling with an influx of penniless student travelers like us. There was nowhere for us to scrounge a decent meal. As the rest of the peninsula still lay in ruins, Gyeongju had become known as a class trip destination; everywhere we looked, there were pairs of students. That evening, the three of us sat in a grove of pine trees on the side of a mountain and watched the sun set. The light from the same sun as yesterday was weakening over the millennia-old stone towers and grave mounds.

Gwang-gil insisted we cross Mungyeong Saejae Provincial Park on foot, making Seong-jin and I grumble as we got off the train. But luck was with us as we found ourselves treated to a picnic lunch in Mungyeong. While walking across an irrigation ditch, we happened upon a group of farmers eating beneath a giant zelkova tree; they gestured and called to us. They shared with us their rice mixed with barley and side dishes made from pumpkin, eggplant, bean sprouts, young turnip kimchi, and chili peppers dipped in bean paste. The *makgeolli* they drank was more refreshing than any soda pop. I would be given such an outdoor lunch again during field training in my military conscript days, but even this tradition disappeared with the modernization of the 1970s.

By the time we returned home, I felt I'd left my boyhood behind. I couldn't fathom the idea of returning to school, to a world that tried to control me with rules and grades.

~

My friends and I began going to the European classical music parlors in Myeong-dong around this time. There was Dolce, where our literary forebears of the 1950s hung out during the war and the national division, and Donghwa, which was located near the Savoy Hotel behind the Chinese embassy. It later changed its name to SS, but we thought that sounded like the initials for the Nazi guards, so we kept on calling it by its former name.

At Donghwa, I befriended boys who were a year or two older; we all treated one another as equals despite the age difference. They, too, seemed to be of a literary bent, although no one really flaunted it. We threw off our school uniforms and put on work clothes or windbreakers and visited bars together where we casually sat around with the adults, smoking.

At the end of the winter, I was hit with some shocking news: we would be notified of our grades and class rankings before the new school year started, and we would have to get them signed off by our parents.

Our homeroom teacher called me and a few other boys separately for interviews. When I entered the meeting room, he was looking unusually serious. "You didn't sit your midterms last semester, correct? Do you know how many days you were absent?"

I stood there, silent.

In the fall semester of 1960, I'd started skipping classes at the drop of a hat. Not that I wasn't interested in learning—I just didn't want to learn what school had to teach me. Most of the days I was absent, I went to the National Library near Midopa Department Store. My homeroom teacher declared that I had flunked. He told me to bring my parents to school, because I was to be held back a year.

Everything went white; my mind was a complete blank. I had never been a bad pupil, and even when I was lazy about getting the grades, I always had this sense that I was really an excellent student underneath. I felt like I'd fallen off the assembly line and was deemed defective before I could even be brought to market. I could almost see the rough fields and shadowy back alleys that I would haunt for the rest of my life.

I stumbled out of school and kept walking as I grew more and more devastated. A group of female students walked by in a row, giggling among themselves. I was going the other way and couldn't bear to raise my head. I was to tread a different path from them from now on.

In the new year, my friends all moved up to the senior class while I stayed behind. A crushing humiliation began from the moment I got on the bus to school. I felt like I was diseased or had something terrible smeared on my face. The nightmare of those few months dominated the rest of my adolescence.

It was May 1961. Around the time we left Yeongdeungpo and moved into the house we'd built in Sangdo-dong, the May 16 coup d'état took place. I was eighteen. Since then, everything important in my life began occurring around the month of May, and my friends and I began to refer to this phenomenon as my "May Crisis."

About a month before the coup, my mother's cousin once removed and his folks who lived in the Samgakji area of Seoul spent the night. They were pious Christians who went to an evangelical church. They said that something big was about to happen and that they needed to cross the Han River and sleep at our place. This was not even a year after the April Revolution, when the postwar Democratic Party administration was still very powerful. We were so unaccustomed to democracy that there was chaos on the streets from daily protests. People kept whispering among themselves, "Wait and see, trouble is coming."

Finally, on the day of the coup, we heard the sound of gunfire all night around the Han River Bridge, and the radio began reporting a coup d'état at dawn. I was still going to school at the time and was passing downtown on the bus. There were tanks stationed here and there and armed soldiers guarding certain buildings and road crossings. Gwang-gil and I sat on Oriole Hill during lunch, talking about the political situation. Ordinary citizens who didn't know any better were saying, "This will be an improvement, it's good the incompetent Democratic Party has fallen." But seizing power by force would eventually turn those weapons against the people. My friend Taek dropped out of school around then, while Seong-jin and Sang-deuk applied for leaves of absence and disappeared.

About a week after the coup, Taek and I met at Donghwa. He showed up in workman's clothes and a towel stinking of sweat around his neck. He was working on the construction site of the UNESCO building in Myeong-dong, which was being built through foreign aid. He said he was moving to the mountains the next day, to this place he'd found. "It's not far. It's a really cool cave. I'm going to take a load of books with me and read all day and try to write something."

I yearned to quit school after failing my previous year. Mother was preventing me from taking the decision, but Taek's words struck a chord in my heart. "I'm going with you," I told him. "I can't stand school anymore." Now that I had decided, I felt a rush of relief.

I returned home late that night and turned off the light as if I were going to sleep. At dawn I went out into the yard and packed my bag with pots and utensils, then raided the kitchen for rice and other food. Finally, I chose the books I would take with me, which made the bag twice as heavy.

I wrote my mother a short letter before leaving home. I said that I did not have the confidence to attend school in the state I was in, that I was going to stay at a temple until I felt like myself again, that she shouldn't worry about me. I folded it, wrote "To Mother" in easily legible letters before placing it on my desk, and left the house in the still-dark dawn with my heavy bag on my back. I had some cash wedged between the pages of a book and wore a watch that I could sell in an emergency, enough to survive on for about three months.

Later on, Mother said this had been the hardest time for her since Father passed away. "You weren't a little boy anymore, but you weren't a man yet either. I didn't worry much about your older sisters. But they say boys your age really need their fathers."

Taek's cave was in a valley behind Hwagye Temple in the Suyuri neighborhood. There was a little path next to a clear, roughly flowing stream, but it was mostly out of the way of hikers. We climbed the ridge behind Hwagyesa's main hall and reached the last hill before the valley. There were a few large boulders on top of each other on that hill; from up there, you could see the adjacent peaks of Bukhan and Dobong Mountains, the carpet of dark-green pine trees below, and the tiled roof of Hwagyesa.

There was a steep slope next to an outcrop that you had to carefully descend. The edge of the rock protruded out like the eaves of a roof; ducking under it, you found yourself in what you might call a courtyard. Inside the courtyard under the over-hang was a little space. It was surrounded by rocks and as cozy as the inside of a dolmen. I used my experience during this time to write "By the dolmen," for which I won *Sasanggye* maga-zine's new writer's prize. In other words, my life as a writer began in that secret headquarters, while in the liminal space of the end of boyhood.

The bear in the Dangun legend survived for a hundred days on nothing but mugwort and garlic, and so we were determined to hold out for three months and ten days ourselves, whether together or alone, one keeping watch in the cave when the other left.

I learned to meditate while in that cave. A young monk from Hwagyesa happened to come along and teach me meditation: how to keep my hips and spine straight, how comfortable it was to support the tailbone with a cushion of soft cloth, how I should keep my eyes half open and my gaze on an unfocused point three palm widths below knee level; how I should see my sitting body not as myself but as my house, and that it wasn't anyone else but me who was breathing in and out.

Sitting on top of the rock in the lotus position, I would first hear the sounds of night birds or the wind rustling through the pine forest, but eventually my breath would deepen and I would begin to hear nothing, my body would feel like a carapace, and the true self living inside my pupils felt as if it were staring out at an alien landscape. As time passed, I felt that I had turned into something exactly like the little stone lying next to my knee. Meditation helped me later, when I was older and in a prison cell by myself; there's nothing like it to take yourself outside of time.

Taek and I whiled away our days in that cave on the ridge of the mountain behind Hwagyesa until summer vacation approached. Whenever our supplies ran low, we couldn't bear to go back home, so we'd call on Sang-deuk, whose family was rich, or Min, or charge into their homes. We sometimes visited the boardinghouse room of a friend from the countryside, to raid his food. We called this our "supply struggle," in the parlance of war, and Taek was much more into it than I was. During those three or four months, I sent a couple of postcards to my mother to let her know I was doing fine. Mother would spend her remaining life desperately waiting for me to come back from something, especially during the Vietnam War. Eventually, her yearning seemed to have granted her some kind of special insight: I would often return from one of my sojourns away to find a special dish or two waiting for me, as if she'd known exactly when I'd be back. When I asked her about it, she replied, "I always see your father in my dreams right before you show up."

She was only in her forties at the time. Thinking back, she was still young and beautiful then. It seems amazing that she never remarried, but still managed to raise four children and send them all to college.

A few years after I married, my mother, for whatever reason, gave her daughter-in-law her old notebooks bundled up in wrapping cloth. These notebooks revealed that there was more to my mother's life than just being my mother. In fact, I discovered that Mother had once had a lover who was not my father. After my parents got married and were living in Manchuria, my father had had to retreat to a place with clean air to recover from a bout of tuberculosis. Mother went back to her parents' home where she sought out "the man," as she calls him in her notebooks; he had been studying in Japan and was a volunteer teacher in the countryside near Hwanghae Province. The record simply states she stayed there for two weeks (two whole weeks!), but it happened to be before I was born, which gave me an odd feeling.

"Maybe this gentleman is your real father?" my wife teased.

All I could do was laugh and say, "Surely not . . . Maybe Mother wanted to be a fiction writer as well when she was younger. And this is the first draft."

She must have kept those diaries during bouts of insomnia through the long nights she spent alone after my father's death. But even so, what of my memory of the man we spent an afternoon with at Changgyeongwon Garden, where my mother took me a year or two before the war broke out? Those melodramatic notebooks aside, the man had clearly said to me: "Hey kid, do you want to live with me?" and "What do you think of me moving in with you?" So was this really my mother's attempt at fiction? And what did the two of them talk about when they met at Changgyeongwon Garden, with me sitting between them?

Even as Mother celebrated the rich lifestyle she enjoyed as a newlywed in Manchuria, she also spoke of how her life had ended when she left her girlhood behind in Pyongyang. During the nights in prison when I lay unable to fall asleep, my heart would ache with belated regret at the thought of all the suffering I had caused her when I was young.

~

One day, after a stretch of living in the cave alone, I went out to the end of the subway line in Miari in the early morning and called Seong-jin. I tried reaching him at Donghwa, but they said he'd moved and gave me his new number. Seong-jin picked up when I dialed, his voice drowsy. He said he was working in a friend's art studio. I wrote down the address. The place stood out even from a distance, being the only two-story Japanese-style house in the neighborhood. The first floor was a cigarette store that doubled as a general store, with a hair salon attached. I could hear Seong-jin singing as I walked up the narrow stairway. Singing was what he did instead of calisthenics before breakfast. There was a rude picture on the door of a thumb wedged between two knuckles, with the English word "OUT" written underneath.

His apartment was one large open space, littered with paints, paint cans, and canvases, with a wooden army cot and a jerry-built chipboard table in the middle. Seong-jin must have slept on the table because there was a crumpled sleeping bag on it. His friend, who rented the place, was sitting there eating. Seong-jin introduced him to me. He had a strange name, Jang Mu, which sounded like it was taken from the subtitles of a Hong Kong period martial arts film. As I repeated it, he added, "My first name, Mu, means 'dense.'"

He was much taller than either of us and very skinny. His hair was closely cropped, and his fingers, arms, and legs were all willowy and long. Mu was preparing a one-man show. He spread his canvas on the floor and painted in his shorts, becoming covered in sweat and streaks. Mu used to stare down at the paintings and say to me, "Writing is probably much easier." To which I would retort, "Colors are easier. And sound even more so."

His paintings were, of course, abstracts. They featured blotches of pigment with little groupings of the kind of bright colors you find in traditional architecture. From the twinkle in Mu's eye to his witty comebacks, I recognized a kindred spirit and immediately took a liking to him.

"So, how's life in the cave?" Mu asked.

"I should be leaving it soon."

Mu gestured with his chin for me to follow. He led me up a small ladder in the corner right underneath the roof to an attic that was crammed with stuff. Mu bowed his head as he edged through the stacks with me close behind him. The sides of the loft were low, but there was an empty space in the middle where you could move around as long as you kept your head down. A ventilation window had wooden slats running across it instead of glass.

"I think this used to be a storage space. Before that, the second floor was a tearoom. You could use this space to work."

It was cluttered and dusty, but I could see that it would be a good space once I had done some cleaning. I answered, cautious of accepting: "It looks fine but it probably gets really hot in the summer."

"That's no problem. Just sit up here naked. All you need is a fountain pen and some paper, right? I'll make you a writing desk."

I decided to pack up the cave first and go home before moving in. The three of us drank soju late into the night. Mu, like me, was the eldest son of a widowed mother. His parents had fled South like mine, and his father had died early, too. His own house, surely enough, was losing what it used to have as his mother grew older, much like a well slowly running dry. Back then, all you needed was to exchange a few words to know someone's life story.

The next day, when Seong-jin and I got to the cave in Suyuri, we found it still empty. I left a short note, packed up, and returned home for the time being. My older sisters were still diligently attending university and Mother seemed as confident and calm as usual, but very tired at the same time. I told her I wanted to write for a bit and would be living with a friend, and then I packed up again and left. I was halfway down the hill from the house when I heard Mother calling me. I set my bags down on the slope and walked back up the hill. Mother handed something to me. "Someone gave this to me. And this . . . Don't waste it on alcohol, buy something tasty for yourself."

Mother handed me some cash and a long box. I stuffed it into my shirt pocket and left. Later I opened the box to find a fountain pen. Of course, nobody had given it to her; she would have carefully picked it out herself. She was always very good at picking things out. I almost started to cry. Perhaps this was her way of gently appeasing me, even while strongly wishing I'd abandon my useless pursuit of writing.

In the attic above Jang Mu's studio, I cleaned up the mess and put down about two *pyeong*'s worth of linoleum. Mu, as promised, built me a desk I could use while sitting on the floor, and it was so sturdy and perfect in height that I took it with me when I eventually returned home, to use exclusively for writing.

As predicted, the attic turned into a steam room in the summer. I spent those hot days reading or lolling about in the little room next to Mu's studio in return for cooking all of our meals. I returned to the attic only after the sun had gone down, to work on my writing until dawn.

Seong-jin entered his competition as planned, Mount and Mu was also nearly done with preparing for his exhibition. I had an idea for two short stories and scratched away at them before repeatedly tossing them aside. On the weekends, it was Mu who scraped together enough money to buy a few bottles of soju so we could go up the hill out back and talk about our plans for life as we got drunk.

Seong-jin actually won a prize in the competition, but his expectations must have been very high because he was still dissatisfied with the outcome. Mu smiled and said, "I'm deigning to hang out with you guys but really you're just a couple of high school students. You've done pretty well, considering."

Looking back, we were barely older than a couple of hatchlings who'd just flown the nest. And yet we were already jaded, like adults who had been through the mill. There was nothing fixed in our future, we had no skill or potential to earn money, and we had only begun to understand a little about our talents.

One day, Seong-jin and I had the studio to ourselves. The monsoon rain had been coming down for days. Staring out at the downpour, Seong-jin suddenly said, "I'm leaving."

"What are you talking about?"

"I'm leaving Seoul." He turned to me and said, "Let's go down to the country. Not my grandmother's house, but someplace I know."

He said we would drop by his grandmother's in Namwon, but where we were really headed was a village near Shilsang Temple. There was a mountain hut there where one of his relatives lived alone; he had cleared a field and was growing crops. Seong-jin said he wanted to help his relative and think of a new way to live: he did not want to go on living this way. I agreed to join him, because I wasn't ready to part company. All that was left to figure out was the money.

"Let's go to my place," I said, thinking of things we could take with us to sell.

We didn't tell Mu our plans in detail, only that we were moving to the country. Mu, who was only two years older, responded as if he surpassed us by decades. "Life isn't that easy. But knock yourselves out. I'd consider it a success if you can come back next year."

We said goodbye to him and headed home. My sisters hardly gave me a glance, resenting me for appearing out of nowhere with Seong-jin in tow, and Mother wordlessly set the table for us. We kept to my room that evening, flipping through books, waiting in silence. Seong-jin, exhausted, dozed off after midnight.

I thought four in the morning would be the best time to make our move, as that was when the nationwide national security curfew ended, and Mother would be sound asleep. I heard a chiming from far away and waited fifteen more minutes before slowly crossing the living room, past the dining room, in front of the kitchen, and slowly opening the bedroom door. My goal was the top drawer beneath a pile of folded blankets in the wardrobe. I knew that Mother kept all sorts of contracts and receipts from utilities payments there, as well as her old-fashioned handbag with the crudely misaligned lock. Mother lay on her side with her back to me. I lay down next to her to wait for a while before pulling at the wardrobe door, which slowly opened. I pulled the drawer and took out the handbag. Just as I was about to push the wardrobe door shut, I noticed a Zenith radio next to the dresser. It was so heavy that my shoulder sagged when I lifted it by the handle.

Seong-jin was still fast asleep when I returned to the room. I shook him awake. Seong-jin's eyelids cracked open as he peered up at me. I grabbed half of the bills from inside the bag and stuffed them in my pocket, leaving the rest, and gently placed the handbag in the middle of my desk.

Seong-jin's jaw dropped when he saw the Zenith radio. That radio was the only bit of cultural apparatus we had in our house.

Televisions were rare at the time, and it was not until the 1970s that record players were included among dowry items like wardrobes and other furniture. It was also the last cutting-edge product of the radio era that we had managed to get, through a leak in the American post exchange, or PX. Under the lid were frequencies for radio channels around the world.

We crept out of the house and decided to finish sleeping at a run-down inn downtown. After a good, long sleep, we woke, went to Namdaemun Market, sold the radio, and went out for dinner.

Late that night, at Seoul Station, we waited for the Jeolla Line night train. People say that once you've committed your first bad deed, you're already on your way to more, and that was true of us. The overhead lights cast a dreary glow over the country folk waiting with us. A middle-aged woman approached, with what looked like a forced smile. "And where are you two students going?"

"To Namwon," I said indifferently, assuming she was going to ask about train lines.

"That train's not until 11:30," she said. "Plenty of time before that. Why don't you have some fun?"

Unlike me, who had no idea what she was talking about, Seong-jin caught on immediately. "Do you have anyone pretty?"

"Of course, they're all fresh today."

Seong-jin gave me a sideways look and said, "It's your graduation day today."

His words made me come to my senses. I'd heard Taek use that expression before. He meant losing my virginity. Seong-jin stood up first with his luggage, and the woman, reading his intention, quickly joined us. "Will you be staying all night?"

"No, we won't be long . . . Let's go."

Up the street where the Gukje Hall restaurant sat across from Seoul Station Plaza were narrow alleys stretching in all directions. After the war, red-light districts had sprung up in Jongno

3-ga Station, Dodong, and Yangdong, and near train stations like Cheongyangri, Yongsan, and Yeongdeungpo, the same as in every other city.

The woman took us to a two-story building that looked more like a pile of cement blocks. A man, who I assumed was a pimp, looked us up and down as we stepped through the second-floor entrance. I couldn't even raise my head. I stuck close to Seong-jin.

Doors lined both sides of the hallway. Women walked by in their underwear, dragging their slippers. The pimp directed me to a room. Seong-jin sat with me for a long time before leaving. In the room was a set of red Cashmilon quilts, two dirty pillows, a small hole cut into the wallpapered particleboard wall, and a cheap light bulb hanging from the hole. The same bulb illuminated both my room and the one next to it. There was a shelf right above the door for shoes, and I put mine there. A small window opposite the door offered a view of the roofs of the shacks down the hill and the lights of the streets beyond.

The door opened and a woman walked in. I quickly sat up straight and backed toward the wall. She was tall with wide shoulders like a man, short hair, and something like a deep knife wound on her cheek. She reeked of alcohol.

"What's this, a first-timer?" she said, snorting with laughter, and lay down on the Cashmilon quilt. She flipped up her chemise, under which she wore nothing. "Hurry up. I don't have a lot of time."

When I simply sat there hugging my knees, she came over to me, threw her arms around me, and pulled me toward her. "Come here. I'll teach you."

"W-wait, let me turn off the light first." I reached over to turn off the light bulb and heard cackles from the other room.

"Who's messing with the goddamn light? Hey, *Unni*, that kid is a virgin!"

"I know, bitch!" The woman on this side cackled as she stripped me of my underwear. "Don't be nervous. Just get on top."

I managed to get excited despite myself, and it was over quickly. The woman pushed me aside and left the room without looking back. My breathing gradually returned to normal as I lay there alone in the dark room. What the hell, I thought, that was nothing. I felt like something grand that had been growing and flourishing inside of me was now tumbling down like an avalanche. I felt a weary sense of disgust and self-hatred, reminiscent of a hangover, as images ran through my mind. Smooth foreheads, sly glances, girls' knees peeking out from beneath the hems of sundresses, tiny white hairs on the cheeks of female students illuminated by the sunbeams shining through bus windows, girlish napes glimpsed between bobbed hair and blinding white collars on the way to school early in the morning, white ankle socks, slim calves . . . vanishing into the sunlight . . .

In the valley near Namwon's Inwolli village lived a distant cousin of Seong-jin's, who was something of an eccentric. Judging from the handful of old law books on the shelf above his desk, he had obviously studied for the civil service exam for several years before changing his mind. Never marrying, he had built a hut out of bricks and brought in some beehives that eventually multiplied to thirty. He had a hundred chickens, five milking goats, and 2,000 *pyeong* of farmland, but without any farmhands he struggled to manage even half of the work. He pointed at the foothills behind his house and said that land, too, was his to cultivate as he pleased—about 30,000 *pyeong* in total. The problem, he claimed, was that no one wanted to put in the work—if he could only turn it into an orchard, he'd have himself a gold mine.

Seong-jin and I were silently unimpressed. We were thinking the same thing: *So what?* The next day, Seong-jin and I began hoeing the remaining fields that had been left fallow. It was the first time I'd ever tried farm work, and turning over 500 *pyeong* of soil was no joke. It took us several days just to clear 200 *pyeong* by hand. The cousin pretended not to have noticed, but soon he leased an ox from some neighbors to plow the remaining land. We planted cabbage and turnip in preparation for the kimchi season. It was only common sense to ready oneself for the coming winter, but I felt strangely resentful at being bound to any future.

I had followed Seong-jin to Namwon, but I couldn't afford to stick around until the kimchi-making season that would follow the first frost and late-autumn harvest. I returned to Seoul just when the Mount Jiri leaves were at the peak of their fall colors.

Mother, as always, simply bit her tongue and waited for me to make the first move.

Then one evening, in the middle of a blizzard, she knocked on my bedroom door after downing a few shots of soju, which normally she wouldn't touch.

She was calm at first. "Fine, I won't interfere with whatever you want to do with your life, whether it's writing or not. But you can't even work in a factory these days if you're a high school dropout. Are you going to go to school or not?"

"I'll just study on my own."

That broke her composure, and she burst into tears. "I promised your late father. I promised him that I would do whatever it takes to send you to college and raise you properly. You ungrateful brat, are you just going to live however you want from now on? Then leave and never come back."

I turned away from her and wept. Her words cut me deeply, but I was already too far outside the normal education system and thought I would never be able to go back. But it was Mother's next words that really devastated me.

"I live because of you. So many times I lie down to sleep hoping I won't wake up in the morning. But I live because I might see you in your uniform again, going to school."

I did go back to school that spring but quit within two months and transferred to another school where I got into a turf war with the other students, prompting me to be transferred again. I went through three different high schools. I wasn't some kind of back-alley bully, but I simply couldn't accept mindless rules and corporal punishment, a remnant of the Japanese colonial education system. I had to fight back, and it was inevitable that either my adversaries or I would end up broken and bruised.

Summer vacation put an end to those trials. And if it wasn't for a certain transition point for my mother and me, my future would have remained as dark and obscure as it seemed at the time. I decided, around then, to finish up the short story "By the dolmen" that I had been working on for a while. I copied what I had so far into another notebook and polished it in places. I was aiming for the most difficult target: the prize for new writers at *Sasanggye* magazine.

My writing had actually appeared in an established publication during my second year of high school. During my freshman year, when I was sending out story submissions wherever I could, I submitted a short story to a writing competition at school. It was titled "Before rebirth" and depicted the two days before Jesus was crucified, told from the perspective of Judas. I wrote it without knowing that Judas and Peter were both part of the Jewish resistance movement against the Romans, and I argued, very seriously, in favor of free will, using Judas's voice. A precocious perspective, thinking back on it now. Someone plagiarized my story and won a new writer competition at a local newspaper. A friend from that region who happened to see it alerted the newspaper and the award was canceled, the real author revealed to be a high school student.

By the time I finished revising my work and sent the story to *Sasanggye*, the hot and tedious summer had passed.

I was sitting at Donghwa with Seong-jin one day when Wu-seok walked in, wearing his old uniform and carrying his school bag. The first thing out of his mouth when he saw me was curses.

"You bastard, you dropped out of school again! Meanwhile Taek's father doesn't care about his education and refuses to send him to school. Don't you feel sorry for your mother?"

Wu-seok had happened to meet my mother once and had never taken my side since. He lectured me for a long time before unzipping his vinyl bag and taking something out. "I borrowed this just for you."

It was a hair clipper. Nowadays they have the ones that run on electricity, but his were manual.

"What are you going to do with that?" I said as I shrank away from him. Wu-seok gave the clippers a few squeezes and said, "I'm going to cut your hair."

Seong-jin pushed us both into the kitchen. The café owner, an old lady, opened her eyes wide and broke off her conversation with the cook. "How dare you come in here!"

"He says he wants to go back to school, so we're going to cut his hair," said Seong-jin.

The owner lady put on a prim expression and nodded. "Good for him. Cut it all off!"

Wu-seok sat me down on a plastic chair in the corner of the kitchen. Now, high school students would normally ask a barber to "use the second level," because a completely shorn scalp doesn't look good, takes ages to grow back, and leaves the skin around your ears feeling strangely bare. The barber would fit a guide onto the blades to leave a little extra length. But Wu-seok had never cut hair before and kept ripping clumps out of my scalp, in addition to leaving me with a buzz cut.

It was a late afternoon in November, cold enough for the first snow to fall, but there I was sitting in a corner at Donghwa, out of uniform, with a woolen monk's cap pulled over my stubbly head. It was probably about five in the afternoon. Around the time the evening papers came onto the streets, Sang-deuk, In-sang, and a few others pushed into Donghwa and greeted me with happy faces. I was wondering what had gotten into everyone that day when Sang-deuk, waving a newspaper over his head, said "Have you see this?" There was an article saying that my short story "By the dolmen" had won the new writer's prize at *Sasanggye*. Three people were awarded, with Seo

Jeong-in's "Transferred to the rear" winning first and mine earning honorable mention. That evening, Sang-deuk took us to the Chinese restaurant next to Midopa Department Store, where we went up to the second floor and drank kaoliang.

I visited the *Sasanggye* offices the next day. No one in the editorial department spoke to me for a long time as I stood there, fidgeting. Finally, the man sitting across from where I stood asked, "What do you want?"

"I got a call." I told him my name.

He stared at me for a while and exclaimed, "Why, you're just a kid with a buzz cut! Did you really write that story? It's not something an older brother wrote?"

This man, the novelist Han Nam-cheol, was to become my friend. He told me later that I looked so young, he'd mistaken me for a middle school student. He told me to sit down, asked a few questions, introduced me to the other editors, and took me to Editor-in-Chief Chang Chun ha's office. Chang wore his hair parted down the middle and kept sweeping it back with his pale fingers. He shook my hand and remarked on how unexpected this was. "The submissions this time around were of the highest quality, so in view of your age it is even more surprising."

When I got home, I saw my mother with a joyful face for the first time in a long while. She called me to her bedroom after my sisters had gone to bed. "My eyesight isn't so good. Can you read this to me?"

She, who read the tiny letters of Japanese pocket editions without effort, held out my story printed in the magazine. As I had done in the old days, I sat down facing her and read out my story. It was late into the night when I finished. Mother brought out roasted sweet potatoes she had placed on top of the coal briquette lid, and we ate them while they were still hot, blowing on them to cool them down. Mother would later say, "I never opposed his ambition to be a writer. But the reason I made him keep a diary and bought him books when he was young wasn't because I wanted him to make a career of it. I just wanted him to be someone who likes books."

Later, when I was having a hard time making ends meet as a full-time writer, I grandly proclaimed to myself that writing was my calling. But now I think of it in more modest terms, as a job I am well suited for. And it is still my belief that a novelist should not be like the classical scholars of yore, who withdrew from the world, but more like a merchant, like one of the traveling storytellers who used to peddle their tales in the market square.

~

I attended night classes at a vocational high school on the outskirts of Seoul for a few months before graduating and going to college. I was two years behind everyone else. My eldest sister got married, and my new brother-in-law was poor but hardworking and clever. Mother, who'd not had an adult man in the house for a long time, seemed to feel more secure with him around. I did not use the usual honorific for a brother-in-law but called him Eldest Brother, as I still do today. He would come on my mother's behalf to retrieve me from Donghwa or my friends' houses, and act as a responsible older brother whenever I was in trouble. Even when I was imprisoned during the dictatorship years, he fearlessly came to visit me at the intelligence offices. He was the one who convinced me to return to school and helped me enter college.

At the time, almost every university save for a prestigious few were more or less the same, and the campuses still bore the scars of war. In some ways, it was better then than it is now to read and study on your own. There were almost no roll calls, and, provided you submitted your papers on time, no one cared if you never attended classes. One student lived far from Seoul, helping out with the family business, and only came up to copy notes and take exams. I had already competed with my friends to read as many books across the arts, humanities, and social sciences as possible, so the content of the classes was nothing new to me. If anything, I found that academic work had narrowed dramatically since the division of the peninsula.

There was about one year of freedom, between the April Revolution and May 16 coup, during which all sorts of books were published; one of them was *Listen, Yankee* by C. Wright Mills. The poet Kim Soo-young had published a few translated excerpts in a magazine and soon the whole book came out. Mills's defense of the Cuban Revolution and critique of America's foreign policy was shocking to us. I felt like a bucket of ice water had been splashed on my face. It was around that time that *Sasanggye* began sharply criticizing our military regime.

Ever since the contents of a secret memo between Korea's intelligence agency chief, Kim Jong-pil, and Japanese Foreign Minister Ōhira Masayoshi had been disclosed a few years earlier, revealing a plan to normalize South Korean and Japanese diplomatic ties, opposition to Korea–Japan talks had been spreading through the universities and society at large. Reparations for the colonial period—a lump sum that naturally included victims of forced conscription, but was also meant to cover both the government and all individuals harmed by colonization—were set at 300 million USD, half of what the Philippines received. They had been labeled "congratulations-on-your-liberation" funds by the Japanese, and "absolution on the cheap" by the Korean side. While done under the guise of normalizing Korea–Japan relations, it was really due to America's unrelenting attempt to secure the last link in the Cold War chain in Northeast Asia. In light of how South Korea immediately began deploying troops to Vietnam after the reparations were agreed, the involvement of the American government in these proceedings was very clear. In fact, no sooner did Park Chung-hee win the presidency over Yun Posun than US Secretary of State Dean Rusk was sent to Korea to publicly browbeat both parties into signing the agreement. From March onward, a coalition of students and religious groups formed, and national protests were held around the fourth anniversary of the April Revolution against Rhee Syngman. Despite belonging to a university in an anti-communist third-world country, Sang-deuk, In-sang, Wu-seok, and Guk-jeong organized a nationwide cultural movement with their upperclassmen at Seoul National University.

The early cultural movement of the 1960s began with a national crisis in which Japanese colonial influence, through American pressure, was reintroduced to the peninsula and South Korean political power was concentrated in the hands of past collaborationists. I call it a *cultural* movement because, looking back among the various paths and methods of social engagement, this was the first time since the war that literature was used for political activism. The funeral held for nationalist democracy at SNU Liberal Arts in 1964 was nonviolent but powerful enough to make an impression on any college student. Some began a hunger strike at the end of May, sparking the student protests that would peak in June.

I was among the many protesters camped out on the steps of the City Hall building, which served as the National Assembly at the time. The protesters read out a petition criticizing the government, and with a cry of "To the Blue House!" we began to push toward Gwanghwamun and the presidential residence. Riot police awaited us around the *Chosun Ilbo* newspaper building and the Gukje Theater, but they were pushed back into the Gwanghwamun crossroads by students and citizens, prompting them to throw tear gas. Gwanghwamun Gate stands there today, but at the time the Central Government Building, which used the old Japanese Government-General Building, stood before us and the street was protected by three layers of barbed wire and barricades, with police standing close together in riot gear, armed with clubs and tear gas dispensers. Behind them, military transport trucks were lined up end to end, forming a wall.

When tear gas canisters came flying toward us, we would grab them right away and hurl them back. We also threw stones as we tried to break through the front and sides. Once we succeeded, the great mass of people entered the back lot of the Gyeonggi Provincial Office that was to the right of the Central Government Building. The workers inside fled as protesters smashed the windows to enter; meanwhile, a stream of people flowed past the building and pushed on toward the Blue House, where the president lived. The police line began to break down. Once the protesters in front managed to move the barricade out of the way, they flowed in like a tide. The line of police quickly retreated to the neighborhood of Jeokseon-dong, near the Blue House, and tried to hold the crowd in the narrow back streets of Gyeongbokgung Palace. The alleyways filled with tear gas. The crowd pushed and was pushed, but eventually some protesters commandeered military trucks and drove off in different directions; it seemed they were going to spread the protest around the city, just like during the April Revolution. Later we learned that their lack of driving skills caused the vehicles to flip over or crash into houses and storefronts.

We got into one of the trucks, shouted slogans in front of the SNU Liberal Arts building, where they were still on hunger strike, and drove around downtown Seoul. Whenever a fellow protester knocked on the roof near the driver's seat and clamored to be taken somewhere, we took off in that direction. "Slow down!" "Stop!" we would all shout in unison, and occasionally the driver would get out and shout at the passengers or passersby, "Do any of you have a driver's license?" One or two would inevitably say that they'd driven in the military, and would change shifts with the driver. Eventually, the jeep ran out of gas or broke down near Yongsan Station. The day had darkened, and everyone was tired and hungry, so we went our separate ways there. Tram services had been suspended, leaving us to cross the Han River on foot.

We had almost reached the other side of the bridge when we saw a barricade, with a small gap for the cars being individually inspected by both civilian and military police. They asked me for my ID. When I said I was a student, they commanded me to stand to the side where there was a group. They repeatedly made us do punitive sit-to-stand exercises before taking us to a nearby police station. They inspected our bags and possessions and discovered fliers printed with the petition protesting our "diplomacy of humiliation."

"You're on your way back from the protests, correct?"

We defiantly declared that we were. Normally, any conversation with the police would begin with a slap to the face, even for an offense as lowly as breaking curfew, but they were very calm this time. A car came for the three of us from Noryangjin headquarters, and that's when we learned that martial law had been declared. After being interrogated late into the night and stamping our thumbprints on written statements, we were held in lockup for two days before being transferred to detention for twenty.

This is where I met the Captain. In the first lockup, I was with two boys brought in for pickpocketing and an old drunk who looked almost like a beggar. The old man was released the next day and I was alone with the two boys when, in the evening, I heard someone arguing loudly with the police officer in charge of registering prisoners.

"Hand over your belongings."

"I've got nothing but my dick. What do you want from me?"

"Then what's this?"

"What are you, stupid? Cigarettes and matches."

As the officer reached into the man's pocket, the man grabbed his arm and twisted it behind his back. "I bought all that with my own money!"

"Let go!"

The other policemen swarmed, pushing him and drowning out his voice, until presently I saw the man approach the lockup with a lit cigarette in his mouth, talking wearily to the policemen.

"You want me to plead with you for my own smokes? Then there's nothing I can do." The cage opened and shut. He shot me a look and said to the boys, "Hey kids, spread out a blanket for me."

The boys were quick to do his bidding as they grabbed a blanket from the stack and spread it out opposite the toilet. I thought the spot nearest the bars was the best place, but that was only true for people like me who wanted to read by the light. The man had chosen a spot where he was invisible to the guard.

He sucked with relish on his cigarette, lay down on one elbow, and said to me: "Let's introduce ourselves. It's not like there's a crowd here, so why not be democratic about it? I'm Jang."

I bowed my head, and he continued: "You look like a student. What landed you in here?"

"I was demonstrating—"

"And those fuckers threw you in for that! It's like the Japanese bastards never left. Hey, have a drag of this." Jang handed me his cigarette. In truth, I'd been craving it ever since I'd caught a whiff.

That first delicious hit of nicotine had me "going to Hong Kong." I asked Jang how he'd wound up here.

"The foreman was messing around with our chits, so I beat him up."

He was a day laborer at the construction site for the second Han River Bridge that had just broken ground. The public works construction projects at the time were handled through hired subcontractors who bribed their way into the work, just as construction projects had been during the Japanese occupation. I discovered from my reportage in the mines during the 1970s that this was still going on. Jang didn't talk too much about this depressing state of affairs and went on to tell the story of his life, dropping jokes in where he could.

He had been honorably discharged from the military as a marine sergeant. In fact he had only three rank insignias, but, owing to his enthusiasm and know-how at the construction sites his fellow workers had promoted him to "Captain." At the time there were few major projects underway, which meant technicians across the country either knew, or knew of, the others. Captain handled his work expertly and had built a good reputation for himself at the *hamba*, the temporary on-site lodgings and canteens for construction workers. The other workers looked up to him as an old hand. He was thirty-three, broad-shouldered and fit, but so tall he actually looked skinny. His hair was curly and his face sunburned, and his unshaven grin recalled the face of Burt Lancaster in a western, riding into town after a long journey.

Captain Jang and I slept side by side for the twenty days in that cage where petty thieves came and went, and shared my lunch box bought with the money Eldest Brother had put in for me. We grew as close as brothers. On sleepless nights, he lay on his stomach and told me all about how he got by in this world.

He had a family, of course: parents, siblings, a wife, and children. Like most independent farming families at the time, his parents had just enough land to cultivate so they would not starve to death. He managed to graduate middle school and left home because he had heard the military would clothe him, feed him, and teach him some skills. His older brother was about to marry, his younger sister had found a job at a hairdresser's, and he didn't want to be a burden to his family. The marines were said to be tough, but it suited his personality to throw himself completely into what was right and absolutely reject what was wrong.

I asked him why he didn't go for first sergeant, chief warrant officer, or actual captain while he was there, and he suddenly turned glum and silent before giving the bars a kick and shouting, "Guard! Hey, whoever's in charge! Get over here."

A drowsy guard approached, rubbing his eyes. "In charge, my ass."

"Now who have we here? Officer Park, serene as the Buddha . . ."

"Stop farting around and get to the point. What do you want?"

"You got my wallet and my cigarettes? Light me one."

The guard grumbled as he complied but, having scrapped with each other before, they seemed to have reached a kind of understanding. In other words, the Captain had become our captain. The guard took out two cigarettes from his shirt pocket, put them between his lips and lit them at the same time, and handed them over.

"Hey, I said get me my wallet, too."

The guard was annoyed. "You give this bastard an inch and he takes a mile."

"What, you little pip-squeak? What are you saying to this elder brother of yours?"

"What do you want with your wallet, anyway? That's against regulations!"

The Captain switched to a serious tone of voice, which I had never heard before. "Officer Park, my wallet contains a photograph of my old flame. This kid wants to see it. And I keep thinking of her."

"Fine." The guard came back with his wallet. "Push it outside the bars when you're done with it. I have to put it back."

As the guard went away, muttering, the Captain drew out a photo from deep within the wallet's folds. We puffed away on our cigarettes as we stared at the photo. There was a moon floating in the sky like a prop from one of those old variety shows, and on a landing or a stairway with overhanging branches stood a young woman wearing a *hanbok* top, a mid-length skirt that was the fashion at the time, and white ankle socks, her hair in braids and a big smile on her face. At the bottom of the photo were white handwritten letters that read, "Memories are forever!" The photo was a bit yellowed and faded.

"Wow, she's pretty. This is your old flame? What happened to her?"

"What kind of a novel do you plan to write like that, rushing straight to the ending? And what do you mean by what happened to her?"

"Well, they say first love ends in tragedy . . ."

"She's not my first love. And what happened was, she became my wife. And that screwed up my life."

That prosaic conclusion took the wind out of my sails. He'd quit the military for her. She owned some rice paddies in the countryside back home, and her older brother had taken on the family poultry farm, where she had suggested they help out for a bit before striking out on their own with some borrowed land and starter chicks.

Around then, the schools were being provided with sacks of wheat flour, baby formula, and corn flour, emblazoned with logos of a handshake, thanks to the UN Korean Reconstruction Agency and US Agency for International Development. Some argued that such measures were undermining the resilience of Korea's agriculture. But the hundreds-of-years-old tradition of planting rice and barley was no longer seeing us through, and now people were trying out all sorts of more profitable farming ventures. Quail was a medicinal fad that ended up crashing the market. Black goats were another, though it lasted a little longer. There was a breed of white chicken called Leghorn that came in through foreign aid; its speedy growth and ability to produce plentiful eggs made it so popular that Korean chicken breeds were pushed out. The Captain left the marines to join his wife at his brother-in-law's poultry farm and got his own Leghorns to set up a business. But a poultry disease soon laid waste to both his brother-in-law's and his own chickens, leaving them in financial ruin.

In the three years since, the Captain had wandered the land alone. The Han River Bridge construction was well underway, allowing him to find work and extend his stay in the city, otherwise he would gladly have left as soon as the azaleas bloomed in the spring. Beyond Seoul there were always municipal infrastructure projects going on, mostly land reclamation or reservoirs or irrigation, sometimes government buildings. When the work was good, he would stay put there until the fall, but usually he left before the midsummer monsoon. Sometimes there would be a good barley harvest, which didn't pay well but afforded him free meals and lodgings at a farmer's house. At the peak of summer, he went to the beach. An easy moneymaker there was to rent a lung-capacity machine as a kind of carnival attraction, enticing people to pay to blow into it to see who had the biggest lung capacity. He went swimming when it was hot and slept in a tent on the beach. Once the currents shifted and cold winds began to blow, schools of cuttlefish would start to make their way down the east coast, from Sokcho to warmer southern waters. That was when Captain Jang would head for the eastern shore, where he would put on a raincoat and rubber boots and rent some fishing equipment and a place on a boat. A cut of his catch went to the captain and the boat owner, and the rest was his.

The work was done at night. The bright light of the fishermen's lamps drew crowds of cuttlefish. The boats headed way out, making the watery horizon glow and dimly illuminating the sky. A turn of the spinning wheel brought up the snagged cuttlefish, sparkling whitely in the artificial light. The fisherman would rip off a flapping cuttlefish with one hand, toss it into a basket, and give the wheel another turn with the other. When dawn broke, a crack of light formed on the faraway horizon, splitting it into above and below. Bands of red and yellow unfurled across the sky.

By the time he had followed the cuttlefish down to Gangneung, Samcheok, and Ulsan, it would be deep into fall. That's when he returned to the countryside to help with the harvest. Eating lunch by rippling fields of gold and napping after a bowl of *makgeolli* was, he said, the best feeling in the world. He returned to the city in the winter. There, he rented a small room and an oven fashioned from an old oil barrel, which he would set up at a bus stop or market to sell roasted sweet potatoes. If he had extra to spend, he could get a covered food cart to sell soju or find another decent construction site and pass the winter nights in the *hamba*.

The Captain's stories made my heart race. His life seemed as free as that of birds migrating with the changing seasons. I imagined that he had no fear of living, that his hardship wasn't so bad. To live, that in itself was a vivid joy. Even suffering is, in the end, a part of this living.

I decided to follow the Captain. I was released about four days before him. When I stepped outside, I saw how the new leaves were now a lush green and the city was basking in high summer. The schools had been ordered to shut down, but the summer break had already started.

By then, even my younger sister had married and left home, so our household consisted of only my mother, my younger brother, and me. Mother had liquidated all of her family property to buy a shop in a market in Heukseok-dong and was selling packaged foodstuffs. My brother and I moved in the merchandise and closed the store when my mother was too tired at the end of the day, which was late at night. The two of them slept in the tiny room attached to the store, and I went up the ladder next to the kitchenette to the attic under the roof.

One night, my brother caught me packing my bags and alerted my mother. She had become so used to it by now that she seemed unfazed. "Going somewhere?"

"Yes. I'm going to stay at a temple to read and write a bit."

Mother scarcely reacted. We didn't have a single quiet moment all day, living as we did in the middle of a market. While I was busy running away from home again, narrowly escaping disaster, and getting shipped off to Vietnam, my brother remained stuck, being raised by a mother who fretted constantly about her other son. Whenever we got into arguments later in life, he would bring up the same thing: that he had suffered because of me, that my needs had overshadowed his, that Mother had no wherewithal to take care of him because she was always concerned about me, that his teenage years had been difficult, that I knew nothing. He resented Mother, because all she could think about, despite his loneliness, was me.

When I set off with my backpack for the first tram, striding out of the shuttered store, Mother saw me to the corner of the market. "Wherever you end up, don't forget to write," she said, and handed me some cash.

I boarded the now-familiar all-stop train with the Captain. Nowadays it takes about an hour to get to Cheonan, but it took so long then that we arrived around four or five in the afternoon. We walked into downtown from Cheonan Station. I saw a butcher at a market close to his neighborhood and bought a *geun* of pork. He bought a bag of sweets from a stand that had piles of *senbei* crackers and striped candies—a modest homecoming.

His house was an old Japanese-style building, where the door on the alley side seemed to be for the landlord while the gate on the main road was for the tenants. Just like the tree of heaven in front of our Yeongdeungpo house, there were a couple of out-of-place plane trees standing guard close to the front gate. Even before we stepped inside, a little girl in a tank top, perhaps a second or third grader, carrying a toddler on her back, hesitated before shouting "Daddy!" and running toward the Captain.

"How have you been? Where's your mother?" The Captain took the sleeping child from the girl's back and held him.

"Mom took the wheelbarrow out to do her selling."

"Look at this runny nose," said the Captain, and deftly swiped away the child's snot and flicked it to the ground before wiping his hand on one of the trees.

His wife appeared around seven, just as the shadows grew long on the ground. The little girl's face brightened at the creaking of the barrow. "It's Mom!"

The woman called her daughter's name as she entered the gate. The Captain, still holding the younger child, was stepping outside just then. They collided in front of the swing doors.

"Oh! When did you get here?" The woman took the child from him and the Captain took the wheelbarrow from her. He unloaded the leftover vegetables and empty bowls and leaned the wheelbarrow against a wall. I fidgeted a bit and bowed. The Captain's wife made no sign of annoyance at finding an unexpected guest as she quickly prepared dinner for us.

The Captain's wife did not go out to sell vegetables the next day. She began cooking early in the morning and went out to buy some mackerel, saying we needed something fatty for the meal. The Captain and I went to a nearby municipal office to see where the biggest public works construction site was, in order to find some work; it happened to be a cigarette factory in Sintanjin.

The next day, the Captain's wife skipped work again so she could accompany us to the station. If she wanted to work, she needed to leave for the fields at dawn to buy vegetables, or hit the big market near the station to buy fish, but she had decided to take two whole days off instead, in order to welcome her husband. At least the Captain had given her some money he had made at construction sites in the city, I thought. She left her daughter with the little one and followed the Captain to the train station. Who knew when he would return again?

"You should go back. We have to get on the train now."

I stood a distance away, watching them try to part. The Captain was consoling his wife as she wiped her eyes with the hem of her skirt. Inside the station, the Captain lit a cigarette and sighed deeply.

~

At the construction site in the town of Sintanjin, the bones of a building were beginning to go up in the empty field, with the site's *hamba*—company store and offices—below. The *hamba* office was a military-issue tent set up in front of cement-block buildings that looked slapped together. There was a mess hall outfitted with tables and long benches made of particleboard, and a convenience store stocked with soju, snacks, cigarettes, soap, and other essentials.

A desk and comfortable-looking office chair were set up in front of the store. An overweight man sitting in the chair greeted us first. "Hey, Captain, what are you doing here?"

"Well, if it isn't Brother Toad. Is the bridge construction done? Did you make some good money?"

"What money? That job ended before we could finish it. Some other bastard became National Assembly member, and it was curtains for that project. Where are you coming from?"

"The second Han River Bridge. I didn't want to spend the summer in the city, so I came here for the scenery. Anyway, it's good to see you again! I'm ready to earn a few coins."

"Hate to break it to you, but we're full up. There won't be any more paydays between now and autumn."

The Captain chuckled and poked me in the back. "Hey, say hello. He's our older brother. This kid here is an uncle to my kids."

I bowed, and Brother Toad looked me up and down. "So, your brother-in-law?"

"Just give us a couple of *hamba* rooms."

Brother Toad tilted his head. "Well, you're an old hand so I know you can do anything. But this kid . . . It's your first time, right?"

I answered yes before I could stop myself.

"I can't give him a full day's worth of chits. He's got to accept a half day."

"Hey, don't do that. Look at how big he is. He's not a child or a woman. Stick him on a battlefield and he'll come home with medals."

"Fine, let's do it this way. Our teams change every two weeks, so we'll pay him half-wages for the first shift. And we'll see how he does before paying him in full the next. If you don't like that, we'll take just you."

The Captain looked at me and nodded. "We accept. We start this evening."

"And don't be late for meals. There won't be any stew left if you are. You're both in Room 3."

It was a single room with holes in the cement wall and plastered with sack paper. Some occupants used military-issue blankets for bedding, or spread open a box and taped it up with electrical tape. There were seven people including us in Room 3, and the laborers who were washing after work immediately began complaining. "Why do they have to put you in our room? Room 8 has just five people, too."

"Why don't we all try to get along? We're all visitors here. I'm called the Captain in these circles. Family name of Jang. Nice to meet you all."

An older laborer by the window said, "You look like a pro. Let's all rub along. There are lots of farmers who come fresh off the fields these days. They don't know anything about the world and they're a pain. You can sleep here." The old laborer had a spot beneath the window where the air was fresh; he pushed away the unattended bedding next to his to make room for the Captain.

I hesitated, unsure of what to do, until the Captain gave the unattended bedding another push farther away from the window and said to me, "Put your things down here."

We sat down and as everyone introduced each other, the man who had been in my spot came in with his laundry. His eyes grew wide when he saw me. "What's this? The rolling stone takes out the seated stone? Don't you have any sense of rank?"

"Why don't you cool it with the big words and work on not snoring instead," said the old laborer, making it clear why he'd given away the man's spot.

The Captain handled it with practiced ease. "Hey, I've spent the last ten years living in *hamba*. Since when does anyone make a stink about who sleeps where? If you want to change rooms, I'll have a word with Brother Toad."

The young man immediately gave in. Just like in prison, changing rooms meant you had to start all over again from the bottom in terms of social rank. And the Captain had implied that he was friends with the foreman. Grumbling, the young man moved his things toward a spot near the wall.

Dinner was a large serving of rice, radish soup, tofu, fried squash, and bright-red kimchi. After, the Captain and I hung our towels around our necks, got our soap and toothbrushes, and went to wash at a nearby river under a steel bridge. The Captain said, "You've got to come on strong at first here. You'll see they're all decent fellows after the first few days. Think about it: what bad person would think to make a living from their own strength? All the bad folks are inside those fancy buildings in Seoul."

Work began the next day after breakfast as soon as the sun rose. There wasn't much equipment in those days; everything was done through sheer manpower. The vehicles were decommissioned military junk. Excavators and cranes were nonexistent, bulldozers a rarity. Instead of today's steel tubes, scaffolding was made from wooden poles about a palm thick and lashed with rope. Planks were fitted between the poles to serve as ramps and catwalks.

Newbies were immediately put to work mixing cement and hauling bricks. As I carried heavy buckets across the shaky planks, I would picture my spine snapping or the catwalk giving away beneath me. I cushioned my shoulders with rags, wore suspenders made of military cartridge belts, and pulled the rope tied to the pail with one hand as I desperately made my way up and down. I could never pause for a second, as there were other workers in front or behind. The plasterer would egg me on for more bricks while from below I was bombarded with complaints about my cement mix hardening. But this was the easier task; the steel-rod-carrying job that came later was even more dangerous and difficult. My hands, feet, and back became riddled with blisters and wounds.

The Captain was so good at his work that he was moved to the better-paying carpentry team. About two weeks after I got my work card, the Captain took me along to carpentry too and assigned me as an apprentice. This was a huge privilege for a newbie. My work now involved minor chores like carrying planks and cutting them as instructed.

Then the rainy season began, and we exchanged our chits for meals as we killed time in the lodgings. When it rained all day, our mouths would be the first to get bored, so we bought noodles, and sometimes we bet on games of *hwatu* cards for alcohol.

The high summer heat began right after the rains ended. Sometimes we ran out of construction materials, and, given the weather, we weren't as productive as we would be in the spring or fall. We accrued debts at the company store. We had to eat to live, and the things we ate became debt that dogged us no matter how hard we tried to outrun it.

The river in Sintanjin was beautiful this time of year. We went there every evening to wash. Sometimes we first contemplated the fish jumping from the mirrorlike surface and the rings that formed in their wake, as the nearby forest darkened. It was almost a shame to disturb the scene by jumping in.

One day after lunch, the Captain, in the middle of a smoke, playfully jabbed me in the ribs and said, "Hey, let's split."

He meant we should just up and leave work. To be honest, despite two months of backbreaking labor, the monsoon and delays in construction had left me with only enough to cover my debts and buy a one-way train ticket out of there. "I'm fine with that, but what about you? Your reputation will be ruined."

He waved away my worries. "I've already talked to the Toad foreman. He'll cover for us by making it look like a construction material loss instead."

According to him, the foremen liked to squirrel away construction material, like cement or rods, and would make a mental note of which workers they could trust. Then they would write off the material as being stolen by workers that had left. It was a mutually beneficial arrangement, especially for workers with *hamba* debts.

During the afternoon break, the Captain and I telegraphed our exit timing through glances and left the work site to collect our things from our room. We left only the blankets and tossed everything else into the tall grass behind the *hamba*. But we had to have dinner before we left, of course, and were sitting in the mess hall tent before everyone else when the Toad called the Captain over. The two whispered on about something for a long time.

We had a great dinner of hot rice mixed with cold water and salty mackerel and radish kimchi, topped off with a cigarette. The plan was to grab our blankets and leave, but the Captain suggested we go to the riverside for some soju. He looked like he was waiting for something.

The lights in the farmers' village across the river were beginning to go out one by one. The Captain took me a short distance from the *hamba* to the material warehouse behind a wide empty space. The guard standing there trained a flashlight on us and opened the door. We went inside and loaded a cart with cement sacks, pushed and pulled it to the hill behind the *hamba*, and tossed in our bags. I went into the rooms alone and fetched our blankets. Everyone was fast asleep in a cacophony of snores and gnashing teeth.

The cart was so heavy it may as well have been loaded with rocks. The Captain pulled while I pushed, and we passed the sandy fields to the road by the river where a truck stood waiting, the Toad perched atop it and smoking. We moved the sacks to the cargo compartment.

The Captain said, "Let's ditch the cart here."

The Toad nodded and stuffed some bills into the Captain's back pocket. "Consider this train fare."

The Captain and I began walking in the dark along the river. At first, the air was loud with frogs, but then it began to rain. This path along the Miho River to Cheongju later became the background for my short story published much later in the 1970s, "The Road to Sampo." It's a desolate story about how dreaming of the past and imagining village life became lost to those displaced by modernization. The migrant laborer Young-dal, the ex-prisoner and itinerant construction worker Jeong, and the debtor fleeing back home from her barmaid life, Baek-hwa, experience a brief moment of solidarity before realizing there is no place for any of them to call home. They become disillusioned, and at the end each heads off into an uncertain darkness.

It was a starless night. The Captain and I crossed a steel bridge and walked the road that followed the river from Seopyeongri. My army boots were drenched with rainwater, and my socks were sticking to my feet. In the distance the occasional goods train passed by, blowing its horn. There were no lights from the villages and no birds calling in the night. We could hear only the babble of the streams nearby. I still remember the pretty names of the villages around there: Seomddeum, Dalyeowool, Darakgol, Gangnaemyun, Saemgol . . .

Our road curved north, and we leapt from rock to rock to make our way across the river. Further inland on the river's other bank was a village, but its lights were out and all we could hear was frogs. It looked almost abandoned. We found a shed, and inside all sorts of farming tools and food stores, sacks rolled up and stacked against a wall, and a ripped bag of fertilizer. The Captain and I each took an empty sack and spread it on a dry spot. The roof was just thatch spread over rafters, and the rain occasionally seeped through and landed on our faces. We listened to the rain for a while, unable to fall asleep at once.

"Is someone in there?" a man shouted as he entered the shack. I quickly stood up. Apparently it had turned light outside a while ago. The farmer, who had come to fetch something, looked around.

"We were just passing by and it began to rain," I mumbled.

The Captain got up and bowed to the farmer, who appeared much older than either of us. "We are sorry for disturbing the neighborhood. It was too late at night to risk bothering anyone at home, so we ducked in here to rest."

"Oh no, it's fine." The farmer got some things from the shed and said, "But what about breakfast? You've got to eat, haven't you?"

The Captain scratched the back of his head and laughed.

"Well," said the farmer, "there's no tavern in these parts. Better follow me."

The farmer led us up the village road to a house where a willow tree stood next to a well. The courtyard was wide, and the house had a nice, long porch that connected all of the rooms.

"Sit down here." He said something to his wife in the kitchen and asked us about ourselves. The Captain said we were itinerant construction workers and asked if there were any building sites around.

We had breakfast there. The soybean paste stew made from greens and freshwater snails netted from the clear waters of the Miho River was so delicious that I shamelessly helped myself to seconds. The farmer's wife had also put great care into preparing dishes of gochujang stew, eggplants, and squash. A middle school boy politely knelt across from us as he ate.

After breakfast, the Captain planned to visit the North Chungcheong Provincial Office to find out about construction projects. If this had been the fall, I would have stayed for a season at this house and eaten that freshwater snail stew to my heart's content while helping out with the harvest. There was a train that led to Cheongju operating at the time, but we tramped the dozens of miles on foot instead. The Captain visited the office and said there was nothing to be had nearby, but North Jeolla Province was running a big land reclamation project.

We found a good tavern in the market and went in for lunch. A woman was boiling freshwater shrimp stew over coal briquettes. We ordered a kettle of *makgeolli* and some of the shrimp stew and proceeded to get daytime drunk. The tavern was typical of those in smaller cities, with long tables and benches and a glass door to the street. Behind us a door opened and a woman in a chemise rushed outside, her rubber shoes scuffing as she went, and threw up in the gutter.

"Stupid bitch, I told her to go easy on the booze." The woman of the tavern grumbled loudly, as if she wanted us to hear. "I can't wait to get her out of here and replace her with something younger. I can't stand her stupid face, just can't stand it."

The vomiting woman turned around and glanced at us from the corner of her eye but seemed to judge that we weren't worth knowing. Perhaps she guessed that we were vagabond laborers. My memories and impressions of the villages near Pohang later fed into "The Road to Sampo," with its character Baek-hwa.

Land reclamation had already begun a year ago in Buan, a county of North Jeolla Province. Back when the Buan project began, Korean farmers were regularly experiencing springtime famines, colloquially known as "barley hill," when food was in short supply. The plan to dam the mouths of rivers to create more fertile land for farming sounded like a good idea.

The Captain and I took the train to Gimje, switched to a bus, and reached the place where there was supposed to be an office for the Dongjin River and Gyehwa Island reclamation project. There was, indeed, construction afoot. My experiences here were used in my novella *Gaekji* (A Strange Land). There weren't any collective struggles or labor protests like in that story, but in these rural construction sites gangsters were often contracted as managers, and there were many conflicts between them and the laborers.

It was such a big project that the *hamba*, too, was bigger and the food much better than in Sintanjin. The work was very hard, but thanks to my experience in Sintanjin, I never got too exhausted and woke up ready for more every morning. We started the day with simple tasks, like carrying soil and rocks, and ended when the stars came out.

I was a city kid, having grown up mostly in Seoul. My parents were also urbanites who had received modern educations. My mother had tried hard to differentiate me from the children of laborers when I was growing up in Yeongdeungpo, because she had certain prejudices stemming from her lifelong distance from such people, as well as a desire to shake off the feeling of rootlessness or lowered class status. I was twenty-two now, and it was a good age to learn the vividness of life through hard labor. I was able to discover the natural beauty of our country and find my true self, far away from any city or village.

Flocks of migratory birds filled the air over the tidelands and the reeds along the Dongjin River, soaring over sky and sea and fields before returning to earth. Autumn was in full swing. During the day shift, I would hike out to the end of the embankment with a pack on my back or pause in the middle of shoveling and look up to discover the sun already setting, the twilight glow dividing the air and water as seagulls and migratory birds flew toward me from a distant sky, calling as they came. I embraced in my heart those who had once been strangers to me.

One day, the Captain and I went downtown, where we had first arrived months ago. We were planning to leave soon. For the first time, I wrote a postcard to my mother and dropped it in a mailbox.

We left the reclamation project before the Chuseok holiday. As we paid off our debt and found ourselves with some money left over, the Captain hesitantly suggested stopping by his house in Cheonan before heading back out to look for more work. In the lockup he had spoken grandly, as if he'd roamed the land without a care in the world, but it turned out that he returned home whenever he had money to give to his family. I boarded the night train with him from Jeonju to Daejeon. The next day, we had an early breakfast of *seollongtang* at Daejeon Station and parted ways. The Captain offered me a night's rest at his house, but I felt I might as well go home, and told him I would continue down toward the south.

~

After the Captain left for Cheonan, I frittered away some time in Daejeon until I could board the all-stop night train for free, just as I had done during my "penniless trips." I had hopped on one without checking, and it turned out to be the Gyeongbu Line. I hunkered down in the connecting corridor and fell asleep. We were in Daegu by the time the sun rose, but it was such a big city that I decided to stay on board all the way to Samryangjin.

I was thinking of going to Masan after changing to the Gyeongjeon Line, mostly because of the Captain's stories and his moving descriptions of the scenery that had greeted him with each new change of season and job. I figured, too, that there would be lots to eat in the countryside around this time and that people would be more generous.

I recalled that one of my high school classmates lived in a farming village near Haman. My plan was to visit, and if he wasn't there, I'd go back to Masan. I got off at Masan and took a bus north toward the Nakdong River. At an elementary school near the village administrative office, an elderly-looking female teacher kindly told me the way. By the time I trudged along and reached his front gate, the sun was setting. As I expected, he still hadn't begun his military service and was helping his father on the farm. I found my friend preparing firewood in the court-yard, crept up behind him, and tapped his shoulder.

"Look who's here!" he shouted in surprise. He was shorter and skinnier than me, but looked tanned and healthy. We hadn't been that close at school and had only spoken a few times. But he seemed glad that I was visiting him in the countryside. I told him I was traveling around, as was the fad for young people, and he scolded me for being so free-spirited when times were tough for everyone.

His father, whom I met at their dinner table, was genuinely happy to see me. "I was about to hire a farmhand!" The Chuseok holiday had fallen right in the middle of the rice harvest, making it hard for him to keep up with his work. He said it wasn't necessary to bring in the entire harvest and that his plan was to maybe get a third in and leave the rest to dry nicely in the autumn sun. Normally it would be considered impolite to enlist your son's friend's help with the farmwork, but as I was a surprise guest at their table, it seemed only fair that I should pull my weight. I suppose, too, you could say that having followed the Captain into the world of manual labor, I had done a lot of growing up and understood something about making my own way. After all, they say that back in the old days even wealthy families would send their teenage children away from home on far-flung journeys to see the world for just this reason.

As soon as the sun rose the next day, my friend, his father, two men from the village, and I carried well-sharpened scythes out to the fields. Waves of gold undulated before us in the wind. We bent our backs, gripped a handful of the stalks, and scythed at an angle. Once you gathered a big-enough load, you left it lying on the field. The work was different from that of construction sites, and my lack of experience showed. While I kept stopping to stretch out the kinks in my back, my friend and the other men were already far ahead. I eventually developed a method of squatting and waddling along as I scythed.

The countryside was indeed more generous in the fall. My friend's mother and sister brought our lunch to the field. We'd had a good breakfast, and lunch wasn't late by any means, but I was ravenous. The lunch baskets arrived, and the families of the men also came to share the outdoor meal with us.

After four days the work was done, and my friend, presumably taking a silent hint from his father, suggested we take a day trip somewhere. We went to a temple on nearby Mount

Mudeung, where there was supposed to be an amazing view, but it was just an ordinary mountain temple. We walked about a bit before finding a tavern in the village below where we drank *makgeolli*. We were quite tipsy when someone walked in and greeted my friend. His face was pale, and he looked as delicate as a gentleman scholar. His name was Oong. We invited him to join us, but he said there was construction going on in the temple the next day and he had to bring the workers their *makgeolli*.

Four days before the Chuseok holiday, I decided to leave my friend's house. I could tell I was overstaying my welcome: his parents had stopped talking to me entirely, and even my friend had taken to eating silently at the dinner table without making eye contact. When I was about to leave, my friend's father stuck his head out the door and asked if he could have the military-issue tent in my backpack. He no doubt wanted to use it as a tarp to cover harvested crops or firewood. As I wordlessly handed it to him, my backpack felt strangely deflated.

My friend followed me out the gate for a few steps and muttered, "I can't go far. Have a good trip back."

I gave him a wave and went on my way. I knew that it was mostly because life was harsh for the poor, but something about how calculating they were behind the lively and generous ring of their voices made me feel sad about the whole thing.

I returned to Masan and headed out again toward Jinju. There, I walked around downtown for a while before finding a room at a shabby inn on the Nam River in Cheonbyeon. I was loitering around the city again the next day when I came upon a job posting on a telegraph pole. The word *bread* caught my eye. The ad mentioned free food and lodgings for workers at a bakery. Back then, Jinju, historically a fortress town, had a small center that one could easily cover, crossing the bridges over the Nam. I don't quite remember where it was—toward Okbong-dong or Sangbong-dong—but once I left the residential area, I found the place in an alley near the market. It displayed a small, square wooden sign saying "Joongang Bakery."

I pushed open the door that led to the work area, which had a coal-burning earthen stove, a large iron oven, two cauldrons, Japanese-style latticed glass doors with good lighting near the front, and a courtyard beyond it. A mound of dough sat on a kneading station built from planks, a little off to the side from the earthen stove. The floor was cement, sticky with wet flour.

The bakery was staffed by two middle-aged women and a man with a towel wrapped around his head. As he forcefully kneaded the dough, he spotted me and called out, "What is it? Do you want some bread?"

"No . . . I heard you were hiring . . ."

"Fancy Seoul accent! Are you from Seoul?"

"Yes."

"Go on in."

Fidgeting awkwardly, I passed through the work area and the glass doors to the courtyard. There was an overweight woman in baggy pants, an apron, and a towel around her head, washing and straining red beans in a basin at the faucet. She looked up as if waiting for me to speak.

"I heard you were hiring."

"Are you a student?"

"Yes, I'm on leave."

"What a pity. I've already hired someone." But she continued to stare at me.

I mumbled, "Oh, all right . . ." and stood there for a moment before bowing and turning to leave.

When I got to the glass doors, I heard her say, "Hey, student, hang on a second." She sat on the edge of the porch next to the faucets. I approached again. "You don't sound like you're from these parts. Where are you from?"

"I'm from Seoul."

"Your parents both alive?"

The usual barrage of questions. I stated: I have a widowed mother, a younger brother, and two older sisters, I took leave from school because I needed to earn tuition money, I planned to go back to school after my military conscription, I wanted to see the world before I did and was visiting a friend when I thought I'd look for a job, I could work for at least six months— it all came tumbling out.

She sighed deeply and said her own eldest son was currently in the military; she had already hired someone a few days ago but since they were still short handed, I might as well suffer, too. With this she laughed so hard that her eyes nearly squeezed shut and her face was as square as a cracker. Oh, my dear Joongang Bakery owner lady, are you still alive today? She urged me to go inside and gave me a little shove through the glass doors.

"Look here, I'm going to put this student to work." That was when I learned the man deep into kneading the dough was the woman's husband. She led me to an annex built right up against the wall across the courtyard, and slid open the paper-screen door. There was a desk and a wooden military-issue cot with a neatly folded blanket. The walls were clean, as if recently papered.

"You can share this room with the Park boy." There was a storage room next door, piled with sacks of flour and powdered milk, with cans of shortening and old baking equipment on the shelves.

I spent the day helping out with minor tasks like carrying flour sacks, going to the taps to refill the water before the tanks ran dry, and arranging cooled loaves of bread into boxes. The Park boy returned from making deliveries, his bicycle loaded with a towering stack of empty boxes. He moved the boxes to a corner of the workroom and parked the bike out front. He kept glancing at me, uncertain of how to take this sudden intruder. The owner man said in an exuberant voice, "Say hello. This is Park, and . . . what'd you say your family name was?"

"Hwang, sir."

In the evening the two middle-aged women went home, and Park and I stayed behind to clean up the workroom. Park brought in water from the courtyard using a rubber hose and cleaned the cement floor of flour and footprints. He also washed the baking tools and the various basins and tubs. Still awkward with each other, we entered the room. Park said he was from nearby Sacheon. He too had taken the bakery job after some loafing around, waiting for his military service to begin. He told me all sorts of things: that the owner lady was a good person, clever enough to land several school-lunch contracts and furthermore helping out an orphanage in dire straits; that the owner man had learned to bake in Busan during the Japanese occupation and his dream was to open a proper bakery, but it was hard getting good ingredients outside of Seoul, which meant that the best he could manage was loaves of white bread. However, they weren't very popular, because "the locals have no taste." The most popular item at the bakery was a bun filled with sweet red bean paste.

I ate at the same table with the owner man and Park. The owner couple treated us like family, because we reminded them of their sons in the military. I helped the owner man with the kneading and took turns with Park going out to make deliveries. It was all I could do to keep from toppling over on the bicycle at first, with even a few boxes, and sometimes I got lost in the unfamiliar city. At night, I took the bicycle and a stack of empty boxes to the playground of a nearby elementary school to practice my balance.

Two months later, Park and I were finally able to liberate the owner man from his work. The owner would put together the basic mix of flour, water, yeast, salt, sugar, shortening, and powdered milk, before stepping back. We would knead it for about half an hour, leave it in the proofing oven to rise, punch it down, and knead it again—after three rounds of this, my face would be drenched with sweat.

We helped the owner lady as well. We boiled the beans, mashed them and filtered out the skins, mixed in sugar, and boiled the mixture over a small fire to make red bean jam. We made pastry cream by mixing sugar and canned American margarine with egg yolks, stirring until it thickened. In the dead of winter, we suggested making steamed buns and dumplings, which would sell better than the red bean–paste buns; it was the owners who had to convince us that taking the winter season off to rest was a better idea.

On a March day when it was still chilly but the scent of spring hung in the air, Park and I went for a walk to Chokseongnu Pavilion. We took a spin within the ancient city walls and were coming down a hill when someone walking toward us asked for a light. I handed him a lighter and he said, "Didn't I see you at Jangchun Temple in Chilwon?"

Ah, this was my classmate's friend whom I'd bumped into at Jangchunsa and the tavern in the nearby village! The young man named Oong.

Oong lived in Jinju. He had been a devout Buddhist from birth, born after his mother had prayed to the Buddha for a son. A sickly child, he was given to the monks at the temple to raise. Oong was on his second attempt to get into university and had gone back to Jangchunsa to prepare. He and Park got along well enough, but it was with me that he really became friends. When Oong heard I wrote fiction, he showed me some poetry he'd been secretly writing. Some were sentimental love poems befitting his age, but the nature poems, thanks to his childhood in a temple annex, were clear and mature. I praised them as well written, and I meant it.

Whenever he visited his parents, he would drop by Joongang Bakery to see me and got to know the owner couple, too. It wasn't a big town. Once the couple learned who his father was, the owner lady began referring to him as "the Eastern medicine doctor's son."

One day, Park had the idea of packing a lunch and going on a picnic somewhere, so I suggested meeting Oong at Jangchunsa.

It happened to be the eighth day of the fourth month of the lunar calendar: the grounds were crowded with women making donations in exchange for paper lanterns that they could write their names in and hang around the temple. We left the main compound and went up a grassy hillock that overlooked the temple roofs. There we ate our lunch and drank *makgeolli*. We reclined on our straw mats and fell asleep; I woke up by myself when I felt a chill come over me.

It was in that moment, my favorite moment of the day, when the sun is on the verge of setting and the horizon is set alight, when a straggler bird sails leisurely through the sky, slowly catching up with its flock, when the world falls silent and the only sound you hear is the breeze rustling through the pine needles—in that moment, I sat up, stared at the darkening mountains and fields, and made a decision: *I need to leave the secular world and become a monk.*

I didn't tell Park of my plans on our way back and merely told Oong that I'd return to the temple soon. A few days later, when I was alone with the owner man and declared my intention to enter a temple, he responded positively, in his usual tolerant and sympathetic manner: "Good for you. If I hadn't had a wife and children myself, I would've become a monk. How great it would be to not deal with this hideous world!"

Asking him to only tell the owner lady that I was going home, I packed my things. The lady immediately teared up when she heard I was leaving and escorted me all the way to the bus station. She pressed some money into my palm and said, "No matter what, you must guard your health. And use this to buy your mother something delicious."

~

Monk Dae-hyun was the abbot of Jangchunsa during my stay there, which had been arranged with Oong's help. A middle-aged man with sharp eyes and a pale face, he seemed to study my every move. No one asked me to, but I helped the old lady congregants by gathering big loads of firewood for them from further up the mountainside. It happened to be vegetable tending season, so I also helped to weed and fertilize the temple's vegetable patch. In the evenings, I sat with Monk Dae-hyun to talk. When I look back on my life, it seems that my elders tended to take a special interest in me. It's not that I tried to curry favor with them; I just tended to be direct with others, possibly to the point of rudeness. But I think this might have endeared me to older people.

Monk Dae-hyun called me to his room one night and asked me to massage his legs. He spoke while I did so. "I became a monk at a young age because, during the Japanese era, I had no other way to survive. The hardest thing was to watch people I knew perish during the war. You will probably leave the temple someday on your own spiritual path, but is there anything you want to say to me before that?"

Oong must have told him of my intentions. I answered without hesitation: "I've always wanted to devote my life to studies that will cultivate my mind and heart."

"That is not a satisfying answer, but if it's what you truly want, I can help you."

"Please help me."

He told me to go to Beomeo Temple in Busan and wrote a letter for me to the teaching monk, Hadongsan. He added that Monk Gwang-deok in Beomeosa had been his guide and suggested that I see him first.

Oong saw me off as I left Jangchunsa and headed for Busan. The area of Busan where the temple was located had bustling hot springs but was otherwise just fields and pine forests.

When we reached the stop for the temple, a boy in monk's robes got off the bus before me. He was handsome, with well-defined features. I was following him when he turned around and asked, "Are you headed for Beomeosa?"

"I am. Do you live there?"

"I do . . . But what brings you to Beomeosa?"

I hesitated for a moment. "I want to become a monk."

The boy monk was not surprised. "Many people come for that reason. But not many are accepted."

"Why is that?"

"It wasn't meant to be." The boy monk spoke as if the answer were obvious.

We reached a path that led into the pine forest of Geumjeong Mountain. As we passed the main gate and entered the grounds of the temple, the boy monk straightened his robes and bowed with his palms together toward the main hall. I lingered behind him until he gestured to one of the buildings and said, "Go in there. They'll help you find whoever you're looking for."

I bowed and walked to what looked like an office. A man in gray monk's robes but without a shaved head was sitting inside. I told him I was there to meet Monk Gwang-deok, and he asked where I was from. When I answered that Monk Dae-hyun of Haman's Jangchunsa had sent me, a young monk poked his head out and told me to follow him. He led me to what looked like a reception area, and soon after, a tall, skinny middle-aged monk entered. He had the forthrightness of a rigorous intellectual, with a gentle gaze and a face that seemed to be holding back a smile.

"You're here to see me?"

This was Monk Gwang-deok, a follower of Great Monk Hadongsan, leader of the Korea Buddhist University Federation, and later the publisher of *Bulkwang*, a Buddhist magazine. He passed away a long time later, a year after I was released from prison.

I handed Monk Gwang-deok my letter from Monk Dae-hyun. He sat quietly for a while before saying, "We can't accept everyone who wants to be a monk. Keep this letter with you and show it to the great monk when he's here." In my memory he never spoke in difficult parables or conceptual language.

I was shown to a guest room. At dinnertime, novices took turns looking in, and the one in charge of food came with dinner, set it down before me, bowed with his hands together, and sat. "Why do you wish to become a monk?" he asked.

I answered honestly. "I don't really know." Something about his attitude made me think he was trying to rile me.

"Are you hoping to find yourself?" Had he read too much Socrates?

"I came here because I had nowhere else to go." That much was true. I briefly thought about the nature of talk. This was something different from the kind of euphemisms my friends and I adopted around each other. It was difficult to speak the truth in a simple way. But the truth itself was not complicated.

After the dinner trays were cleared, it was time for bed. At dawn I heard the sound of chanting, but I didn't get up. Someone had to come in and wake me, and I reluctantly roused myself, washed, and ate the breakfast they gave me.

Gwang-deok took me to Monk Hadongsan's quarters, which were in a separate, quieter spot. A straw screen was drawn over the door. A boy monk emerged, rolled up the screen, and invited me inside. I sat down on the floor and the boy monk opened a sliding door. Inside sat the great monk himself. I did the three *sambae* bows as I'd been taught and handed him the letter. The old monk, who had aged as softly as a child, gave it a glance before pushing it aside. "So, how long do you intend on being here?"

I couldn't answer and only sat there with my head down. The old monk was also silent. Before I bowed again and left his presence, I said, "As long as I have nowhere else to go, I shall stay."

This was an interview of sorts. Outside, Gwang-deok asked me, "What did he say?"

"He asked me how long I was going to be here."

Gwang-deok did not ask me anything else, not even what my answer was. That meant I could stay. I went back to the guestroom and stayed another night.

After breakfast, another monk came to me and told me to bring my things outside. He didn't say anything as he walked briskly along. I followed with my bag. We went down some stone steps and to a path through a thick pine forest. Here he said: "Wait here, another monk will come and fetch you."

I waited for a long time, crouched on those stone steps. The birds twittered noisily as they flew from treetop to tall treetop. Somewhere close by I heard the sound of young people on an outing and a woman's laughter. A young man started to sing in a tenor voice:

> Standing on the old hill where I played,
> this unchanging scene is just a poet's dream.
> The great pine tree of old is felled and gone.

The lyrics, which had always sounded trite to me before, pierced my heart. A middle-aged monk with a beggar's sack on his back and a straw hat on his head came down the stone steps and stopped to look down at me.

"Are you the one Monk Gwang-deok told me about?"

I said yes.

"Follow me."

I awkwardly stood and gathered my bag.

"I don't know what they were thinking when they put you in my care, though. They told me to come get you since you have nowhere else to go. But my hermitage is very small. We can't afford to keep you with us long."

The bus shook for hours as it drove toward Ulsan. We got off, followed a path that ran alongside a beach, and after many miles reached a hermitage that had a main hall, a kitchen attached, and one room that served as living quarters. Despite its small size, it had its own Buddha statue inside. There were straw mats on the floor—who knew how old they were? It had been built very close to the cliffs; the sound of powerful waves striking the rocks made my ears ring at first.

The monk who brought me said the temple had been left empty for a long time and needed to be cleaned out. He put me to work with a rag. Helped by my memory of cleaning the class-rooms in elementary school, I ran the rag in lines along the floor. The monk then instructed me to light the stove and make rice. When it was done, he took a pair of aluminum lunch boxes from his sack. Inside were sweet potato shoots, greens, kimchi, preserved turnip, and other side dishes that he must have obtained from the Beomeosa kitchen. We ate by candlelight with a bowl of rice each, and it tasted like heaven.

I had thought there was only the one room, but past the hall that housed the Buddha statue lay another, longer, narrower room with earthen walls. The floor was dirt, with a straw mat so old that it, too, was coated in dirt. I hardly slept due to the noise of the waves. Suddenly the door burst open and the monk shouted: "You little parasite, you say you want to dedicate your life to the Buddha but you're just lying here asleep because you don't even know it's prayer time!" Saying I deserved a beating, he began to kick me where I lay. I jumped up and fended him off, running away to the yard past the main hall.

"Look at that bastard go! Leave, then!" He mercilessly tossed my things into the yard. I rushed to put on my shoes and grab my belongings, only to realize that I had no idea where to go at that time of night. The monk ignored me and began knocking on his *moktak* and chanting.

After standing there for a long time, I made my way back down the dark mountain path. Day began to break as I stumbled along. Tears ran down my face. "That son of a bitch, that bastard of a monk . . ."

There's an old story about a young monk who complained to an elder monk after being beaten at a temple where he had been sent on an errand. In answer, the old monk scolded him. "Don't you see they were doing you a favor?" Later, when the young monk became a novice himself, he learned that it was a kind of rite of passage for initiates.

It was evening, dinner long ended, by the time I managed to reach Beomeosa. I sat at the store near the gate of the temple, appeased my hunger with bread and a drink, and entered through the gate, exhausted. No one paid me any attention. There was not a soul in the empty courtyard of the main hall, but then I noticed a familiar youth sitting on the porch of the living annex. It was the handsome boy monk I'd spoken to on my first visit there. In the outside world he would have been a high school freshman. I wonder if he's a great monk now.

I sat down next to him. He didn't seem to know I'd just been somewhere far away. When I described how I had been cast out by a fierce monk, he smiled and said, "Have you noticed that to reach the inner temple you must first pass through three gates?"

I immediately understood what he meant. "And how did you decide to become a monk?"

He answered as if it were nothing: "Nowhere else would feed me."

That night, I went back to the guest room. The monk in charge of guests entered early in the morning, grumbling as he looked around the room, and told me to wait by the stone steps again after breakfast. With no choice in the matter, I waited just like the previous day. There were many monks going in and out of the temple that day. I stared at them and they stared back but passed me without a word. It wasn't as if I could ask, "Are you looking for me?"

I couldn't have lunch and was starving by the time dusk rolled around. But no one came for me, and none of the monks going in and out talked to me. Though it was early summer, night was already falling. Finally an old monk walked down the stone steps, looked surprised, and cleared his throat. "Huh, you gave me a fright just now. Who are you?"

I bowed without a word, and he stood for a moment before saying, "Aren't you the boy they asked me to teach the ways of the temple? Come with me."

We walked the long path to the paved road and rode the night bus to downtown Busan. The old monk wordlessly cut through the crowds. He moved so fast that I could barely keep his robes in sight and didn't realize I was in Busanjin Station at first. It was only when we reached a waiting room that I saw it was a station. I kept looking around us.

The monk sat down heavily and gestured for me to join him. As I sat, the hunger and thirst of the entire day nearly overwhelmed me.

"Go buy some drinks from that shop over there. You have money, right?" Ah, yes, I mumbled as I ran over and got two bottles of soda. I gave him one and drank the other, feeling a burn in my empty stomach as I did so. The monk took a few hearty swigs and paused to catch his breath. "Why are you trying to be a monk? Look at how many monks there are. Everyone has their own path to walk."

I knew that making any kind of response to this would be my loss, so I continued staring at the floor.

"Forget the whole thing and go home." He drank half the bottle, stood, and placed it on the table. "I'm getting tickets. Don't go anywhere." His robes swirled into the crowd.

He never came back. I waited a full hour before suddenly becoming suspicious. I jumped up and scanned the lines of people waiting for tickets, trying to catch a glimpse of monkish gray fabric. But all I saw were scores of soldiers on leave. I went to the other waiting areas, but the monk was nowhere to be found.

I was like a gourd bottle with a snapped string, sitting in that waiting room chair. I began watching the people running to catch their trains, or smiling as they saw familiar faces. Everyone had someone waiting for them or a place to go to. Where was I to go? How was I to find this monk? Who would come looking for me at Beomeosa, where they wouldn't even feed me anymore? Should I give up and go back home?

I had to eat something first. I crossed the plaza and ordered a stew filled with rice in a restaurant across the street. As I scraped the bowl clean, my eyelids began to droop.

I came back out to the station plaza and wandered without a goal. Thinking about how that old raccoon of a monk had schemed to get rid of me from the start, my resentment reached all the way to Monk Gwang-deok. Those bullshit monks really had it in for me.

Someone came right up to my face and whispered, "Do you want to have some fun?" An old, heavily wrinkled woman stood there smiling.

"Forget fun, I'm dying of sleep. Take me to a room where I can spend the night."

"There's a clean, quiet room nearby." It wasn't too far from the red-light district. I saw drunken people and soldiers in uniform in the maze of alleys. The women were practically in their underwear. The madam brought me to an empty room and asked for money upfront. "Bring your shoes indoors."

An acrylic blanket and a dirty pillow were spread out on the linoleum floor. I latched the door and lay down. Judging from the cackling and moaning coming from the rooms on either side, business was brisk. I tossed and turned but could not fall asleep. It was not until the curfew lifted at 4 a.m. that the hellish neighborhood quieted down enough for me to sleep, only to be awakened around nine by the sound of loud radio music.

I left the alleys and walked the main street without knowing where I was going. When I reached Gukje Market, I bought a bowl of blood sausage stew and glimpsed a barber's sign, which gave me an idea. It was so early that there wasn't a single customer, and the barber was pretending to read the paper as he stared at the young woman in charge of shaving.

I sat down in one of the chairs.

"How do you want it?"

"Shave it all off."

"All of it . . . with a razor?"

"Or clippers or whatever. Take it all off."

"You'll regret it . . . Wait, are you going into the army?"

I didn't feel like explaining, so I nodded.

"Ah, then you have the right idea. It'll get you into the right mindset, too." He talked about how the soldiers would rip out new conscripts' hair with their clippers, just to haze them. My hair had grown quite long by then; as he lifted it up at the crown to shave it off, the ends fell across my face. With my scalp as bald as a monk's and my face clean-shaven as well, I felt much cooler in the heat.

I took the bus, walked the long path back to Beomeosa's main gate, and entered the inner temple. Just as on the first day, I went to the reception room, and the monk who had been there the first time saw me and came out.

"I would like to meet with Monk Gwang-deok today."

"Didn't you leave with that monk the other day?"

"He abandoned me at the station."

I could sense him closing ranks. "That can't be right. Well, Monk Gwang-deok is not here. In any case, you should have a long talk with him this time." There was, apparently, a meeting scheduled between the Beomeosa's affiliated temples and their abbots, and his advice was for me to latch on to one of them and follow.

I didn't wait by the stone stairs this time. I sat in the reception room instead. The abbots had been arriving in the morning one by one, and it wasn't until well after lunch that their meeting finally drew to a close. Taking pity on me, or perhaps it was another of Monk Gwang-deok's schemes, the reception room monk took me to a tall monk. He had just put his shoes on and was getting up from the stone step in front of the porch.

"Monk, please take this man. The housekeeping monk's request."

"What? This is the first I've heard of this."

They continued to whisper between themselves awhile, until the reception room monk beckoned me and said in a low voice, "Go with him. And *stay* with him, even if he tries to cast you out."

I was wearing a shirt and worsted trousers, but my shaven head probably made a better impression on the monks than before. I followed two steps behind him. He looked back a few times but didn't say a word.

We reached Haeundae's Geumgangwon Temple, rumored to have strict training and rules. The monks were young and full of righteousness. I was a little nervous about its proximity to Beomeosa and how quiet and regimented it seemed. The abbot made me wait in a courtyard while he called a monk to say, "Give him a change of clothes. He's a new novice." That was the moment when my place was finally decided.

I went into the novice room in the living annex and changed into gray robes. From that day on, my task was to clean the temple with the other novices. The monk in charge of keeping the novices in line and managing their daily lives interviewed me. He informed me of the rules and asked for my name and my ID. I gave him my legal name. He wrote some things down and then announced: "We'll call you Novice Suyoung. *Su* meaning 'to train,' *young* meaning 'path.'" All he did was change the Chinese characters in my existing name, but I liked it.

Now that the magnolia, forsythia, azalea, guelder roses, and wisteria had bloomed and withered in turn, it was early summer. I began to enjoy tending the vegetable patch. I learned the monastic style of mindful eating and of keeping the physical body alive. I woke at the break of dawn, wiped the temple floors, and swept the courtyards all the way to the main gate as daylight brightened. The sweeping was hardest in autumn, when leaves fell, and in winter, when snow fell. Still, clearing the path in the softly fallen snow so that others could walk unimpeded calmed and humbled my heart. On my own, I gathered the robes of monks who had gone into winter practices and washed them.

All the monks kept their wooden eating implements stored in a wrapping cloth on a shelf in the large hall. During meals they spread it out and sat with their backs against the wall. First, they rinsed their bowls with water and took only as much rice, stew, and garnish as they could eat in one sitting. The stew was always vegetable soybean paste stew, and the side dishes two kinds of greens and kimchi. On special days or events, we might get fried side dishes that smelled of sesame oil. We had to eat everything in our bowl; at the end of the meal, we filled the bowl with water and drank every drop. Then we filled it again, drank, wiped everything down with a dry towel, and packed it all back up in the wrapping cloth.

My tasks consisted of cleaning and small errands. After a few months the monks sent me into town on various errands, such as posting mail, exchanging messages with congregants, or buying things for prayers and services. Whenever I set out, the monks gave me a bit of spending money on top of what I needed to complete the errand.

One day, about six months into this life, I had an errand to run and went into downtown Busan for a change. I finished around noon, with plenty of time before I had to return in the evening. I went into an old Chinese restaurant and ordered *jjajangmyeon*, black bean noodles. I was only a novice but I sat there in my monk's robes, and after finishing off a bowl of noodles, there was still time, so I checked out the movie posters on the telegraph poles and walls and picked one. A black-and-white film called *One Hundred Men and a Girl*, it was about an unemployed trombone player who gets an orchestra together and convinces the famous Leopold Stokowski to conduct them in order to help his daughter, an aspiring singer with a pure soprano voice. I remember the last scene where the girl sings and the conductor passionately waves his baton, hair tossing this way and that.

I was being swept out with the rest of the crowd when someone grabbed my shoulder and stopped me. "Aren't you Sok-yong?" I turned and was dismayed to see it was a friend of Eldest Brother. He had studied commerce and worked at a bank, and occasionally visited our house. I gave him a quick bow and tried to run away, but he grabbed my wrist and demanded, "Where have you been? Do you have any idea how hard your mother and brother-in-law have been looking for you?"

I lied and said, "I've been in Jinju."

"Jinju?"

I broke out of his grasp and escaped into the crowd. He didn't follow. I thought of my mother for a moment and sighed deeply and tried to shake the thought off. I was glad I'd said Jinju. I'd named it at random, but in fact I had sent my mother a postcard from Jinju last Chuseok.

One morning, nearly a month later, I was sweeping the courtyard of early fall leaves when a monk came up to me and said, "There's someone here to see you. They say they know you well."

I wondered who it might be as I reluctantly made my way out of the temple. On either side of the path were tall pine trees and past the main gate through the forest was a souvenir store selling handcrafted wooden bells, walking canes, fans, and towels embroidered with the temple's name. Standing across the road from the store was a familiar person. It was the kind of blurry familiarity you might feel from looking at someone through a heat shimmer, or glancing out the window on a day of misty rain and seeing the indistinct outline of someone you know. Mother wore a *hanbok* made from worsted fabric with a cardigan thrown over her shoulders. I paused for a moment, and then my footsteps quickened. I came to a stop when we stood facing each other. We did not hug, like in the movies, but she came to me and wrapped an arm around my shoulders. "Let's go home!"

My mother led me past the store and down the wide road.

"I roamed all of South Gyeongsang Province looking for you. You're coming home with me, right?"

My eyes flooded with tears, and I said, "Yes, Mom, let's go home."

We were on our way to the bus stop when I sensed someone following us. I looked back and was surprised to see Oong.

"What are you doing here?" I asked, but Oong only smiled.

Mother said, "If it wasn't for that boy, I never would have found you."

Eldest Brother's friend had told Mother that he'd met me in Busan and that I was somewhere near Jinju, which reminded her of the postcard I'd sent. I hadn't written the address properly, only the street number, but Mother had managed to find Joongang Bakery all on her own.

The owner lady hadn't forgotten me. She'd heard from her husband that I'd joined a Buddhist order, and felt sorry for my mother. She told Mother about the Eastern medicine doctor's son and went to see the doctor herself, to get the name of the temple where Oong was staying in Haman.

Mother went to Jangchunsa and found Oong, who in turn told her I was at a temple in Busan and went with her to look for me. She had Oong go up to the temple alone, but the monks rebuffed him and wouldn't tell him where I was. They merely said I had come wanting to be a monk and had stayed for a brief while, but they didn't know which monk I had followed or which temple I had gone to.

Oong and Mother went searching through the temples around Busan. A monk advised them, "If he's a novice, he's probably still somewhere near Beomeosa." Mother made up her mind and went to the reception room at Beomeosa and cried floods of tears, begging them to tell her where I was. Monk Gwang-deok presently appeared. The first thing he said was, "He has already given himself as a child of Buddha, why do you search for him still?" Mother wept again as she reasoned with him, saying she was a widow who had lost her husband at a young age, that I was all she had left, that I was Christian from birth, that Christ's and Buddha's teachings were a little different but the fundamental sympathy with the world was the same, that her son had run away and never asked her permission to enter the order.

Monk Gwang-deok listened to all of this without a word and nodded at the part where she said I had run away. He said to her in a low voice, "Then this is what you must do. Meet him. If you meet him and he follows you, he is your child. If he does not and returns to the temple, he is Buddha's child, and you must never search for him again."

I learned of all this later on, of course, and I did sometimes regret following her and not returning to the temple. But perhaps it was my fate that I would return to the outside world and become a writer.

The first thing Mother did was take me to Gukje Market to get me some street clothes. I think she was worried that if she let me keep my robes on, I'd go back into the temple. We went into a nice restaurant in front of Busanjin Station; when I ordered bibimbap, Mother insisted she needed to thank Oong for his efforts and ordered the more expensive bulgogi instead. When I was at the temple, the smell of meat would turn my stomach, but that day, the meat broth flowing into the reservoir of the domed grill was so delicious, I fought with Oong for every bite.

The sight of Mother's face as she fell asleep on the train from Busan to Seoul broke my heart because it had changed so much. I went out to the vestibule and smoked, accompanied by the rhythmic *takada ta takada ta* sound of the steel wheels running over the seams of the rails. When the train passed over a bridge, the open air below us made it sound like *walgurang tang walgurang tang*. My ears ached as the crisscrossed steel beams flew by outside. The bridge soon came to an end and we were rolling over the ground again. *Walgurang tang, walgurang tang, walgurang tang . . . takada ta, takada ta, takada ta . . .*

The clear change in sound was like the death that would have met me if I'd jumped off the train then, or like the division between my life as it had been and what was to come.

~

I returned to the attic room in Heukseok-dong Market. I slept like the dead for a long time and then started to write again. Whether I was acting the novice at a mountain temple or undergoing an existential crisis in the attic room of a Heukseok-dong shop and doing nothing but writing all day, the world continued to turn in a hurry. Despite the continuous protests against the Korea–Japan diplomatic talks, the agreement went ahead, a measure passed for the deployment of Korean soldiers to Vietnam, and the first wave of the Fierce Tiger Division was sent to Southeast Asia.

While I was living in the attic above the kitchenette behind my mother's store, I traversed the border between life and death more than once. A furnace for coal briquettes was right next to the attic ladder; if I wasn't careful, the occasional gas leak would seep into my room. That winter, I nearly died of carbon monoxide poisoning. I wasn't conscious but somehow managed to open the door to the attic and urinate below; I think someone had told me that if you urinated after being exposed, you survived. The sound woke my mother, who managed to drag me down. For two days I was barely conscious, but slowly recovered with the help of various remedies and by drinking kimchi brine.

For some reason, after that incident, whenever I went down to the Han River, I was possessed by the urge to join the flowing water disappearing into the distance. The cars and people on the street looked like surreal scenery from a silent movie. The sound of cars seemed to come from very far away.

One night, on my way home from downtown, I felt this urge again. I think I got off the bus near Namyeong-dong. I went to a nearby pharmacy and bought some Seconal, then traveled a few more stations and bought some more. I kept doing this all the way to Yongsan Station until I'd acquired a considerable number of pills. I knew that right across the Han River bridge in Noryangjin there were plenty of bars frequented by people heading home from work. I must have drunk two bottles. In truth, the amount of alcohol I drank then was what saved me. I stumbled home and ignored my mother complaining about how much I had drunk and went up to the attic to collapse on my bed. I was so drunk that I'd forgotten to take the pills.

I was woken around two in the morning by a desperate scream. I knew who was screaming. There was a crazy woman who wandered the market alone; she slept in the public toilet inside the market.

Her scream brought back the memory of the pills I had bought. The fluorescent light buzzed; it had been on all night. I sat at my desk, wrote my mother a farewell letter, and rummaged through the closet for a pair of clean underwear. Then I got dressed as if I were going out. Yes, I was off on a long journey. I stuffed over thirty pills in my mouth and swallowed them with some water. I turned off the light and lay down, but I didn't really feel like I was about to die.

In the morning my brother came up to the attic to get his books and schoolbag, which is what saved my life one more time.

"Mother, there's something wrong with *hyeong*."

I was taken in an ambulance to the emergency room at Yeongdeungpo Municipal Hospital. The doctor examined my pupils and wordlessly began emergency measures, bringing out an oxygen tank and placing the mask on my face. My eldest sister flipped through the clinical chart and saw how every category was "Undetermined" except for the heart, which was labeled "Possible." According to the doctor, I was fortunate to have been found in time.

For four days I lay unconscious until I finally began to stir. They said I had seizures so powerful that the entire family had to hold me down on the bed. I woke up on the afternoon of the fifth day. The doctor decided it was safe enough to discharge me, and Mother moved me to my eldest sister's rented place in a quiet residential neighborhood.

Eldest Brother and my sister were both schoolteachers and were out for most of the day. Mother waited until I was sleeping peacefully and decided to slip out, too, to buy some groceries. I was lying close to the wall; when I opened my eyes, I couldn't see anything except for a blurry light to the right. I instinctively wanted to go to it. The light looked like a wide, open space. I stood up slowly, holding onto the wall for support, and felt my way around the room. Even when I was standing in front of the blurry light, I still couldn't see anything at first; it was like standing inside a dense fog.

I started to discern lines within the fog. The light turned a weak yellow, then deepened. I was standing in front of a large window. The lines of houses, land, bare winter branches, all started to emerge from the yellow they'd been buried in. For a long time, I stared at the world-changing colors. It was only when that color divided itself and turned into multiple other shades that I could see that snow had fallen the previous night and the sky was clear and blue. That deep yellow had not been a real color.

Things went back to normal as if nothing had happened. I met up now and again with friends, who were still voracious readers, and bluffed my way through those conversations. I said nothing of my wanderings or of nearly dying.

Now and then I heard from my artist friend Mu, or bumped into him in a tea house. I don't remember if it was right after I came back from wandering the southern peninsula or after I came back from my suicide attempt, but I did receive a postcard that left an impression on me.

I was idling my life away and had nothing to really look forward to, spending all my time loitering around the city or sleeping in my attic room until late in the afternoon. Like a submarine hatch, the only exit from the room was the trapdoor; my mother's head would pop up from time to time.

"Look, someone sent you a lovely postcard a while back."

One side showed a watercolor painting of a blue ocean, pine forests, and clouds on the horizon. Above it was written: "In keeping with the song 'Gaudeamus igitur,' I am commemorating my springlike youth. From the beautiful beaches of Gapo . . . Mu."

A year earlier, Mu had gone to the Catholic hospital in Malli-dong for his tuberculosis. When Seong-jin and I went to visit, the first thing Mu did, skinny as a rake in his hospital gown, was ask for a cigarette. He seemed so normal that we thought he would be discharged soon, but instead his condition wors-ened, and he was transferred to another hospital for further treatment in Masan.

I have a portrait of myself done by Mu. He drew it in profile on a sketchbook page the size of a paperback, with the emphasis on strong cheekbones and chin. I pinned the page on the particle-board wall of the attic room.

I was going to write a belated reply to his postcard when I remembered that his place wasn't that far from mine. I decided to make a day of it and visit him in person at his house, which was next to a quilt shop, a place that looked like a good location for a restaurant. The front of it was all glass doors, but that day the doors were covered with wooden planks and only the side door was open. I called out "hello" and knocked for a long time until I heard footsteps and a woman who resembled my mother came out.

"I'm a friend of Mu's. He sent me a postcard . . . I just wanted to see how he was doing."

The woman's irritated expression vanished, and she covered her mouth as she murmured, "He passed away . . ."

"Oh . . . I see . . ." I backed away, bowed, and was about to leave when Mu's mother called out to me.

"If you still have that postcard . . . Might I see it?"

I took the postcard from my pocket and showed it to her. Her hand didn't leave her mouth as she stared at it.

"Please take it," I said, but she quickly waved no and handed it back to me.

"No, you should keep it."

I knew that Mu's mother was a widow as well. She was so similar to my own mother in appearance that I wondered if she, too, had once been part of the enlightened class of Pyongyang.

She probably had not been happy with Mu being a painter, either. Like my mother, she must have spent every last coin she had to acquire the shop she owned now.

I trudged back home with the postcard in my hand. In the battlefields of Vietnam, I often thought of the sentence Mu had written on it, in which he bade farewell to his springlike youth.

My mother gave up her business at the market and moved to a small rental in Daebang-dong. Just as she did right after Liberation in North Korea, Mother turned to making clothes, one of her many talents. She hired some women and opened a *hanbok* store.

I returned home one day to learn from my brother, now in middle school, that a policeman had come looking for me to deliver a military conscription notice. The notice said that I had failed to respond to two notices for physicals and would have to report to the police station, on pain of arrest—very threatening stuff. I had apparently missed the notices during my lost months of wandering.

I'd heard somewhere that not showing up for physicals after three notices would land you in jail for six months, after which you would immediately serve out your conscription. I happened to pass a marines poster on the street that said they took in several applicants every month, and so I applied. I swiftly passed the IQ test and physical exam, and the very next month was served my conscription orders.

In August of 1966, I rode the all-stop train from Yongsan to the south once more. The emergency money Mother had given me as I left the house that dawn was hidden in my underwear. Just as she had done when I had a school picnic, she made *kimbap*, rice rolls, late into the night and packed them for me to eat later, and never showed any tears. No one saw me off at the still-dark Yongsan Station at dawn, of course. And that was how I bade farewell to the first half of my youth.

10

Prison V

As the summer of 1995 approached, a number of writers and other concerned citizens signed a "Petition for the release of Hwang Sok-yong" and sent it to the Kim Young-sam administration. The petition proposed that the first civilian administration to come to power after the military dictatorships should use this fiftieth anniversary of Liberation as an opportunity to promote harmony and work toward reunification and democratization by pardoning political prisoners. Around this time, it was reported that there were 454 prisoners of conscience and North Korean POWs still behind bars, and that since Liberation, around 10,000 people were still incarcerated under the Anti-communism Law, the National Security Act, and restrictive labor laws. The Kim Young-sam administration released a number of prisoners, including corporation heads but not labor activists, stating that these pardons were for the purposes of national unity and were restricted to persons who showed a clear intent to rehabilitate themselves. At this, political prisoners in all thirty-two prisons nationwide launched a hunger strike on August 7, demanding "the release of all conscientious prisoners and the repeal of the National Security Act." The hunger strike continued for ten days but, of course, no additional prisoners were released.

I had been in prison for two and a half years already. It was unlike anything I'd ever experienced. When I thought back on what my life was like before becoming a writer, it seemed that I'd always been starting something new or living in a state of anxiety. First I had opposed the military dictatorship with my literary allies when I became famous as a novelist, and had struggled to depict reality in my writing while simultaneously fighting for my right to express myself. *Jang Gil-san* is a ten-volume historical novel that took me a decade to complete, because I had to write and do my activism at the same time. It was inevitable that things I experienced in life would appear in my fiction, or that a scene from fiction would be recreated in real life; my writing and my activism had become one.

The past few decades had been a series of crises interspersed with periods of recovering from those crises. I relearned the lessons of my past in my own way, using them to survive my forced reformation in jail.

The reason I was trying to retool my prison life as it entered a third year was that I was afraid of losing my health, and, more than anything else, I was intent on preserving my identity as a writer. As a National Security Act violator, I was imprisoned apart from the regular inmates, and my repeated hunger strikes and complaints added to my isolation. I also believed I should fight censorship and read as much as possible—this was what "democracy activists" were supposed to do in prison. But what I ended up doing was completely different, since daily life inside a prison was much harsher than life as an ordinary civilian. For example, I needed a knife to eat fruit and vegetables, but such things weren't allowed for prisoners. I needed to put in a request if I wanted to use a knife, use it only under observation, and return it immediately after I was done with it. This was such an inconvenience that it became easier to just fashion my own crude blade instead. During exercise hour, I went around looking for cans or pieces of chimney caps. Or I would ask the working prisoners for an exchange of goods. Once I had a can, I cut a piece from the side, hid it under the sole of my shoe, and snuck it into my private cell. Avoiding the gaze of the guards, I sharpened it for days against the cement wall and hid it under the floor boards or between the pages of my Bible in case of inspections. This would make ten days go by like a shot.

There was no one to talk to in the private cell, and I never exchanged more than a few words with the guards. I began to forget how to speak; proper nouns were the first to go. I once spent a week trying to remember the name *Antigone*. I developed a habit of talking to myself. I'd fart and mumble, *Good for you!* I'd talk to myself when I got up in the morning. *Hey, you should clean up today. Look at how dirty the floor is! Such a mess.* I muttered to myself all day long. I borrowed a Korean dictionary from the library and read each word out loud, following along with my finger. But I soon realized that reading in prison was not proper reading. Books needed to be read with others and communicated with others in order to be properly understood. The content of the books I read alone in my private cell became like a pillar blocking the wall. I stopped reading altogether. I forgot about my identity as a political prisoner or an intellectual and befriended the regular criminals, laughing at their jokes, breaking the rules, and behaving like one of them. I had the notion that my survival as a writer was more dependent on the details of real life as I lived it with the regular prisoners. These efforts helped me adjust to life outside prison after just a month, whereas others spent years after their release suffering from the side effects of solitary confinement.

Gongju was a fair distance from Seoul, and the prison wasn't near any train stations, but my ex-wife, Hong Hee-yun, brought my eldest son, Ho-jun, with her once a month to visit me, and I got the occasional drop-in visits from various writers and activist friends.

My visits were held not in the regular visiting room but in the office of the division in charge of reforming political prisoners, and sometimes in the special reception area of the national security division. Visits from PEN International, the UN Human

Rights Committee, Amnesty International, foreign presses, and other foreign dignitaries and Korean politicians were mainly conducted in the special reception area, but when it came to friends and family, we usually met in the aforementioned office. These were all, in a sense, "special visits," because the Ministry of Justice had forbidden me from having any visitors other than immediate family once a month; if any of my literary friends wanted to see me, they had to contact the prison beforehand and have a National Assembly member accompany them.

The persons authorized to visit me as family were my eldest son, Ho-jun; daughter, Yeo-jeong; their mother, Hee-yun; my in-laws representing my then wife, Kim Myoung-su, in the US; and my eldest sister and her husband. Hee-yun and Ho-jun lived in Gwangju and visited once a month with one or two Gwangju people in tow. My father-in-law also visited once every two or three months, always smuggling in a snack he discreetly slipped to me.

When Myoung-su learned that my ex-wife was coming to see me with Ho-jun, she became suspicious. I wanted her to come back to Korea with our son, but she wanted him to be educated in America and refused to come back. Physical distance and time apart led to distrust and misunderstandings between us, aggravating our conflicts past the point of no return. When I heard from my father-in-law that Myoung-su had entered a dance school to extend her stay in America and become eligible for a green card, I congratulated her in my letter but resented her for it, nevertheless. As our conflict crested, her letters ceased for a time, and I begged her in mine to be patient and endure, our future wouldn't always be so dark; once I was out of prison, I would be a good husband and father. Myoung-su explained how much effort it cost her to involve all sorts of people in the campaign for my release at the same time as rehearsing for her performances. She told me that, if only for the future of our child's education, I needed to be clear on where the royalties for my best-selling work, *Jang Gil-san*, were to be paid: to her, or to my ex-wife and other children. In her eyes, this was not just a matter of money but of her rights and pride as the author's wife.

After two years of torment over the issue, I finally had the publisher give her half of the royalties generated from *Jang Gil-san* that had previously gone to my ex-wife and my two older children. The psychological pain of this time was greater even than what I experienced in the punishment cell. All these things culminated in a years-long divorce dispute after I was released. The thing about divorce is that the longer it drags on, the worse the mudslinging becomes, with both sides devoted to ruining the other. Any trace of guilt or sympathy is oblit- erated. Ho-seop, whom I parted with when he was five, went through his rebellious teen and college years and became a grown man in my absence. When I think of him as I write late into the night or lie in bed unable to fall asleep, I still think of him crying "*Appa!*" as I left him behind at the airport in New York.

Unlike the four seasons of the outside world, prison has only winter, which is cold, and not-winter, which is not cold, and surviving each long winter was a great struggle. Winter in prison lasted from October to March. It was around the start of this time, when padded blankets, vests, and hot-water bottles started appearing in preparation for the long freeze ahead, that the Hiltmanns visited me from Germany.

When I entered the reception room, Jochen and Song Hyun- sook rose from the sofa to greet me. We made light conversation at first, asking after each other's families and plans in Korea, until Jochen, normally so serene, suddenly began to cry, wiping away his tears with both hands, which prompted Song Hyun- sook and I to shed tears as well. Through her sobs, Song Hyun-sook continued to interpret for Jochen. He said it was the prisoner number sewn on my tunic that had broken down his restraint. He knew many stories of the Nazi concentration camps. As a professor of the arts, the sight of a writer wearing a prisoner's uniform was a great shock. Song Hyun-sook interpreted:

—Artists should not be locked up in prison and made to wear blue POW uniforms.

I told them that I was called No. 1306, pointing to the cloth tag as I explained that the numbers referred to my cell block and room.

—He says that Germany managed to reunify, but it will take a long time for East and West Germans to get along with each other. And he apologizes for Germany reunifying ahead of Korea.

Song Hyun-sook had an exhibition in Korea and was staying for a while. They told me about being denied entrance to Korea while I was in the US. The Hiltmanns had helped me during my exile in Germany, taken me in when I had nowhere else to go, and put me up in their house on an island in the North Sea so I could write. When this became known, the Korean Embassy's intelligence officer had responded with threats and even came to Jochen's school to investigate my whereabouts. Denied entry at Gimpo Airport, the Hiltmanns were questioned and held in a narrow cell for a sleepless night until their flight back to Germany. Jochen had cried like a baby then, and continued to cry on the plane. I knew the same thing had happened to Professor Itō Narihiko when he tried to visit in order to invite Paik Nak-chung and the poet Ko Un to Japan, and there were many other instances of overseas Koreans being turned away the same way; but with the Hiltmanns I felt especially guilty. They had managed to finagle an interview with me through the help of the Germany Embassy of Korea and the Goethe-Institut. Later, when Korea was the guest of honor of the Frankfurt Book Fair and I met them again at a literary event in Hamburg, I felt strangely sad to see how the three of us had aged. Despite the years that had gone by, the world hadn't changed much, and there were still wars going on.

Postcards, newsletters, and books began to arrive a few days after—a result of PEN America, Japanese PEN, and German PEN making me an honorary member, and Amnesty International designating me a prisoner of conscience. I was also sent a magazine called *International Socialism*, perhaps having been mistaken for a Western socialist. I read it with the aid of a dictionary, thinking it would help me with my English, but gave up, much to my subsequent regret.

Dutch people from all parts of society sent me postcards, and many came from a kindergarten that one of the Amnesty members apparently taught at; by Christmas I had a stack of hundreds. I used bits of leftover rice to stick them on the wall, which made the bare cell look more festive with their colors. The children's drawings made my heart swell. I managed to find, in the pile of letters, one from a woman around my age who seemed to be the head of the kindergarten, and I wrote her a letter of thanks. In the early 2000s, when "Mr. Han's chronicle" was published in the Netherlands and I visited Amsterdam, I imagined those little children grown up into young adults and visited the Dutch offices of Amnesty International to give them my belated thanks.

The poet Lee Si-young faithfully visited once every two months, bringing news of the outside world. One day, he whispered that he was confident I would be included in the Liberation Day pardons. I laughed it off, saying how could he know such a thing, and asked whether he'd had a glass of soju with President Kim Young-sam. He said that the novelist Lee Mun-ku had obtained a promise to that effect. A certain female poet in the Association of Writers for National Literature happened to be high school friends with the wife of President Kim's son, Kim Hyun-chul. Lee Mun-ku had visited Kim Hyun-chul's house along with his wife. Unofficially, it was to plead for my release. Kim Hyun-chul had smiled and said he had been too busy to think about pardons, but promised to include me in the next Liberation Day list.

The news made me believe I only had a few months of my sentence left, which got me so excited that I gave away my books and useful things. But Kim Hyun-chul, far from pardoning anyone, ended up getting arrested himself for the Hanbo Steel incident. President Kim Young-sam threw him in prison to show he was different from the military dictators of the past. Expecting a pardon in that situation was absurd. I was a bit disappointed after my brief high at the prospect of imminent release. I managed to retrieve my dictionary, my knife fashioned from a scrap of can, and a few other things I'd prematurely given away.

Cho Se-hui, who is remembered by generations of readers for his novel *The Dwarf*, came to visit me to talk about old friends and of the funeral of playwright Jeon Jin-ho, who died a lonely death in the US. He proposed we create a literary magazine together after my release. He took out a cigarette, ranting about how we needed to sweep away the sycophants of the dictatorship era, and didn't even glance at the guards in the reception room as he offered me one. I was genuinely not intending to start smoking again. I hadn't had so much as a whiff of secondhand smoke in years. I shook my head, and he lit up, saying,

—Did you know white people are calling cigarettes drugs now? The world is so boring, we may as well enjoy at least one drug, no?

He held the cigarette between thumb and forefinger and took a blissful drag. Watching him made me long for my lost freedom more than any cigarette. It was my determination to use this opportunity to quit smoking once and for all, especially considering my health.

This resolution, however, broke down only a few days after I was released. The poet Lee Si-young took me out for drinks at a Japanese restaurant to congratulate me; he ordered *hirezake*, made from charred blowfish fin, and smoked so enticingly as he drank the hot *hirezake* that, before I knew it, I'd smoked one too. Lee Si-young reminded me of an incident I'd forgotten: one evening as I sat shivering in my cell and a snowstorm raged outside, I'd had near-hallucinations of a guard opening the food hole and offering me a warm shot of *hirezake*. I was on my second smoke when Lee slipped out to buy me my own. He tossed the carton on the table and said:

—Who wants to be alone and bored after everyone else has gone? Let's smoke all we want, and go when it's our time!

That's how I went back to being the hopeless nicotine addict I was before I went to prison. Lee Si-young, on the other hand, whose liver deteriorated, successfully quit.

Speaking of the people who came to visit me in prison, I can't leave out the story of the mural in the exercise yard. Gongju Correctional Institution was divided roughly into two blocks, with a steel fence running left and right between and a connecting corridor down the middle. Administrative buildings were at either end of the corridor, which again gave way to another corridor leading to the outside wall and the gate of the prison. The outside wall wrapped around the inner wall in a circular fashion, with lookouts posted along the top. The left block had the prison factories and in front of it the large exercise yard, while to the right were four cell blocks with one on the very end for political prisoners and felons and the smaller yard that we used in front. The smaller field had a track for jogging and an ad hoc tennis court in the corner.

It was in this exercise yard that the gangsters bowed to me my first day there. The sight of these tall, muscular young men bowing to me was the first surprise, and the giant mural along the long wall was the second. I could guess, as soon as I saw it, whose work it was. For one thing, the style was known as *minjung* art. It depicted the four seasons of the agrarian cycle: plowing and sowing in the spring; weeding the fields and lunches eaten outdoors in the summer; harvest and dancing to *pungmul* drums in the fall; and scenes from Lunar New Year, spinning tops, and games of *yut* in the winter. The artist apparently wanted to show prisoners a healthy life of work and play, but it didn't quite fit with the difficult lives and complex emotions we all felt behind bars, and looked as didactic and preachy as some church pamphlet. Maybe a well-intentioned warden had deemed the long white wall too stark, indeed, detrimental to the prisoners' reform? I laughed on the inside: the painting looked as imprisoned as I was.

The poet Cho Chae-hun of Kongju National University, a member of the prison's civilian steering committee, came visiting a few times with other cultural notables, including the painter Kim Jeong-heon and another professor from the Korean department. I had to tease Kim, for I knew that it was he, as an art professor, who had designed the mural.

—Your painting is making my sentence even worse than it is. I have to spend my precious exercise hour looking at the same tedious images every day.

But he had come prepared to be made fun of.

—Are you kidding? I was barely able to do that much. They wouldn't stop butting in, telling me I can't draw this, I can't paint that. And don't even get me started on all the interference from the folks hanging out their cell windows, trying to put in their two bits. Hey mister, why don't you draw that skirt a little shorter? Make her boobs bigger, too, while you're at it.

I couldn't resist.

—Aside from the content being boring, it's downright badly painted.

He turned red in the face and I realized I had gone too far. I had to backtrack.

—What I mean is, it's just as trapped as I am. I hope they let us go.

In fact, the painting was in peril of disappearing along with our smaller exercise field. A new warden appointed by the Ministry of Justice decided to build a nondenominational worship space for Catholics, Buddhists, and Protestants on that ground. There were just three political prisoners at that time—a union rights activist, a student, and me—and the prison authorities tried to convince us first. After negotiations, they agreed to put in table tennis and badminton in the empty lot between the third and fourth cell blocks, and, even more importantly, allowed political prisoners to grow vegetables on a small plot. This was how the *soji* and I came to cultivate vegetables in prison.

Around this time, five students and two civic group activists, sentenced for unlawful assembly and protest, were transferred to my prison, bringing the total number of political prisoners to ten. They were all held on the second floor of the cell block in the private cells. Before they arrived, the three of us had been a cozy group. The union activist worked at one of the faddish radical labor groups, and the student, Jong-ho, was from Gwangju in Jeolla Province and attending Dongshin University. Jongho had developed a social conscience from an early age, having followed his father to work at construction sites where his father operated heavy equipment. He said that when he got out he would continue to work hard to provide for his family, but he was also determined to participate in the labor movement.

The three of us played table tennis during the exercise hour and extended our stay outdoors into the lunch hour with our little "farm." Calling it a farm is a bit generous, but it was precious to us nonetheless. The empty lot in front of the fourth cell block was fairly wide, and faced south; there was a little slope below the path, ensuring good drainage. The prison hadn't simply given us some bare land to cultivate—it had provided a former flower bed. Our tools were a shovel, hoe, and sprinkler; we'd been worried about plowing the whole thing by hand, but one of the long-term prisoners brought along a tiller and plowed it for us in the blink of an eye. Our furrows were almost straight.

Growing vegetables was dubbed a "sentence killer," and it was true: an entire season would zoom by while watching the garden grow. After exercising, we fetched cups of water to sprinkle on the crops; when the roots got stronger, we borrowed a hose from the prison greenhouse workroom to water them. In a few months we were eating fresh lettuce, kale, and mugwort with our meals, dipping the green chilies and perilla leaves into *jang* paste or making *jangajji* preserves using soy sauce and gochujang. The regular prisoners had their own patch in front of the factory and ate fresh vegetables every summer. It was true: the joys of the daily ritual of watering and harvesting made us forget we were in prison.

On the first day that Jong-ho and I planted seeds in the patch, we were startled to hear someone shouting behind us. Well, I was startled, but Jongho seemed to know what was going on, as he pointed to the shouter and called him Mr. Candidate. We politely called each other "political prisoners" but the guards still called us by the old term, "spies," or even "red commie thieves" when they were angry. The second floor of the fourth cell block was for political and private prisoners, with the first floor an infirmary of sorts, and the windows of half the first-floor cells were covered in steel pipes behind which they held prisoners with mental issues, such as Mr. Candidate. The prisoners of the fourth cell block were well aware of the sounds the lower-floor prisoners made.

Mr. Candidate had a life sentence. He'd been dragged off to the Samcheong Reeducation Camp, created under the guise of "socialization" when the Shingunbu "new military faction" came into power, and had resisted the guards. He was transferred to Gongju after being tortured. While working in the prison factory, he'd had a psychotic breakdown and beat another prisoner to death with a hammer. During his episodes of mental instability, he ranted endlessly about the people who were out to destroy him and protested his innocence. The sound of his

screaming at night was devastating. The other prisoners shouting that they couldn't sleep and the guards trying to shout down
the chaos turned the entire prison into pandemonium in the wee
hours of the night.

He'd start shouting all of a sudden as we watered our plants.
He always began with "Citizens, please listen to me," and went
on to expound his political views, ending with, "Please vote for
me as your National Assembly representative." He would holler
former president Chun Doo-hwan's name, along with slogans
advocating his removal. At first the enraged guards would try to
shut him up but after a certain point they just left him alone. On
days when his symptoms worsened and his nerves were on edge,
he'd lie in wait with feces in his food bowl and throw it at
patrolling guards.

In the vegetable patch, we would occasionally look up from
watering to see his face in his bathroom window. He seemed to
be gazing into the distance and not at us. For the most part he
would eat his meals, but sometimes he threw his food around
and smeared feces all over the cell; the *soji* kids who had to clean
it up were furious. He occasionally was taken to a prison with a
psychiatric ward and would come back a little calmer. This went
on for about three years, until one day he didn't return. I asked a
guard what had happened. He smirked and murmured,

—He probably got out.

—How can that be? He has a life sentence. Did his family
take him? And is Korean law so backward as to leave mental
patients in prison?

The guard replied nonchalantly.

—I mean if he's out it's because he's dead.

There was another young man there everyone called Telegraph
Pole. He was in his early twenties, knew who I was and what I
was in for, and was clearheaded enough to ask me for books to
borrow. He wasn't in the inner, steel-shuttered side of the first
floor but an outer room. In other words, he was a little disturbed,

but not too seriously. He was as tall as a basketball player; the other prisoners would lament how good he would have been at prison sports if he'd only been right in the head. But he always made a fuss when the warden or auditors or anyone high-ranking came around for inspections, cursing them or spitting at them as they took turns peering at him. It took three or four guards to hold him down and bind him with leather belts and ropes, and once he came out of that, exhausted, he would kick the cell door some more. Telegraph Pole also visited the prison with the psych ward once every six months, growing quieter every time. His exuberance turned to silence, and he became thin as a rail. The youthful spirit in his eyes vanished. He already looked like a middle-aged man. One day I asked the exercise-hour guard about him as we watched the bedding being carried out to dry in the sun.

—Telegraph Pole seems different. He has no spirit.

—They say he's better. He's not ranting anymore, right?

I thought differently. He had gone to another world he could never return from. After three visits to the other prison, his body seemed emptied of any soul. He no longer remembered me at all. In any case, he served out his six-year sentence and disappeared.

We all have lines we shouldn't cross. In prison, these moments of crisis are inevitable. When you first start your sentence. When you've spent a few years in your private cell. When a few years turns to nine or ten. When your wife leaves you. When a family member, but especially your mother, dies. When your children are sick or something bad happens to them. When a guard you hate is reassigned to you. When you're wrongfully punished. When you're scooping up dog food with your mouth in a windowless, dark cell with your hands tied behind your back. When such things happen, you cross a certain boundary. A soul that can't withstand it leaves the intolerable space of the body and creates a new, lonely world for itself.

~

After the three-and-a-half-year turning point had passed, the authorities relaxed their grip on me. With regular prisoners, they would raise their ranks or move them to easier positions in the factory. With political prisoners, they'd start by being strict with us and eventually, after we "adjusted," would raise us to "model prisoner" level. Of course, once inspections began, the rules for prisoner management would briefly change. It was the authorities who decided what *adjusted* meant. It was too much to ask a "democracy activist" to change his stripes over-night, but as long as a prisoner wasn't too combative and could discuss compromises with the authorities, there was a chance that treatment would improve. I felt like a military conscript in his final months, trying to stand outside the rules for the last lap of his term.

We'd call the rich and powerful prisoners "tiger skins" and their opposite "dog skins." Prisoners who broke the rules were known as "foul hitters" and their opposite were "straight hitters." I was moving from hitting straight to hitting fouls. They say that tiger skins and dog skins originated from rich prisoners wrapping themselves in expensive blankets in winter, while the poor ones huddled under old military-issue blankets; however, it's not just blankets that make the military and prison similar for me. Insofar as military service means obeying strict rules and regulations for a set amount of time, it, too, is a prison that confines us at the peak of our youth. Just as a prisoner waits for their release date from the moment they are sentenced, so a military conscript awaits the date of discharge, ticking off the days one by one. An optimist would say that anyone who successfully endures a prison sentence might come out stronger than before, much as an awkward young man after a three-year conscription may emerge as a true adult. The point is that, whether in prison or the army, what matters is your capacity to endure it.

11

Deployment

1966–69

Eight weeks of boot camp in Jinhae and four weeks of infantry training in Sangnam will turn anyone into a rough and tough "man of the seas." The training methods were modeled after the US Marines, but life inside the barracks was drawn from the Japanese military, where harsh discipline, or *bbatda*, was the rule. On a nearly daily basis, the drill sergeant indoctrinated us to see ourselves and our fellow soldiers as an ironclad band of comrades, whereas the enemy was no more than a ragtag mob.

There were all sorts of slogans posted around the barracks. We had the classic "Once a marine, always a marine," as well as "The ghost-catching marines," "Invincible marines," and "You toughed it out another day, brother" written in yellow paint against a red background. In less than two weeks, the trainees, steeped in an overwhelming feeling of solidarity and belonging, shouted in unison that the marines were the greatest of all the military branches.

When I was in the US during my exile, a Korean man who lived next door and owned a dry-cleaning service asked me to come "say a few good words" to the local Korean marines' association. I protested that the whole world knew I was a "troublesome element" who had been to North Korea and back, and I still remember his answer: "Once a marine, always a marine, and there can never be a troublesome element in the marines."

It's common to think that military policemen look dapper in their uniforms when directing the traffic or patrolling the streets. But behind that façade is a barracks life that's built on tears and sweat. If you don't shine your shoes until you can see your face in them before morning inspections, you have to lick the sole. The brass buckle of the cartridge belt must be polished every day so your face leers back at you like a fun house mirror. You have to crease your trousers just right, taking care to stick a rice grain on the inside before ironing so the crease stays tight. None of your superiors do these things.

Once I finished with specialization training, bringing my total time in training to a year, I started from the bottom of the ladder in my unit. Until a new recruit came in below me, I was in charge of taking care of all my superiors' uniforms. My eyes opened automatically at 4 a.m., and I began my day by shining shoes and ironing uniforms. If they thought their shoes weren't shiny enough, they made me lick the soles and ordered me to "plant my head." This meant bending over to form a triangle, supporting myself with my feet and forehead, my hands behind my back, in a position we in the marines called "Wonsan bombing." "Begin bombing!" they'd shout, and we'd reply, "Yes, sir!" and assume the position.

Of all the disciplinary measures I was subjected to, the most creative was "stick to the bunks," "nylon sleep," and "mosquito banquet." The first of these were usually issued a day after family visits. Trainees, when the first leg of training was over, were allowed one family visit. My mother and older sisters brought meat. Training makes you crave not only meat but things you wouldn't have thought twice about before, like rice cakes and pastries, whatever fills your stomach. You barely say hello to your visiting family before swiftly unwrapping their packages and gobbling up the food, and you're so full later that you stumble through the group runs, barely managing to shout your refrains and sing along. The staff sergeants knew this, and because there'd been cases of conscripts getting sick overnight from overeating, they made us all throw up after returning from visits. They stood us in a row, admonished us for a bit, and ordered us to "stick to the bunks," which meant placing your booted feet on the bed frame and bending over. Three minutes of this was usually enough to bring up whatever we'd eaten. We went to bed only after we'd cleaned up the mess and been assigned a week of bathroom-cleaning duty.

Eventually I got my transfer orders: the combat division in Pohang. Farewell, "Misery Corps!" I thought. I slung my duffel bag over my shoulder and left for Pohang, not knowing that my new division had already been designated for deployment to Vietnam. Combat training began as soon as I arrived. We put on our field gear and powered around the East Sea in a tank landing ship and went up and down mountains in search of North Korean operatives, who were said to pop up in Gang-won Province at the time. Then came August of the following year.

Our entire battalion was ordered to enter a special jungle-combat training program. We knew where we were headed after this. I was posted as a rocket artillery gunner in the company weapons section. The company leader was a graduate of the Naval Academy. He once mentioned a short story he'd read in *Sasanggye*, and I blurted out that I was its author. He seemed mildly impressed.

The weapons section had a reputation for being one of the easier posts. It was draining to run with cartridge belts slung across your shoulders, and the equipment and artillery were very heavy as well. But the rocket launchers were light, aluminum cylinders that could be disassembled into two parts and slung over either shoulder. While the other troops panted up the hills during high-ground attacks, chasing after tanks, all we had to do was set up the launcher and rest for a bit. If an officer asked what we were doing, all we had to say was, "Yes, sir, we have assembled our rocket launchers and are standing by to fire."

One morning, on the way to combat training, we were passing the division's south gate near downtown when I noticed a woman dressed in *hanbok* standing at the three-way intersection. As the trucks slowed down and snaked around her, I realized it was my mother. Later, I heard that she had requested a visit but was told to return after the evening's tasks were over, so she had decided to stand near the gate and see if she might catch a glimpse of her son.

I leaned out of the truck and shouted, "Mother! I'm here!"

My mother ran a few steps toward me, waving her hand. The ranking officer on our truck took pity and ordered it to stop.

I shouted again, "We'll be back in the evening! Request a visit at the guardhouse over there!"

"All right! Have a safe trip!"

My eyes were hot with tears. In some ways, this good-for-nothing son of hers was the only man in my mother's life, at least up until I married and had children of my own. She wandered everywhere just to keep track of the child who had been thrown into this bitter world. Even when I thought she had run out of strength, she somehow always managed to travel a long way to find me. Seeing my mother aging by the day, her shoulders narrower than I remembered, I would curse myself under my breath: *You rotten bastard.* That evening I sat across from my mother at an inn, a home-cooked meal set between us. Pulling the bones from the fish for me, she said, "When you're on the battlefield, make sure you pray to God. I will pray, too. The Lord will make it so that not a single hair on your head is harmed."

She gave me a pocket-sized Bible before she left. This was the first time she had explicitly urged her faith on me. The older she became, the more she relied on her religion.

My rocket launcher training partner was a guy nicknamed the Chieftain; he had dark skin and a nose like an eagle's beak. He would later lose both arms stepping on a booby trap in Vietnam's Batangan Peninsula. I will never forget the sight of him, usually so bright and carefree, screaming in pain as he was flown out on a helicopter, his poncho spattered with blood.

There's another soldier I think of when I think of the Chieftain. He was a short, smart signalman named In-su who always begged me to tell him funny stories during breaks. Even in the transport ship to Vietnam, he was quick to lift a bit of bread or ham for a discreet snack in the middle of the night. In-su would die during an ambush operation in Vietnam, his whole body shredded by shrapnel, when the drowsy soldier marching behind him accidentally fired his grenade launcher into the air. The three of us had been best buddies since jungle-combat training. Never will I forget the few months we had together.

The Chieftain and I first became friends during the night-combat training course. We shared a two-person tent. We were always hungry; we would lay there at night talking about all the things we used to eat. Because he worked in the mess hall, I guess, the Chieftain had a knack for describing foods so vividly that he could practically conjure them up from words alone. We would get so absorbed in his stories that by the time the food was ready and headed for the table, we'd be nearly out of our minds. Having survived the ordnance unit, on top of all the other hardships he'd suffered in life, the Chieftain was skilled at soothing others even when he himself had nothing.

We ate chicken for the last four days of the night-combat course. The Chieftain had snuck out to a poultry farm a good ten or so miles away and brought back six chickens. We hid them in a secret storage locker in the squad, which involved hanging them by the feet between the pine trees, covering them with a poncho, and having others take turns guarding them with the promise that they'd get a share of the meat. We got up in the middle of the night to fry the chicken in our steel helmets. At night when we went out for map-reading or nighttime ambush training, the Chieftain would do his best to procure whatever he could for us to eat, like turnips the size of our forearms, unripe watermelons, and young sweet potatoes.

He shook me awake one night when the rain was pouring down. Underneath his poncho were three pairs of brand-new army boots, never worn. I rubbed my fingers along the sharp edges of the soles and wondered if the Chieftain had raided the actual division ordnance warehouse.

"The Signal Corps got fresh supplies today." The Signal Corps was across the street from the training grounds. He must have slipped into the barracks and snatched the boots. "I hid them underneath the plank and was so scared someone would discover them that I haven't eaten all day." I realized that a joke he had played earlier, lying on a plank in the tent and pretending to be sick, had been because of the boots.

A deployment party was held as soon as we boarded our ship at Busan Harbor. As always, the officers, staff sergeants, and others went down to the pier and stood in a row as bureaucrats and other important people gave speeches, with high school girls waving flags and a military band playing a triumphant march. I was lying in my assigned bunk on the ship. The other soldiers leaned over the rail, watching the Oryukdo Islands and Busan Harbor disappear over the horizon.

Most of us had no idea why we were going to war. We were probably relieved to escape the pressures of barracks life and excited to be setting off for some place new. Some were looking forward to the deployment pay. And to the food. All we were fed in the regular units was bean sprouts in a salty broth, rice with flat barley mixed in, and pickled turnips; but the deployment training grounds served bean sprout soup with fish and what we jokingly called a "whole chicken"— a hard-boiled egg. That was a lot in those days. The strict rules had turned into friendly cajoling, and while training itself was hard on the body, it was less stressful on the mind than trying to make a living.

The ideas embodied in martial lyrics such as "I marched to the jungle to stamp out the red scourge with our colors held high" did not change until soldiers came home in ruins; for some, the ideas never lost their shine, even as they themselves became old reserve soldiers. When veterans returned to their hamlets with their pathetic discharge boxes containing C-ration cans and a few electronic appliances, their fathers would sing drunkenly about "the Southern Cross of this southern country" and lament to their permanently crippled sons, "How is this any different from when those Japanese bastards dragged me to the South Sea Islands during the Pacific War?"

There was a friend of a friend whose name I've forgotten, but let's call him Im Cheol for now. Cheol was majoring in English at some university; I'd met him only a couple of times over drinks, on nights when he'd tagged along with one of our other friends. I vaguely remember talking with him about George Orwell's participation in the Spanish Civil War and the film *For Whom the Bell Tolls*, based on the Hemingway novel. Someone mused, "If we'd been in Spain, it stands to reason that we would have sided with the anti-fascists. And during the Pacific War, student conscripts should have deserted or actively served the Allies. So what does that mean for us in Vietnam?"

We didn't say anything more but were silently agreed: *It's the same here as during the Japanese occupation.* Then Cheol said: "In any situation, there is a limit to how much you can take. As similar as our situations were, Korea was still divided into North and South, and we couldn't make the same choices we would have made in Spain in the 1930s."

I remember him to this day because of his death. I'd just transferred to another battalion when I happened to run into him, in Vietnam of all places. It was a Sunday morning, when everyone had gone out to the city and I was alone doing laundry and writing letters. I was about to cross the street to the store for some military-issue *makgeolli* when a truck stopped right in front of me. "Why, isn't this Hwang-*hyeong*!"

I didn't recognize him in uniform. Only when he said his name did it finally dawn on me who he was. He had been conscripted to provide additional soldiers to marines deployed in Vietnam. Luckily for him he spoke English, which placed him in a US Marines unit. He worked at the American barracks near the division's eastern gate. I visited him there on the weekends. They had good mess hall food, and his office was big and quiet. He would have the radio on low and read stacks of books. I had seen him only a couple of times after entering special training and had forgotten about him by the time I was in Vietnam.

After I was moved from the Chu Lai front to Hội An, I met an administrative soldier I knew who worked at brigade head-quarters. He was in the US Military Assistance Advisory Group and belonged to an intake below Cheol's. I asked him how my friend was doing, and he answered in a low voice, "Didn't you know? He died after entering special training."

Facing a shortage of English speakers in deployment, the Korean leadership had ordered an increase in language special-ists, which resulted in Cheol being forced to apply for active service. He had to receive special training; it seems he made up his mind during the week of night-combat training. He must have squirreled away an extra bullet at the firing range. On the day he received his orders, he went down to the training camp at Molgaewol, got drunk, locked himself in one of the toilets at the far end of the sports field, put the barrel of the M-1 rifle in his mouth, and fired. They say he pulled the trigger by fitting a wooden stick through the trigger guard and stepping on it with both feet. "The unit kept it all under wraps and things were pretty dark for a time. I think it was dismissed as a shooting accident." Up until that point, I'd thought of Vietnam as merely another post that I'd happened to stumble into while being swept up in whatever situation was at hand; but the news about Cheol set off quiet ripples of change inside of me. Soon, I was taken out of the infantry and put into investigations at Danang, and would only come face-to-face with Cheol again in the naked truth of war. What I remember about the boat ride to Danang is the taste of the fist-sized oranges, their rinds stamped "California" in black letters, and stealing a tub of ice cream and sharing it below decks. After the Korean War, anything made in America was like treasure from heaven. I remember, too, the Western cigarettes we bought from the PX the first time we received American military chits as on-board spending money, and the footprints on the toilet seats from soldiers unused to sit-down toilets. The Filipino crew members whistled at us and taunted us for being no better than circus animals.

The transport ship arrived in the harbor city of Danang, and the next day we switched to a tank landing ship to reach Chu Lai. This was where the combined forces of the US military command were based; on its outskirts were the US Army's Americal Division. One of that division's platoons, under the command of Lieutenant William Calley, would later be responsible for the Mỹ Lai massacre. The first thing that greeted us was the hot, humid air of the tropics and the deep, ominous green of the jungle.

The American base, built on sandy coastal fields, formed a huge city of its own. As we made landfall, I gazed in awe at the mountains of scrap metal. Bombshells, broken equipment, and empty ration cans lay in rusting piles everywhere, and dark wisps of smoke rose all around from burning food waste and feces from latrines.

On my first night in Vietnam, I saw from the ship the many lights of another Asia across the darkness: not the lights shining from house windows but searchlights, flares, exploding bombs, and helicopters endlessly taking off or landing. I sat on a hanging chain on the deck like it was a swing, calming the edge of expectation and excitement in my heart, sensing the cries and pain of that unknown land being carried to me on the waves. At dawn, when the unfamiliar sun rose from the sea, the first thing I smelled on the wind was not salt or the scent of the jungle but gasoline.

~

The route from the military harbor in Chu Lai, past the American base to the navy brigade command, was Vietnam's Highway 1. This is a long road running north and south, connecting Saigon and Hanoi. On either side were thick jungles with sparse clusters of interconnected villages and towns.

Armed transport vehicles raised dust in front of and behind us, while we in the middle truck carried our rifles loaded and pointed at the jungle. After unpacking my things in our temporary billet at brigade headquarters, I lay awake all night, unable to sleep amid the ear-piercing din of bombings and endless machine-gun fire coming from somewhere nearby.

War and poor villages had been familiar to me since I was little. It was probably the same for any Korean soldier around my age. There wasn't much difference between the farming villages in the country that we'd left behind and the hamlets dotting the jungles of Vietnam, but the ubiquitous rice paddies above all, the sight of planting and harvesting, would have reminded us of our families and neighbors back home. The new arrivals were sent off to their new regiments and assigned by their battalion into companies and platoons. According to rumor, a rookie private could become part of an advance detachment after six months if he managed to survive his first three months without incident. No unit left their men on the front for more than eight months. If a tour of duty lasted ten months, at least the last two of those months would be spent at a "cushion" (encampment) at the company or battalion base. But most newbies died in the first three months or were shipped out, giving rise to the superstition that "if you make it past a hundred days, you'll make it out."

In any case, you couldn't forget that whenever a superior asked you anything, you had to answer with a smart "Yes, sir! I will see to it!"

We were getting our assignments when an officer looking through our personnel files called some of us out separately. He was picking soldiers who'd had a college education. When it was my turn, I went up and stood to attention in front of the desk where he and a sergeant sat side by side. They asked me about my studies before demanding, in an almost accusatory tone, whether I spoke any English.

"Yes, sir! I will see to it!"

He wrote something down in my file and motioned with his chin for me to go outside. I joined a group of soldiers who had already finished their interview, standing around and whispering together. The men here were said to be headed for either dispatch positions with the American troops, or liaison positions at headquarters. The work could include coordination with the Americans concerning firepower and radio helicopter support, detachment at an American unit that supported Korean troops, or reassignment altogether into the American military. These roles encompassed everyone from infantry to drivers and cooks; it was said that if you were lucky, you might not even see another Korean until you were back from your tour.

Everyone said I was medium-lucky when they learned I was headed for the Chu Lai base. The worst position was assisting the American troops' signalman, and the best were in places far from the fighting, like the US Air Force or Navy divisions.

I will never forget how I lost my way while searching for my new unit after being put on patrol duty. I didn't know where to go and was wandering around the docks where everyone was busy offloading the ships. I was wearing my still new-looking jungle-colored uniform that still had its clear stripes and carried an M-1 rifle hanging loosely from my shoulder, a weapon that was already a relic from World War II. I was also dragging an old-fashioned duffel bag filled with provisions. I poked around the boxes near the A-ration warehouses. Sweat poured from under my helmet down my forehead and temples, and I kept having to hitch up the straps that slid from my shoulders.

An American soldier who had been watching me came up and asked if he could help. I stuttered out the name of my division, and he smiled and said this was a warehouse and my unit was very far away. Lights were already beginning to come on around me, and soldiers carrying canteen cups and frying pans were heading for the mess hall. The American soldier kindly went out of his way to make some phone calls and got a car to come for me.

In the meantime, he let me wait inside the checkpoint. I remember thinking as I sat there that I might never see home again. When the American soldier heard that it was only my fourth day, he gave a low whistle. This young man with chestnut-brown hair said I reminded him of himself a year ago.

My job was to support the American road patrol. The Korean sergeant in charge of our team led six people, including myself, which was not even half of a full squad. In shifts, we patrolled the roads around the base, directed traffic, and inspected the safety of the guardhouses and bridges every hour. The region I was responsible for was Highway 1, the farthest away and most dangerous. Every day I shuttled back and forth from the base at Chu Lai past the navy brigade headquarters to Quảng Ngãi. Wearing plastic goggles that sagged over my nose, I directed the parade of heavy equipment and armored vehicles, tanks, and caravans to safe roads. Every day, during the early hours, we slowly inspected the roads with the help of a search squad and a mine detector, crossing with the other team who came from the opposite direction. In the afternoons, along with two American patrol soldiers, we sat in the back seat armed with 30 mm machine guns and made the round trip on Highway 1. We received POWs from teams that patrolled the hamlets, transported Vietnamese civilian informants, and closed roads and contacted the engineers when we found buried booby traps. In the evenings, my exposed arms and neck and the parts of my face not covered by goggles would be covered in red dust. I once scraped it together, out of curiosity, and ended up with a lump the size of a walnut. The threat of death was always close. I faced death more directly during later missions, but even around Highway 1, my continued survival was a daily miracle.

On my patrol route, near Bình Sơn, was a little store where I would stop by for a Coke, just to get away from the heat. That day, I asked for a wet towel to wipe my face, drank my ice-cold Coke, and had just left when I heard an explosion behind me. A plume of smoke was rising from the store. We carefully turned our car around, readied our rifles, and approached. Half the structure was gone, and there were bodies lying everywhere. The injured lay twisting and screaming. Someone had fired a single shot with a short-range rocket launcher before quickly retreating. They had clearly targeted, in broad daylight, a store frequented by the American military.

The fact that the Americans came to say that "any Vietnamese civilian walking around on two feet is an enemy" testified to how they'd conceded early on that this was an unwinnable war. Around that time, all of Vietnam was declared a free-fire zone by the US Army General William Westmoreland.

There were two kinds of US patrol drivers: those who drove at reckless speed over bumpy unpaved roads and those who crouched over their steering wheels, shoulders tense, slowly making their way. It didn't matter whether you drove fast or slow over a booby trap; once it exploded, you were dead. Still, it was true you were more likely to survive if you drove at top speed through an ambush or over a mine with a command wire. This was why we'd get into arguments with slow drivers and get out of their truck to go ride in another.

Heavy-hearted days that turned into sleepless nights usually started with bad news from home, or sightings of women or boy soldiers in the POW camp, or stumbling across signs of mass killings in the narrow paths through the jungle, or transporting the corpses of our men in the back of our patrol vehicle. What bothered me the most, though, was the pressure coming from the staff sergeant of the dispatched Korean unit. He ordered me to use a forged card to buy refrigerators and televisions from the PX, and urged me to "plant seeds" within the supply corps, by which he meant sniff around for someone who might be a useful contact for him. He disciplined us by making us crawl across the sand every morning, destroying our morale. We felt deeply inferior compared to the American troops. Every day I regretted not being an officer and not having volunteered for combat duty.

The mobile company's main role was to patrol the base and its environs and secure the roads, but it also connected the Korean and South Vietnamese troops, making it a de facto part of the American contingent. Vietnamese patrollers, therefore, were among us. They usually accompanied Americans on their patrols around the villages near the base. There was an airstrip on the beach, protected from easy invasion, our quarters were within the airstrip grounds, and guards were posted at the wire fence and watchtower outside. Further from the airstrip were independent defense zones divided into strategic units where daily ambush and search patrols took place. Nevertheless, the Northern Vietnamese and local guerrillas still managed to infiltrate the villages and strategic zones every day.

One day during the rainy season, enemy troops invaded a swath of territory from downtown Bình Sơn up to the southern edge of Tam Kỳ. This was the first time our transport had been attacked in the middle of Bình Sơn, which included the county seat and POW camp. It was internally guarded by Vietnamese and Korean security companies, with American troops drawing a line of defense on the outskirts.

A unit member who'd been returning from a patrol in Bình Sơn said that they were passing by the market downtown when he saw a crowd of locals gathered in a circle. He parked and they approached with rifles at the ready, to find a Vietnamese soldier being beaten up by a group of youths. Such soldiers were not in the Vietnamese military but were part of a militia of sorts, hastily trained to do police work or guardhouse duties. Neither the Americans nor the Koreans trusted them much. When tasked with guarding the ambush checkpoint, for instance, they often left when they felt like it or snuck off in the middle of the night. Still, such beatings couldn't be allowed, so the patrolling soldiers broke it up and tried to arrest one of the youths. Unafraid of the Americans and their weapons, the boy shook off his restraints and raced away, and an angered American seemed to have shot a blank. During the subsequent chase to a corner of the market, the locals scattered and hid, and someone began firing an AK-47 from a rooftop. An American soldier, running ahead of the others, was hit. His companions fired back and managed to escape with their injured squad member, carrying him out of the market on their backs. Something about the incident felt ominous, and sure enough, around midnight, guerrillas who'd been hiding out in the houses in town used the distraction to invade and take over the POW camp and county seat. Some of the Koreans were not taken and stood their ground all night, while the company managed to retreat to behind the line of defense and avoid a total rout. But the navy company leader who gave the coordinates and ordered his soldiers to "shoot above my head" died in the battle.

On the same day, I went patrolling in Tam Kỳ. A Vietnamese sergeant named Nguyen went with us, someone whom we teased for having a concubine in every place he worked. Nguyen, unlike his best friend Cao, was a big man and cheerful, easily trading jokes with the Americans. I tended to trust him more than Cao.

Tam Kỳ was the kind of town that sprang up around American bases, a sight common enough in South Korea. Along both sides of the main street were crude houses thrown together from cement blocks and planks that had flowed into the town from the base, along with restaurants, stores selling drinks, souvenir shops, bars, and brothels. This was a small downtown area, not even a kilometer wide, but every shack was stocked with cigarettes, rations, beer cans, and Coca-Cola from the black market. Tam Kỳ was attached to the western side of the base, and across from it was the battalion defense region, making it hard to infiltrate. However, if Tam Kỳ were taken by the enemy, the airstrip would come within the range of rocket launchers, a threat that prompted the authorities to set up barricades on the southern and northern entrances to the road and lock the village in every evening at sundown.

Our daily patrols included slowly cruising up and down the wide road next to the town and watching for irregularities, as well as parking the car somewhere and checking around inside the village. Two patrol units were tasked with this: one manned by the Vietnamese Sergeant Nguyen and two American soldiers, and one by me and two Americans.

Nguyen took the lead and entered a bar, which was empty. Since we were on duty, we only ordered a can of soda water each. Nguyen checked the back and returned looking puzzled. He asked the proprietress where all the girls were. The lady said they were working in a neighboring town, where a big party was being held.

We walked out to the main road again, and Nguyen, after visiting another house, said it was strange how empty the neighborhood was today. Then an auntie from another house smiled and waved at Nguyen, who followed her into the building. When he didn't reemerge for a long time, one of his American counterparts went in after him. The American came out, cursing and laughing. Nguyen had reunited with an old flame and decided to spend the night in Tam Kỳ. We laughed it off and left Nguyen behind.

That very evening, fighting broke out around Tam Kỳ and went on all night. A call came in the morning, and our patrol unit put on full gear and set out for Tam Kỳ. The village had already been taken by the Americans. Parts of the village had been destroyed and were still smoking, despite the misty rain, from the trench mortars. The streets were littered with bodies, including the corpses of thirty guerrillas who had attempted to invade the battalion defense zone, now displayed at the entrance to the village. They all wore black pajamas, like farmers, and rubber "Ho Chi Minh sandals." Their weapons and ammunition had been removed, leaving the empty-handed corpses in all sorts of poses. Legless poses, armless or headless poses, relatively neat corpses with only bullet holes, corpses so mangled it was hard to say whether they weren't just lumps of meat, corpses with half their bodies burned black, corpses with legs and torsos showing blue-black rot from the monsoon rain that had fallen all night. These were things I would keep seeing in my nightmares later in civilian life. What I realized too late was that I did not even feel pity for them. All they were to me were strangely shaped objects.

I did not think of how those youths were Asian, like me, and had their own families and friends and dreams of the future. The American soldiers were even more callous. The white ones especially, who sneered about "yellow bastards" living in huts made of leaves and mud that Americans wouldn't house their livestock in back home, who ate weird food that smelled worse than garbage—what souls could they possibly possess?

I was later surprised to learn that the word *gook*, which Americans used to refer to the Vietnamese, originated from Korean—from *hanguk*, in fact, the Korean word for Korea, or *migook*, the Korean word for America. It had spread among the Americans during the Korean War. Even now, *gook* is still used among American troops as a derogatory term for Asians.

We were anxious to know if Nguyen was all right. The other sergeant, Cao, shook his head as he accompanied us to where we'd last seen him. He told us that the women disappearing from the bars and brothels had been a clear and early sign of what was to come.

The Vietnamese soldiers were already investigating the house. It looked like grenades had been thrown inside: the windows were all shattered and three bodies riddled with bloodstains and shrapnel wounds were lying on the cement floor around a table. They were local Vietnamese security guards, who appeared to have been ambushed while drinking together late at night. Their guns and bulletproof vests were stacked up on a chair right next to them, but they wouldn't have had a chance to use them. The guerrillas had pulled it off without harming a single one of their own civilians.

Finally, in the backyard, we came upon Nguyen's body. He was in his underpants. They seemed to have taken turns to stab him, as there were clear bayonet wounds to his back and side. That was only a foretaste of what I would see in this war. Later I served in combat, in body recovery, and witnessed even worse scenes of slaughter.

And then came my turn to spend a night in Tam Kỳ. A guy in the same patrol squad as me, who'd arrived in the country six months earlier, said he'd worked on a military base in Pyeong-taek. A sergeant, he spoke English well and was clever but never took undue risks. He behaved pleasantly to everyone lower in rank, which meant that everyone wanted to work alongside him. One day he whispered to me: "Let's go out to Tam Kỳ and have some fun, like the Yankees do."

"But what if we get caught by the gunnery sergeant?"

"Don't worry about it. He spends every weekend with the main forces. And remember, some of us are getting sent out on a mission next month."

What he meant was that a large-scale joint operation with US forces was starting in a month, and rumors were spreading that the base soldiers would be ordered to report back to their original units. We finished our work that afternoon, skipped the 6:30 dinner, and headed out the west gate to wait. A Korean civilian who worked for Pilkor Electronics showed up in an army truck and stealthily made his way to the checkpoint. The sergeant waved; I assumed they knew each other well. With his discharge date approaching, the sergeant was probably working with the civilian to make some cash on the side to take home.

We got in the truck and headed into Tam Kỳ. Technically speaking, entering the village was prohibited after dark, but as long as you made it back before midnight when the gates were locked, everyone looked the other way. If you weren't specifically ordered to stay in the base, then that was as good as getting permission.

The civilian headed straight to a building that I took to be his regular spot. The owner and a group of men who had been waiting inside came out and quickly unloaded the truck. There were cases of beer and Salems—given the heat, menthol cigarettes were the favorite of the Vietnamese. The deal complete, we were led inside, where I saw several partitioned rooms with curtains for doors.

Five women dressed in áo dài stepped out and lined up in front of us, and we each took our pick. Our selected partners sat next to us, and we drank beer and talked in a mixture of awkward English and Vietnamese and hand gestures. I still remember the name of the woman I chose: Song. I wonder if it was based on a Chinese character. We went into a room dimly lit by a candle and lay next to each other on a bamboo bed.

As night deepened, the sounds of a nearby ambush rang out. I heard star shells being fired from 81 mm mortars, the rat-a-tat of machine guns, and the whomp-whomp of helicopters flying back and forth. In other words, a quiet night on the front lines.

Through our limited communication, I learned that Song's husband was a Vietnamese soldier somewhere on the front. But each time his platoon moved, he changed wives or took on an additional family. Song had a newborn daughter who was being cared for by her parents. She had just turned twenty.

Her work complete, I lay still as she kissed me all over my face and said, "Sleep. Sleep. Don't worry." She seemed to have noticed that I'd grown more nervous as the sounds of fighting grew closer. She blew out the candle, rested her head on my chest, and reached up to stroke my hair. I soon fell fast asleep. We slept in each other's arms until the sergeant came to get me the next morning.

A few days later I found out I had the clap. I wasn't mad about it, though. Instead, all I could think about was wanting to take some medicine to her, too. I was given a week's sick leave, since this sort of thing was practically a daily occurrence on the front, during which I got regular shots and hung out in the barracks, racking my brain for ways to help her get treated. Following inspection, my patrol leader rewarded me with ten punitive swats. The pain in my groin had me waddling around with my butt sticking out, much to the amusement of my fellow US soldiers, who whistled and mimicked my walk.

Four people in my unit were ordered back to HQ to be sent out on field operations. There was Sergeant Im from the Jeolla region whose face was tanned dark, Sergeant Park from Busan, Corporal Shin, and me. We were placed in a battalion that went inland from the eastern coast of the Quảng Ngãi front, with Americans to the east and Vietnamese to the west. This operation, on the Batangan Peninsula, probably involved securing the region of the port cities of Danang and Hội An from attack. With battalion headquarters personnel and the last tank landing ship, we went up the shoreline of the peninsula. There were two warships off the beach acting as bombardment reinforcements.

The first thing we had to do was establish the battalion head-quarters on the beach, after the three company units had finished their missions and gone in. We dug a trench facing inland and built a bunker with sandbags in front and behind. We placed our heavy artillery there, installed a circular wire face in the front, and buried Claymore land mines back and front. It was a bunker and rest stop in the safest part of the beach. A company of soldiers took turns guarding this base. I was lucky, having arrived later than the rest, and was given guard duties for a month. Whatever happened after that, I had a month of guaranteed safety.

We were posted in the front dugout and bunker only at night, for guard duty; one squad remained during the day for guard duty, with the rest killing time around the bunker. The four of us were placed in the same platoon and spent most of our time together. During ambushes, we dug into the sand to stomach-level, put up posts and a roof of palm leaves, and covered the ground with ration boxes and ponchos. Over that we put down mats acquired from a nearby village and a military blanket and liner.

When we came back from guard duty, we would relax, cooling ourselves in the ocean breeze for a moment before sleeping all morning. We woke around lunchtime, which meant ripping up a ration box for fuel and cooking rice and stew in a cartridge box. Our food consisted of both American and Korean rations. The American stuff we ate as snacks, or added the canned meats, like ham or sausage, to the Korean kimchi and mackerel pike cans, thus creating a fusion stew that would later be known as *budae jjigae* (army stew).

One day, when I happened to be in charge of the food, I woke at noon and put some rations together over a fire, then went up to a sandy hill with a spade to do my business. It was a perfect place for that purpose, because you could see the ocean for miles and the breeze carried away the smell.

I had dug a hole and was leisurely going about it when I saw that the cartridge box below was about to boil over. Damn, I thought. I had forgotten to leave the lid open a crack to let the steam escape, and now all that good stew was about to explode.

I had quickly done up my trousers and was running down the sandy hill when I heard a sharp whistling sound. I instantly hit the ground and heard a sharp, dry crash, like hundreds of windows shattering. My back was covered in sand. I lay there for a while with my face down as wet clumps of sand continued to rain down around me. When I looked up, the air was white with gunpowder smoke and stank of sulfur. I couldn't hear a thing. I thought it was too quiet all of a sudden. Only when I saw the cartridge box lid flip open and pieces of kimchi scattering all over the place did I realize I'd gone deaf.

I could see Im and Park running and shouting. I collapsed on the sand. Only then did it occur to me to turn around and look at the hill I'd run down. To my astonishment, the hill was gone, replaced with mounds of sand and fragments of palm trees. The other soldiers ran up to me and shook my shoulders, but aside from my sudden deafness, I was okay. We stayed low as we scrambled back to the bunker.

We learned much later what had happened: a warship near the shore had accidentally fired its cannon. It was a targeting error. After we learned it wasn't an attack, we went back to where the hill had been to find a big pit. Had I paused one second longer or been on flat ground, I would have been incinerated. But the soft sand and slope of the hill had absorbed the explosion, and the shrapnel had scattered much higher up and gone into the ocean instead of into me. My hearing slowly began to recover after an hour. The pit ended up being used to burn trash.

Though we were only defending a minor coastal base, there was always the possibility of an enemy attack at night, which necessitated taking shifts one squad each on the line of defense, spending all night in the front dugout. But aside from two surprise attacks that did not amount to much—as the guerrillas of the liberation front were seasoned veterans who knew to reserve their energy for more strategic battles—the only time I saw our so-called enemy in the flesh, albeit at a distance, was during a patrol in the middle of the day. Our company was divided by squadrons before being sent into different zones; the jungle broke off into a stretch of green rice paddies before becoming jungle again. In the middle of the rice paddies squatted a guerrilla having a bowel movement. We could tell he wasn't a farmer, despite his black pajamas and conical hat, because of his gun and cartridge belt.

As the entire platoon hit the ground and began to shoot, he leaped up and zigzagged down the paddy at full sprint. Despite all the ammunition he was carrying, he vanished into the jungle in no time. The soldiers were always saying how hard it was to target a moving man. When they joked that he didn't even have time to wipe himself, I laughed, too. To us, he was not so much a human being as an animal that we'd missed while hunting.

~

At the battalion I was reunited with the Chieftain and In-su the signalman, with whom I'd become friends during special training. The Chieftain and I were both corporals, and In-su was a sergeant. One day, a leading platoon that had returned to base to replenish personnel and supplies came back with a body in a poncho. The bloody mound of flesh was In-su. It had been a peaceful day with no fighting. They had almost arrived at their trench when someone accidentally set off a grenade launcher; the grenade flew into the air and fell straight back down, landing near In-su. The others suffered only minor injuries. That's how absurd fate is in war.

A month later, it was my company's turn to go out on operations. We were to assist the American and South Vietnamese troops in clearing the settlements and jungles that ran from the western outskirts of Quảng Ngãi to the eastern part of Highway 1. Three companies were also taking turns setting up their defense trenches and securing the environs. Unlike the army, the marines avoided using large amounts of ammunition to sweep wide regions but instead made surgical encroachments on the ground. This meant the sacrifice of many men and the need to be constantly on the move.

In general, booby traps were buried around the villages that soldiers were likely to pass through. The guerrillas used everything for their booby traps, from grenades to all sorts of handmade bombs, shells captured from our side, and anti-tank mines. They were designed to explode when stepped on or when triggered by a trip wire.

The guerrillas also used more primitive booby traps. The most common were bamboo spikes smeared with poison, a method they had used since their resistance against France. One wrong step and a bamboo spike would pierce the sole of your boot and go clean through your foot. This quickly led to debilitating swelling and, given the tropical humidity, rapid gangrene. Even if you made it to medical care, you usually lost your entire foot. But at least that only affected the person stepping on the spike; if the danger were a land mine, entire platoons marching nearby could be wiped out. Consequently, the rule was always to advance in three platoons: left, right, and center. If a village came into view, whichever of the left or right platoons was better positioned would break formation, go around, and cut off one side of the village. The other platoon broke to cut off the other side, while the center platoon prepared to invade.

Platoons remained connected by radio. Each platoon advanced in similar fashion, in which a more experienced soldier led from the front, covered by a couple of other troops behind him. As it progressed, the platoon divided further into squads and a rearguard, since no one knew from which direction the attack might come.

The lead soldier's primary mission was to look out for booby traps. If one was spotted, he would raise his hand for the others to halt and then go to work with a helper to disarm it. He also had to watch for signs of ambush ahead. Though taking the lead meant being the first exposed to the dangers of booby traps, it was actually less dangerous as a position when the enemy was in front of us. Normally the enemy would wait until our troops came closer and allow the lead to pass through their initial defenses. If the lead did not find any traps along his own path, it was not uncommon for a clumsy soldier to set off a different booby trap only a few steps away.

When a booby trap did go off, the jungle filled with noise, screams, and gunpowder. Everyone dropped to the ground in surprise. Once we got back up, we would see the victim mangled, his limbs perhaps hanging from the branches, and whatever remained of him screaming and trembling. We would quickly administer first aid and radio a helicopter to lift him out. Our eyes would fill with blood and murder. In this state of near insanity, we entered the villages.

During the peace talks in Paris launched in 1968, North Vietnam and the National Liberation Front (NLF) presented several cases of civilian massacres conducted by the American troops and coalition forces. But it was difficult to distinguish regular military behavior from guerrilla warfare in regard to the atrocities carried out in the countryside and cities. In the mid-1960s, the US military undertook a combat strategy in which all jungles, paddies, and even villages located outside of US-designated safe areas were declared free-fire zones. The roads were simply broken lines between points of defense.

Every foreign soldier knew that, at night, anything he aimed his rifle at, or basically everything outside his trench, was enemy territory. General Westmoreland described this aspect of his operations as "leopard spots." By this he meant that he viewed not only armed fighters but also hostile Vietnamese citizens as the enemy, and that foreign troops were surrounded by them. However, no war that brands a whole people as the enemy can ever be called a just war.

To this day, I still cannot freely talk about everything that I witnessed. But even the American reportage coming out of the region at the time makes it clear what we did. There were soldiers who collected the ears of those they claimed were Viet Cong—for all we know, they were just ordinary farmers—and wore them around their necks, and young soldiers who took photos of themselves holding up severed heads. Women were raped and murdered, and there were even cases of grenades being pushed inside women's vaginas and set off, or live snakes being shoved inside of them. Like hunters on safari, machine-gunners in helicopters on patrol would bet on how many farmers they could down as they walked along their irrigation ditches.

The Mỹ Lai massacre was just one of the many acts of cruelty on a mass scale that were perpetrated during the Vietnam War. Such acts were also committed by Korean troops. I believe it was the internalized violence from the Korean War and onward, exacerbated by the Vietnam conflict, that enabled the slaughter of civilians in broad daylight several years later during the pro-democracy protests in Gwangju. Korea's lack of reflection on our role in the Vietnam War is especially shameful in the light of our eagerness to point out Japan's atrocities, when condemning the violence of one Asian nation against another.

"Fry them all!" was an order often issued when we suffered a higher number of casualties than usual. Some units made a point of setting an example by killing every living thing in the village, not only all the people but every cow and pig, even the chickens.

Here, I must ask myself: does the fact that I was a mere witness to atrocities exempt me from moral judgment? Is it possible to objectively witness any of the many atrocities going on in this world? In battle, I firmly believed that there were no such things as ghosts. But when I was discharged, and returned to civilian life, and interviewed the witnesses of the Sinchon Massacre to write *The Guest*, I changed my mind about the existence of ghosts. Those "hauntings" are nothing less than the memories and guilt we have buried within ourselves, the other face of history that has been erased from our lives.

When the Chieftain was blown up by a booby trap and both his arms were torn off, his scream pierced the jungle's canopy and went up into the sky. His cries soon subsided to whimpers. After first aid, he was taken away in a helicopter, and we found the village we'd invaded was empty. Thankfully so, otherwise we wouldn't have left anyone alive.

We scattered and followed the layout of the village to find appropriate cover like houses or rocks or half-fallen walls, securing the area in waves. There was a tiled structure in the middle of the village that looked like a town hall or a temple, which a sergeant and I were the first to approach. The sergeant covered the entrance as I leaped inside, firing off a few shots before taking cover. As I ducked down, I felt a humming, like a machine being turned on, and the interior, about twenty *pyeong* wide, abruptly turned pitch black. The air filled with a mass of flies. Inside the temple were about thirty corpses of men, women, and children that were decaying into all sorts of unrecognizable forms; the flies covering them had lifted when I came bursting in.

After the initial sweep, the breaking company entered the area for cleanup duty, which was usually given to lower-ranking soldiers and newbies just arrived in Vietnam. The bodies and body parts were picked up and deposited in a hole dug with a forklift. The relentless rain and heat accelerated the decay, often swelling legs to twice their normal size; they burst like plastic bags full of black liquid when accidentally stepped on. The brains splattered on walls like tofu had long since dried, making it hard to wash away their traces. Our double layers of work gloves ended up soaked through with a thick black fluid that resembled soy sauce. The more bodies piled up, the more red-black everything turned, and the swarm of gathered flies would grow so thick that the pile seemed to be covered by a moving blanket.

"Work over; at ease!" Once that order came through, we would gather to drink water from our flasks and chomp down on ham and sausages from our ration cans. If someone happened to walk up to the pile, we frantically shouted, "Go around! Go around!" but it would be too late. The flies rose into the air and attacked our rations before settling back down on the bodies.

But we soon learned to accept and adapt. That was the mark of those who'd survived. Flies were a mere annoyance; we would shoo them off with one hand and tear at our rations with the other.

The war perpetrated by the Americans in Asia was a more direct and material hell than the metaphor of civilization in William Golding's *Lord of the Flies*. The teeming flies and the hot sun were both the form and content of the Vietnam War. Compared to this, humanity was a luxurious abstraction.

When you open your eyes at dawn and peer out of the trench as the damp fog lifts in the heat of the rising sun and your field of vision slowly widens, you begin to make out bodies in the dimness. Large rats and lizards dart in and out of the ragged holes torn in the corpses. Anyone who has seen such surreal sights cannot recreate them, even in dreams. The subconscious rejects it; only the active senses take them in before distorting and erasing them, to allow the viewer to continue with every-day life.

In prison, too, the subconscious files away difficult experiences by resorting to metaphor. At some point, when I started to forget certain words and had trouble finding the words for what I wanted to say, an older woman began appearing in my dreams.

I can't see her face. It's covered in darkness, like black ink on a photograph. She stands inside the cell door and laughs some-times, talks to me sometimes, and crawls in under my cold blanket. When I wake at dawn after sleeping beside her, I feel queasy and am seized by a mysterious feeling. She isn't my first love, or the kind of actress one sees in the magazines that are available in prison; this plain, stout woman with no face who comes looking for me is no ordinary dream.

Rattled, I went out on exercise hour to consult some of the long-term prisoners who were at their cleaning shift. These were model prisoners who had received sentences of more than ten years.

—This middle-aged woman keeps appearing in my dreams. Does that ever happen to you?

—Oh, that woman? She shows up about three to four years into your sentence.

—I can't see her face.

—You're in for a treat. She's probably the guardian spirit of this area. All the long-term prisoners know her.

I found it reassuring that I wasn't the only one who knew her, but the uneasy feeling intensified.

In dreams, I wandered through countless rooms and corridors and went through numerous gates and doors, trying to find a way out of prison. At the end of a dark tunnel and stairwell, I would come across a place that looked like a shop in an express bus terminal. The faceless woman was the owner of this store. When I asked her how to get out of there, she cackled heartily.

—You've still got plenty of time left on your sentence, what's the rush? Have a little more fun with me first. Ha ha!

After my release, it occurred to me to do some research on her. As I wrote a few lines about the vision in the middle of the night, I suddenly realized with a shock who she was. She was my mother, rooted in my subconscious. For long-term prisoners, the last person to come visit them could only be their mothers. Just as we called for our mothers whenever we were afraid as children, the subconscious calls up the one woman we can rely on through the long years of isolation and loneliness, erasing the face of this "haunting."

The internalized wounds of war are no doubt wrapped tight and stored deep down inside my memory. To this day I am scared to death of large, blue dung flies. In my dreams, they hum on the windowsill and blot out the sun.

I was reassigned to an ambush squad that had secured a small traffic post. Since our brigade had shifted north, the boundaries of our defense zone had expanded, requiring additional personnel to secure the larger area. The monsoon arrived, and with it came enemy attacks; we received orders to keep moving north to defend some of the region's major cities. HQ's idea was to hand over the area we'd already secured to South Vietnamese troops.

The withdrawal planned since the beginning of the month had begun, and the entire brigade was sent into different areas, company by company. As the marine brigade began moving from Chu Lai to Hội An, the men leaving later were to defend the brigade's headquarters before handing it over to the South Vietnamese government; I happened to be one of the last to leave. This was my final combat experience in Vietnam, described in my short story "Tower." But unlike in the story, our mission was not to guard the tower. It was to secure a traffic point where Highway 1 and another strategic road met, ensuring the safe passage of the South Vietnamese troops.

We held the guardhouse for two days as guerrillas attempted to infiltrate every night. On the first night, they merely approached to a certain distance and fired at us until dawn. On the second, a larger contingent arrived with rockets around midnight. We set up a line of defense, with Claymores and a semicircle of barbed wire, putting our men in a horseshoe-shaped formation. We had automatic rifles, grenade launchers, and two M60 machine guns for personal firepower, and the brigade headquarters supplied us with 81 mm mortars. The artillery fired flares and pounded the coordinates we called out for them. We could hear the rifle shots of the enemy so close by that they were echoless and raw.

At dawn, the enemy bypassed us, blew up a nearby bridge, and retreated. Our squad likewise withdrew back to brigade headquarters when the American forces' highway patrol appeared. We'd been in trenches around the guardhouse, but two rocket blasts had injured three soldiers. We put them on a truck, returned to headquarters, and left with the last of the retreating forces by helicopter to Chu Lai's piers.

Only when we arrived at the new brigade base, located just outside Hội An, did we realize that the Tet Offensive, as it became known, had been launched by the North Vietnamese. Day after day, enemy shells flew into our as-yet unsettled line of defense. We jumped into the trenches whenever a bombardment began, trenches that were filled with rainwater up to our chests. Three or four hours we would spend in that long bath, sometimes dozing off.

On the side of the company that provided food and ammunition to each battalion and company base lay a wide, sandy expanse with the jungle beyond; this company always sustained the heaviest attacks. We called out coordinates, and our rockets mercilessly rained down 105 mm mortars that gave off a terrifying sound. The enemy would go quiet, then start broadcasting in Korean. At night they played popular Korean songs and appealed to us in quite convincing fashion: "Why must you become Yankee mercenaries just for a few measly dollars? Tomorrow you must lay down your guns and go back home. Next, we'll play Nam Jin's 'Did I come here for the tears?' for you."

Into the brief lull where no rockets fell would come a song. We listened in silence, staring out at the jungle beyond the sands. All we saw was darkness.

At that point an officer would come to his senses and shout, "What are you all doing! Call out the coordinates!" The coordinates would be called, and the battle would resume. The deafening noise continued, lights flashed, and smoke billowed from the jungle. During the next quiet interval the speaker babbled on again: "Please, let us cease our rockets. Let us not slaughter innocent civilians!"

In the midst of all this, we were informed that the North Vietnamese troops had occupied downtown Hội An and we were pegged to fight them. My fellow soldiers and I were cleaning our guns at the time. We were going to enter the city by helicopters and trucks. The 105 mm mortars continued to hit targets across the river. But these were only loud bangs, and above the empty sand fields and the barbed-wire fence and the forest was just white sunlight coming down in waves. Several companies and battalions were connected by narrow military roads that were flanked by low walls of sandbags and barbed wire on either side between the remaining copses of jungle, which looked like paper boats floating on water. We heard a menacing burst of fire coming from a tall tower, the kind installed at every traffic control point on the roads. A jeep blew dust as it ran through the passage between the sandbag walls toward our company. It came to an abrupt stop in front of the barricade, which a soldier pushed aside. As the dust settled, I could see the occupant. He wasn't wearing camouflage. He was in the dark pajamas the Vietnamese wore, combined with the wide-brimmed hat worn by the Burmese special forces. The driver was dressed the same way. There was a machine-gun seat in the back with no one manning it; the magazine had been taken out and the gun was swaying at an angle.

"What's the meaning of this?" demanded the company commander of the man in civilian clothes with no insignia or uniform. The man did not remove his opaque sunglasses or salute the officer as he proffered a document. "We're here to fetch a transfer."

The company commander scanned the papers. He called out my name, and I clambered out of the trench. My hair was pressed flat from the steel helmet and I was looking about, confused, as I walked up to them. My knees were showing over my boots where the hem of my fatigues had been cut, and thread was coming off them like tassels.

The commander waved the papers in his hand. "This puts me in a bad position . . . If you take all our experienced soldiers, who will fight the battles? We don't have anyone who can take the lead now." He was speaking to the man in the jeep as if he were head of military personnel. I was already in full gear, except for my helmet.

The man took off his Burmese hat and fanned his chest with it. "Any man who crosses the firing line becomes experienced."

I have described leaving the front and transferring to an investigative desk job, where I would confront an even more elusive truth about war, in my novel *The Shadow of Arms*. I had been suddenly plucked from hell, without a clue as to what was going on. At the front, no one can predict their immediate future. That afternoon, in the battle to recapture Hội An, the largest number of casualties was sustained by the brigade that I had left barely an hour before it was sent to fight.

Later, I learned what had prompted this sudden transfer. My mother had seen the address on my letter from the front and realized my duties were particularly dangerous. She recalled that a young man who used to live in our neighborhood was now a colonel or captain on Baegnyeong Island, in the western sea. She went to see his family for his current address and somehow managed to get a seat on an irregular ferry that crossed the passage once or twice a month.

Our former neighbor was amazed to see my mother turn up at what was then the western front against North Korea, where civilians were rarely authorized to visit. He promised her to do what he could to mobilize his connections and get me transferred. That was the end of the previous year, only two months prior. Since I had gained previous experience at the American base in Chu Lai, my transfer to Danang's Korea–US joint investigative unit was not difficult to accomplish.

If I witnessed extremes of death, violence, barbarism, and the human condition at the front, my work as an investigator of Danang's black market led me to realize the full scope of the war America was waging.

My first duty at the joint investigative unit was to understand how the PX really worked. Next, I was given the task of monitoring Danang's underground commerce. I was, to borrow my colleagues' phrasing, dropped slap into the middle of a "*dokkaebi* market."

Danang was an island surrounded by the North Vietnamese People's Army and the NLF, and daily life on this island was governed by a special economic system. The most powerful currency was the US dollar, but it was the vouchers issued by the US military command that ruled the market. The occupation forces and their environment were bound to replicate American consumerism, and the PX was the source of all luxury and consumer goods. In addition, the supply depot held the very survival of the city in its grasp with its control of vegetables, meat, tea, coffee, chocolate, alcohol, and cigarettes.

In the marketplace, the warring sides had no choice but to trade and conspire together within the rules. The darkest form of trade involved weapons, but a whole range of various goods was involved in the hierarchy of the market. A-rations referred to uncooked vegetables, fruit, and meat, while B-rations indicated lightly processed or prepared foodstuffs. C-rations were completely processed foods like cans and field rations. There was often corruption by individual Americans working at the PX, but I became sure there was also a separate financial office dealing with the economic operations. They used A- and B-rations, as well as prized products like beer and cigarettes, to manipulate prices.

As operations continued for two months, the supply of fresh vegetables and other staples from the countryside dwindled, sending market prices through the roof. The people living in Danang were military families, bureaucrats, merchants, and ordinary civilians. They participated in the black market for a taste of American consumerism. The American military used the profits from these under-the-counter transactions to pay their local workers' wages, and occasionally switched vouchers to recover dollars that had disappeared underground.

Soldiers and technicians from third-party nations also jumped into the black market. The South Vietnamese forces and managers dealt in combat food and weapons; their customers were, of course, the NLF who collected taxes from merchants. During the monsoon season, the coalition forces and NLF opened C-ration cans together even while fighting each other. If, for example, the South Vietnamese forces were issued new weapons like grenade launchers, a few always got sold on. When America's peace settlement construction project was underway, countless aid goods flooded the market. Cement and slate for houses, powdered grains and animal feed, food, and enough weapons and gunpowder to arm a neighborhood militia poured in. I learned much of this from my predecessor and became aware of it myself on the job.

I used to sit in a corner of the marketplace wearing fatigues, but with no rank insignia or cap. Sometimes I wore a shirt and cotton pants, or Vietnamese civilian wear, and sat in a teahouse or tavern in the market. I was taller than most Vietnamese, and the children would follow me around calling me *pileukddang*, which means "Filipino."

I got to know a middle school teacher at a teahouse in Danang. When he learned I was Korean, he probably thought I was a civilian technician or similar; he once brought up an article in an English-language paper and demanded, "Why are you murdering poor Vietnamese children in the countryside?"

"First I've heard of it."

"It was reported in our English-language newspaper. Everyone is angry about it."

"Do you support the Viet Cong?"

"I hate anyone who kills innocent civilians."

Our conversations went nowhere. I couldn't think of anything to say to him. Such exchanges kept me awake at night. I regretted having come to Vietnam.

We bumped into each other at the teahouse in the afternoons, and once we became better acquainted, we criticized the Americans together. We both thought the other had got the better end of the deal. He spoke of how the peace settlement plan had seized land from subsistence farmers, driven them out, and made powerful people the new landowners. At the market,

I began to understand the true face of this war. This is what I wrote in *The Shadow of Arms*:

What is a PX? A Disneyland in a vast tin warehouse. A place where an exhausted soldier with a few bloodstained military dollars can buy and possess dreams mass-produced by industrial enterprises. The ducks and rabbits and fairies are replaced by machines and laughter and dances. The wrapping paper and the boxes smell of rich oil and are as beautiful as flowers.

What is a PX? A place where they sell the commodities used daily by a nation that possesses the skill to shower more than one million steel fragments over an area one mile wide by a quarter mile long with a single CBV. A nation capable of turning a three-hundred-acre tract of jungle into a defoliated wasteland where not a single plant or animal can survive, in under four minutes.

What is a PX? It's Uncle Sam's attic, the old man who makes appearances at villages the world over garbed in the Stars and Stripes, a Roman-style dagger in hand as he brandishes a shield with the motto: "America is the world's largest and greatest nation." It is the general store of the cavalry fort, frequented by whores and ministers and arms smugglers who join hands in transforming the natives into ridiculous puppets, intoxicating them and exploring new frontiers of vileness.

And the PX brings civilization to the filthy Asian slopeheads who otherwise would go on living in blissful ignorance on a diet of bananas and rice. It teaches them how to wash with Ivory soap, how to quench the thirst and ease the heart with the taste of Coke. It showers down upon the bombed-out barracks perfumes, rainbow-colored cookies and candy drops, lace-fringed lingerie, expensive wristwatches, and rings graced with precious stones. Cheese appears on the smelly meal tables of Asia, and condoms slip out from between Asian girls' thighs and dance on children's tiny fingertips.

Anyone who has ever been intoxicated, even once, by that taste and smell and touch, will carry the memory to his grave. The products ceaselessly create loyal consumers who are at the mercy of the producers. Those who lay hands upon the wealth of America will have the label US MILITARY burned into their brains. Children who grow up humming their songs and eating their candies and chocolates off the streets trust their benevolence and optimism. The vast purchasing power in the market, the booming business in the city, and the enthusiasm and ecstasy in the back alleys are all in proportion to the intensity of the war. The PX is a tempting wooden horse. And it is America's most powerful new weapon.

As I came to realize that the Americans were no more than mercenaries in Vietnam, I felt guilty living among the Vietnamese civilians in Danang. I used to glance at my reflection in the windows as I walked into the market with an American, with whom I'd come in an investigator division's car disguised as a private company vehicle. My real mirror, in the end, was the Vietnamese people themselves.

12

Dictatorship

1969–76

My tour of duty in Vietnam lasted longer than the customary year; I was discharged from the marines after a year and a half. All I brought home were some cigarettes and toiletries in a small Boston bag. I also vowed never to cause direct harm to anyone ever again. But after settling back into civilian life, I realized my resolutions were little more than words. It did not take me long to understand that such idealistic notions were the product of a limited sense of self that was, in turn, the product of a land divided by ideology. In reality, the homeland I had returned to was a military dictatorship under the powerful influence of the United States.

As I got off the train at Cheongnyangni Station and made my way to my mother's new address, I was filled with anticipation and anxiety. She was frailer than ever, and my younger brother was now a senior in high school. I would have to go back to college, but we couldn't really afford that. I had returned to my depressed youth, full of dread about the future.

Mother had taken a sewing job as a last resort and had, with much trouble, managed to get a small, three-bedroom working-class house in Daebang-dong. She left for work at dawn and returned in the evening; her only pleasure in life was to sit in front of the black-and-white television at night to watch the soap opera *Assi* (Lady).

I lived for a while in one of the rooms in the back, the curtains drawn in the middle of the day, which was much better than the attic room in Heukseok-dong Market. My brother was preparing for the college entrance exam; I could hear him muttering things with his friend as they studied by rote memorization. I suffered from insomnia. When it wasn't the sound of my brother's studying, it was the buzzing of the fluorescent lights that filled my skull.

I met up with many of my friends right after I returned. There were some who had just left the military, like me, and some who had stayed, married, and found jobs. They seemed to find it baffling that I'd come back from Vietnam without any money.

I was quieter than before and would sit for long stretches of time staring into space. I would fall asleep in the middle of a rainy scene in a movie theater and not wake until late at night, or linger in teahouses where old men sat killing time, skimming discarded newspapers for hours.

I was so tired of everything. I had begun to pick up books at used bookstores but didn't feel able to start writing again. I was numb to everything, and at the same time I would find tears rolling down my cheeks while listening to popular songs or watching TV dramas.

If I couldn't fall asleep, I simply stayed up. Then, after a couple of nights, I would fall asleep in exhaustion. But it was seldom a deep sleep; I could sense every footfall in the next room and outside beyond the wall. I dreamed a lot, usually nightmares. I would be walking down a foggy road alone. Suddenly, the road would be littered with body parts and decaying corpses. I would trip over the hand of a corpse or accidentally kick a severed head, and sometimes drown in dead bodies. I could clearly smell rotting flesh, which smelled like soy sauce being made, a smell so disgusting that it would jolt me awake even from the deepest sleep. In one dream, I was burying the bodies underground. But no matter how much earth I added, I still kept seeing a toe or a fingertip, or a tuft of black hair poking out of the soil. Another nightmare involved our escape during the Korean War. I was passing the rubble of downtown, separated from my family. Smoke rose from the devastation; no one else was around. Suddenly, I was surrounded by unfamiliar soldiers. They laughed loudly and started shooting at me. I stumbled over rubble as I fled. Bullets tore through my body, a bomb went off nearby, and my limbs flew off.

The sound of screaming woke me, and I shuddered at the strange sight of my room. My brother was there, wailing, his head covered in blood. A vase lay shattered on the floor, the water drenching everything. My brother had entered my room when he heard me flailing and, in my sleep, I had smashed the vase against his head. He ended up getting twenty stitches at the hospital. I finally came to terms with the fact that I was unwell.

One day, I woke up late and stared at my face in the mirror before shaving off my eyebrows. Without them, I looked as if I had no expression or soul. I continued to stay in the house, and at night I would sit by myself before sleeping almost twelve hours during the day. I felt completely alone. I had no one to talk to. My mother and brother tried hard not to disturb me; when I slept for hours with the curtains drawn, they would quietly come in to check that I was breathing before creeping back out.

I would wake up at night, wander around the house, eat rice mixed with kimchi, and read the books stacked by my bed. One evening, I came upon a contest-winning short story entry in a magazine. I had no idea who the author was, what she looked like, or how she spent her time, but I decided to write her a letter anyway. That first letter led to more, and I would find myself rising at dawn to go out into the dark, empty street, slide another letter into the mailbox, and go back home.

It was a truly isolated time for me. I was starved of self-expression. Oddly, what made me overcome those bleak days and begin writing again was the power of writing love letters to this woman, about whom I knew little more than her address.

~

That winter, my eyebrows finally grew back, and I escaped the dark room. My short story "Tower" and a play, *Hwanyeongui dot* (The Phantom Sail), written over several weeks, won contests: I was back into writing. The woman writer I had been corresponding with had helped me reconnect with the outside world. Over the next year, I began publishing older works that I had stored away as well as new stories.

Early winter, November 1970. The day was overcast. I was shocked to hear the news on the radio. A laborer at Pyeonghwa Market named Jeon Tae-il, after appealing to the authorities to uphold labor laws, had poured gasoline over himself and set himself on fire in order to tell the world about Korea's inhumane treatment of workers. In his last testament, which began with the line "Friends, and all who know me, and all who do not," he said: "I wish I had at least one friend with a college education. Then he could help me to understand our complicated labor laws," a lament that pierced the hearts of many. In particular, his final words as the flames engulfed him—"Uphold the Labor Standards Act, we are not machines!"— sent shock waves throughout the universities and intellectual society. To this day, we hear of activists who claim their lives were changed by his terrible self-immolation; such was the effect of his sacrifice all throughout the 1970s and 1980s upon the labor and democratization movements.

Beginning in November, I spent three months working on my story "A strange land." It was based on my experiences during the 1960s with the reclaimed land projects and *hamba* living, but life in South Korea hadn't changed much since then. The so-called Five-Year Economic Development Plans, pushed by the military regime, began with restructuring labor-intensive piecework as factory work. As the countryside began to unravel, the next to follow was the Saemaul (New Village) Movement, which uprooted the sharecropping class and small-scale landed farmers and turned them into factory labor. Slums expanded around the cities, just as they did around factories in the West during the Industrial Revolution a century earlier. "A strange land" was greatly influenced by Jeon Tae-il's death.

I didn't know where to submit the story when it was finished. The poet Choi Min told me about the *Quarterly Changbi*, where he had just published a poem, so I sent it there. A month later, an editor there asked to meet me. I went to Cheongjin-dong to the journal's offices.

Little of all this remains now, but Cheongjin-dong used to be full of taverns selling *haejangguk*, *bindaeddeok*, and *makgeolli*. There were many large and small publishers set up in the old Japanese-style buildings or in compact two- or three-story offices. At the time, the development of the land south of the Han River was still in the planning stages. Old residences were being knocked down to make way for nicer, single-family homes, with mass housing constructed on the outskirts. The people who lived in the "nice" homes were fond of shiny mahogany furniture and television sets with wooden paneling next to record players and shelves lined with sets of hardcover books that were never read. These book sets were printed by a handful of successful large publishers who sold them on lucrative installment plans. The books contained classics from both East and West and sported thick, gilded covers. Almost everything about them, from editorial planning to content, was modeled on Japanese book sets, and many of the translations were second-hand from the Japanese as well. No one cared about copyright or publishing rights; the publishers cranked out set after set in high-quality hardcovers and hired temporary contract workers to sell the monthly plans.

In contrast, the little publishing houses clustered in Cheongjin-dong were run by the so-called April Revolution generation, mostly up-and-coming intellectuals who had studied foreign literature and the social sciences. They focused on promoting new writers making their debut in the 1960s and 1970s, printing their work in quarterly magazines before publishing them in book form, a practice that breathed fresh life into the literary market. The literary establishment had no faith that these single-title books and poetry collections would ever break even, let alone one day become as profitable as the reprinted classics sold in sets on monthly installment plans. And no one could ever dream of being a "full-time writer." No one dared question the minuscule manuscript fees doled out by editors, let alone expect royalties. More often than not, payment consisted of a round at the bar, which the writer had to simply accept, unable to demand money instead. A writer after the 1950s was little more than a member of the lumpenproletariat, wandering from teahouse to tavern, scribbling bits here or doing hourly work for publishers there, like a part-time employee. The best one could hope for was landing a full-time gig as a schoolteacher or news reporter.

The editor I befriended at *Changbi* was the critic Yeom Mu-ung. Though only two years older than me, he carried himself with mature aplomb (though he would later prove to be quite the comedian) and spoke little. He published me in the magazine but was anxious about it. The authorities tended to persecute the editor rather than the writer for problematic stories, and "A strange land" was the first to deal with labor rights issues directly.

In the fall of 1971, I was married off at last. Now that I was starting a family, I could not go on living in my mother's house— not with a wife. I tried working at a publisher, for the sake of having a regular job, but felt suffocated by the meaninglessness of editing other people's writings. After a few days, I left the office during lunch hour and phoned in to say that I quit.

To concentrate full-time on writing was the height of foolishness in those days. Few publications paid the author, and what they did pay was hardly enough to cover living expenses. Even if I published a short story every month, I would never make enough to put food on the table. And who could crank out a story a month? In neighboring Japan, it was possible around that time to maintain a middle-class lifestyle for about three months on the publication of a single short story. In other words, you could live a full year on just four short stories. Then you published a short-story collection every three years, kind of like settling accounts.

Later, when the fight for freedom of expression became more heated, the dictatorship moved to subsidize manuscript fees at magazines, cut taxes for arts workers, provide mortgages, and even bring in foreign investment as "carrots" to keep writers in line. But those benefits only went to the artists who complied with official policies.

I wanted to finish my new novella, "Mr. Han's chronicle," which I'd been working on until just before my wedding. I sensed a certain mood of decadence and a new wind of change in East Asia, and wanted to explore it in fiction. Henry Kissinger visited China, and the Park Chung-hee administration was proposing talks with North Korea through the Red Cross. A year later, in 1972, the July 4 North–South Korea Joint Statement was announced and the Yushin dictatorship began, heralding new relations with the US and China.

I'd been a middle school student when I first learned about the ideological discrimination suffered by my eldest maternal uncle, who had fled from the North alone, and my mother's isolated efforts to support him in prison. I got the story again in exact detail from my mother, who was a born storyteller, and decided that the neglected lives of common people during the war was the right topic for my novella. Many of the first generation of divided families were still alive, giving my work a contemporary and universal appeal. In this battle of Korean against Korean, it was the blameless common people whose lives had been torn apart.

I laid out Mother's testimony in chronological order and filled in the gaps with my imagination. I wrote the first draft in a room at a vineyard in Gwacheon, by the foot of Mount Gwanak. It was in a remodeled three-room shack that had been used to house farming tools and manure. The other two rooms were occupied by students studying for the national civil service exams; I'm sure my weird work of "writing fiction," which had driven me to retreat to a quiet, peaceful place, struck them as freakish and useless at once.

I had left my mother's home with my wife, Hee-yun, but it hadn't taken long to realize that having no job and hoping to write fiction for a living was a foolish dream. First of all, there was nowhere to go. We didn't have enough to cover living expenses, let alone a deposit for a place of our own. All I had was the advance for my novella and some money from short stories, which was just enough to support us for two months if we kept to a strict budget. A few authors were declaring themselves full-time writers around then, but they generally had working wives, or they wrote movie scripts.

After asking around, we rented a bungalow on the slopes of Bukhan Mountain that we'd eyed during a hike, and moved in during the winter. Hee-yun was pregnant with our first child. We bought some household goods at Suyuri Market as well as a small, low table. That table was where I did my writing, after we'd sat around it on the floor for our dinner.

The bungalow was one of ten built in the Ui-dong valley near the Bukhansan hiking trail. A rich man's mistress was said to have inherited these houses and rented them out to hikers and vacationers. I remember paying 5,000 won—the equivalent of $4 today—in monthly rent for the entire house. The structure was simple, with the front door leading to a narrow hall with doors to the kitchen and bathroom, and a sliding paper-screen door to the bedroom. There was no electricity or running water; the floor was heated by a wood-burning *agungi* built into the outside of the house. As my pregnant wife curled up to sleep, I lit an oil lamp by the window and worked on "Mr. Han's chronicle" through the night, until the break of day.

~

That winter, the Ui-dong valley would get snowed in once every few days, with especially harsh winds from the north. Even behind the windowpane, the flame of my oil lamp would whip about as if it was about to go out. There were only maybe four hours in a day where sun shone on the valley, and the wind was relentless; fuel became our biggest problem. There were no coal deliveries this far up the slope, and the *agungi* could only handle small amounts of wood. The landlord had stocked the wood-shed full of pine cones, old leaves, and sticks, and so our house on the hill was always giving off white smoke. The landlord brought in some wood once or twice, but it was so expensive that there wasn't much of it and we went through it quickly.

I finally went to a junk shop and bought an axe. If I sweated for about half a day, I could chop down enough firewood to last four days, but I was unused to the labor and injured myself frequently; once I slipped from a tree and was bedridden for a few days. Not only that, the mountain stream we drank from would freeze over, and breaking the ice every morning was a difficult chore. I once slipped and fell while carrying a pail of water in each hand. My trousers were soaked, and I had to fetch the water all over again, shivering like a doused rat.

As Hee-yun's stomach grew bigger, I began hearing from publishers that my novella, with its political themes, would be impossible to publish. We were beginning to see soldiers standing guard in the streets, looking down in contempt at people from their tank turrets. That winter was cold and tedious. I'd write into the night, and go outside for a smoke, shivering in the cold air, and see the Sunwoongak *gisaeng* house shining across the dark valley. The city seemed as if it were buried somewhere deep below.

Writing line after line about the torn fate of our times while blowing on my fingertips to warm them, I would eventually hear the sound of a band playing in Sunwoongak valley around dawn. I would turn the lamp off when the sun began to rise. As I sat in the dimness, a bird would wake underneath the eaves and cry mournfully. What depths of the forest did it fly from? What wanderer built its nest under that eave? I wondered if this was the bird of legend that lived in the snowy mountains, the one said to shiver all night, crying that it will build a nest when the day breaks, but forgetting once the morning comes. The one that asks, *why build another home when here I am unharmed?* yet regrets it each day when night falls.

The valley that winter was full of strange experiences. A shaman moved into one of the nearby bungalows. One day, my wife said, "That woman keeps saying strange things. Like that the mountain god comes down here and circles our house."

There were days when I went downtown and returned late at night, and I worried about my wife sitting in our house alone. The thought of this shaman woman filling her with fear upset me. I marched down to see her. There were handmade paper lotus blossoms and other complicated shamanistic designs plastered on the walls. This being a shrine, she had set up a pair of candles near one wall and put some incense and a white porcelain bowl filled with clear water before them.

I stood in front of her door and said loudly, "Stop filling my wife's head with nonsense! She's pregnant!"

"Now just hold on," she said. "I'm speaking the truth. Hear me out."

The candles flickered in the draft of the open door. I went inside and crouched next to the sliding door inside. The shaman woman lowered her voice and said, "It's true. When I sit here and look at your house, I sometimes see two lights like lanterns wandering around the hill and disappearing."

"But that's . . . How do you know that's a mountain god?"

"I just do."

"The god of Bukhan Mountain?" My mischievous nature overcame my irritation at this point, and I was teasing her.

"No, from farther away. Something to do with coming from Guwol Mountain in Hwanghae Province and having a look around here before going back."

"Well, never speak of such things to my wife again."

With that, I headed home and reassured my wife that the shaman had simply hallucinated during one of her prayers. The road up to the house from the last bus stop at Ui-dong went through a thick, pitch-black pine forest, with a steep slope on the left and a stream flowing over rocks on the right. I would weave up this path when drunk, singing to myself.

One night, I heard the sound of a woman crying in the pine forest. I could clearly make out someone who was trying to swallow her tears but found her sobs overflowing, nonetheless. Everything else was dark. I'd been told that a man and a woman had swallowed some pills and died in the snow, and the man was said to have taken off his coat to wrap around the woman. It was, truly, an eerie winter.

One morning, when the snow had come down in great mountainous drifts, Choi Min and three other friends came to visit me in Ui-dong. We got drunk on ten bottles of soju and dozed off around dawn.

"Hello there, come on out! Come on out, hurry!"

It was the shaman from next door. My wife and I got up to investigate. The shaman kept pointing at the ground around our house and crying, "Look! These are signs that the mountain god was here!"

Indeed, there were footprints the size of my palm. My friends, woken by the ruckus, were also looking around in wonder. The footsteps really did go around the house and up the ridge behind us. We went back into the house in a daze.

"It does kind of look like animal footprints . . ." Choi Min said.

I tried to dismiss what he was saying. "So it's a dog or wolf or what?"

Choi Min shook his head. "Too big for dog-paw prints. And they're in a straight line."

"A straight line?"

"Big cats walk like that. One foot in front of the other."

Mountain gods are associated with tigers, and so, all of a sudden, the shaman's talk seemed less far-fetched.

After we left the valley in the spring for a two-room house in the village, the painter Kim Gi-dong used it as studio space. He told us about other strange things that happened afterward. He had nightmares every night, for a start. Across from the house flowed a stream from a different set of tributaries from our own stream, and it fed into a pool surrounded by boulders. I used to go there to collect pails of drinking water. There was a little waterfall between the rocks, behind which was a space wide enough for two people to sit. Offerings of rice or fruit or half-burned candles were often left there, probably by someone who had prayed all night. Kim said that vegetables or rice he had washed and set aside for later had a way of disappearing. We learned that the valley had been turned into shaman territory for *gut* ceremonies and devotions, and in the folklore there was a separate term—*shilmul*—for the disappearance of foods in devotional lands.

~

For three years in the early 1970s, while I kept on writing short stories and novellas and trying to make it as a full-time writer, the Park Chung-hee administration was tightening its grip by getting rid of tenure limits on the presidency. The self-immolation of Jeon Tae-il, the publication of Kim Chi-ha's incendiary poem "Five Bandits" and my "A strange land," and the first post-division North–South contact at Panmunjom took place around that time, while in Seoul a garrison decree was issued, armed soldiers marched into university campuses, and subcontracted laborers protested before the Korean Airlines building demanding restitution for unpaid wages. While North and South Korea came up with an agreement, Park Chung-hee dismissed the National Assembly and declared martial law across the nation, inaugurating what would be known as the October

Yushin era—referencing Park's authoritarian Yushin Constitution. Soon afterward, North–South talks ground to a halt.

I joined a group of pro-democracy writers to petition against the changes to our constitution. For four days, we collected signatures from sixty-one people, read out the declaration on the steps of Myeong-deong Cathedral, participated in the subsequent protest, and were all arrested by the KCIA. Each signatory author was interrogated, and five were arrested under trumped-up charges in a fabricated "literary spies" incident.

Night after night, we poured ourselves rivers of soju at taverns in Cheongjin-dong, where we grilled fish and pork over coal briquettes. Around that time, any intellectuals possessed of a modicum of critical thought would gather to talk of democracy and death and resistance against the dictatorship. We would drink all night, and many of us would remain blood brothers for decades to come.

The magazine *Quarterly Changbi* began after the April Revolution, directed by Park Yoon-bae. With his short hair and sharp eyes, he gave the impression of never having done anything as delicate as reading a novel. The first thing he wanted to do when we met was to tell me his thoughts on "A strange land" and "Mr. Han's chronicle." I don't recall his exact words but the gist was as follows: "'A strange land' is impressive for being the first labor fiction since the Liberation, and this is an important achievement. But it is a little overeager in its zeal for the struggle."

To be honest, I'd had similar thoughts. There were many works written in the 1980s that dealt with the so-called labor problem, but this writing tended to be didactic. Looking back, I was still on my way to finding my own approach as a writer, and while I had put together my *hamba* experience of the 1960s with Jeon Tae-il's death, I was not as mature as the characters in my own work.

"Writers must throw themselves into the real world as fully as they throw themselves into their craft," Park Yoon-bae told me. "Coupling activism to writing is crucial."

I believed him and believed in him. We spoke of many things as we kept on seeing each other. He was an avid reader and had learned Japanese in order to expand the scope of his reading. Later I visited his house and realized the full extent of his learning when I saw his shelves, full of books from various fields; yet he wore his reading lightly. He would go on to take care of Lee Bu-young, Kim Chi-ha, and many other young writers after me.

Around the time that I was seeing him frequently, I came to a decision, which I discussed with my wife. I wanted her to earn her own income while I joined the labor movement. My wife decided to run a clothing store near Ewha University, and we moved to a two-room apartment in a poor neighborhood in Sinchon.

The sprawling area from Daerim-dong to the five-way intersection at Guro-dong and Garibong-dong houses the Guro Industrial Complex and its laborers' living quarters. I walked about Guro Market, Guro Theater, and the bus stop dressed in scruffy laborer's clothing. There were small taverns and drinking stalls by the side of the big road from the complex, where several factories were clustered. I decided to go to the busiest stall to kill time. A middle-aged couple were running it; they sold noodles in fish broth and side dishes to accompany drinking, such as skewers of chicken gizzards and hearts, *injeolmi* and red bean rice cakes. It was busiest around 9 p.m., when the laborers leaving an overtime shift would decide it was too late to go home to make dinner and would instead order a bowl of noodles and some skewers and call it a night. There were factory girls who bought fish cakes and rice cakes before going in for the night shift. After four days of killing time in that stall, I offered a shot of soju to the owner, and without my having to ask, he proceeded to tell me his life story and treat me as a friend.

His name was Kang. He'd been a tenant farmer, but it was too difficult to support his family and old parents on land that was barely ten *majigi*, or about one acre, wide. The military dictatorship boisterously promised to write off his loans, but the creditors showed no mercy. Abandoning the thatched cottage he couldn't even give away, the family fled to Seoul in the night. They settled down in a single room in a neighborhood in the mountains, and the young couple went to work in factories doing all sorts of manual labor. But his parents died one after the other, and his wife injured her back at a factory and died after a year of being bedridden. His eldest son was conscripted into the military and ended up staying to make a career of it, while his eldest daughter declared she would become a hairdresser and left home; she had not been heard from since.

Kang became a junk collector, trading taffy or popped rice for old equipment destined for the scrap heap. He met his second wife while working in an alley in the market. His wife had a child of her own, he had a younger daughter from his previous marriage, and his youngest was already six years old. They followed the trail of manual labor gigs into the complex when it was first being built. After it was finished, a township of shacks sprang up along the stream on a nearby strip of land that began at the edge of a tilled field. I later described this town in "A Dream of Good Fortune."

When he heard I was looking for work and a place to live, Kang promptly offered his spare room to rent. He added that many foremen visited his stall, and he could grab any one of them to ask about a job for me.

I decided to take a look at his place first, so I waited until they closed up the stall before curfew to accompany them to the shantytown. Kang roped the rear of his bicycle with empty basins, pails, and liquor bottles and pedaled slowly in front, while his wife followed carrying on her head a Styrofoam box containing the day's leftovers packed in ice. I took up the rear, carrying containers sloshing with broth, bottles of sauce, and more leftovers.

Faint lights began to shine in the dark as we walked along the walls of the complex and crossed a makeshift bridge of a few stacked sheets of metal. They lit up one by one beyond the dark stretch of empty land. I suddenly felt as if I were back in my childhood days right after the war. As my eyes adjusted to the dark, I could make out the movement of lit cigarettes and hear the sounds of babies and children. Most of all, the warm scene of a candle's flame dancing in the rectangle of a window brought back dim memories. It looked like the recreation of a neighborhood during the evacuation period.

Kang's house was the first one facing the vacant lot, so it was better placed than others. It had good air circulation and space enough in front of the gate for his wife to plant lettuce and green onions. As there was no porch, the papered-over sliding lattice doors acted as gate and front door combined. Despite the cold, their son Geun-ho had left the door open as the kids waited for their parents. As soon as he heard footsteps, he hurried outside and helped his parents put away their things.

Geun-ho was a nineteen-year-old middle school dropout. He'd lived in an orphanage before his mother married Kang. After quitting school, he apprenticed at a factory to become a lathe worker and now was a master in his own right. His mother was immensely proud of his having a regular job, and Kang also respected him to some extent as his own man.

Geun-ho, like most workers around that time in the complex, worked twelve hours a day, with only Sundays off. The factory ran in two shifts from nine to nine, and the day and night shifts switched places every week.

I asked Geun-ho that night, "What is the best way to get work?"

"What skills do you have?"

"None."

Geun-ho smiled and nodded. "Well, even if you had any, they'd be useless now. There's so much specialization these days, and the machines are different at every single factory. On top of which they switch them out at the drop of a hat."

He was right. Large slogans saying "Work is battle" or "We can do it" were plastered on the buildings of the complex offices, with smaller ones below saying "Labor 80%, machines 20%." In other words, the work at the complex was still largely labor-intensive. Most of the profit came from exploiting low-wage labor for subcontracted work commissioned by Japan.

Japan at the time, much like South Korea today, employed the strategy of farming out labor-intensive manufacturing work to Korea and Southeast Asia, while keeping the high-value-added, technologically advanced jobs at home. Modernization in South Korea was a vicious cycle: landless farmers were made to leave their homes in the country, keeping wages down across the nation, which meant that the price of crops also had to be kept low in order to feed the masses of factory workers in the city. In other words, parents who were farmers had to break their backs producing rice to be sold for a pittance so that their urban, factory-worker children could just about afford to buy the rice on their low wages.

The military dictatorship at the time believed in "build first, distribute later." Koreans still say that today, only now we call it "increase the pie before sharing it." But despite becoming one of the top fifteen richest countries in the world, the fact that we still have one of the lowest levels of spending on social welfare tells you bluntly how much of this sloganeering has been just one big lie.

Naturally, we on the activist left began to discuss whom exactly we were referring to with the label *minjung*, "the common people." Eighty percent of the population were still farmers right after the war, but at some point people started talking about the "ten million laborers." The number of tenant farmers and subsistence farmers fell, with only landed farmers remaining in the countryside, while the number of urban poor working in service jobs or small businesses increased. The majority ended up being laborers, farmers, urban poor, or the middle class. It seemed obvious that these groups needed to support each other and organize if they wanted to fight the dictatorship. Later on, anyone who managed to rent a room in the city and put a little rice on the table imagined themselves to be middle class, but this illusion would be dispelled around the mid-1980s.

Following Geun-ho's advice, I decided to aim for a factory job that required a bit more skill and paid better than others. Geun-ho thought that since I was post-military, and a bit older, I might tire more easily, and six months of hard apprenticeship was sure to lead to new skills and higher pay. He said such workplaces also had a friendly atmosphere, since most of the skilled workers were older and educated. Here, *educated* meant a high school diploma. Workplaces with low wages and large numbers of workers tended to be full of young people and also more hostile.

I slept in Kang's small room for a few days. That weekend, Kang, Geun-ho, and I ripped up all the flooring in the house and replaced the heating stones. Now I had a place to stay. In addition, having Geun-ho around was as fortifying as having a strong younger brother. He had Kang introduce me to someone for work.

I was waiting at the stall when a man with a sun-darkened face and a gray factory uniform jacket came in. Kang's expression immediately changed as he introduced us. The man was smiling and apparently unassuming, but his gaze was not simple, like a country bumpkin's. He seemed to know something of the world.

"Foreman Lee is the highest-ranking man in these parts. He started when this place was built, you see."

Lee inquired without hesitation: "You're looking for work, right?"

"Yes, I couldn't find anything after I left the military."

He asked me where I had served, and when I said I was in Vietnam as a marine, he said he'd been there, too, and was discharged as a sergeant. It's easy for men to keep talking once they start on their military experiences. Foreman Lee said his home was in Gangwon Province, where he'd worked as a farmer for two years before realizing he would never turn a profit; so he had come with empty pockets to the city for work. He had tried his hand at every form of hard labor in factories before getting a job at the complex. Now he was the foreman at the lens grinders' division, the most popular of the production lines. He had married a factory girl who worked a sewing machine, and they had a child. His dream was to buy a house and for the company to succeed in its exports, so that he would make plant manager.

He introduced me to a lens-grinding division at an optical factory that was doing well at the time. I got the job thanks to my high school diploma, proof of military service, and hand-written CV. If I had graduated from my first, prestigious high school, the cat would have been immediately out of the bag. But because I had ended up graduating from night classes at an industrial high school, specializing in construction, no one suspected me of political infiltration.

Later, when I'd quit the job, a police officer came visiting. He stared at my citizen's registration card for a long time, stated, "Someone reported you," and left. It wasn't until much later that I learned the man who had reported me as a labor-activist infiltrator was the very man who got me the job: Foreman Lee.

The grinding division was divided into three groups. The first ground glass circles into their initial shape, the second polished them to a flawless shine, and the third fitted the glass on a grinding mold. The round, wooden grinding molds were coated with coal tar; when the surface turned malleable with heat, the lenses were stuck on one by one and plunged into cold water to fix them in place, before slotting the molds into a machine. When this process was complete, a worker removed the lenses from the molds and stacked them to one side so they could be transported to another factory for more grinding.

I started off as an apprentice, of course, and was put on the initial grinding unit. The master was a fat young man with bad skin. I don't remember his name, but he would hum the songs of Na Hoon-a or Nam Jin as he worked: *The man who took a look back at the end of the stone wall path, another look as he crossed the stepping stones, before departing for Seoul . . .*

Soon I moved on from assisting to fitting the machine myself, but it was not as easy as it looked. The machine did the work of grinding the glass that had been fixed to the wooden molds, but if the glass was tilted even slightly, the lens would shatter instantly. The cost of that was, of course, taken out of your wages. The moment one lens was done, the next had to be placed in the grinder immediately. The machine never stopped, and the slightest hesitation meant a shattered lens. The grinding mold also needed to be refilled with a fine abrasive powder and constantly dunked in water. By the afternoon, my fingers would be aching. We were expected to work at these monotonous tasks for twelve hours a day. I wanted to whoop with joy whenever we were told there was no overtime that day, but the other workers would curse in disappointment, because it meant that much less pay.

I asked the old hands at the taverns and stalls whether there had been any labor disputes in the past. They told me there'd been a big one at a famous sewing factory. The workers had sealed off the building and managed to hold off the authorities for a while but were eventually chased out. They took refuge up a nearby hill, where they continued their protest for two more days before it was suppressed. There had also been short-lived conflicts in electronics and food-packaging factories. But these old hands, despite the disputes unfolding in plain sight, had only gazed blankly at them or went to play volleyball during lunch. And even these stories were whispered to me in a park near where I worked, not talked about openly.

There's one particular man I befriended who sticks in my memory. His nickname was Madoros. He used to work at corporate before being sent down for some mistake or other, and he was now fitting lenses onto molds. I envied his easy job at first but, apparently, this was the work of a master. It was that difficult to attach the lenses to the round molds without an iota of tilt. I've forgotten his real name because we used his nickname so much. A navy man, all he talked of was the sea. And because his military affiliation had been so close to mine, we had a lot to talk about.

Madoros told me a little bit about himself once over drinks. He'd worked in a company before joining the navy. After he was discharged, he hoped to join a ship's crew and scoured the ports of Incheon and Busan, but no one wanted to hire him. There were too many men like him who'd been in the navy and were looking for the same work. But then his father, who ran a bicycle store in a small town, was hit by a truck and lost the use of his legs, and Madoros could no longer afford to be choosy. As eldest son, he had to get any job he could and at least contribute to the monthly pharmacy bills. He ended up asking for a job at the same company he'd started out in.

He told me that the current division leader at corporate had been his foreman when he first entered the company, and they had been at odds from the start. The man had pretended to be drunk during a company drinking session and beat him up. Also, just two months after he began work, he was sent down from corporate to the complex for being one of five workers involved in instigating a labor dispute. "We were too hasty, and few of the others joined us."

It was he who told me about the social groups the employees had formed. At work, if you so much as mentioned labor unions, your coworkers, whom you knew next to nothing about anyway, would instantly clam up and avoid you. So, getting people together to socialize outside of work wasn't easy. Whoever put a group together had to have a reputation for being a responsible worker. No one trusted a worker who acted like a gangster. It helped, too, if they were skilled at their job. Some companies had been extending overtime into Sundays and holidays, but churches and religious groups began to object, which meant laborers could use Sundays to meet up. The social groups tended to divide along gender lines, with women getting together for church, books, or music appreciation, and men getting together to hike, fish, or play soccer or volleyball.

Sundays at the Guro-dong workers' residential area usually involved napping until lunch, doing the laundry, watching base-ball, or going to the theater with a date. Some people belonged to social groups with their coworkers, but I didn't see too many of these.

One weekend, I suggested to Madoros and my master engi-neer that we go see a show. I wanted to check out the culture in these parts. Madoros was reluctant. "We're a little too old . . ." But the master engineer said he had been meaning to go but didn't want to go alone. He invited the factory women as well and found out what was playing: the Ha Chun-hwa show was in town at the Guro Theater.

The next day at our meeting site near the tram station, the engineer showed up in a tan suit, complete with necktie, while the other three or four factory men and women in their twenties also came in smart suits and dresses, waving their hands as they crossed the street toward us. The show was on in several the-aters at once, and performers had to rush between different venues in central Yeongdeungpo, Guro, Siheung, and the out-skirts of Anyang. As a result, the order of appearance was always being switched around, depending on who showed up when. Sometimes you'd be treated to a nice, long performance from one of the headliners, whereas other times you'd be stuck with an intermission because they couldn't make it on time. In any case, the inside of the theater was filled to the rafters, almost all young factory workers. They whistled, sighed, applauded, and cried their eyes out.

When we came out into the dark street after the show, the young workers disappeared into the market alley, saying they were going to have a few beers and shake their bodies to the earsplitting disco at the music teahouse. Madoros said, "It's the only way they can endure another week of overtime."

The young factory workers were either scattered and lonely individuals or stranded outside of the consumer market without a penny to their names. I reckoned that cultural communication made it possible for individual laborers to raise their consciousness and gather together to enact change; political communication could come after. During this period, thoughtful people in the organized religions began proselytizing in industrial areas; in time, night classes were opened for laborers. It was around then that the idea of on-site cultural activism was born.

Foreman Lee, who had introduced me to my job, was in a different workplace and somewhat hard to get hold of; I had the feeling he was keeping me at a distance. Instead, I became friendly with Foreman Hong, who oversaw all three grinding divisions. We bumped into each other a few times during meals and sat together. Normally we would pay for our own lunch in the factory cafeterias, but on overtime days dinner was on the house, including a midnight snack.

"Read any good books lately?" Foreman Hong said out of the blue.

I was perplexed. "Do I look like someone who reads books?"

Hong smiled. "Hey, give me a break here. I'm as tired of living in this world as you are. Even if I am a bit too quirky for the independence movement. But you've been to college, right?"

He asked so bluntly, I had to reply. "I had no money . . . I gave up trying to go back after military service."

"That guy over there says you want to create some kind of social club?" Hong pointed his chopsticks at Madoros. I was glad there were only two of us at the table, but I was still anxious because I didn't know what Hong's intention was. *Ah well, whatever*, I thought, and decided to trust his kind smile. "Let's form a union. How else are we going to make a dignified living?"

He grinned. "You're just going to stir the pot and leave us to deal with all the work?" He stood up with his cafeteria tray. "What are you doing on Sunday? Come join us at the teahouse in the corner of the Guro intersection."

When I went there on Sunday, he was wearing hiking clothes and a backpack instead of his navy jacket with the company logo. He was with two other men in their thirties. As I approached, they all got up, and we moved the party to a pork rib place nearby. I learned over soju that they were foremen from other factories. Theirs was a hiking club, with twenty members, that met every Sunday to climb Mount Gwanak. "If we're in a group like this, higher-ups pay more attention, and our voices count for more," Hong said. "No one needs to break the law, but it's a good way to talk about our companies . . . Who knows? If we include people like you, then you can take the blame for some of the stuff we do. Doesn't that sound good?"

Over the next two months, I went on hikes with Foreman Hong and learned a lot from him. "I've seen many people older than me who've worked in the labor movement all their lives. Change doesn't happen overnight. You have to sacrifice your whole life to it. There are people who have staked their entire families on their company, but when people like you leave here, they just go back to where they were and that's that."

I moved out of Geun-ho's room and became roommates with Madoros, living in a laborer's hive house for about two months before getting a room of my own. I reconnected with Sohn Hak-kyu at this time, a college activist whom I had met earlier through my political writer friends. At the time he was attending Jeil Church, frequented by industrial evangelists and the first generation of cultural activists like Hong Sehwa, Kim Min-ki, and Im Jin-taek, and wanted to work among the people with me.

I asked Geun-ho to find out which factory in the complex had the worst, most problematic working conditions and where the laborers were most concentrated. We researched an electronics factory subcontracting for the Japanese and decided to get jobs there. Sohn Hak-kyu didn't tell me this at first, but he and a few of his college club friends were likewise trying to spread themselves out to infiltrate different workplaces.

Sohn Hak-kyu and I rented a room in the neighborhood across from Guro Market. It was too hard to predict who we might run into in the crowded hive houses and how much attention we might draw. Our new place was further down an alley with a private entrance, an *agungi* burner next to the door, a kitchenette, and some utensils the previous tenant had left behind.

Lodgings secured, we sent our CVs and graduation certifications to the electronics factory during the end-of-the-month hiring period. On interview day, we joined the sea of waiting candidates. We were on the older side, with everyone else, men and women alike, being in their teens or early twenties. Again, my Vietnam experience and night school diploma from an industrial high school made me stand out. The problem was Sohn Hak-kyu's educational background. The world knows him now as being part of the Kyunggi High School Three Musketeers, along with Kim Geun-tae and Cho Young-rae, who protested the ongoing Korea–Japan talks and whom everyone knew to be anti-dictatorship activists. Sohn was also a Seoul National University graduate, which flagged him as a labor activist infiltrator from the start. He later made his credentials even worse by studying at Oxford. To avoid detection, he had no choice but to submit only his Kyunggi Middle School diploma.

The interviewer didn't say anything to me, but when he saw Sohn's CV, he gave him a hard look. "Do you really want to work here? If you went to Kyunggi Middle, then you must have also gone to Kyunggi High, and that means you ended up at Seoul National University, no? What's your real reason for being here?"

Sohn was branded a person of suspicion right then and there, his application rejected. On the way back, my dispirited friend joked, "Those crappy schools I went to can't even get me a job!"

This joke continued to perpetuate itself among our friends and was the basis of Sohn's "Kyunggi Night School" routine, about how all the activists with prestigious educations who were working on-site were dubbed "the night schoolers."

I couldn't face working in that factory on my own, so we decided to look for something else. Park Yoon-bae, who would do anything for a friend, got us fake diplomas from Dogye Middle School near the Dogye Mines. He also strongly advised us to wear tattered work clothes to interviews. The fake diplomas seemed to do the trick, as we were accepted right away and began work in the carpentry team.

At the time, record players and televisions were treated like high-end furniture. The console the record player was housed in received more attention than the machine itself. The material ranged from the best-quality mahogany to plywood, and decorative flourishes, like leaves or stripes, were added. Television boxes were also made of high-quality wood, with doors that closed across the screen. Newbies like us were not put in the decorative carpentry line but in simple and repetitive tasks. I was, once again, an apprentice, as in the last factory. My work involved trimming legs down to the correct lengths or cutting plywood for the backs of the consoles. The foremen responsible for each line called us together before we were sorted.

"Your daily tasks must be completed, even if it means staying late. The slightest deviation in working the material means the entire product must be discarded, and the worker responsible must pay for it. Negligence on the job leads to industrial accidents. You must turn off the machine in between pieces by stepping on the switch. The saws can take out a finger, which is also the responsibility of the worker and not the company, who has already provided safety equipment and training. You have already sealed your contract with your thumbprint, meaning you accept these terms."

To put it another way, industrial accidents were bound to happen, and they were always already our fault. At least our division only had to cut wood and plywood; the factory women's work applying glue to the boards, hammering, or boring holes was extremely monotonous, and their pay was accordingly very low. The part of the company dealing with machine assembly was on the other side of the factory building.

In the mornings, we began work right after the master carpenter retrieved the day's supply of plywood and planks from the materials division, along with the necessary measurements written on a piece of paper.

To create console legs, I cut the wood to size and the master carpenter tapered them. They were then sent to the next division to be smoothed with sandpaper or an electric planer.

The apprentice measures a piece of wood and marks it with a pencil, prepares a sample, and places it above his workstation. At first he's nervous and awkward, turning the saw off for safety after each piece, but later he keeps it spinning. At some point, his mind moves from the monotony of work to thoughts of that girl he met last weekend, the show they saw at Guro Theater, or his little brother's letter from the countryside. He might briefly look up to see the foreman coming or have his thoughts clouded by the memory of another pretty factory girl, which brings his hand too close to the blade. The blood splatters, the pain is like a hammer coming down, and the severed finger wriggles a bit before it stills. They said it was the same for lathe or casting workers. Geun-ho lost three fingers during his apprenticeship.

Pay was calculated once a week, based on your time card. You had to punch in on the machine next to the security guard when you arrived and punch out when you left.

Sohn Hak-kyu worked hard at his assigned station. Although the work itself was tolerable for us, making friends with the other workers and earning their trust to organize them into unions seemed impossible. Sohn and I were in different divisions, meaning that while normally we worked at the same times and cooked dinner and cleaned our room together, sometimes when production deadlines loomed and we had to do overtime, our hours did not coincide. Just like any other people living together, I began seeing the good and the bad in my roommate; one of the bad things was that Sohn was no good at replacing the coal briquettes, so the heat would often go out. I would come back from overtime at 9 p.m. to find our room freezing cold. Opening the *agungi* would reveal the spent briquette, the embers on their last glow. Of course, I was tired enough that I could have just given up at that point and dozed off, but I had to eat something, and since we didn't have portable gas burners back then, even a simple bowl of instant noodles required fire.

In most ordinary neighborhoods, one could ask a neighbor to borrow a spark of fire to start cold briquettes with, but there was no concept of neighbor in that place. Everyone was a vagabond in the same boat. This was probably why a little store nearby would sell lit briquettes at three times the price of unlit briquettes. I remember it being even more expensive in the winter.

I would grumble at Sohn for forgetting and buy a lit briquette to restore the fire. Another problem was that while I was a night owl myself, Sohn was even worse and would read his goddamn books until dawn, even when we had to work early the next day. On Sunday mornings when I was doing the laundry and cleaning up, he'd be lying in bed reading a book. I made endless fun of him for being a hopeless nerd.

We shared a wall with the next-door room, occupied by two women who worked at bars. They would come home even later than we did and blast the radio or have loud shouting matches with their pimps. We'd put up with it for a while before banging on the wall, which quieted them only briefly. They were always fighting about money—how much their cut was, how much they'd taken last time. It had been the same when I lived with Madoros in the hive house: the driver couple next door would argue almost all day about money. If the wife made some spare cash from hand-beading bags for days, the husband would take it from her and spend it on booze.

"Damn them, why don't we just take over a bank and print some money and throw it at them. They never let up!"

At least the weekend meetups with the keener laborers let us feel some hope for the future. However, the prospect of an alliance of trade unions across the entire complex seemed like a distant dream. I now understood why Jeon Tae-il had resorted to using his own body to light the way.

One morning after a night shift, I found Sohn waiting for me instead of leaving for work. He looked anxious. "Something happened to someone I know around here, and we've all decided to retreat. You might get mixed up in it, so you ought to split right now."

"What happened, what did they do?"

"Got caught at a book club session."

I sent him away first and, seeing as we'd already paid rent for that month, decided to simply disappear. The landlord would see for himself eventually that we had left. I packed my things. All the little objects I'd accumulated during my sojourn amounted to two large bags.

~

When I got home again, Hee-yun was about to go out of business and, to make matters worse, her landlord wanted to redecorate and was hassling her to move out. The little courtyard bustled with the cooking and washing of people who owned small shops in the building. I had to make some money somehow, to contribute to expenses, so I pulled out the manuscripts I'd started while hiding in Masan for the Guro Complex incident to blow over. I was even able to get a makeshift writing studio to work in, albeit just a tiny, cramped shelter cobbled together from cinder blocks in the corner of a court-yard normally reserved for food storage. My wife and son lived in a room across from that. Since there was no kitchen, we would cook outdoors in the courtyard under a plastic tarp next to the cement steps. I wrote "The Road to Sampo" there. *Shindonga* had commissioned a manuscript, but I had procras-tinated until the day before the deadline, when the editor finally issued an ultimatum. I got to work at seven that evening. Twelve hours later, as the sun rose, I wrote the final line: "The train raced toward the darkened fields where the snow flew in thick flurries." It felt like I'd written the whole thing in a single breath.

I wrote "A Dream of Good Fortune," based on what I saw in the factories at the Guro Industrial Complex, the next day. Hee-yun had talked the landlord into letting me use a bigger room in another wing. I hung a heavy blanket over the paper-screen door to block the noise of people bustling around outside, but that left the room airless and so hot that I had to strip down to my underwear. My sweat fell on the paper as I worked, but I was too absorbed in the story to care.

Poor Hee-yun didn't have a day's peace, thanks to her struggling-writer husband with his passion for social justice. Ho-jun was affected, too, as Hee-yun had to leave him with a string of babysitters while she worked. One time, he acciden-tally spilled some water; despite no one scolding him, he immediately went and sat with his face to the wall. One of his babysitters must have punished him that way. Hee-yun and I sat for a moment in silence before deciding together that I would return to writing full-time and give up on labor organizing, for the good of our family. We moved back to Ui-dong.

I met the poet Cho Tae-il on the day I published "A strange land" and got my writer's fee. Han Nam-cheol had taken me to a bar on the corner near Gwanghwamun, where the Kyobo Book Centre is now. The late dramaturge Park Young-hee was also there with us.

It was the day opposition candidate Kim Dae-jung had lost the election to Park Chung-hee's military dictatorship. The bars were full of melancholy people. Writers had participated in a national election-observer movement, sending people across the country. Cho Tae-il had just come up from Gwangju. He gulped his *makgeolli* like he might swallow the bowl as well. He got drunk quickly. Normally quiet, he showed himself to be a true poet as his emotions turned violent when he drank. On upswings, he would sing a song: "I'd dearly like to see that face again . . ." His friends would urge him to go on, to sing again "That face again."

Cho Tae-il was once imprisoned, around the end of the dictatorship era. He had been on his way home after a long night's carousing. But for some reason, upon arrival, he stepped up onto a cement platform outside his house and started railing against Park Chung-hee's militant dictatorship. He shouted, "Down with the dictatorship!" over and over, waking his peacefully sleeping neighbors. The neighborhood dogs began to bark, lights turned on one after the other, and people poked their heads out of their houses. His wife, a teacher, begged him to stop as she ushered him down from the platform. He shouted all the way to his bed, whereupon he fell fast asleep. Before his wife left for work the next day, the police paid them a visit. He was arrested for a violation of martial law. He learned later that a busybody local barber had ratted on him.

He had benefited from our normally troublesome literary group. The authorities were already under international scrutiny after locking up our friend Kim Chi-ha for his dissident poetry. During this period, reporters were often thrown in jail for ranting about the same things in a taxi or on the street, and many city dwellers and even country farmers were arrested for the mistake of ranting while drunk. The authorities would have been reluctant to toss the name of another poet into the fray. That was how we met.

And so, just like in *Water Margin* and *The Chronicles of the Eastern Zhou Kingdoms*, people of different talents began gathering in Lee Mun-ku's Cheongjin-dong office, literary types who could not stand their frustration and hunger. Changbi Publishers and Moonji Publishing had already moved into the neighborhood, but Lee Mun-ku's office was the best place for these misfits to gather. The writers would play *baduk*, betting on drinks, and any time one of us got paid, we'd bet that money, too, since it was never enough to cover our bills anyway.

In the fall of 1972, the Yushin Constitution was passed by Park's dictatorship, and every form of expression, not only political but also artistic, was banned—to be replaced by the advent of "youth culture." We had hardly managed to drag ourselves into the modern world, but already the first signs of consumerism were appearing in Seoul's hot spots and around its college campuses.

There were three major symbols of youth culture, as declared by the commercial press: draft beer, acoustic guitars, and blue jeans. Around the late 1960s and early 1970s, American culture remained on the margins, while important changes were occurring in Europe. It was a radical movement, declaring that all thought and material reality within any systemic frame-work, left or right, must change. In America, this attitude was expressed through the peace movement in opposition to the Vietnam War. From the establishment's point of view, all of this—from the hippie subculture to pacifist, counterculture folk songs, to draft-dodging and anti-establishment community activism—was pathetic and destabilizing. And so, the establish-ment's response to the restless stirrings of disenchanted young people was to slap it all with the label of "youth culture."

Around the same time, the "military look" came into vogue, featuring clothes that looked like uniforms, complete with rank insignias, when Vietnam vets went to college with their army jackets thrown over their shoulders. The fad soon crossed the Pacific, but it ditched any ideological implications halfway across the ocean and haunted Korea as an empty shell of its former political self. What did youth culture even mean, when criticism of the Yushin Constitution could land a young person in jail?

1972, in a Cheongjin-dong pork rib joint. Kim Jun-tae was back from Vietnam and writing poetry, and Cho Tae-il, who had bought him drinks and was also a regular at that place, was shouting at him as they ate. Han Nam-cheol, Yeom Mu-ung, and I were having a drink when Han said, "Hwang, my friend, I met this historian guy and he said something pretty interesting. You know how Hong Gil-dong and Im Kkeokjeong are about the only bandits we know from the Joseon Dynasty? Well, apparently, there was another bandit that could've had both their asses on a plate for dinner."

I didn't think anything of it at first. This historian, according to Yeom, was a junior scholar named Jeong Seokjong. His essay on the Hong Gyeong-nae rebellion that was to appear in *Quarterly Changbi* was supposed to be quite interesting, but I hadn't paid much attention to it.

"But you know, the really interesting thing about that bandit is, he used to be a jester or something."

I woke at dawn one morning in the Ui-dong house, my mind suddenly filled with a spine-chilling tale I'd heard once from Paek Ki-wan. It had to do with the Hwanghae Province folktale about the Jangsan Cape hawk. I gulped some water I'd placed near my pillow the night before, shook off my hangover, got up, and lit a cigarette.

I once held a training session for on-site activists at a Christian association in Busan. Paek Ki-wan, me, and Chae Hee-wan, who practiced *talchum* dance in college, set out as instructors. After the session, we were on our way back on the Gyeongbu Line train when Paek Ki-wan, excited about something, delivered a long inspirational speech. Chae Hee-wan and I listened open-mouthed to his Hwanghae Province–inflected thoughts.

"Culture, you know, it's all connected. It's all bundled up with the life that we live. The *jing* that you play, that's not a *jing*. What's the difference between that and the noise of hitting a can? *Jang, jang, jang*, it's the same. There are good villages down below Guwol Mountain in Hwanghae, they have landowners who have so much land. There are wells and a fence around it. Inside one well is a large chamber pot, hidden deep inside. The landowner's wife's ass is as large as a rice sack. She lifts one cheek and thunders out a fart, and one piss is like a squall in June. Every morning, a maid has to collect that chamber pot, rinse it out, polish it until it shines, fill it with water, and hide it behind the fence. The male servants are always looking for it. They want to put a rope through it and use it as a *jing*, because one hit with it makes a nice *jiiiing* sound. You're not supposed to just hit the thing. You have to hit it with the hundreds of years of sorrow of the lower caste, hit it like you would the face of that landowner bitch. *Jing, jing, jing*, that's the deep sound of the *jing*. They're harvesting early barley and beating it, and the muscly servant takes his top off and strikes at the barley, he automatically begins to sing, *ong-heya, ong-heya, ong-heya*. That's not just a man hitting something but the servant hitting the landowner's head over and over again. He's sweating like he's in the rain and the barley hulls stick to his skin.

"They wash themselves in the stream and have a bowl of cold *makgeolli*. They catch a dog and cook it over a fire. They decide who gets to eat it with a show of strength. Here we go, a wrestling match. The others hit the *pungmul* drums and kick up a storm. *Jenga-jenga-jeng*, now *this* is culture, OK? Damn, I'm thirsty, here comes the drinks cart."

I remember that Chae Hee-wan and I hastened to buy five bottles of beer and a dried squid so Paek Ki-wan wouldn't stop talking. And that's how he came to tell me about the Jangsan Cape hawk.

I thought I could put together a tale from the mood and tone of the story, and decided I'd go out to see Jeong Seokjong as soon as it was day. An adjunct college instructor who hadn't found a home yet, his rented room was as shabby as mine. He was short and looked younger than his age, but his eyes lit up whenever he talked about "the bad guys."

Social change in the late Joseon Dynasty was his area of interest. Around this time, his historian cohorts were striving to expand the academic reach of Korean social history in order to overcome the mainstream colonialist thinking entrenched in schools. Older historians, like Kim Yong-seob or Kang Man-gil, were examining transitions in social status by combing caste records and family registers, concentrating on economic changes in rural localities. At that time, Jeong Seokjong was digging through the mountainous records of the Goryeo-Joseon dynasties' Uigeumbu judiciary in the Kyujanggak royal library.

The Uigeumbu records were untrodden, virgin territory. He suggested I go through them on my own first, but embarking on my research I figured out a more cunning method. I paid a few graduate students to look through the material until they found something I might use. In any case, he'd given me hundreds of pages on Jang Gil-san alone—from both *The Annals of the Joseon Dynasty* and the Uigeumbu records. I had no idea where to start.

I began my research and visited Jeong once a month to discuss it with him. My rapid assimilation of the material seemed to surprise him. The younger researchers specializing in history seem surprised to this day by my imaginative powers: many times they thought I was being absurd, only to discover for themselves that my conjectures were right.

I used any spare time on research trips for short journalism articles to hunt for material for this book project in the antiquarian book markets of Insa-dong and Cheonggyecheon. I had no money to buy expensive rare editions, so I would simply read the book while standing in the shop.

~

Kim Chi-ha disappeared after we sixty-one writers participating in the anti-Yushin petition were arrested and eventually released. The authorities were looking for him, and we were trying to get word to him to flee. Many others in our barely-months-old planning committee for a cultural activist organization were arrested, and still more went into hiding.

Seoul National University Student Association representatives and drama club students came to see me. The first to do so was the actor Kim Seok-man, followed by the dancer Lee Ae-ju, *sori* musician Im Jin-taek, singer Kim Min-ki, *talchum* dancer Chae Hee-wan, traditional musician Kim Young-dong, and later the future movie director Jang Sun-woo. They had been told that if the "Bandit" disappeared, they were to work with me. The "Bandit" was a nickname for Kim Chi-ha. These artists were later referred to as the first generation of the cultural activism movement, and they would eventually give me a nickname, Gura Hyeongnim, which I guess you might translate as Bullshit Brother. I probably earned that moniker for the stories and gags I'd learned from watching snake-oil salesmen spin their yarns in the marketplaces.

Looking back, Park Chung-hee's Yushin era brought about the nationwide spread of a mainstream nationalist student movement and the organization of intellectuals, of a kind that had disappeared after the Japanese occupation and throughout the wars. It also incited solidarity movements between laborers and farmers to converge across the nation. During that single year of 1974, national student heroes were made; the literary group we had been preparing was launched as the Council of Writers for Freedom and Practice; and this news was spread along with free press declarations of reporters from the *Dong-a Ilbo* and other papers, including the *Chosun Ilbo*, which is now a conservative paper. I spent those fraught years during the 1970s and 1980s with most of these fellow activists in joy and happiness.

~

It was around this time that my first short story collection, "A strange land," was published by Changbi. It was, I should say, the spark that ignited the age of volume-publishing. Mineumsa and Moonji followed suit with collections of Korean contemporary short fiction of their own, although none of us had any confidence yet that readers would actually purchase these books. Thanks to word of mouth among students, my collection circulated rapidly.

Hee-yun was pregnant with our second child, but our financial situation was still dire, and we were always out of cash. The baby was nearly due by the time my story collection came out. When my literary friends found out I'd received an advance, they clamored for me to buy them drinks. A national curfew was still in place, which meant we were always pressed for drinking time between dusk and midnight. We had to drink quickly. After midnight, many of us gave up on going home. A few whose families were already angry at them for staying away too many nights would call up reporters they knew who were on night shift to accompany them home, or bribe a garbage truck to swing by their houses, pinching their noses the whole way, or even beg a ride in a police car. Some who couldn't be bothered would simply walk into a police station on their own and spend the night in lockup.

Had I pocketed my advance and gone home right away, I would have proved a decent family man. But my friends had shaken me down, going from this tavern to that, and when I finally showed up at the Changbi office after a bowl of hangover stew, looking pathetic, Paik Nak-chung sat me down for a scolding. "I moved heaven and earth to get you that advance so you could use it for your wife's impending hospital bills, but you never even went home! Don't you know what's happened? Your wife just had the baby. She's in the hospital. Go see her." He gave me another advance on my royalties. Still perturbed by my sorry state, he sent me on my way with a final warning. "Don't do anything stupid on your way home!"

Hee-yun had given birth to a daughter, Yeo-jeong. Even now, whenever my eldest son brings up that day, all I can do is shut up and listen. Ho-jun was only three at the time. Daddy was out and Mommy was going into labor. Hee-yun had no choice but to leave him crying in the courtyard and take a taxi with the landlady to a hospital in Suyuri. We barely had enough for the rent at the time, let alone for hospital fees. She called my eldest sister, who immediately came running with her husband.

Ho-jun still remembers everything that happened that day. After his mother suddenly disappeared in a car, he went down to the bridge over the stream and cried until nightfall. The landlady came back from the hospital, found him, and took him to see his mother. She had already given birth. The poor boy had to spend the next few days in the hospital room beside his mother and new little sister.

During my time in a dark prison cell, I would abruptly remember certain buried memories, things I could never take back, and it's this incident, and the fact that I could not be by my mother's side when she passed, that break my heart the most. I went about the entire country as if possessed, not even properly supporting my wife and children, and in the end left them nothing but hurt.

One spring, I published a few short stories in Lee O-young's magazine, *Munhak sasang* (Literature and Thought), which had launched a couple of years before. Lee was fond of sitting visitors down and lecturing them. He would mock my realist tendencies in a roundabout way but, according to others, had always recognized my talents. Something about having no manners but being a good writer. True, I wasn't the obsequious type, but that didn't mean I was completely without respect.

I visited him because he was talking about serializing a full-length novel in the magazine. I happened to be gathering information on Jang Gil-san at the time. He listened to me hold forth for a while and then said, "That doesn't sound like it can be contained in a novella or a novel." But he must have told the *Korea Times* about the project without letting me know, because I was soon contacted by Chang Ki-young, the paper's owner.

Chang was shouting on the phone when I was led into his office along with one of the department heads. I stood awkwardly as my escort bowed without a word, and Chang gestured for us to sit down on the sofas.

Chang Ki-young, having reputedly built up the *Korea Times* from nothing, was said to have a military-issue cot on the floor above the editors and to share night shifts with the reporters. There were enthusiastic slogans hung up in the stairwells, like "Think while you run." The *Korea Times* kept calling itself "a young, new newspaper" in those days.

He sat down and read the synopsis of *Jang Gil-san* that I had written for him. "A good bandit has to make us feel better in these harsh times. He's got to punish this bastard and that one, he's got to use his power the way he wants to."

I asked him, as a kind of test, "There's been a lot of censorship lately. Can you guarantee it won't happen to my story?"

"Why? Are you going to get all anti-government?"

"The bandit shackles the rich and rebels against the king."

"That's fine, that's fine. Just don't go overboard. If you do get caught, I'll beg them to release you. You know, when Hong Myong-hui was serializing *Im Kkeokjeong* for the *Chosun Ilbo* during the Japanese occupation, he missed his deadline so many times that on days when we had nothing to run, we'd tear up the newspaper in the bathroom and curse out the Japanese governor general. Historical fiction needs to be simple and savory, you know? That way everyone will enjoy it." He then added something he would come to regret: "The important thing about a writer is that he has to do as much research as possible."

I blurted out, "Then give me as much money as possible to spend on research." My escort, the department head, tapped my knee, but I ignored him. "If the readers don't like what I write a year from now, I'll give it all back to you."

Chang laughed until his face turned red. "Research money! I didn't think of that . . . How much?"

"I'm just a young, penniless writer, so getting one of those low-income, publicly funded houses shouldn't be too hard. I'll need a room full of books, after all, if I'm going to come up with a good story."

Chang started chortling again. "Fine, fine. The house is on you—use the money you make from writing—but a library's worth of books, I can give you that."

He cut me a check then and there, and there was actually an extra zero at the end of it. Without exaggeration, it was enough to buy half a house. He wanted to see some pages immediately, but I pushed for six months from then, and we settled on three.

Rumors that I'd received a large sum of money spread throughout Cheongjin-dong. To be honest, I was the one who couldn't contain himself and blabbed about it at Lee Mun-ku's office as if I'd just won big by gambling. For a week after, I had a new set of drinking buddies every day as we drank like fish. Choi Min drank so much for such a tiny man that he would stay to the end of the night. Later, I stayed out so late that a couple of my drinking friends would go to the market and buy us all fresh socks and underwear that we'd change into, roaring with laughter. There were late brunches of hangover stew, after which we'd go to an inn to sleep it off and wake up when the sun began to set, our eyes shining and our feet pointed toward another tavern to do it all over again. At the end of this bender, the research money was nearly all gone, but I gave what little was left to my wife out of what I laughingly would call my pride as the breadwinner. Then my anxiety over actually acquiring the research material came down on me like a mountain.

"Oh well. What can I do? I'll just have to buy those expensive editions somehow."

I dragged myself back to Chang Ki-young. It would take ages to go through the editor who was managing me, so I simply walked up to his office and asked his assistant to tell him I was there. He must have had some free time because he let me in. He asked how the writing was going, and I said I had spent the money on drink because my writer friends and I were so poor.

"You mean you drank all that money?" Chang Ki-young sighed. He wrote me another check and scribbled something on the back of a business card. "This time, buy the materials you need. Here's my card. I wrote the address of a bar on the back. I'm a regular there. Don't go drinking anywhere else. And put it on my tab."

The department head who had introduced me to him flew into a rage when he found out what I'd done. The staff would talk about it for years over drinks. I bought all the rare books I needed for the project; there were so many books in our cramped little house that we barely had room left to sleep. The reporters told me later that Chang Ki-young had ordered them to get me whatever I needed to get the job done.

When I went an entire week over deadline—the first such incident in the history of newspaper serialization—then-newbie reporter Kim Hoon was sent all around town to find me. Such were the days of that eventful project. But Chang Ki-young always told people to let Hwang do whatever he wanted, and that it was excusable for a writer to miss deadlines when he had writer's block.

There were no photocopiers back then, so reporters would have to go all the way to Kyujanggak to take black-and-white photos of old books and put them in scrapbooks for me, scrapbooks that followed me wherever I moved in those days. I started *Jang Gil-san* when I was thirty-one (1974) and finished when I was forty-two (1984). Ten years! I had no idea it would take that long when I began. My friends opine that but for the *Korea Times* and Chang Ki-young, there would be no *Jang Gil-san* today. Chang Ki-young died before the serialization was complete, and it had to be paused several times, but his spirit seemed to continue supporting the work after his death. There were many days when the next installment would be replaced with this message: "Serialization has paused due to unforeseen circumstances." And during the 1970s and 1980s, when I was running all over the country engaged in political activism, I'd often find myself writing the next installment on the spot and sending it off with strangers who had come looking for me on behalf of the paper.

In 1975, the Park Chung-hee administration administered a yea-or-nay vote on the new constitution while releasing violators of martial law from prison. Kim Chi-ha, as soon as he was released, published "Penance, 1974" in the *Dong-a Ilbo*, who had recently made a strong declaration for freedom of the press. His new work described how he went into hiding, his arrest, and the fabrications surrounding that arrest on false charges. After the firing of the *Dong-a Ilbo* reporters, Kim Chi-ha was arrested again.

Students began protesting again in April, emergency rule was reinstated, and the eight people imprisoned over the second People's Revolutionary Party incident—when the Korean CIA created a fake seditious organization in order to falsely accuse and imprison prominent democracy activists—were executed. What I still see in my mind's eye, as those framed, blameless people were put to death, was how yellow dust tinged the sky over Seoul. The blue above turned yellow, like during a monsoon or sunset, and the sunlight was blotted out by the descending cloud.

A few days later, Seoul National University College of Agriculture student Kim Sang-jin read out a declaration of conscience and committed suicide by disembowelment. Kim Chi-ha's declaration of conscience was smuggled out of prison, and law graduate Cho Young-rae and cultural organization worker Shin Dong-su added to it before disseminating it in the colleges. The art critic Kim Yoon-su, involved in this operation, would be arrested for it along with some other students and the future founder of Physicians for Humanitarian Action, Yang Gil-seung.

I was living in an old-fashioned *hanok* house near the Ui-dong bus station at the end of the line, not far from the plot of land that would become Duksung Women's University. The house had a shed and an outhouse either side of the main gate, with the kitchen and main rooms arranged around a courtyard, much like the *hanok* of the middle classes in the olden days.

One night around nine, I heard someone pounding on the gate. I put on my shoes and went up to it, asking who it was. "My friend, it's me." Shin Dong-su was standing outside, with another person carrying a large bundle. I brought them into the house and was introduced to Shin's acquaintance. This was Kim Geun-tae, his face as white as a sheet. He'd been on the run after Yushin was declared and had kept in contact with Shin, an old friend from high school. He had been working in the factories and organizing workers in the Incheon industrial zone. They were preparing a memorial protest for Kim Sang-jin, the student who had disemboweled himself and become another icon of the labor movement, like Jeon Tae-il.

A month earlier, the US had given up on Vietnam and retreated, and the South Vietnamese government had imploded as Saigon was overrun. The Vietnam War was over, but soon we were hit with the "state of Vietnamese defeat" in Korea. The Yushin administration set up pep rallies and displays of our defense across the country, and passed security laws, civil defense codes, military spending statutes, and other legislation. They also declared Emergency Measure No. 9, outlawing any kind of dissent against the Yushin Constitution. Yet the students began protesting a mere ten days afterward. The literary and drama activist groups were preparing their own protest. That day, Shin Dong-su and Kim Geun-tae asked me to write a declaration for the protest, an elegy for Kim Sang-jin that would move the hearts of the people. They asked me to write it in one night, make copies, and pass them out on the scene.

I worked on it while they slowly sipped their soju. I had composed countless such declarations throughout the 1970s and 1980s, words that didn't pay a cent, words that could easily have sent me to prison for years. Later collections of activist martyrs' writings and their bibliographies would include texts that had, in fact, been authored by me.

They took the declaration I spent all night writing and disappeared at dawn. Kim Geun-tae's reserved, calm manner left a lasting impression on me; I would later work alongside him in Seoul during the last days of the Yushin years. The main organizer for the protest was the literary critic Chae Gwang-seok. Working with him were the poet Kim Jeong-hwan and the critic Kim Do-yeon (who died in a car accident when I was in prison). Kim Do-yeon inherited the *Community Culture* newsletter I founded with Kim Jeong-hwan, and also ran a publishing house. When he learned that I had written the declaration he read aloud that night, he jokingly grumbled, "I don't care who wrote it, but it took three and a half years to get through the damn thing. I demand you compensate me for that lost time." After I was moved to the prison in Gongju, the older guards told me that all three had been incarcerated there at one point.

This first protest by cultural activists during the Yushin era was very significant. It was a joint effort by artists from the spheres of literature, dance, and drama. Throughout the 1970s and 1980s they would become more organized, developing true forms of cultural activism. Above all, the seeds sown in Gwangju would soon yield further resistance.

13

Gwangju

1976–85

When I discussed with Hee-yun the prospect of moving south to Jeolla Province, she readily acquiesced, noting that being there would help me concentrate on writing *Jang Gil-san*, rather than staying in Seoul where I was constantly surrounded by friends. We decided I should go down first to find somewhere to live.

My good friend, the painter Yeo Un, had a widowed mother who was the principal at a girls' high school in Haenam, and Yeo Un's good friend Kim Dong-seop was also living there after a stint in Seoul. I went to look at a place they'd both recommended: a stately old house with a well-maintained, 1,000-*pyeong* traditional garden. In the middle of the property was a separate two-room southern-style house, similar to servants' quarters, sitting on 100 *pyeong* of land and surrounded by its own stone wall. It had good natural light, but best of all I liked the sound the wind made rustling the leaves of the great zelkova tree in the yard. The house had sat empty for years. I asked Kim Dong-seop to find someone to fix it up and decided to move in.

A month later, in the fall of 1976, I sent my family ahead on an express bus while I drove the removal truck. Yeo Un, who had done so much to find the Haenam place, accompanied me. There was a highway between Seoul and Gwangju, but the road between Gwangju and Haenam wasn't even paved. The dust rose like clouds and the holes in the road bounced us off our seats every now and then. But the mountains and rivers outside the window were breathtaking, and as we passed Naju, the view of Mount Wolchul dramatically rising up from the middle of the flat fields was a sight to behold. I knew this road had been famous for centuries, known as the "Thousand-*li* Road of the South." When I decided on Haenam as my own place of exile, I was thinking of making this southwestern corner of the country my base for writing and a center of a new *minjung* cultural movement. No one had banished me here, but as my friends joked, I was about to embark on a life of self-imposed exile.

Heading southwest again, Yeo Un and I drove past the lovely mountains, fields, and streams of Okcheon to the Useuljae hill road that led to Haenam. After breathless twists and turns through the mountains, the village of Haenam appeared below. Smoke from cooking fires rose above its roofs in the glow of the sunset as the villagers prepared their evening meals. This warm tableau made us fall silent. Anyone from this village who was returning from a long sojourn away would be in tears at this point of the journey. After moving to Haenam, my heart would fill with impatience to see my family whenever we reached the Useuljae road coming back from a trip to Gwangju or Seoul.

I saw a big propaganda poster on the hill: "Look again to see if your neighbor's visitor is a spy." It seemed to mock us for having been so charmed by the beauty of the sunset a moment ago. Yeo Un and I broke our silence as we collapsed into laughter. Yeo Un jabbed me with his elbow and said, "I think they're talking about you." The truck rattled as it descended into the village.

There were a few reasons I decided to move down to Haenam. First was the fact that, while writing *Jang Gil-san*, I realized how little I knew about country life, having grown up in cities. I couldn't rely solely on other people's material and my imagination. My boyhood had not been spent catching frogs or grasshoppers in a rice paddy or rustling through straw-thatch roofs looking for sparrows' nests. My only rural memories were of visiting friends for a few days. The only reason I could tell a rake from a hoe was because I'd seen pictures of them. I needed to be where there were still traces of traditional life.

My second reason was that there was a big controversy among students and young activists over the question of "the intellectual vanguard vs. the common people." As sociopolitical oppression had worsened in the early 1970s, arguments had arisen between those who believed a small vanguard had to be set up to recover our democracy, even if by illegal means, and those who believed we had to live and organize alongside laborers, farmers, and the urban poor if we wanted the movement to have any meaning. I had realized my mission as a writer only after working at the Guro Industrial Complex, and I believed that any movement had to involve "the people." Kim Chi-ha and I discussed establishing a cultural activist movement within the larger democracy activism scene, one that could incorporate the traditional culture clubs that were already beginning to pop up around the universities.

The cultural movement of the 1970s began with college plays and *talchum* (narrative masked dance) performances, which fused into a form we now know as *madanggeuk*. *Madanggeuk* required a director, actors, a writer for scripts, and artists for painting the backgrounds, creating props, and making the masks. *Madanggeuk* had the added advantage of being able to be performed guerrilla-style in any open space, such as empty lots on campuses, with only the light of a torch. *Madanggeuk* were staged under conditions of censorship and monopolized cultural control to criticize the dictatorship and inspire resistance in students, citizens, workers, and farmers. Cultural education was crucial if the movement was to leave the campus and establish schools in the country, help out during planting season, or align with church groups that aid people in the countryside. Catholic and Protestant organizations were the first to work with cultural activists, enriching their own religious outreach programs directed at farmers and laborers.

Those who participated in the *madanggeuk* process naturally joined in on activist work, and the different cultural
genres combined into one. Support in the countryside swelled
as those who came to the plays or helped on location became
allies of the movement. The thing about book clubs or
consciousness-raising meetings was that they required a lot of
time and people, and the effects were minimal compared to
the risks. One only ended up with small, limited groups. But
the *madanggeuk*'s preparation process itself stood in for organizing and consciousness-raising, in a fast and effective manner.

The cultural activist movement within the larger pro-
democracy sphere was often looked down upon or derided as
"cultural reformism." Cultural activists called themselves
ddanddara—jesters—not to mock themselves but as a badge of
pride. What made the connection between the universities and
the outside world possible was almost entirely the work of the
cultural movement; by the late 1970s, cultural education became
a crucial element in pro-democracy activism.

As we entered the 1980s, the experiences of the cultural activists were enough to endow the larger democracy movement with
confidence. We first created bases for cultural activism in the
towns and then provided support to the cultural activists,
mostly workers and farmers, who spontaneously organized
themselves in factories and farms all over. The people in the
towns were teachers, office workers, religious people, middle-
class married homemakers, doctors, pharmacists, and nurses
who formed urban intellectual book clubs to support night
schools and education programs in the countryside. This
madanggeuk, an art form that seemed amorphous at first
glance, kept producing more and more kinds of collective action.
For example, once a *madanggeuk* produced a singing group,
that group would record an album on cassette tape. The art
groups knew how to mass-print material at short notice and
taught themselves to use an 8 mm film camera to create documentaries. With the development of media technology, the

movement's reach expanded overseas where the same methods were used to multiply ideas and actions.

I chose the remote village of Haenam to live in so I could work on cultural activism in my spare time away from writing *Jang Gil-san*. But once there, I discovered that Haenam was already losing its old rural traditions, due to the destructive effects of the Saemaul "New Village" Movement that was sweeping the country. Far from being revived, villages were emptying out. Today some regard the Saemaul Movement as Park Chung-hee's jewel in the crown, but everything that's light has a dark side. On the ground, the policy seemed deliberately designed to devastate tenant or subsistence farmers, concentrating resources with richer landowners and attempting to increase production and specialization to raise revenue for Korea's agricultural economy. The poorer farmers ended up abandoning the countryside to become factory workers in the city, and their former homes and lands were razed and tilled to make way for mass industrial farming. The poorer farmers became the urban poor, clinging to the outskirts of towns, or low-income, unskilled laborers.

Right behind the house I moved into, the side of the mountain had been cut away. In the house behind ours lived a boy named Il-lang, who became friends with my son. Il-lang's home looked more like a classical tenant farming household. The father had once found occasional work as a carpenter or a plasterer but lately had taken to drink; his wife made money by helping out with farm chores around the village. The eldest son and daughter had long left for the city, and a middle school–age daughter remained, along with six-year-old Il-lang. This daughter, of course, had only graduated elementary school and helped her mother or occasionally babysat for Ho-jun and Yeo-jeong, which was Hee-yun's pretext for giving the family some money every month. Then, one day, the daughter left home, saying she planned to become a hairdresser. Scattered to the winds, the family left Haenam a few years later. I do not know which city slum they disappeared into.

Our house had a little entry path next to the stone wall; there was no front gate. We had a view of the main house, which was large with a traditional tiled roof and looked like the master's quarters to our servants' dwelling. When I greeted the owner, he struck me as the grandchild of a once-great landowner. He was in his late forties or early fifties and, much like others of the landowning class who had fallen into ruin, looked sadder and more tattered with each passing year.

Two weeks after we moved to the gateless house, someone came to visit. The man's face was tan as a farmer's but, incongruously, he wore horn-rimmed glasses. As I came out to the yard, he bowed and said, "My name is Kim Nam-ju."

I was familiar with the poet's name, of course. He had been arrested and imprisoned for political publishing, and debuted as a poet in the *Quarterly Changbi* when he was released. One of his poems memorialized the moment in which an intelligence officer held a gun to his forehead during an interrogation, an incident he related to me again when we met. The hole in the muzzle of the gun had looked so big, he'd felt like a cannonball would burst out of it and shatter his head. His poems were so modern and sharply satiric that it was hard to imagine he was born in a simple farming household. In a later poem he would describe his father as a farmhand on a landowner's estate.

Kim was obsessed with books from a young age, but his father would scold him for wasting the lamp oil. His father used to say that if only one of his sons would become a forestry official and the other a civil clerk, he would have nothing to fear as a farmer. His idea of paradise, in other words, was to chop all the firewood he wanted and not be bothered by the pesky laws and regulations that seemed designed by low-level government officials to thwart the peasantry.

He studied on his own, passed his high school equivalency exams, and was accepted to the English department at Chonnam National University. He'd grown too accustomed to studying by himself to attend classes regularly by then. One time, during a Shakespeare lecture, he suddenly stood up, laughed out loud, and left the class. After he was released from prison, Nam-ju opened a bookstore called "Kafka" so he could write poetry and support young writers. Park Seok-mu had Changbi and other publishers send him stock without Kim paying a deposit, but the bookstore soon closed anyway. It was bound to fail: there were always four or five young people who practically lived on the premises. They would go out drinking late into the night, which meant the bookstore would be closed all the next morning, and what business could thrive like that? Nam-ju was subsequently nicknamed Mulbong by his friends, for his inability to resent anyone or say anything bad about someone else. A *mulbong* is a Haenam-style sweet potato boiled until it's very soft and sweet; the nickname was given to anyone in that region who was especially softhearted and easily pushed around. But the mainstream would dub him "Warrior Poet," for never relenting against the Yushin dictatorship.

I told him of my wish to move to the country and added that the dictatorship would never fall unless we joined forces "with the *minjung*." I cited examples from revolutions in other developing countries. We talked about Mao Zedong in China, Frantz Fanon in Algeria, Ho Chi Minh in Vietnam, and Fidel Castro and Che Guevara in Cuba. I pointed out that half of their time preparing for revolution had been given to teaching and raising the consciousness of their *minjung*, an effort that continued right up to the uprisings. I remember introducing him to *Black Skin, White Masks* by Fanon, Aimé Césaire's poetry collections from Martinique, Lee Yong-ak's poetry collection *Nalgeunjip* (An Old House), and Oh Jang-hwan's hand-copied translations of Sergei Yesenin's poems. Kim Nam-ju could read English, having majored in it, studied Japanese on his own, and eventually learned German so well that he would translate Heinrich Heine's poetry.

Kim Dong-seop brought someone to our home around this time. His name was Jung Gwang-hoon and he was five years older than me, but everyone called him Deacon Jung. He was always dressed in old work clothes and forever seemed to be just waking up, but his eyes had a clever twinkle and his mind was so keen he could understand any book immediately and retain its contents for a long time. After high school, he had been a signalman in the army and an electrician after that. He learned his trade by taking apart and reassembling radios, televisions, and refrigerators on his own, becoming the only working electrician in Haenam. He attended the biggest church in the village, and was so diligent and easy to get along with that he acquired the "general problem-solver" title of Deacon. He had inherited no land or money from his parents, which meant he made his living from skills learned on his own.

As the handyman of the village, Deacon Jung would come running with his only tool, a screwdriver, if anyone called for help with their fuse boxes or sockets or radios. He also worked as an electrician on construction projects. I immediately sensed he was a salt-of-the-earth type. He was a born organizer who did not use the language of intellectuals but could explain the content of books in an accessible manner. He read a truly astonishing number of books and always had one in his hand. I introduced him to Kim Nam-ju.

Later he became chair of the National Federation of Farmers' Associations and threw himself into international solidarity activities, allying with farmer activist groups in other emerging nations. He even flew to Mexico as part of the resistance movement against the WTO's liberalization of grain markets.

Early spring in Haenam made itself known by the warm sunlight that fell on our cold necks and the gentle spring breeze that seemed to wake the barley sprouts. In early March, Park Seok-mu brought Kim Sang-yoon, who had been above him at the National Democratic Youth and Student Alliance, and the novelist Song Gi-sook to see me in Haenam. I took them to a tavern near Daeheung Temple. We had just raised our glasses when a burly, rough-looking man entered the tavern and demanded to know which of us was Hwang Sok-yong. I reluctantly said it was me, and he told me to follow him, without so much as a greeting.

There was a black jeep parked outside. The man said he was an intelligence officer with Haenam Police and that I needed to get in the car, because we were going to the police station for a bit. I was taken to the intelligence division room. I could hear barked commands outside. The officer had just said he'd heard I'd moved here, and wished to take this opportunity to introduce himself, when a man in his fifties, dressed in a sharp suit, entered the office. The policemen of lesser rank all sat up ramrod straight and saluted. He gave me a piercing look and sat down in the section chief's chair.

"I'm the intelligence coordinator for the area. This is Mr. Hwang Sok-yong, correct?" He glanced around the room and everyone answered for me: "Yes, it is." Later I learned that the KCIA had spread their operatives around the country, calling them coordinators. This one was in charge of Jangheung, Gangjin, and Haenam. "I have no time for this," he groused. "I suppose it'll be dawn by the time we're finished?" He took some papers from an envelope as the other detectives left the room. What he said was simple. At Myeong-dong Cathedral, a group of religious persons and independent intellectuals had distributed a petition for the striking down of the Yushin Constitution and the release of those detained for the March 1 pro-democracy declaration. My name was on this petition.

"Everyone involved is being investigated for espionage. Do you want to get arrested yourself?" That was when I realized what had happened. I had moved to the boondocks, but my friends had probably needed a famous name to attach to their petition and so they'd used mine. I told him that while I had no idea how my name had ended up on the petition, I was sympathetic to striking down the Yushin Constitution. Further, Park Chung-hee's elimination of presidential term limits was against the democratic principles of our original constitution.

He went on to question me about every single thing I'd done over the past few years, my reasons for moving to Haenam, my contacts there, and what I planned to write. I stated that because I had so many friends in Seoul who were constantly bugging me to do things with them, I wanted to move somewhere quiet where I could concentrate on writing. He wrote up my statement on what looked like a novella's worth of paper, handed me a single sheet, and instructed me to write down what he said. It was a kind of pledge that I would do no more than write, and not participate in any political activity. "If you were in Seoul right now, you'd be arrested for violation of martial law. That's at least three years in prison. Be thankful I'm not arresting you now."

I assumed he would attach my declaration to my statement and submit it to KCIA headquarters. It was one in the morning when he finished and left for Jangheung. The next morning, Park Seok-mu and Song Gi-sook came to see me, having worried the night away at a nearby inn. We went for some hangover stew and Park Seok-mu joked, "My word, it's hard to even get a drink with Mr. Hwang now."

From then on, the big detective who looked like a wrestler became my handler and visited once a week. Sometimes, it was the calm and fastidious chief of intelligence. They told me to let them know if I ever needed anything while living in Haenam. I was in my thirties at the time and therefore still in the reserve force. The training sessions were far more frequent than in Seoul. I asked them if they really wanted me to attend military reserve training, walking about criticizing the Yushin administration and the president. The chief said, "Of course not!" With that, I was immediately exempted from training. I learned the name of the burly detective from Deacon Jung, who also told me that, despite his intimidating appearance, he was actually rather lazy and not very bright.

Gathering people together was like building a snowman. You start with a small, hard ball of snow and roll it around to make it bigger; then, when it reaches a certain size, you roll it in as wide an area as possible until it takes on the shape of a snowman. I thought the sponsor group and the activist group should be organized separately. If we had about ten each of rural activists and intellectual activists, we would have enough for a good organization. There were little churches dotting the countryside at the time, mostly affiliated with the Presbyterians. Among Protestants, the ones who practiced *minjung* theology—led by graduates of Hanshin University and part of the Presbyterian church—were critical of Korea's development-based dictatorship, and believed that the way back to Jesus's original intentions was to return to the lives of the *minjung*, to live and think with them and assist the less fortunate. The Presbyterians already went into shantytowns or factory zones and were just beginning their evangelism in rural areas. While not all Presbyterian affiliates were as enlightened, the ones who had ventured into the countryside showed at least some sympathy toward the *minjung* movement.

One day, I heard from Jung Gwang-hoon that the Okcheon Church's pastor seemed interested in the movement, which made me cross over Useuljae to pay him a visit. I met him in the living annex of the church. He was very welcoming and invited me to have *ssambap* lettuce wraps with him. I was already good at making friends with new people, and it helped that I was by then a well-known writer. In fact the pastor wasn't thinking too much of activism at that time, concentrating on increasing the number of his congregants.

The church was full of elementary school children listening to a story being told by a volunteer. Because the annex was right next door, I could hear the story as we ate. It was about a small insect who was made fun of by the other insects for being born in a dung pile, but one day it shakes off its chrysalis and shines its bright light in the dark night sky. The story had such a delightful sense of narrative to it that I became curious about the storyteller. His name was Yun Gi-hyun, a subsistence farmer with only an elementary school education, who was supporting his widowed mother. The pastor introduced us, and I asked him where he had heard such a beautiful story. He answered shyly that there were no books at home or anywhere to hear stories, and that he had come up with it as he did his farmwork while thinking about what children would like to hear. He was fond of dreaming up stories as he worked in the fields, combining this strand with that.

"Have you thought of writing fairy tales?" I asked.

He looked confused. "What's a fairy tale?"

I had no idea how to begin, and simply said they were stories for children. "You just have to write down exactly what you told those children just now."

Yun Gi-hyun visited my house on his way to market in town and started to write fairy tales as I'd suggested. I taught him how to use manuscript paper, but Hee-yun more considerately coached him on proper punctuation and spelling. In just a few months, he finished two fairy tales. I introduced him to Lee Oh-deok, a fairy-tale writer and children's educator. Yun Gi-hyun continued to write and submit to magazines, won a literary award, and debuted as a children's author. He avidly borrowed books from me and had such a capacious intellect that his learning seemed almost effortless. The singer and activist Kim Min-ki would be so moved by his first book of children's stories, *Seollu gan heosuabi* (The Scarecrow Who Went to Seoul), that he adapted it into a musical, titled *Sarangui bit* (The Light of Love).

I asked Kim Dong-seop to introduce me to any college graduates he knew around town, and he connected me to various people including school friends and drinking buddies. There were middle and high school teachers, a military clerk, a pharmacist, a veterinarian, the owner of a general store, and even a former fighter back from a life outside his hometown. I met them in twos and threes at first, and when a pocket edition of my book was published, I invited them all to a restaurant to give them personalized copies. A high school teacher who was already in cahoots loudly suggested we might as well set up a *gye* association, a common funds-and-credit-sharing arrangement, which developed into a book club.

On market days, when the farmers came to gather in a local store, they would instead be led to my house; soon about twenty farmers knew about our place and around ten of them would come over directly, every market day.

Kim Nam-ju and I started out by talking about the current sociopolitical situation and its corporate, or *chaebol*-focused, modernization. Then, there would be an open discussion on "Why is life so hard for farmers?" Farmers complained about the things petty bureaucrats had done to them, how landowners would threaten them, how the National Agricultural Cooperative Federation wasn't owned by farmers but by its executives, and how the cooperative decided the price of crops. Farmers' objections to why they had to have an outside authority set the price of their crops, when a street vendor was free to set the price of his junk food, was helpful to us in seeing where we had to start with our activism. We couldn't simply explain books we had read to them; we needed to listen to their stories and learn, visit where they lived and worked, if we wanted to find a way to help.

The Catholics, who had already started to organize farmers in the 1960s, formally established the Catholic Farmers' Movement in 1972, raising their campaigning to the national level. There were several reasons why the *minjung* movement centered on churches during the military dictatorship of the 1970s and 1980s. Firstly, if *minjung* activism in the post-division South was in danger of being persecuted by anti-communist interests, organizing under the umbrella of religion was relatively safe. The second reason was that the Catholic church had a strong hierarchy and international backing that stretched all the way to the Vatican, while the Protestant churches had almost as many followers as the Buddhists and could attract solidarity from overseas as well. Thirdly, we could lean on the churches to raise the funds needed for on-site activism.

We decided to set up a three-day farmers' education meeting and borrowed a prayer center run by a Christian organization in Okcheon. We excerpted or summarized works that we thought farmers should know about for course materials. Lacking access to a printer, we ended up using a mimeograph machine through sponsorship of the YMCA for handouts.

In the midst of all this, I was still sending *Jang Gil-san* installments every day to the *Korea Times* in Seoul. At night, I went to my study in the neighboring house to write, and in the morning, Jung Gwang-hoon would transform into Deacon Jung and take the manuscript to the bus station. He would grab anyone going to Gwangju and ask them to drop off the manuscript at the Gwangju branch of the *Korea Times*. Once dropped off, the manuscript was transmitted by telex to Seoul where an editor on the receiving end would decode the English into Korean letters before setting it into my column space. I was so late on deadlines that, on some days, Hee-yun had to run to the Haenam post office with the manuscript herself, borrow the headpiece from the switchboard operator and dictate the entire manuscript to the Seoul editor on the other end. Telephone sound quality was not great between Seoul and the rest of the country. She had to shout out the scenes from *Jang Gil-san*, a bandit's story rife with curses and other rough language, not to mention sexual allusions.

"Hello? Yes, quotation marks, it's dialogue. Stop right there, you scumbag! If you run, I'll catch you and rip your balls off!"

"*What is he ripping off again?*"

"His balls, his balls!"

The switchboard ladies would collapse into giggles, my wife would blush scarlet, and the female reporter on the other end would be too mortified to ask anything more. I was told the reporter had been teased so much by the male editors while loudly reciting these embarrassing lines that she burst into tears more than once. It was always some newbie reporter on the cultural beat who was saddled with this task, making me a sworn enemy of the cultural section, from the chief all the way down to the newest recruit.

The ten years it took to finish *Jang Gil-san* and all the episodes and difficulties during that time are too much to detail here. I had to run around going to protests and declarations during the serialization, often carrying my research notes and manuscript paper into inns. But I don't think my activism harmed my novel. I tried hard to reflect the highs and lows of contemporary society in the novel itself, striving to recreate the conditions and challenges of today's *minjung* in the lives of our ancestors from long ago.

We began our first organized consciousness-raising at the prayer retreat in Okcheon, with fifty farmers. We gathered a bit of money, and the rest was paid by Kim Dong-seop and the book club in town. A few felt the endeavor was too risky and begged off in the middle, but the ones who remained continued to sponsor the farmers' school.

We contacted the Christian Academy run by Pastor Kang Won-yong, of Kyungdong Presbyterian Church in Seoul, to send instructors. The ones I remember best are Professor Lee Woo-jae, who specialized in agricultural economics and veterinary science, and Professor Hwang Han-sik, who was an economist. They didn't have tenure at the time but were dedicated to teaching those who most needed it. I was deeply impressed by their ability to strip difficult subjects down to easily digestible chunks for the farmers; their everyday language and gestures helped students understand their own plight.

In the fall of 1977, we created the Haenam Farmers' Association and celebrated by holding a farmers' festival. We didn't hold conferences or lectures or write up some manifesto and distribute roles like we would have done before, but instead held a fun event for the farmers, having already decided what our organization looked like. This became the basis for the later South Jeolla Province Christian Farmers' Association and would ultimately evolve into the Korean Christian Farmers' Association Alliance, founded in 1982.

Thus, I had established a base of operations for my fieldwork in Haenam and planned a center of cultural activism for the entire region, including Gwangju. I discussed it with other cultural activists in Seoul beforehand. For the festival, instead of asking professional musicians to provide a visiting show, we wanted events the farmers could easily participate in and be the center of. The professional artists, in other words, would only consult, and the performers on-site would be the farmers.

We decided to hold the festival in the wide lot in front of the YMCA, across from Haenam's administrative office. The YMCA building, converted from a Shinto shrine dating to the Japanese colonial era, was surrounded by large zelkova and cherry trees—perfect to hold a *madangpan* festival. The farmers gathered days in advance to prepare. The traditional music bands had all been dissolved by the government's modernizing Saemaul Movement, but the *jing, janggu, kkwaenggwari*, and other instruments had been carefully stored away; it took only a few measures for the rusty farmers to remember the old rhythms.

Someone suggested we reenact a traditional country wedding as a comedy, something everyone had experience of; but another suggested that the tragedy of a country funeral would be better for creating a "dignified joy." This was called *sangye-onori*, in which the funeral procedure and bereavement were turned into spectacle and, when the funeral procession was underway, street performance. The farmers and I sat in a circle and discussed whose funeral it should be. The farmers were all using loans from the National Agricultural Cooperative to pay for pesticide, fertilizer, and roof repairs; as in any rural region, the administrators liked to throw their weight around. It was decided that the cooperative would be the main target of criticism and the subject of the funeral. The farmers recounted what they had experienced at the hands of the cooperative and divided their stories into categories. Each category became a skit. The connecting theme would be how powerless the farmers were in the face of injustice. We needed three teams for the skits and the farmers fought to be the ones to perform. A fat and mischievous-looking farmer got the role of the cooperative; he was undeniably the star of the show. With the aid of balloons, he would grow fatter and fatter throughout the skits as he exploited the other farmers, and his stomach would "pop" at the end. He was teased for his role throughout the production and given the nickname Fatty. Decades later, when I asked Yun Gi-hyun about him, I learned that this nickname had followed him for the rest of his life. "Oh, Mr. Fatty? He's doing very well. He owns a restaurant now and has a new grandson."

The bier was borrowed from a neighboring village, wrapped in five-colored cloth and decorated with paper flowers and the satiric slogans of the wishes of the farmers. The coffin-bearers were the farmers and performers from Seoul. Lee Kang and Kim Sang-yoon brought students from Chonnam National University and Chosun University to Haenam. There were many attendees from both town and country who, having expected an ordinary festival, seemed overwhelmed by the spectacle. Who knows who invited them, but the wife of Haenam's mayor also came, as did the wife of the pastor of Haenam Church, seemingly perplexed that there were no separate seats reserved for them. All we did was give everyone a mat to place on the ground as we sat in a circle.

It was only when the street performers loudly beat their drums as they marched through the main street and the curse-filled and occasionally racy skits started that the community leaders and their wives slunk off the scene, allowing the real festivities to get underway.

The fat "cooperative" character expired, and the funeral procession began. The singer in the front called to the pallbearers in back, who responded in unison, the sound sweeping through downtown to every corner of the market and residential areas as the procession progressed. It was actually a farmers' protest. But no one could rightly object to it, as it preserved the form of a farmers' festival and performance.

At around the same time, it came to light that the rice mill and the local administrators of Haenam had conspired in the process of buying grain, and the farmers organized to boycott the buyer and demand their grain back. The mayoral office, afraid the situation would escalate, forced the factory to make the necessary repayments. The farmers saw with their own eyes how each of them received exactly what they were due, right down to the last kilo. This did wonders for morale. Since this happened right after the farmers' festival, the number of farmers in our group skyrocketed, and similar groups popped up all over the little towns of South Jeolla Province.

~

In 1976, the year I came down to Haenam, the US House Committee on International Relations began an investigation into rumors that the Korean American lobbyist Tongsun Park had engaged in bribery of US legislators under orders from the Park Chung-hee administration. Kim Hyong-uk, the former head of the KCIA living in the US in exile, also denounced Park Chung-hee's corruption. The American press dubbed the incident "Koreagate." All through that year, activists, minority-party legislators, college professors, and students put out endless petitions and statements, held protests, and got arrested. Professors who'd been fired formed an association and published a manifesto for democratic education.

Those arrested for violations of martial law decided to protest on March 1, 1978. Kim Dae-jung was being held on sedition charges at Seoul National University Hospital. In June, students from Seoul National University and Korea University held a surprise demonstration demanding the end of the Yushin administration and, for the first time since the dictatorship was installed, managed to make it all the way to Gwanghwamun in central Seoul, close to the presidential Blue House. Park Chung-hee was once more "elected" as president, following a superdelegate vote of the National Conference for Unification, held in a gymnasium. He was probably intent on keeping himself in power in this fashion until he died.

At the end of June, the novelist Song Gi-sook called me and asked if I had any plans to come to Gwangju. When I took the hint and went there, Song said he had just been to Seoul to meet with dismissed professors, including Paik Nak-chung, editor of the *Quarterly Changbi*, and Sung Nae-woon. They feared that the number of expelled and arrested students would rise again with the new semester, in which case the professors promised to immediately join together to issue a statement of condemnation. At Chonnam National University, professors were held accountable for any protests in the school and expected to keep an eye on students at every gathering on campus. In other words, staff were tasked with becoming informants and policing students. What's more, the authorities made professors pair up with detectives to prevent students from attending events in the city. Song Gi-sook said the academics, unable to bear the humiliation and political pressure, had decided to join the student movement to bring down the Yushin government.

During the Yushin era, a National Education Charter modeled after the Education Decree of the Japanese colonial era, was proclaimed. Every student from elementary school to college, not to mention soldiers and civil servants, had to be able to recite it at the drop of a hat. Soldiers were punished if they couldn't; office workers had to stay at work until they finished memorizing it; and students' grades were docked if they failed to perform it perfectly. Song Gi-sook was planning to make a statement against the charter. Professor Sung Nae-woon came to Gwangju with the declaration Paik Nak-chung had written. He was determined not to let the semester pass without taking action. About fifty people had signed it in Seoul, but there was no consensus yet, which made them decide that eleven professors from Chonnam National University would sign first, and the petition taken up nationwide once something came of it. Kim Nam-ju and I were not indifferent to the affairs of the Council of Writers for Freedom and Practice. As a founding member, I contacted Park Taesun, Lee Mun-ku, or Lee Si-young whenever something happened in Seoul. Kim Nam-ju was in Gwangju to manage the Minjung Cultural Research Center. I spent a few days a week in Gwangju with him and traveled around other regions like Daegu, Busan, Masan, and Jinju in the name of solidarity. We drew quite a crowd at my lectures and Kim Nam-ju's poetry recitals. Nam-ju would recite a few of his poems and several translations of Neruda and Heine.

As Kim Nam-ju ran the Minjung Cultural Research Center with Kim Sang-yoon's help and the Nokdu Bookstore as its base, he put together a seminar and rendered into Korean the Japanese translation of a book on the Paris Commune. One day, a student lost his bag; the police somehow got their hands on it and found some fliers and the Japanese copy inside. They caught the owner and brought him in for questioning. When they learned that Kim Nam-ju had taught him, Nam-ju fled to Mokpo.

In any case, the Chonnam National University professors were ready to be arrested as soon as the students set out on their protests. Since this was the first major demonstration since the April Revolution and was expected to bring instant solidarity between activists and students, most organizers were raring to go. Naturally, the main organizers were the recently launched cultural activist clubs of Chonnam National University and Chosun University.

As soon as the Chonnam National University professors made their declaration and were arrested by the KCIA in Gwangju, I went to Song Gi-sook's house with Yoon Han Bong. Song's wife was a demure woman of few words, who seemed unfazed by her husband's latest exploit. Yoon Han Bong went to the city accompanied by pastors, lawyers, feminist activists, and Christian activists in Gwangju, and I used Song's phone to notify Seoul of our developments and to ask them to gather in Gwangju. For two days, Paik Nak-chung, Park Taesun, and Paek Ki-wan from Seoul met with various people in Gwangju, figuring out what our next move should be. We were confident these movements would pressure the authorities, and torture seemed unlikely now that the foreign press was catching wind of what was going on.

A meeting was held at a YMCA downtown. My wife handed me the phone on the afternoon our petition for the professors' release went public. It was Song Gi-sook. "They said they'd let me go once the investigation was over. I think you can stop agitating." However, he was arrested for violating martial law, sentenced to four years, and sent to Cheongju Prison. The other professors like Sung Nae-woon who participated in the preliminary meetings were also arrested and sacked. Student protesters took to the streets to demand the reinstatement of their professors, walking down Geumnamro Street, but the organizers of the protest fled. A few of them were taken in by cultural activists in Seoul.

Ten days later I had returned to my house in Haenam when I received a surprise visit from Kim Nam-ju and Choi Kwon-heng. The patient and considerate Choi Kwon-heng, along with Lee Hae-chan, was part of the younger generation involved in the National Democratic Youth and Student Alliance, and also a scholar of French literature. He was blood brothers with Kim Nam-ju and Park Hyoung-seon from the early days, and the three were very close. Choi Kwon-heng and Lee Hae-chan ran a nonfiction publishing house called Hanmadang in Seoul. The three of us were drinking soju when Kim Nam-ju suddenly said, "I can't stand it anymore. This Yushin dictatorship will not fall if we pussyfoot around like this! It would be better if we did nothing at all. I want a real fight." I asked him what he meant by that and he said, "Let's put out an underground newspaper."

"The three of us?" I said. "Don't we need an organization?" Kim Nam-ju said we could make the newspaper first and the organization would form later. I said that we had just started a mainstream movement and needed to wait a little longer—it would take time for the effects to spread into the general populace. "Look at how the Haenam Farmers' Association became the South Jeolla Farmers' Association." But Kim Nam-ju said that as soon as he got his fee for the translation he was working on, he would go to Seoul.

The next day, as we parted, he gave Hee-yun something wrapped in a handkerchief as a present. It was a copy of Che Guevara's farewell letter to Fidel Castro as he left Cuba.

> All sorts of thoughts are entering my head now: meeting you in María Antonia's house for the first time, you asking me to join your group, the tension we felt when we were preparing for our journey, when we decided who would send word of each other's deaths when the time came, when all that potential suddenly became our reality.

That famous letter. On another page was a copy of the letter he left for his beloved young daughter, Aleida:

> I write you a letter today though it will be far in the future when you read this. But please remember that I have never forgotten you for a single moment . . . Remember the endless struggle before us. When you're grown up, you will join the struggle. Prepare, always, to become a revolutionary person when you grow up . . . Mother's kisses will fill the time that we cannot see each other.

Kim Nam-ju must have given me Che's letters to show he was decided on moving to Seoul. In the meantime, he was going to avoid the police by hiding out in Mokpo, where he translated Frantz Fanon's *The Wretched of the Earth*. He finished his manuscript soon after and moved to Seoul.

My eldest sister in Seoul informed me that Mother was on her way to Haenam. I had decided she should come live with us. My wife and I had been discussing whether to buy a house or rent a bigger one. Mother arrived in Haenam with very few belongings. I cleaned up the spare room for her, reproaching myself for having neglected her for so long. A few days later, the Haenam police intelligence officer asked to meet me. He wanted to know if I was aware that my house was in the plans for a new urban renewal project. It wasn't supposed to happen for a few more years, but there would be a road going through the house and I would lose out if I didn't sell the place now. I smiled and said, "Are you telling me to leave Haenam?" His eyes grew wide as he waved his hands and protested, "No, no, not at all, I'm just trying to do you a favor here. A citizen of this nation has the right to live anywhere he chooses . . ."

I went on needling him. "The thing is, my mother has come to live with me, so I'm looking to buy a bigger house anyway. Someplace downtown? I love it here so much that I think I might settle down."

The officer caved. "Oh, Mr. Hwang, please don't pull my leg. My phone is practically on fire because of people calling about you! It's killing me! My superiors have it in for you. They're trying to get you to leave Jeolla Province."

I joked again, "Well, if you can get someone to sell my house, I can offer you a cut of the price."

"There's no need, I'll take care of it immediately."

I wanted to ask him if it was even true, what he'd said about the new road, but thought better of it.

Yoon Han Bong called saying he'd found a good house in Gwangju, and, just like before, I sent my mother and family ahead on the bus while I loaded up a truck with our things and crossed over Useuljae.

~

Yoon Han Bong and I decided to open our office in Gwangju. We renamed it the Modern Cultural Research Center, so as to not raise government alarm with the word *minjung*. Fundraising was to be done on a rolling basis, but no one was going to give money to the pro-democracy movement just like that. You could be prosecuted for aiding and abetting criminals. Many people had been imprisoned already for helping activists and students go underground.

I came back to Seoul and talked with my trusted friend Yeo Un again. He knew everyone who was anyone—writers, reporters, and businesspeople. He first suggested selling some work by painters that he knew, but then he had a better idea. Making and selling celadon vases decorated with paintings and handwriting of famous painters and artists was sure to raise a lot of money. We made them and displayed them at the YMCA in Gwangju; fundraising ended only days after. The buyers had an inkling as to what the money was for, but no one was bothered about it.

Yoon Han Bong got us space in the building next to the Nokdu Bookstore. Our purpose was to coordinate the different religious groups and activists. Various groups were created around this time among youth and cultural activists, volunteer teachers, and wives of political prisoners. Regional activism in Gwangju grew steadily up to 1978, and many of the groups had overlapping memberships, with almost every volunteer giving their time and effort to two or three organizations. We all knew or knew of each other, just like villagers living in the same village.

I was working as part of the Gwangju branch of Council of Writers for Freedom and Practice; they would contact me whenever there was a need for solidarity or petitions. The list of arrested figures was long: Kim Chi-ha, Moon Ik-hwan, the poet Yang Sung-woo, Song Gi-sook, and the critic Lee Young-hee were all in prison, and there were many protests demanding their release.

Whenever I went up to Seoul, I'd meet with Kim Nam-ju. We stayed together once in Suyuri, the plan being to obtain some money from my publishers and give him some of it. We'd had lunch and were about to part ways, so it would have been early in the afternoon. I saw a poster for the Daeji Cinema and said, "Look, a double feature. I'll be back by the time you're done watching."

Nam-ju took a look and chuckled. "A melodrama, followed by a kung fu movie? Guess that'll make me a true scholar-soldier."

I bought him a ticket and went downtown. By the time I was done meeting with everyone I had to see, it was late, far past dinnertime. I grabbed a taxi and rushed back to the Daeji, where a voice from a dark corner greeted me: "I thought I was going to starve to death. Let's go." He was sitting on the steps by the ticket office.

My guilt made me irritable. "Why are you sitting out here? If I was late, you should've waited at the motel."

Annoyed himself, he said, "As if I had any idea where that was." He prattled on as he followed me. "How does anyone know where anything is in Seoul?"

"A revolutionary who can't even find his way around Seoul," I teased.

"Eh, who cares if I don't? I'll burn it all down, anyway."

He was in some kind of anti-government organization around this time, doing underground propaganda work. He seemed to have been deeply moved by the leaders of this group, whom he believed to be of such faultless moral standing and selfless dedication that a wretched unknown poet like him was worthless in comparison. It brought him to tears every time he saw a white-haired elder among them running the mimeograph machine by hand as if it were nothing. He whispered, "I'm not always in agreement with their thinking. They're more extreme than we are, but definitely against the dictatorship. I'm scared and shaking all the time. But I also feel alive for the first time."

Each cell moved as a team, one full member and one half member, with the full member leading. They would leave fliers in telephone booths; when it was observed to be safe, they put more fliers in other nearby booths. Sometimes they would leave them on benches in university parks or classrooms. The fliers had simple slogans: "Down with Park Chung-hee" or "End the lifetime dictatorship." The teams would also wear long coats with holes in the pockets from which they'd surreptitiously scatter leaflets while walking around at night. The text of the leaflets varied depending on the situation. When the price of cabbage and turnip spiked during kimchi-making season, the leaflets read, "We can't eat kimchi because of Park Chung-hee," and were dropped all over the markets. They sought to instill into the public mind that the most important thing was for Park Chung-hee to step down. They signed each of their handouts with their name: the South Korean National Liberation Front. Nam-ju urged me to join their "operation" (his military word for it) as well, saying if I showed my allegiance by obeying their rules and commands, I would eventually be given full membership. I had already read many books about revolutionary activism around the world and had a sense of what was going on. I couldn't bring myself to agree with their approach, but I thought there might be situations where I could help them.

In April of 1979, the world was turned upside down. Kim Nam-ju and others broke into the house of the Dong Ah Construction Company CEO, Choi Won-suk, to fund their movement, but were foiled by his guards and assistant. One was arrested at the scene, while the others ran. Kim Nam-ju, already wanted by the police, was suddenly a person of interest, and the heat was being turned up on him.

I was especially anxious around that time. If I hadn't been serializing *Jang Gil-san* and establishing the Modern Cultural Research Center, I would have gone the same route as Nam-ju. Minority party leaders Kim Dae-jung and Kim Young-sam were also stepping into radicalized political struggle, and college students protested in the streets, fearless of arrest or persecution. Intellectuals and religious people were being arrested left and right, and the workers' struggles on the shop floor were getting more brutal by the day.

In August, 877 unionized women at the YH Trading Company began their protest in a lecture hall at a Mapo district administrative building. The police mobilized 2,000 men to break up the protest and forcefully disperse them, killing a worker named Kim Gyeong-suk in the process. Kim was twenty-one, a sewing machine operator and union organizer. The letter she had written to her mother before the event shows us the gravity of the situation:

Dear Mother,

I miss you. YH Trading Company, where I live and work, is a very large corporation. The rich owner has run away to America, and the bosses have abandoned us laborers. They only care about themselves. They are shutting down the factory and have put out redundancy notices. But weak as we are, we have banded together to fight.

There is something I especially need you to remember. It's that the company owner is an evil man who will stop at nothing to get what he wants. Do not believe anything anyone else says in a letter, unless it is from me.

It was revealed that company staff had visited the families of the protesters and told them they were being led astray by communists and were committing a heinous crime against the country. They had also made indirect threats about the family being held liable if their daughters did not desist immediately.

The workers were being pressured by the company, government, police, and secret agents. The ruling party headquarters was so well guarded that activists instead visited the newly appointed head of the opposition party, Kim Young-sam, to plead for the women to be allowed to continue their protest. Kim Young-sam listened for just five minutes and understood immediately, promising: "We will protect and support the female workers." In response, the government arrested the activist leaders and stripped Kim Young-sam of his National Assembly member status. This incident would become the first crack in the wall that would bring down the Yushin government.

Religious leaders went into protest mode, demanding the Act on Special Measures for National Security Integrity be struck down. There was a protest at the Gwangju YMCA as well. I was asked to write up a petition and ended up making the declaration. It was a clear breach of the very act we were trying to strike down, but it was unavoidable. I had just returned from the event when the police arrived and ordered me to stay at home until further notice. I later learned from another writer that, of all the petitions, the one from Gwangju had been the most strident. No wonder I ended up under house arrest.

I was so frustrated that I briefly wondered whether I should take part in an "operation," as Kim Nam-ju had done. I asked to borrow a mimeograph machine from a pastor at a nearby church, saying it was to publish an anthology of young writers. Yun Gi-hyun came up from Haenam just as I had set up the mimeograph machine. I told him what I was really thinking and wrote it up. It was basically a call to fight the Park Chung-hee administration. The two of us printed fliers all night, put them in a closet, and went to sleep. Yoon Han Bong visited us in the morning. He saw our faces and whispered, "I saw Pastor Kang just now. He is very worried about you." When I said nothing, Yoon pressed, "You borrowed a mimeograph machine from him, didn't you? What are you going to do with it?"

I had no choice but to tell him how humiliated and vengeful I'd been feeling lately, and that I'd rather be an honest man in prison than a free traitor. He looked over my fliers and sighed. "Do you think you're the only one who feels this way?" He reminded me that it was always darkest just before the dawn. He waved a ream of leaflets in the air. "This never happened. Let's burn them all."

Our house in Gwangju's Yanglim-dong was two stories high, with a cement staircase and a slab rooftop with a narrow court-yard below. Yun Gi-hyun, who'd been sitting quietly until then, grabbed the leaflets from Yoon's hands and said, "I'll do it." He burned them all in the flower patch, next to a wall draped with grapevines, and buried the ashes in the soil.

The Modern Cultural Research Center was shut down soon after. Plainclothes police were always loitering in town. We also began seeing strange men near the alley leading to our house.

On October 9, the Ministry of Home Affairs announced the arrest of the members of the South Korean National Liberation Front (Namminjeon). The charges were more outlandish than we'd expected. It seems that, in naming the project, the investigators had changed the group's name to "Liberation Line for South Joseon Nationals" and then added the phrase "Preparatory Committee" to the title during subsequent arrests, to make the group seem as seditious and sinister as possible. As the investigators explained the title change to arrestees: "That's what you were going for anyway, right?"

Once the press made their rounds, the entire democracy movement was calling it the "Namminjeon incident." Spurning the accused group's claim to be "a socialist and progressive nationalist group modeled after the National Liberation Front for Southern Vietnam," the authorities dubbed them "North Korean spies trained to instigate riots in the nation."

The head of the Namminjeon was forty-five-year-old Lee Jae-moon. He had been a passionate advocate for independent reunification since the April Revolution and was imprisoned for his participation in the first People's Revolutionary Party incident, in which the KCIA fabricated a fictitious seditious organization and accused socialist and progressive activists of belonging to it.

After the People's Revolutionary Party inmates served their time and were released, they would gather occasionally to talk about the state of the nation. In 1974, during student anti-dictatorship protests, the KCIA fabricated another People's Revolutionary Party incident by claiming the later protesters were trying to revive the organization. The KCIA surprised the world with its bald-faced cruelty, sentencing the accused to death and executing all of them the next day in what is still called an act of "legal murder." Lee Jae-moon, about forty at the time, had managed to flee. His hair had turned completely white. He made a promise to himself. He had only one life to live, and the only dignified choice he could make was to fight on, even if it meant death. Through the wives of his executed comrades, he had gathered the underwear the men had worn in prison to sew together a flag of the Namminjeon.

The prosecution stated: "While it is unrealistic to think that Kim Il-sung had a direct hand in supporting the accused, they are still, clearly, an organization of North Korean operatives." The official written arraignment, however, only says that: "The Namminjeon is not a South Korean revolutionary force under the command of Northern spies but an independent revolutionary group composed of South Koreans; but, had there been any contact with Northern operatives, the Namminjeon would have been a leader in North Korean espionage." In other words, our own authorities admitted that there was no connection with North Korea. They were, however, highly motivated to show that the Namminjeon was intent on overthrowing the military dictatorship and establishing a socialist system.

On October 16, about 5,000 students from Pusan National University marched, demanding the end of the Yushin government.

Students from the local universities as well as citizens smashed police stations and other public buildings, leading the government to declare martial law in the city on October 18. Undaunted, the citizens continued their protest into the night. Masan's college students also poured into downtown along with the laborers of the free-export zone, in what was later dubbed the Busan-Masan resistance. The government declared martial law in Masan and Changwon on the 20th as well, and by the 24th, Daegu's students were also protesting in the streets.

A while after the Namminjeon incident, Yoon Han Bong was dragged away and harshly tortured by the police. I began hearing rumors that the Modern Cultural Research Center was being tied to the Namminjeon and that our activist friends were going underground. There were rumors of an even bigger fabricated spy incident on the horizon. Lee Kang and other farmer activists were thrown in jail for being on the Namminjeon list. The South Jeolla Province region was hit by a wave of arrests.

I discussed the state of affairs with Hee-yun, packed a bag, and laid low in a boarding house near Bulgap Temple. It was a classic *hanok* house with three buildings surrounding a courtyard. I sat on the porch every day and listened to the news on the radio. The Busan-Masan resistance was not being reported and so I had no idea it was happening, but at least I was writing my manuscript and sending it off regularly to Seoul.

One morning, a loud, urgent voice pierced my waking dreams. Then some grand music played on air before the news came back on again. Unable to go back to sleep, I got out my toothbrush and stepped into the courtyard. The landlord's son asked me in an agitated voice, "What if there's another war?" Still barely awake, I asked him what on earth he was talking about. "President Park Chung-hee has been shot. He's dead."

I thought I'd misheard him and turned my attention to the radio. The minister of culture and information was unmistakably announcing the death of the president, in a voice choked with sobs. I listened numbly until I felt a sudden chill all over my body. I immediately went to my room to pack my bag and leave for Gwangju.

Park Chung-hee's death had changed the entire world. The television showed nothing but reports on the incident and images of people expressing their condolences. Many who had been in hiding began gathering at our center's offices, and we hoped that Yoon Han Bong and other martial law violators would be released soon.

That day, when the sun broke through the clouds of the Yushin era, my writer friends and some youths drank through four crates of beer on the slopes of Mount Mudeung. The Modern Cultural Research Center was being managed by someone new, and Yoon Han Bong's place was also being kept warm by another labor activist. We were going to strengthen all of our activities, from teaching and youth organization to cultural outreach. The cultural activist group was performing *madang-geuk* all over the country by then, with participating students later moving on to perform in the countryside or factories in the Gwangju region.

Seoul's activist community and minority party leaders were demanding that the next president be directly elected by the people, the Yushin Constitution struck down, prisoners freed, and the powers of the government transferred to the people. They decided to issue their demands through a declaration on November 24, registering the event as a wedding at the Myeong-dong YMCA, as protests were banned. Various activists, politicians, religious people, academics, fired journalists, writers, and youth gathered to make their declaration, and the police moved in to beat up and arrest the participants. They were taken to a military post in Yongsan to be tortured. Ham Sok-hon had his beard pulled out; Paek Ki-wan never did recover his health. Hyun Ki-young, known for his novel *Sun-i Samch'ong*—about the April 3 Massacre on Jeju Island, which had taken place under American rule after Liberation—was especially mistreated by the military investigators. He suffered from the aftereffects of his torture for a long time.

Hearing what had happened in Gwangju, we had hastily written a declaration ourselves. It demanded the striking down of the Yushin Constitution, the end of martial law, the release of political prisoners, and direct elections to the presidency—in other words, for the military to give their power back to the people. These were all things that would have had us thrown in prison only a few months earlier if we had so much as uttered them. We thought the military government wouldn't dare to arrest us now. The declaration was to be read aloud at the Gwangju YMCA, among a crowd of religious leaders, intellectuals, and lawyers, with some reporters watching. I wrote the declaration, but Professor Myeong No-geun, one of the dismissed academics, was to read it.

We were all arrested that evening. I wrapped up against the cold before getting hustled out. Everyone who had signed the declaration was at the police station. We spent a night in lockup and were taken to a military intelligence branch—Honam Gongsa—the next day. Their guidelines must have been different from Seoul's, because while we were roundly insulted and humiliated, we weren't tortured. Half of our group were pastors, including Kang Shin-seok and former resistance activists from the Japanese occupation. About ten main instigators were identified and imprisoned separately at a military prison in Gwangju's Sangmu. We were charged with violating martial law.

The military prison was a semicircular structure, with a watchtower in the middle and two military policemen surveilling the narrow, fan-shaped cells. I shared a cell with a pastor whose name I don't recall. We were the only two civilians; the rest were soldiers. The most common crime was desertion, but there was a mix of soldiers in for causing traffic accidents, stealing, and assaulting a superior officer. They were all in their twenties, with a few thirty-something officers. The pastor in the cell with me had his congregation in Gangjin; he had once joined a walk to Seoul in protest when Park Chung-hee declared the new constitution.

Each cell was the size of a schoolroom and housed thirty to forty men. Those from Gwangju were divided into groups of twos and threes and placed in different cells. We spent about a month there. I attracted the attention of young military police on duty there who happened to be fans of my work. The higher-ranking ones, especially those nearing the end of their conscription period, fought to get me to sign their autograph books. A scrawl would get me a bag of crackers. The prison served an early dinner, with lights out around nine. The pastor and I would wait patiently until then to break open the crackers, making as little noise as possible. But no matter how quiet we tried to be, we could hear our fellow prisoners nearby swallowing their saliva at the slightest rustle.

Around December 15, a conscript who treated me well beckoned me to the bars at the beginning of his shift. He informed me that on the twelfth, Army General Chun Doo-hwan had mobilized a military force and, after a gun battle, managed to arrest Army Chief of Staff Jeong Seung-hwa and take power. This was the December 12 coup d'état. Change was on the horizon. I was soon released on suspension of indictment.

The new military administration decided to install Choi Kyu-hah, the man they had appointed acting president, as actual president through the still-extant National Conference for Unification. His appointment triggered the release of all martial law violators, and many youth activists, including Yoon Han Bong, were free again.

We thought, considering the precedent of Park Chung-hee, that this transitional phase of the military government would continue for another year, now that the new administration had appointed Choi Kyu-hah as president. We planned to establish a theater that would support the work of the Modern Cultural

Research Center. We got some underground space near the Nokdu Bookstore and Center and began remodeling in April of 1980. I had to figure out the deposit, remodeling fees, and lights and sound equipment. I saw no alternative but to ask my publishers for another advance.

Chun Doo-hwan had Choi Kyu-hah appoint him head of KCIA and commander-in-chief. Now that Chun held all the de facto power, it became clear that he would soon push Choi aside. Other politicians, including Kim Dae-jung and Kim Young-sam, had reignited their political careers, invigorated by their pardons, but no one knew how long this reprieve would last. That April, in the universities, it was as if decades of suppressed yearning for freedom were exploding all at once. Nineteen universities were closed because of protests, sit-ins were underway at twenty-four schools, and twenty schools were demanding the dismissal of government-appointed professors.

I met Yoon Han Bong, Choi Kwon-heng, and Lee Hae-chan in Seoul while I was there to wrangle another book advance to fund the center. Lee Hae-chan, a Seoul National University representative at the time, was trying to fulfill his pro-democracy movement duties while managing the expectations of radical underclassmen who were itching for a fight. We felt in our bones that a pivotal clash between the administration and the democracy movement was looming. Yoon Han Bong said that the military leadership, having tasted power and now wielding arms, would never cede to civilian rule. We had just had lunch and were near the red-light district of Miari when Choi Kwon-heng suggested we get our fortunes told. I was about to share my thoughts on an ominous future anyway, so we picked one of the fortune-teller shops around that neighborhood.

Yoon Han Bong asked for his fortune first. The shaman channeled the spirit of an innocent who had died young; she shook some bells, opened her eyes wide, and her voice changed to that of a little girl. She said that Yoon's father had died of sorrow because of his son and that Yoon needed to buy him a set of clothes and burn them before his grave. Everyone knew that Yoon's father had passed away while Yoon was imprisoned during the National Democratic Youth and Student Alliance incident. She said she saw blood in his future. She mumbled that blood would flow like a river. He needed to be careful, very careful, if he wanted to avoid death.

The fortune was so disturbing that Choi Kwon-heng and I didn't even ask for ours. Yoon, as we walked the street, said there was nothing strange about it. Hadn't we already had the feeling that something like that was about to happen? The Miari shaman's prediction that "blood would flow like a river" left a deep impression on us.

~

When I was running a farmers' school in Haenam with Kim Nam-ju and Jung Gwang-hoon, the National Council of Churches invited me to give a talk in Busan at a conference for church workers in industrial zones, slums, and the countryside. I became acquainted with many activists in that sphere, including Lee Cheol-yong. Lee had only graduated from elementary school and limped from the aftereffects of arthritis from tuberculosis. He was still a feisty character, with a criminal record that grew longer and longer, and lived in the slums of Miari.

Lee Cheol-yong was a born organizer of the slums. He felt that students or pastors who preached to the poor were full of it, that the poor did not trust flashy words from gentlemen and ladies. Lee took a different approach. In his neighborhood, there was a problem with raw sewage being discharged on the street, which stank in the summer and dangerously froze over in the winter. So Lee's strategy was to wait until the meanest lady of the neighborhood came out onto her doorstep, and then pour sewage right in front of her house.

The woman shouted, "Who is this asshole dumping his sewage in front of my house!"

Lee matched her stream of curses with his own. "Stupid bitch! There's no sewer around here, where else am I supposed to dump it?"

"You bastard, how is that my problem? And how is it my fault we don't have a sewer?"

The people of the neighborhood gathered. At some point Lee said: "Then stop blaming me and let's take it to the district office."

"After you, asshole, let's go!"

"Hey, everyone! This is no way to live! Don't we pay taxes like everybody else? Just because we live in a slum, doesn't mean we aren't citizens! Let's all go to the district office!"

And just like that, he had the whole enraged crowd on his side.

I remember an incident during President Carter's visit on June 29, 1979. Activists started a petition against his visit to Hwashin Department Store in Jongno and were arrested after a brief protest. Only religious gatherings were permitted at the time, so a "protest prayer" was held at the National Council of Churches offices on Jongno 5-ga. Heo Byeong-seop and Lee Cheol-yong decided to burn down the decorative arches welcoming Carter. There was one on the second Han River Bridge on the way into Seoul from Gimpo Airport, and another in front of the *Dong-a Ilbo* offices in Gwanghwamun. Burning down an arch didn't hurt anyone physically and yet would have significant symbolic impact.

Pastor Heo's team took the arch on the bridge, and Lee took two students for the one in Gwanghwamun. Heo's team had a gasoline can but it happened to be raining at the time. The arch was made of particleboard on a steel structure, both of which refused to catch fire. Lee's game plan was different. He got two small cans of lighter fluid and hid them in the inside pockets of his jacket before setting off. It was early in the evening and rush hour, so there were plenty of people on the streets. Lee, with his bum leg, was to go up inside the arch and spray the lighter fluid while a lookout stood underneath to keep passersby away, with the third

person setting the flame. Everything went to plan until the deci-
sive moment: the arch immediately exploded, sending the third
man to the ground. As the fire attracted a crowd, the lookout ran
straight through the intersection, while the one holding the lighter
foolishly stuck to the sidewalk only to be caught by some virtuous
pedestrian. He said later that he'd sprained his ankle in the fall
and couldn't keep running. Lee watched it all unfold from nearby
and returned to the slum. His house was at the top of Miari, where
the houses were so close together that it would be easy to jump
from roof to roof if he had to flee. It was also not a middle-class
neighborhood, and no one cared if strangers went in and out. I
heard all of this from him at Heo's church.

The arch had been repaired by the next day and not a single
journalist reported on the incident. There were no repercussions
despite the arrest; it turned out that the American Embassy
had dropped the matter, as they did not want to attract attention to it. From the Americans' perspective, having just dealt
with the Koreagate bribery scandal, Carter's Korea visit was
perceived as an attempt to pressure Korea on issues of democracy and human rights.

Several students and activists took down Lee Cheol-yong's
life story, and I used the notes and recordings to weave them
into a narrative that became my story of Korean poverty,
Eodumui jasikdeul (The Children of Darkness). This was
around the time that *The Autobiography of Malcolm X, The
Children of Sánchez,* and *Eoneu dolmengiui oechim* (Shouts
from a Stone), on the lives of Korean laborers, were published.
My story was published in a magazine and the edition sold out.
I gave all the rights and royalties to Lee, of course.

Beginning in early May of 1980, the members of the cultural
activist troupe Gwangdae began borrowing a conference room
at the YMCA for rehearsals, in preparation for our theater
opening. It was a version of my own work, "Mr. Han's chronicle," which I'd adapted myself.

On May 16, a Friday, I went up to Seoul to get further funding for the theater construction. The publishers said the banks were about to close and wouldn't open until Monday, which meant I had to spend the weekend in Seoul. On Saturday 17, I was sitting in a bar near Sinchon Station when a young man I knew ran inside and told me that a meeting of the student government representatives of Ewha Womans University had been broken up by the police and the members arrested. I called up Ko Un, Rhee Young-hee, and Moon Ik-hwan. They had all been arrested around the same time at their homes. I called the Nokdu Bookstore in Gwangju, and Kim Sang-yoon's wife said that he and various local activists had also been taken into custody.

On May 18, we began hearing news of protests in Gwangju, with the first death reported at Gwangju Express Bus Terminal. The activists who had managed to escape arrest were either fleeing to Seoul or going into hiding. On Monday, May 19, the situation worsened, and I consulted with those around me as to whether I should go back to Gwangju or stay put. The novelist Park Taesun declared that this was exactly like the Donghak Peasant Revolution in 1894 and that it was my historical imperative to join the revolution, while Choi Kwon-heng, Pastor Heo, and others urged me to stay in Seoul to organize support, as it was obvious I would be immediately arrested upon my return.

For the next few days we attempted to start protests in Yeongdeungpo, Jongno, and other districts of Seoul, and a few people were arrested. Then, a young activist named Kim Uigi stood on the sixth floor of the National Council of Churches building on Jongno 5-ga, scattered a ream of fliers out the window, and threw himself to his death.

We decided to produce an underground newspaper that would tell the citizens of Seoul the truth of the popular uprising and state repression in Gwangju. Because of martial rule, not a single line about the incident had made it into the Seoul papers, despite more innocent citizens being killed every day. Heo

Byeong-seop and I went to the "House of dawn," Pastor Moon Dong-hwan's church. They had a semiautomatic printer that Pastor Heo said they weren't using.

Heo must have contacted Moon's wife, because she came home while we were at work in Moon's study. She was an American whom he had met while studying in the US. She spoke Korean well and had grown very familiar with Korean society and emotions. She told us that, while away on business in Australia, Moon had heard that his colleagues were in preventive custody; he had gone to their New Jersey home instead of returning, and she was going to join him there. She worked in the library of the United States Army stationed in Korea and was up to date on what was happening in the country. According to her, the American authorities were going to keep silent about the new administration's violent suppression of the rebellion in Gwangju. She packed a bag, saying she would stay with an American friend before departing the country, and left the house.

Pastor Heo and I were devastated by the news of American complicity in the violent suppression of Gwangju's citizens. There were all sorts of fliers on the table that had come from Gwangju. One was an eyewitness account in the name of Chosun University's student council. Their words were like a message in a bottle, pleading for rescue from a lonely island in the distant seas, carried to us over the waves from that far-off place. I kept myself together as I tried to write something that would move people's hearts. I drafted slogans and statements while Heo checked them over and set the printer. We printed hundreds of copies and crawled onto the sofa to sleep only when the sun began to rise.

Over the next three days, Lee Cheol-yong and Shin Dong-su organized five underground newsletter teams made up of twelve volunteers. Seven were women workers that Lee Cheol-yong had been introduced to; they were members of a credit union in Mugyo-dong that had been formed by the fired female laborers of Dong Il Company Textile, in the brief period of freedom after Park Chung-hee had died and Choi Kyu-hah was acting president. The other five were students and activists who'd responded to a call put out by Shin Dong-su. We all paired up, one person tasked with distributing fliers and the other with keeping a lookout and ensuring they had a quick exit ready. Each team took a different area; Lee Cheol-yong offered to take the Samsung headquarters, *JoongAng Ilbo*, and Seosomun, where there were many offices. We targeted the highly trafficked neighborhoods of Gwanghwamun, the Jongno intersection, Myeong-dong, and Sinchon first.

Pastor Heo and I bagged up the day's portion of fliers and headed for a restaurant next to the Daeji Cinema. It was usually pretty deserted after lunch and had private rooms and tall booths that were perfect for secret meetings. We chose a room, and every half hour or so a team would come in and take a packet of fliers. Shin Dong-su showed up sharply dressed in a dark suit and tie. When it was over, Shin went to a third location where he made sure everyone was accounted for.

At one point, a fired female worker and a male Seoul National University student, who'd partnered up to flier an underground passage in Myeong-dong, got into an argument over who would do the actual distributing. Having reluctantly taken the lookout job, the woman was flabbergasted to see the student stop halfway down the stairs and drop the entire ream down on the people in the passageway. He was so nervous that he simply dumped the whole stack and ran off without looking back. The woman courageously hurried down the steps, grabbed the fliers and pressed them into people's hands to make sure they wouldn't be ignored or overlooked, and hurried out of the passage. She had caught a taxi and was headed toward Euljiro when she saw the SNU student sprinting by with his hair blowing in the wind. "Get in, get in!" she shouted, but it took him a moment to hear her, and he practically collapsed into the taxi, his body drenched in sweat. He stopped coming to meetings, and the woman said she needed a new partner, as the college boy was not suited for this work.

On the same day, I followed Lee Cheol-yong out to Seosomun because I wanted to see him in action. He glanced around and said, "You better just sit tight and watch." He sat me down at a bakery with a good view and slowly walked up the steps to a nearby overpass. He threw the fliers off the steps to the pedestrians below and quickly came back down. Then, among the gathered crowd picking up the fliers, he cocked his head and picked one up, looking at it intently. Note that this was after a state of emergency had been declared nationwide and there were tanks stationed next to every newspaper company, broadcaster, and administrative building, and soldiers standing around everywhere with bayoneted rifles. In the midst of this repressive climate, I couldn't help but be amazed at his brashness.

According to *The Kwangju Uprising*, in which I recorded my memories of the incident, the special forces had moved into Gwangju on the night of May 17 and taken over the various administrative and college buildings, especially in Chonnam National University and Chosun University, where they arrested students in libraries and student council rooms. There was a clash between the special forces and students at the gates of Chonnam National University on May 18, which triggered a student protest that spilled over into the city and pulled in ordinary citizens. Martial forces spread throughout Gwangju and started to beat and kill citizens with batons and bayonets, while students fought back with stones and Molotov cocktails. Faced with the military's violent crackdown, it became a fight for the very survival of the citizens of Gwangju. There had already been preemptive arrests of activists in Gwangju and Seoul on the 17th, but the cultural activists and volunteer teachers still at large used their emergency network to take on the role of organizers. Kim Tae-jong, Jeon Yong-ho, Kim Seon-chul, and others printed fliers with eyewitness accounts of what had happened and scattered them in residential areas. This was the beginning of the "Combatant newsletter." Yoon Sang-won and Kim Sang-jip made Molotov cocktails at the Nokdu Bookstore. After the 18th, tanks and armored vehicles appeared on Geumnamro Street, Gwangju's main road, and the whole of Gwangju turned into a resistance zone. Countless students and citizens were killed. The youth took up wooden planks, steel pipes, and Molotov cocktails, and from the afternoon of the 19th, the citizens began to fight back. They fought because of the massacre they had witnessed the day before. The mass killings in front of the Catholic Center, in particular, had made them realize that they needed to arm themselves. There were citizen barricades everywhere, and everyone was prepared to fight to the death. Even high school students, girls and boys alike, jumped into the maelstrom of protests.

The gymnasium at Chosun University and auditorium at Chonnam National were full of injured citizens and students who had been grabbed off the street by soldiers. Helicopters spouted propaganda and surveilled the movement of the protests. Later, there were reports of armed helicopters firing into the crowds. It appeared that the first shots on the ground were fired around 4:50 p.m. on the 19th, from an armored vehicle surrounded by protesters. There were eyewitness accounts everywhere of the army's violence; taxi drivers who had been beaten with clubs for trying to stop soldiers from pulling out their young customers and arresting them were planning a car protest. At night, the protesters set fire to arches and cars and police stations.

At 10:20 a.m. on the morning of the 20th, right in front of the Catholic Center on Geumnamro 3-ga, thirty men and women were stripped down to their underwear, lined up, and put through discipline drills. Almost all were young people in their twenties with a few who looked to be in their thirties. Many of the women wore high heels. Ten or so soldiers surrounded

them with batons, while someone who looked like a sergeant shouted commands in the middle. "Make an arch. Lie on your back, lie on your side, roll five times, crouch, jump with your hands on your ears, crawl forward, stand on one leg." Anyone who couldn't keep up was immediately beaten with batons. The humiliation of the women was especially hard to see. I would rather have suffered it myself than have to watch it. Think of a young woman in her panties and brassiere forced to do such things in the middle of the street. This was witnessed by many citizens. From the sixth floor of the Catholic Center, Archbishop Yoon Gong-hee and Father Cho Bi-oh were looking down, and from the diocese offices, nuns and administrators. Father Cho later stated at a military law tribunal: "I may be a man of God, but if I had a gun next to me then, I would have shot them all." Archbishop Yoon later stated: "I happened to notice a young man being beaten in a nearby alley while that was going on. I don't know what they beat him with, but he was bleeding profusely from the head. It made me think he would die if no one helped him. But I was too afraid to go down and try to stop them. I do wonder if he survived or not, but I also wonder why I didn't go down there myself. As a man of God, it is a sight that haunts me to this day and stops my heart. Since then, I have begged God again and again to forgive me."
—Kim Young-taek, *roilganui chwijae sucheop* (Notes from Ten Days of Coverage), Sakyejul Publishing, 1988

On the afternoon of the 20th, three brigades and ten battalions' worth of soldiers were called into the city with orders to suppress the rebellion. Clashes between protesters and soldiers broke out all over the city. Around 3 p.m., the citizens started to converge on Geumnamro Street in the city center. Tear gas canisters would go off and they would briefly retreat only to surge forward again, over and over, while the crowd swelled to tens of thousands until there were seas and mountains of people. But the soldiers swarmed on them like bees, swinging their batons mercilessly. The peaceful sit-ins turned to blood-shed, and yet more and more people poured into the street. Students started a sit-in protest at the intersection of Geumnamro and Jungangno Streets, near the construction site for the new underground shopping center. When a citizen stood up and suggested purchasing a microphone and speaker, the crowd instantly took up a collection and it was bought. One person held the speaker, another the battery, and a third shouted into the microphone: "We are ready to die here and join those who have gone before us!" The protesters' morale soared, and the throwing of rocks reached fever pitch. Waves of citizens surged down the six roads that led from the plaza in front of the Provincial Hall. The protesters at the front tipped oil drums and large planters on their sides and rolled them toward the soldiers' line of defense as they advanced step by step. Each road was blocked by rows of soldiers and police offi-cers, and amid the tension the soldiers started to move against the protesters with their bayonets.

Around 7 p.m., bus and taxi drivers, incensed at the deaths of their colleagues and the massacres occurring all over the city, drove their vehicles to Geumnamro Street in the hundreds, buses and large trucks leading the way, their blaring horns and flashing headlights breathing new life into the protest. The sense of defeat in the face of ruthless state repression trans-formed to strong feelings of solidarity and confidence; it was an important turning point in the citizens' defense of their city against martial forces. The protests continued all night, and the buildings of broadcasters MBC and KBS—which kept report-ing falsehoods throughout the events—were set on fire, as well as other buildings, including the Labor Administration and the National Tax Service. Gwangju became a war zone: protesters fought fiercely hand-to-hand near the Provincial Hall and Gwangju Station, and cars fitted with loudspeakers spouted propaganda all over the city. The entire region, but for Provincial Hall and Gwangju Station, was in the hands of the enraged citizenry. The authorities fired into the crowd at Gwangju Station, killing about thirty, but elsewhere the citizens managed to take back their city (except for the Provincial Hall and Gwangju Station). That night, all the phone lines going in and out of the city were disconnected. The martial forces' line of defense started to break down, prompting them to open fire, and around 11 p.m. they began firing at the crowd of 20,000 to 30,000 people demonstrating in front of the Provincial Hall. Citizens staunchly continued the protest into the night.

The morning of the 21st dawned. Geumnamro overflowed with protesters who had moved on from Gwangju Station. More conscious than ever of the need to arm themselves after the many casualties of the previous day, the citizens had rushed to the Asia Motors factory and driven off with numerous vehicles, including armored cars and military trucks. They drove around the outskirts and transported citizens to the center, and also ventured beyond the city to spread news of what was happening. This was the beginning of what became known as the "blockade of the cars," as drivers tried to use their vehicles to keep protesters safe. The news spread ever faster, and there was strong solidarity among the citizens as everywhere people were provided with rice balls, *kimbap*, and soft drinks. The protesters in front of the Provincial Hall had elected their own leader and were negotiating the retreat of the martial forces. But even as the military used the provincial governor to pretend to consider the protesters' demands, they were at the same time flying ammunition in by helicopter while ferrying out dead bodies and secret documents. The military began to fire upon the crowd at Chonnam National University, a little off from the center of town. Shortly after twelve o'clock, in front of the Provincial Hall, they shot a young man who was driving toward them in an armored vehicle, unleashing a massacre as the soldiers then let rip into the crowd, protesters bleeding where they fell. Snipers on rooftops even took aim at citizens who crawled into the streets to try to rescue the wounded.

That afternoon, when the martial forces started firing at civilians all over Gwangju, protesters who had fanned out to Hwasun, Haenam, Naju, and other outlying regions were spreading the word of the horrors taking place in Gwangju, before returning to the city center with guns raided from police stations and armories. These weapons were distributed around 3 p.m. to Gwangju citizens, creating the militia we know as the "citizen army," equipped with guns and live ammunition. They fought to the death to guard Gwangju. It was a fight between an ill-prepared civilian army and an elite unit armed to the teeth. It was on this day and in this battle, in front of the Provincial Hall, that the largest number of deaths occurred during the Gwangju Democracy Movement. Citizens lined up in front of the hospital downtown to give blood, while others continued raiding weapons in order to resist the indiscriminate slaughter by martial forces. At the same time, a voluntary combat leadership team was formed to regulate the weapons and vehicles circulating haphazardly around the city, while also imparting basic weapons and military training on the fly before assembling a commando unit of veterans and reservists who knew how to handle a gun. With the appearance of this armed militia, and the power of the light machine gun on the roof of Chonnam National University Hospital, the martial forces hastened to withdraw.

Around 5 p.m. the same day, the forces occupying Chonnam National University and Chosun University retreated to the outskirts of the city and began closing Gwangju off from the outside. The "Liberation of Gwangju" lasted all of seven days, from the evening of May 21, when the citizens took back the city, until the 27th, when the martial forces retook Provincial Hall. But on the outskirts, intermittent clashes between the martial forces and the citizen army continued. A committee was convened to discuss next steps, with one side arguing that the weapons should be returned and the other saying they needed to fight on until martial law was lifted and an apology was issued. The protesters occupying the Provincial Hall formed a leadership committee under the name of "Committee for Democratic Struggle." On the plaza in front of the Provincial Hall, a propaganda arm of this committee held daily morale-boosting rallies while a mobile strike team patrolled the city. At dawn on May 27, the martial forces went on the offensive again, overpowering the citizen armies that had been posted to Gwangju Park, the YWCA, and the YMCA, and finally killing or arresting the remaining men who'd guarded the Provincial Hall with their lives, thus putting an end to the uprising.

All throughout this, I was unable to get to Gwangju and was stuck in Seoul, receiving calls and trying to hide the young men and women who had managed to escape from there. Yoon Han Bong stayed with Lee Cheol-yong for a while before going elsewhere, the women were hidden at a convent, and some were taken to the homes of relatives. I was finally able to contact my wife, Hee-yun, through a friend who lived nearby, as we did not have a telephone at home. Hee-yun had experienced much of it firsthand, including giving a speech at one of the rallies to urge our fellow citizens to rise up, and cooking for the citizen army as they occupied the Provincial Hall. She sobbed over the phone as she informed me of the deaths of friends and colleagues. A team of detectives had come to the house on the 17th to arrest me. Mother had shouted at them to take off their shoes, but they had searched the entire house before leaving. Hee-yun also bade me not to come to Gwangju for at least a month, until things had settled down.

For a while, I kept in contact with and managed the living arrangements of Yoon Han Bong, Park Hyo-sun, and other fugitives. When I returned to Gwangju in mid-June, many people I knew had either been killed, were on the run, or were in jail. It was like the aftermath of a war. Mother went out that winter, slipped and fell, and never got out of bed again.

575

One day, a high school friend of mine paid an unexpected visit to our house. He was a military judicial officer and had come down to investigate the "Gwangju incident," quite pleased with himself for having gotten rid of a thick file of reports involving me. He said it would take three months to finish his investigation. At first he advised me to leave, and wondered aloud why a Seoul man would come all the way down here in the first place. When I told him my mother was too sick to be moved, he said I, at least, should leave the city for the time being. He also said martial law would be partly lifted and that the tourist zone of Jeju Island would be safer. After discussing it with Hee-yun, I headed to Jeju to restart the *Jang Gil-san* serialization that I'd put on hold during the events in Gwangju.

There I established another cultural activism group, Sunurum, and founded the Jeju Issues Research Center. With some Jeju National University students and teachers, we created the Sunurum Troupe and moved the lighting and sound equipment from Gwangju to put together a small theater.

Mother died while I was in Jeju. A typhoon prevented me from visiting her on her deathbed, a failure that haunts me to this day.

~

Two years passed since the massacre at Gwangju, during which the government did everything it could to represent the uprising as a riot instigated by North Korean spies and to suppress the facts of the massacre. Chun Doo-hwan became president in 1981, and when Kim Dae-jung and other prisoners of the Gwangju Democracy Movement were released during the annual Liberation Day pardons, some of the Gwangju cultural activists were freed as well. I saw to my mother's funeral, went back to Jeju, and returned to Gwangju in the fall of 1981. By then, films and videos made by foreign correspondents who had witnessed the events of May 1980 were circulating throughout the country via religious channels. As soon as the movement had been suppressed, we felt a need to amass documentation to publicize the truth of what had happened, and various teams had already started on this work. I got my younger friends together to help and also looked for ways to use cultural activism to spread the word of the Gwangju Democracy Movement.

Most of the people who died during the incident were buried in a cemetery in Mangwol-dong, and the government prohibited any gatherings there, let alone any event of any kind. With permission from the relatives of Yoon Sang-won, who was killed as part of the militia leadership at the Provincial Hall, and Park Gi-soon, a female factory-laborer activist who had died before the incident, we decided to hold a symbolic "wedding of the souls," thus allowing the bereaved families to come together in a kind of protest. I wrote a musical titled *Neokpuri* for the occasion. I knew we couldn't perform it in front of an assembled audience, but I thought we could at least distribute cassette tape recordings.

Our house in Gwangju's Unam-dong was at the end of a hilly path and surrounded by woods. We recorded the group performance in the second-floor living room, with curtains drawn and windows locked. I insisted on making the production as collaborative as possible, like a *madanggeuk*, to make it feel that many people had a hand in putting it together. The lyrics were written by committee and, as befitting a collaboration of this nature, I edited, erased, and corrected as I saw fit. I inserted a Moon Byeong-lan poem as a recitation interlude, and also used part of a Kim Jun-tae poem. The theme song of the production, "March for the beloved," was fleshed out from a section of a Paek Ki-wan poem. *Neokpuri*'s narrative dealt with the beauty of youth, the death of youth, the healing of the survivors, the mothers of Gwangju, the coming together of a community; it culminated in a march for freedom.

We learned our songs first with Kim Jong-ryul's accompaniment and rehearsed in the afternoon. We recorded the work three times and chose the best version, which was still flawed because there was some barking coming from our yard. Someone also said they could hear a train whistle. But it had the best-sung version of the finale, "March for the beloved," so I insisted it had to be that one. The ambient noise would only help to convey the urgency and passion of a nonprofessional group. Jeon Yong-ho and I made three tapes. One we stored, and two we sent off to a Christian organization in Seoul, who made 500 copies and spread them around universities, factories, and the countryside. "March for the beloved" became not just a resistance song for Gwangju but also for laborers and college students. For a long time after, the song served as an anthem of freedom for the people of Asia, and was adapted and translated for labor activist organizations in Japan, Taiwan, the Philippines, Thailand, China, Vietnam, and Indonesia.

One night in the late fall of 1982, Hee-yun was suddenly wanted for interrogation by the police. She told me to contact Seoul as she was being taken away, and it was only when I did so that I realized the gravity of the situation. Our contact Choi Kwon-heng had been taken to Lee Geun-an's infamous Namyeong-dong police interrogation facility, along with Yoon Han Bong, the painter Hong Jeong-gyung, who hid him, and Lee Cheol-yong, who had hidden so many others in the slums.

I didn't ask for details, but I assumed that Hee-yun was involved in arranging the exile of Yoon Han Bong, the last man still at large concerning the incident in Gwangju. Hee-yun was the director of Songbaekhoe, a women's organization in Gwangju, and it was an unspoken rule between us that we shouldn't know too much about each other's activist work.

I couldn't sleep a wink that night, as I racked my brain for a solution. I left the children with the painter Hong Seong-dam and, with the help of a long-time reader employed at the American Cultural Center in Gwangju, I met the head of the center. She was a middle-aged woman with a vivacious spirit, who had reputedly helped Archbishop Yoon Gong-hee to communicate the truth of what happened in Gwangju to the American government.

With the lifting of martial law in January 1981, Chun Doo-hwan, under pressure from the US, commuted Kim Dae-jung's sentence from execution to life in prison, and US president Ronald Reagan authorized Chun's visit to America as a reward, de facto recognizing him as Korea's head of state. Still, the Americans knew that the arson incidents against the American Cultural Centers in Busan and Gwangju were in protest against US government policies that either condoned or blatantly supported the massacre in Gwangju, and they were probably discomfited by the rise in anti-American sentiment among the student activist community and the citizenry. This led to the illegitimate administration's continued existence with the political help of the United States.

I kept these points in mind when I met with the American Center director. I told her about Yoon Han Bong's exile to America assisted by the Robert F. Kennedy Human Rights organization, that several people had been arrested for aiding him, and that, if nothing was done about it, I would write to as many media companies as possible to disseminate the truth. She understood that this would be a tricky political situation for her. She asked for another meeting that evening. On arrival, I found her with two men in sleek suits. Their business cards declared they were from the political section of the American Embassy. I explained the situation to them once more. They said it was a politically sensitive matter, gave each other a look, and said they would take care of it. Around midnight, I was called up by the authorities to collect my wife. Hee-yun looked exhausted. We were told over the telephone that Choi Kwon-heng and all the others who had been arrested in Seoul had been released as well. But the teachers of Gunsan and Jeonju, who had been detained before them, were still being interrogated, and the newspapers soon trumpeted the fictitious story of a captured leftist cell of revolutionaries called Osonghwe.

The Osonghwe incident began when five teachers from Gunsan Jeil High School went up to the hill behind their school, to hold a service in memory of the April Revolution and Gwangju Democracy Movement and to read aloud a political declaration. They were subsequently accused of being an anti-governmental organization and given heavy sentences. Among them was the poet Lee Gwang-ung, a close friend of mine and of my wife, who had helped Yoon Han Bong when he was in hiding. The police had woken up to his part in Yoon's hiding and were cooperating with Namyeong-dong to link it to another fabricated spy incident that covered Gunsan, Jeonju, and Gwangju. But now that the Gwangju inmates had been freed and they had only the five teachers left, the Chun Doo-hwan administration had no choice but to name it Osonghwe—"meeting of the five under the pine tree." It remains the most infamous fabricated incident of its kind during the Chun era. As absurd as it sounds, I had saved my friends and the mother of my children by asking for help from the Americans.

After the release of *Neokpuri*, we used the project as an opportunity to create an underground media group called Voice of Gwangju. Jeon Yong-ho did most of the work, scrounging time from recording studios where live bar musicians worked, copying hundreds of tapes. He borrowed a small room in an alley behind the market and assigned a graduate student named Kim Yeong-jeong from Chonnam National to sit there all day and manually replace each tape in the four decks as they finished copying.

Then, in 1983, the regrouped team of cultural activists consisting of Hong Seong-dam, Jeon Yong-ho, Kim Tae-jong, Yoon Man-sik, and Kim Jeong-hee gathered once more to form the cultural activist group Work and Play. We built a permanent theater and got half of its activities funded by a German church group. We also published an irregular magazine titled "Work and play." Hong Seong-dam did the photography and made prints and paintings of Gwangju, while the Work and Play theater continued to produce *madanggeuk* and spread the experiences of the group far and wide. Within about a year we had helped establish cultural activist groups in Jeju, Mokpo, Jeonju, Jinju, Masan, and Busan. In Seoul, Chae Hee-wan, Im Jin-taek, and other organizers began a network of thirty-three cultural activist groups that stretched across the country. This grew into an interdisciplinary media movement built on solidarity across literature, art, photography, movies, theater, and music, in which collaboration became essential as the movement latched on to the most effective distributive mediums of the day: recorded music, in the 1980s, to be followed by film and video documentaries. But the *madanggeuk* constituted the origin of all of these later experiments. We established a national cultural activism association in 1984, and I joined the executive committee. We still felt an obligation to spread the truth of Gwangju far and wide, both inside and outside Korea. Many teams had been gathering information and materials since the moment it had ended, but because it had to be done out of reach of the government's watchful eye, it took longer than expected. The media was heavily censored under martial rule and many journalists had been dismissed. Occasionally team members would disappear because they were wanted by the authorities, which delayed production for another few years. Meanwhile, I had to somehow finish *Jang Gil-san*, which I had been serializing since 1974. At long last the final episode was printed, exactly ten years later, in the summer of 1984.

Early that winter, Jeong Sang-yong and Jeong Yong-hwa, who were among the survivors of the massacre at the Provincial Hall, came to see me. Jung Yong-hwa had run the Modern Cultural Research Center since Yoon Han Bong's exile and was also in charge of putting together the record of the Gwangju Democracy Movement. Hee-yun would regularly collect material from him, show it to me, and hide it. The two Jungs came to see me to discuss the management of these records. Jung Sang-yong had met with a couple of archivists, but they had refused to help, knowing they would be immediately arrested if word got out. I still felt a sense of debt to the people who had died in Gwangju. Chance had placed me elsewhere during the height of the uprising, and it always weighed on me that I was not there to stand with the people of Gwangju in their hour of need. This, at least, was work I could do as a writer and something that might lessen that guilt. I wholeheartedly accepted but told them I would need time to go through it all and write it up into a book. Jung Yong-hwa explained that a few people were working on it already, the first draft would be ready in the spring, and all I would have to do was edit a little at the end. I understood: they needed to borrow my name for legitimacy with the public, and I would have final responsibility for the work.

The manuscript began making its way to me in pieces the next spring. Cho Bong-hoon drew timelines of what had happened during the incident. I later learned the names of a few of the recorders, but at the time I only knew that Jung Sang-yong, Jung Yong-hwa, and Jeon Yong-ho were involved. Jung Yong-hwa put it simply: "Everything is your responsibility. You don't need to know anyone else." I understood what he meant. It was a dark time, and we needed to be prepared for the worst. It was like cutting off a limb in order for the whole body to survive. I might be arrested, but I wouldn't have enough information to take anyone down with me.

Pulbit's Na Byung-sik offered to publish the book. We brought together some influential activists to discuss how to go about publishing it and dealing with the fallout.

In mid-April of 1984, manuscript in hand, I left Hee-yun and the two children in Gwangju. Hee-yun saw me off, doing her best to hide her worry and exhaustion. We knew that once *The Kwangju Uprising* was published, I would be on the run for who knew how long.

During our years together, in the lonely times when I was away, she'd been tasked with raising our children alone, caring for my sick mother, and watching over her as she died. I'd had countless friends over for dinner. She'd once cooked for a hundred people, all without a single word of complaint. Emotionally, though, she was still stuck in the Provincial Hall along with her vivid memories of the uprising. I was not a rock to her but a burden. Leaving was a way to escape both my sense of debt to the people of Gwangju and my guilt for not having been with my family during that difficult time. By then, I'd grown used to being away from home for one reason or another.

The night train to Seoul left Gwangju and raced through the darkness. Before me lay a long journey from which I would never return.

14

Prison VI

The seasons changed, and it was back to the tedium of winter. The *soji* boys helped me with the harvest of our vegetable patch. I wrapped the cabbages in newspaper to help them last through the long winter ahead. Just before my fourth Christmas behind bars, I received a letter from Kim Myoung-su. With the *Jang Gil-san* royalties still in contention for over a year now, we had stopped writing, except for the occasional missive whenever it felt like the other was about to let go of communication entirely. My heart still couldn't decide, and I wanted to be rid of the whole business altogether. But the guilt and pity I felt toward the mother and son I had left behind in another country made me chastise myself time and again. I carefully read the part about Ho-seop that Kim Myoung-su had scrawled in her nearly illegible handwriting:

Pulbit Books sent a twenty-volume *manhwa* version of *Jang Gil-san* that Ho-seop likes very much. I can hear him laughing as he reads it aloud to himself before bed. He asks about the names. He said Daddy promised to meet him before Christmas and keeps asking me about that, too . . . His teacher says he talks about you a lot. Ho-seop is very fond of his teacher. Not at first, but with time Ho-seop has opened up to him quite a bit. He's also inviting friends over more and being invited over himself. He's very much into music and will get to play the trumpet in the school orchestra next year. He took lessons for an hour after school every Tuesday and passed the audition. His best friend's father is in the Metropolitan Opera, which is why he wanted to go into music, too. It's just like that saying, "If your friend goes to Gangnam, you go, too."

I imagined my child playing the trumpet. I had missed out on seeing him grow up, ever since he'd turned five, and could not picture what his face looked like now. No matter how I stared at the photos they sent me, all I could recall was my last moment with him. I had never, not once, created a loving home for my children. This Christmas, like their other Christmases, would be spent on their own, scattered here and there without their father. Ho-jun and Yeo-jeong were all grown up, but I couldn't even say whether Ho-seop still believed in Santa Claus.

On December 26, 1996, the day after Christmas, the conservative New Korea Party snuck through the Agency for National Security Planning Act and labor law reform bills. The New Korea Party politicians had received phone calls from their party whip on the evening of the 25th, gathered at four hotels in Seoul, and discreetly took tour buses to the National Assembly. They took their seats, and at 6:00 a.m. sharp, in the absence of their opposition colleagues, swiftly passed eleven bills in less than seven minutes. The opposition party was of course up in arms, and artists strongly objected to the revival of the ANSP's right to prosecute the crime of "praising North Korea," with its potential to suppress freedom of expression. Censorship statutes against movies and music were judged to be unconstitutional, but these modifications in the ANSP Act had enabled government control over an even wider range of creative activity. There were no clear standards of what constituted "praise," which meant that the authorities had carte blanche to brand almost anything pro–North Korean and therefore illegal. Cultural activists voiced concerns that the new laws could be used against any kind of artistic work that was critical of the government.

They would deincentivize creativity altogether, throwing us all into a "mental prison."

Myself and the nine student protesters and activists in Gongju Correctional Institution decided to enter resistance mode, as defined by the nationwide Committee of Prisoners of Conscience. Our activities—consisting of hunger strikes, shouting every morning and evening, declarations, and disobedience to prison rules—ended after a week, but as a result young Jong-ho and the missionary were transferred elsewhere. I could only listen to them yelling slogans from afar as they were dragged away from our cell block.

The warden requested a meeting with me, as the de facto leader of the prisoners of conscience, to clear the air and propose a future of discussion and mutual compromise. I told him I'd talk to the prisoners to see how far we were willing to negotiate with our demands.

The regular prisoners' demands mostly had to do with food and censorship of their letters. The political prisoners wanted to be allowed the use of a library, audiovisual education, and to read books without censorship. But because most of the demands had to do with meals, I decided to write up a proposal centered on food to garner maximum support from my fellow prisoners. In addition, if we couldn't have uncensored letters, the prison could at least inform the senders of why their letters weren't forwarded so they could rewrite and resend them. As for books, the new civilian government had promised that any book published in Korea, including translations, would be allowed. There was a library in the prison, and the students were to come up with a list of books that any prisoner could request and read. Another demand was to let political prisoners have library time, like regular prisoners had religion time.

I asked that any personal books left behind by released prisoners be automatically donated to the library. I also wrote to my publishers to donate some volumes. Soon enough, the publishers sent hundreds of books to the prison.

~

As Gongju Correctional Institution housed only a thousand inmates, it had a smaller budget than the prisons of big cities. But it was above all the long-held relationship between the prison and subcontractors that made their food so expensive to buy. We wanted the prison to create daily menus according to the season, post the expenses for materials and fuel on the walls of the blocks, and choose one person per block to assist in the selection of these seasonal menus. We also asked that prisoners be consulted on what could be sold in the prison commissary, and for suppliers to be replaced if their goods weren't up to par. These were detailed, almost trivial demands, but so obvious that it was astonishing they hadn't been adopted earlier.

The authorities agreed to everything we asked for, but as time went by they slipped further and further back into their old ways and it was eventually all for naught. The warden, who had started at the bottom of the ladder of the prison workforce, was now facing retirement. He could be generous from time to time but was a cunning old fox in the end. He was experienced enough to know that the mundane can easily wear you down.

For a while, though, we had a bit of relief. We tended the vegetable patch during exercise hour and went to the library. The warden rented a video for us every week from downtown. The udon, ramen, and other snacks that the working prisoners had been given for sports day were also given to our cell block guards for safekeeping, and we made ourselves lunch with the materials in the shower room.

There was a Chosun University student who had been a cook in the military; he made good *sujaebi* stew. He knew how to knead the flour beforehand and let it rise for a night on a windowsill, and made broth using anchovy and kelp, tossing in some chopped kimchi. The regular prisoners had special visits from their families in the exercise yard or auditorium twice a year; it was a big festival like those in military training camps. Some families brought pots and pans to cook dishes on the spot and would invariably make so much food that the leftover *ddeok* would come all the way to our cell block. Political prisoners weren't given this privilege, but after I raised a bit of a stink with the commissary and kitchen, the prison authorities started allowing our families to feed us during visits, provided it wasn't a broth. The guards began to overlook our carrying in *kimbap*, *ddeok*, dumplings, meat, and *jeon* after our visitors had left. The young political prisoners all wrote to their families, and we were able to supplement our diets thanks to the home-cooked food that came in once every two months.

Inspector Lee Ju-hee summoned me to the political prisoners' management office. Like others of his rank, he was a "nobody," as he put it, having started from the bottom as a two-leaf guard, but he was a hardworking and honest civil servant, nonetheless. I thought he was a little too square at first, but we eventually understood each other better and I was able to discuss matters with him whenever there was a crisis. We talked a lot about our respective families. Lee once visited me in solitary during a hunger strike and tearfully begged me to stop. He had two clever sons, the eldest of whom got accepted to Seoul National University the year I was released. I once went to visit him at Gongju Correctional Institution after I left, and when I built my house in Deoksan in Chungcheong Province, he came to see me with a pot of honey as a gift. He retired as a decorated chief inspector. We exchanged news on occasion; he called once from a hospital to tell me he had cancer. A few months later, when I was overseas for an event, I received a message saying he had passed away.

One day, Lee said I would have a special visitor the next day. I asked who it was. They had told him not to warn me beforehand, but Lee figured it was more important that I was willing to see them, and revealed that they were from Daejeon's ANSP office. I grinned. I wondered aloud why they would bother to come to see me, because if it was about my release they would have sent someone from the Ministry of Justice. I added that I had no more business with the ANSP anymore. Lee nodded and said I didn't have to see them if I didn't want to. I said I would, curious to find out what they were after.

The next day, two middle-aged men in suits were waiting for me in the political prisoners' management office. They were not courteous and kept talking down to me. They had all the arrogance of fancy civil servants deigning to speak to a prisoner. They started by asking me about my health and life in prison, and I did my best to deal with them as if it were any other prison visit. Then one of them cut to the chase.

—You've served just over half your sentence already, haven't you? You've been inside longer than Pastor Moon.

I kept my response calm and nonchalant.

—So why not let me go? It's torture for a writer not to write.

The other agent pounced.

—That's why we're here, to help you.

They went on to explain that they had come to ask for my collaboration. Kim Dae-jung had recently reentered public life. He was sure to bring instability to society and had to be stopped from engaging in political activities, for the sake of national unity. Since I knew so much about him, I should write a book criticizing him, and they would surely pardon me soon enough. They offered to provide me with as much research material as I needed and would give me a good writing space to work in.

I burst out laughing at their naïve proposal. I was tempted to give them a piece of my mind—to the effect that I hadn't thrown myself into democracy activism and gone to North Korea to do politics; I chose literature because it was my calling; anything I did aside from that came from my sense of duty as a public intellectual, and was part of my literary life; coercing me to write something so nakedly political and contrary to what I believed in was exactly what they made writers in North Korea do; I was fighting this fight to change all the things they held dear about our current sociopolitical system—but I said the following instead:

—I'm not going to write that.

The two men looked at each other, and one of them, angry now, spat out his next words.

—Then you're going to be here for the full seven years.

The other one jumped in.

—You must like the jailbird life.

I held my temper in check and tried to sound as contemptuous as possible.

—I don't know who put you up to this, but you're barking up the wrong tree. If you wanted to talk pardons, you should have come two years ago. Now that I've gotten through a decent amount of my sentence and learned to have a little fun here, you come crawling to offer me a *potential* pardon? Who do you think you're dealing with?

Apparently deciding there was nothing more to be said, they abruptly stood up and left the room. Lee, who had been pretending to take notes nearby, piped up.

—I couldn't have put it better myself.

We laughed about this incident for years afterward.

Then came my fifth summer in prison. I was allowed outside visits for the first time. I needed to go to the general hospital downtown because of an ear infection. It all started from the cold water I kept pouring over myself to keep cool. Water must have gotten deep inside my ear, as I kept hearing a sound like a monk's *moktak* when I knocked on my head. It annoyed me and I kept digging into my ear with my finger, which led to an infection. I woke up one morning with my ear inflamed and the swelling traveling down my cheek. What was a light ache at first soon began to pulse with every beat of my heart. In the infirmary, they went through the motions of disinfecting the ear and giving me antibiotics. I had nightmares that whole night. A couple of days later, I was finally granted outside medical treatment.

Before I could leave, I was taken to the same room where I'd been brought when I transferred there, was given a body inspection, and changed from my blue prisoner's uniform to the gray uniform of transferred prisoners. I was made to wear rubber shoes with the heels sawn off. They put handcuffs on me, tied my arms, and then bound my upper arms to my body. The end of the rope extended from my back like a leash, which was held by a guard. I wasn't even to dream of eating on the outside, as we had lunch before setting out. That was the first time I saw my guards wearing civilian clothes. They looked like friendly neighbors in their suits and jackets without insignias, their heads bare of caps.

A jeep waited for us with its engine running. I sat in the back with one guard while the other sat next to the driver. It felt like a miracle when the jeep drove through the open gate. The guard next to me unwrapped a stick of gum and popped it in his mouth, then unwrapped another and held it out in front of my mouth, and I snapped it up.

We crossed a bridge. It was the rainy season and the river was brown with sludge, threatening to overflow the embankment. The day was overcast but dry. I stared closely at the cars of unfamiliar shapes and at the people inside. No one looked back at me. The passengers sat side by side, talking, laughing, or simply gazing ahead without expression.

The jeep parked a hundred meters away from the hospital. The guard in the front wound the lead rope around his fist, and we set out. I wondered how I looked to others, being led around by two men in civilian clothes. They must have thought I was a violent criminal. I saw the glass doors of the hospital in the distance. A woman came out of a shop holding the hand of a small child. The child was whining, but when we passed them in the street, the child's face went from puckered to awed. The woman was also staring. The heelless soles of my shoes made a slapping sound on the ground. I had to take small steps to keep them from coming off. The child tugged at his mother's hand and asked:

—Mom, who is that man?

The woman didn't answer but instead gripped the child's hand tighter and pulled him away. I couldn't help but turn to look. I saw them both standing in the street, staring at me. I tried to smile at the child, but the woman quickly turned and pulled the child along after her.

Inside the hospital was a reception area with sofas and chairs. One of the guards went to see the doctor I had an appointment with, and the other guard sat me down on one of the sofas. There were all sorts of people waiting there, none of whom would look at me. They were trying to act casual, but I could tell they were making an effort not to meet my eye. They all had the same look on their faces. No one sat down next to us. Two teenage girls entered, giggling over something. I happened to be looking in their direction. They walked toward the sofa, absorbed in their conversation. It was only when they noticed me that they stopped in their tracks and exchanged a look.

I kept telling myself that all I'd done was resist the immoral power of the government. I was no sinner. Nor was I an outcast. I'd simply rejected what was offered and walked out on my own two feet. But there were no tags on my uniform, not even one saying I was prisoner 1306. I was denied anything that would identify me as an individual. I had been erased.

It was a depressing outing. Even if I were to be released, I was always going to remain a prisoner in some form unless the outside world changed. I now knew what society thought of me.

The poet Lee Si-young, of Changbi Publishers, was more of a brother than a literary colleague in the way he took care of me while I was in prison. As I have mentioned, he went to jail for publishing my North Korea travelogue, written during exile in Germany, in the *Quarterly Changbi*. You would think he'd resent me for it, but he came to see me in prison once every two months as soon as he was released. He pitied my boredom, since I'd been prevented from writing during my imprisonment, and suggested I try my hand at translating *The Romance of the*

Three Kingdoms. Our generation studied Chinese characters in primary school the way students in the West once mastered Latin, and our college textbooks regularly mixed Chinese characters with Korean letters. I had also taken private lessons from Hong Jin-pyo in preparation for writing *Jang Gil-san,* which made me think I could take on the task of translating from classical Chinese.

I asked if he could get me a copy of the Jeongeumsa Press edition of *Romance,* which was the version I had read as a child in the 1950s. He had it sent to me. I thought it would be interesting work to compare different translations and better pass the time in my cell, the perfect task for prison.

I asked Inspector Lee, of the political prisoners' management office, if it would be possible. I wouldn't be writing creative work that required going through the Ministry of Justice censors, and *The Romance of the Three Kingdoms* was a classic that Koreans of all ages enjoyed. It would reduce some of the tedium of my sentence and help me improve my classical Chinese and writing chops. I wanted to write *something.* I bought several dictionaries of both Korean and classical Chinese, and read the edition of *Romance* that was popular at the end of the Joseon Dynasty and throughout the Japanese occupation. It helped me revive my reading comprehension of classical Chinese that had grown rusty since my *Jang Gil-san* days. Another edition, sent by Choi Won-suk, happened to be the source text used in all subsequent Korean editions of *Romance,* and so I used it as my own source. The first sentence goes: "It has been known for generations that what has been divided shall be united, and what has been united shall be divided."

I slowly translated two volumes in prison, eventually finishing the entire task some five years after my release. Inspector Lee Ju-hee had the carpentry inmates fashion a low desk and legless chair for me, and provided notebooks, pens, and colored pencils. The Ministry of Justice was able to tell the outside world that I was "being allowed to write," and while that was a compromise for me, I didn't complain. The prison, when they heard I wanted to translate, was happy to move me to a quieter cell.

My new cell was in the block for remand prisoners. Between the inner and outer walls of the prison, where no convicted inmates were allowed, were the prison offices, workers' cafeteria, meeting rooms, and two detainee cell blocks. These blocks housed those who weren't technically criminals, as their cases were still being tried, and yet were not free, either. The second floor was completely empty. This meant there were fewer prisoners still on trial than there was room for them in the prison. My room was in the middle of the second floor and was normally occupied by seven or eight inmates. It was twice the size of the private cells I was used to; best of all, it had a south-facing window that enabled me to see beyond the prison gates, all the way to the city and mountains and forests. I was all alone on the second floor, and no one came to do checks in the mornings and evenings.

I missed cultivating the vegetable patch and exercising with the younger inmates like I used to, so I did those things with the *soji* assigned to me, instead. My *soji* there was a former car dealer who'd accidentally killed someone while drunk at the wheel; his sentence was nearly at an end. His nickname, because of his tippling, was Strawberry Nose. He vowed to me again and again that he would never touch a drop after he was released. His repeated assurances made me suspect that he really, really wanted that drink. We created a vegetable plot by the wall in the backyard. Just like before, we planted lettuce, kale, mugwort, and chili, using seeds and seedlings provided to us by the guards. My exercise with the young inmates was replaced with badminton in the yard with Strawberry Nose, using a set provided by the inspector.

I began to see my old cell block with new eyes whenever I happened to visit. I finally read the slogans plastered on the walls, which my eyes had blurred over before. I even read them out loud. "You don't know life if you haven't cried into your bread." "Lead, don't be led." "What have I done for my family today?" "Mother, your son is being reborn."

I once went over to the halfway house to cook stew with the *soji* when the stove in my cell block's hallway was put away for the summer. The halfway house was a real house, with a kitchen and four rooms and no bars on the windows. No one was staying there at that time. We quietly entered through the front door and cooked our stew using an electric heater placed over the sink. I looked around the rooms. The walls were black with writing. There were the dates and names and comments of people being released. The words crowded the walls at eye level. What were these traces of their souls they had wished to leave behind? "Dear Sook, tomorrow I go to you." "Thirteen years of bloody tears." "My dead father, your son is finally going home." "That bastard guard Park Il-dong, you're my sworn enemy until the day I die." "Oh, my youth that has passed me by." "Young ones, obey the law." "This place is a trash can of humanity." "Money ruins lives."

Like in the old tales where there's a river or chamber of oblivion between this world and the next, a space where we lose all of our memories of the life before; or like the midway points in the ocean where deep-sea divers must linger before surfacing if they want to avoid decompression sickness, regular prisoners spend two to four days in this place before they are set free. It is already halfway outside the prison walls, which means your body as well as your mind is halfway out of captivity. During those few days, the prisoner must forget all that has happened in prison and prepare to connect their past to their future. It may seem strange to them, however, having accomplished this task, to find that the world continued to go its way while the prisoner himself was in prison.

The outside world was in turmoil with the upcoming presidential elections in December. Kim Dae-jung had come out of retirement and returned from exile overseas to declare his candidacy. A campaign for my release was still going on in the midst of election fever. Just as pardons were being discussed for former presidents Chun Doo-hwan and Roh Tae-woo, in prison for high treason, writers and intellectuals who were petitioning for my release cited the need to "obtain justice for those imprisoned for resisting Chun Doo-hwan and Roh Tae-woo, whose crimes have been confirmed and are about to be pardoned by the law."

The day of the election, December 18, was warm for early winter. The prison did not provide televisions, but we could listen to the radio in the evenings—especially when there were major sports events, which they let us listen to late into the night. I believe they broadcast the election night results as well. My cell block was allowed newspaper subscriptions but had no broadcast facilities. Even so, I was meeting with family or my lawyer almost every day at that point and was bound to be updated on any important developments.

I'd heard that the opposition party candidate was favored to win. I couldn't sleep on election night, knowing that my remaining time in prison would be determined by whoever won. Around midnight, I heard a roar go up in the other cell blocks, just like when the Korean national soccer team scored an away goal. They had all been listening to the radio. It made me jump out of bed. The guard on duty downstairs ran up to my cell and shouted joyfully to me:

—Kim Dae-jung has won! Sir, you're going to leave this place soon!

On Christmas Eve, political prisoners across the country embarked on a hunger strike to protest the Christmas presidential pardoning of Chun Doo-hwan and Roh Tae-woo. Normally the doors would be opened during exercise hour, allowing me to meet up with the student prisoners in the other cell blocks during hunger strikes. But that day, the guard came up to the floor where I was held alone and stayed there until evening, without once opening my cell door.

I learned what had happened at the Gongju Correctional Institution only later, when I read about it in the newspaper. My fellow writers had arrived at the prison as a group to publicly proclaim a "Protest for the Freedom of Hwang Sok-yong," aimed at the government and President-Elect Kim Dae-jung. Fifty writers had come to visit me from Seoul, Gwangju, and Daejeon, only to be prevented by the prison authorities, where-upon they staged a protest instead.

The writers went on to participate in "prison allowance solidarity," where they paid the 30,000 won daily quota for prison allowance transfers. They decided to contribute a 500-won coin each so that everyone could have a hand in it, with some even giving extra 100-won coins to max out the quota. At 4 p.m. the smiling writers waved goodbye to the twenty or so guards blocking their way at the prison gates and climbed aboard the bus for Seoul. This bus, according to Lee Soon-won with his usual writerly eloquence, was "meant to take Hwang Sok-yong back to Seoul with us," the newspapers quoted him as saying. "The light was as bright as the sun shining on a country elder's birthday banquet, but the walls of the prison were still too high."

We finally entered the new year, and I received some New Year's cards, including a letter from Yeom Mu-ung in Daegu:

> It's 1998 already. How fast time flies. It's as if I am not living my life on my own time but being dragged around by a time outside of myself. I feel this is the case more and more every day.
>
> During the events of the end of last year, I thought of where you were, that very place I spent six years of my middle and high school life. I also thought of the dawn climbs during the winter at Suyuri twenty-five years ago.
>
> How is your health? Now that you are in your midfifties— how awful the thought, one's midfifties!—you must be feeling it

597

in your bones. I've had diabetes for the past ten years and feel that I have less strength with each passing day. I feel a helplessness, as if I was being pushed down a mountain by a power beyond my control. All this, however, must seem trivial to you where you are.

I am sure that I will meet you in the outside world before spring. The past five years will be a springboard for creative life in the coming years.

Please take care of yourself.

They say that *gwishim*, the desire to return home, is as keen and swift as an arrow, but instead time wore on and spring dragged its feet. Finally, on March 13, 1998, Kim Dae-jung issued a presidential pardon on my behalf.

Normally I should have been let out after midnight, but it took some time for the paperwork to come down from the Ministry of Justice to the regional prisons. Inspector Lee had been transferred to another prison and there was only Inspector Park, with whom I had not gotten along since the beginning of my sentence. He was the one who handed me the changes of clothes and shoes that I'd been sent from outside.

I peeled off my prisoner's uniform. First went what inmates jokingly called the "People's Army" jacket, padded with cotton like the Korean War–era Chinese soldiers, then the trousers that were held up by a string as thick as my finger. I took off the thermal long johns with their now stretched-out knees and stood in my undershirt and underpants, feeling untouched by the cold of early spring. I put on the shirt, the suit, and lastly the shoes. Inspector Park, who was standing nearby, chuckled and said I was fit to be a model.

I retrieved my things from prison storage: a photo of my mother taken before she died, one of Ho-seop sent from America, photos of Ho-jun and Yeo-jeong from when they were small, and my faded brown leather wallet. I had visited the storeroom before, to change my blankets every season, and I knew very well where my things were lying in wait. There, in lockers with perforated doors, labeled with each prisoner's number, were objects that held the traces of their incarcerated owners. There were pairs of shoes that had trod unfamiliar streets and alleys, smeared with their dirt, the heels worn on one side. A faded laborer's jumpsuit with a *makgeolli* stain, an eyeglass case, tattered summer clothes now no better than rags, mesh-top slippers that were trendy some summer past, thick-soled hiking boots, all sorts of hats, rings, necklaces, watches, and other baubles—all the objects that had disappeared from life the moment their owners were arrested, tied up in string like the old memories of people long dead.

Inspector Park handed me my release notice and informed me that I was technically on parole and needed to report to the nearest police station within a week of my homecoming. He shook my hand.

—Congratulations on your release. I hope you become a fine, upstanding member of society.

He saluted me, and I bowed in response. I was a little surprised at how his gesture washed away the resentment I'd felt toward him. We walked to the prison gate together and stopped in front of the small side door next to the guard post.

—All right, then. Beyond here is where the world starts. Have a good life.

I nodded and walked through the gate.

Friends and scores of reporters were waiting outside. Standing by the gate, my eldest son, Ho-jun, and daughter, Yeo-jeong, were the first to greet me. I told the reporters:

—It feels as if I have now completed the long journey that began in Gwangju in 1980.

The reporters returned to Seoul on their chartered bus, and I left in a car provided by my in-laws. Light snow began to fall. By the time we reached the highway, the spring snow was coming down so heavily that it was accumulating on the edges of the windows. As the car sped down the highway my ears began to go numb, and soon everything sounded very far away. As if I were alone in the mountains, with the sounds of the city coming to me from somewhere deep in the valley. I felt no sense of speed. My body, having lived in a private cell for so long, was trying to protect itself. My years in prison already seemed like a distant memory. It was like that feeling at dawn when you're not quite over the previous night's drinking.

I must have dozed off, because next thing I knew the car was slowing down. We were passing through the tollgates into Seoul. I stared out at the unfamiliar streets flowing past me into darkness.

Epilogue

December 3, 2016. The weather was harsh and cold. I dressed in layers and took the subway to Gyeongbokgung Station. There was nowhere to sit because the train came loaded from Ilsan, and the station itself was crowded with passengers standing on the platform and moving up and down the stairs. Everyone fell in line and waited patiently for their turn. The five main roads that fed into Gwanghwamun Plaza were jammed with crowds. For the previous protest, on November 12, we had bought candles with paper-cup guards, but now these were replaced by electric candles with batteries. My wife had stuffed her backpack with blankets and mats, but we couldn't even step foot in the plaza. We stayed at the edges instead. We had walked around before the march began, looking at the different sections of the crowd that were each protesting in their own way. Young students, Won-Buddhists, movie stars, farmers, labor union members, Catholics, feminists . . . There were all sorts of people there, including many elderly couples, mothers pushing baby carriages, whole families with parents holding their little ones' hands, and middle-aged office workers handing out homemade signs. There were also quite a few groups of homemakers, calling on their phones to locate each other in the crowd, their cries of joy and *long time no see*'s bringing a smile to my lips. And I kept bumping into people I hadn't met in decades, acquaintances I used to see often who had changed jobs or moved to different parts of the city, friends I would think of from time to time. The protest was a party, a true festival.

There were many young volunteers helping out. Some wandered through the crowd collecting money, and many people willingly opened their wallets. The heat from the million candles and the mass of people was enough to stave off the cold. In Gwanghwamun Plaza and its surrounding streets, and in cities all over Korea, an estimated 2.32 million people came out for the candlelight protest against President Park Geun-hye, daughter of the former dictator Park Chung-hee. An unprecedented number of people had turned out that day, because the National Assembly was set to vote on the president's impeachment. A right-wing politician had said dismissively, "Candles go out the moment the wind changes," which merely incited more citizens to take to the streets, telling their friends and family to come out as well, anxious to see through a successful impeachment vote. Many others had come out to the protest when they found they couldn't bear to just sit at home and watch.

The citizens did not throw stones at the police buses that blocked their way but slapped stickers on them instead, and when it got late the young volunteers swept the streets clean and even ripped the stickers off the buses. They did so because they were worried that the riot police, conscripts around the same age as themselves, would have to spend hours doing it themselves.

I followed the march into Hyoja-dong, past the Jeokseon-dong alley that I had walked down every day in middle school and high school. There was another roadblock in front of the public administration center at Hyoja-dong; because this was the closest point to the presidential Blue House, a great many protesters were gathered there. They were nearly all passionate young adults in their twenties and thirties. President Park would have been in earshot of their shouted slogans. Demonstrators and police had already battled over the protest in court, where the police would try to block the protest and a judge would remove that block, over and over again. The older folks from the 1980s anti-dictatorship protests, unused to such genteel methods, shouted from the taverns that we needed to charge at the cops with Molotov cocktails if we wanted this to be a real revolution. But nonviolence has always been the order of candlelight protests.

The organizers were cultural activists with considerable experience in civic groups. They never handed over the microphones to famous personages or politicians. Except for the musicians who had come to perform, no one was automatically entitled to address the crowds. Instead, the microphone was passed between nameless citizens, seniors, middle school students, anybody with a story they needed to tell, who proceeded to share their experiences with the crowd as best they could. If someone got overexcited and attempted to scale the wall of buses, the crowd would calm them by chanting, "Come down, come down! Nonviolence, nonviolence!" and the person would come down with the support of those below. The sight of everyone acting strong but wise, angry but, as individuals and yet deferential to one another, was as beautiful as the candlelight itself. In the plaza, I experienced a new country, a completely different community from what had been before. I do not always like the word *citizen*, but a new citizenry had appeared before me.

We wandered until dawn and returned home, whereupon I immediately lay down with the chills and a fever. I had come down with the flu. I'd had a flu shot in the fall, free for all senior citizens, but it didn't seem to have worked. It was in this state of sickness that I watched as the National Assembly voted to impeach Park Geun-hye on live television. Congratulatory messages flew in from all over. Finally, we were beginning to emerge from the long, dark tunnel of Park Chung-hee's legacy of dictatorship. His daughter had picked up his historic karma and was being kicked off the political stage. I was nineteen years old when Park Geun-hye's father seized power, and now I was seventy-five.

~

The policies of the Park Geun-hye administration, which had taken office in 2013, were ill suited to the current times, leftovers from the Yushin dictatorship as they were. The Korean peninsula remained divided; we were still subservient to world powers and at the mercy of their actions. Because we had pursued modernization within the framework of dictatorship, we were bad at balancing different opinions or taking care of the disenfranchised. The power of capital was stronger than ever and its control over politics ever more subtle. South Korea seemed to top every negative ranking in the OECD: suicide rate, irregular employment, work-related accidents, labor hours, youth unemployment. The two conservative administrations of Lee Myung-bak and Park Geun-hye, through their hostility and Cold War attitudes toward North Korea, had wiped out all our efforts to transform our system of armistice into a system of peace, pushing the Korean peninsula back to the brink of war.

Most of the people I met at various events agreed that Korea was in crisis, both domestically and internationally. They believed that it was a crisis across politics, the economy, and diplomatic relations, and that we might not be able to overcome it even if all the disparate and dissenting voices in our society managed to come together as one. As usual, the brunt of this crisis would be borne by ordinary people, and wounds much deeper than those sustained during the Asian Financial Crisis would appear in our society. The widespread consensus was that, late as it was, we as a community needed to find a way to survive.

Park Chung-hee, who seized power through a military coup in 1961, imposed a development-oriented dictatorship to modernize the country, the aftereffects of which are still present in our lives today—wearing the fashionable clothes of democracy over one half of a body that remains divided by a militarized border. Despite two democratic governments in between, the reactionary remnants of the past successfully installed the Lee Myung bak and Park Geun-hye administrations. The daughter of the dictator Park brought back the cronyism between government and industry that had been common practice during her father's time. Every social system began reverting to the past, conformist thought-policing returned, and surveillance of those in the arts and academia was conducted with even more guile than before.

In my own case, there had been veiled threats from the government alongside offers of leadership positions in pro-governmental organizations; every year they looked into my bank records and sent mailed notices of having done so. Members of right-wing organizations also posted about me on social media, twisting the former KCIA's reports about my North Korea visit and labeling me a communist and a spy. These subtle and malicious forms of harassment and surveillance had trickled on for some time until—immediately after the *Sewol* ferry disaster in April 2014, which killed hundreds of school students—turning into a deluge, which leads me to believe that the *Sewol* incident was the true preamble to the fall of the Park Geun-hye administration. As voices criticizing the government's incompetent and confused handling of the *Sewol* increased in volume, those who spoke up were labeled as radical leftists or impure elements threatening national security, and got added to a secret blacklist that was only later revealed. I was used to that kind of treatment, but I can imagine how difficult it must have been for younger writers and artists. But I still believe that, no matter what kind of oppression or difficulty ensues, the social function of the artist must begin from a critical point of view. The relationship between the government and the arts must be that the former supports, but does not control, the latter. A society where artists have lost their faculty of criticism and submit unconditionally to power is well on its way to losing its democracy.

I could not keep my promise to my publisher of delivering the manuscript of this book by the end of the year. I was too sick

from an unending flu, and too exhausted from being sick. I rang
in 2017 in this state. Soon, my right shoulder was in such pain
that I temporarily lost use of the entire arm. My whole life I had
insisted on writing all my manuscripts by hand, to the point
that I'd suffered from a severe case of frozen shoulder during my
exile in Germany. The pain in my right shoulder kept recurring,
and the only real treatment was to stop working long enough
for it to heal. This time, however, was different. When I was
young, I had once caught a middle-ear infection after swimming and couldn't sleep for days as I cried from the pain, but
this pain was much worse. Being an adult, it wasn't as if I could
cry all night anymore; all I could do was lie in bed with my eyes
open and moan. The pain pulsed with the beating of my heart;
it was all but audible. It got to the point where I couldn't lift
my cutlery; my wife had to feed me. When I finally got checked
by a doctor, he declared that the flu must have developed into
pneumonia before receding, leaving behind a swollen and
infected shoulder joint, long devoid of any cartilage. He drained
the fluid from my shoulder and prescribed a regimen of pills and
physical therapy, which had me in and out of the hospital all
winter long.

I was born left-handed. I've seen American presidents sign
documents with their left hands, which makes me think the
West doesn't really discriminate against left-handed people. But
in the East, there is a strict tradition of doing anything involving
eating or writing with the right hand. Whenever I held a spoon
or a pen with my left hand as a child, my mother would slap my
hand or scold me. Even the word *right* has the moralistic meaning of correct, proper, or normal. Is the left hand, then, the
"wrong" hand?

After much correction and practice, I learned to eat and write
well enough with my right hand. But when I threw a ball, or
swung a fist in anger, or drew a woman toward me after I'd
learned how to love, it was my left hand that reached out. My
blood called for my left hand, but I was thwarted many times.

The world is full of objects for the right-handed. Even in the military, the old-fashioned M-1 rifles were designed for right-handers, which made me a bad shot and subject to much disciplinary action. Through this constant conflict with objects for the right-handed, I developed a perspective that was different from most people's. This isn't such a bad thing to have when you're a writer. But this long-standing conflict had now compromised my body at a key moment. Was this a sign telling me not to use my right hand anymore, or a sign that I did not deserve to use my right side anymore?

A whole twenty years have passed since I was released from my five-year sentence. Looking back, I cannot think of a single year of my life that might be called easy, but those particular years of exile and imprisonment now seem, from this side of seventy, like they were at least brief.

When I left prison, South Korea was in total economic chaos because of the Asian Financial Crisis. There were mobs of homeless people around the train and subway stations, large corporations declaring bankruptcy, and soaring numbers of layoffs. The world was being reformatted into the neoliberal order following the end of the Cold War. My own greatest concern was trying to make a living again as a writer. Quite a few of my colleagues whispered behind my back that old Hwang would never be able to write again.

The first thing I did was go into a big university hospital to get a full-body checkup. Fortunately, no major illnesses were found, but my eyesight had gone quite bad and my gums were in such terrible shape that I needed new molars. They said it was from stress and malnutrition. I was told that I might suffer from insomnia, agoraphobia, and intense introversion—symptoms that could persist for three to four months or even up to a year before slowly returning to normal. I did begin to feel better with time, but meanwhile I would get dizzy and my heart would pound when I was on the subway, or a wave of panic would wash over me when I was in crowded places like shopping malls, forcing me to step aside until I felt able to move again. These were all symptoms of having spent so long in a private cell, I was told. Writing *The Old Garden* and *The Guest*, however, helped me overcome these symptoms and bring me back to my old self.

Writing an autobiography was something I really did not want to do. I had made it a rule to work only on fiction, but, more than anything else, I hated the thought of talking about myself. In 2004, when I was living in London, I was approached about serializing my life story in the *JoongAng Ilbo*, but I ended up cutting it short for those same reasons. As I chronicled my childhood and youth, the closer I got to the present, the worse I began to feel. It became harder and harder to see myself objectively, and I found myself inadvertently presenting myself in a favorable light or making excuses for the hurt I had caused—and this was not a gratifying discovery. I thought I needed more time to see myself from a distance. I would have given up entirely if it weren't for the fact that I'd signed a contract with a publisher. I kept putting it off for ten years until the rights went to a different publisher, who was much more persistent in demanding that I either hand over a manuscript or return the advance. I was used to sweating under one deadline or another anyway, so I gave them the rough draft that I had been working on before I'd canceled the serialization. That draft had ended at the part where I go down to Haenam to finish *Jang Gil-san*, and the remaining narrative was filled in with an "interview" chapter. When Kang Tae-hyung, editor and director of Munhakdongne, heard this, he scolded me, saying that my story was not just the story of an individual but a valuable resource for all of Korean literature, and how dare I mistreat it that way. He returned my large advance, managed to wrangle back the rights, and waited three more years for me to finish.

I reread the manuscript I had put in storage for ten years and broke into a sweat at the thought of what I had almost done. I decided to start again. As I resumed work, I chastised myself for not respecting autobiography as a literary form and for nearly making a foolish mistake. This past year of looking back at myself and thinking about my life has been a precious experience in my twilight years.

I became famous at a young age and was cared for by many people. Talented people are arrogant: many of them rest on their talents and have no knowledge of their selves. What is more, I was always rushing headlong toward some new destination. I would reach that place only to turn and head off to somewhere else, leaving behind people and places the moment I'd grown accustomed to them. I had a habit of moving on to the next project when I'd reached the midpoint of my current project, finishing off the latter in a hurry. So you can imagine what my personal relationships were like.

One day, when I was living in Paris, I was on my way home from a walk with my family. I remember holding my adult daughter's hand as we crossed the Pont Mirabeau. A cool breeze blew over the river and boats passed by under the bridge. My daughter was excited to be on a trip. Our palms were sweating. It was getting uncomfortable to walk that way, so I let go of her hand. She shot me a sidelong glance and said, "Of course you'd be like that." Sometimes I will take such criticisms to heart, but for the most part I overlook them. Then, later, I fall into moments of deep regret. By that point, the person I've hurt will have already moved on, as far away from me as a shot arrow, with no way for me to make amends. How many people have I hurt like this? How many friends did I walk away from, and what have I been running toward? All those people, both inside and outside Korea, who helped me in my times of need—I had never missed them more until that moment. Late as it was, I called each of their names in my heart, sending them my gratitude.

Spring seemed to be coming slowly. The pain in my shoulder receded just as slowly. Coincidentally, the new edition of *The Kwangju Uprising* was being published at the same time as this work, and while I was revising the edits of both books, the mass Candlelight Revolution against Park Geun-hye lit up our hearts again in Korea. Finally, on March 10, Park Geun-hye's impeachment ruling was certified. The Constitutional Court's declaration was a long time coming, but it showed how much our society had grown up.

On the day of the certification, I looked out into my front yard and saw it was white with apricot blossoms. My shoulder is now much stronger and more flexible than before. Since my sickness, I have discovered that I am ambidextrous. I can hug from both sides. In my old age, I have finally grown up.

It is thanks to Kang Tae-hyung that this autobiography was reborn. I also wish to thank Yeom Hyun-sook who managed its publication, Lee Sang-sul, and the entire editorial team at Munhakdongne for working so hard to make this, my true release from prison, a reality.

And if it wasn't for my wife, Kim Gil-hwa, and her daily encouragement, reading and editing the manuscript scores of times through many sleepless nights, I would still be trapped in the past somewhere, like a prisoner who cannot find the way out.

Having spent my life as a writer in the prison of time, language, and this Cold War museum that is the divided Korean peninsula, I know the fragility of this freedom in which I live.

About the Translators

Anton Hur studied law at Korea University and has translated works by many authors, including Shin Kyung-sook and Park Sang Young. He currently resides in Seoul.

Sora Kim-Russell is a literary translator based in Seoul. She has translated *At Dusk*, *Familiar Things*, and *Princess Bari* by Hwang Sok-yong, in addition to works by other authors, including Pyun Hye-young, Kim Un-su, and Jeon Sungtae.